SIOUX CHIEFTAIN

SOUTH DAKOTA

A GUIDE TO THE STATE

Compiled by the Federal Writers' Project
of the Works Progress Administration

Second Edition Completely Revised
by
M. LISLE REESE

AMERICAN GUIDE SERIES

ILLUSTRATED

Sponsored by the State of South Dakota

HASTINGS HOUSE · Publishers · NEW YORK

FIRST PUBLISHED IN 1938

SECOND EDITION PUBLISHED IN 1952

PRINTED IN THE UNITED STATES OF AMERICA

Library of Congress Catalog Card Number 52-7601

SOUTH DAKOTA

A Guide to the State

Preface

South Dakota: A Guide to the State is both an enlargement of and
and sequel to the earlier *South Dakota Guide* which was published in
1938 as one of the first volumes in the popular American Guide Series.
This book's predecessor has long been out of print and a collectors'
item.

Having been the editor of the original *South Dakota Guide,* as well
as State Director of the Federal Writers' Project while it was being
prepared and published, I have derived a large measure of satisfaction
in preparing this new and up-to-date edition. The main body of the
book, as well as its original flavor has been retained, but a great deal
of new material, pictures, and maps have been added.

South Dakota, although it still has the aspect of a pioneer state, has
changed considerably in the last fourteen years. There are a thousand
new lakes, a network of improved roads, and scores of newly established
State parks and recreation areas. The great cultural adventure in the
sculpture of Mount Rushmore National Memorial—America's Shrine
of Democracy—has been completed, and the State is in the midst of an
economic excitement surrounding the series of dams being built across
the historic Missouri River. Nor has South Dakota's fabulous Black
Hills region ever been greener!

Even so, the three early-day nicknames given the State in a sense
describe it — the Sunshine, the Blizzard, and the Coyote State. To
these has been added, in the State's tourist literature, the euphemistic
"Land of Infinite Variety." Perhaps its official name, Dakota, taken
from the Sioux language and meaning "an alliance of friends," is the
most characteristic. South Dakota believes in its State motto "Under
God the People Rule"; it was the first State to introduce the initiative
and referendum in State affairs, and it has one of the lowest illiteracy
rates.

This book seeks to describe faithfully, interpret honestly, and present
as entertainingly as possible the background and way of life in South
Dakota. For the traveler as well as the native South Dakotan, an
attempt is made to point out unusual settings and activities—Sioux
Indians on and off their reservations, gold mines and ghost towns, pheasant and deer hunting spots, historic sites, scenic retreats, wide open

spaces and towns that have the flavor of the old wide open frontier days.

Valuable advice and assistance have been given by numerous consultants and agencies. Especially helpful were the University of South Dakota, South Dakota State College, the State School of Mines and Technology, the South Dakota Department of Game, Fish and Parks, the National Park Service, The United States Forestry Service, and the United States Indian Service.

It is appropriate also to give special acknowledgment to A. H. Pankow, director of publicity for the State Highway Commission; Col. Will Robinson of the South Dakota Historical Society; Lora Crouch, Sioux Falls librarian; Lincoln Borglum, Mount Rushmore sculptor; Hoadley Dean, manager of the Black Hills and Badlands Association, and Archer B. Gilfillan, Black Hills author and raconteur and Walter Frese, president of Hastings House, whose love for Americana made this new edition possible.

M. LISLE REESE

Sioux Falls, South Dakota
April, 1952

Contents

Illustrations

Sioux Chieftain—*Frontispiece*

Page

Maps

How to Use the Guide

General Information contains practical information for the State as a whole; specific local information is given in the introduction to The Black Hills recreational area, and to each city and tour description.

The introductory essays are designed to give a composite, yet comprehensive, survey of the State's contemporary scene, natural setting, history, and social, economic and cultural development. Frequent cross-references are made to further information on these subjects elsewhere in the book, particularly in the Tour section; these are found by reference to the index. *SOUTH DAKOTA: A GUIDE TO THE STATE* is not only a practical travel book; it will also serve as a valuable reference book.

The guide is built on a framework of tour descriptions, written in general to follow the principal highways from East to West, or from North to South. They are easily followed, however, in the reverse direction. In many cases the highway descriptions are equally useful to travelers on railroads. Whenever railroads parallel the described highway the fact is stated in the tour heading.

As a matter of convenience, several of the towns in South Dakota are described separately in the Cities section.

The tour descriptions contain cross-references to other tours crossing or branching from the route described, and to pertinent material found elsewhere in the book.

Important routes, with terminals, are listed in the Contents and are indicated on the tour key map. Each tour description follows a single main route. Descriptions of routes branching from the main routes are in smaller type. The long route descriptions are divided into sections at important junctions.

Cumulative mileage is used on main and side tours, the mileage being counted from the beginning of each section or, on side tours, from the junction with the main route. The mileage notations will vary somewhat from future driven mileages because of an extensive road-building program in South Dakota which is eliminating curves and avoiding villages. The construction of dams across the Missouri River at four points will cause slight relocation of some trans-State highway and railroad bridges, and such changes are noted in the tours.

The list of descriptive titles of tours gives the nearest out-of-State cities on the routes, important South Dakota cities on them, and State and Federal highway numbers of routes.

Points of interest in each city are arranged in the order in which they can conveniently be visited, and the numbers correspond with those on city maps.

Standard abbreviations are used throughout.

General Information

(For highways and other transport routes, see State map panels following TOURS section.)

Railroads: Chicago, Milwaukee, St. Paul & Pacific (The Milwaukee); Chicago & North Western (North Western); Chicago, Burlington & Quincy (Burlington); Chicago, Rock Island & Pacific (Rock Island); Great Northern (GN); Illinois Central (IC); Minneapolis & St. Louis (M&StL); Minneapolis, St. Paul & Sault Ste. Marie (Soo Line). (*See TRANSPORTATION.*)

Bus Lines: Northland Greyhound (Minneapolis to Aberdeen); Overland Greyhound (Omaha to Sioux Falls); Burlington Trailways (Denver to Black Hills points); Jackrabbit (Fargo, N.D. to E. South Dakota points); Inter City (Sioux City, Ia. to Rapid City); Kyote (N.E. South Dakota to Black Hills). Several intrastate and feeder lines.

Air Lines: Mid-Continent Airlines (Kansas City to Minot, N.D.) stops at Sioux Falls, Huron, and Aberdeen, with route from Huron to Minneapolis via Watertown and a direct route from Sioux Falls to Minneapolis; Northwest Airlines (Chicago to Seattle) stops at Rapid City, Black Hills Airport (Spearfish-Lead-Deadwood), Pierre, Huron, and Brookings; Mid-West Airlines (Omaha to Huron) stops at Yankton, Sioux Falls, and Mitchell. (*See TRANSPORTATION.*)

Highways: Ten Federal routes. US 12, 212, 14, 16, and 18 cross the State E. & W., about evenly spaced; US 77, 81, 281, 83, and 85 cross it N. & S., mostly in the eastern section. Most of the arterials are oiled; some are graveled in part. During winter, roads in Black Hills often are slippery. No inspection at State borders. Roadside markers indicate points of interest.

Trails: Horseback and hiking trails in Black Hills. Maps available at National Park Service office in Rapid City, and U.S. Forest Service offices in Deadwood (Black Hills) and Custer (Harney).

Motor Vehicle Laws: Speed limit 60 m. during day and 50 m. at night. Speed for curves, hills, school zones, and towns as marked Hand signals. State maintains Highway Motor Patrol. Car license plates bear two numbers separated by dash, the first two numbers designating the county in its alphabetical order.

Accommodations: First-class hotels in larger cities and in Custer State Park. Modern tourist camps in most towns and throughout Black Hills area. Cabins available in Black Hills and NE. Lake Region. Roadside picnic grounds in forest areas.

Recreation Areas: Chief recreational regions are the Black Hills and the Lake Region (*see RECREATION*). Twenty-eight State parks and recreation areas operated by South Dakota Game, Fish and Parks Department widely scattered throughout State (*see TOURS and MAPS*).

Big Game Hunting: Deer and elk seasons and limits vary each year, as prescribed by State Game, Fish and Parks Commission, Pierre. Hunting confined to Black Hills area (excluding parks) except occasional special seasons for deer in certain Eastern counties when animals become menace to farming. Licenses: Resident, $7.70; non-resident, $35. Antelope hunting permitted some years in certain West-river counties, with public drawings to determine by lot who may hunt. License: $7.50. For infractions of hunting laws, Game Wardens are empowered to confiscate guns. (*See RECREATION.*)

Small Game: The following fur animals may be taken during seasons prescribed by State Game, Fish and Parks Commission: raccoon, mink, skunk, badger, oppossum, and muskrat.

Upland Game Birds: State is noted for Chinese ringneck pheasant shooting (*see RECREATION*). Seasons, limits, and counties in which birds may be taken are prescribed each year by the State Game, Fish and Parks Commission. Licenses: Resident, $1; non-resident, good for 10 consecutive days, $25. Hunting guides (licensed and bonded) are available. Grouse hunting permitted some years in certain West-river counties.

Migratory Waterfowl: Hunting of ducks and geese prescribed by State Game, Parks and Fish Commission; some years no out-of-state hunting permitted. (*See RECREATION.*)

Fishing: Trout, May 1 to September 30, 10 per day, 20 in possession; wall-eyed pike, northern pike, pickerel, crappies, perch, bluegills, sunfish, rock and silver bass, May 1 to February 28, limits variable in different counties; black bass, June 15 to February 28 in certain counties, limits variable. Advisable to secure current fishing regulations from State Game, Fish and Parks Commission, Pierre, or any county treasurer or license agent. Licenses: Resident $1 (women and children under 18, no fee); non-resident (regardless of age or sex), $5; Special 10-day visitor's license, $3.

Forest and Prairie Fire Rules: Dropping or throwing from any vehicle burning matches, cigarettes, cigars, or other burning substances is a misdemeanor, punishable by fine or imprisonment. Setting of grass fires or failure to extinguish camp fires also punishable under State laws.

Precautions: Rattlesnakes occur W. of the Missouri R. Most prevalent on dry, rocky hillsides. Rattlers usually give a short, strident buzz as warning. If person is bitten, tourniquet should be applied above wound, then each fang mark criss-crossed to depth of ¼ in. Suck the wound to induce bleeding. Poison ivy is common in wooded sections, recognizable by green-white flowers or fruit and trifoliate leaves.

Liquor Regulations: Both "on sale" (by the drink) and "off sale" (by the package) systems of dispensing intoxicating liquors. Local option may determine whether city or town shall permit on or off sale, both, or neither. Municipal ownership of liquor stores and/or saloons in some places. No liquor sales after midnight nor on Sundays. Beer of 3.2% or less alcoholic content sold under more liberal licenses, including Sunday sales. Possession in public place of bottle of liquor with seal broken subjects violator to minimum fine of $200 or 90 days in jail, or both.

Public Information Service: Publicity Director, South Dakota Highway Commission, Pierre; Greater South Dakota Association, Huron; National Park Service, Rapid City; U.S. Forest Service offices, Deadwood and Custer; Chambers of Commerce.

Calendar of Events

Jan.	1st wk.	Pierre	Inaugural Ball (odd years)
	2nd wk.	Aberdeen	Northwest Snow Queen Festival
Feb.	*nfd	Lead	Terry Peak Ski Meets
	nfd	Sioux Falls	Mardi Gras
Mar.	nfd	Rotative	State "A" and "B" Basketball Tournaments
	4th wk.	Sioux Falls	Made in South Dakota Exposition
Apr.	nfd	Aberdeen	Aberdeen Relays (track meet)
May	1st wk.	Sioux Falls	Dakota Relays (track meet)
	20th	Rapid City	Armed Forces Day (air show)
	4th wk.	Vermillion	Horse Show
June	1st wk.	Spearfish	Strawberry Festival
	15th-Sept	Deadwood	Trial of Jack McCall (semi-weekly)
	4th wk.	Pierre	Days of '81 Celebration
	4th wk.	St. Onge	Rough Riders Rodeo
July	1st wk-Sept.	Spearfish	Passion Play (twice a wk.)
	3-4-5	Belle Fourche	Black Hills Roundup
	4th	Sioux Falls	Elks Running Races (pari-mutuel)
	4th	Martin	Sioux Stampeded
	4th	Ft. Pierre	Ft. Pierre Rodeo

* nfd—No fixed day.

	2nd wk.	Hot Springs	Miss South Dakota Beauty Pageant & Pari-Mutuel horse races
	3rd wk.	Sheridan Lake	Boat Races
	4th wk.	Spearfish	Black Hills Airfair
	4th wk.	Custer	Gold Discovery Days Pageant
Aug.	1st wk.	Deadwood	Days of '76 Festival
	2nd wk.	Sturgis	Jack Pine Gypsy Tour (motor cycle) and Races
	3rd wk.	Rapid City	Greater Rapid City Shows
	3rd wk.	Hill City	Heart o' the Hills Celebration
	3rd wk.	White River	Frontier Days (rodeo)
	3rd wk.	Sioux Falls	Sioux Empire Fair
	4th wk.	Madison	Welcome Neighbor Days
	4th wk.	Vermillion	Days of '59 Celebration
Sept.	1st Mon.	Lead	Labor Day Celebration
	1st wk.	Aberdeen	Dakota Open Gold Tournament
	2nd wk.	Huron	State Fair
	3rd wk.	Watertown	Little World Series (amateur baseball tournament)
	4th wk.	Mitchell	Corn Palace Festival
Oct.	*nfd	Huron	Baseball Pheastival (Major League players day before pheasant hunting season)
	nfd	Aberdeen	Gypsy Day (Northern State Teachers College)
	nfd	Springfield	Founders Day (Southern State Teachers College)
	nfd	Spearfish	Swarm Day (Black Hills Teachers College)
	nfd	Sioux Falls	Tepee Day (Sioux Falls College)
	nfd	Rapid City	"M" Day (S.D. School of Mines)
	nfd	Madison	Homecoming (General Beadle Teachers College)
	nfd	Sioux Falls	Viking Days (Augustana College)

* nfd—No fixed day.

*nfd	Huron	Powwow Days (Huron College)
nfd	Mitchell	Blue and White Day (Dakota Wesleyan)
nfd	Yankton	Pioneer Day (Yankton College)
nfd	Vermillion	Dakota Day (Univ. of S. D.)
last wk.	Brookings	Hobo Day (S. D. State College)
Nov. 3rd wk.	Sioux Falls	Automobile Show

* nfd—No fixed day.

South Dakota Today

VISITORS who come to South Dakota for the first time expecting to see near-naked Indians, gun-toting cowboys, and Calamity Janes will be disillusioned. Although there are as many Indians as there were a hundred years ago, when the early white adventurers found them living in their natural state, today they live peaceful and interesting lives, foreign to war whoops and breechclouts. There are cowboys, but not of the motion picture variety. Recurrence of such early hardships as drought and grasshoppers, with the addition of a new one, the dust storm, for a time arrested prosperity and progress, but it failed to discourage the tenacious people.

This tenacity paid off in the 1940s with unprecedented prosperity. The land was never more productive. Towns became citified. Reflecting confidence in honors that only a prairie State may appreciate, the cattlemen pointed proudly to South Dakota in 1950 as having more wild hay acreage than any other; the farmer smiled as his radio announced that his State was second in durum wheat crops. Even to the old prospector, busy seeking newly important strategic minerals in his Black Hills haunts, it came as no surprise that South Dakota was leading all other States in the production of gold.

To know whence the South Dakotans came and why, is to begin to understand them. When the land west of Minnesota—Dakota Territory until 1889—was thrown open to homestead settlement, school teachers, lawyers, farmers, merchants, and bright-eyed youths turned to the new country to stake their claims, their hopes, their lives. From eastern cities and long-established communities, from Yankee and old frontier families, these adventuring homesteaders brought with them to the Middle Border a deep-set cultural tradition and training, coupled with a determination to achieve economic independence.

The serious task of making a living in the undeveloped country

THE HUSKING BEE

occupied the minds and hands of its people, leaving little time for
the enjoyment of esthetic pursuits. The soil was turned by men
dripping sweat; store counters were worn smooth by calloused hands.
In young South Dakota there were no operas, no symphonies, no
dramas. When the corn was picked and the earth left to sleep for
the winter, father unpacked his fiddle and uncle his harmonica,
mother baked a cake and the children "buggied" to the neighbors
with invitations—a husking bee tonight. To lively tunes learned
"back East," a dance was started and the corn was husked. And so
it has been with South Dakotans through the recent pioneering
years: combining work with pleasure, making their own entertainment, and still keeping an appreciation of the finer arts.

Not always physically strong, these homesteaders were mentally
alert and formed the bases of ambitious communities. Then came an
influx of foreign groups, men of the soil—Germans, Swedes, Norwegians—strongly built and strong of will. The assimilation was
fast, the Yankee pioneers and foreigners uniting in business and
marriage.

All this has happened within a lifetime. Many of that famous
homesteading cavalcade are still living. They are the grey-haired,
weathered men and women who love to recall their hardships; yet
they keep their sons at home to run the farm or the store because

"we've had mighty good crops, and they'll come again." That second generation makes the State of today. Whether in professions, business, politics, or the kitchen, South Dakotans want it known that their parents or themselves originated farther east, but that they themselves have lived here most of their lives. Now the third generation is taking root.

Even the drought years of the 1930's failed to dislodge the lingering spirit of pioneers. South Dakotans went to work damming creeks to create more than 1,000 artificial lakes, and even more stock ponds. New schools, which now loom as the largest building in many towns, were built confidently. In the Black Hills, depression-born projects were parlayed into a general face lifting—new roads, bridges, park hotels, recreation areas, and tourist attractions.

The World War II exodus to war fronts and industrial centers was followed by a substantial return, plus veterans who had been stationed at the numerous airfields in South Dakota. The 1950 Census showed an increase over the preceding one, in contrast to some of the other States in the region.

A new era of Missouri River development is underway, with Federal agencies planning to spend a billion and a half dollars in South Dakota to provide hydro-electric power, irrigation, and flood control, through a series of dams and gigantic reservoirs.

Although settled in comparatively recent times by men and women of eastern origin, South Dakota by no means lacks western color. In this State, as large as Indiana, New Hampshire, and South Carolina combined, there are wide variations in activity and scene. There is the broad, flat farming region, the rugged ranching country, the mountainous mining and recreational area, each having its own type of citizenry and culture. The widely differing regions divided by the Missouri River are known locally as East-river and West-river.

The eastern half of the State is a continuation of Iowa and Minnesota farm land, with the latter's recreational lake region duplicated in the northeastern section. In the James and Sioux River Valleys, the barns are large and well-stocked; radios and motor cars are as common as plows; and their owners are politically conservative and deeply religious. Diversified farming and cooperative societies have made for prosperous communities. Schools and churches are large and numerous. Here one will find small cities not unlike Oshkosh, Terre Haute, and Hackensack. Outside the long, narrow valley-lands, the farms are newer, smaller, and farther apart; the people are busy fighting the elements for a living. Dust storms raised havoc in this region of huge plowed fields without windbreaks.

Across the Missouri River the large fringe of the Middle West's rich farming region merges into the first long reaches of the western cattle and mining empire. While in eastern South Dakota, groves of trees around the farmhouses stand today as monuments to the homestead period in which ten acres of trees were planted and nursed to secure the land, farther west, beyond the Missouri River, abandoned shacks stand in dejected silence to give testimony of over optimism and the unwise use of land. Here the legendary "wide open spaces" roll away as far as the eye can see. There is something about the vast expanse that appeals to strangers and holds the scattered inhabitants. In the northwest part of the State, the original pioneer ranchers still color the homestead tide that swept over the country in 1909 and 1910 and receded for the most part in the years following. Today "honyock," or farming homesteader, and old-timer live peaceably side by side, and each has learned much from the other. The old-timer taught his neighbor the art of stock raising on the range, and the honyock convinced the old-timer that some forage crops could be raised and that it was not good economics to ship out a carload

WHERE OLD AND NEW MEET

Introducing South Dakota

SO FAR AS THE EYE CAN SEE

STATE CAPITOL, PIERRE

SOLDIERS' & SAILORS' WORLD WAR MEMORIAL

STATE MUSEUM OF NATIVE STONE

BADLANDS NATIONAL
MONUMENT AREA

BLACK HILLS
GRANITE NEEDLES

MAN-MADE SYLVAN LAKE

STATE-OWNED SYLVAN LAKE HOTEL
TERRACE FACES HARNEY PEAK

FAWN

of cows and at the same time ship in a carload of condensed milk.

Although largely unfit for farming this region is being utilized for ranching with further potentialities undeveloped. In this range country inland prairie towns still retain their hitching posts and general stores.

Farther on in the Black Hills a current mining boom suggestive of the gold rush of 1876 gives an increased prosperity to towns clinging like swallow's nests to the mountainsides. Lawrence County has regained its position as the greatest gold-producing area in the United States, but the minor minerals, such as beryllium, which is used in the atomic energy field, and lithium, a raw ingredient for hydrogen bombs, are getting new attention in a region where gold has long been king.

The Black Hills people, strangely worldwise though isolated, are in the midst of an artistic, scientific, and industrial awakening. To the visitor, the general knowledge of these native South Dakotans, so far removed from cities and culture, is puzzling. The explanation lies in the fact that, with spasmodic discoveries of valuable minerals, the Hills like a magnetized needle attract financiers, engineers, prospectors, gamblers, and entertainers from the world at large. Artists, writers, and sculptors come here for the color; scientists come to study the secrets of earth and air. From contacts with the famous and notorious, idealist and realist, great and near-great, these people have absorbed a cosmopolitan atmosphere. Whether in new tweeds or ragged jacket, the man who is confronted by a visitor will probably be a composite of many men who have come this way before. He may seem at first a merchant, a rancher, or a prospector, then a woodsman or hunter; as the day wears on he may reflect the artist who stopped off the previous year to paint wild animal life, or the paleontologist who came to track down a triceratops. Next summer he may have also the characteristics of his recent visitor.

Throughout South Dakota, a stranger will notice in the cities and along the highways a human familiarity like that of a small village. On the streets the resident speaks to nearly everyone, and calls by their first names half of those he meets. Visitors will often find themselves being greeted on the street by natives with whom they have had only the most casual contact. South Dakotans pride themselves on the number of their acquaintances over the State.

While the transition from the "firsts" to the modern scene is reflected in nearly every town and city, it is more clearly marked in the West-river region. There an unpainted, frame, false-front store with its board sidewalk and porch stands alongside another building of brick, steel and concrete; wide-brimmed, tent-shaped hats and high-heeled boots are worn with cravats of Park Avenue style;

grizzled prospectors pick the earth in the shadow of million-dollar gold mine shafts.

Culture, in the urban sense, has had to wait on the unhurried assimilation of external elements impinging on a society essentially pioneer in character. When Hamlin Garland wrote of the endless drudgery and loneliness of life on the prairie in "Main Traveled Roads" and "A Son of the Middle Border," his homesteading neighbors would have nothing to do with him or his books. It was fifty years before he was accepted as a native son. Meanwhile, South Dakota furnished settings and characters for many novels, among them Rölvaag's "Giants in the Earth," Stewart Edward White's "Gold" and "Claim Jumpers," and Rose Wilder Lane's "Let the Hurricane Roar." Today there is a serious effort to acquire culture. Farm families meet weekly in rural schools to discuss new books furnished by the State's free lending library; villages have active literary societies and imported lecturers; people in cities turn out en masse to band and orchestral concerts, to local and road-show dramas, operas and art exhibits. In nearly every town are libraries and historical museums, in which are proudly exhibited collections of Indian relics and those of pioneer days.

South Dakota has been, and still is, a pioneer State.

Natural Setting

SOUTH DAKOTA is a rectangular tract of land, about 370 miles long by 210 wide, lying approximately in the geographical center of the North American Continent. It is about equidistant from the Atlantic and Pacific Oceans, and about midway between the North Pole and the Equator. It is bounded roughly on the north by the 46th and on the south by the 43rd parallels of latitude, on the west by the 104th meridian of longitude and on the east by Traverse and Big Stone Lakes, the 96th meridian, and the Big Sioux River. It embraces an area of 77,615 square miles, or nearly 50,000,000 acres of land, being larger than the combined areas of the New England States, and one and one-half times as large as England. It ranks fourteenth among the States of the Union in size. North Dakota lies along its northern border, Montana and Wyoming bound it on the west, Nebraska has a common boundary line with it to the south, and Iowa and Minnesota lie directly to the east.

TOPOGRAPHY

The Missouri River, which flows through the middle of the State from north to south, divides South Dakota roughly into two parts —East-river and West-river. The Missouri marks the western edge of the vast ice sheet that in prehistoric times covered the north central portion of the United States. In fact the Missouri was forced out of its original course, possibly the present James River valley, and in rounding the edges of the ice-sheet it cut the extremely narrow valley in which it now runs. When the ice receded, the river had already cut through the height of land in the southern part of the present State, and so could not return to its former course.

But while the ice-sheet had no effect on the West-river country, other than to define its eastern border, it had a literally transforming effect on the eastern half of the State. The ponderous mass of ice leveled off eminences and filled in valleys, and over all it spread a thick layer of glacial soil brought from every point along its route. This soil was deposited sometimes in large terminal and lateral moraines that are clearly defined today, and sometimes as a rich and fertile covering that needed only the stirring-plow of the settler to release its wonderful strength into corn and grains. But the ice had still another effect. From its receding face the James, the Vermillion, and the Big Sioux rivers flowed south to join the Missouri, through a rich and gently sloping plain left by retreating ice.

The northeast corner of the State, as abandoned by the ice-sheet, had very little slope and correspondingly poor drainage. The result is that this whole section is dotted with lakes and marshes. It is likely that in some places masses of ice were left buried when the ice-sheet retreated; and that when this buried ice melted it left lakes, ponds, or marshes, according to the depth of the depression. All this has resulted in making this region today a playground for the inhabitants of the eastern part of the State, and of sections of Minnesota and Iowa. Fish are plentiful in the lakes, which are stocked by the State fish hatcheries. The marshes abound with wild fowl that summer there, and afford excellent hunting in season.

Just south and west of the Lake Region life the James and Sioux River Valleys, constituting perhaps the richest agricultural section of the State.

West of this region, the Missouri River flows between high bluffs for almost its entire course through the State. It's swift current is still cutting a channel, its present course being so new that it has not had time to make a wide valley for itself, as has the much smaller James River. The land bordering the river on both sides is a mixture of farm and ranch land, reaching westward to the semi-arid ranching country.

This section, lying just east and north of the Black Hills, is an area like no other part of the State—a region of buttes and bad-lands, semi-arid, thinly populated. In the southern part of it are the unique Badlands (*see Tours 6 and 6A*). To the north is a long and wide belt of "gumbo."

One more giant movement of Nature's forces, comparable in importance to the ice-sheet, was to affect profoundly the future State. In the extreme western end of what is now South Dakota, some internal convulsion of the earth caused a gigantic upheaval or upthrust and formed the Black Hills.

The lowest point in the State is in the northeast corner at Big Stone Lake, 965 feet above sea level. But the slope in this portion is very gradual. The James winds its lazy, snake-like way across the

State with the dubious distinction of being "the longest unnavigable river in the world." West of the Missouri River, the story is quite different. At the extreme western border are the Black Hills, crowned by Harney Peak, a granite crag with an elevation of 7,244 feet, the highest point in the State and the highest point in the Nation east of the Rocky Mountains.

CLIMATE

South Dakota is known as "The Sunshine State"; the sun shines nearly every day of the year. Its climate is subject to extremes of heat and cold, but the high, dry character of the terrain makes this heat and cold less noticeable than in damp and muggy climates. The highest temperature ever recorded was 115°, and the lowest, 46° below zero. Such extremes, however, are rare. The average temperature for January, the coldest month, is 10° above zero; and the average for July, the hottest month, 71°. The year-round average is 44°.

The rainfall of the State varies from less than 15 inches in the extreme northwest corner to more than 25 in the southeast portion. In general it may be said that the rainfall increases as one goes eastward. The average for most of the West-river territory is from 15 to 20 inches; east of the river it is from 20 to 25. Average annual rainfall for the entire State is about 20 inches. Three-fourths of this occurs during the growing season, and this feature of the climate makes the crop production equal to that of many regions having a much higher annual precipitation The rainfall, however, varies greatly from year to year, producing good crops one season with perhaps a complete crop failure the following year.

The last killing frosts rarely occur after May 10, and the first serious frosts of autumn do not come before September 15. The average growing season for the State is 135 days, but various sections show differences in this regard as they do in rainfall. The high plateau of the Black Hills has a growing season of less than 105 days. From this point the growing season lengthens as one crosses the State from northwest to southeast, till in the latter region it exceeds 145 days.

One feature of the climate which has received wide publicity is the blizzard, a combination of snow and high wind. The violence of these storms can hardly be overestimated, but their occurrence is very rare. In South Dakota, as in the surrounding States, the historic blizzards were those of 188 and 1949.

How paralyzing prairie storms can become was demonstrated in 1949, when much of the West-river area and parts of adjoining States were buried under snow for several weeks. Following a mild

Holiday season, during which Rapid City's golf course and tennis courts were reopened, a blizzard struck on January 3. A 70 mile-an-hour wind swirled 23 inches of snow into mountainous drifts. Second floor windows became exits. But that was only the beginning. One snow storm piled up on another. Chinook winds brought thawing, followed by February days when the mercury dropped to 31 degrees below zero. For 21 days no trains moved into or out of the Black Hills. The Fifth Army's "Operation Snowbound" moved in with bulldozers and amphibious vehicles to dig out roads to isolated ranch families. The Air Force organized a "haylift" to drop feed to livestock. It was April before the country was dug out, and cattlemen's losses were severe. No human lives, however, were lost in South Dakota.

The average winter has two or three storms, but not approaching this one in severity. Too little snow is often as great a problem as too much. The average depth of snow is not nearly as great as that in the wooded areas of the North Central and Northeastern States.

Dust storms and drought played their part in the State's recent history. In the central and south central portions in 1934, dust-laden winds left freakish piles of granulated soil in ditches and along fences. Fences and farm machinery in the so-called "Dust Bowl" were frequently covered beneath drifts of shifting soil. In South Dakota, as in other States of this area, a period of drought is likely to be followed by occasional dust storms. Drought was combatted by the construction of hundreds of artificial lakes and stock-water dams; and the effects of the dust storms have long since disappeared because of soil conservation and irrigation projects, shelterbelts, and the return of plowed submarginal land to pasture. The introduction of new drought-resistant grasses and crops is an important factor.

GEOLOGY

Ancient Black Hills: In order to realize the age of the region, one must first consider the Black Hills. They are the key to the geology of the whole State of South Dakota and much of the adjacent territory.

The Black Hills were ages old before the Rocky Mountains were uplifted. They existed long before the Alps, the Caucasus, the Pyrenees, the Apennines, and while the site of the Himalayas was still a marsh. All these great mountain ranges were still level land when the Black Hills first began to rise in a great dome 150 by 75 miles in extent.

This huge dome or batholith, somewhat like an overturned wash basin, gradually rose through several million years. It is not certain that the Hills are through rising yet. But, however long the process took, it accomplished an enormous task; all the rest of the strata, from the bottom to the top of the geological column were pushed aside out of the way of this rising knob. The deepest and oldest rocks are now the highest.

It will be noticed in the Black Hills that all the layers, or strata, of rock run at about the same level in concentric rings completely around the Hills—a streak of red here, a strip of yellow there. Nearly every stratum, except the softer and more easily weathered ones, forms more or less of a cliff, facing the central backbone of the Hills and sloping downward and outward toward the plains, the successive layers roughly resembling shingles on a roof. This pattern is repeated so that one entering the Black Hills traverses the following formations of shales, limestone, and sandstones: Lance, Fox Hills, Pierre, Niobrara, Carlile, Greenhorn, Granerous, Dakota, Fuson, Minnewasta, Lakota, Morrison, Unkpapa, Sundance, Spearfish, Minnekahta, Opeche, Minnelusa, Paha Sapa, Englewood, Whitewood, and Deadwood. The highest and innermost are the Algonkian schists and granite core. The slender pinnacles known as the Needles, worn by weathering and erosion, are remnants of this granite center or core.

Plains Section: From the eastern border of the State, between Watertown and Redfield, is found the Pierre formation, running westward to the James River. Here, running northeast from the southwest corner of the State, a long arm of the Niobrara, a whitish chalky material, extends to Redfield; this formation varies in width from 12 miles at Redfield to 72 miles east of Chamberlain. From Flandreau southward through Sioux Falls, covering parts of Moody, Minnehaha, McCook, and Hanson Counties, is an arm of the Sioux Falls quartzite, a hard flint-like rock used extensively as building material. West of these two formations, the Pierre stretches to the Black Hills uplift just east of Rapid City, covering about three-fifths of the whole State; it is bordered on the northwest by the Fox Hills formation from the point where the Missouri River enters the State to Belle Fourche. Its gray to bluish shade distinguishes it, and its gumbo clay properties in wet weather are notorious. In the extreme northwest corner of the State is the Lance formation, in which are the Hell Creek Beds.

PALEONTOLOGY

The Dinosaurs: Huge monsters wallowed along the shores of tropical swamps in western South Dakota more than forty million years ago, and skeletal remains of these long-extinct dinosaurs come to light each year through erosion and scientific excavation. During the Mesozoic era, or age of reptiles, the lumbering *triceratops,* resembling a combination of elephant and rhinoceros, waged mortal combat with the swift-moving, kangaroo-shaped *tyrannosaurus rex;* while perhaps the *brontosaurus,* largest of all prehistoric reptiles, watched the battle from aloft, his long neck rising 30 feet above the earth. Fossilized bones of the *brontosaurus*—he of the 15-ton body and two-ounce brain—have been found in the area surrounding the Black Hills. In the so-called Hell Creek Beds, in the northwest corner of the State, expeditions from various museums have excavated many fine specimens; an almost perfect head of the great "frilled" dinosaur, *triceratops,* was obtained by the State School of Mines in 1927 in the region of the West Short Pine Hills, south of Camp Crook. Along White River and in the Badlands National Monument, many interesting fossils are found annually. Here are fossilized bones and teeth of the giant rhinoceros, *titanothere;* mountain sheep, *oreodon;* three-toed horse, *mesohippus;* tiny camel, *poebrotheium;* giant pig, *leptauchenia;* and saber-tooth tiger, *dinictis squalidens.* Snow, rains, and wind erode the surface clay, so that each spring new fossils are found protruding from the banks.

A major paleontological collection is exhibited in the Museum of the School of Mines and Technology (*see RAPID CITY*), and smaller exhibits may be seen at the University of South Dakota Museum, Vermillion (*see TOUR 8*), and the Custer State Park Museum (*see TOUR 5, Sec. C.*). Reproductions of five prehistoric creatures have been formed in concrete in Dinosaur Park (*see RAPID CITY*).

Marine Fossils: Most of the State is covered by the Pierre formation. It is a dark clay, gray-blue in color, and weathers to a yellow or light gray shade; in many localities where it emerges it is called gumbo. Scattered through the gumbo are thousands of iron-like clay concretions, containing fine fossil remains of marine creatures. The nautilus, a round, thin-edged, coiled fossil in the shape of a snail, is common; and ammonites of the same shape, but sometimes as much as 24 inches in diameter, have been dug up along the rivers in western South Dakota. A long jointed fossil known as the baculite, an ancient ancestor of the present devilfish, is also found. All of these marine fossils are especially prized because, on shaving off the soft shell, the scales show all the opalescent colors of the rainbow, and beneath that layer is a fine lace-like pattern. Oyster and clam shells, cup corals, and fishbones are also frequently found, along with imprints of ferns and sea lilies.

NATURAL RESOURCES

Both the development and conservation of the State's physical resources have been accelerated during recent years. The scientific uses and strategic needs for hitherto secondary minerals have re-evaluated the unexploited mineral wealth of the Black Hills. The harnessing of the Missouri River for power and irrigation, a serious search for oil, and the conservation of the State's greatest resource —its land—chart the way to new activity.

Since 1947 the South Dakota Natural Resources Commission has been in operation, primarily designed to coordinate research activities and to promote "home grown" industries.

Minerals: Much of the rock of the Black Hills holds hidden fortunes, and prospectors who roam the hills hunting for gold, silver, and precious stones occasionally find veins of rich ore. One "mother lode," the Homestake at Lead (*see LEAD*), has yielded more than 500 million dollars' worth of gold; new mines are springing up throughout the Hills and old ones are being reopened. Altogether, there were 68 Black Hills gold mines operating in 1949, which produced gold in the amount of 457,000 troy ounces, valued at $16,221,699. South Dakota followed by California and Utah, are the top three gold-producing States.

But the mineral resources of this mountain region are not confined to gold and silver. Twenty-nine different minerals are being mined in sufficient quantities to be classed as commercial production. The U.S. Bureau of Mines has established a research and testing laboratory at Rapid City to develop methods for mining and treating essential minerals for strategic and industrial uses. Uranium, or pitchblende, has been found in the Hills, but not in quantity. Deposits of lithium ore, which may be used as a concentrate in connection with the H-bomb, and commercially for such products as chipless enamel, air conditioning equipment, greases, alloys, and anti-histamine pills, has been under special investigation since 1942. A large producing mine is near Keystone (*see Tour 5*).

The Black Hills area is the nation's principal source of beryl. Beryllium has numerous applications in the atomic energy field, as a moderator and reflector of neutrons, and is used in X-ray tube windows, airplane sparkplugs, television, and numerous industrial combinations. Feldspar is mined and milled in the Keystone and Custer areas (*see Tour 5*), finding its way eventually into homes as the enamel on bathtubs, dishes, glassware, and tile. Mica, also conspicuous in the Hills, has gained new prominence in the electrical appliance and insulating fields.

Ranking second to gold in output is bentonite, a clay found on the flats surrounding the Hills. Pioneers who used to curse the "soap holes" into which their wagon wheels mired would be startled to know that this mud now brings in about two million dollars annually. It is used principally in filtering and decolorizing oils, revivifying molding sand in foundries and steel mills, and in oil-drilling operations.

The high yellow limestone cliff that rims the Black Hills, known as the Paha Sapa formation, is used in cement, as a filler in certain kinds of paper, for plaster, and even to clarify beet sugar juice. Manganese is also present in this formation, and is used for painting outdoor iron and other metal work. One of the strangest of minerals is bentonite, found in the Belle Fourche region. In its natural state it appears to be a bed of dried yellow clay; a foot underground it becomes wet, and still deeper it is like stiff butter. Just as it is found, it can be used as a soap that will wash off black sticky motor oil from one's hands; it has 96 commercial uses, including its employment in the manufacture of face powder and in the outside chocolate-coating of candy to prevent melting. Hidden in some small cavity in the heart of a chunk of beryl that has rested for millions of years locked in a dike of granite, there may be a glass-clear, deepwater green crystal—the emerald. Or perhaps a dirty grayish rock protruding from the ground may expose, when broken, a ledge of corundum, the second hardest mineral in the world; in this ledge may be also a transparent crystal of blood-red color—the ruby; or it may be, instead, a blue or straw-colored gem—a sapphire.

One of the largest reserves of crude manganese in the country is located in a 40-ft. bed of shale, topping a 60-mile stretch of bluffs along the Missouri River north of Chamberlain (*see Tour 5*). The Bureau of Mines, which set up a pilot mill there, estimates that there are over 100 million tons of low-grade manganese in this deposit.

In 1950 more than two million acres of land were under lease in the western part of the State for oil exploration. Oil-bearing structures were discovered, but no producing fields were found.

Forests: Although most of South Dakota is a plains region, there are three national forest areas. In the Black Hills are the Harney and Black Hills National Forests, covering 1,185,647 acres. Merchantable timber is estimated at nearly three billion board feet, equivalent to the lumber needed to house a half million people in six-room bungalows. Most of it is ponderosa pine. The annual increase produced by growth is about 40 million board feet; while the U.S. Forestry Service permits an average annual cut of timber of 27 million board feet.

The Custer National Forest is divided into four groups, all in Harding County—the Slim Buttes, Cave Hills, and the East and West Short Pines; no lumber operations are carried on in these reserves. To perpetuate the supply of timber in the Black Hills, stagnated stands of young trees are thinned and the defective, diseased, and weaker trees removed. After 35 years' growth, mature trees are cut to make room for a new growth. In addition to the stately ponderosa pine, there are lodgepole and limber pines, western white spruce, Rocky Mountain red cedar, ground juniper, aspen, cottonwood, balsam, poplar, birch, burr-oak, hackberry, ash, elm, willow, and ironwood.

Water: The importance of water to a plains State such as South Dakota can hardly be exaggerated. Water rights have formed the basis of much litigation in the Black Hills mining region; the fencing of water holes by homesteaders broke up the big West-river cattle empire; and as recently as 1941 the City of Mitchell obtained the right to all waters of Firesteel Creek to protect that city's water supply in man-made Lake Mitchell.

It may surprise even residents of South Dakota to realize how many water courses and lakes there are. For instance, 1,105 rivers and creeks can be listed, although many of them are in the embarrassing position of being without water during parts of each year. To augment the 257 natural lakes, dams have been constructed across hundreds of creeks and draws to form artificial lakes and ponds. As a result, South Dakota now has 1,185 new lakes ranging in size from a few acres to more than a thousand, plus some 10,000 nameless stock-water ponds. Nearly all of these new bodies of water have been formed since the 1930's under the water conservation programs conducted by various city, county, State and Federal agencies. A notable exception is the Belle Fourche Reservoir which dates back to 1906 and provides water to irrigate sugar beet fields (*see Tour 3*).

Utilization of the waters of the Missouri River, long talked about in the State, moved forward with the Flood Control Act of 1944, in which the U.S. Congress authorized a comprehensive program of development in the upper river basin which includes South Dakota (*see History*). The Missouri River passes through South Dakota for a distance of 547 miles, of which 417 miles will have bottom land flooded by four large reservoirs. More than 600,000 acres will be used for water storage behind the dams.

A project to irrigate 750,000 acres in the Huron area is also included in the Federal program (*see HURON and Tour 4*).

An artesian basin underlies the central portion of the State, and water for farm and city use comes from this source. Nearly every farm in this region has an artesian well, with force enough to pipe water without pumps.

FAUNA AND FLORA

Animal Life: The coyote is a native of South Dakota, and is the State university mascot and the State animal. At one time South Dakota was known as "the Coyote State." These animals are still quite numerous in western South Dakota, where it has been estimated by professional hunters that there is an average of one coyote to each square mile.

Until 75 years ago, great herds of buffalo roamed the plains and river breaks of South Dakota, but with the coming of white men they were slaughtered by the thousands and became nearly extinct. However, a herd of 350 buffalo is kept in Custer State Park, and the Wind Cave National Park game refuge has a herd.

Elk and deer are numerous in the Black Hills, both in and out of the game refuges. Beaver, porcupines, squirrels, racoons, and bobcats are also found in the Black Hills. Antelope, jackrabbits, and prairie dogs are plentiful in the West-river section; the State maintains an antelope preserve in Harding County (*see Tour 2A*). Badgers, weasels, skunks, muskrats, jackrabbits, and gophers are numerous in the eastern section of the State, especially along creeks and lakes.

Bird Life: Nearly 300 species of birds are found in South Dakota, this large number being due mainly to the State's varied regions, such as mountains, forests, and prairies. The Missouri River is an important route of the north-south migration of waterfowl; and each spring and fall flocks follow this watercourse. In addition to ducks and geese, flocks of pelicans and occasional swans nest in the Lake Region; while herons, cranes, cormorants, sea gulls, and snipe are common. A waterfowl peculiar to the Black Hills is the water ouzel, which dives into the mountain streams and feeds and swims against the current.

Chinese pheasants, prairie chickens, and Hungarian partridges are plentiful in the eastern section of the State; and toward evening the highly colored ring-necked pheasants are seen as they come out to feed near the road.

In the eastern section of the State the meadowlark, with its cheery song, is the best known of South Dakota birds. The robin, red-winged and yellow-headed blackbirds, flicker, goldfinch, swallow, kingfisher, humming-bird, and brown thrush are the most common birds in the East-river section; in the Black Hills there are catbirds, bluebirds, wood thrushes, rock wrens, warblers, crossbills, wood peewees, and woodpeckers. Of the larger birds, bald and golden eagles are frequently seen west of the Missouri River, especially in the Badlands; magpies are common to the Black Hills and buttes sections; turkey buzzards and prairie hawks are seen in the cattle country; and barn, screech, great horned, and burrowing owls are found throughout the State.

Wild Flowers: The State flower is the pasque, a purplish, fur-petaled prairie blossom that shows itself at Easter time on sunny hillsides. The pasque (also called crocus, mayflower, and anemone) is the first to bloom in the spring. Early in June, the pink wild rose and evening primrose blossom profusely in the fields. In the Lake Region are yellow and white lilies in the creeks; and pink beard-tongues, yellow and purple violets, buttercups, and blazing stars are found in grassy sheltered places. In the central part of the State, the wild orange geranium grows on the prairie, with an occasional black-eyed-susan, Mariposa lily, and prickly poppy. Native to the Missouri River "breaks" and westward is the soft wax-like gumbo lily, growing out of bare gumbo. In this region is the yucca plant, also called Spanish bayonet and soapweed, with its sharp spears and delicate white flowers blossoming on a tall spike. The cactus plant, common in western South Dakota, has waxy yellow flowers flecked with pink, which may brighten an entire hillside. In the Black Hills are scores of flower species, including the blue-flag or fleur-de-lis, yellow lady slipper, wood orchid, bluebell, larkspur, monkshood, woodland star, bog-violet, shooting star, baby's-breath, and forget-me-not. In autumn, the goldenrod and sunflower are common throughout the State.

Chokecherry, wild plum, gooseberry, and currant thickets are frequent in the eastern part of the State; and wild grapes, raspberries, and wild strawberries are found along creeks and lakes. Buffalo-berry bushes grow thickly in the "draws" of the western section.

There are also several noxious plants and weeds such as nettles, poison oak, and poison ivy; likewise barberry, creeping-Jennie, leafy spurge and dodder.

Indians and Indian Life

LARGE areas of South Dakota are still Indian country. There are 26,500 Sioux, or Dakota, Indians and 9 reservations (or agencies)— the Pine Ridge, Rosebud, Cheyenne, Standing Rock, Crow Creek, Lower Brule, Yankton, Sisseton, and Flandreau. In remote sections of the Pine Ridge and Rosebud Reservations live bands of Sioux who cling to old customs, language, and crafts; in more populated regions the assimilation with whites has resulted in a strange group of people, red-haired and light-skinned, their Indian features dominating their evident foreign heritage. Bands of Indians in various stages of culture may be seen on the reservations; archaeological remains of tribes who preceded the Sioux may be seen elsewhere in the State.

The U.S. Bureau of Indian Affairs maintains an area office at Aberdeen which supervises the reservations and agencies in the Dakotas and in Nebraska. An excellent Sioux Museum is operated by the Indian Bureau at Rapid City (*see RAPID CITY*).

Mound Builders: Traces of a primitive people, presumably part of the great race of mound builders that at one time inhabited the Ohio valley, are found in eastern South Dakota. How long they lived here or what became of them is not known. They vanished, leaving only their burial mounds as evidence of their presence. These earth mounds, some round and others almost square-sided, are filled with bones and implements of this early race. From the artifacts, it appears that the mound builders knew little of agriculture and were mainly a carnivorous people. Their first craftsmanship was displayed in the making of weapons, which were gradually improved from crude, rough stones, through the stages of stone hatchets and knives, to those made of hammered metal. Their pottery shows some measure of ornamentation, chiefly in linear form. In one instance, in the investigation of a mound in Hutchinson County, an attempt at color decoration was found, pottery burned to darker shades. Personal ornaments in the form of beads were made from shells and bones. In the Brandon mounds, near Sioux Falls, shell beads were found made from the columnella or conch shells. The outstanding characteristic of the mound builders was their veneration of the dead. In the few mounds opened in South Dakota by archaeologists, the burials had been made in groups. The bodies were placed in varying positions—some lying straight or with flexed limbs, others in sitting postures—and they were covered with clay and rock. Above them other burials were made, the bodies covered with another stratum of soil, making a huge mound, erected with all the toil involved in the use of the rudest implements—the shoulder blade of an animal to dig with and a small basket to transport the earth.

Skeletal remains and artifacts from the mounds are on display at the University of South Dakota Museum at Vermillion (*see Tour 8*), and in the Pettigrew Museum at Sioux Falls (*see SIOUX FALLS*).

The mounds of this vanished race are found in South Dakota principally along the Big Sioux River and Big Stone Lake. Sites have been located in the following counties: Roberts, Grant, Deuel, Brookings, Moody, Minnehaha, Marshall, Day, Codington, Kingsbury, McCook, Hutchinson, Clay, Yankton, Charles Mix, Brown, Spink, Jerauld, Davison, Lincoln and Faulk. More detailed descriptions of certain mound areas are given in other sections:

City of Sioux Falls, Sherman Park, a small group of mounds well-preserved and accessible to visitors. (See SIOUX FALLS.)
The Brandon group eight miles east of Sioux Falls between the Sioux and Split Rock Rivers, comprising 38 mounds. (See Tour 5.)
Hartford Beach on Big Stone Lake, a large group situated in a stand of natural timber. (See Tour 2.)

Arikaras: The second known inhabitants of what is now South Dakota were the Arikara, or Ree, Indians. Closely related to the Pawnee Indians of Nebraska, the Arikaras came up the Missouri River early in the seventeenth century. From Yankton northward they built large villages, planted gardens of beans, corn, squash, and tobacco, and hunted buffalo along the Missouri to supplement their vegetable diet. Increasing in numbers, they built other villages, always tending northward. The Arikaras occupied the river banks unmolested until 1750, then for 40 years they were engaged in war with the invading Teton Sioux who drove them up the Missouri and into virtual extinction. It was near Mobridge that the Lewis and Clark Expedition of 1804 found the pursued Arikaras, who were friendly and eager to trade.

The Arikara villages were made up of from 10 to 50 dirt lodges, circular, with rounded tops. The frame for the huts was made of poles set in the ground, around which sod was banked. At the height of a man's head the poles were bowed toward the center. Covered with skins, dry grass, and dirt the dwelling was warm in winter and cool in summer. A hole left in the side formed the door, with a buffalo hide to cover it, and niches around the interior of the walls, with robes hung in front, formed the sleeping cubicles. The size of the lodges varied, some accommodating as many as three familes. Beside each dwelling were refuse heaps with pieces of pottery, arrowheads, and scrapers which have since been helpful in studying Arikara culture. In the center of the village would be a large council lodge. The villages, usually facing the river, were protected by trenches on the other three sides. Village sites are identified along the Missouri River by the circles made by the lodge walls and the rubbish heaps.

Remains of an Arikara village are visible at Lake Mitchell (*see MITCHELL*) where one of the lodges was reconstructed in 1939. Pieces of broken pottery, garden tools, and animal bones may be found in the area. In 1950 several sites along the Missouri River were excavated to precede flooding by the reservoirs formed by the Fort Randall and Oahe dams. The expeditions, under the direction of the Smithsonian Institution and the University of South Dakota, removed the artifacts for preservation and study.

Some of the major sites, in addition to Lake Mitchell, are:

Crow Creek site, east side of Missouri River where creek enters. Traces of deep trench with redoubts may be seen. (See Tour 4-A.)

De Grey site, 18 miles east of Pierre, State 34, one-half mile west of De Grey on Grandle and Bowman farms. Series of sites may be seen by careful examination.

Fort Pierre site, high terrace nine miles north of Fort Pierre just outside buffalo pasture. Bluff gradually being washed away into Missouri. (See Tour 4.)

Fort Sully site, across dry creek from abandoned Fort Sully, 23 miles northwest of Pierre. Circles and rubbish heaps visible. (See Tour 4.)

Lewis and Clark site, west bank of Missouri and on both sides of Elk Creek. Located six miles east of Wakpala. (See Tour 2.)

Mobridge site, east side Missouri near Milwaukee Railroad bridge, one and a half miles north of Mobridge. This is a Mandan Indian village site. (See Tour 2.)

Mitchell site, on south shore of Lake Mitchell, with rings visible and mounds to west. (See MITCHELL.)

Excellent collections of Arikara pottery are housed in the University of South Dakota Museum, Vermillion (*see TOUR 8*), and the State Historical Museum (*see PIERRE*).

The Sioux: The Sioux, or Dakota, Indians, who had resided in Wisconsin and Minnesota, were forced out on to the prairies by the more numerous Ojibways when the latter were given firearms by the French. The Sioux were a nomadic people, following their food supply, principally buffalo, and ranging westward to the Missouri River. Here they found the Arikaras and promptly attacked them. The Sioux were a virile race, splendid specimens physically. They were unusually mobile with their herds of ponies, and accurate marksmen with bow and arrow.

Taking the country for themselves, Sioux bands spread from the lake region of what is now northeastern South Dakota, south to Yankton and westward to the Black Hills. Then the Sioux began encountering occasional white men—trappers and fur traders. In 1775 Pierre Dorion, a fur trader, married an Indian woman and made his home in the Sioux country near the present site of Yankton. Explorers and missionaries followed and found hospitable entertainment. Trading posts were established and, with the coming of the steamboat, trade multiplied between the Indians and whites; white blood was fused with that of the Indian, and the Indians adopted the white man's dress.

During the War of 1812, the Sioux, friendly with the British through long association with the English fur companies on the upper Missouri, joined forces against the Americans. With the treaty of Ghent, signed Dec. 24, 1814, the Indian tribes were left to make their own terms with the United States. Governor William Clark, who had met the Sioux during the Lewis and Clark expedition in 1804–06, called a great council of Indians from the Upper Missouri and Mississippi at the confluence of the two rivers, July 19, 1815. All the Sioux tribes came in full regalia. Separate treaties were made with the Sioux of the Lakes, one having been handed down through the family of Walking Buffalo. The document, yellowed with age and worn with much folding, is still in the possession of South Dakota Indians. The thumbprints of the several Indian chiefs were in blood. The treaty reads as follows:

A Treaty of Peace and Friendship made and concluded between William Clark, Vivian Edwards and Auguste Chouteau, Commissioners Plenipotentiary of the United States of America, on the part and behalf of the said States of the one part; and the undersigned Chiefs and Warriors of the Sioux of the Lakes on the part and behalf of their Tribe, of the other part.

The parties being desirous of reestablishing Peace and Friendship between the United States and the said Tribe; and of being placed in all things and in every respect on the same footing upon which they stood before the late war between the United States and Great Britain, have agreed to the following Articles.

Art. Ist   Every injury or act of hostility committed by one of either of the contracting parties against the other, shall be mutually forgiven and forgot.

Art. IInd   There shall be perpetual Peace and Friendship between all the citizens of the United States of America, and all the individuals composing the said Tribe of the Lakes, and all the friendly relations that existed between them before the war shall be and the same are hereby renewed.

Art. IIrd The undersigned Chiefs and Warriors for themselves and their said
        Tribe, do hereby acknowledge themselves and their aforesaid Tribe to
        be under the protection of the United States, and of no other nation,
        power or sovereign whatsoever.

        In witness whereof the said William Clark, Vivian Edwards, and
        Auguste Chouteau, Commissioners aforesaid, and the Chiefs and Warriors
        of the aforesaid Tribes have hereunto subscribed their names and affixed
        their seals this nineteenth day of July in the year of our Lord one thousand
        eight hundred and fifteen and of the Independence of the United States
        the Fortieth.

        Done at Portage des Sioux   Wm. Clark (Seal)
        in the presence of
            R. Wash, Sec'y to the Commission   Vivian Edwards (Seal)
John Miller   (Louis Decouagne Auguste Chouteau
Col. 3rd Inft.   (Louis Dorian
A. Paul C. I. of the C.   (John A. Cameron
Edw. Hall Lt. late   (Jacques Mette
28th Inft.   (John Hay
J. B. Clark   (Ta-tan-ga-manie
Adjt. 3rc Inft.   (The Walking Buffalo X (Seal)
Manuel Lisa, Agt.   (Hai-san-nee—The Horn X (Seal)
Thomas Forsyth, I. Agt.   (A-am-pa-ha—The Speaker X (Seal)
Jno. W. Johnson, U. S. L. & I. Agent   (Na-ree-sa-ga-ta
Marin Blondeaux, land. Agt.   (Hai-bo-haa
                                           (The Branching Horn X (Seal)

In 1862 the bands in Minnesota had a desperate war with the
whites. Scouts and soldiers forced the Indians back across the
Minnesota border, broke up their villages, and herded them into
encampments near forts. The names of these old army posts cling
to spots along the Missouri River, where all signs of established
life have vanished and grass grows again on upland prairie benches.
Among the forts were: Fort Randall, Fort Lookout, Fort Thompson, Fort George, Fort Pierre, Fort Sully and Fort Bennett. The
only permanent one, Fort Sisseton, has been restored. (*See Tour
1A.*)

Some of the most dramatic events in western Indian warfare
occurred after the treaty of 1867, in which the Sioux agreed to retire
to reservations before 1876. Reservations were established in 1868,
and the Sioux were moved into these confines at the same time that
homesteaders were moving into the open land of Dakota Territory
after the Civil War. The discovery of gold in the Black Hills led to
a rush of prospectors and settlers, protected by the U.S. Army, thus
violating the treaty. The Sioux, in defence of their rights, were led
in an uprising by a talented strategist—Red Cloud, chief of the
Oglala Sioux. In a series of swift campaigns he forced the U.S. Army
to abandon its forts and roads north of the treaty line, and to close
the Bozeman Trail. This is almost the only occasion in American
history where an Indian leader, fighting U.S. regular soldiers on
equal terms, defeated them and procured his own demands. Red
Cloud retired to a reservation in South Dakota to live peacefully.

His brilliant achievement was preliminary to the encounter on the Little Big Horn where Gen. George A. Custer's foolhardy advance led to the "massacre" in 1876. Twelve years later, land allotments were made each individual Indian and attempts were made to establish them on farms. Then in 1890 the Messiah War broke out, climaxed by the last warfare between the Indians and whites at Wounded Knee when about two hundred Indians were killed by soldiers.

After the homesteaders' invasion, other stockmen and farmers came into the reservation, buying and leasing land. In 1934 considerable reservation land was designated as sub-marginal, repurchased by the Government from bankrupt whites, and turned back to the Indians.

Tribal Organizations: Thirteen recognized tribes of the Sioux Nation now live within the borders of this State. Each tribe claimed descent from a common family whose exploits were exalted in legend and song; each tribe was held together by a set of tribal fetishes and common taboos. These tribal divisions still remain. If Pete High Elk from one tribe marries into another division and makes his home on his wife's land amongst her tribe, he will be spoken of as an outsider after years of residence there.

When Indian reservations were established in 1870, the groupings closely followed recognized tribal divisions of the Sioux Nation. Today these tribes are living in largest numbers in the following localities.

1. Mdewakanton—(Mday-wah-kan-ton) "Mystery Lake village" located at Flandreau.
2. Wahpekute—(Wah-pay-koo-tay) "Shooters among the leaves (of deciduous trees)." Combined with Mdewakanton.
3. Wahpeton—(Wah-pay-ton) "Village among the leaves (of deciduous trees)." Sisseton Reservation.
4. Sisiton—(See-see-ton) "Marsh village." Sisseton reservation.
5. Yankton—(Ee-angk-ton) "End village." This tribe is closely related to the Yanktonais tribe. Yankton Reservation.
6. Yanktonais—(Ee-angk-ton-aye) "Little-end village." Upper Yanktonai—Standing Rock Reservation. Lower Yanktonai—(Hunkpatina Crow Creak Reservation.
   Teton—(Tee-ton) "Dwellers on the prairie." The largest division of the Sioux. There were seven divisions of this tribe.
7. Sicangu—(Si-chang-hu) "Burned thighs." Also called Brule. Rosebud Reservation. Lower Brule Reservation.
8. Itazipco—(Ee-tah-zip-cho) "Without a bow." Also called Sansarc. Cheyenne Reservation.
9. Sihasapa—(See-hah-sah-pah) "Black feet." Cheyenne River and Standing Rock Reservation. (Not to be confused with tribe in Montana which is not of Siouan stock.)
10. Miniconjou—(Miniikanyedan wojupi) (Mnee-ko-jou) "Those who plant beside the stream."
11. Oohenonpa—(O-o-hay-non-pah) "Two boilings," called "Two Kettles," Cheyenne Reservation.

1ᵃ. Oglala—(O-glah-la) "To scatter one's own." Pine Ridge Reservation.
1ᵇ. Hunkpapa—(Hung-kpah-pah) "End of the circle." Standing Rock Reservation.

Within each tribe were numerous bands; these were firmly knit family groups who lived together in winter villages and had economic and social independence. Each band was led by a headman and the name of this leader became the name of the band. When the Indian social structure came to grips with military rule in the Dakota Territory in the 1860's, the headman's name was translated into English. This became the final name of the band as marked down in the Government records. There is the Drifting Goose Band in the Yanktonais tribe and the Red Cloud Band of the Oglalas, named for the chief who led the war in 1866. He-Dog on the Rosebud Reservation and the Iron Nation Post Office on Lower Brule Reservation mark the spots where these headmen camped with their kinfolk about them. The names of the bands may be found in the current conversation of the people, and traceable, too, are the personal traits and the family characteristics of a band.

Chiefs: Those who come to find chiefs on the reservations of South Dakota will find them as numerous as colonels in Kentucky. In olden days the wisest headmen formed the chief tribal council and these were called "chiefs." None of them was given arbitrary power in the council, where the vote of the majority ruled. Rather these chiefs were fathers to their bands; their duties were to study the welfare of their people, to counsel wisely after deliberation, and to set examples of bravery and generosity. But for years the "chiefs" have been named by the white men for either economic or sentimental reasons. When the white trader or soldier came into Indian country he picked out the leader most amenable to his interests and by favors and gifts marked him out and called him "Chief." At fairs and shows and during visits to Washington, the "chiefs" come into their own. At home they are "on a par" with the rest and are called "Tom," "Charlie" or "Joe."

Family Life: During the past century the old pattern of home life disintegrated, with only a few customs remaining. A hundred years ago the men's work was to protect the home, provide materials for food and clothing, make bows, arrows, and household implements, and supervise political activities. The first two occupations, war and the hunt, kept the young men busy; the others, craftwork and the holding of councils, were left to the elders.

Three generations formed the family unit and each generation had its appointed and accepted tasks. The women's work was the preparation and care of the food, including the drying of meat, wild fruits, vegetables, rice and herbs; gardening, which meant raising squaw corn and drying it; storing and transporting all the food; making clothes and tepees from the hides of buffalo by dressing the skins and decorating them. The care of the young children and the instruction and protection of the young girls fell to grandmothers. Children gathered wood and carried water; the boys hunted small game, the girls sewed on hides and learned to decorate them with porcupine quills and beads. For the children there was always understanding sympathy, affection, and respect.

When wars, hunting, and fur trading passed, the Indians moved into log cabins and small frame houses. The men took up meager farming and stock raising, without enthusiasm for work that kept them alone in the fields all day. During this period, payments under treaties and from sale of lands, together with regular money from land rents, came to the Indians in large sums of fairly even distribution. It was money from these sources and rations of food from the Government which supported family life for fifty years. For this half century the cost of children to the family group was practically nothing, because the children were at Government or mission boarding schools where everything was provided without direct payment by the parents.

When payments became rare and leasing dropped off, when drought and mismanagement made it difficult to raise a crop, the standard of simple living adopted in 1870–80 began to go down.

Shortly after the close of World War I, the Indians of South Dakota entered a pitiable struggle for existence. They bartered their heirlooms, their beautifully beaded-and-quilled robes, their rare head dresses. Families moved out of the houses as they fell into disrepair, and into second-hand Army tents. They sold their household goods and, in great poverty, their prized rifles. The women picked wild fruit; the men fished. The only jobs on the reservations would be a few weeks on road crews, and a few glorious days helping white ranchers at roundup time.

Their land, which is semi-arid even in lush years, was hard hit during the drought years. What few cattle remained were slaughtered and butchered on the spot, reminiscent of buffalo-hunting days. Government work projects revived their spirits; and when large groups gathered, the old dances and community living returned.

On Rosebud Reservation, a repayment cattle program has put many families back into ranching. Cattle are issued to young men on the promise that, as the herd is increased, part of the increase will be returned, until full repayment is made in cattle. These, in turn, are issued to some other deserving young men. From 1935 to 1948, the number of cattle owned by Indians on the reservation increased from 3,144 to 17,338.

World War II found Indians being lured off the reservations as cheap labor. They joined construction crews at Army installations, worked in sawmills, and as waitresses. More than two thousand moved to Rapid City, setting up their tents along the river. At war's end, instead of returning to the reservations, they were in demand as skilled and semi-skilled workers.

The Sioux, who have retained their horsemanship and their tribal dances, have also found themselves in demand, as entertainers. The Oglalas of the Pine Ridge Reservation not only appear at rodeos and pageants in the Black Hills each summer, but are transported to various settings for motion picture productions.

Another new source of income has come to the families on the Cheyenne River Reservation. In 1950, about 25,000 acres of tribal and allotted lands held by Indian families were leased for oil exploration.

Arts and Crafts: Through the years of transition the Sioux satisfied his need for adornment by decorating all kinds of useful objects. The preparation of materials for art work as well as the execution of each piece took days of work; creative art filled the leisure hours. The Indian's sense of limitless time and his devotion to a task until it was completed made him undertake large pieces of fine design and patiently work out every technique needed to produce a thing of beauty. He excelled in geometrical design made interesting by a combination of bright colors. His pictorial representations of events are sparing in the use of line; in pictorial art the Sioux does not excel but he has left interesting records of his way of living pictured on tepees and saddle blankets.

Early decorations were made on hide with porcupine quills, colored with native dyes. Symbols were worked on tepees, clothing, saddle blankets, baby cases, and tobacco bags.

Examples of this earliest art can be seen in the Pettigrew Museum in Sioux Falls, in the State Historical Museum in Pierre, in the Sioux Museum in Rapid City, and in collections on display at the various Indian agencies and schools. Outstanding exhibits include a buffalo hide tipi, in the Pettigrew Museum; a "bull boat" made of hide, in the State Historical Museum; and a "winter count" hide, graphically recording tribal history back to 1796, in the Sioux Museum.

When the fur trader came bringing beads, the medium of decoration changed. Beads in place of porcupine quills were used in later designs and pictures. Beaded moccasins are made on every Sioux reservation today and worn by many members of the tribe. This skill is being passed on to the younger generation; but a knowledge of the technique of quill work is dying because quills were flattened between the teeth of the workers and eventually the teeth were worn down. The younger Indians will not subject their teeth to this punishment.

SIOUX SYMBOLS

HOGAN HUHU
FISHBONES

PTE HE KARYA
BUFFALO *FEMALE* SKULL
'LIFE'

WAPA HASAPA
BLACK *WAR* BONNET
'AUTHORITY'

TATANKA OYE
BUFFALO TRACK–SIGN OF PLENTY
'FEASTING'

MARPIYA WAKANKDI
HEAVENLY MANIFESTATION
'MYSTERY'

MATO OYE
BEAR TRACKS

TAHOHMUN–OHMUN
FAINT TRACK IN NEW SNOW
'SUBTLETY'

EYAYA–THEY ARE GONE
'BROKEN ENCAMPMENT'

WA
SNOWFLAKE

ZITKA OYE
BIRD TRACKS

T'ATE WICOTI
CAMP OF HOSTILE BUFFALO
HUNTERS

KIMIMI
BUTTERFLY
'JOY'

The younger people are, however, learning from the old men the art of carving. Pipe stems, ceremonial bowls, and bows and arrows were rudely carved before knives came to the Indians. With a good knife in his hand the Indian man grew skillful, and worked long hours decorating pipestone and wood. This craft has brought money to the Indians in recent years and is being worked at steadily by a number of present-day craftsmen.

Craft work is opening up in several reservation centers; Indian dolls, beaded belts, souvenirs, and excellent reproductions of old pieces are being made. The Indian people draw, paint, carve, and bead for fun—arts and crafts are a great resource in their leisure time and an economic asset, as well as an expression of their appreciation of beauty.

Legends and Songs: Legends and songs of the Sioux were repeated through so many generations that all the people came to know them well. As soon as white men came among the Indians they devised a phonetic writing of the Dakota language and wrote down legends and songs. Because of their meter and rhythm the songs have been easier to preserve in the original form than the legends The story-teller varies the wording with each retelling.

WANAGI WACIPI OLOWAN	SONG OF THE SPIRIT-DANCE
Ina, hekuye,	(Mother)
Ina, hekuye,	Mother, oh come back,
Misunkala Seya-ya omani	Mother, oh come back,
Misunkala Seya-ya omani	Little brother calls as he
Ina, hekuye,	seeks thee, weeping.
Ina, hekuye.	Mother, oh come back,
	Mother, oh come back.

Reservations: To see Sioux Indian life, one may visit the various reservations on the following tours:

Sisseton Reservation ....Tours Nos. 1 and 10
Standing Rock Reservation ....Tour No. 2
Cheyenne Reservation ....Tour No. 3
Crow Creek Reservation ....Tour No. 4A
Lower Brule Reservation ....Tour No. 4A
Pine Ridge Reservation ....Tour No. 7
Rosebud Reservation ....Tour No. 7
Yankton Reservation ....Tour No. 8
Flandreau Reservation ....Tour No. 9

History

THE State of South Dakota derived its name from Dakota Territory, which in turn was named for the Dakota Indians, who were the inhabitants of this region when the first white explorers came. Dakota means "allied" or "many in one." From a loose confederation of Indian tribes came the connotation of an "alliance of brothers." The name of the Indian nation became that of the new Territory; and when the Territory was divided in 1889, the resulting States were called North and South Dakota respectively.

Although South Dakota belongs to that group of States more recently admitted to the Union, it has a history reaching back to Colonial days. Thirty-three years before the declaration of Independence was signed, white men stood on the banks of the Missouri within the present confines of this State and left indisputable evidence of their presence.

Although never glimpsed by white men, the first known inhabitants of South Dakota have been identified as the so-called Mound Builders, who occupied roughly the eastern third of the present State. Of the tribes with which the white men came in contact, the first were the Arikara or Ree Indians, who lived in villages along the Missouri River. The Sioux, driven from the upper Mississippi valley by the Ojibways, in turn drove the Rees from the present State by keeping the buffalo at a distance from the river and by harrassing the river villages until, about the year 1800, the Rees finally left the region and retreated up-river into what is now North Dakota.

Early Exploration: There is some question as to who was the first white man to enter the boundaries of the present State. It is fairly well established that the Spanish explorer, Coronado, came as far north as the River Platte in 1540, but there is no evidence that he visited what is now South Dakota. Le Sueur, the French trapper and trader, wintered near the site of Mankato, Minn., in

1699; and he afterward furnished material for a geography of the upper Mississippi, including what is now eastern South Dakota. But there is no direct proof that he entered the present State.

The first indisputable visit of white men to this region was that of the Verendrye brothers in 1743. On March 30, of that year they climbed a "gumbo" hill above the present site of Fort Pierre, and took possession of the country in the name of the King of France; and in proof of this, they buried an inscribed lead plate and raised a cairn of stones over it. This plate lay undiscovered for 170 years (*see Tour 4*).

In 1775 Pierre Dorion, who afterward guided the Lewis and Clark Expedition, settled among the Yankton Sioux on the lower James River and married one of their women. He thus became the first white resident of the State. In 1794 a school teacher, Jean Baptiste Trudeau, came up from St. Louis with 10 men to engage in trade on the upper Missouri River, and he built the "Pawnee House" under the chalk cliffs in what is now Charles Mix County (*see Tour 7*). This was the first house erected in the State. That same year Jacques d'Eglise pushed up the river as far as the Ree villages at the mouth of Grand River; and in 1796 Registre Loisel built a fortified trading post on Cedar Island, just above Big Bend in present Hughes County.

On March 9–10, 1804, at St. Louis, the Louisiana Purchase was formally transferred to the American Government. On the afternoon of May 14, the Lewis and Clark Expedition set out up the Missouri River. The purpose of this expedition, sent out by the Federal Government, was to discover the shortest feasible water route to the Pacific Coast, to gauge the trade possibilities of the region through which they passed, and to make treaties of friendship with the various Indian tribes. On August 22, at Elk Point, the expedition made its first encampment in what is now South Dakota. On August 27, it arrived at the mouth of the James River. Learning that there was a large Indian encampment near by, the leaders invited the Indians to a feast and a council. This lasted several days, in the course of which Lewis took a new-born Indian babe, wrapped him in an American flag, and prophesied that he would become a distinguished leader and a great friend to the Americans. Both these prophecies were fulfilled, for this was Struck-by-the-Ree, who was afterward instrumental in saving the white settlement at Yankton.

On September 8, the party reached the "Pawnee House," and on the 22nd the Loisel Post on Cedar Island. On September 24, it arrived at the mouth of the Bad River, where some trouble developed with a band of Teton Sioux under Black Buffalo. At the mouth of the Cheyenne the expedition encountered a French trader who said he had spent the previous winter up the Cheyenne River, near the Black Hills. On October 8, the party reached the Ree villages at the mouth of Grand River, where it was entertained for several days. From that point it passed out of present South Dakota.

Two years later, almost to the day, the expedition crossed the present South Dakota line on its return trip from the Coast. It again visited the Rees on Grand River, but passed by the Teton Sioux at the present site of Fort Pierre. After stopping briefly with the Yankton Sioux, the party set off for St. Louis, arriving there in September. The guides for the trip had been Charbonneau and his wife, Sacajawea (*see Tour 2*).

On the return trip, Lewis and Clark had persuaded Big White, a Mandan chief, to accompany them, and later they took him to Washington. They had agreed to give him safe conduct back to his own country; so in the spring of 1807 he was assigned a place with a party of traders (under Pierre Chouteau) and soldiers bound for the upper Missouri. All went well until they reached the Ree village at the mouth of Grand River. Here the Indians suddenly turned hostile; there was fighting and three soldiers were killed. This was the first armed conflict between soldiers and Indians on what is now South Dakota soil. The expedition was abandoned, and the party returned to St. Louis.

The Fur Trade: In the spring of 1811, Walter Price Hunt, leader of the so-called Astorians and an agent of John Jacob Astor, the leading fur merchant of the day, set out with a party up the Missouri on his way overland to establish a trading post at the mouth of the Columbia River. About the same time, Manuel Lisa, fearing Hunt's rivalry in the fur trade, left St. Louis in pursuit. Lisa, born in New Orleans of Spanish parentage, was one of the leading fur traders of St. Louis. He had done much work in cultivating the goodwill of the Missouri River Indians, and he did not like the idea of an outside trader or company reaping the fruits of his labor. In the vicinity of Springfield, Hunt was overtaken by a messenger from Lisa, who proposed that he wait for him so that they might travel together for mutual protection. Hunt replied that he would, but he had no intention of doing so and pushed on with all speed. He met Black Buffalo and his Sioux, but on convincing them that he did not seek trade on the Missouri he was allowed to proceed. Just above Big Bend, Manuel Lisa overtook Hunt, and for a while there were strained relations. However, when they arrived at the Ree villages and each saw that the other was not interfering with his purposes, they came to a friendly agreement.

They stayed at the Ree village many days. Hunt bought horses of the Indians, who promptly raided the herds of neighboring tribes wher they ran short of animals with which to supply his needs. Lisa traded out his goods and returned south. Hunt set out straight west up Grand River and on the way traversed the present upper tier of counties—the first white man to pass through this part of the present State.

At the outbreak of the War of 1812, Capt. William Clark, formerly of the Lewis and Clark Expedition and now superintendent of Indian Affairs for Louisiana Territory, raised $11,000 on his own responsibility and sent Manuel Lisa up the Missouri with a large outfit of goods to trade with the Sioux and keep them friendly to the American Government. Clark appointed Lisa a sub-agent for the Sioux of the Missouri valley. Lisa first built Fort Manuel (1812)— near the present North Dakota line; and when the Indians destroyed this fort, he moved south and built another at Big Bend. Through cunning strategy he caused the defection of the Mississippi Sioux from the British cause, kept the Dakota Sioux friendly, and contributed in no small measure to the final outcome of the war and the retention of American sovereignty in the West.

After a temporary set-back on account of the War of 1812, the fur trade revived; and in 1823 Gen. William Ashley, Lieutenant Governor of Missouri Territory, organized a trading party and set out up the Missouri River. He reached the Ree village at the mouth of Grand River in safety, and traded with the inhabitants for several days. But the night before he and his party were to leave over the Grand River route, they were treacherously attacked by the Rees, a number of them were killed, and the rest were forced to retreat down the river. The Rees were later punished by a detachment of the United States Army under Col. Henry Leavenworth, commanding officer of the district, and they left the State,

OLD FORT PIERRE

retreating up-river into what is now North Dakota (*see Tour 2*).

In 1817 a French-Indian trader named Joseph La Framboise established a trading post at the junction of Bad River with the Missouri. This became the first permanent white settlement within the present border of the State. In 1822 it was rebuilt as Fort Tecumseh; and in 1832 it was again rebuilt and named Fort Pierre Choteau, which was afterward shortened to the present Fort Pierre.

In 1831 the first steamboat on the upper Missouri, the *Yellowstone,* ascended the river to Fort Pierre, and a new era dawned in the fur trade. A journey that formerly required a whole season could now be accomplished in a few weeks. The following year Pierre Choteau took a steamboat up to the mouth of the Yellowstone. The revived impetus which this gave to the fur trade lasted till the Civil War. By that time the buffalo herds were becoming smaller, and the supply of other furs had greatly lessened. The Civil War, with its disruption of trade and its frontier Indian troubles, practically ended the fur trade in this region.

First Agricultural Settlement: Up to this time trade and settlement had been confined to the Missouri River and had been related to the traffic in furs. But in 1857 it became apparent that Minnesota would be admitted as a State without the eastern portion of future South Dakota, which it then included as a Territory. Therefore far-seeing men in Minnesota Territory and Iowa formed land companies with the idea of getting control of desirable sites for settlement, which might be sold at advanced prices when the influx of settlers began. The Dakotah Land Company was formed by Gov. Medary of Minnesota Territory, and a party was sent to establish a settlement at the site of Sioux Falls. But when the settlers arrived, they found the falls themselves in the possession of the Western Town Company of Dubuque, Iowa. However, the newcomers appropriated for themselves the power available above the falls, and the two groups cooperated in perfect harmony. Settlements were also made at other nearby points including Flandreau and Medary. By the organization of the Territory of Nebraska, May 30, 1854, and the State of Minnesota, May 11, 1858, a great tract of country lying to the north and west was left without legal name or existence. So the settlers on the eastern fringe of what is now South Dakota, in their eagerness to obtain government and recognition, resorted to political strategy of a most unusual character. In order to set up a Territorial government and to give an impression of substantial numbers, the 30 or 40 inhabitants of Sioux Falls split up into groups of three or four and set out in different directions; and whenever they stopped to rest their teams, they set up election precincts, appointed one another judges and clerks of election, and proceeded to vote for themselves, their relatives, and even their distant friends. The total vote was quite respectable in volume, if not in quality. Shortly after this, the "rump" Legislature thus chosen convened and elected a Governor and one or two State officers, including a Delegate to Congress. That body, however, refused to recognize him. In 1859 the settlers again held an election, choosing a new Legislature and a Governor and Delegate. But again Congress failed to set up a Territory.

By the treaty of Traverse des Sioux in 1851, the Indians ceded to the United States all lands east of the Big Sioux River in present South Dakota. On July 10, 1859, the Indians tacitly accepted a treaty by which the land between the Big Sioux and Missouri Rivers was opened for settlement. Having previously refused to vacate this territory they were told by the tactful new Indian agent that a feast was being prepared for them in their new home. Yankton Reservation, which had been set aside for them farther west. Thereupon they followed along the river bank, while the agent's steamer forged upstream. A great crowd had been waiting on the Nebraska side of the river; and as soon as the Indians had left for the reservation, the settlers poured across. They took up farms and established the townsites of Bon Homme, Yankton, and Vermillion. This region thus became the first permanent agricultural settlement of the State.

The people of Bon Homme erected the first schoolhouse within the State in 1860. It was built of logs and had a dirt floor. Ten pupils attended during a school term of three months. South Dakota's first church, of the Presbyterian denomination, was established at Vermillion in 1860.

Territorial Days: There are two quite remarkable points about South Dakota's history. The first is the very small population it had when it became a Territory, and the second is the large population it acquired before it became a State. One of the last official acts of President Buchanan was to sign the bill creating Dakota Territory, which consisted of the present States of North and South Dakota and those portions of Montana and Wyoming lying east of the ridge of the Rocky Mountains. The act was signed on March 2, 1861. At this time there were only 2,402 white inhabitants of this vast region. One of the first official acts of President Lincoln was to appoint his family physician, Dr. William Jayne of Springfield, as the first Territorial Governor. The latter selected Yankton as the temporary capital, and called an election for the choice of a Legislature and a Delegate to Congress. The *Weekly Dakotan,* which still survives as the *Press and Dakotan,* was established June 6, 1861. Pursuant to the proclamation, the first Legislature, nick-named "The Pony Congress" on account of its small size in comparison

Pioneer Trails

GORDON STOCKADE

A Treaty of Peace and friendship made and concluded between
William Clark, Ninian Edwards and Auguste Choteau, Commissioners
Plenipotentiary of the United States of America on the part and behalf of
the said States of the one part, and the undersigned Chiefs and Warriors
of the Sioux of the Lakes on the part and behalf of their tribe of the
other part.

The parties being desirous of re-establishing Peace and friendship
between the United States and the said Tribe and of being placed in all
things and in every respect on the same footing upon which they stood
before the late war between the United States and Great Britain have
agreed to the following Articles.

contracting parties against the other shall be mutually forgiven and

Art. II. There shall be perpetual Peace and friendship between all the citizens
of the United States of America and all the individuals composing
the said Tribe of the Lakes and all the friendly relations that existed between
them before the war shall be and the same are hereby renewed.

Art. III. The undersigned Chiefs and warriors for themselves and their said
Tribe, do hereby acknowledge themselves and their aforesaid Tribe to
be under the protection of the United States and of no other nation,
power or sovereign whatsoever.

In witness whereof the said William Clark, Ninian
Edwards and Auguste Choteau Commissioners aforesaid and the
Chiefs and Warriors of the aforesaid Tribe have hereunto subscribed
their names and affixed their seals this nineteenth day of July in
the year of our Lord one thousand eight hundred and fifteen and of
the Independence of the United States the Fortieth.

Done at Portage des Sioux

Wm Clark
Ninian Edwards
Aug. Choteau

R. Wash, Secretary to Commission

John Miller
Col. 3 Infty

Lewis Decoigne
Louis Drivon
a Cummins

Jacques Mette
Sam Kay

B. Paul C. S. of the C. S.

Camp Hale Pto Lte
33th Infty

WO Clark
Infty 3 Ky

Manuel Livenguest

Thomas Forsyth I. Agt
Jno W Johnson US Ind. Agent
Maurice Blondeau Interpreter

Ta tan ga mane The walking Buffalo X
Hae san mee The Horn X
A om pa he The Speaker X
Na ni ton ja ter The Hard Stone X
Hae la haa The standing horns X

INDIAN BLOOD TREATY

CUSTER WAGON TRAIN, 1874

BUFFALO

23462 Tallyho Coaching at the Great Hot Springs of Dak.
Photo and copyright by Grabill, 1889.

THE STAGE

SIOUX SUN DANCE

SITTING BULL'S
NEPHEW AT HOME

INDIAN CHAPEL,
WOUNDED KNEE
BATTLEGROUND

with the National Congress, convened on St. Patrick's Day, 1862, with nine members of the council and thirteen of the house. After a strenuous contest, Yankton was chosen permanent capital of the Territory. The Legislature was in session two months.

South Dakota took little active part in the Civil War. Although a company of militia was raised by the State and tendered to the President, it was deemed advisable to keep the unit in South Dakota for use in possible Indian hostilities. In 1862 occurred the War of the Outbreak, when the Santee Sioux in Minnesota rose and massacred the whites. Though most of the fighting took place outside the State, two men were killed in a hayfield near Sioux Falls, and Gov. Jayne immediately sent soldiers to remove the inhabitants of that place to safety at Yankton. The Indians pillaged and burned the deserted settlement, and it was several years before any further attempt at settlement was made, although Fort Dakota was built there in 1865. In the same year a great council with the Indians held at old Fort Sully officially ended the War of the Outbreak.

This was no sooner settled than the Red Cloud War began. The Government had determined to open a new road to the gold fields recently discovered in Montana. It proposed to survey a road from Fort Snelling west, and from the California Trail north from Laramie through the Powder River valley. Red Cloud, chief of the Oglala Sioux, saw that this would mean the ruin of the last buffalo ranges left to his people, and he therefore resisted the survey. As he was debating the proposal with white leaders, Red Cloud saw a company of soldiers approaching. "What are these men for?" he asked. He was told that they were troops sent to guard the proposed road. Red Cloud held aloft the rifle that was in his hand and said "In this and in the Great Spirit I put my trust!" Whereupon he and his followers immediately withdrew from the council.

Notwithstanding, the survey was undertaken with the protection of the military. A company of 80 of these was ambushed by Red Cloud and massacred. A council was thereupon held to which Red Cloud sent representatives. He demanded the abandonment of the forts which had been established in the Powder River country. Although this was agreed to, Red Cloud refused to come in and sign the treaty until the abandonment had actually been carried out. According to the terms of the treaty, all the land between the Big Horn Mountains on the west, the Platte River on the south, and the Missouri River on the east and north was to be reserved to the Indians as a permanent hunting ground. No white man was to be allowed in that region except on business connected with the Indians. Furthermore, this treaty could not be altered without the consent of three-fourths of the Indian braves affected.

In 1865 occurred the first of several serious grasshopper infestations, commonly referred to as "plagues." They have been a sporadic menace to agriculture ever since that time, a particularly severe visitation occurring in 1877.

The first railroad entered the State in 1871, a short stub of the Winona & St. Peter Railroad, operating only as far as Gary just within the State line. The following year, the Chicago, Milwaukee, St. Paul & Pacific built into the State through Elk Point and reached Yankton in 1873, when the panic of that year put a temporary end to railroad building.

Discovery of Gold: In 1874 occured the most important single event in South Dakota's history—the discovery of gold in the Black Hills by a military expedition under Gen. George A. Custer. The first find occurred near the present town of Custer on August 2, 1874, and the discoverers were Horatio N. Ross and William McKay, prospectors with the expedition. Word of the discovery was immediately sent to St. Paul. On October 6, the so-called Gordon Party left Sioux City for the Black Hills. The group numbered 28 persons, among whom was Annie D. Tallant, who thereby became the first woman to enter the Hills. After a trip lasting three months and entailing much suffering, the party arrived at Custer and built a stockade in which it spent the rest of the winter. A reproduction of this stockade may be seen near Custer today (*see Tour 5*). But early in the spring the military arrived, put the members of the party under arrest and took them to Fort Laramie, since it was contrary to the treaty for whites to be in the Hills.

In the fall of 1875 the Sioux were summoned to meet at Red Cloud's agency and arrange for the leasing of the Black Hills to the whites. The plan was that the whites should be allowed to extract the gold and other precious metals and then abandon the territory to the Indians again. But it was soon evident that no agreement could be reached and less than the required three-fourths of the braves were present; so the council broke up without accomplishing anything. Immediately after this the military, realizing the futility of doing otherwise withdrew all opposition to the entry of whites into the Hills. Gold seekers poured in and in the winter of 1875–6, there were several thousand men in the vicinity of Custer.

In the late fall of 1875, John B. Pearson of Yankton discovered rich placer diggings in the northern Hills between the present cities of Lead and Deadwood. When news of this "strike" reached Custer, it depopulated that place almost in a day, leaving fewer than 100 people in the town. In the summer of 1876 there were more than 25,000 people in Deadwood Gulch. At that time they had no legal government, since they were squatters on Indian land; but they maintained a kind of rough justice of their own, after the manner of mining communities. The town of Deadwood was laid out that summer, along both sides of the single trail up the gulch. In the same year gold was discovered at the head of Gold Run Gulch, on the site of the present city of Lead, and that prosperous mining town was born.

The discovery of gold in the Black Hills was important not only to South Dakota but to the country at large. For Black Friday of September 1873 had plunged a large part of the country into bankruptcy; and this was the first ray of light that heralded the coming of a brighter day. Both in its actual and its psychological effect, it was instrumental in bringing about recovery from the panic.

The battle of the Little Big Horn in which Custer and his command were annihilated, occurred in June 1876. Following this, Gen. Crook, who had been unable to take an active part in the battle of the Little Big Horn, was on his way from Fort Abraham Lincoln to protect the settlers, when he unexpectedly encountered a band of Indians in the Slim Buttes of what is now Harding County. Thereupon followed the Battle of Slim Buttes (*see Tour 2A*). It was on Sept., 8, 1876, that the advance guard, under Maj. Anson Mills, contacted a small band of Indians in Reva Gap of the Buttes. He held them off until night, when he was reinforced by Gen. Crook and the main body of the troops. But the Indians also received reinforcements during the night from portions of Crazy Horse's band. The Battle of Slim Buttes was fought all the following day. At the conclusion of it three whites had been killed, two soldiers and a scout, and a dozen or more of the Indians. Several of the latter were also taken prisoner. The battle resulted in more or less of a stalemate but the Indians withdrew during the ensuing night. The following morning Gen. Crook burned what was left of the Indian village and buried his own dead, causing the entire command to tramp over their graves as they broke camp.

In the fall of 1876, a peace commissioner visited the various reservations and obtained the signatures of the Indian leaders to a new treaty ceding the Black Hills to the whites. The Indians claimed later that they were merely ceding mineral rights, as they had been asked to do before, and that the treaty did not have the requisite three-fourths of the signatures. However, a regular and legal government was now established for the whites in the Black Hills region.

Following the discovery of gold in the Black Hills came the great boom period of the Dakotas. People came for gold, but many of them remained to take up farms. Two railroads, the North Western and the Milwaukee, built their lines halfway across the State, arriving at the Missouri River by 1880—at Pierre and Chamberlain respectively. Beyond this they could not go, for the West-river region, with the exception of the Black Hills, was still Indian country. People poured into the eastern part of the State, and within five years Brookings, Madison, Mitchell, Huron, Pierre, Watertown, Redfield, Aberdeen, Webster, and Milbank had become important towns. Rivalry between various communities was keen, especially with regard to the location of county seats. In one instance, the militia had to be called out to preserve the county records.

Commerce west of the Missouri River was carried on by stagecoach and ox train. There were main trails leading into the Hills from Pierre, Chamberlain, Sidney, Neb., Cheyenne, Wyo., and Bismarck, N. Dak. But the coming of the railroads to the Missouri meant the end of the steamboats. Thereafter they survived on the upper Missouri only as ferries at the principal crossings, until the building of the State bridges many years later.

The winter of 1880 was a memorable one for this region. The snow fell heavily in a blizzard in October, and did not disappear until the following spring. Train service was interrupted and the roads were practically impassable. In the resultant thaw in the spring, a great amount of damage was done, especially on the lower Missouri in the southeastern corner of the State.

The Fight for Statehood: When Dakota Territory was created in 1861, it included what is now North and South Dakota, much of what is now Montana and most of present Wyoming. But with the creation of Montana Territory in 1864 and Wyoming Territory in 1868, Dakota Territory was reduced to the present size of the "Sister States."

As early as 1872 there was some agitation for the division of Dakota Territory into two equal parts as at present; but nothing came of it. In 1879, however, an attempt was made to buy the school lands of the State at a low figure; and through the influence of the superintendent of public instruction, Gen. William H. H. Beadle, it was determined to combine the fight for the division of the Territory with a demand that no school lands should be sold for less than $10 an acre. A convention of citizens was held at Canton in June 1882, and a committee was appointed to further both these ends. The committee carried the matter to the Legislature the following winter and the latter passed a bill calling for a constitutional convention. This bill, however, was vetoed by Gov. Nehemiah G. Ordway. The executive committee thereupon called a delegate convention to meet at Huron in June 1883. Every county in South Dakota was represented by its strongest men. An ordinance was passed providing for a constitutional convention to be held in Sioux Falls on September 4. In the meantime delegates to the convention were elected. At the appointed time they met in Sioux Falls and drew up a constitution, in which was inserted the $10 school-land provision. This constitution was submitted to the people at the November election, and was adopted almost unanimously. A committee was appointed to present it to Congress, together with a petition for Statehood; but Congress did not see fit to act.

The next Legislature provided by law for a new constitutional convention to be held in Sioux Falls in September 1885. The constitution framed by this convention again with a $10 minimum clause was ratified once more by the people at the November election; and a complete set of State Officers together with a Legislature and Congressman were elected at the same time. The Legislature elected two United States Senators and these men and the Governor carried a petition to Congress. But the National Administration was at this time Democratic and the leaders did not favor a plan that would be sure to introduce four new Republican Senators to cut down the Democratic majority. They favored the admission of the whole Territory as one State and the National Administration brought pressure to bear to the same end. But every time the question came to a test vote the people of the Territory voted overwhelmingly for division.

In 1888 the Republican National Convention made the admission of the two States a campaign issue. The Republicans prevailed in the fall elections and the Congress then in session yielded to the inevitable and passed the enabling act on Valentine's Day 1889. It was approved on Washington's Birthday. A new constitutional convention met in Sioux Falls on July 4, with power only to amend and resubmit the constitution of 1885. At a special election on October 1, this document was approved; and on November 2, 1889, the long fight was ended and proclamations were issued by President Benjamin Harrison admitting North and South Dakota to the Union. At the time of its admission, the State of South Dakota had a population of more than 300,000.

An interesting method was employed in preparing the proclamation for the Chief Executive's signature. The President desired to give neither State priority, but to admit both as "Sister States." Before the Presidential signatures were attached, therefore, the two proclamations were placed on the President's desk with the texts covered and only the lines for the signature showing. As a further precaution, after the signatures had been attached, the documents were thoroughly shuffled by another person. This made it impossible to tell which State was admitted first. It can only be said that the two Dakotas are the thirty-ninth and fortieth States.

As a matter of courtesy, when it is necessary to rank the States, South Dakota yields to North Dakota, which has a prior position in alphabetical order.

Immediately after entering upon Statehood, South Dakota experienced its last Indian trouble—the Messiah War. A Nevada Piute Indian named Wovoka claimed to have had a vision following an eclipse of the sun in 1889. From this he evolved a religion which was a curious mixture of Christianity and Indian religious thought. The gist of it was that he, as the Messiah, had come to drive out the whites, restore the land to the Indians, and bring back the buffalo. This was to be accomplished by means of a religious dance called the "Ghost Dance," during which the dancers wore a "ghost" shirt, which was supposed to render them immune to the white men's bullets. The dancing craze spread till it was inflaming the Indians to a dangerous degree. Sitting Bull was killed resisting arrest on the eve of setting out for the Ghost Dance with his band; and orders were given for the arrest of Big Foot's band, which was also on its way to join the dancers. The band was overtaken and apparently submitted to arrest; but during the night they escaped into the Badlands. A young captain named John J. Pershing was among the troops maneuvering to isolate Big Foot, although he was not present at the ensuing battle. The morning following its escape, Big Foot's band was overtaken on Wounded Knee Creek. Again they surrendered and the soldiers began to disarm them. This angered the Indians and they were further inflamed by a medicine man named Yellow Bird who, speaking in the Sioux tongue, exhorted them to resist and reminded them that they were wearing the bullet-proof ghost shirts. Finally, as a soldier pulled aside an Indian's blanket to see whether he was armed, another Indian fired at the soldiers and was joined at once by all the rest of the Indians. The soldiers immediately fired in return and at point-blank range the carnage was frightful. Then the Hotchkiss guns of the artillery raked the Indian village, setting fire to the tipis and killing women and children indiscriminately. The superior arms of the soldiers and their artillery could have but one result. Only a few of the Indians escaped to the hills and the draws, and the soldiers cut down those whom they could overtake, women as well as men, leaving their bodies scattered for a distance of two miles. The Wounded Knee massacre—for it was that, rather than a battle—resulted in the death of nearly 200 Indians, men, women, and children, and some 60 soldiers. It was caused by the use of green troops, led by inexperienced officers. Shortly after this, Gen. Nelson A. Miles arrived, restored order, and composed the last of the serious differences between the whites and Indians.

The first Legislature of Dakota Territory made provision for a Territorial university; but it was not until twenty years later that the university became an accomplished fact. The story goes that after Pierre had won the capital, Sioux Falls had the next choice of State institutions, and chose the penitentiary; then Vermillion had to take what was left, and got the university. The University of South Dakota was established at Vermillion in 1882, through the enterprise of the citizens and the people of the county. In 1883 the State College of Agriculture and Mechanic Arts was founded at Brookings.

The Capital Fight: The question of the location of the Territorial and later of the State capital was one that agitated the people for years. Although Yankton had won the honor in 1861, the fact that it was in one corner of the vast Territory led to agitation for removal of the capital to some more central location. Finally, in 1882, the Legislature appointed a capital commission to select a permanent site. They chose Bismarck, largely because of the inability of South Dakotans to agree upon a site themselves. Although many subsequent attempts were made to remove the Territorial capital from Bismarck, they were unsuccessful for the same reason.

The constitutional convention of 1885 submitted the selection of a capital to popular vote, and Huron won. The enabling act of 1889 again required that the people should designate a temporary capital. This brought on a hard-fought struggle in the summer of 1889, with Pierre, Huron, Watertown, Sioux Falls, Mitchell, and Chamberlain as contestants. Pierre won by a large margin. Under the constitution, the permanent capital was to be selected at the election of 1890. This time Pierre and Huron were the only contestants. Pierre again won by a large majority.

Despite this decisive outcome, agitation still continued for the removal of the capital to some other city. In the Legislature of 1901, the other candidates agreed to abide by the result of a caucus, and Mitchell won. An attempt was made to submit a constitutional amendment, but a filibuster blocked this. At the session of 1903, the caucus plan was again adopted and again Mitchell won. The Legislature passed the submitting resolution by a large majority in both houses. During the next two years a strenuous campaign was waged. It became a contest between the State's two principal railway systems. The Milwaukee backed Mitchell and the North Western, Pierre. At first the railroads gave influential citizens throughout the State passes to visit their respective candidates for capital. Finally the situation developed to a point where the railroads felt obliged to transport free anyone who wished to visit either of these cities; and in the summer of 1904 they carried upwards of one hundred thousand people to the rival cities, a mass movement unprecedented in the history of the State. The election resulted in a victory for Pierre by about 18,000 majority. The Legislature of 1905 made provision for a permanent capital building, which was dedicated in 1910.

During the Spanish-American War, South Dakota raised and equipped a regiment for service. It went to the Philippines, participated in the hardest fighting in many battles, and won great distinction, several of its members receiving the highest military award, the Congressional Medal of Honor; and on its return it was reviewed by President McKinley at Aberdeen.

In the year 1907, the Milwaukee and the North Western railroads continued their lines from Chamberlain and Pierre, respectively, through to the Black Hills at Rapid City. Earlier, about 1890, the North Western and the Burlington had built their lines to Deadwood from their Nebraska terminals—the Burlington through the heart of the Hills and the North Western up their eastern edge. At the same time, the Milwaukee extended its main line west from Aberdeen to Lemmon.

State Enterprises: During the period from 1915 to 1925, the State engaged in a number of experimental ventures into business and finance. Some of these the State administered directly and some it controlled. The first of these ventures was the State Bank Guaranty Law of 1915. Under the provisions of this act, the State undertook to administer a fund, contributed pro rata by the banks, to liquidate closed banks and thus protect the depositors. This plan worked satisfactorily during prosperous times, and the first few banks which failed were liquidated promptly. But with the coming of the depression the financial strain proved too great, the fund was soon exhausted, and the law fell into abeyance.

In 1917 the Rural Credits constitutional amendment became effective. This provided a means whereby landowners could borrow money directly from the State, from funds secured by the sale of interest-bearing bonds. As it turned out, the administration of Gov. Peter Norbeck tended to provide loans on the basis of political expediency rather than business security. The department made 12,116 loans which by 1925 amounted to $47,500,000. Although no further loans were made, neither were many payments. Interest on the bonds piled up and the credit of the State took a hard jolt.

By 1939 only 1,281 of the original 12,116 loans were in good standing. The State had become owner of 7,000 tracts of property containing 2 million acres. The Legislature of 1939 gave the department five years to liquidate its holdings. In 1947 a plan was worked out to retire the remaining bonds by 1954, and taxpayers settled for a $57,000,000 loss on the Rural Credit venture.

Another State venture was the purchase in 1919, of a coal mine at Haynes, N. Dak., for $200,000. The vein of coal pinched out, and the mine was sold in April 1936, for $5,500, which was insufficient to pay outstanding obligations against the property. In the winter of 1933–4, the State opened a strip coal mine at Firesteel, S. Dak. (*see Tour 2A*), but this work was halted when it was discovered that coal could be purchased elsewhere for less than it could be mined at the State project.

A method whereby farmers could receive the benefits of hail insurance was the objective of another State-promoted venture. The act provided that every farm should be automatically covered; and if the beneficiary did not wish protection, he was obliged to file an application for exemption. Although farmers in the areas subject to hail storms reaped benefits, the fact that the average farmer did not wish to carry this insurance led to the repeal of the law.

Gov. William H. McMaster rose to Nation-wide prominence in 1924 when, announcing that the oil companies were charging too much for gasoline, he ordered the State to engage in the gasoline business. The result was that motor fuel prices dropped sharply. The public praised the step, and a little later McMaster rode into the United States Senate on a wave of popularity. The act was later declared unconstitutional.

A State-owned enterprise that still is in operation is the South Dakota Cement Plant at Rapid City (*see RAPID CITY*). It was started in 1925 with a bonded indebtness of about $1,200,000. During the next 25 years it turned $1,500,000 in profits over to the State's general fund and $337,000 to the State Highway Department. The bonds were paid off from earnings in 1943.

To double its production during the post-World War II construction boom, the cement plant was authorized to issue $1,350,000 in bonds for internal improvements. By 1950 the plant had gross annual sales amounting to about $2,000,000. Much of the success of the plant has been attributed to the on-the-spot availability of all raw materials, coupled with the fact that the same management survived through the terms of eight governors.

The 1920's and '30's: Until the 1920's, there were no highway bridges across the Missouri River to unite the two halves of the State. All vehicular traffic had been by ferry. In 1919 the citizens of Yanktown decided to bridge the Missouri to Nebraska (*see Tours 8 and 10*), and funds were raised through subscription and a bond issue. At about the same time, the State began building five bridges which were located, from north to south, at Mobridge (*see Tour 2*),

Forest City (*see Tour 3*), Pierre (*see Tour 4*), Chamberlain (*see Tour 5*), and Wheeler (*see Tour 7*).

In the summer of 1927, the State for the first time had the honor of providing the summer home of a President of the United States. President Coolidge occupied the State Game Lodge in Custer Park (*see Tour 5*) for the season, and maintained business offices in the high school at Rapid City.

While Coolidge was in the Black Hills, he became interested in the sculpture work which Gutzon Borglum was starting on Mount Rushmore (*see Tour 5A*). The President dedicated the memorial which was being financed by voluntary contributions; and later helped in getting Federal funds for the project.

The Federal order in 1933, increasing the price of gold at United States mints from $20.67 to $35 an ounce, by changing the dollar's gold content brought a revival of mining activity in the Black Hills, the renewed operation of many mines that had been closed as unprofitable, and, for the first time in many years, a revival of placer mining. While no outstanding "strikes" occurred, it developed that placer mining could be made to yield a fair day's wage and that was important at a time when jobs were scarce.

When Tom Berry came off his 30,000-acre cattle ranch to become governor in 1933, he inherited not only a period of depression but one of drought and dust storms as well. A close friend of Will Rogers, Berry brought a homespun philosophy into the State government and a determination to utilize every resource available. In every county men and women were put to work on special projects.

In July 1934 occurred the first stratosphere flight from the Stratosphere Bowl, 12 miles west of Rapid City (*see Tour 5*). This and the succeeding flight were sponsored by the National Geographic Society and the U. S. Army Air Corps. The 1934 flight did not succeed in breaking the record, although the balloon, Explorer I, attained a height of over 60,000 feet. At this point the fabric began to rip and the descent was begun. The flight ended near Holdredge, Neb., when the balloonists were forced to resort to their parachutes to save their lives.

In the early summer of 1935, a second attempt to penetrate the stratosphere was made; but an hour before the time scheduled for the take-off, the already inflated balloon burst at the top and the charge of helium escaped. Nothing daunted, the sponsors of the flight repaired the balloon, Explorer II, and on Armistice Day, 1935, their efforts were crowned with complete success; for on that day the greatest balloon ever made by man reached the greatest heights ever attained by man. The giant bag arose to a height of 72,395 feet, remaining in the air eight hours. The descent was as felicitous as the rise and the balloon made a perfect "egg-shell" landing near White Lake, S. Dak., 240 miles southeast of the rock-walled starting point. Capt. Albert W. Stevens commanded the flight and Capt. Orvil A. Anderson was the pilot. Both men became important Air Force officers in World War II, as did the affable young lieutenant, H. H. "Hap" Arnold, who had flown President Coolidge's mail back and forth to Washington in 1927.

In 1938 an oil-topped highway (US 14) was finally completed across South Dakota to the Black Hills. It was the result of a campaign promise made by Leslie Jensen, first governor to come from the Black Hills region.

That same year, with the rumble of war in Europe, the Luenen Passion Play company settled in Spearfish, and carried on the seven centuries old, father-to-son tradition. (*see Tour 4*).

World War II: The South Dakota National Guard's 147th Field Artillery regiment, which had made a distinguished record in France during World War I, this time went westward. On the day Pearl Harbor was attacked by the Japanese, the men of the 147th were on a transport between Hawaii and the Philippines. There were some uneasy days on board, as well as at home, until the troops were diverted to Australia to become the first American soldiers there. Col. Leslie Jensen, the former governor, was their commander. The 109th Engineer regiment of the State's National Guard became a part of the 34th Infantry Division which saw action in Africa and Europe.

During World War II, nearly 60,000 South Dakota men and women were in active service. Many became national heroes. To make a permanent record of the individual participation of South Dakotans, the State Legislature appropriated $25,000 to publish a history.

Meanwhile, at home, a number of military establishments were developed. At Sioux Falls, the Army absorbed the municipal airport and 1,500 acres to build a huge Air Force Technical Radio School (*see SIOUX FALLS*). A $25,000,000 Air Force base was built near Rapid City, and satellite fields were built at Mitchell, Pierre, and Watertown (*see CITIES*). Ft. Meade, which had been a cavalry post since the Indian wars, became a training center for mechanized and airborne units (*see Tour 4*). The Black Hills Ordnance Depot, near Edgemont, became a $73,000,000 installation covering more than 30,000 acres (*see Tour 7*).

For a time, during World War II, the Black Hills lost the use of its most precious possession—gold. In a region where gold dust was king, the closing of all gold mines by the Federal government came as a hard blow. With the diversion of its workers to more vital war production, the giant Homestake closed down except for some special war plant contracts, and the city of Lead was virtually deserted (*see LEAD*).

The need for war materials, however, stimulated the mining of other minerals in the Black Hills. The feldspar mines, which had blossomed with the repeal of prohibition to provide an ingredient in making glass bottles, now worked overtime. The region became the nation's largest producer of milled feldspar. Mica mining also boomed. Sheets of the transparent, isinglass-like mineral were in demand in the war-expanded electronics industry. Lithium, tungsten, tin, bentonite, gypsum, and other minerals were processed for use in making implements of war and as substitutes for unavailable materials.

During the war period, the State was governed by Harlan J. Bushfield, who later became a U.S. Senator, and by M. Q. Sharpe, each serving under a wartime economy that restricted governmental activities.

Recent History: When George T. Mickelson took over as governor in 1947, he embarked on a double-edged program of stabilizing the State's fiscal policy and, at the same time, revitalizing the State's institutions and run-down highway system. Four years later, when he announced his retirement from office, the State had undergone the greatest construction and public improvement period in its history, had financed the payment of a veterans' bonus, and had arranged to rid itself of the heavy rural credit indebtedness plaguing the State for more than 25 years.

A unified budget plan was introduced to eliminate pressure groups and the bartering system, whereby institutions and departments with the strongest lobbies fared the best. State schools, institutions, highways, and various departments had gone for years on slim budgets, first because of the lack of funds prior to the war and then because of the ban on construction during the war years. At long last, by careful planning there was money on hand to catch up on urgent needs.

The State's educational and eleemosynary institutions received $8,500,000 in new buildings and equipment by 1951, together with a long-range plan based on priority rather than rivalry.

More than 1,200 miles of new hard-surfaced highways and 100 bridges were included in the expenditure of $35,000,000 between 1945 and 1950 by the State Highway Commission, in conjunction with the U.S. Bureau of Public Roads. Public welfare, health, and other State programs were expanded to meet current needs.

A veterans' bonus amounting to $27,424,797 was paid on 57,878 claims, for an average of $473 to each veteran. In contrast with the

World War I bonus fund of $6,000,000 in bonds, which cost the State an additional $7,200,000 in interest over a 20-year period, the 1949 bonus bonds of $21,000,000 can be paid off in less than three years at a cost of approximately $250,000. A program of self-repealing taxes underwrote the World War II bonus plan, and the interest rate on the bonds averaged only one percent.

Governor Mickelson also undertook to wipe off the rural credit debt, which had saddled the State government since the ill-fated venture began in 1919 (*see above*). With a $6,000,000 investment, a program was set up to repurchase and retire the last of the bonds by 1954, to make the State debt free.

Meanwhile, in September of 1950, the South Dakota National Guard again was called into active Service, and was designated as the 197th Regimental Combat Team. The State also has an Air National Guard, commanded by Col. Joe Foss, the former Marine ace and Congressional Medal of Honor winner (*see SIOUX FALLS*).

Missouri River Program: When the Congress passed the Flood Control Act of 1944, it authorized a vast network of projects in the upper Missouri River valley. Through joint efforts of the U.S. Corps of Engineers and the Bureau of Reclamation, together with the affected States, the Missouri River Basin Development Program embraces hydro-electric power, irrigation, flood control, storage of water for navigation on the lower reaches, and development of recreational areas.

For South Dakota, the scheduled program calls for an expenditure of $1,500,000,000 in Federal funds. One unit, the Oahe reservoir and irrigation project, which was started in 1949, represents a cost greater than the total of all appropriations made by the State legislature since Statehood. Another unit, the Fort Randall dam, construction of which was begun two years earlier, includes a hydro-electric plant capable of producing 320,000 kilowatts of power. This is more than twice the regular generating capacity in the entire state. When completed, the four dams in the Missouri River in South Dakota will form almost continuous reservoirs, extending from the Nebraska line near Yankton well into North Dakota (*see Natural Setting*).

These Federal projects are: Oahe, near Pierre, (*see Tour 4*); Big Bend, near Fort Thompson, (*see Tour 4A*); Fort Randall, near Lake Andes, (*see Tour 7*); and Gavin's Point, near Yankton, (*see Tour 8*)—all in the Missouri River. Also part of the Missouri River Basin program in South Dakota are several flood control-irrigation projects in which dams have been, or are being, built across tributaries. These include the Angostura Reservoir in the

Cheyenne River, S. of Hot Springs, (*see Tour 7*); the Deerfield dam in Rapid Creek, W. of Rapid City, (*see Tour 14*); the Bixby dam in the Moreau River, NW. of Faith, (*see Tour 3*); and the Shade-hill and Blue Horse dams in Grand River, S. of Lemmon and McIntosh, respectively, (*see Tour 2*). The major irrigation project, designed to serve 750,000 acres in central South Dakota, is associated with the Oahe reservoir (*see Tour 4 and HURON*).

STATE GOVERNMENT

With a total population equivalent to that of such cities as Milwaukee, Wis., or Pittsburgh, Pa., South Dakota must support 6,000 miles of trunk highways, seven State colleges, various charitable and penal institutions, and the increasing demands upon State governments.

The State government normally receives about 60 million dollars a year from taxes and other sources, including approximately 14 millions in Federal aid. Nearly half of the Federal funds are for matching local funds in highway construction programs and the next largest share, about one-fourth, is in public assistance participation.

The bicameral Legislature convenes at Pierre on the first Monday after the first Tuesday in January of odd-numbered years, for a limited session of 60 days. State senators and representatives are elected every two years. Special sessions have become increasingly frequent.

South Dakota was the first State (1899) to provide by statute for the initiative and referendum. By petition, new measures may be initiated or existing laws referred and placed on the ballot for popular vote. This method is used quite often.

The salary of the Governor has been $8,500 a year since 1947; previously the $3,000 salary was the lowest paid to any State executive in the Union. Constitutional officers receive $4,800 a year, while some of the appointive officers range somewhat higher.

South Dakota has five judges in its supreme court. Originally there were three, but the number was increased in 1909, by an act of the Legislature. The judges are elected every six years by a vote of the entire State, and vacancies are filled by appointment by the Governor. The court has both original and appellate jurisdiction, although most of its cases are appellate. The only appeal from its decisions is to the United States Supreme Court. Salary of the judges is $7,200 a year, with additional allowances for expenses.

Twelve circuit judges, elected by districts every four years, preside over the tribunals that hear most of the civil and criminal cases arising in the State. They have original jurisdiction over all cases except those of probate, city ordinance, and Federal character. The salary of circuit judges is $6,300 a year.

The trend of South Dakota's finances is toward a decrease in bonded indebtedness. In 1927 the percapita net bonded indebtedness was approximately $88.66 and by 1936 it had been reduced to $63.56. This included Rural Credit bonds which in 1936 constituted 91.8% of the total net bonded indebtedness while contributing only 16.1% of the total amount in the interest and sinking funds. In 1951 surplus balances in the State's general and sinking funds were more than enough to offset all existing indebtedness, but some of the outstanding bonds were not callable.

INDUSTRY AND LABOR

South Dakota is preeminently an agricultural State, but manufacturing, mining, and lumbering are also important in various sections. Since 1940, a marked increase has been shown in the expansion of established industries and the development of new ones.

There were approximately 500 manufacturing plants in 1951, turning out foodstuffs, building materials, and varied commodities valued at $100,000,000 and employing about 10,000 persons. By comparison, in 1933, there were 348 manufacturing establishments with an employment of 4,731 persons.

The processing of agricultural products takes precedence over all other manufacturing in South Dakota. Ten meat packing plants produce $50,000,000 in frozen and canned beef, pork, and mutton each year. Nearly half of the State's livestock is processed in these plants. High-grade flour is manufactured from locally-grown hard spring wheat in 14 mills scattered through the State. Creameries, sugar refineries, feed mills, produce plants, and bakeries are also important local industries.

Among newer manufacturing plants are those fabricating metals and assembling farm equipment. Building materials, particularly cement and granite, have become increasingly important. A State-owned cement plant is operated at Rapid City.

Mineral production adds an additional $25,000,000 annually to the industrial income of the State, with four-fifths coming from the gold mines in the Black Hills. However, in recent years South Dakota has become a leading producer of bentonite, feldspar, lithium ore, mica, and beryl. Large deposits of lignite coal exist in the northwestern part of the State, but as yet they remain inaccessible to transportation. Manganese deposits of low-grade ore are found along the Missouri River and are undergoing pilot mill tests.

With producing oil wells in the surrounding States of North Dakota, Wyoming, and Nebraska, nearly all land west of the

Missouri River in South Dakota has been leased for exploration. Several test wells drilled prior to 1951 failed to produce, but exploration continues.

Although known as a prairie State, there are 26 sawmills and planing mills which turn out lumber in the Black Hills. An average of 30 million board feet of pine timber is logged off each year in the Harney and Black Hills National Forests. In 1951, the U.S. Army Corps of Engineers began operations along the Missouri River to make commercial use and sale of about 90 million board feet of cottonwood timber on land within areas to be flooded by the huge government reservoir projects.

The Federal government's Missouri River flood control, irrigation, and hydro-electric dams in South Dakota will have a producing capacity of 1,100,000 kilowatts when completed. The dams are part of the Missouri River Basin Development Project (*see Natural Resources and above*).

Labor: As early as 1886, three years before Statehood, a charter was issued to Typographical Union No. 218 in Sioux Falls, and even before that there were local organizations of railroad men, bricklayers, stone masons, and other tradesmen within the Territory.

By 1920, when the first convention of the South Dakota State Federation of Labor met at Huron, there were 55 local unions represented. The labor movement developed slowly until the early 1930's, during which time membership in all locals was about 3,000. By 1950 there were approximately 12,000 members belonging to operating locals of the A.F. of L. in South Dakota. Nearly 2,500 others, mostly in communications, are affiliated with the C.I.O. and other organizations.

All the large industries in the State, except mining, come under major union organizations. These include meat packing, milling, trucking railroading, and publishing. The major unaffiliated union is at the Homestake Mining Company at Lead where, in an election supervised by the National Labor Relations Board on March 9, 1951, the gold mine employees rejected the United Steel Workers of America (CIO) as a bargaining agent by a vote of 901 to 587. In the building trades throughout the State, about 75 percent of all the men are organized.

Of all union members in the State, about 60 percent live in Sioux Falls, the largest city. The Morrell Packing Company alone, employs an average of 2,500. There are 35 locals affiliated with the Sioux Falls Trades and Labor Assembly.

There has been little serious labor trouble in the State. Major disputes have been at the Homestake and at Morrells. The South

Dakota National Guard was called out during a strike at the Morrell plant in 1935.

Trades and labor councils are maintained in Sioux Falls, Huron, Mitchell, Watertown, Aberdeen, and Rapid City.

The problem of migratory labor has lessened in recent years, with the advent of the combines to thresh the grain. The demand for farm workers to do summer work usually exceeds the supply throughout the east half of the State.

During the drought and dust storm years of the 1930's, thousands of destitute farm and town families required Federal aid for the necessities of life. Government-supplied employment on permanent improvements, such as water conservation dams, soil erosion projects, roads, and public buildings, provided a tremendous boon to business and agriculture. It was the biggest factor in South Dakota's battle against the lean years.

Agriculture

THE process of transformation from raw and unfinished prairie lands to a relatively developed countryside began in 1857, in the extreme southeastern corner of the State, and the last raw land was opened for settlement as late as 1910, in the opposite section, in the counties of Harding, Perkins, and Butte. During this period of agricultural and commercial expansion, there was a modest but determined growth in education, social welfare, and the fine arts, so that today economic and social development keep abreast in South Dakota.

With nearly one half the soil in its virgin state, untouched by the plow, the agriculture of South Dakota might be considered still in the infant state of development. However, this balance of crop and grazing areas provides a stability to agricultural income. Although South Dakota ranks high among all states in raising durum wheat, oats, rye, corn, and flaxseed, two-thirds of its normal cash farm income is derived from the marketing of livestock and livestock products.

Stock feeding is becoming more important each year. Baby beefs from the range are fattened in feed lots nearer the markets. Crops needed for feed and forage have become increasingly important. The diversity of the State's agriculture is being broadened; for instance, poultry raising brings an income more than double that obtained from gold, although South Dakota ranks at or near the top each year among all gold-producing states.

The development of irrigation may bring new changes. The Missouri River dam projects are designed to bring 1,000,000 acres under irrigation. Use of impounded waters will not be completely new to South Dakota. The Bureau of Reclamation has operated a project since 1908, north of the Black Hills. Sugar beets, processed in a nearby plant, and alfalfa are grown successfully in the Belle Fourche Valley (*see TOUR 3*). Also irrigated is the Spearfish Valley, noted for its fruit orchards, truck gardens, and roadside stands (*see TOUR 13, Sec. A*). The Angostura dam on the Cheyenne River, completed late in 1949, was the first major unit of the so-called Missouri Basin projects (*see TOUR 7, Sec. B*).

Progress of farming in the State has been necessarily slow. Indian troubles disrupted the first settlements. The call of free land beckoned many Easterners who were unprepared for prairie farming, much less for pioneer hardships. The lack of railroads was another handicap, and it was not until after the attainment of statehood that much thought was given to settling beyond the Missouri River. The West-river region began as stock country, with large trail herds brought up from Texas to feed on the lush buffalo grass. After being engulfed for a decade, homesteaders who came, were conquered by the elements, and left, the land reverted to open range. But tractors were to make further invasions.

During and following World War I, wheat was king in South Dakota. Buffalo grass was turned under and sloughs were drained to get more wheat in the ground. Nature seemed to add approval as rains were well-timed and harvests were bountiful. In 1920, with wheat at $2.11 per bushel, the average value of South Dakota farmland was $71 an acre (as compared to $12 an acre average in 1940). The bonanza did not last long. Wheat prices dropped in a glutted market. The land, which was robbed for quick and easy profit, failed to produce. Farmers, who stayed with their land, turned to varied crops and to more livestock.

Then, in the 1930's came wind, drought, heat, and dust, accompanied by hoardes of grasshoppers. Ushered in by the famous and devastating "black blizzard" of November 1933, the dust storm scourge, which was something new to Dakota prairies, swept much of the top soil from hundreds of farms. Dirt from the fields was deposited like brown snowdrifts along fences. In 1930, 17,800,000 acres of farmland were harvested; in 1935 only 4,800,000 acres. Of the 83,000 farms in the State in 1935, 69,000 reported crop failures.

With Federal help, farmers and ranchers fought back the drought. Conservation practices, ignored for 20 years, were introduced. Eroded lands were returned to grass, stock dams were built, hillsides were terraced, trees were planted. Herds of cattle again roamed the rolling West-river range and much of the East-river prairie. Drought-resistant crops came to the fore. Hybrid corn seed was utilized.

The demand for food during and after World War II found South Dakota in another period of productivity. This time, however, grain was secondary. In 1948 the cash farm-ranch income was

$650,641,000, not counting government payments, of which live-stock and livestock products produced $385,409,000 of the total. Wheat accounted for 106 million dollars of the $265,232,000 in crops; flaxseed 46 million, and corn 41 millon. Oats, barley, rye, and hay followed in that order. During the same year, cattle and calves brought a cash income amounting to 158 million dollars, and hogs produced 141 million. In 1949, however, cattle receipts jumped to 183 million dollars while wheat dropped to 73 millions.

Among other states, South Dakota in 1949, ranked second in durum wheat, third in other spring wheat, but fifteenth in all wheat. It ranked third in rye and flaxseed, fifth in barley and oats, and eleventh in corn. In wild hay acreage, the State ranked first. It was eighth in alfalfa seed, tenth in sweet clover seed, nineteenth in soybeans, and forty-fourth in Irish potatoes.

A new cash crop for the prairies is the development of blue grass seed. Thousands of acres have been turned to the Kentucky import. Largest operations, which began extensively in 1950, are between Brookings and Pierre where the seed is stripped, cured, and baled in the fields.

In more than half of the State, ranching predominates. In 1950, there were 27,000 livestock brands on record, an increase of 8,000 in seven years. Some of the older cattle ranches, such as the Double X and the Diamond A, continue to operate spreads covering as many as 30,000 acres. The average ranch, however, has 1,464 acres.

Cattle raising in South Dakota is carried on under three general systems. Two of these, dairying and the feeding of beef cattle, are practiced mainly east of the Missouri River. Since dairying is carried on much the same everywhere, there is no need of describing it in detail. In the feeding of beef for market, young steers are purchased from the range country to the west of the river and fed intensively for a short period on the surplus corn of the eastern and southeastern sections; after which they are shipped the comparatively short distance to Midwestern markets.

The third system, the range raising of cattle, is necessarily confined to the range sections of the West-river country. The 20 years from 1880 to 1900, were the halcyon days of the big cattle outfits, with thousands of stock run under a single brand, frequently with absentee ownership. Little or no provision was made for winter feeding of such vast numbers, and cattle raising under such conditions was a gamble. If the winter was an open one, the stock came through in fine shape; if it was severe, the ranges were cleaned.

But with the turn of the century, the prosperous days of the big outfits came to an end. There were probably many factors contrib-

SQUATTER'S CLAIM

uting to this, but the chief was perhaps the "nester." Some cowhand with the makings of a good stockman, becoming tired of
working for someone else, would start up for himself. He knew
all the favorable ranch locations on his range, and would file on a
piece of land with shelter and water; if possible, some hay bottoms.
There he would build up his herd—some say at the expense of outfits so large that all their unbranded stock could not be rounded up.

But the reign of the "nester" was short. Just as he had driven
out the big outfits, so the homesteaders drove him out, or at least
curtailed his activities. As the wave of homesteading swept over the
land, shacks, dugouts, and sod shanties appeared overnight on
every quarter-section. The homesteaders for the most part had little
knowledge of farming and none of ranching, but they had an exaggerated idea of the value of the grass. The "nester," now become
the cattleman, could not meet their terms and survive. Some sold
out, some were cut down, some made arrangements with the more
reasonable homesteaders. Those who survived made good, for the
homestead wave receded—not so rapidly as it rose, but just as surely.
Today in the West-river country there are cattle ranches of varying
size, with a small nucleus of deeded land as the core, with a larger
body of homestead and State land, surrounding it, and always
with a fringe for which the cattleman pays neither rental nor tax.

In South Dakota sheep are raised either on farm plots or in
range flocks. The farm flock may be found anywhere in the State.
It numbers all the way from one "bum" lamb to two or three hundred head of sheep. If carried on as an adjunct to farming, it is
profitable, like raising chickens or milch cows. The range flock, on
the other hand, averaging from 1,500 to 1,800 head, usually represents the total investment of its owner and his whole means of livelihood.

It is axiomatic to say that sheep raising on the range can be carried on only in a natural range country. Certain conditions must be
present before sheep can be raised in large numbers, and the first
is an abundance of grazing space. The three northwestern counties
meet this requirement, having the lowest population density in the
State.

The second requisite is cheap land. In the northwestern corner
of the State this condition also exists. The land there may be leased
from the government and from private individuals at a minimum
of six cents an acre a year, the rental varying in different counties.
Another requisite for range sheep-raising is feed and shelter. This
region has an abundance of natural grasses of various kinds, including buffalo, wheat, blue-stem, and sand grasses. Grass in this
region cures on the ground in July and August and, unlike the

grasses in moist climates, is as nutritious in winter as it is when first cut and stacked. Shelter is found along creeks and draws, and it is in these places that stockmen usually build their ranch houses and sheds, and feed their flocks during the winter.

The final requisite is water supply, at least during the summer months. Sheep, like horses, will eat snow in the absence of water and survive, whereas cattle must have water, winter and summer. This particular region has a number of streams that run the year around, and others that at least have waterholes along their courses. The result is that this northwestern corner of the State, an area of roughly 100 miles square, supports an enormous number of sheep. Harding County alone, for example, showed a production of more than 68,000 spring lambs in 1931. Butte and Perkins counties also produce many sheep by the range method, but few others employ this system.

Different sections of the country find different breeds of sheep best suited to their purposes. In the range section of South Dakota, almost the only breed found is the Rambouillet. It is a dual purpose sheep, valuable both for wool and lambs. The range wool in South Dakota ranks with the best, comparing favorably with the high grade wool of the Montana ranges.

With the acknowledgement among most farmers that the best way to sell grain is "on the hoof," hog raising in South Dakota, as elsewhere, is complemented by the production of corn and other grains. This is true especially in the eastern section, where alfalfa and clover fields furnish pastures to supplement the corn ration. Western South Dakota ranchers and farmers usually raise some hogs, but not with the care and attention to scientific formulas that characterize those in the eastern section.

Poland-China, Duroc-Jersey, and Hampshire breeds have been the mainstay of the farmers of the State, Hampshire being more popular in the West-river country because of its hardiness and ability to rustle for its living. It is the leading type of bacon hog raised in the State.

Although seldom raised exclusively, poultry, principally chickens and turkeys, are raised on nearly every farm where diversified agriculture is practiced. Poultry and egg houses buy the products from farmers and ship them to Eastern markets.

This brief general picture of South Dakota shows a State with wide diversification in farm crops and methods, each section peculiar to itself. Farmers are learning, after years of uncertain fumbling, that particular areas are adaptable to particular crops and products, and that the land is generous to those who observe this rule; unsympathetic and unyielding to those who do not.

Education and Religion

EDUCATION

THE early settlers of South Dakota believed no community was complete until a school had been built and a teacher engaged. The first school building was erected by public subscription in Bon Homme County in 1860; the school operated only three months, however, because the building had to be torn down when more logs were needed in a stockade for protection against the Indians.

The second school was built at Vermillion in 1862, by soldiers of Company A., U.S. Cavalry, following a public meeting called by Capt. Nelson Miner to discuss the needs of the frontier community. The 16x20-ft. structure was erected at the foot of Ravine Hill, and one of the soldiers, Amos Shaw, was assigned to teach the eight pupils. Indians peeped in the windows, but there was no trouble. The first permanent schoolhouse in Dakota Territory, the old log building, served also as the town's first church, community hall, and balloting place. A marker is at the original site, and a reproduction of the schoolhouse has been built on the campus of the University of South Dakota (see Tour 8).

William Jayne, first Governor of Dakota Territory, signed the original law in 1862, establishing a school code and a common school District. In 1864 Gov. Newton Edmunds appointed James S. Foster as first superintendent of Public Instruction. It proved to be a happy choice, for this educator, grounded in the school of Horace Mann, through three successive terms laid the foundation of the present school system of the State. By 1870, there were 83 schools in the State, with approximately 1,800 children in attendance.

The school district system was originally modeled after that of New England. Later the township system was introduced, with one school board having control of all schools within the township. The two systems have existed side by side since that early day, and later legislation was enacted to permit communities to change at will from one form to the other.

The decade 1870–80 was marked by the installation of the first course of study, the enactment of much school legislation, and the raising of the qualifications for the office of county superintendent. In this time the enrollment in schools increased to more than 13,000, with 464 teachers employed.

LOG SCHOOLHOUSE, VERMILLION

The years 1880–90 saw a complete recodification of school laws. Courses of study were revised and United States history, temperance, physiology, and hygiene were added to the curriculum. From 1890–05 the important developments were the advent of the first grade teaching certificate, the strengthening of the compulsory education laws, and the advocacy of uniform textbooks and consolidated schools. The period from 1906–16 saw the establishment of the State Certificate, the raising of teacher requirements and the founding of consolidated schools.

The period of greatest expansion was from 1917–1929. During this time 80 percent of the rural schools of the State were built, State aid was made available for rural schools, free textbooks were provided and $6,500 was appropriated for a State-wide educational survey. In 1919 a revision of elementary and secondary school courses was completed. In 1926 the peak of teaching salaries was reached, the high salaries attracting a class of better qualified teachers.

Between 1929 and 1940, economic conditions forced many

charges, including drastic reduction in teaching salaries, and the closing of some rural schools, as families moved away. At the same time, however, many town and country schools were built through WPA and PWA aid. The depression-born schoolhouses stand as the largest building in many towns and cities. It was fortunate that so many schools were built at the time, for following World War II enrollments jumped greatly, together with building costs.

By 1950 there were more than 7,000 grade and high school teachers for the more than 113,000 public school students in the State. School districts maintained 3,837 schools, including 81 large consolidated school centers serving large areas, and 302 accredited four-year high schools. In addition there were 60 parochial schools, 13 of which offer high school courses.

To provide further educational facilities for the youth of this new frontier, the first Territorial legislature, at its first meeting at Yankton in 1862, passed a measure to create a university in Dakota Territory. The act provided for a board of 18 regents with authority to appoint teachers, form courses of study, fix tuition, and grant degrees. The legislature was given power to determine salaries. But it was not until 20 years later that the university buildings were actually started.

As the State developed, and its agricultural, commercial, and industrial activities expanded, its school system expanded also. The interest of the State became more clearly defined, and the types of educational institutions needed, became more evident. To meet these recognized needs, there are now in the State, in addition to the grade and high schools, sixteen institutions of higher education, seven of them State-supported and nine, including junior colleges, privately supported. W. H. H. Beadle, Superintendent of Public Instruction from 1879 to 1885, was greatly interested in the common schools of the State, and in the problem of supplying teachers for them. As a result, normal schools were established at Madison, Spearfish, Springfield, and Aberdeen, during the next few years.

The first institution of higher learning in South Dakota was established by the Congregational Church in 1881 at Yankton. It is known as Yankton College. The University of South Dakota was founded at Vermillion in the following year, 1882, through the aid of people of the town and county. At present the university is divided into eight major divisions: College of Arts and Sciences, College of Fine Arts, School of Business Administration, School of Education, School of Law, School of Medicine, the Graduate School, and the Extension Division. There is also the Black Hills School of the Theatre, operated in connection with the university's summer Black Hills Playhouse (*see Tour 5, Sec. C*).

Since the founding of the university, more than 6,700 men and women have been graduated. The average annual enrollment since 1946 has been 1,775, and the teaching faculty numbers 130. Many members of the faculty are known as the authors of textbooks and scholary publications, or for their contribution to scientific research. Among the distinguished graduates is an internationally recognized scientist, Ernest O. Lawrence, who developed the atom-smashing cyclotron, and was the winner of the Nobel Prize in Physics for 1939.

Since its founding in 1883, the State College of Agriculture and Mechanic Arts at Brookings has had a wide influence in the advancement of South Dakota, both through the activities of its graduates and through scientific service rendered. The work of this institution falls into five major divisions: agriculture, engineering, pharmacy, home economics, and general science.

It is only natural in an agricultural State such as South Dakota that major emphasis should be given to this subject in a State educational institution. The four-year college course provides instruction in agronomy, animal husbandry, dairy husbandry, horticulture, agricultural engineering, veterinary medicine, poultry raising, entomology-zoology, and farm economics. In addition, students are given broad training in English, mathematics, chemistry, biology, modern languages, history, and political science.

One of the greatest services State College performs for the farmers is the continuous research carried on through its experiment station farm at Brookings which has 1,200 acres devoted to experimental use. Here crops are tested for adaptability to soil and climate; feeding and breeding experiments are carried on for all classes of animals; fruit varieties are originated and tested; and destructive plant diseases and insects are studied to develop methods of control and eradication.

One of the potent forces in carrying to the people the information derived from these experiments is the agricultural extension service, with its corps of specialists, county agents, and home demonstration agents in the field.

The first of the teachers' colleges, Eastern State Normal School, recently renamed General Beadle State Teachers College, was opened at Madison in 1883, and in the same year, Sioux Falls College was founded at Sioux Falls by the Baptist Church. In 1884 the Episcopal Church established, at Sioux Falls also, a school for girls, known as All Saints' School. The following year, 1885, witnessed the founding of two more major educational institutions: Dakota Wesleyan University, a Methodist school, at Mitchell, and the Black Hills Teachers College at Spearfish.

The South Dakota School of Mines and Technology at Rapid City, established in 1887, is ideally situated among the Black Hills. The great variety of minerals, ores, and rock formations; the streams available for experiments in light, power, and irrigation; the nearby manufacturing plants; the forests, and the fossil-bearing Badlands —all these give to the School of Mines and Technology scientific and engineering advantages such as few other technical institutions possess.

In recent years it has expanded its engineering departments to include the latest developments in mechanical, industrial, hydraulic, and civil engineering. The school undertakes extensive paleontological and geological expeditions each summer, providing outstanding exhibits for its museum in Rapid City (*see CITIES*).

Augustana College at Sioux Falls, largest denominational liberal arts school in the State, was created by uniting Lutheran schools of Canton and Sioux Falls, which had been founded in 1889. An extensive building program following World War II was undertaken to accommodate the increased enrollment. It is supported and controlled by the Evangelical Lutheran Church.

Southern State Teachers College was established at Springfield in 1895 and, in recent years, has specialized in industrial arts and vocational training. In 1902, the Northern Normal and Industrial School, later changed to Northern State Teachers College, was started at Aberdeen and soon became one of the Northwest's largest teacher-training schools.

In 1898 the Presbyterian University, founded at Pierre in 1883, was moved to Huron and became known as Huron College.

Among the educational institutions of more recent development are Wessington Springs College established in 1923; and Freeman Junior College established in 1927. The school at Wessington Springs is sponsored by the Free Methodist Church, and that at Freeman by the Mennonites.

Mount Marty, a girls' school at Yankton operated by the Benedictine Sisters, added a four-year college course in 1950, to its high school and normal training classes. Notre Dame Junior College, which had been part of a Catholic academy at Mitchell for 28 years, was transferred to Aberdeen in 1951, and renamed the Presentation Junior College, a school for girls.

Special institutions operated by the State are the School for the Blind at Gary, the School for the Deaf at Sioux Falls, the State Training School at Plankington, and the School and Home for the Feeble-Minded at Redfield.

With no educational facilities for the more than 2,400 educable but physically-handicapped children on the State Board of Health's register in 1948, a citizens' movement in the East-river area raised a half-million dollars to build the Crippled Children's Hospital-School at Sioux Falls. It is governed by a board of directors representing the more than 50,000 contributors, and has no governmental, denominational, or fraternal affiliation. A school for crippled children is also operated at Hot Springs in connection with the West River Polio Center, a Lutheran institution.

More than 5,000 Indian youths attend schools on the various reservations and at large government boarding schools maintained at Pierre and Flandreau. For many years, the churches carried the brunt of education among the Sioux, and they still have some of the largest and most efficient schools. There are six elementary and four high schools at Catholic missions. Especially interesting are St. Paul's at Marty, St. Francis at Rosebud, and Holy Rosary at Pine Ridge, all of which are on or near US 18. The Episcopal school, St. Mary's at Springfield, is the only exclusively Indian girls' high school in the United States.

RELIGION

Among the earliest explorers of the region which is now South Dakota were the Jesuit missionaries, who worked among the Indians, converting many to the Christian faith. Rev. Thomas S. Williamson and Rev. Stephen R. Riggs, with their wives, were the first Protestant missionaries to make their homes among the Indians in this region. In 1840 Dr. Riggs made a journey to Fort Pierre and while there conducted a religious service, the first Protestant service conducted in what is now South Dakota.

Working together, Williamson and Riggs translated the Bible, *The Pilgrim's Progress,* several hymn books, and other literature into the Eastern Sioux language. Dr. Riggs was the author of a valuable Dakota-English dictionary, giving the Sioux words and their English equivalents.

The work of the early Catholic missionaries was confined at first to the wandering bands of the Sioux, rather than in settled missions. The first Mass in the State was held on the James River in Bennett County in 1842 by Father A. Ravoux. On the same trip he visited the French-Canadian trappers and their families at Fort Pierre. In 1839 Father De Smet made the first of many visits to the Dakota Sioux. He visited the Badlands of the White River on this trip and found a band of Sioux there. He returned in 1851, and many times thereafter until 1866. The first Catholic Church was erected at Jefferson in 1867.

The earliest Protestant religious movement in Dakota Territory (including what is now the States of North and South Dakota) was begun by Baptists in 1852, when they established a mission at Walhalla for the evangelization of the Indians. Its leaders were Elijah Terry and James Tanner.

In the southern half of Dakota Territory, the missionaries came with the pioneers to the earliest settlements, especially those at Yankton, Vermillion, Elk Point, and Bon Homme. They risked the dangers of frontier life in their desire to preach the gospel to those who, with them, were laying the foundation of a new State and endeavoring to shape its character and destiny.

In January 1860, Rev. Charles D. Martin, a missionary connected with the Presbyterian Church, reached Yankton and preached the first sermon to a congregation of white people in Dakota Territory The congregation was large and enthusiastic. His text was, "Who so despiseth the Word shall be destroyed; but he that feareth the commandment shall be rewarded" (Proverbs 13:11). He preached from an upturned whiskey barrel, the only available substitute for a pulpit.

Rev. Martin seems to have been familiarly called "Father Martin," and to have come at that time from Dakota City, Neb., a distance of about 70 miles. In October 1860, he solemnized the first marriage recorded after Dakota Territory was opened for settlement, that of Miss Robinson to Mr. Jacob Deuel.

One incident of early days reveals the attitude of many of the rougher pioneers in what is now western South Dakota. It is related that an Easterner, visiting Fort Pierre, asked, "Does the stage to the Black Hills run on Sunday?" A man from Deadwood, who happened to be going on the same stage, replied, "Stranger, there ain't no Sunday west of the Missouri River and no God west of the Cheyenne. If a man dies west of the Missouri, they don't bury him; and if he dies west of the Cheyenne, the coyotes won't eat him."

Two other figures of importance in the religious development of South Dakota were Rev. J. W. Cook, an Episcopal minister, who located at Greenwood in 1870, and Jedediah Smith, a young minister of the Methodist Episcopal Church who is said to have been the first person to perform a public act of worship within the confines of the State of South Dakota.

The heterogeneous nature of the population of the State has resulted in the establishment and growth of numerous religious organizations. The Norwegians, Swedes, and Germans brought with them Lutheran doctrines and ideas and established their Lutheran churches the Irish, French, and Germans established Catholic organizations. Other groups with varying religious doctrines organized themselves in like manner.

Today nearly all common religious faiths are represented in South

Dakota. The Lutherans have the largest membership, with the Catholics second. The State census report of 1945 showed these two at 147,448 and 91,836, respectively, followed by the Methodists with 65,577. Other larger groups were the Presbyterians, with 26,579; the Congregationalists, with 26,150; the Baptists, with 17,001; the Episcopalians, with 10,771; and the Reformed, with 10,592. The Evangelical church membership was reported at 5,216; the Mennonite church at 4,475; the Christian church at 4,062; and the Seventh Day Adventist, 1,816. Nearly all common religious faiths are represented in South Dakota, and in recent years there has been a marked increase in the evangelist movements. The Assembly of God, Church of the Bible, Gospel Tabernacle, Church of God, and others, have many fine new edifices throughout the State.

Most of these denominations have their young people's organizations and meetings. Summer institutes for young men and women are held annually by the Methodist, Congregationalist, Baptist, and Presbyterian groups. Most of the groups meet in the Black Hills in the latter part of June and the early part of July, in their various church camps.

Transportation

SOUTH DAKOTA has the framework of an adequate transportation system. The northeast and southwest corners of the State are cut by transcontinental railroads. Two lines traverse the State from east to west, and other lines run north and south through the eastern and Black Hills regions. Ten Federal highways cross South Dakota, five from north to south, and five from east to west. Three major airlines and a feeder line serve the State. (*See GENERAL INFORMATION*.)

The State's first highway was the Missouri River, which flows south through the approximate center of the State and then curves out of it at the southeast corner. Up this broad highway, in the early days of the white man's settlement, came the explorer and the trader, the trapper and the priest. They came by canoe, by boat, by barge, and finally by steamer. When the first farms fringed the eastern border of the State, the covered wagon and the ox team brought the settlers in from Iowa and Minnesota, and the agricultural frontier was pushed slowly westward.

Gold was discovered in the Black Hills and immigration swept the State. Railroads that had just touched the eastern border sprang into life and leaped halfway across the State. The Chicago & North Western stopped on the river at Pierre, and the Chicago, Milwaukee, St. Paul & Pacific at Chamberlain. Farther than that they could not go, because beyond was Indian country. But gold lay 250 miles to the west. Long winding bull trains began to thread their way from Pierre westward, from Sidney and Cheyenne northward, from Bismarck southwestward to the Black Hills.

Oxen, however, were too slow for passengers, so the stagecoach was added to the crowded thoroughfare, and the still swifter pony express carried the mail. Boats, competing with the railroad, carried the heavy freight up the broad Missouri from Yankton and Sioux City, and unloaded at Chamberlain and Fort Pierre. Ten years later, the Chicago, Burlington & Quincy and the North Western came from the south into the Hills, and the bull trains vanished.

The first railroad to enter the State was the Winona & St. Peter, afterward part of the North Western system. In 1871 this railroad was built as far as Lake Kampeska, but for seven years it was operated only to Gary, just within the State lines. In 1872 the Dakota Southern, afterward acquired by the Milwaukee, built into the State from the south, through Elk Point to Vermillion. In 1878 the Worthington & Sioux Falls Line was built, connecting Sioux Falls with Sioux City. Thus prior to 1880 there were short stubs of railroad projecting into the State at three points.

The discovery of gold in the Hills brought in the Great Boom period, and with it the building of railroads. In the year 1880 both the Milwaukee and the North Western extended their lines to the Missouri. The same year the Milwaukee began to build its transcontinental line across the northern border counties of the State.

The eighties saw much railroad building. In 1884 the Minneapolis & St. Louis began building lines in South Dakota, eventually to reach half across the State; and in the same year the Chicago, Rock Island & Pacific entered Watertown from the southeast. In 1886 the North Western built north from its Nebraska lines to skirt the eastern and northern borders of the Black Hills, putting an end to the picturesque old trails, from Sidney, Neb., from Cheyenne, Wyo., from Bismarck, N. Dak., and from Fort Pierre. In 1887 the Great Northern built one of its two lines reaching into the State from the northeast, and the Illinois Central reached Sioux Falls. The following year the Burlington built across the extreme southwestern corner of the State, and three years later extended a branch line up through the center of the Hills to Deadwood. This compelled the North Western also to build up into the Hills from its terminus at Whitewood.

The depression of the early 1890's put an end to railroad building in the State for a time. It was not until 1902 that the Sault St. Marie built a short line into the Lake Region in the northeast. In 1906 the Rapid City, Black Hills & Western constructed a scenic line up Rapid Canyon for 35 miles. In 1907 the North Western and the Milwaukee extended their lines from the Missouri River to the Black Hills, and the railroad picture was practically complete.

However, the picturesque Rapid Canyon line was foreclosed and dismantled following World War II, and some of the other railroads have adopted track-driven vehicles for branch line service.

The railroad history of the State is unique in many respects. The transcontinental lines do not traverse the central part of the State. Pierre, the capital city, is served by a line of the North Western

ending in the Black Hills. The reason is twofold. The Indian reservation to the west blocked railroad building till the first decade of
this century, and the Black Hills furnished a natural barrier, becoming a terminus in themselves.

There has been a marked rivalry between the North Western and
the Milwaukee systems. Both built their roads to the Missouri
River in the same year, and both completed their lines to the Hills
at the same time; but the rivalry did not stop there. In the first five
years of the present century, when the question of a permanent site
for the capital was still being agitated, the North Western backed
Pierre, and the Milwaukee backed Mitchell.

The Black Hills Region, with its wealth of scenic and historic
features, is served by the North Western, the Burlington, and the
Milwaukee. While, due to the difficulties of the terrain, the railroads do not approach the more impressive areas, they connect at
convenient points with adequate bus services. One of the railroads,
the Burlington, conducts its own motor tour of the Hills. The Badlands are skirted on the south by the Milwaukee. The Lake Region
is touched by practically every line that enters the State.

South Dakota has been slow in building modern highways.
Long distances and limited finances held up construction of trunk
highways for many years. The first automobile trip from Pierre
to the Black Hills was made in 1905, by Peter Norbeck, who later
became governor; he followed the winding, deep-rutted Deadwood
Trail abandoned by the bullwhackers. The prairie trails were gradually converted to motor use, but in the Black Hills the hell-for-leather
stage coach routes and toll roads were something else. Funds to
build highways penetrating the mountain recesses were a long
time coming for the farmer-dominated legislatures favored farm-
to-market roads. The solid granite upthrusts of the Harney Range
also discouraged roadbuilding in the central mountain area until
Norbeck personally directed construction of the Needles Highway
(see TOUR 14A). Four engineers-in-charge resigned before the
14.5-mile road was completed between US 16 and US 85A.

The State Highway Department was not organized until 1918.
Its first improved road was 13.2 miles from Watertown east. It
was not until 1938 that travelers could cross South Dakota on a
dustless, oiled highway, US 16. A network of highways now crisscross the State, with most of the main traveled routes being hard-
surfaced. There are a number of scenic roads, particularly in the
Black Hills, but the most spectacular is the Iron Mountain Highway
—US 16, through part of Custer State Park (see TOUR 5, Sec. C).
Like the Needles Highway, which was built with a combination
of artistry and pure cussedness, the Iron Mountain Highway provides

a series of unusual views. It has one of the longest spiral, or pigtail, bridges in America, and three tunnels that frame the figures of Mount Rushmore in the distance.

Passenger bus and motor freight lines have kept pace with highway development. These lines connect many points not otherwise served, and provide fast and frequent service for intrastate traffic as well as interstate connections. A fleet of sight-seeing busses, with convertible tops, are operated in the Black Hills.

The first regular air service was established in South Dakota in 1928, from Rapid City through Pierre and Huron to Watertown. All the larger cities now are served by commercial airlines (*see GENERAL INFORMATION*). Modern airport terminals are maintained at Sioux Falls, Huron, Watertown, Aberdeen, Rapid City, Pierre, Mitchell, Yankton, Brookings, and the Black Hills Airport which serves Spearfish, Lead, and Deadwood. In addition, there are numerous airports serving local and transient aircraft. Nearly every county has at least one such field.

Although the Missouri River has played an important part in the history of the State and formed its first great highway, there is no commercial traffic on its waters within the confines of the State today.

Architecture

ALTHOUGH no type of architecture is peculiar to South Dakota, there are wide variations within the State, owing to the character of the country. Materials and styles differ in the farming, ranching and mountainous sections, each showing influences brought from surrounding regions, coupled with the utilization of the earth, timber, and stone at hand.

First the Arikara Indian went to the river banks to build his hut of sticks and mud, inside of which were living quarters for his several wives, children, and horses. Then came the Sioux Indian with his portable tent of buffalo hide, well-tanned and stretched on poles. When the first white settlers began pouring into the new country, they laboriously built log houses where trees were available; but as most of the State was treeless, the earth was made to serve as the building material. These pioneers who came to file claims on the virgin prairie found that by hitching their oxen to a plow, it was comparatively simple to loosen furrows which could be cut into blocks five or six inches thick, a foot wide and two or three feet long. The dirt was so interwoven with the strong roots of prairie grass that the chunks were solid enough to be carried easily and laid, brick-fashion, into place. Damp dirt was used to fill in crevices and around the windows, which were usually high and small. Roofs often were made of limbs, brush and hay with a covering of dirt; usually, however, cheap slab lumber covered the sod shanties. In the late 1870's and for a few years the land seekers were content to live in their drab, squat sod houses while they proved up their claims; those people became known as Soddies.

That was more than a half-century ago, but on the Indian reservations, particularly the Pine Ridge and Rosebud, sod houses are still being occupied by white families as well as Indians, and it will be some time before the complete transition to modern homes will be effected. Today there is a revival of interest in utilizing the

70

prairie soil as building material. The use of rammed earth is being proved practical as well as economical through experiments at South Dakota State College, and its use in small towns and on the farms is gaining favor again. Dirt with a high content of sand is placed in molds and compressed, simple tire jacks often being used in the operation. Rammed earth walls afford excellent insulation, holding the heat in winter and keeping it out in summer; the mottled soil has a lovely natural color and the walls increase in strength with age. Such structures are conveniently used for chicken houses and livestock barns.

Along the rivers and in the Black Hills logs were the most available building material in the eighties when much of this frontier area was young. Rivers were banked with large cottonwood trees and the soft wood was hewn square, notched at the ends, and chinked with clay. The use of logs was not confined to home-building; in fact, the first schoolhouse in the State was made of logs in Bon Homme County in 1860, and many business establishments combined logs with "store" lumber to save money. When the Black Hills were suddenly populated during the gold rush of 1876, log buildings were put together as simply and quickly as possible. Ponderosa pine logs were peeled, notched a few inches from the end, laid up and chinked with either plaster or slabs; exceptions, however, where the logs were carefully hewn and notched so that the ends were flush at the corners, still stand while the others have fallen to disrepair. An old cabin in Custer which was built in 1874, shows the intricate system of notching logs, and the axe marks where the log was evened give indication of the tedious labor expended by the pioneers (*see illustration*). Stone fireplaces in those days were held together with mud instead of cement; an example of such a fire place, still in good condition, is in the cabin on the floor of Stratosphere Bowl (*see Tour 5, Section b*).

Log cabins are still popular in the Black Hills. There along creeks and under crags an almost endless number of cabins are built attractively of native pine logs. But the style has been adapted to a new taste and expression; from the rectangular, hand-hewn, one-story cabin, the home-builders have evolved bungalows and huge, rambling residences of stained, peeled logs, with stone foundations and trim.

The character of the wind-swept plains country, coupled with the background of homesteading groups, resulted in some peculiar designs in the eastern section of the State. Most of the pioneers, both in town and country, built square, four-room, frame houses, which invariably were painted white; then as the family and income grew, an addition was tacked on the house, or a second story built.

Since then have come the second and third generations, adding a porch or sun parlor to meet their increased demands. Into the north-central section of the State, around Eureka (*see Tour 1*), families from Eastern Europe came to homestead. Economical and practical, these Germans who had previously emigrated to Russia constructed long, low, frame buildings combining the house, granary and barn. By dividing the building into three sections—the first for the family, second for the grain and third for the livestock—wall space and heat were conserved. Such houses still stand, but the families have grown and prospered, and the customs have changed so that the original practice is no longer observed. One of the features of early residences in South Dakota was the cupola perched on top of many houses. Because of the frequent snowstorms that often reach blizzard proportions, combined with the lack of landmarks on the flat prairie, the cupola, like the Old North Church, was used to hang lanterns in so that members of the family, neighbors and strangers could find their way on stormy nights. The extreme weather has had its effect on architecture. Windows and doors facing north are avoided, especially in the open country where icy wintry blasts seem to penetrate even the sideboards. And protection in summer against the bright sun is acquired by means of wide porches and awnings.

Borrowing their designs from more easterly States, there was a strong predilection during the nineties for frills and fringes carved out of wood around windows and porches. This was the "scroll-saw" period and townsmen and farmers alike had curliques dropping from the eaves and around porch pillars. Houses long deserted in ghost towns of the State may have sideboards flapping in the wind, but the slightly askew wooden lacework still reflects that gay period.

The use of native materials in public buildings is prevalent; in fact, the State owns and operates a cement plant (*see Rapid City*). It has several quarries of granite and sandstone, and the Black Hills yield quantities of lumber. A new trend is shown in the Black Hills where several public buildings are of rock taken, virtually, from their own back yards. An outstanding example is the new, modern-styled Sylvan Lake Hotel, high on a pine-capped granite cliff overlooking the lake and facing towering Harney Peak. It was designed as an inhabitable continuation of the gray rock ledge, by Harold Spitznagel, Sioux Falls architect, who ordered that no moss be removed from the rough rock (*see Tour 14*). The low, massive Indian Museum in Rapid City was built from irregular ledge formations, some weighing more than a ton, (*see RAPID CITY*), and the soft yellow limestone in the buildings of the Black Hills Airport came from the cliffs further down the road (*see Tour 4*). In Custer State Park, uncut boulders with moss intact have been rolled up to form a rambling museum, and in several Black Hills cities native stone is being utilized for public buildings. While the trend in the Black Hills is to make public buildings blend with the natural scene, cities in other sections of the State have coupled economy with local pride and rolled boulders, residue of the glacial period, off nearby hills, and cut and chipped them to make business and monumental buildings. In Pierre, for instance, the county courthouse, a new, attractive structure, was built of colorful reddish-gray flecked rocks from the hillsides, costing only the trouble of moving; sandstone from Hot Springs is used for trim. More of this easily cut sandstone is found in the State Soldiers' and Sailors' Memorial Hall where it is used for exterior and interior, its soft texture allowing effective carvings (*see PIERRE*).

The trend toward combining local materials with a rambling design where building space is plentiful was followed in the new Governor's Mansion at Pierre. The building has two large wings, one at the front and one at the rear so that it forms a modified letter-Z. Native lumber, brick, and cement were used exclusively, and the fireplaces were made of petrified wood from the Badlands.

The plan for the State Capitol was taken from that of the National Capitol, and the stone imported from Indiana. Most of the county courthouses, built in the early 1900's, have copper domes, long weathered black; the wings of the buildings which were patterned after the State Capitol were of such abbreviated proportions that the desired effect was lost; examples of this type are at Webster (*see Tour 3*), Brookings (*see Tour 4*), *and* Onida (*see Tour 12*). The newer courthouses, however, are modern in design, usually with an addition on the roof, looking like a penthouse but used as a jail. These are found at Ipswich (*see Tour 2*), Redfield (*see Tour 3*), Pierre (*see PIERRE*), and Mitchell (*see MITCHELL*).

In Sioux Falls, the State's largest city, many of the buildings are of a durable pink rock, quarried barely outside the city limits. The county courthouse, with its church-like spire, and a new million-dollar high school, two stories high and covering a block are examples of the use of native stone. There are no skyscrapers in South Dakota; the highest building is the 11-story Alex Johnson Hotel in Rapid City. With so much space available, buildings of more than four stories are few in all the cities of the State.

In the large towns and cities the style of the architecture is lost in a maze of variations. A Dutch Colonial house is neighbor to a California bungalow; public buildings are patterned after those in older States. The college campuses have buildings of many styles and materials.

Small prairie towns almost invariably present the picture of a high, black-bowled water tower, three or four tall, red grain elevators lined up along the railroad, a few one-story brick buildings on Main Street, false-front and unpainted stores on the side streets, spired churches—one brick and others wood—a large imposing brick schoolhouse, located proudly on the highest rise of ground, and four out of five houses painted white with open porches in front and coal sheds at the rear. The false-front, frame store buildings, many of which have second-story porches protruding over board sidewalks, are still found in most towns of western South Dakota. The so-called false-front buildings are those with fronts extended squarely upward beyond the ridge of the roof, giving the effect of an extra story.

White farmhouses and large red barns which splotch the South Dakota plains are characteristic of the entire Middle West. It is an established axiom that architectural priority is given the barn in preference to the house. Out in this farming country, the hip-roof barns are huge, and the chicken coops, hog barn, granary, garage and outhouses are grouped together to break the wind in winter. Unlike surrounding grain belt states, there are few silos; but windmills dot the prairie.

Unlike the farm buildings which are almost always built on the highest rise of ground available, the ranches in the western part of the State are located in draws, and out of the wind. The cattle ranches are distinguished from farms by the usually unpainted, rambling house, low barn, bunkhouse and corrals. Every first-rate ranch has at least two corrals; one is round, the other square, each made of poles and posts. The round corral has a stout snubbing post in the center of it, and is used in roping and branding horses and cattle; the square corral is for confinement purposes and serves also as an adjunct to the round corral. Few buildings are needed for a ranch, as only saddle horses and a few work horses and cows are kept in the barn, and the feed is piled in stacks out of doors. A sheep ranch differs from a cattle ranch with regard to the style of barns and corrals. A sheep shed is about 100 by 30 feet, has a high board fence which extends south from the west side, and a wire fence completes the rectangular corral with the shed and board fence furnishing shelter against the northwest winds. Many of the old cattle and sheep ranch houses are made of logs; they are likely to follow a certain type—long and low. The building, of heavy cottonwood, cedar or pine logs hauled from a distance, is the width of one room with the length governed only by the number of rooms required. To save on materials the eaves begin little higher than a man's head, the roof slopes only slightly, and the windows are set low. In a long house of several connecting rooms, there are usually two outside doors, both on the south side. The main door leads into an entry which connects with the large kitchen, the most important and most-used room on the ranch. As a ranch prospers, a new frame house is built and the old log house is relegated to storehouse purposes, or becomes the bunkhouse. The new home is usually square and painted the ubiquitous white with green trimmings.

Attempts are being made to evolve a type of architecture to fit the prairie sites of this plains region. The U.S. Indian Service, in constructing hospitals at Sisseton, Wagner and Rapid City, designed rambling, one-story stucco buildings with large windows and roof gardens. The Rural Rehabilitation Corporation in planning houses for farming communities featured five-room cottages made of pine boards, 10 inches wide, running up and down, rows of windows to the south and east, and a storage tank for water in the attic to provide plumbing facilities. Simplicity rules in the design of new buildings and the material used is that at hand.

Except for the engineering feat of blasting and drilling out the features of four Presidents on Mount Rushmore (*see Tour 5B*), the erection of impressive monuments must await sufficient time and funds in South Dakota. Large boulders, with bronze tablets, mark most of the historic landmarks, awaiting the time when suitable monuments, replicas and restorations can be made.

Folklore and Folkways

ORIGIN of Folkways: When large groups of people migrate from one country to another, they tend to take with them and perpetuate in the new country the language, customs, and traditions of the old. They retain their group identity and are slow to assimilate with their new fellow countrymen. An example of this is the twice-transplanted German-Russians. Originally German they migrated to Russia where they remained for several generations. From there many of them migrated once more to the plains of North and South Dakota and settled in large groups. But in spite of their double migration, they still retain their racial purity, a partial use of their language, and many of their old world characteristics and customs. Conversely, when people migrate as individuals and scatter out in the new country, they tend to assimilate quickly. They forget their childhood language and lose their racial identity. In South Dakota the principal groups retaining their folkways are the Finns, the Scandinavians, and the Russian-Germans. It goes without saying that the largest body of people within the State having their own peculiar customs and ways of living are the Indians, but they are dealt with in a separate article in the present volume.

The Finns have the reputation of being somewhat clannish, and State statistics of racial strains show that they tend to settle in large colonies, more so than any of the other racial elements. They show a persistent attachment to their native tongue, which is unlike any other North European language and very difficult to understand or acquire. With them Finnish is the universal language of the home. While the children learn English in school and speak it without accent, at home they use the language of their elders. Finns are likely to take the same side on questions of public policy, and to vote as a unit.

One trait of the Finns is their exceeding fondness for coffee. In a Finnish household the coffee pot is literally never off the stove.

When a guest enters a Finnish home, he is immediately offered a cup of coffee; and even in the absence of guests, the family is likely to drink coffee at least once between each two meals. The Finns also use skis to a greater extent than the Scandinavians and their skis are somewhat different in shape and appearance.

Probably the most characteristic custom existing among the Finns today is their system of bathhouses—"Finlander hells," as they are popularly known. These bathhouses are detached buildings of sod, stone, or any other convenient material, built as nearly airtight as possible. There will not be a bathhouse for every house but perhaps two or three to a community. On a set day a fire is built in the bathhouse under a flat rock or rocks, and when the rocks have been thoroughly heated, the fire is raked outside the building and as many as wish to bathe, or as many as the hut will hold, enter with pails of water and close the door tight. Water is then poured on the heated rocks, and immediately the place is filled with steam. The amount of steam can be accurately regulated by the amount of water thrown on the rocks. The Finns, through practice, can endure a great amount of the hot vapor, but others would be well-advised to proceed with caution. Since rocks hold heat for some time, those who have bathed give their places to others until all have had their turn. Sometimes the baths are prepared for men and sometimes for the women and girls, since the whole community follows this custom. The Finns are very hospitable in inviting those not of their race to avail themselves of these baths and, although in principle a Turkish bath, it is an experience not often to be met with in such a setting.

The Scandinavians, while not so clannish as the Finns, have a strong feeling of racial solidarity. This is more true of the Swedes and Danes than of the Norwegians. The racial tables show that the Danes, more than the other two, tend to settle in large colonies. The Swedes and Norwegians are scattered generally throughout the State. But all these races have certain characteristics in common, among them a fondness for coffee. It is a Scandinavian custom to have a lunch in the middle of the forenoon and again in the middle of the afternoon, consisting of coffee and cookies or cake. The men come to the house, if they are working nearby; but if at a distance the women take the lunch out to them in the field.

On Easter Sunday the men stage a contest to see who can eat the greatest number of eggs. The Norwegians celebrate their independence day on the 17th of May with games, sports, and community picnics.

Another Scandinavian characteristic is their fondness for the cooking of the homeland. In Beaver Valley near Sioux Falls and in many other Swedish communities there is still to be found the

smorgasbord, an array of "appetizers" of all sorts, often forming
the evening meal. The Scandinavian fondness for fish is proverbial,
and of the many varieties *ludefisk* or *lutefisk,* cod cured in lye,
seems to be the favorite. The *ludefisk* season extends roughly from
the first day of November until after the Christmas holidays. At
Storla, south of Woonsocket, there is a huge annual *ludefisk* dinner,
to which people come from all that part of the State. In addition,
almost every Scandinavian church in the eastern part of the State
has its annual *ludefisk* feast.

Perhaps the most strongly-minded community in the State is the
Mennonite colony at Rockport (*see Tour 5*). It is a religious group,
held together by ties of both faith and race, since it is a segment of
the Russian-German immigration. The Mennonites have certain customs which tend to set them apart from their neighbors. The men
never shave after they marry. Previous to that they live in large
dormitories with others of their kind. Both men and women wear a
dress sober in the extreme, eschewing the use of bright colors and
jewelry. The sect does not believe in the use of liquor or tobacco
in any form, nor in shows, dances or other light amusements. All
property is held in common, and anyone voluntarily withdrawing
from or marrying outside of the sect loses all his financial interest
in the community. For the rest, these people are frugal, industrious, peaceable (their strong pacifist belief has been the principal
cause of their world-wide wanderings), and inclined to settle their
difficulties among themselves. They are good neighbors and welcome visitors to their community, but have a strong aversion to
having their pictures taken. They prefer to have their own schools,
since their children's difference in dress from the other pupils sometimes subjects them to petty annoyance.

In the northern section of Aberdeen is a large community of so-
called Russian-Germans. Although they are to a very large extent
Americanized, their houses, painted in many brilliant hues, still show
an old world influence, as does the use of their native language in
the home and of head kerchiefs by the older women.

Folklore: In a State not yet fifty years old and with a population
drawn from a dozen States and as many foreign countries, it is
obvious that there cannot be any one body of folklore common to
the various groups. As men gather around the campfire or before
the bar, the grizzled prospector dreams of hidden gold and future
wealth; the leathery-faced rancher harks back to the days of the
sheep and cattle wars; and the lumberjack recalls the tales of Paul
Bunyan that he heard in the Minnesota and Michigan woods. The
largest and most authentic body of folklore in the State is of course
the great storehouse of Indian legends, accounting for the phenomena

of Nature, the path of life which the Indian treads, and even the origin of the Indian himself. But first listen to the lumberjack as he tells of the origin of the Black Hills, according to the best traditions of Paul Bunyan mythology, in the story of *The Mountain That Stood On Its Head*.*

According to this tale, Paul Bunyan, the mightiest of all logging bosses, came to the Dakotas to log off the strangest of all forests, on the Mountain That Stood On Its Head. Paul had just obtained the help of Hels Helsen, the Big Swede, whom Paul christened Bull of the Woods and appointed him his foreman. As long as the logging operations were confined to the ground beneath the mountain, the industrious but unimaginative Hels managed the work successfully, leaving Paul Bunyan free to do the book work he detested but which had to be done by someone.

Now the Mountain That Stood On Its Head rested on its peak instead of its base and its slopes flared outward from the bottom, shadowing the ground beneath; and on its slopes the trees grew head-downward with their tops pointing to the earth. The rim, or base, of the mountain was two miles above the plain and on top of this base was another plain, covered with the finest standing timber and one hundred and twenty-seven miles in circumference. There were High Springs in the center forming a Lofty River, which tumbled from the rim two miles to the plain beneath in a mighty cataract called Niagara, a name which was later given to a little waterfall along the Canadian border.

Now when the trees beneath the five-mile slope of the inverted mountain had all been logged off, the Big Swede began to have trouble with his loggers. He insisted that they should go on logging the inverted slope just as they would an ordinary one—in other words that they should stand on their heads, supported by wire cables that ran from tree to tree. But while doing this all the dirt and sawdust fell into their mouths and eyes instead of to the ground and the blood ran to their heads and altogether the conditions were so unusual that they returned exhausted from each day's labors. So each day found the work going more slowly until finally there was only one tree cut per man for each seventy-two hours of work. But while the unimaginative Swede was being bested, Paul Bunyan was working out his own solution of the problem.

One morning when Bunyan awoke he found that none of the loggers was starting for the woods. He inquired the reason of the Big Swede and that taciturn individual made a speech of unaccustomed length:

"Sye forgot tal you, Bunyan, but aye goin' move dar camp. No

(*Paul Bunyan, by James Stevens, 1925.)

use to try har no moore noo aye tank. Logger can' stan' on head mooch lonker har. Aye don' tank so, Bunyan. We move new yob noo."

Paul Bunyan was enraged both at the Big Swede's assumption of authority and his familiar form of address. Raising his voice in a shout that tumbled the loggers from their bunks, he ordered them to follow him to the Mountain That Stood On Its Head. On his shoulder was a double-barrelled shotgun that he had fabricated for the job, the barrels of which he used later as smokestacks for his first sawmill. In his belt were cartridges loaded with vast amounts of powder and with sheets of steel two feet square. Arrived at the base of the mountain, actually its peak, he took aim along its inverted slopes and pulled both triggers. A thousand pine trees were sheared off and dropped straight to the ground, their tops sticking in the earth and their bare trunks waving helplessly in the air. All day the mighty Paul cleared the slopes of trees and at evening a new forest stood beneath the inverted cone, promising easy work for the loggers on the following morning.

But next day Paul saw the Big Swede going alone to the inverted mountain. With Paul Bunyan in hot pursuit the Bull of the Woods clambered up the shelving slope, crawled over the rim and began tearing up the standing pine with his bare hands. Enraged at this independent logging system, Paul took a flying leap at the rim but missed his hold and took considerable of the edge with him in his fall. A second leap and he gained the upper plain and lay there resting before what he knew would be the battle of his career. The Big Swede came toward him.

All day that epic battle raged. The sound of the blows struck could not be told from thunder and the stamping of the giants made the earth tremble till the frightened loggers crawled into their bunks and stayed there. Whenever the contestants neared the edge, great masses of earth would crumble off and fall to the plain below. Whole acres of standing pine were flattened as one or the other of the fighters felled his opponent with a mighty blow. All that day and all that night the battle raged and finally at sunrise the next morning there came a shock that overturned every bunkhouse. Shortly afterward Paul Bunyan appeared, carrying on his shoulder the vanquished Bull of the Woods.

"You're going to be a good foreman now, Hels Helsen!"

"Aye tank so, Mr. Bunyan."

"You *know* so, Hels Helsen."

"Yah, Mr. Bunyan."

But the Mountain That Stood On Its Head was no more. That titanic struggle had demolished it and spread it out over the plain.

Only a few heaps of blood-darkened dust remained, a series of mounds that are called the Black Hills today.

Gold: What magic there is in that four-letter word! How many men has it sent into the frozen Arctic and the burning African wastes. Men in all ages have lived for it, fought for it, died for it. Perhaps as much or even more sudden wealth has come from oil, but there is not the same glamour about it that clings to gold. It was gold that filled the Black Hills with tens of thousands of people drawn from all parts of the country that gave to the State an impetus which still is felt. And now that the various "strikes" have been made, the placer deposits worked out, and gold mining has passed from the individual to the industrial phase there linger tales of the early days—of mysterious mines that no one but the owner ever saw, of gold dust cached in large quantities, to remain forever lost because of the sudden death of the man who took it from the earth, of gold taken in hold-ups of treasure caches, hastily concealed and never reclaimed. All these tales are a "second crop" in any gold country. They represent the hopes of those who know that gold in its virgin state is no longer to be had. But where buried treasure exists, anyone may hope to find it, even a child; hence the appeal is universal. Many of these legends are current in the Black Hills, and there is a tale of buried gold along the banks of the Missouri at Pierre, and some in the Lake Region of the Northeast.

Sioux Legends: One of the important contributions of the Sioux Indian is a body of legends that have furnished inspiration to many of our American poets besides Longfellow. The following legend of *The Red-Eyed Quail* might find its counterpart in the Bre'r Rabbit stories of Uncle Remus.

Once upon a time a lone traveler was making his way across the plains. He had traveled many days and was becoming tired and hungry. Suddenly he saw in the distance a beautiful lake. He made up his mind that this would be a nice place to rest and procure some food. As he approached the lake he saw a large group of ducks, geese, prairie chickens and quail feeding and resting at the edge of the water. The sight of the birds increased his hunger, but he had to determine just how he could approach them without scaring them away. So he sat down and thought for some time. Finally he spread out his blanket and filled it with sticks until he had a large bundle. Throwing it on his back, he went on his way hoping that his plan would work. Suddenly the birds saw him and asked where he might be going and what he was carrying in the bundle. He told them that it contained songs that he was taking to his people. The birds all became interested and asked him to stop and sing them some of his songs, so that they might dance. He told them that he would have to put up a tent and that they would all have to go inside with him and dance as he sang. They all agreed.

So he used his blanket and put up a tent and they all went inside. Then he told them that they must close their eyes and dance in a circle around him and the first one that opened them would have red eyes. The birds agreed to this and the dance began. The traveler sang as loud as he could and as a large goose came within his reach, he seized it, twisted its neck, and pushed it under him and waited for another to come near. As he repeated his trick, a quail opened its eyes and seeing what was going on, shouted to the rest to flee. And this is said to be the reason why quails have red eyes.

Hexism: There is a difference between the harmless little superstitions which we all pretend to accept and a belief in witchcraft and magic that may influence the deluded person to commit acts of folly and even violence. Most persons think that a belief in witchcraft has not existed in this country since early New England days, but the superstition still persists. In some parts of the State today there is a belief in hexes or hexism as the following stories from the vicinity of Sioux Falls illustrate.

About thirty years ago a man and his son were returning home one night with a team and wagon after doing their trading in a nearby town. All of a sudden, for no apparent reason, the team stopped. It was a dark night, but suddenly there was a shower of falling stars. Looking about him as best he could, the man decided that this was the place where the evil spirits had often manifested their power. He knew that this power must be concentrated in some particular object and he got out to see what it was. He found it. One of the wheels, instead of the regulation twelve spokes, had a thirteenth, made of bone and gleaming white. With a heavy ax that he had in the wagon he smashed the bone spoke and immediately the team was released from the spell and the wagon moved. The next day it was found that a certain woman, suspected of being a witch, had suffered a broken leg and refused to say how she received it.

Another story concerns a man who had been ill for some time, under the care of a nurse. Finally his wife suspected that he was being bewitched. She investigated and found that the feathers in his pillow were bunched in such a manner as to assume the forms of birds, rats, and other small animals. She took the pillows and all the rest of the bedding out into the yard and burned them. The man immediately recovered, but the nurse, presumably a witch, suffered burns.

There are certain beliefs, principally theories about weather, that are prevalent in the range sections of the State. One of the commonest is that if the horses and cattle grow long winter hair early in the fall, it is a sign that there will be a hard winter. An early flight of migratory birds is said to have a similar meaning. An early flight north in the spring is taken to be a sign of an early spring. Sundogs are said to be a sign of approaching cold weather. A bright aurora borealis, one reaching high towards the zenith, is said to be a sign of approaching storm. One of the commonest beliefs is that ninety days after a fog there will be a rain. When horses run and play or when small birds swoop in flocks without apparent reason, it is said a storm is approaching.

Language of the West: Every trade and profession has its own nomenclature but the language of the West is distinctive in many ways. Farm, cattle ranch, sheep ranch, and mining camp each speaks its own vernacular. The following are some of the terms employed in these various fields of work.

On the Farm.

BANG-BOARD: a wide board rising above the side of the wagon, against which the ears of corn are thrown as they are tossed into the wagon.

BREAKING: to turn virgin prairie.

BUNDLE PITCHER: one who pitches bundles from the field into the rack and from the rack into the separator.

FANNING MILL: a contrivance for blowing the dust and chaff out of seed grain.

HOUNDS: the braces that hold the wagon tongue steady.

LISTING: plowing a field with trench-like furrows to conserve moisture.

NIGGER WOOL: a grass with tough fibrous roots that resist decay.

ROUGHAGE: forage crops.

SNAPPING: picking corn without removing the husks.

SUMMER FALLOW: to let a field lie idle for one year to absorb moisture.

WAGON HAMMER: an iron pin that holds the evener to the tongue.

With the Prospectors.

CLEAN-UPS: final separation of gold from dirt.

DISCOVERY: the place of finding the vein, or "pay."

GRUB STAKE: to provide the prospector with food in return for a half interest in what he discovers.

A LOCATION: a mining claim.

LODE: a lead or vein of ore.

PLACER (Pronounced plasser) MINING: the washing of gold from sand deposits, either through hand panning or the use of hydraulic machinery.

SOURDOUGH: refers to the prospector himself, from his weakness for sourdough biscuits.

STRIKE: hitting pay dirt.

In the Cow Country.

BRUSH UP: used of cattle, to hide out in the brush.

BUNCH-QUITTER: an animal that voluntarily quits the herd.

CAYUSE: an Indian pony.

CLOSE SEAT: steady and firm seat in the saddle.

DALLY: to wind the rope around the saddle horn.

DOGIE (pronounced with long "o"): a young steer two or three years old; formerly used of cattle shipped in from the South.

FALL-BACK: a horse which deliberately falls backward with his rider.

FENCE-CRAWLER: a breachy animal that cannot be held in a fence.

FREE MARTIN: female of mixed twins, unlikely to calve.

HAYBURNER: a horse of little value.

KYACK: saddle.

LONG YEARLING: an animal, a horse or cow, several months older than a year and not yet two.

NIGHT HAWK: the man who watches the horse herd at night.

OUTLAW: a horse that cannot be broken.

PELTER: an old horse.

PILOT OR POINTER: rider preceding the herd to show the way.

PITCHING: same as bucking.

POINT RIDERS: horsemen on each side of the herd near the front to point the herd in the right direction.

POKE: a wooden collar to restrain the fence-crawler.

SEEING DAYLIGHT: the rider leaving his seat so that daylight appears between him and the saddle.

SLICK-EAR: an animal that has not had its ears notched or split.

SPRINGER: a cow heavy with calf.

SUNFISHER: a bucking horse which twists in the air, first to one side and then to the other.

SWAPPING ENDS: a horse making a half-circle in the air.

SWING KICKERS: horseman on each side, back of the point men, to swing the main body of the herd.

TO TAIL UP: to raise weak cattle by the tail.

TRAIL HERD: cattle cut out and ready to be driven to the railroad.

WHITE FACE: a Hereford.

In Sheep Country.

BEDGROUND: the spot back of the wagon where the sheep bed every night.

BLACK-FACES: any one of several shire breeds.

TO BOG DOWN: used of a band of sheep that bunch up and refuse to move.

BRAND: in the case of sheep, a mark stamped with paint on the wool.

BUM: a lamb raised by hand.

TO BUM A LAMB: to take it away from its mother and raise it by hand.

CAMP TENDER: the man who keeps the herder in supplies and moves the wagon; or, an old ewe who picks up scraps around the wagon.

CUT-BACK: a lamb or ewe that is rejected on account of size or condition.

TO DOCK: to earmark, amputate tail and castrate lambs.

A DRAG: an individual sheep too weak to keep up with the bunch.

THE DRAG: the rear end of a moving band of sheep.

DROP BUNCH: the ewes which have not lambed yet.

DRY BUNCH: the ewes which will not lamb in a given year.

EARMARK: to notch or split the ears to indicate age.

TO FLAG A BUNCH: to place scarecrows about it to scare away coyotes.

LAMBER: one of a crew assisting at lambing time.

LAMB-LICKER: derisive term for lamber.

THE LEAD: the fore end of a moving band of sheep.

MARKER: usually a black sheep, but may be any unusual one used in checking up on possible lost sheep.

PEEWEE: a late or stunted lamb.

SHEEP HOOK: a long pole with a steel hook to catch a sheep by the leg.

SKINNY: an old ewe.

STONE JOHNNY: a monument of piled rocks, usually erected by a sheepherder.

WETHER: castrated male sheep.

WOOL-BLIND: a sheep with wool grown over its eyes, shutting out its sight.

WOOL TRAMPER: one who tramps fleeces into wool sacks.

WRANGLER: one who moves small bunches of ewes and lambs; or, who fills and empties pens for shearers.

General Terms.

BREAKS: rough or broken country along the present or former course of a stream; caused by erosion of softer soil.

BUTTE: abrupt hill rising from comparatively level country.

CHINOOK: warm wind in winter from the southwest, causing snow to vanish very quickly.

CUT-BANK: a perpendicular bank of earth, originally cut by running water, but may be any distance from existing stream bed.

COULEE: a canyon with steep sides.

DRAW: any swale or depression down which water drains or "draws."

GALLOPING GOOSE: a gas propelled, combined express and passenger railroad car, distinguished by striped front.

GUMBO: extremely sticky black clay, known geologically as Pierre clay.

HARDPAN: extremely hard clay, impervious to water and almost impossible to till.

HONYOCK: slang term for homesteader.

MUD BUTTE: a butte of pure clay and gumbo, devoid of vegetation and rising abruptly from the plain.

PROVE UP: to submit proof to the Government that the law governing homesteading has been complied with.

SQUAW SIDE OF A HORSE: right side, due to squaw's preference for mounting from that side.

Recreation

POSSESSING a wide and diversified range of recreational opportunities, South Dakota is best known for its pheasant hunting (as many as 3,500,000 birds are shot during some seasons). The State also offers mountain big-game hunting, and some excellent goose and duck shooting. There is every kind of fresh-water fishing:—trout in mountain streams; pike, bass, and other game fish in the lakes; and catfish in the Missouri and tributary rivers.

Major recreation regions are the Black Hills, along the western border, and the Lake Region, in the northeastern part of the State.

Since 1945 there has been an extensive program to develop public recreation areas throughout South Dakota. In addition to the well known Custer State Park in the Black Hills, seven more State parks, nine recreation areas, and twenty "recreation development areas" have been established under the jurisdiction of the State Game, Fish and Parks Commission. Generally, the plan is to set aside a recreation area in each of the prairie counties to provide camping, picnicking, fishing, and swimming facilities.

Those with the most developed recreation facilities are: Custer State Park, (*see Tour 5*); Farm Island State Park, (*see Pierre*); Fisher Grove State Park, (*see Tour 3*); Hartford Beach State Park, (*see Tour 2*); Lake Herman State Park, (*see Tour 10*); Newton Hills State Park, (*see Tour 7*); Oakwood Lakes State Park, (*see Tours 4 and 9*); and Union County State Park, (*see Tour 9*).

Designated as State Recreation Areas—primarily for use by the people of the surrounding communities—are: Lake Corsica, (*see Tour 7*); Lake Hiddenwood, (*see Tour 2*); Lake Iroquois, (*see Tour 4*); Lake Louise, (*see Tour 4*); Lake Molestad, (*see Tour 2*); Lake Osceola, (*see Tour 4*); Lake Pierpont, (*see Tour 2*); Richmond Lake, (*see Tour 2*); and The Palisades, (*see Tour 9A*).

Of the twenty so-called Recreation Development Areas, nearly all of them consist of tree-planting projects around artificial lakes which, in future years, will provide prairie dwellers with a shady spot to picnic, fish, and relax on Sundays.

HUNTING

Big Game. Every fall deer hunting draws hundreds of sportsmen to the Black Hills. Both the white-tail and the black-tail deer are numerous, particularly in the area known as The Limestone—a remote and rugged region along the western slope of the mountains (*see Tour 14, Sec. A*). Hunting camps are maintained each fall, and the various State lodges are opened during deer season, which usually begins about November 1. Regulations are prescribed each year by the State Game, Fish and Parks Commission (*see GENERAL INFORMATION*). In normal seasons, about 4,000 deer are killed. This represents success for about 60 out of every 100 hunters.

Elk and antelope hunting is restricted to South Dakota residents, and drawings are made for a limited number of licenses. Because outlaw bull elk and a few cows escape from Custer State Park and make damaging forays among neighboring ranches, open seasons are allowed most years. Especially sporting is the hunting of the swift antelope on the prairies adjacent to the Black Hills.

Buffalo roundups are held occasionally in the Custer State Park game refuges to cull old bulls from the herds. Visiting dignitaries are given a chance to shoot selected buffalos, and the meat is given to the Indians who are invited to add color to the hunt.

Pheasants. Climatic conditions, natural haunts, and good feeding grounds have brought South Dakota pheasants, Chinese ring-necks, a reputation of superiority. Every fall sportsmen invade the hunting grounds, with as many as 90,000 out-of-state hunters taking out licenses. The area east of the Missouri River and around Winner, in the south-central section, have the heaviest pheasant populations. For a ten-year period, an average of three million birds were killed by hunters each season. Next to buckshot, blizzards are the biggest hazard to a full life for the pheasants. Thus, every few years a short season is declared; however, the increase is so rapid that no pheasants have been planted since 1918, and no breeding farms are maintained.

Airports at Winner, Mitchell, Aberdeen, Huron, Pierre, Watertown, Sioux Falls and other towns accommodate hundreds of visiting sportsmen who fly to the State from distant points. Lockers for freezing and shipping pheasants are maintained throughout the area, and most restaurants will cook the game birds to order. (*For hunting regulations, see GENERAL INFORMATION*).

Grouse. These once plentiful birds almost disappeared some years ago, but closed seasons and other methods of protection have restored their numbers to a large extent. Unlike the pheasant, grouse are most abundant in the counties west of the Missouri River. Open seasons are generally set in late September. Ruffed grouse, or "fool hens," are confined mostly to the Black Hills. Their lack of fear of human beings makes them rather easy to kill.

Ducks and Geese. With many natural haunts—lakes, marshes, favorable shelter where food is abundant—northeastern South Dakota is a favorite halting place for hordes of ducks that remain to propagate their families in sheltered spots, and for transient birds that stop to feed on wild rice, wild celery, or duck potato before continuing their long flight southward.

About half the ducks hatched in South Dakota are blue-winged teal, pintail, and mallards. Others most common here are shovlers, gadwells, baldpates, redheads, ruddy ducks, scaup, and canvasbacks. Biologists estimate that the Lake Region breeding area produces about 46 birds per square mile.

Numerous duck passes—the most noted of which is Hedtke Pass Public Shooting Grounds, near Webster—between long chains of lakes provide hidden vantage points for hunters, who lie in wait for the fast-moving waterfowl on their way from one body of water to another. Boats and blinds are both popular with duck hunters. Many cottages and lodges are situated near the lakes, where every fall sportsmen spend several weeks hunting and fishing.

Among the better known habitats for ducks in the Lake Region are Rush Lake and Kettle Lakes and the chain known as Waubay Lakes.

Because the goose likes both water and food within easy reach along its route on the long flight southward, the Missouri River range section, that extends across the State from north to south, is a favorable hunting strip for sportsmen waiting to ambush the waterfowl that "honk high of night."

Following World War II, the State restricted waterfowl shooting to South Dakota residents. Because the heavy invasion of pheasant hunters took their limits of ducks and geese, coupled with the situation which found wealthy out-of-state sportsmen buying up the best hunting areas, and often outbidding the State for public shooting grounds, the legislature passed laws designed to halt the exploitation, at least temporarily.

FISHING

Mountain Trout. In the Black Hills three varieties of trout—rainbow, Loch Leven and brook—in numerous well stocked streams furnish opportunities for the angler to match his skill against the elusive fish that frequent the cold mountain waters. While there are other kinds of fish in the Black Hills region trout is the principal variety; it is found in every creek of appreciable size.

Lake Fish. In the northeastern part of the State, where ducks abound in the fall, Nature has provided one of her most picturesque playgrounds, the Lake Region. Bordering the northeastern line of South Dakota are the twin lakes of Traverse and Big Stone. Big Stone Lake's setting is one of the most beautiful in the entire State. Black Bass, as well as wall-eyed pike, northern pike, crappies, and other pan-fish are plentiful here.

Watertown is the center of an extensive Lake region, the chief of the group being Lake Kampeska, long noted as a summer resort and amusement center. Other important fishing and pleasure centers include Lake Andes, Lake Preston, Buffalo and Four-Mile Lakes, and Blue Dog Lake. Probably the most popular fishing resorts in the State are at Pickerel Lake and Enemy Swim, both north of Waubay. All of these and many others have ample fishing facilities, and at most of them cabins may be rented.

River Fish. Of all river fish, the catfish is the most sought after as a delicacy. Every year the Missouri River and its tributaries give up thousands of pounds of five varieties of catfish. The spotted channel "cat" is most frequently caught and most highly prized. Other river fish are sturgeon, pike, bass, and bullheads. (*For fishing regulations, see GENERAL INFORMATION.*)

SUMMER SPORTS AND ATTRACTIONS

Rodeos. The tide of homesteaders that sounded the death knell of the open range glory of the large cattle outfits 25 years ago also put an end to a unique pioneer figure—the cowboy. Suddenly swept from the free prairie life he had been used to, the cowboy, except in scattered sections, was forced to accept what little remained of his once colorful existence.

As an outgrowth of demands for a reenactment of spectacles and scenes from a day that is past, fragments of the old West have been salvaged through annual rodeos (pronounced "ro'-dee-os" in South Dakota) in which young men and women who have learned their skill from a past generation, compete. The Black Hills Round-up held annually in July at Belle Fourche is well worth seeing.

Numerous professional and amateur rodeos are staged each summer throughout the State, often in connection with celebrations (*see ANNUAL EVENTS*). Some of the most exciting are on the Indian reservations and in the ranching country, with local talent vying for prizes.

Summer Theatre. The former Luenen, Germany, Passion Players perform three nights a week at Spearfish. A huge amphitheatre, with an 800-foot stage, provides an impressive setting for the play that attracts thousands of visitors for each performance, and is considered the most professional "Passion Play" in the United States.

The Black Hills Playhouse at Legion Lake, near Custer, produces summer stock under the sponsorship of the University of South Dakota.

Hiking and Riding Trails. Camps and outdoor clubs have been established in response to the demand of multitudes of pleasure seekers who throng the Black Hills each summer. The camps are situated in spots where there are trout streams, lakes and bridle paths. Harney Peak, accessible alike to the hiker and horseman, should not be missed because of the panoramic view of the entire Black Hills area to be had from the mountain's granite peak.

Hostel tours are also made through the Black Hills.

Swimming and Boating. Public pools or beaches are maintained in most of the larger cities and several smaller towns. The Lake Region offers the best swimming, together with sail, motor, and rowboat rentals. Most of the Black Hills lakes have boat renting facilities, and the speedboat races at Sheridan Lake are a summer feature (*see ANNUAL EVENTS*).

Golf and Tennis. Drawing as many as 200 players from all parts of the State, the South Dakota Amateur Tournament, held during the latter part of June, is the major golf event each year. On Labor Day, Aberdeen holds the Dakota Open Tournament in which players from North and South Dakota and Minnesota may compete. This popular event draws an average of 100 entrants and comes as a climax at the end of the season.

Golfing fever is not confined to the larger cities. Most small towns have courses, and even in the Black Hills, where hazards are numerous, golfing is popular.

Tennis is the only minor sport that has gained much recognition on college and high school campuses. It has been played to some extent since the State was admitted into the Union in 1889. The year's chief event is the open State championship tournament held in Sioux Falls the third week in July.

Horseshoe Pitching and Corn Husking. These two farm sports are popular in South Dakota. Attracting thousands of people, a State corn husking contest and occasional national contests are held in the eastern part of the State each year. Horseshoe pitching courts are found on nearly every farm and contests are held at county fairs and celebrations.

Baseball. South Dakota takes its baseball seriously and, although it has contributed only a few players to the major leagues, it was the birthplace of American Legion Junior baseball (*see Mil-*

bank, TOUR 2). The Northern League (Class C) which operates in Wisconsin, Minnesota, and the Dakotas has professional teams at Aberdeen and Sioux Falls. There is a State League of eight teams, several semi-pro teams, and more than thirty amateur leagues that send their champions to a State Amateur Tournament at Watertown each fall. Another outstanding feature is a "Baseball Pheastival" at Huron each fall the day before the opening of the pheasant hunting season; major league stars play a team composed of minor league stars.

Other Sports. Football and basketball are the major sports of the colleges and high schools. The University of South Dakota at Vermillion and South Dakota State College at Brookings play a few intersectional contests each year, but their top games are saved usually for each other. With Augustana College at Sioux Falls they are members of the North Central Conference. Other colleges are members of a State conference. College-high school track meets have become increasingly popular, and special events are held annually at Aberdeen, Sioux Falls, Mitchell, and Pierre.

WINTER SPORTS AND ATTRACTIONS

Skiing. What once was the longest ski slide in the United States and the scene of State, regional, and national ski-jumping championships at Canton, prior to World War II, is no longer operated. However, interest in skiing has boomed in the Black Hills, which has both the terrain and climate for the sport. A beautiful four-mile run has been developed at Terry Peak, near Lead, with a power tow, warming lodge, and a professional instructor. Classes in skiing are part of the curriculum at Lead and Deadwood high schools.

Ice-Skating. With the growing popularity of figure skating and hockey, rinks are being developed in most cities and towns. Until recently, ponds and creeks had to suffice. Ice-boating is an exciting addition to winter sports on some of the larger lakes, such as Kampeska and Poinsett.

Cities

IF you are a person who believes that it takes more than 50,000 inhabitants to constitute a city, then South Dakota has only one city and several large towns. West of the Mississippi River, it is said that towns become cities early in life. In South Dakota, the term "cities" often applies to those municipalities which were optimistically platted fifty or sixty years ago to become metropolises, and sufficient time has not yet passed for them to do so. Some of the prospective cities have become quite "citified," as much so as larger and older places in the East; others have become ghost towns, but they still carry names such as Crook City, Central City, or Silver City.

There were several cities which could not be conveniently described in the Tours section on account of the amount of historical matter and the number of points of interest. The six largest—Sioux Falls, Rapid City, Aberdeen, Huron, Watertown, and Mitchell—augmented by Pierre, the State Capital, and the colorful Black Hills twins, Deadwood and Lead, are described here. It is no reflection on any city, nor its Chamber of Commerce, if it is not included in this section; other large towns will be found in the Tours section.

If early-day anecdotes do not always agree with those you have heard or read, it is because the sources—reference files and pioneers themselves—also differ. Short tours to points of interest on the outskirts of some of the cities have been arranged.

For population figures see Table of Contents.

Aberdeen

Railroad Stations: C. M. St. P. & P., Main St. & Railroad Ave.; G. N., Main St. & Railroad Ave.; C. & N. W., Pennsylvania St. & 2nd Ave. S.; M. & St. L., Main St. at 11th Ave. S.
Bus Station: Main St. & 6th Ave. for Greyhound and Kyote lines.
Airport: Saunders Municipal Airport 2.7 m. E. on US 12, for Northwest Airlines and Mid-Continent Airlines.
Traffic Regulations: Standard regulations prevail. Parking meters. Free parking lot on Lincoln St. at 1st Ave. S.
Street Numbering: Main St. divides city into E. and W. sections while Milwaukee RR. is dividing line between N. and S. street numbering. Streets to W. of Main St. numbered from 1 upward. E. of Main St. names prevail.
Accommodations: Four hotels; numerous motels and tourist camps.
Information Service: Aberdeen Civic Association, 518 S. Main.
Newspaper: American-News (*daily*).
Radio Station: KSDN.
Theatres: Auditorium-Arena, Washington & 2nd Sts., has road shows and concerts. Five motion picture houses; outdoor drive-in theatre.
Swimming: Wylie Park, NW of city, and Moccasin Creek park, E. 6th Ave.
Tennis: Melgaard Park, State St. & 17th Ave. S.
Golf: Hyde Park, extreme W. end of 8th Ave. N.; Country Club, 1 m. W.
Annual Events: Northwest Snow Queen Festival, mid-January. American Legion Pari-Mutuel Horse Races, July.

IN Aberdeen (1,229 alt.) every one of the thousands of trees has been planted by hand, thus achieving a degree of forestation on a treeless prairie not surpassed by many cities on forest sites. Pioneer builders of the city were largely from wooded areas in the Eastern States, and this gave them the urge to plant trees in large numbers.

Aberdeen, third largest city in South Dakota, is situated in the fertile James River Valley, the site once a part of the ancient Lake Dakota, with a slope so gentle that drainage can be attained only by careful engineering of street levels. There is an air of financial, commercial, and political importance about the city not often found in urban communities of similar size in the more populous sections of the Nation. The fact that it is the largest city between Minneapolis, Minn., and Butte, Mont., a distance of more than 1,000 miles, accounts for its local importance.

While some manufacturing is carried on, a recognition as a commercial center is substantially built upon distribution of manufactured goods. Its retail territory extends in a rough circle approximately 100 miles in diameter; its wholesale activities cover much of the State, as well as parts of North Dakota and Montana. The four railroads employ the greatest number of workers in the city, with wholesale distributors second.

ABERDEEN   95

In architecture, city planning, schools, and social life, the city is typical of the Midwest. There is little difference in the dress of residents of Aberdeen and those of cities farther east. A mixed population of native American stock from the Eastern and Central States, together with Russian-German and Scandinavian immigrants, has built the city on a firm foundation. Evidence of the foreign element are the annual "Ludefisk" public dinners given by Scandinavian church groups and the German dinners sponsored by groups of German birth and descent. The German-Russian influence is still seen in the picturesque wedding dinners in the tradition of the homeland on such occasions.

The so-called German-Russian section on the northeast side of the city, about six blocks from the Milwaukee tracks and east of Main about the same distance, was settled almost exclusively by immigrants from southern Russia. Their forbears emigrated from Alsace-Lorraine during the Napoleonic Wars of 1808–10 to the lowlands of the Dniester River at the invitation of Duke Richelieu, French Royalist refugee, then serving as governor of Odessa. Although they lived in Russia for two generations or more before emigrating to the United States, they preserved their language, traditions and racial purity. They settled in Aberdeen beginning in 1884 and many of the immigrants still reside here. The neighborhood has lost most of its foreign atmosphere, but many houses are painted in bright, contrasting colors, front yards are planted with vegetables and flowers, and the older women still wear silk head shawls and flowing skirts. The older people use their native language, but the tongue is restricted almost entirely to the home. The typical old style wedding, with feasting and merry-making for two and three days is sometimes celebrated.

It is probable that no white man crossed the site of Aberdeen before the coming of the government surveyors in the closing years of the 1870's. Military trails and the routes of voyageurs and trappers were to the east and west, following the James River on the east and the Missouri to the west. Perhaps the first actual settler, on the site was Friedrich Fenske, a part of whose homestead was on the original city plat.

First to consider the site as a future city was a party of 12 who drove overland from Watertown in the spring of 1880. In the party were the Rice Brothers and Charles Boyden. The party chose a spot where the survey of the Chicago, Milwaukee, St. Paul & Pacific Railway crossed the Chicago & North Western, two miles south of the center of the present city. A store was built there, a post office established, and the new town was named Grand Crossing.

Later in the summer, Charles H. Prior, immigration agent for the Milwaukee R. R., had the present site of the city platted. By July 6, 1881, the Milwaukee ran its first train into the city, named Aberdeen in honor of Aberdeen, Scotland, the native city of Alexander Mitchell, then general manager of the Milwaukee.

It was soon evident that Aberdeen, and not Grand Crossing, was to be the future city so the store erected by Rice Brothers and Boyden at the latter place was moved into Aberdeen. Here, John Firey occupied it as a drug store, one of the first in the new town. The building, now the Lacey Drug store, was still standing at Main St. & First Ave. S. in 1937.

Characteristic of the men whose leadership was to build Aberdeen into the second city of the State was Major Samuel H. Jumper, who arrived ahead of the rails to act as agent for Prior, the owner of the town site. He is said to have preceded his party on foot in order to be the first to sleep on the town site.

The settlers were largely young men who sought new homes and intended to build a new community. Wisconsin, Michigan, Illinois, Minnesota, and Iowa contributed the majority of the new settlers. There were almost no soldiers of fortune, no adventurers, nor any of the Wild West bad man type.

Almost the entire population was young, a circumstance well-illustrated by an anecdote. When Gen. Nelson A. Miles passed through the city in the eighties, he was feted and driven through the streets lined with people to greet him. Seated beside him was Mayor S. H. Jumper. Turning to Jumper the general said, "Where are the old men, Mr. Mayor?" "We have no old men, General," was the answer.

The city was incorporated in May 1882. A special charter was passed by the Legislature in 1883, providing for an aldermanic form of government, which continued until 1911, when electors decreed a change to the commission form.

With the coming of the Great Northern Railway in 1886, another spoke in the railroad wheel centering in Aberdeen was formed.

Shortly before World War I, Aberdeen gained considerable notoriety for its Home Guards. In the fall of 1916 the I. W. W. (Industrial Workers of the World) established headquarters in Aberdeen. Within a few weeks five murders and several damaging fires were attributed to the I. W. W., so young Aberdeen business and professional men organized the Home Guards, raiding the headquarters of the I. W. W. and ordering all members to stay outside the city limits. The I. W. W. in retaliation put a boycott on South Dakota in an attempt to hamper harvesting operations,

Cities of the "Middle Border"

CITY HALL, SIOUX FALLS

CORN PALACE, MITCHELL

CLOSE-UP OF CORN DESIGN

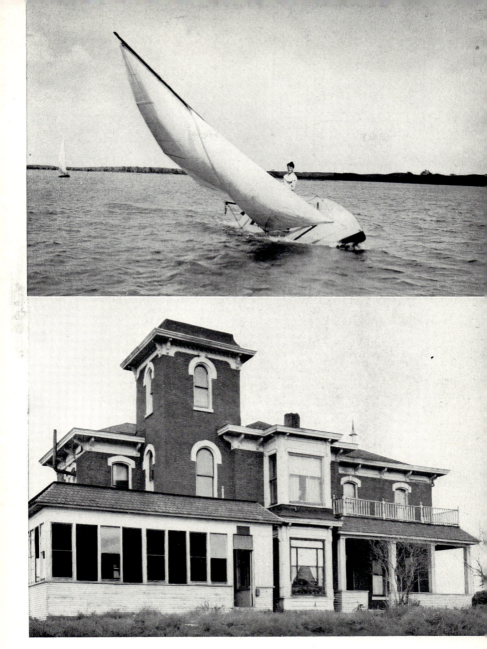

LAKE KAMPESKA, WATERTOWN

THE MELLETTE HOME

UNIVERSITY OF SOUTH DAKOTA, VERMILLION

STATE COLLEGE CAMPANILE, BROOKINGS

NORTHERN STATE TEACHERS COLLEGE, ABERDEEN

GARDEN TERRACE
THEATRE, YANKTON

PACKING PLANT
SIOUX FALLS

but local clerks and business men turned out to help the farmers and the crops were harvested.

Two men who resided in Aberdeen during its formative years gained literary recognition. One was Hamlin Garland, author of *Main Traveled Roads, A Son of the Middle Border, A Daughter of the Middle Border, Afternoon Neighbors,* and many other books. Pioneer residents recall the persons who were prototypes of characters immortalized in his novels (*see Tour 11*). L. Frank Baum, author of a series of children's stories known as the Oz books, lived in Aberdeen as a youth and young man. As editor of the *Saturday Pioneer,* a weekly newspaper, he poked fun at local citizens and officials. He often filled his columns with hilarious and fantastic stories, but these failed to impress the mortgage holders and the sheriff took possession. Baum's next literary effort was *The Wizard of Oz,* which had a phenomenal run in New York as a musical play and later became a successful motion picture.

Among native Aberdeen artists is Frances Crammer Greenmen, who has done portraits of Mary Pickford, Ella Wheeler Wilcox, and others. Frank Ashford of the Rondell community and Aberdeen has done portraits of President Calvin Coolidge, Senator Peter Norbeck, Dr. Frank Crane, and many persons of State prominence.

Best known is Syd Fossum, whose one-man shows and paintings of Dakota scenes, have been in galleries throughout the country.

World War II brought national prominence to at least three Aberdeen people, for widely different reasons. General Laverne "Blondy" Saunders, one-time Aberdeen and West Point football star, became a heroic flying commander, whose exploits have been dramatized on national radio programs and in the magazines. With one leg missing, he returned to Aberdeen after an absence of more than twenty-five years to become a successful businessman. The municipal airport bears his name.

For two young girls, whose father was the long-time pro at the Hyde Park golf course, the war meant moving and being unable to defend the local and State golf titles they were winning. By 1949, however, Marlene Bauer had been named the Woman Athlete of the Year in the U.S. and, with her sister Alice, had gone far from the home course.

In 1951 the Presentation Junior College, a school for girls, was established in connection with the Presentation Sisters' Motherhouse (*see page 99*). Future plans call for building a high school and college on a 109-acre tract at the N. end of Main St.

Although Aberdeen showed a healthy growth following World War II, it lost its position as second largest city in South Dakota to Rapid City in the 1950 Federal census. As a result, the Aberdeen businessmen entertained the Rapid City Chamber of Commerce at a banquet where the hosts ate crow.

POINTS OF INTEREST

1. The SITE OF THE DRUG STORE in *Main Traveled Roads* by Hamlin Garland, is at the corner of Main St. and First Ave. S.E., across from the Alonzo Ward Hotel. In this frame building the drug store clerk who "chased a crony wth a squirt pump" worked for John Firey, Aberdeen pioneer.

2. The AUDITORIUM-ARENA, Washington and Second Sts., is a modern structure used for civic and school affairs, having a seating capacity of 4,700 for arena events and 1,600 for theatrical productions. It is the scene of athletic contests, road shows, concerts, indoor circuses, conventions, meetings, and dances.

3 FEDERAL BUILDING, Fourth Ave. between Lincoln and Washington Sts., was dedicated by Postmaster General James Farley in 1937. This five story building of buff brick and limestone was designed to begin a "new trend" in government structures. Of particular interest is the "mahogany granite" from the Milbank quarries (*see Tour 2*) which is used around the mammoth doors.

4. ALEXANDER MITCHELL LIBRARY, cor. Lincoln St. and Sixth Ave., was originally established two years after the founding of Aberdeen, when 150 citizens subscribed $2 each and loaned 100 volumes. The first library was housed with the telephone exchange. In 1900 Andrew Carnegie provided $15,000 for a building on the condition it be named for his friend, the railroad executive (*see above*). The building held out until 1950 when its 30,000 volumes and heavy use caused it to be condemned. Books were distributed to various rooms about the town so that lending could continue while efforts were made to provide a new, streamlined building.

5. The buildings of NORTHERN STATE TEACHERS COLLEGE, cor. 12th Ave. and Jay St., form a quadrangle. On the E. side are Spafford Hall, the Administration Building, and the Mechanic Arts Building; on the S. is Central Hall, to the W. women's dormitories, Graham, and Lincoln Halls. The new Seymour Hall, a men's dormitory, is to the south of the quadrangle, and the athletic field is to the east.

The school was founded in 1902, to provide industrial training and teaching certificates. It is now an accredited four-year college, offering a Bachelor of Science degree. During World War II special technical courses were taught. The enrollment at Northern State usually exceeds 1,000 students, with a growing percentage of men taking courses.

Gypsy Day, in mid-October, is the annual, homecoming celebration, when students don the garb and habits of gypsies and revel throughout the day and evening.

The FATHER ROBERT HAIRE MONUMENT, on the campus, was erected in honor of the pioneer priest of South Dakota. Father Haire came to Dakota Territory in 1880 and built a sod church by his own efforts, near Columbia. He founded St. Luke's hospital in Aberdeen, was a member of the State Board of Regents and was active in the move to place the initiative and referendum law on the statute books of the State.

6. A reproduction of the LONGFELLOW HOUSE is at cor. of N. Main St. and 12th Ave. The yellow frame house, with its green shutters and white trim, was built from a copy of the original plans of Longfellow's home in Cambridge, Mass. The owner, Harvey C. Jewett, Jr., has also furnished the interior in the manner of the original.

7. PRESENTATION SISTERS' CORPORATION, State St. bet. 2nd and 4th Aves., Motherhouse of the order, includes ST. LUKES HOSPITAL, the CONVENT, the CENTRAL SCHOOL OF NURSING, and temporarily, the PRESENTATION JUNIOR COLLEGE. The four-story main hospital building was constructed in 1920 and the first hospital, built by the Sisters in 1900, is now the Convent. The large five-story wing across the street to the N., which is connected to the main hospital by an overhead archway, was moved intact from the city's business district, when the Sisters purchased the Lincoln Hospital. St. Luke's is a 225-bed hospital and serves a large area.

8. THE CITY BASEBALL PARK, State St. and 14th Ave. S., accommodates State and National amateur baseball tournaments. The park was sponsored by the city in 1936 and built by the WPA. It is also the home ground of the Aberdeen Pheasants, a professional team in the Northern (Class C) league.

9. MELGAARD PARK, State St. at S. edge of city, is a recreational city park comprising the tree claim of Andrew Melgaard, pioneer, whose statue is in the horseshoe flower bed. The figure is cast in bronze and is the work of Alice Letting Siems, Chicago. The park has a band shell, where the municipal band presents weekly concerts. It also has tennis courts, a playground, a picnic area, and tourist camp.

CIRCLE TOUR 1—4.1 *m.*

L. from Main St. on 12th Ave. N.

10. HYDE PARK GOLF COURSE (*public; nominal green fees*) is an 18-hole course with built up hazards. It was here that the Bauer Sisters—Marlene and Alice—began their golfing careers that took them through the top amateur tournaments before turning professional (*see above*).

11. THE ABERDEEN COUNTRY CLUB has an 18-hole course with natural hazards, a clubhouse and polo field. The Club sponsors the Dakota Open Golf Tournament each Labor Day, a 72-hole medal contest, in which players from North and South Dakota compete.

R. from Country Club on gravel road.

12. WYLIE PARK, 2 m., has an artificial lake and bathing beach (small admission charge). The lake is called Minne-eho, or Water Behold. The park consists of 25 acres, part of which is a zoo with buffalo, deer, elk, bears, coyotes, foxes, monkeys, eagles, pheasants, and waterfowl.

R. from Wylie Park to junction with US 281.

13. FAIR GROUNDS, NW. of city limits, were originally built to serve parts of three states. The large exhibit pavilion is used as a livestock auction and sales barn, the scene of relatively new but interesting weekly stockmen's sessions. There are pari-mutuel races held at the track during Fourth of July week.

Deadwood

Bus Station: 33 Deadwood St. Bus connections to Burlington R. R. at Newcastle, Wyo.
No Railroad Station. Chicago & North Western R.R. at Rapid City.
Airport: Black Hills Airport, 11 m. N. on US 85. Western Airlines.
Traffic Regulations: Main St. is very narrow, with parking flat to curb. All streets
are steep; drivers are cautioned to brake cars while parked.
Information Center: Chamber of Commerce, Franklin Hotel, Main St.
Accommodations: Five Hotels; numerous motels and tourist camps.
Radio Station: KDSJ (1450 kc.)
Newspaper: Deadwood Pioneer-Times *(daily)*.
Theatres: One motion picture house. Dramatic production of "Trial of Jack McCall"
at Old Town Hall, four times a week, June 15 to Sept. 5.
Rodeo Grounds: Deadwood Amusement Park, E. end of Main St.
Riding Stables: Riding horses for hire, both downtown and at camps, by the hour
or day.
Golf: Tomahawk Country Club, 8 m. S. on US 85A. Public; green fees.
Ice Skating: Blacktail Indoor rink, on Central Road.
Skiing: Terry Peak Ski Club *(see Lead)*.
Annual Events: "Days of '76" Celebration, 1st week in August.

DEADWOOD (4,630 alt.) is the most famous town not only in the
Black Hills but in the State; people all over the country have heard
of this historic mining community of the Old West. Deadwood has
always been associated with gold, the gay life, the frontier characters;
the latter—Calamity Jane, Wild Bill Hickok, and their crowd—are
now only memories.

Deadwood has a most unusual location. No one who has stood
on the rocky ledge of Mt. Moriah cemetery and looked down into
Deadwood Gulch can easily forget the sight of this little city where
the closely set pine trees vie with dwelling houses for possession of
the steep slopes on both sides. Deadwood is a town of one main
street, the narrow bottom of the gulch having no room for more; and
that one street is needed for the business section. So the houses must
climb the steep sides of the gulch on either hand and the roads that
lead to them form so many terraces. Where the gulch divides toward
the upper end of town, the buildings follow both valleys, the business houses below and the residences above; while at the lower end
of town, the valley becomes so narrow that the road itself is forced
to leave the stream and wind its way up the almost perpendicular
hillside. Above the famous Mt. Moriah cemetery, with its graves of
Wild Bill and Calamity Jane, tower the glistening pinnacles of the
White Rocks, from which, northward, can be seen the gleaming
line of the Slim Buttes, 100 miles away.

Deadwood's prosperity rests on a very substantial basis, due to various factors. To begin with, it is the seat of Lawrence County, which contains three cities, rich farming land, irrigated orchards, and valuable mining properties. Then it has a Nation-wide fame and is a magnet for every tourist who enters the Black Hills. In fact it would be unthinkable to leave the Hills without seeing historic Deadwood. In the third place, it shares in the prosperity of its larger neighbor, Lead. And lastly it has the reputation all through that region of being a liberal, more or less "wide open" town, a reputation it has held from the beginning. It has, it is true, spasms of virtue at times, but, like many another penitent, it finds it difficult to hold to the narrow way.

Its saloons and brothels are landmarks, some of the latter having added neon signs to beckon the miners, cowboys, sheepherders, and soldiers who come to town. Following World War II there was a State crackdown on Deadwood's open gambling rooms, and the roulette wheels and dice games were moved out of sight.

Once a year Deadwood goes all out in a revival of the boisterous gold rush, during the "Days of '76" celebration. For three days and nights in the first week of each August, the streets are filled with games of chance, saloon keepers throw away their keys, and ghosts of Mt. Moriah live again. Each morning a mile-long parade rumbles over the cobblestone Main St. which follows the same course that the first placer miners picked out through the gulch. Ox teams, covered wagons, stage coaches, a prospector with his pack mules, Sioux Indians, Boots and Saddle Clubs, military units, and rodeo performers thrill the crowds in which men in buckskin jackets rub elbows with those in Harris tweeds. In the afternoon a rodeo and pageant are highlights, and in the evening the realistic re-enactment of the Miner's Court trial of Jack McCall, who shot Wild Bill but was acquitted (see below) takes place.

"The Days of '76" is the subject of a two-reel technicolor film made by a Hollywood studio (Warner Brothers) and is shown throughout the country.

In 1874 Custer's expedition discovered gold on French Creek, near where Custer stands. At once various parties set out for the Hills, but many were turned back by the soldiers since this was, at that time, Indian country. But in the fall of 1875 the Government, after a fruitless parley with the Indians, no longer offered any objections to the entry of white gold seekers and the latter poured into the Hills from every direction in the turbid flood which only a gold rush knows. Most of them went to the southern Hills, where gold had first been discovered. But late that same fall John B. Pearson of Yankton penetrated the northern Hills and discovered rich placer diggings in Deadwood Gulch. That winter the snow was very deep, with little communication, and perhaps Pearson kept the good news to himself. At any rate it was March of the next year before word of the rich gold strike got out. At this time Custer was said to have a population of 7,000. When word of the strike in Deadwood Gulch reached it, the town was depopulated almost overnight. It is said that less than 100 people remained. There was a mass movement northward through the Hills and Deadwood was born, taking its name from the gulch in which it lay, which in turn was named for the dead timber of some forgotten fire.

There were 25,000 people up and down that narrow gulch before the end of the summer, and the new town had to meet their needs. It would probably be impossible to overdraw the glamour of those early Deadwood days, and that first summer in particular. There were the usual accompaniments of a gold strike—saloons, dance halls, brothels, and gambling houses. There was an unusually colorful assemblage of individuals, even for that time and place. Wild Bill, Calamity Jane, and Preacher Smith walked the streets, together with an assortment of men who were glad to be there because their presence was undesired elsewhere. The most momentous happening of that summer, and indeed of all Deadwood's history was the shooting of Wild Bill (*see Motor Tour 2*). Next in importance perhaps came the killing of Preacher Smith, by the Indians, while on his way to Crook City (*see Tour 4*). Of the three most noted personages of that summer, two died in their prime, and the third, Calamity Jane, out-lived her environment. (*See Motor Tour 2*).

In the early years of Deadwood's prosperity profits were high, and gold plentiful. Each miner carried his buckskin sack filled with gold dust, which he squandered recklessly. One big miner scattered the contents of his gold sack on the streets to see the people scramble for it. Flour cost $60 per 100 pounds, wages were from $5 to $7 a day, while mine owners made small fortunes in a short time.

By the year 1879 the town had outgrown the canyon and had already started climbing the mountainsides of Deadwood and Whitewood gulches. On the night of September 25th, a fire which originated in a bakery on Sherman Street spread to a hardware store next to it. In the latter was stored a great deal of black powder which exploded, sending cinders all over the wooden buildings of the little gulch. Having no water system, miners and merchants alike stood helpless and watched their town burn. But in spite of the fact that it lay hundreds of miles by wagon road from its nearest base of supplies, the town was soon rebuilt.

During the winter of 1883, the snowfall had been unusually heavy and had melted but little; then followed warm rains, swelling

Whitewood and Deadwood Creeks until the town was flooded and much damage done. Strong retaining walls have since been built on Deadwood Creek, harnessing the stream, black with mill tailings, to its course through the heart of the city.

As with all boom mining towns, Deadwood's greatest glory was in her first years. When the placer diggings became exhausted, many miners left. A new gold strike in Lead, which was later absorbed by the Homestake Mining Co., attracted still other inhabitants of the older town (*see LEAD*). But in 1887, with a silver boom in the nearby towns of Carbonate and Galena, Deadwood experienced a rejuvenation. In like manner, in 1894, when the price of silver declined, Deadwood slumped in population to a total of 1,600. Later a smelter was built and the Golden Reward erected its plant and reduction works in the town. A cyanide plant was constructed for the Rossiter Mill. These activities brought about a revival of prosperity for a time. But this came to an end with the strike of 1909, which closed all the plants, and only the Golden Reward opened again.

With the headquarters of the Black Hills National Forest in Deadwood, together with the advent of the motoring tourists, the town held its own. The nearby Homestake Mine at Lead, only three miles away, paid good wages and its prosperity was reflected in Deadwood.

In the 1930's Deadwood was the liveliest town in the Hills. When the United States went off the gold standard in 1934, the price of gold rose substantially. At the same time the repeal of prohibition legalized the open sale of liquor. A new rush was on, and Deadwood was in the middle of it.

During World War II, the soldiers stationed at Fort Meade and at the Rapid City Air Base quickly discovered Deadwood. They gave it some descriptive names, which the Chamber of Commerce refined to "South Dakota's Playtown."

Just as all residents of Reno do not patronize their divorce courts, so it is that Deadwood has a more virtuous side. Its schools, churches, library, museum, and societies work doubly hard to excell in their fields.

POINTS OF INTEREST

1. The ADAMS MEMORIAL HALL MUSEUM, cor. of Sherman and Deadwood Sts. (*open weekdays 10:00 a.m.—9:30 p.m., Sun. 2–6 p.m.; free*), is one of the outstanding features of the city of Deadwood. For many years it had been the hope and dream of some of the far-seeing citizens of the Black Hills to establish a place

of safety for the fast disappearing records and relics of the early days. The gathering of such mementos is laying a foundation for a complete history of the struggles of the early pioneers.

To Fred D. Gramlich of Deadwood goes the credit for originating the idea of a museum, but it was W. E. Adams who realized this dream. He was a pioneer, and in memory of his family and of the pioneers who together with himself had helped to make the city of Deadwood the flourishing community that it is, he gave the Adams Memorial Hall. This Memorial forms a link between the pioneer life of more than half a century ago and the Deadwood of today. The Hall was dedicated October 4, 1930.

The most important exhibits in the Adams Memorial Hall are: a book containing the laws and rules that the Gordon Party (*see Tour 5*), laid down in writing on February 23, 1875; the Theon Stone, which was found by Louis and Ivan Theon at the base of Lookout Mountain and is the only record of six Missourians, who, otherwise unknown, left the first authentic record of white men in the Hills, dating the stone 1834; a saddle and a pair of boots which President Theodore Roosevelt used on his ranch at Medora, N. Dak., and later gave to Captain Seth Bullock in October 1908; a saddle used by Quincy Turner, a cowpuncher, when he came with the first trail herd from Texas into the Black Hills; the first locomotive in the Black Hills, which arrived in August 1879 by bull team from Bismarck, N. Dak.; more than 100 shotguns and rifles dating from the pioneer period to the present day, also ox yokes, grain cradles, sluice boxes, rockers, broadaxes, bear traps, gold scales, and spinning wheels, which were all brought in during the early days; a collection of Indian saddles belonging to High Bearers, Two Moons, and Plenty Coups (High Bearers and Two Moons were in the Custer fight); a letter from the Messiah, a Piute Indian, Wovoka, who had emissaries among the Sioux and spread the religious rite of the ghost dance (*see Tour 7*); original marriage certificate of the only couple married by Preacher Smith while he was in Deadwood; and a most complete collection of early photographs of Deadwood and the Black Hills.

2. At the lower end of Main Street is that area which in early Deadwood days was known as CHINATOWN. At one time included in Deadwood's population was a considerable element of Chinese. They rapidly assumed the dress and manners of Americans. Chinatown extended E. from Siever St.

Besides their usual occupations as laundrymen and restaurant keepers, there were merchants and doctors who conformed to the American fashions in all except their "cues," to which they religious.y clung. The women and girls adhered to the native costumes. The Chinese had their own place of worship which they called the Joss House.

Most of the Chinese came under contract, which stipulated that their bodies be sent back to China. After six or seven years, allowing sufficient time for decomposition, a Chinese undertaker would go to the cemetery, disinter the bodies, separate the bones, wrapping each in a newspaper and muslin with proper labels, and place the package of bones in a small zinc-lined box 10 x 14 x 22 inches, which was sealed and shipped to San Francisco where with 1,700 or 1,800 more it would be sent to the Orient.

Mrs. Wong was the last Chinese woman to rear a family in Deadwood. An opium pipe which belonged to her is on display at the Adams Memorial Hall. Also on display at the Museum is a picture of the Chinese Hose Team of America which won the Great Hub and Hub Race in Deadwood on July 4, 1888. There is also a picture of the Chinese Sunday School class and some of the teachers. There are very few Chinese in Deadwood today, but this part of the city is still called Chinatown.

3. The site of the old GREEN FRONT, the most famous brothel of the Deadwood of early days, and one of the most notorious in the entire West, extended from what is now 591 to 601 Main St. It was in existence from the early days of Deadwood until 1911.

4. At 613 Main St. is the site of the GEM THEATRE, probably the first and only legitimate theatre of the eighties in this western land of cowboys, miners, and gamblers. It was known as having excellent stock companies at that early day.

5. At 620 Main St., was the famous old NO. 10 SALOON, where Wild Bill Hickok was shot by Jack McCall (*see Motor Tour 2*). McCall ran across the street and hid in an old barn which was next to a pool hall.

6. DEADWOOD AMUSEMENT PARK, S. from E. Main St., is an arena with a huge native log grandstand in a pine-clad setting where the "Days of '76" and other programs are staged. It was developed in the 1930's as a WPA project.

TOUR 1—3.7 m.

W. from Main St. on Shine St.

7. BLACK HILLS NATIONAL FOREST (entrance at 1 *m.*) covers practically the entire northern Hills area, as the Harney National Forest covers the southern portion. (*See BLACK HILLS RECREATIONAL AREA.*) At some points along this road the

mountain side slopes away from the highway at a very sharp angle and careful driving is necessary.

8. ROOSEVELT MONUMENT is at the summit of Mt. Roosevelt (5,676 alt.). This circular tower is 35 ft. high, set in a solid base, the whole being built of native diorite found on the hill where the memorial stands. A bronze tablet placed on the monument bears the following inscription:

In Memory Of

Theodore Roosevelt

"The American"

The idea of a monument was conceived by Captain Seth Bullock (*see Motor Tour 2*), an intimate friend of Theodore Roosevelt, and was carried out by the Society of Black Hills Pioneers in 1919, when the memorial tower was erected; and the mountain, formerly known as Sheep Mountain, was dedicated to the former President of the United States.

From the summit of Mt. Roosevelt it is possible to see four States, North Dakota, South Dakota, Wyoming, and Montana; and in the foreground to the south and west are the Black Hills and to the north and east rolling plains.

TOUR 2—0.9 m.

S. from Sherman St. on Van Buren Ave.

WHITEWOOD CREEK, once a crystal-clear, tumbling mountain stream, now a dirty leaden color, literally a flow of liquid mud, caused by the tailings from the Homestake mine at Lead, flows through the center of Deadwood. It is said that this one small stream carries down four million tons of tailings annually to the Belle Fourche River. The stream leaves the Hills in a continuous series of rapids with a flow too swift to deposit mud at any point within the Hills; and it remains turgid and heavy with mud all the way to the Belle Fourche. Livestock will drink the water along the lower reaches; but no animal life is possible in it.

9. MT. MORIAH or "BOOT HILL" CEMETERY is visited annually by thousands of tourists, curious to see the graves of four famous Western characters, Wild Bill, Calamity Jane, Preacher Smith, and Seth Bullock. Of these, easily the most famous was Wild Bill, or as he was christened, James Butler Hickok, "the Prince of Pistoleers," one of the handsomest men on the frontier, and admittedly the quickest and best shot on the turbulent border in its most turbulent days. Born in Illinois, he was fired with a determination to emulate the career of his hero, Kit Carson; and going out to the frontier while still a boy, he became successively a

freighter, hunter and trapper, stage driver and station-tender, and sold er and scout in the Union Army, penetrating the Confederate lines three times in disguise. After the Civil War he was a scout on the plains for various units of the United States Army, then an actor (a poor one it must be admitted), and finally marshal of some of the roughest towns of the old West and the entire country. It was the last-named activity that brought him his greatest fame. As one after another of the Kansas towns became the head of steel and consequently the shipping point for the herds of wild Texas cattle driven up from the South by equally wild cowhands, these cow towns became the Mecca for gamblers, prostitutes, and bad men who congregate wherever money is freely spent. It was the business of the town marshal to protect the merchants and law-abiding citizens and it was usually necessary to remove permanently from society the worst of the bad men in order to accomplish this. Wild Bill is generally credited with having killed 27 men, although he himself would never discuss the subject. It was this reputation of his as a law-enforcement officer that led directly to his killing. Although he came to Deadwood to make a stake for the bride he had just taken, the lawless element of the town feared that he would be appointed marshal and put an end to their activities. They therefore bribed a weak character, Jack McCall, to assassinate Wild Bill, promising him $300 to accomplish the deed and filling him up with cheap whiskey to give him courage. Wild Bill was indulging in his favorite pastime of a friendly game of cards in the old No. 10 saloon. For the second time in his career, he was sitting with his back to an open door. Jack McCall walked in, shot him through the back of the head, and rushed from the place, only to be captured shortly afterward. Wild Bill's dead hand held aces and eights, and and from that time on this has been known in the West as "the dead man's hand." Jack McCall was tried before a packed jury and acquitted. He later went to Custer and Cheyenne and bragged of the killing, but was arrested by a United States Marshal in Cheyenne and taken to Yankton for trial before the District Court. His plea of "double jeopardy" was disregarded on the ground that the miner's court had no jurisdiction; and he was convicted, sentenced, and hanged. Although Wild Bill was technically a killer, he killed only in self-defense or in the line of duty as a peace officer. His grave in Mt. Moriah is surrounded by an iron fence and marked by a red sandstone, life-sized statue of dubious artistic merit which has suffered considerably from vandalism.

In the adjoining enclosure is the grave of another famous character of early Deadwood, Calamity Jane, or Martha Jane (Canary)

Burke. Born at or near La Salle, Ill., May 1, 1852, she drifted west with her family and at an early age was left an orphan. She became a hanger-on of construction camps, bull trains, army expeditions, and gold camps; and according to some accounts she served at times as an army scout or mail carrier. She dressed by preference in men's attire, frequently a suit of fringed buckskin, and few persons ever saw her in women's apparel. She was credited with a vocabulary of extraordinary breadth and richness, even for a time and place that was not entirely lacking in self-expression. There exists the widest divergence both in the accounts of her life and estimates of her character. Time has made of her a legendary figure and the different accounts of how she gained her sobriquet, "Calamity Jane," are not very authentic. Although she had been a wanderer up to the time she reached Deadwood in 1876, at the height of the gold rush, she seemed to find that region to her liking, for she made it more or less her home for the rest of her life. She took trips to Montana and to the East, and for awhile was a midway attraction at the Pan-American Exposition in Buffalo. But she always returned to the Hills, and there passed away in a boarding house at Terry, Aug. 1, 1903, almost twenty-seven years to the day after the shooting of her friend, Wild Bill. In accordance with her last wish she was buried beside him. Her funeral is said to have been the largest ever held in Deadwood; and South Dakota remembers her colorful career rather than her human frailties.

A short distance up the hill from the graves of these two is another lifesize red sandstone statue marking the last resting place of another pioneer, Preacher Smith (*see Tour 4*).

Somewhat apart from the other graves, on a slight elevation, is the grave of Seth Bullock. Originally a cowboy with the big outfits, he organized Theodore Roosevelt's Rough Riders and was immediately appointed captain. After Roosevelt became President, he appointed his old companion-at-arms United States Marshal for South Dakota, a position which he held for many years. He also served as first sheriff of Lawrence County and was the first Forest Supervisor of the Black Hills forests. Before he died he asked to be buried where his grave would be in sight of the monument erected to his hero, Theodore Roosevelt. That request was the reason for locating the grave where it is.

POINTS OF INTEREST IN ENVIRONS

Cabin and Grave of Deadwood Dick 2.3 m.; Preacher Smith Monument, 3.3 m., (*see Tour 4*).

Huron

Railroad Stations: The Chicago & North Western R. R., Dakota Ave. and Second St., and the Great Northern R. R., Dakota Ave. and First St.
Bus Station: Union Depot, 424 Wisconsin S.W.
Airport: W. W. Howes Municipal Airport, 2 m. N. on Dakota Ave. (State 37). Mid-Continent, Western, and Mid-West Airlines.
Traffic Regulations: Standard ordinances. Parking meters.
Information Service: Chamber of Commerce, Marvin Hughitt Hotel, Dakota Ave. & 4th St.
Accommodations: Two hotels; numerous motels and tourist camps.
Newspaper: The Huronite and Plainsman (daily).
Radio Station: KIJV (MBS—1140 kc.).
Theaters: Huron Auditorium for road shows and concerts. Two motion picture houses. Outdoor drive-in theater.
Athletic Area: Memorial Park, 4th St. N.E., for baseball.
Swimming: Ravine Lake, 4th St. N.E., public bathhouse.
Golf: Meadowbrook Golf Course (public), N. of Airport, 9 holes; Country Club (by invitation), N. on State 37, 9 holes.
Tennis: Public courts, bet. 5th and 6th Sts. on Oregon St.
Annual Events: South Dakota State Fair, 1st week in Sept. for 6 days; Baseball Pheast val, day before opening of pheasant hunting season; National Hereford Show, last week in Oct. for 4 days; Memorial Day Auto Races, May 30; Thrill Derby, July 4; Huron Rodeo, mid-July.

HURON (1,288 alt.) is situated on the west bank of the James River in the center of a broad, level region that spreads, fan-wise, in all directions. As the hub for the numerous small towns that lie within the confines of a mythical wheel, Huron draws trade from a large agricultural area. Good highways, airlines, railroads, and hotels have combined with the city's location near the State's center of population to make it popular as a convention city, as well as the home of the State Fair.

The city is most widely known, however, as pheasant hunting headquarters. Each fall thousands of sportsmen converge here, many coming by chartered airplanes and special railroad cars. Major league baseball stars are special guests of the city which furnishes their out-of-state hunting licenses in return for a baseball game to start off the season. *Holiday* magazine has called Huron the "pheasant capital of the United States."

Huron's future is tied closely to a 750,000-acre Federal irrigation project undertaken as part of the Missouri Basin development plan. The project calls for the channeling of water from the Oahe dam in the Missouri River at Pierre into the James Valley, irrigating an area extending from Huron north to Aberdeen and west to Miller. The Bureau of Reclamation, which has charge of the project, has its headquarters in Huron. Construction of the Oahe unit was started in July 1950.

Largely dependent upon agriculture and allied pursuits—dairying, poultry raising, grain, and livestock farming—the city also has industries to process the farm products, including a meat packing company and produce plants.

Huron has always been known for its strong labor organizations. There are 23 trade and labor unions in this small city, and they maintain the Huron Central Labor Union Hall for their activities. The first labor organization was the Brotherhood of Locomotive Firemen whose charter, issued July 13, 1883, was signed by Eugene V. Debs, one-time candidate for president of the United States on the Socialist ticket.

Called an "overgrown country town" in 1910, Huron has lost many of the characteristics of a small town. Up-to-date structures have replaced the old frame buildings in the business section, and a new courthouse, city hall, school buildings, and airport show the recent progress.

Although named for an Indian tribe, Huron was born to the accompaniment of squeaking wagon wheels, humming hay mowers, and locomotive bells. The history of the present site of Huron, dates back to 1879, when John Cain, among others, staked out a claim on the east bank of the James River. Shortly afterwards a party of surveyors of the Chicago & North Western Railroad arrived and camped near there. At the direction of Marvin Hughitt, general manager of the line, the west bank of the river was selected as division headquarters of the railroad. This was in reality the first step toward bringing the city of Huron into existence. The railroad company through its subsidiary, the Western Town and Lot Company, gained title to 880 acres of land on which final entry was made September 11, 1879. The railroad company built depots, a roundhouse, shops and offices covering a building space of 38,000 feet. Either Mr. Hughitt or someone in the Chicago office of the railroad gave the new town its name.

Huron was a busy place in the summer of 1880, with building operations going on and settlers coming in to seek land. Perhaps it was for this reason that the first July 4th celebration was staged in Huron a day late. The event was none the less important. Journalism, like the new town, was informal—yet personally vital. Following is an example of it, as carried in the columns of a newspaper on July 6, 1880, reporting the belated celebration:

"The grand success of Huron's first celebration of the Nation's birthday is the general topic of conversation among her citizens, and the occasion of their mutual congratulations.

"At the first indication of the rising sun on the morning of the 5th, he was greeted by the National salute and an extra gun for

Huron, fired under the supervision of M. Chase. Pistols, shotguns and firecrackers made music in the air until afternoon, when a crowd assembled to witness a game of baseball on a ground which had been prepared near the city. Two nines were selected by Messrs. Fairbanks and Parkhurst, and play was commenced with Lon Hartis as umpire and A. L. Church as scorer. Before the nine innings were played, the last bat in Huron was broken and the game could not be finished.

"Shortly before sundown two running races took place over a course west of Wright's Hotel, one of which was won by Williams' gray mare and the other by a horse belonging to a young man in Wright's employ."

The dry summer and hard winter of 1880–81 retarded the growth of the town, but a boom began the next year as settlers continued to stake claims nearby and require implements, household necessities, and entertainment. The War Department installed a signal station in this prairie town in 1881; it has since become important as a weather bureau for the State. Cutting hay on Huron's present busiest thoroughfare—Dakota Avenue—took place in 1885, when Hollard Wheeler, pioneer druggist, mowed the foot-tall grass in front of his store to improve appearances. The present brick structure that houses the Wheeler Drug Store had just been built when "haying time" began on the street.

In the late eighties, crop failures, coupled with a period of depression, again temporarily checked the growth of the city. As times picked up, Huron was selected as the site for the State Fair in 1904. Following the World War came another period of growth, when headquarters for oil, utility, and wholesale companies were established in Huron. From 1933 to 1935, drought and dust storms ravaged the crops in the rural regions surrounding Huron, and crippled the sources of income. This area, which was more affected than any other in the eastern half of the State, was the scene of roadside ditches leveled with wind-driven topsoil and deserted farmsteads. Fence posts actually were attacked by hoardes of grasshoppers unable to find anything edible in the fields. Dispirited farmers and merchants took heart as Robert D. Lusk's *Daily Huronite and Plainsman* waged a crusade to stick with the land and the city. A large artificial lake was formed within the city limits, bare patches of ground were planted to grass for parks, and new farm crops were tested and developed. The U.S. Department of Agriculture established the State offices of the Soil Conservation Service in Huron and began shelterbelt, land use, and erosion projects. Today hardly a trace of the dust storms is to be found.

POINTS OF INTEREST

1. THE SOUTH DAKOTA STATE FAIR GROUNDS, on 3rd St. bet. Nevada and Indiana Sts., (*Adm.: Adults, 25c, children under 12, free.*) comprises 150 acres where the State Fair is held early in September beginning on Labor Day. The race track and grandstand are used for several other public events during the spring and summer, including auto races, pari-mutuel horse races, and a rodeo.

The grounds and buildings have been described as the most disreputable of any State Fair in the country, but at Fair time no one seems to mind as thousands of people jam the livestock pavilions, exhibits, midway, grandstand, and political headquarters.

A plot of ground, conveniently located and enclosed to afford police protection, is set aside by the State Board of Agriculture for the exclusive use of families desiring to camp while attending the Fair. No charge is made and parties may bring their own tents or rent one on the grounds. Maintained on the grounds as additional service for visitors are an express office, post office, rest cottage for women and children, check rooms, dining halls, telephone and telegraph offices.

2. HURON COLLEGE, on Illinois Ave., 7th and 19th Sts., was founded at Pierre in 1883, by Harlan Page Carson as Pierre University. Soon afterwards, 1898, it was moved to Huron and established as a Presbyterian college, starting with three students. Today it comprises one main building—Ralph Vorhees Hall—a girls' dormitory and a large gymnasium and auditorium, all set deep on a broad, well-landscaped campus. For many years students from Oriental countries—China, Korea and Japan—have attended Huron College. This is largely due to the efforts of George Shannon McCune, former president, who spent much of his life in the Far East. The college is developing the group system of studies and a correlation between high school and college work. It has added all the pre-requisite courses in engineering, medicine, dentistry, journalism, and law.

3. CHIC SALE HOUSE, 643 Illinois Ave., S.W., was the boyhood home of "Chic" Sale, as he was known to the theatrical and literary world, but whose real name was Charles Partlon Sale. He was born in Huron in 1884, the son of Dr. Frank O. and Lillie B. Sale who came to Huron in 1882. "Chic" spent the first 11 years of his life in the new prairie town and attended the school on the present site of the Huron High School. The publication of *The Specialist* was "Chic" Sale's debut into the literary field and it

became the "mirth of a nation," over a million copies being sold. This was followed by *The Champion Cornhusker* and *I Tell You Why*.

4. ST. JOHN'S HOSPITAL, 4th St., and Iowa Ave., S.E., was completed in 1947, at a cost of over one million dollars. It is operated by the Franciscan Sisters. The five-story, 150-bed hospital has a school of nursing in connection.

5. HURON AUDITORIUM, 5th St., S.W. between Wisconsin and Illinois Aves., is the largest in the State with a seating capacity of 6,000. The $760,000 building was constructed in 1950, by the school district for combined school and civic use. The architect was Harold Spitznagel, Sioux Falls.

6. RAVINE LAKE, 4th St., N.E. at Beach Ave., covers 100 acres and provides swimming and water facilities for the city. There is a public bathhouse. The lake was formed by holding back run-off waters heading for the James River. Tree plantings and an island make it a scenic spot.

7. MEMORIAL PARK, 4th St., N.E. at Jersey Ave., is the site of the annual Baseball Pheastival in which players of the Major leagues meet stars of the Minor leagues in a game to start off the pheasant hunting season. The idea was originated in 1944, by James Meagham and usually follows the World Series. The ball park was built into a hillside along the James River and is of major league dimensions. It has 160 lights on eight 90-ft. towers. The grandstand accommodates 1,600 people. It is also used for tournaments and State League games.

8. ARMOUR AND CO., 4th St., S.E., is a meat packing plant and main South Dakota branch of the Chicago firm. An average of 350 persons are employed.

9. LAMPE MARKET, Dakota Ave. S. at the edge of the city, is an example of the idea of the "vertical trust" in commerce, the inclusion of all the processing steps in the converting of raw material to the finished product within the confines of a single organization, with consequent elimination of profit-taking on the various steps of manufacture and marketing. The Lampe Market raises its own meat on its 900-acre farm, kills it, packs it, and markets it.

The Lampe Market was first opened by Albert Lampe, Sr., in 1887. A native of Wernigerode, Germany, he came to Huron in 1882. Improvements in the plants were made in 1907, and the market was enlarged to accommodate increased business. The improvements were of such a character as to cause the market to be described in the newspapers of that day as "the best market in the Northwest." It has moved twice to larger quarters.

On request the visitor is shown "behind the scenes" where there are large ranges for delicatessen cooking, ovens for bakery goods, and the meat department where sausage, bacon, ham, and lard are prepared. The basement is a complete packing plant with exception of the slaughter house and fertilizer department. There also are thousands of square ft. of cold storage rooms.

10. W. W. HOWES MUNICIPAL AIRPORT, Dakota Ave., N. at the edge of the city, is the terminal for three commercial airlines, and is the hub of air transportation in the State. The airport was named for W. W. Howes of Huron, who succeeded James A. Farley as Postmaster General under Franklin D. Roosevelt, and was built with the aid of the Works Progress Administration. All the buildings are substantially constructed of hand-cut native stone and all have cement floors. The hangar is 108 ft. long, 94 ft. wide, and has a 19 ft. ceiling.

The administration building, west of the hangar, has two stories, a full basement, and an observation lookout on the roof from which the activities of the airport are directed. The offices, waiting rooms, and lunchroom occupy the ground floor.

POINTS OF INTEREST IN ENVIRONS

Huron Mennonite Colony, N. on State 37 (*see Tour 4*).

Lead

Railroad Stations: Bus connections with Chicago, Burlington & Quincy at New-castle, Wyo.
Bus Station: Highland Hotel.
Airport Black Hills Airport, 14 m. N.E. Western Airlines.
Traffic Regulations: Main St. is a stop street, with severe penalties for violation. No U turn on Main St. within city limits. Parking only flat to curb. No double parking.
Information Service: Highland Hotel.
Accommodations: One hotel; several lodges and cabin camps nearby.
Newspaper: Lead Daily Call.
Theater: One motion picture house. Other programs in Recreation Hall Auditorium, Main St.
Golf: Lead Country Club, W. of city, by invitation.
Swimming: Recreation Building, Main St.
Skiing: Terry Peak Ski Area, 6 m. W. on US 85.
Ice Skating: Blacktail indoor rink on Central Road.
Annual Event: Labor Day Celebration.

LEAD (pronounced Leed, 5,320 alt.), is the seat of the Homestake, the largest gold mine in the United States, and the greatest gold producer in the Western hemisphere. Lead takes its name from the famous Homestake "lead," meaning lode or vein, which has yielded over $500,000,000 worth of gold, and in 1950 was still producing at the rate of more than $15,000,000 a year. Lead is the Homestake and the Homestake is Lead; the two are inseparable.

The contrast in the physical appearance of Lead and Deadwood, three miles apart, is remarkable. While the latter is packed into the bottom of the gulch, Lead, at the head of Gold Run Gulch, is spread out, a mile high, over the tops of the surrounding hills. The two towns have one feature in common, the almost total lack of level ground. But Lead is the hillier of the two. The porch of one residence is often on a level with the roof of the one in front of it.

Lead residents live a mile above sea level, and those who work at the lower mine levels are a mile from their homes—straight down. There are about 120 miles of underground tunnels, extending more than 5,000 feet below the city.

Lead is what might be called a town on the move, for with shafts and tunnels undermining the city, large areas are in danger of sub-siding and have been cleared of buildings. On top of the highest hill in Lead a new residence section has sprung up, where the underground workings are not likely to undermine it. Because of cave-ins and shifting earth, together with the prosperity of the city, there are few old buildings in Lead and no high ones.

The upper end of Main Street apparently leads into the sky, while the lower end drops steeply into the canyon of Gold Run Gulch on its way to Deadwood. On one side of Main Street rises the tall and silver-colored slenderness of the Yates, Ross, and Ellison shafts and on the other side is the yawning chasm of the Open Cut, the most striking single physical feature of the City of Lead.

Unlike most mining towns, Lead has no night life. Night clubs and taverns are forbidden and presumably Deadwood reaps a rich harvest from this ruling. Only the sale of beer is permitted.

The foreign element of Lead is diverse, the population being divided among 18 nationalities. Seventy percent of the inhabitants, however, are native born. The population is stable, because Homestake jobs are obtained with difficulty and held tenaciously.

Practically all the land in Lead is owned by the Homestake, but any employee may build on a site and occupy it rent-free, as long as it is not needed for mining purposes.

The Homestake operates its own hospital and medical department, free to employees and their families; also a large club building free to both employees and the public. Sanitary, well-appointed dressing rooms with shower baths are available for the men coming off-shift.

It was when the late winter snows began to melt in 1876 that Thomas E. Carey, a mining pioneer, left his claim in Deadwood Gulch, crossed over the divide to Gold Run Creek in search of gold, and, finding the swollen stream and surrounding soil rich with the precious yellow metal, staked his claim and sent word of his discovery to Deadwood Gulch.

On July 14, 1876, the first town lot was recorded, Lot 1, Block 1, at 100 Mill and Pine Streets. The first meeting of miners to organize Lead City was held July 26, 1876. On Feb. 28, 1877, the Black Hills area was ceded by the Indians to the United States, and on Sept. 21, 1877, the first mineral application to the Land Office was made.

A few weeks subsequent to the founding of Lead, the town of Washington was laid out not far from it by a different set of locators. The two towns had a separate existence for a number of years; but Washington finally became an addition to Lead.

In this same year, 1877, the first gold-bearing quartz from the site of the present city was treated and recovered by the Manuel Brothers, Mose and Fred. To test their finds, the Manuel brothers hauled 4,000 tons of quartz to Whitewood Creek. They built a rude home-made crushing mill called an "arrastra" (a Mexican term), and the ore yielded so richly that the fame of Lead spread to all

parts of the country. Promoters and big-time prospectors became
vitally interested and from Alaska, down the western coast to
Mexico, traveled the news that gold lay in the Black Hills. From all
parts of the United States came the gold seekers, showmen, adventurers, and seasoned miners. So it was that George Hearst, Lloyd
Tevis, and J. B. Haggin, members of a San Francisco syndicate,
sent Samuel McMaster, a mining engineer, to Deadwood early in
1877, to report on silver mines there. But gold was god of the Hills
at that time, so McMaster recommended the purchase of two
claims, the Homestake and the Golden Star in Gold Run Canyon.

The Homestake Mining Company was incorporated in 1877, at
San Francisco, and the group, headed by George Hearst, bought the
mines for $77,000. As the property was developed, it proved to be
a rich investment and provided a family fortune for Hearst's son,
William Randolph Hearst, whose interests were in newspaper and
magazine publishing.

Under the guidance of the company, Lead grew into a city which
at one time was the largest in the State. In 1950 it ranked tenth.

In early days a small stream called Gold Run ran through
Lead and down to Pluma where it was lost in Whitewood Creek.
Today no stream is to be seen in Lead until a point below the
Homestake regrinding plant. Much of the water that now runs
down Gold Run Gulch is from Spearfish Creek and is piped by
the Homestake Company over a rise of hundreds of feet to Lead.

The first dance in Lead City was held on the night of July 4,
1877, in the second frame building, known as Jentes Corner. There
were but seven women present, the total feminine population of
Lead at that time.

A little log cabin was the city's pioneer school in the year 1877.
It was a tuition school.

In 1879 the first hospital, a log cabin, was erected. At first a
physician was selected, satisfactory to both employees and the management, to render aid to employees and their families. In 1906
the company took charge of the department and the service was
extended to include general medical, surgical, and obstetrical cases,
free of charge to all employees of the Homestake and their families. A two-story frame building was erected in 1889, and the present hospital, a three-story brick structure, modern and completely
equipped, was completed in 1925.

On the morning of March 8, 1900, occurred the most disastrous
fire in the history of the city. It destroyed a quarter of a million
dollars' worth of property. The fire burned the entire business section of Lead and a part of the residence section also. The wind sent

clouds of sparks whirling across Bleeker Street to the frame buildings which line Pine and Mill Streets, threatening the Hearst store
and the Star Mill of the Homestake Mining Co. After hours of
hard work the fire was stopped in its course up Mill Street. With
the aid of dynamite it was kept from spreading to the mills.

On March 25, 1907, between 4 and 5 o'clock in the morning, the
timber stoping on the 500-ft. level of the Homestake Mine caught
fire. The air pipes, through which water was run in case of fire,
had been removed on this level. An attempt was made to put the
fire out with two hoses, each having 200-lbs. pressure. Pipes were
laid to carry water and men were doing good work with them,
when the stope began to cave in behind them and this method had
to be abandoned.

Steam was next tried. The drift was tightly closed, and this took
many days. Steam was then turned in for seven and a half days. The
gases were by this time so strong that all work had to be stopped
except at the extreme north end. After the steam was turned off the
fire was still raging, and the rock in the vicinity was at a temperature
of about 1500 degrees F.

As a last resort it was decided to flood the mine, and on April
18th the water was allowed to fill the lower workings instead of
draining off as usual. This, too, proved inadequate and therefore
two tunnels were built and a small stream was turned through them.
During 23 days these tunnels carried 19 million cubic feet of water
into the mine.

After the fire had been smothered by this means, the task of "un-
watering" began. This required the removal of over 300 million
gallons of water. The machinery in the mine was rusted but was
soon made usable, while the mine itself needed but few repairs to
put it in working condition again. The blow to the community was
only temporary. In a very short time, owing to the resources of
the company and the energy and devotion of the men, Lead's prosperity was restored.

Owing to world conditions the price of gold increased from
$20.67 per ounce in 1933, to $34.00 per ounce in January 1934, and
by reason of the Gold Act of 1934, the price was fixed at $35.00
per ounce. This brought immense prosperity to gold producing regions. Wages went up in the gold mines, business was stimulated,
and the mines made greatly increased profits; and, in the case of
the Homestake, this prosperity was shared with the men in the
shape of increased wages and semi-annual bonuses. In 1936 each
employee received a $50 bonus in June and $100 at Christmas.

A fine City Hall was built in 1937, with a PWA grant; but the city's pride is the half-million dollar high school built in 1940. Nearby is an athletic field, well over a mile high, which was constructed by blasting off the tops of two mountain peaks.

Then, during World War II, all gold mining was suspended by the War Production Board. Lead was hard hit. The windows of many houses and a few business places were boarded up as people moved away. Another blow came when the big company store, the Hearst Mercantile, burned to the ground. For a time it looked as if Lead were about to join the ranks of the other Black Hills ghost towns

When the Homestake reopened, Lead came back to life. During normal times approximately 2,200 people are employed by the Homestake and the annual payroll is about $6,000,000.

Lead has become the winter sports headquarters for the Black Hills. The Terry Peak Ski Area (*see Tour 13*), developed by the Bald Mountain Ski Club since 1947, provides skiing for the novice and expert. There are three slides, each with motor-operated tows, a four-mile ski run, and a warming house. An indoor ice skating rink is operated in an old Homestake cyanide plant on Central Road.

POINTS OF INTEREST

1. The HOMESTAKE MINE, Main St. bet. Mill St. and E. city limits, consists of two parts, the underground workings, or the mine proper, and the hoists, mills, and plants above ground (*guide service provided for surface workings; tour requires an hour*). Here one can see the giant hoists that haul up nine-ton loads of ore at three times the speed of the fastest elevators of New York sky-scrapers, and follow the various steps in separating the precious minerals. Genuine gold bricks are the final result.

The Homestake employs both the mercury and cyanide processes in extracting gold from ore. When the ore arrives at the mouth of the shaft, it is hauled to the stamp mill. Here, amid a din that renders even shouted conversation impossible, huge stamps reduce the ore to fine proportions. It is then ground in rod mills and mercury is added. The mercury unites with the free gold and the resulting amalgam is collected in amalgamators. The mercury is later driven off by heat and recovered, and the gold remains. The residue of the ore is then reground till it is as fine as flour and leached in huge vats or in filter presses by a weak cyanide solution. The cyanide dissolves what little gold remains and forms a chemical combination with it. The bottoms of these vats are composed of canvas, through which the cyanide and gold filter and are drained off. This compound is chemically treated, the cyanide driven off and recovered, and the gold remains. The residue in the vats, now free

of all but the faintest trace of gold, is washed into Gold Run Gulch
to find its way, via Whitewood Creek, to the Belle Fourche River.
So thorough is this process and so adapted to the handling of ore
in vast bulk that treatment costs are low and over 95 percent of the
gold in the ore is recovered. The average yield of the ores treated
is one-third of an ounce per ton.

2. The OPEN CUT is best viewed from the S. end of Mill
Street near the Ross shaft. It is an immense gash in the earth
where there was first an open pit mine, out of which enormous
riches were taken in the early days, and where later the underground workings of the mine caused the surface to cave in and
add still further to the immense cavity. The Open Cut changed the
whole topography of Lead. As it kept increasing in size and depth,
the rest of the city retreated respectfully before it.

North Mill St. was at one time the leading business street of
Lead, boasting the largest buildings in the city and most of the
business activity. Formerly about five blocks long, now only one block
remains and there are no buildings on it. The rest of the street has
dropped into the Open Cut. But even then the Open Cut was not
satisfied. In advance of its yawning cavity, the lower end of the
new Main Street became unsafe. Its buildings were condemned,
including the abandoned North Western depot, and business retreated W. along the sloping thoroughfare. Today the lower end
of Main St. is denuded of buildings and next to this vacant space
stand those which have been abandoned but are not yet torn down.
The upper end of Main St., however, which is the present business
center, stands on land which will not be subject to caving, and the
same is true of the newest residence section on the hill above. But
in the pavement of lower Main St. from time to time new cracks
appear; and portions of the street have sunk several feet below
their former level.

3. GRIER PARK, named in honor of T. J. Grier, a former
superintendent of the Homestake Mine, is at the west end of Main
St. and joins the city on the south. It is one of the highest hills in
Lead and comprises 13 acres. In it are swings and other playground equipment, a large pavilion for dances and meetings, and
what is probably one of the most unusual baseball diamonds in
the world. Well over a mile high, it was built by the Homestake at
a cost of $50,000 by blasting off two sharp peaks. Only by such
means as this could level ground be obtained anywhere in Lead.

Grier Park is also the scene of an annual Labor Day celebration,
consisting of various sports and contests. Formerly the feature of
the celebration was a series of turtle races. Every Homestake employee bet on a turtle decided by lot. The race was run off in a num-

ber of heats, until the winner was determined. The turtles were numbered and released in the center of a large ring and left to their own devices. The first turtle to cross the circle at any point was the winner of that heat. A more fair (and a more uncertain) race could hardly be devised. It was more of a gamble even than the "wild horse race" of the rodeo. The proceeds of the Turtle Day Races, minus the prizes that went to the winners, were devoted to the welfare of Homestake employees.

4. The RECREATIONAL BUILDING, on the south side of Main Street, is a clubhouse built by the Homestake for the use of its employees. On the ground floor is a large room with chairs, tables, and periodicals, a place for general visting. On the second floor is the FREE LIBRARY, established in 1894, and today ranking with the best in the State. In the basement are bowling alleys, for the use of both men and women, and a swimmng pool. All these are free to employees. There is also in the building a motion picture auditorium.

5. In the basement of CHRIST CHURCH (EPISCOPAL) on the south side of upper Main Street is a FREE KINDERGARTEN, established in 1900, by Mrs. Phoebe Hearst, mother of William Randolph Hearst.

POINTS OF INTEREST IN ENVIRONS

Terry Peak Ski Area, 4th highest peak in the Black Hills, 6 m. and Spearfish Canyon, fishing & scenic retreat, 10 m. (*see Tour 13*).

Mitchell

Railroad Stations: Chicago, Milwaukee, St. Paul and Pacific R. R., S. end of Main St.; Chicago and North Western R. R., Main St. and Eighth Ave.
Bus Station: Union Depot, 203 1st Ave. W.
Airport: Municipal Airport, 3 m. N. of State 37. Mid-West Airlines.
Traffic Regulations: Standard ordinances. Parking meters; free parking in Corn Palace area on N. Main St.
Information Service: Chamber of Commerce, Corn Palace building, N. Main St. at 6th Ave.
Accommodations: Two hotels; several motels and tourist camps.
Newspaper: The Daily Republic.
Radio Station: KORN (MBS).
Theaters: Local productions and road shows at Corn Palace; three motion picture houses. Outdoor drive-in theater.
Swimming: Lake Mitchell Municipal Beach, 2 m. N. of city.
Tennis: Hitchcock Park, E. Hanson St. bet. Gamble and Foster Sts.
Golf: Lakeview Municipal Course, Lake Mitchell, (public) 9 holes; Country Club, E. on US 16, (by invitation) 9 holes.
Annual Event: Corn Palace festival, last week in September.

MITCHELL (1,312 alt.) is situated in the James River Valley and is widely known for its Corn Palace, the only one of its kind in the world, where the city each year stages a six-day festival as a climax to the harvest season. The town's location in a diversified farming region has made it an important trade center. The principal industries are meat and poultry packing, butter and cheese making, and livestock and grain shipping; tons of frozen eggs are shipped to eastern markets annually.

Dakota Wesleyan University contributes to the life and culture of the community which takes an unusual interest in musical and artistic activities.

Following the trend of architecture begun in the nineties, most of the long main street has brick structures, although several of the old wooden buildings remain. Mitchell, lacking in natural recreational areas, was one of the first plains cities to create a large artificial lake to supply its demands. The city is also proud of its canopy of shade trees which began with two hackberry sprigs carried in the valise of a settler's wife. The old trees now stand on the corner of Rowley St. and 4th Ave.

A piece of driftwood and an engineer's farsightedness were the factors responsible for Mitchell's location. In the late seventies a town called Firesteel was started on a creek about two miles from the present site of Mitchell and early residents hoped the village would be permanent. But in 1879 the Chicago, Milwaukee & St.

Paul R. R. sent an engineer to locate a town site. In examining the ground near Firesteel the engineer picked up a piece of driftwood, "This will never do for a town," he declared emphatically. "Where water has been it may come again." The report convinced the railroad company and Mitchell was platted. Although Firesteel residents laughed at the engineer's deductions at the time, two years later a flood completely inundated what remained of the town. However, 32 residents had moved meantime to the new town which had been named for the railroad's president, Alexander Mitchell.

The disastrous blizzard of 1880 left the town stranded for 16 weeks without a train and virtually no communication from the outside world. Church services continued regularly, however, in a hall used also for dances and parties. During services one Sunday, after the trains had been blocked for weeks, a man walked into the hall engrossed in reading a letter. Believing the long belated train had arrived with welcome mail, the congregation, one by one, slipped out until only one person, a woman, remained. No sermon could compete with a letter from home.

Unlike most frontier prairie towns, Mitchell's first residents included many college graduates. The reason was that the Government in 1880 opened a land office and employed only college-trained help. Some were married but among them were 15 eligible young bachelors. The group organized a dramatic club, and gave as its outstanding production "East Lynne." As stage properties were often lacking, audiences were implored to use their imagination. Until 1881 there was but one meeting place for all types of gatherings—a hall over a saloon on Main Street. Here public dances, private parties, and religious services were held, the seats consisting of plank boards supported by beer kegs. When prospects of the town's growth prompted the erection of permanent church buildings, the first was the Presbyterian Church, in 1881.

As the Corn Palace celebration, which was started in 1892, brought Midwest recognition to the growing city, citizens of other East-river towns began booming Mitchell to oppose Pierre for the State Capital. In 1903 Mitchell even erected a capitol building of reddish South Dakota granite with stately white pillars. Although thousands of people visited Mitchell on free passes issued by The Milwaukee Railroad, Pierre won, and the would-be capitol became the city hall; it stands at the corner of Rowley St. and 2nd Ave.

During the 1930's, while other cities were retrenching, Mitchell extended itself. One of the finest courthouses in the state was built of Minnesota cut stone and aluminum trim; the Corn Palace was given fancy towers and minarets plus a large new Armory building adjoining it. Parks were created, sewers extended, and Federal Government offices secured. State WPA offices were established at Mitchell in 1937, and it became the headquarters for the Federal Art and Writers' projects sponsored by the University of South Dakota. The artists' efforts were particularly lasting, for murals in the court-house, recreation center, bus depot, and library continue to draw admirers.

The U. S. Air Force built and operated a base here during World War II. It is now the Municipal Airport.

POINTS OF INTEREST

1. CORN PALACE, Main St. and Sixth Ave. (*open weekdays, free; Corn Palace week, admission fee*), was conceived in 1892 to advertise the principal products of the locality. The Corn Palace each year attracts thousands of visitors from all parts of South Dakota and adjoining States.

There is a wide contrast between the frame building that housed the first Corn Palace crowds in the "Gay Nineties" and the spacious modern structure erected in 1921, at a cost of $300,000 with a capacity of 5,000.

Its exterior and interior are decorated with corn, two to three thousand bushels being used each year, and some 40 tons of other grains in bundle form. Flax, oats, millet, proso, and cane are all com-bined to picture a different theme each year. Designs are changed from time to time. One year, for example, in portraying local tra-dition, an interior panel showed an Indian chief beside his prairie tipi, buffalo meat roasting over the fire, while with misgivings he pointed toward the next panel, the sod shanty of a settler. Next came a house and barn of the nineties, followed by a large field with stacks of grain and finally a modern farmstead. Two large exterior panels, 14 x 35 feet, supplemented by smaller ones, depict other scenes. Ten separate shades of corn are used in imparting a lifelike appearance to the scenes, many of the colors having been developed for specific use near Mitchell. When unprecedented drought ruined crops in most parts of the State in 1936, boughs of evergreen trees from the Black Hills were employed as a substitute for the regular materials to aid in carrying out the scheme of the design.

In pursuing their policy of getting the best entertainment ob-tainable, the committee had some amusing experiences. In 1904, wishing to engage John Philip Sousa's band, they wired his manager to inquire if this famous band were available for the week of the celebration. The manager's return wire reported that no city, in-cluding Chicago, was large enough for Sousa to play a week's en-gagement. However, the committee was not discouraged and asked that the cost be quoted. The manager's telegram read "$7,000" which he thought would end the matter. By return wire, the two Mitchell banks guaranteed that amount. When Sousa arrived with his band on a special train, he caught sight of the muddy and rutted Main Street stretching north to the Corn Palace; he refused to allow any of his men to leave the train until the bankers delivered the cash to his compartment. Before the week was out, Sousa had rearranged an unprecedented program of three concerts a day, with numerous encores. He was so delighted with the response, that for the next 25 years he made frequent and enthusiastic visits.

In recent years, it has been the policy to engage a well known dance orchestra, a screen or radio personality, and have several stage acts. Entertainers have included Bob Crosby, Marion Hutton, Bert Lahr, and Joan Edwards; among the orchestras are those of Harry James, Paul Whiteman, Tommy and Jimmy Dorsey, and Lawrence Welk, the latter having started his career in this vicinity. The Corn Palace has had as special speakers Franklin D. Roosevelt, Theodore Roosevelt, Herbert Hoover, William Howard Taft, and many other prominent men.

Of the proceeds for the week, $10,000 is turned over to the city and the balance goes into a sinking fund for improvements and future entertainments.

During the rest of the year, the Corn Palace is used for college and high school basketball games, dances, conventions, music festivals, and public meetings.

2. RECREATION CENTER, 616 N. Main, adjoins the Corn Palace. It is a three-story building of concrete, following a Spanish style of architecture. It was built in 1938, as an armory for the National Guard units, and in the basement is a rifle range. The main and second floors open into the Corn Palace and are used during exhibits and conventions. On the main floor is the city recreation center with billiard tables, ping pong games, crafts, and a soft drink bar.

3. DAKOTA WESLEYAN UNIVERSITY, S. Sanborn at McCabe St., began in 1885, with the erection of Merrill Hall, which was destroyed three years later by a fire that took the lives of four students. Constructed of Sioux Falls granite, the present group of buildings is set in a picturesque 20-acre campus.

Governed by the Methodist Conference, it is a four-year College of Liberal Arts and School of Music. In addition, a combination college and professional nurses' training course is offered in conjunction with the Methodist State Hospital in Mitchell.

The *a capella choir* of 60 voices tours the State each year, and glee clubs, quartets, and stringed trios add to the musical life of

Cities of the Black Hills

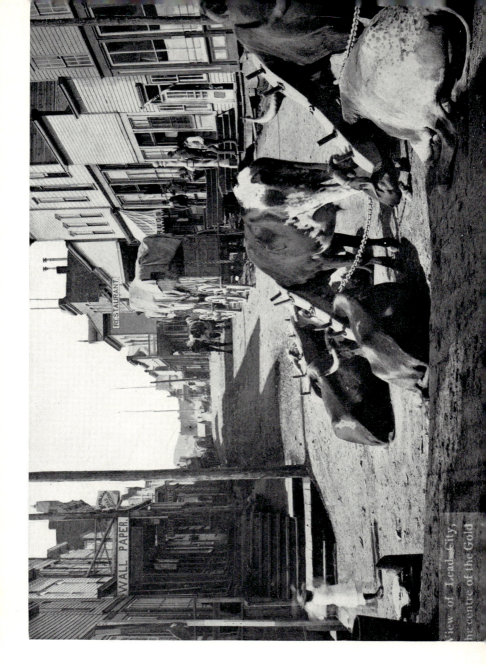

EARLY
LEAD

View of Lead City,
the centre of the Gold

WALL PAPER.

RESTAURANT

HOMESTAKE
GOLD MINE
AT MIDNIGHT,
LEAD

FLOUR MILL,
RAPID CITY

"DAYS OF '76" CELEBRATION, DEADWOOD

DEADWOOD FROM MT. MORIAH

1875

FREE MUSEUM

CUSTER MUSEUM

NATIVE POTTERY

RIVER AVENUE, HOT SPRINGS

the city. A Little Theatre group, known as the Prairie Players, present dramatic productions during the school year.

Dakota Wesleyan athletic teams, called the "Tigers," have been especially outstanding in basketball.

4. FRIENDS OF THE MIDDLE BORDER MUSEUM, on the campus of Dakota Wesleyan, was founded in 1939, by a group interested in preserving upper-Midwestern history and culture. The incorporators included Hamlin Garland, whose books of the "middle border" country suggested the name, and Stewart Edward White, authors; James Truslow Adams, historian; John Dewey, philosopher; Gutzon Borglum, sculptor; and Clinton P. Anderson, U.S. Secretary of Agriculture.

Manuscript and galley proof collections of O. E. Rölvaag, John Neihart, Rose Wilder Lake, L. Frank Baum, Hamlin Garland, Feike Feikema, and of two South Dakota Writers' Project publications, are housed here.

The latter are *The Hamlin Garland Memorial,* a biography with excerpts of Middle Border scenes, and *Our Landlady,* an annotated transcript of L. Frank Baum's Aberdeen newspaper columns, that preceded his "Wizard of Oz" series. The art gallery includes paintings by Oscar Howe, resident artist, and Levon West, Harvey Dunn, Jes Schlaijker, and others. A music collection of folksongs, cowboy ballads, and Sioux songs is being developed. There are also collections of Indian artifacts and pioneer items, including costumes, furniture, utensils, and implements.

5. ABBOTT HOUSE, 1111 W. University Ave., is an attractive home for neglected and orphaned children maintained by the South Dakota Children's Aid, a philanthropic organization. It was built in 1950.

6. CARNEGIE LIBRARY, Rowley St. and 3rd Ave., was built of granite from the Spencer quarries east of Mitchell. In the dome is a mural of Sioux symbols painted by Oscar Howe, noted Indian artist; and the building houses an excellent collection of South Dakota materials.

LAKE TOUR—2.2 *m.*

N. from 6th Ave. on Main St.

7. LAKE MITCHELL, Main St. and Lakeshore Drive, was formed by damming Firesteel Creek and impounding the water in the creek bed. The city planned, financed and constructed the dam and spillway as a park improvement. It is popular in summer for fishing, boating, and swimming.

L. from Main St. on Lakeshore Drive

8. In GRACELAND CEMETERY, L. of the Road, is the ISRAEL GREENE MONUMENT, a large, red stone marker bearing the coat of arms of the Greene family—Nathaniel Greene of Revolutionary War fame and Israel Greene who captured John Brown at Harpers' Ferry in 1859, while a lieutenant under Gen. Robert E. Lee. When the Civil War was over, Israel Greene came to Mitchell as a surveyor, living there the rest of his life.

9. An OUTDOOR AMPHITHEATRE is situated in a natural depression beside the lake on the west bank, and has a heavy green turf which is used in summer for city band concerts (*free*) and entertainments.

10. ARIKARA INDIAN VILLAGE SITE, marked by a large sign (R) (*see Indians and Indian Life*), includes several acres of concentric rings, 10 to 20 feet in diameter, indicating where mud huts stood sometime prior to 1700. Pieces of broken pottery and flint scrapers are still found in remains of rubbish heaps on the grounds. A double defense trench forms the NW. boundary of the village.

POINTS OF INTEREST IN ENVIRONS

Rockport Hutterite Colony, 18 m. (*see Tour 5, Section a*).

Pierre

Railroad Station: Chicago & North Western R.R. Pierre Street and Pleasant Drive.
Bus Station: Union Depot, 416 Pierre St.
Airport: Municipal Airport, 3 m. N.E. on US 14. Western Airlines.
Traffic Regulations: Turns may be made either right or left at intersections. No U turns on Pierre Street. Drive through Statehouse grounds is one-way.
Accommodations: Three hotels, and tourist camps.
Information Service: Chamber of Commerce, 105 W. Dakota Ave. Tourist booth (summer) Pierre St. below C. & N. W. overpass.
Radio Station: KGFX (630 kc.).
Theatres: Two motion picture houses.
Swimming: Municipal pool in Riverside Park, Dakota Ave. and Crow St.
Golf: Country Club, Broadway and Madison Aves., nine holes, green fees.
Tennis: Public courts opposite Statehouse.
Riding: Vera Fusan Stables, 515 N. Illinois; Tyler Polo Ranch, on Farm Island Road.
Annual Events: Days of '81, 4th week in June. Oahe Days, 3rd week in Sept.

PIERRE, (pronounced "peer," 1,442 alt.), second smallest capital city in the Nation, is in the approximate geographical center of South Dakota and North America, and stands where the East-river farming section of the State merges with the West-river ranching country. At this natural and geographical "transitionary" point lies Pierre, neither eastern nor western. Here the West-River rancher with his typical broad-brimmed hat, dark shirt and high-heeled boots rubs elbows with the East-river farmer, the business man, and the Government official, giving a dual character to the town.

Pierre is spread out along the broad Missouri River, with rock and yucca-covered gumbo buttes bordering the town to the north and east. In the center of town on a plateau is the State Capitol, its dome dominating the landscape. Part of the town is on a rise of ground between the river bottoms and the buttes; the reason for Pierre being so spread out is the result of rivalry between early land promoters. Owners of land "on the hill," the section of town north of the railroad tracks, battled the owners "on the flat." Each sought to encourage expansion their way, but the town insisted on growing up between the two sections.

A new era of expansion began in 1950 when the U.S. Army Corps of Engineers began construction of the $281,000,000 Oahe dam across the Missouri River just north of Pierre. The Oahe project (*see Tour 4*) is part of the Missouri Basin Development Plan approved by the U.S. Congress to provide irrigation, power, and flood control.

A large housing project was built on the northern fringe of Pierre, causing the removal of the popular Polo Barns and the historic Hyde House, a mansion with white cupolas that stood for 60 years as an expensive sentinel of earlier boom days.

In spite of years of progress and development, Pierre remains a frontier town in many respects. Progress, with its backbone of brick and steel, has made substantial headway, but a walk through the business district, where modern brick stores have as neighbors squatty, false-front frame buildings, emphasizes the old-new compromise.

Pierre claims to be the only city on the Missouri River owning its entire stretch of waterfront, which it has converted into parks. The city also owns and operates its own light and power plant, natural gas business, water system, liquor store, auditorium, tourist camp, swimming pool, and a recreational park at Farm Island.

Although much of the city's revenue is furnished by State and Federal pay-rolls, the basic source of its prosperity is the livestock industry. Pierre's citizens, according to their sources of income, are divided for the most part, in either of two groups: those who hold State or Federal positions, and those who have permanent homes and businesses. The first group is migratory, changing with each administration; the other consists of early settlers, their grown children, and business and professional men who have been attracted by the steady incomes. The social life is centered around the State and political balls. There are numerous social clubs and those for recreation such as country clubs, polo and riding clubs, and skeet shooting organizations.

The town received its name when J. D. and Anson Hilger of Bismarck consigned a shipment of lumber and household goods down the river in 1880, to "Pierre, on the east side of the river, opposite Ft. Pierre." At that time Pierre was simply a ferry landing for the bustling town of Fort Pierre across the river (*see Tour 4*). Upon the arrival of the Hilger barge, Napoleon Duchneau and two other ferrymen paid a social visit while the brothers had gone off seeking a likely-looking homestead claim. A three-gallon keg of whiskey was discovered among the boxes, and a jamboree was staged in the absence of the owners, after which the ravine was promptly called Whiskey Gulch. The incident in Whiskey Gulch, north of the present railroad bridge, typified the spirit of the early eighties, as whiskey and guns were staple articles of trade and figured in many land deals and purchases of food and clothing. Joseph Kirley, who with Duchneau ran the ferry, paved the way for the first railroad by trading his squatter claim along the river to the Chicago & North Western railroad for a double-barreled shotgun. Before the first train arrived in 1880, the little town was recog-

WHISKEY GULCH

nized as a convenient stopping-off place when making the long stagecoach or ox-train trip to the Black Hills. And with the coming of the railroad, Pierre became the mecca for bull-whackers, soldiers, gamblers, prospectors, ranchers, settlers, and notorious outlaws. With persons of every description contributing to Pierre's prosperity in the early eighties, law and order battled with turmoil and confusion. A severe blizzard marooned the town from the world for five months, while pent-up emotions of outlaws found release in riotous plundering of limited supplies. Citizens formed the Pierre Vigilantes, rounded up the desperadoes, and sent them down the river.

In 1881–82 the town boomed as the surrounding country was settled and Pierre became the center of a large trading area as well as the terminus of the railroad. Nearly $1,000,000 were spent in one year as the rival land promoters fought tooth and nail for choice building lots, speculating as to where the railroad would build its bridge across the Missouri. Mostly unpainted and with protecting porch-effect roofs extending over board walks, Pierre was a thriving frontier town when incorporated in 1883.

After losing to Bismarck in 1883, for the Dakota Territorial capital, Pierre set out to be the State capital and won in 1889, when South Dakota was admitted to the Union. Once possessing the distinction, Pierre had to fight to keep it. A bitter struggle developed when Mitchell tried to wrest the seat of government from Pierre. The railroads serving the two towns got into the thick of the battle. Thousands jammed Pierre and Mitchell on free railroad passes; hotels and rooming houses were packed. When the smoke cleared away after the 1904 election Pierre settled down to a well earned rest, still the Capital City.

In 1907 the North Western railroad extended its line west to Rapid City. This, with the opening of the Sioux Indian lands west of the river, increased Pierre's business. It was not until 1927, however, that a highway bridge connected Pierre with the ranching country. Three years of drought 1934–36, while making inroads into the prosperity of most South Dakota cities, affected Pierre only slightly in comparison, the large government payrolls acting as a financial stabilizer.

During World War II, the U.S. Air Force built a base on a plateau east of Pierre for use as a satellite field in training fighter pilots. When it was turned back to the city, the buildings became the headquarters for the U.S. Army engineers in charge of building Oahe dam and the Pierre housing project.

POINTS OF INTEREST

1. The STATE CAPITOL, Capitol Ave. E. (*open weekdays 8 to 5; guide on first floor*) was begun in 1907, and occupied in 1910. It was constructed at a cost of $1,000,000 under the supervision of State Engineer Samuel H. Lea. O. H. Olson was the architect. By 1931 the needs of the State demanded more office space, and an annex was added to the north side of the building at a cost of $250,000, doubling the office capacity.

Although the design suggests the Capitol at Washington with its central rotunda flanked by legislative wings, it is in no sense a copy of the older structure. The corridor of the first floor runs the entire length of the building, the walls of which are decorated with portraits of personages notable in the history of the State.

The lower portion of the building is constructed of sandstone; the walls above are of Bedford limestone. Native granite steps in front and door cases add trimming. A broad marble staircase leads to the main floor above which rises the 165 ft. dome. Around the walls of the rotunda are four allegorical paintings by Edward Simons, each with a feminine figure representing respectively the family, mining, agriculture, and the livestock industry.

The first suite of rooms on the south side of the west wing is for the use of the governor. A painting by Edwin H. Blashfield, called the "Spirit of the West" is in the main reception room.

At the head of the staircase leading to the legislative floor is a painting by Edward Simons representing the beginning of State commerce—a white man bargaining with an Indian for a pelt. In the wing to the west is the Senate Chamber, and to the east is the House Chamber.

The FREE TRAVELING LIBRARY is housed in the annex. The library furnishes books to readers and clubs in small towns and rural communities.

East of the Capitol is picturesque CAPITOL LAKE, resembling a large sunken pool in a vast, well-kept lawn. The lake, fed by warm artesian well water, is the home of numerous wild waterfowl that remain summer and winter. At the east end of the lake, is GOVERNORS' GROVE, in which a tree is being planted to honor each governor of the State. Another new feature is the GATE OF COUNTIES, an entrance made up of polished stone markers from each county in the State, each inscribed with the date of organization. Each stone has some local significance, such as gold-bearing quartz from Lawrence county's famous Homestake Mine, mahogany granite quarried in Grant county, and Sioux Falls pink quartzite from Minnehaha county. Across the lake is the GOVERNOR'S RESI-

DENCE, a rambling white house built of native lumber, brick and stone with the aid of the Works Progress Administration in 1936.

2. MEMORIAL HALL, opposite the Statehouse on Capitol Ave. (*open weekdays 8 to 5; offices of State Historical Society on main floor*), is dedicated to South Dakota soldiers and sailors who lost their lives in World War I and houses the State Historical Society, Department of History, and State Museum. The cornerstone was laid in 1930, and the building was occupied in 1932.

Constructed of Hot Springs, S. Dak., sandstone, the building is stately and of classic design. Six large Ionic columns support the temple-like entrance; an elaborate frieze borders the top of the building, forming a sharp contrast to the pale sandstone walls. Windows are at the first story only, the second being served by skylights. Steps of Milbank granite lead to the entrance. The architects were Hugill and Blatherwick of Sioux Falls, S. Dak.

In the curve of the retaining wall is a large rock in which is visible the imprint of a human hand, believed to have been chiseled there with a sharp rock by an Indian.

The sandstone interior of Memorial Hall is carried out in the same classical manner as the exterior. A broken column, symbolic of the lives given in battle, stands with a girdle of four burning torches at the top of the first eight steps of the stairway to the second floor. In the background is a memorial window of cathedral glass, beneath which is a bronze tablet inscribed "In Flanders Fields." Each of the three side walls of the lobby has a carved stone slab bearing the symbols of the divisions with which South Dakota troops were identified.

In the Museum is the lead plate planted by the Verendrye expedition in 1743, claiming the land for France. It was found on a hill overlooking Fort Pierre in 1913, and represents the first authentic record of the presence of white men within the present confines of the State. (*See HISTORY*.)

Souvenirs from the U.S.S. South Dakota, "Battleship X" of World War II, are prominently displayed. The ship took part in most of the Pacific island invasions and fired the first salvo from a surface vessel against the Japanese homeland.

Other exhibits include a gun collection, a collection of skulls of historical characters, relics of early days in Dakota Territory, geological specimens, and mementoes of World Wars I and II.

On the second floor is the INDIAN MUSEUM. Here are several of Sitting Bull's relics—his sacred buffalo head, flutes, medicine bag, and peace pipe. Tomahawks with human hair streamers are displayed. A buffalo skin "bull boat" used by the Sioux in crossing the Missouri River is particularly interesting. Artifacts of the mound builders, Mandans, and Arikaras, excavated from various sites in South Dakota, are shown in wall cases.

The HISTORICAL LIBRARY is housed in the right wing and in the basement of the Memorial building. In addition to accessible vaults for the newspaper, manuscript, and document collections, microfilm service of early-day records is available. Photostatic reproductions of the first newspapers in Dakota Territory are on wall panels. This library is a depository for official documents of the State and Federal Governments. The State Historical Society attempts to obtain everything in print pertaining to South Dakota, or written by present or former South Dakotans; it is considered to be the best collection of such material in existence. Many of its possessions, especially pamphlets and records, are the originals.

In the Library office is a bust of Doane Robinson, first State Historian and originator of the Mount Rushmore National Memorial project. The bust is the work of Gutzon Borglum who created the Rushmore sculpture. The lifetime efforts of Robinson in preserving historical materials and sites has been carried on by his son, Col. Will G. Robinson.

3. STATE OFFICE BUILDING, Capitol Ave. across from Capitol Lake, was built in 1950, to accommodate an overflow of departments in the Statehouse. The building is of soft yellow brick to harmonize with Memorial Hall to the west. Built on a hillside, the structure is two stories high facing the street and has three stories in back. A block-long tunnel connects the office building and the Statehouse. The Department of Game, Fish and Parks has interesting wildlife displays.

4. HUGHES COUNTY COURTHOUSE, Capitol Ave. and Pierre St., is a modern four-story building with brick walls, faced with native granite boulders gathered from the hillsides near Pierre. It is trimmed with Hot Springs sandstone, the entrances carved by Joseph Auer. A stone slab from the first building marked "1883 Hughes County Courthouse," is built into the wall on the first floor.

5. AMERICAN LEGION CLUBHOUSE, at the foot of Pierre St., is constructed of native cottonwood logs. On the grounds is a marker where Alexander Putello, alias Arkansas, was killed by a posse of vigilantes on Nov. 18, 1880, ending the period of lawlessness in this area. He had violated an order to cease shooting in the streets and business houses of Pierre. Behind the clubhouse is one arm of the Missouri River as it flows around La Framboise Island, site of a Lewis and Clark Expedition camp, Sept. 24, 1804, and the La Framboise fur trading post in 1817, and Fort Teton in 1828.

6. AUDITORIUM, Dakota Ave. between Highland and Chapelle Sts., is the scene of State and civic functions, including the Governor's Inaugural Ball. It was built as a WPA project.

7. ST. MARY'S HOSPITAL, E. Dakota Ave., was founded in 1889, when five Benedictine Sisters with a capital of $50 arrived in Pierre with the intention of founding a school. Shortly after their arrival, Dr. D. W. Robinson persuaded them to found a hospital instead. The Sisters expended their little capital in furnishing one room of an abandoned hotel; and as their funds slowly increased, they furnished the remaining rooms, one after another. The original building, which adjoins the modern structure on the west, was thus slowly remodeled from a hotel to a hospital. It now serves as the nurses' home.

8. RIVERSIDE PARK, extending from the highway bridge to Belleview St., has a swimming pool (*open daily except Mon. in summer, and every evening; free*), municipal tourist camp and picnic grounds. In 1928 Mayor John Hipple obtained the first Federal permit of its kind—allowing the use of old automobile bodies to make dikes to keep the Missouri River's current from eating away the shoreline, reclaiming and enlarging the strip of parking along its banks.

9. THE THREE SISTERS, Missouri Ave. and Crow St., were originally three, now survived by two, towering cottonwoods in Riverside Park. They are believed to mark the spot where a ship loaded with bullion sank in the 1860's. The legend connected with them has several times caused excavations and shaft drilling for the lost gold. The story is that a ship carrying gold from the mines in Montana came down the Missouri River with its precious cargo years before settlement was begun on the site of Pierre. The ship sank in the treacherous river near where three large trees stood close together. A search was made for the Three Sisters along the river bank, and these trees were believed to be the ones mentioned in the ship's dispatches. In 1922 a company was organized and a shaft sunk, but neither gold nor ship was found. The shaft, sunk in solid ground where the shifting river used to flow, can still be seen, covered with boards.

Pioneers recall having seen Indian bodies in these trees, in accordance with their custom of disposing of the dead high above ground.

TOUR 1—4.8 m.

E. from Capitol Ave. on Lewis and Clark Road (State 34).

10 The PIERRE INDIAN SCHOOL (R), (*open; adm. free; liquor prohibited*) is a Federal institution with several large buildings, occupying 300 acres of land along the Missouri River. Here some 250 Indian boys and girls live and engage in agriculture, livestock raising, domestic science, music, and athletics, in additon to their academic subjects. Music plays an important part in the school's curriculum, most interesting of all being the endeavor to

perpetuate the old Indian songs and dances. Dormitories house the boys and girls who attend the school, some of whom remain the year around. The institution was secured for the city by Charles H. Burke of Pierre while Commissioner of Indian Affairs at Washington, and one of the buildings bears his name.

The students, for the most part, are young orphaned children or those coming from broken homes. Observation of the children about the campus reveals a striking variation in racial characteristics. Some of the youths are from homes of full-blood parents, some show partial Indian traits, while many, through intermarriage of their forebears with the whites, have lost every semblance of their Indian heritage, there being some children with blond or reddish hair.

Before reaching the campus proper the road passes a sunken garden (L) and recreation grounds. The gymnasium-auditorium is directly ahead as the road turns R. in a tour of the grounds. It is near the gymnasium that the bones of three Indians were unearthed in 1934 during road-building operations. Following the road west the last building in the group is an Episcopal chapel built by the Indian students. For a continued circle about the grounds, turn L. east of the chapel and continue, ultimately returning to the campus entrance. On the way are the power plant, dining room, machine shop, barns, and two dormitories. The largest dormitory, Morgan Hall, was destroyed by fire during the summer of 1936, resulting in a loss of nearly $100,000.

11. RODEO AND POLO GROUNDS (L), walled by boulder-studded hills, provide the setting for the annual Days of '81 rodeo program and the practice field for the Pierre Polo Team which plays matches throughout the country. It usually participates in the U.S. Polo Association 12-goal tournaments, often representing the Northwest states. The horses are trained at the nearby Tyler Ranch.

R. from Lewis and Clark Road on Farm Island Road.

12. TYLER HORSE RANCH raises polo ponies. Three generations of the Tyler family have played on Pierre polo teams.

13. The SITE OF OLD FORT SULLY, marked by a monument L. of the road, is called Old Fort Sully to distinguish it from another of the same name, 30 miles north of Pierre, which replaced the first one (*see Tour 4*). Old Fort Sully was built in 1863, amid the unrest caused by Indian disturbances during the Civil War. Named for Gen. Alfred Sully, the fort was never a garrison, but was merely headquarters for troops stationed in the vicinity. The structure was more or less temporary with none of the substantial buildings of its successor.

14. FARM ISLAND STATE PARK covers a large island in the Missouri River. It is a heavily-timbered stretch of land three miles long, connected with the mainland by a dam. It is popular as a

recreation point and for its picnicking facilities. So named because in the early days soldiers of Fort Pierre and fur traders used it for farming purposes, the island now has little resemblance to the sandy, brush-covered strip on which a party of the Lewis and Clark expedition hunted deer and elk in 1804.

The dam connecting the island with the mainland was built in 1934 by CCC boys, who accomplished what many engineers thought impossible—the taming of the impetuous surging waters of the river. Thirty-five thousand cubic yards of earth and rock were required to dam this arm of the stream. When finished, it created a still body of water, named Hipple Lake, in honor of Mayor John Hipple of Pierre, who was an energetic force in promoting Farm Island improvements. The dike provides the road to the island.

On the island are two large picnic areas with native stone and pine log shelters, fireplaces, tables, water pumps, and ample supplies of firewood. A swimming beach along Hipple Lake is midway along the north side of the island. The lake is stocked with perch, blue gills, wall-eye pike, black bass, and catfish to provide good fishing.

The park is a natural sanctuary for wild life, and hunting is prohibited. Deer, pheasants, grouse, and numerous song birds make the island their home. There are many varieties of wild flowers, among them gumbo lilies, wild roses, and morning glories. Visitors are forbidden to pick the flowers or wild fruit—buffalo berries, grapes, chokecherries, and plums.

The State Game, Fish and Parks Department maintains its park headquarters for the eastern half of South Dakota in the buildings originally constructed for the Civilian Conservation Corps camp. The Izaak Walton League, Boy Scouts, and Girl Scouts maintain lodges and camps on the island.

In 1804 hunters with the Lewis and Clark expedition killed four elk on the island during a brief stop, and a monument commemorates the visit. Later, about 1832, the American Fur Company maintained gardens on the island. In 1889, by act of Congress, the island was given to the city of Pierre on the condition that it be preserved as a park. It was not until 1933, that the city paid any attention to the island, and by 1946, it was found that the upkeep was too great for the local government. It was then transferred to the State of South Dakota for park purposes.

POINTS OF INTEREST IN ENVIRONS

Oahe Reservoir Project, Center of South Dakota Monument, Snake Butte Indian Mosaic, Municipal Airport, Fort Pierre (*see Tour 4*).

Rapid City

Railroad Stations: C. & N. W., Rapid St. between 8th and 9th; C. M. St. P. & P.,
7th and Omaha Sts.
Bus Stations: Burlington American Buslines Depot, 410 6th St.; Airbase Bus, leaves
from corner of 7th & St. Joe Sts.; Black Hills Tours, Black Hills & Western Lines,
Alex Johnson Hotel lobby.
Airports: Municipal Airport, 12 m. E. on State 40 for Western Airlines; Rapid City
Air Force Base, 11 m. E. on US 14-16, military aircraft only.
Traffic Regulations: Standard. Parking Meters. No free parking lots.
Information Center: Chamber of Commerce, Alex Johnson Hotel. During summer,
booth at E. Boulevard & St. Joe Sts. (US 14-16).
Accommodations: Three hotels; more than 50 registered motels and cabin camps.
Wide range of rates.
Radio Station: KOTA (CBS—1380 kc.; FM—94.7 mc.).
Newspaper: Rapid City Daily Journal.
Theatres: Three. Outdoor drive-in theatre. Special programs in Municipal Audi-
torium, 711 7th St.
Swimming: Canyon Lake, W. edge of city; Municipal pool, Roosevelt Park.
Golf: Meadowbrook Golf Course, public, green fees.
Tennis: City Recreation Center, Main Ave. at E. Boulevard; Wilson Park, S. 8th St.
Ice Skating: Same as above.
Dog Racing: Black Hills Kennel Club, 6 m. N. of US 14, 6 evenings a week, July 1
to Sept. 1.
Annual Events: Armed Forces Day, mid-May; Greater Rapid City Shows, mid-August.

RAPID CITY (3,231 alt.) is the second largest city in South
Dakota and the metropolis of the Black Hills region. Between 1940 and
1950 it almost doubled in size, passing the 25,000 population mark.

As the eastern gateway to the purple-hued mountains which rise
to the west, Rapid City also forms a link between what are known
locally as "the Northern Hills" and "the Southern Hills." Both sections vie for the tourist traffic that funnels through Rapid City.

The bustling young city derives its name from Rapid Creek, the
mountain trout stream that races through the heart of town toward
the broad expanse of prairie stretching eastward almost 200 miles
to the Missouri River. While the business section was laid out on
flat ground, the residential area sprawls over the foothills and into
the canyons, with many beautiful homes in pine or cliffside settings.
One large hilltop has been sliced off to make an attractive, plateau-
like residential grouping which, when it was built in 1941, was the
largest private home-building project in the nation. By contrast,
only a block or so from Main Street is another picture—Indian
families living in tents and shacks, cooking out-of-doors the year
around. Their lot is gradually improving, however, as they become
more skilled workmen in local industries.

The broad streets, laid out with a pocket compass, teem with uniformed airmen from the nearby Rapid City Air Force Base (*see Tour 4*). Weathered ranchers, occasional prospectors, and students at the School of Mines and Technology mingle with townspeople and tourists, while Sioux Indian families cluster in front of store windows or watch from their parked cars.

The local industries reflect much of the economic pattern of the region. Here are modern plants which manufacture or process flour, meat, cement, gold jewelry, lumber, saddles, dairy products, and tourist novelties.

That its centralized location and comparative accessibility would some day make this the disturbing center of a great portion of the State west of the Missouri River was the vision a group of disheartened prospectors had over a campfire on the outskirts of the present site of the town on February 23, 1876. Out of that conversation the town was born; for two days later four leaders of the little party, Sam Scott, John R. Brennen, John W. Allen, and James Carrey, all of whom had been in nearby mining camps, realizing that they were better suited for this work, began to lay out the new city.

Settlers immediately began to erect log houses and to consider how they could persuade business enterprises to locate there. Word reached the embryo city that a man from Bismarck was entering the Black Hills with a sawmill. A committee at once set out to meet him and induce him to set up his mill near Rapid City. Other men coming into the Hills with stocks of merchandise were persuaded to stop at Rapid City.

White settlement in this Indian territory would violate treaties signed by the Indians and the United States Government. So the latter declared all white persons in the Hills to be trespassers, ordered them to leave, and stationed guards on all trails to stop further immigration. The Indians, realizing that the white men were trying to usurp their last domain, began to use extreme measures as a right of self-preservation.

Still immigrants sifted through. Guards were placed on the trails from Sidney, Neb., Pierre, S. Dak., Cheyenne, Wyo., and Bismarck, N. Dak. The Indians lurked along the trails and the outskirts of the settlement to kill helpless travelers. By summer food and ammunition were getting scarce. Hundreds of discouraged settlers began to leave.

On August 23, Rapid City had 200 residents. The Indians were becoming bolder. The next day four white men were killed west of town. A freighter between Deadwood and Pierre stopped at Rapid City on the morning of the 25th. Citizens borrowed his team and wagon to get the bodies of the men killed the day before. They returned at noon with the bodies and found wagons loaded and lined up ready to start for Pierre with most of the population.

That afternoon a roll call was taken and only 19 men and one woman remained. The following morning the residents were notified by a traveler from Hill City of another death. The situation by this time was serious enough to cause another vote, to discuss whether or not the rest should follow the migration to Pierre. They voted to "stick it out" and work was immediately started on a blockhouse for protection. The new structure, 30 feet square and two stories high, was built at the present junction of Rapid and Fifth Sts. A well was dug and preparations were made for stubborn resistance.

The month that followed put the pioneers to an extreme test. Indians appeared every day, and none of the settlers dared leave even to hunt or fish. Guards were stationed day and night. Food and ammunition became extremely scarce. When hope was almost abandoned a small party arrived from Ft. Pierre with the news that the Government had withdrawn its blockade. Residents took new courage and attention was at once turned toward developing Rapid City.

The largest factor in that development was probably transportation. Stages from Ft. Pierre and Sidney, Neb., served the new town and gradually its favorable location brought results. At first dubbed the "Hay Camp" by the mining interests in the Hills, Rapid City carried this title for several years.

The first railroad to enter Rapid City was the Fremont, Elkhorn & Missouri River, from Gordon, Neb. July 4, 1886, was the day set for the first passenger train to arrive. As the train pulled into the station, a faked stagecoach hold-up was enacted in sight of the passengers and the throng that had congregated to see the first train come in. The holdup was a joke for the "bandits," but a serious episode for passengers on the stage. Dr. Pierce, driver of the stage, had previously arranged with nine other men to rob the passengers as he drove a four-horse team up to the depot just as the train pulled in. He had persuaded 10 or 12 unsuspecting young men who were generally well supplied with cash to ride with him on the stage to the depot. As the stage pulled up to the depot one "outlaw" grabbed the lead team and "buckled" it, so that further progress was impossible. The other "desperadoes" with six-shooters in their hands ordered the passengers out, lined them up, and took their cash, turning them all free after the job was completed. That afternoon and evening the former "desperadoes" were busy treating everybody, especially the innocent passengers.

The Government established a post office in Rapid City, April 18, 1877, and all mail for the Black Hills came through this office. Soon after the first newspaper was established; its first edition was published by Joseph and Alice Gossage Jan. 5, 1878, and called *The Black Hills Journal*. On Feb. 2, 1886, it was made a daily. Since then, the *Rapid City Daily Journal* has become the spokesman for the Black Hills in State affairs, and its Sunday edition is read widely in the region.

In 1907 Rapid City was the goal of two great railroad systems— the Chicago & North Western and the Chicago, Milwaukee, St. Paul & Pacific. In an effort to reach the Black Hills first, both companies started construction at the Missouri River and at Rapid City. The North Western's golden spike was driven near Philip, and the first train arrived from Ft. Pierre July 10, 1907. The Milwaukee drove its golden spike July 18, and the first train from Chicago reached Rapid City on July 20.

By 1920 Rapid City had overtaken the gold-mining city of Lead in the race to become the Black Hills' largest town by the narrow margin of 5,777 to 5,013. During the ten years that followed, Rapid City doubled its population while Lead was standing still.

During President Coolidge's visit to the Black Hills in 1927, the high school building on Columbus St. was used by him and his staff as the SUMMER WHITE HOUSE OFFICE, the President driving back and forth each day from the Summer White House at the State Game Lodge (*see Tour 5*).

The influx of visitors during 1927 was followed by others who came to see Gutzon Borglum at work carving the Mount Rushmore figures, or to watch the U.S. Army-National Geographic Society stratosphere flights in the 1930's. Tourist camps, filling stations, and taverns sprung up in and around the town.

For a period, projects with tourist interest took priority over civic needs in Rapid City. While streets, sewers, and public buildings were neglected, the city went all-out for tourist attractions and facilities. One such project was Dinosaur Park, in which life-size reproductions of prehistoric monsters overlook the city from Skyline Drive (*see below*). Dinosaur Park draws many visitors, but to local residents it is best known as "Dam Eye-Sore" park.

During World War II, the Army built a bomber base costing $25,000,000 which absorbed the WPA-built municipal airport east of the city (*see Tour 4*). In 1950 a new municipal field was built south of the military base, on State 40. While Rapid City gained new airfields, it lost a railroad. The Rapid City, Black Hills & Western R.R. up Rapid Canyon to Mystic, which had been built in 1906, was sold for junk following World War II.

Several Federal agencies maintain special field stations here, including the National Park Service, U.S. Bureau of Mines, and U.S. Indian Service. Rapid City has two large hospitals, Black Hills General and St. Johns, in addition to the Sioux Indian Sanatorium.

Major annual events are the Greater Rapid City Shows in August which combine the former West River Horse Show, Black Hills Range Days, and the Rapid City Exposition. The Black Hills Players, with headquarters at Legion Lake each summer, also perform in the Baken Park Pavilion on a circuit schedule. Dog Racing, with pari-mutuel betting, is sponsored by the "40 et 8" (a fun and welfare organization connected with the American Legion) at the track north of the city (*see Tour 4*).

POINTS OF INTEREST

1. SOUTH DAKOTA SCHOOL OF MINES AND TECH-NOLOGY, East St. Joe St., was established by law in 1885. During the earlier period of its history the institution was largely devoted to the teaching of mining and metallurgical engineering and the study of the mineral resources of western South Dakota. As the demand for training in engineering subjects developed, the curriculum of the School of Mines was gradually expanded. It now offers a variety of courses in technical and scientific fields. Teaching activities are not confined to the campus, as field expeditions do extensive exploration, and a study is made of the mines, hydroelectric plants, and other industries of the mountain States. Its scholastic standards are high, and its graduates are scattered throughout the world.

The MINES MUSEUM, in O'Harra Hall, (*free guide at curator's office*) features outstanding exhibits of minerals, gems, and fossils. Specimens of ores and minerals from every country are marked in neat showcases. Relief maps indicate mining activity in the Black Hills, and also show timber and water resources. There are several unusual displays of gems and geological formations from the Black Hills and Badlands. Of special value is the paleontological exhibit which includes the fossilized remains of various types of life long since extinct, such as the ancestral camel, saber-tooth tiger, three-toed horse, giant pigs, a deer no larger than a rabbit, and a mother oreodon with unborn twins. Dinosaur skeletons and embedded footprints, marine discoveries, and tropical plant life excavated from the surrounding area, turn back the pages millions of years.

O'HARRA STADIUM, at the SE. edge of the campus, is reported to be the first "drive-in" college athletic field in the country. Built in 1938, it has three terraces on which cars can be parked so that spectators can watch football games on cold evenings without leaving their automobiles. There is also a grandstand to accommodate 1,500 persons.

Athletic teams are known as the Hardrockers, stemming from the gold mining tradition. The annual homecoming program is called M Day.

2. ALEX JOHNSON HOTEL, cor. 6th and St. Joe Sts., is the tallest and most elaborately furnished privately-owned building in the State. It was completed in 1928. This 11-story building of early English design is the first one to be seen on approaching the city. Indian pictures and decorations are displayed throughout. In the banquet hall hangs an oil painting of Alex Johnson, one time president of the Chicago and North Western R.R. (1920–29), by John Doctoroff, a Russian artist.

On the top floor is a roof garden and the studios of radio station KOTA. Here also is a solarium of helio grass, from which is an excellent view of the city, the immediate Black Hills, and the distant Badlands.

3. PUBLIC LIBRARY, cor. 6th and Kansas City Sts., features a large collection of Black Hills materials, including books, reports, and newspapers. Annals of early Rapid City have been compiled for easy reference. There is also a shelf of the *Black Hills Engineer,* School of Mines and Technology quarterly.

4. U.S. INDIAN MUSEUM, W. Blvd. bet. Main and St. Joe Sts. (*free; open daily*), was built of uncut limestone in 1937, as a WPA project to house the rare Rosebud Sioux collection of John A. Anderson. Later it was placed under the supervision of the U.S. Indian Service, and the collection was enlarged. The personal belongings of many of the leading chiefs of the Sioux Nation are on display, together with panoramas of Indian life in various phases. The feature item is a tribal calendar, or "winter count," in which the history of one tribe is recorded through events drawn on a buffalo hide. This pictorial calendar shows the annual highlights of the tribe beginning with 1796.

5. HALLEY PARK LOG CABIN, in the triangle where Main and St. Joe Sts. join, is the oldest building in Rapid City. The squat, cozy-looking structure was built in 1876, near its present site. Beside the door is a stone with the inscription:

> I was built in the olden, golden days,
> When this was an unknown land;
> My timbers were hewn by a pioneer,
> With his rifle near at hand.
> I stand as a relic of "Seventy-Six,"
> Our nation's centennial year
> That all may see as they enter the Hills,
> The home of a pioneer.

HANGMAN'S HILL

6. HANGMAN'S HILL, W. Quincy St. up Skyline Drive, is the setting of a true tale of the early days of Rapid City. On June 21, 1887, the sheriff was notified that his services were required north of town. He called for volunteers and 10 men responded. After an absence of about two hours the posse returned with three strange men and five horses that bore the Sidney Stage Company's brand of "LV." There was no jail and while the sheriff was deliberating where to hold the men for investigation a crowd gathered. One of the witnesses heard the youngest but largest of the three remark: "If they had not caught us asleep, they would never have taken us." He talked continuously, while the older men said nothing. A witness identified the "LV" brand.

The prisoners were put in a granary and armed guards stationed outside. Shortly after the prisoners were lodged in the granary, the Deadwood stage arrived with the superintendent of the Crook City barn. He immediately identified the horses as the ones taken from their barn the night before. Considerable interest was manifested that night over the affair and around the post office spectators heard the phrase, "Whiskey drinks are free tonight, Stage Company's treat," passing from mouth to ear.

The next morning the attention of citizens was drawn to a tree on a high hill just west of town, where the bodies of three men were visible hanging limply from the limbs. A coroner's inquest was held that morning with about 50 men present, and the witness heard the testimony of the guards. "Hung at midnight by unknown parties," was the verdict signed by Roscoe Burleight, coroner. The original tree has long since disappeared, but one that stood close by it has been preserved in a casement of stone and cement to commemorate the first sentence meted out locally to criminals for so serious an offense as horse stealing.

The story is that during the night the three prisoners were placed on two horses with their hands tied and ropes dangling from their necks. The right arm of one and the left arm of the other of the two men that rode the one horse were tied together. In this state the horses were led up the hill to the big pine tree that had limbs extending far out in opposite directions, just high enough to let the horses and men pass under. A horse was led on either side and when the riders were just beneath the limbs the horses were stopped, the ropes thrown over the limbs, and made fast. Those details being attended to, the horses were led away and back down the hill, leaving the men to atone for their crime.

The original Hangman's Tree has long since disappeared but because so many people ask to see it, another gnarled, lifeless tree has been embedded in cement at the roadside for all to see.

7. DINOSAUR PARK (open) has five life-size prehistoric reptiles modeled in cement on the hillside. The reptiles are believed to have inhabited this region more than 40,000,000 years ago during the Mesozoic era. The idea of the park was conceived by Dr. C. C. O'Harra, late president of the State School of Mines and nationally known authority on geology and paleontology. Sponsored by Rapid City, the park was built with Works Progress Administration aid. The monstrous prehistoric creatures represented are the Triceratops, Tyrannosaurus rex, Brontosaurus, Stegosaurus and Trachodon. E. A. Sullivan, Rapid City Attorney and sculptor, was the designer; Dr. Barnum Brown, curator of the American Museum of Natural History, served as consultant. Fossils of these reptiles have been found in the Black Hills and Badlands regions of South Dakota; footprints of the Tyrannosaurus rex were found two miles N. of the park on the same range of hills and removed to Dinosaur Park.

At the right are the lumbering TRICERATOPS and TYRANNOSAURUS REX waging combat. The Triceratops, with features resembling the present-day rhinocerous and elephant, was a land reptile with heavy scales on its back; as reproduced it is 27 ft. long and 11 ft. high, with 40-in. horns. A head of this reptile was found in the Badlands 40 miles SE., and is on exhibit at the School of Mines Museum. The Tyrannosaurus rex, resembling a kangaroo, was the only carnivorous reptile of the group; swift-moving on its large hind legs, it probably roared through the swamps in pursuit of small animals. It had from 64 to 70 teeth, some of them six inches long. The figure has been reproduced 35 ft. long and 16 ft. high with a head 41 in. long. The BRONTOSAURUS, center, was the largest of prehistoric reptiles, and this reproduction is larger than any previous. However, there is no exaggeration, since it is reproduced exactly to the measurements of fossils in the American Museum of Natural History. This amphibian lived in the water, weighed about 15 tons, had a two-ounce brain and a smooth skin. It was a peaceful reptile and was preyed upon by smaller animals. As reproduced it is 80 ft. long and 28 ft. high, and can be seen for 35 miles. The STEGOSAURUS (L) was a smaller reptile with large dermal plates protruding from its back, and from four to eight horns on its tail for protection. Comparatively little is known about this peculiar looking reptile which has been reproduced 11 ft. long and seven ft. high. The TRACHODON, known as the "Duck Bill," has some features of both a duck and a kangaroo. It was a herbivorous reptile with web feet and a large bill; the reproduction is 17 ft. high and 33 ft. long.

8. "M" HILL, N. Oshkosh St., also known as Cowboy Hill, bears a stone and cement letter "M" 112 feet high, 67 feet wide on the hillside. In 1911 the students of the South Dakota School of Mines began building the letter with freshman labor on "M Day," annual homecoming event. Each fall freshmen are compelled to relay sand and gravel in 30 pound sacks up the steepest slope, then each boy is required to carry 15 gallons of water up the longest side, followed by a relay of 35 sacks of cement, while upper classmen urge them on. The job of keeping fresh coats of white paint on the giant letter also falls to the new students.

9. SOUTH DAKOTA STATE CEMENT PLANT, NW. edge of city, is a State-owned enterprise begun in 1925, which has virtually monopolized the cement business in South Dakota. Located where materials are easily accessible, the plant has been financially successful. State cement is specified in all contracts for highway and building projects in which State funds are used. This guarantees a market. However, the post-World War II building boom caused production to be doubled. The original bonds for the plant, amounting to two

million dollars, have long since been retired and earnings are turned in to the State Treasury. Between 1925 and 1950, the gross returns amounted to 29 million dollars.

Cement is made from lime rock, shale, and gypsum. The limestone is quarried just back of the plant from a layer of rock 45 ft. thick. The shale is from the State's own bed five m. E. of town. Gypsum is purchased from the U. S. Gypsum Co. of Piedmont (*see Tour 4*).

Lime and shale are ground together in proportions of 80 and 20 percent. After the mixture is "burned" and prepared as "clinkers," a small percentage of gypsum is added to govern the time it takes cement to set.

The plant owns two railroad engines, one of which is a narrowgauge that is used in the quarry; 12 railroad cars haul the shale.

10. SOUTH DAKOTA NATIONAL GUARD HEADQUARTERS, W. Main St. bet. Tilford and 37th Sts., formerly part of the Indian School property, the 84-acre plot was set aside as a permanent camp for the State's National Guard. Construction began June 25, 1934, and the work was carried on by relief organizations. The offices of the Adjutant General of South Dakota are housed in the Administrative Building (center). During the defense period prior to World War II, the camp was developed and used, but since that time the military units have outgrown the facilities. A BASEBALL FIELD has lights for night games and is used for city league and semi-pro games. Most of the buildings are used for storage.

11. SIOUX INDIAN SANATORIUM, on Canyon Lake Drive, is a Federal hospital for tubercular Indians from reservations in South Dakota and surrounding States. The older buildings are part of an Indian boarding school established in 1897. The present institution not only provides excellent medical facilities, but has an outstanding native crafts department. As Rapid City grew beyond the sanatorium, the Indian Bureau's lands separated two parts of the city until an act of the Congress provided for use of property along Rapid Creek.

12. CANYON LAKE AND PARK, Canyon Lake Drive, is municipally-owned and includes a city-operated beach, bathhouse, and picnic grounds. The lake was formed originally in 1890, when a crude dam was built across Rapid Creek. It was washed out a few years later. In 1932, Dr. R. J. Jackson of Rapid City donated 45 acres of land on the condition that no motor boats would ever be permitted on its waters. Rowboats are rented at the bathhouse. A favorite local sport is feeding the ducks that live here the year around.

In the park is a "fish fry" constructed of native rock and logs, with a cooking range 22 ft. in length for use by large gatherings.

POINTS OF INTEREST IN ENVIRONS

Rapid City Air Force Base, 11 m. (*see Tour 4*); State Fish Hatchery, 3 m. (*see Tour 4B*).

Sioux Falls

Railroad Stations: Chicago, St. Paul, Minneapolis & Omaha Ry., 421 E. 8th St.; Great Northern Ry., 519 E. 8th St.; Chicago, Rock Island & Pacific Ry., 210 E. 10th St.; Illinois Central Ry., 304 E. 8th St.; Chicago, Milwaukee, St. Paul & Pacific Ry., 5th St. and Phillips Ave.

Bus Station: Union Depot, Dakota Ave. & 7th St., all lines.

Airport: Municipal Airport, N. end of Minnesota Ave. Mid-Continent and Mid-West Airlines.

Traffic Regulations: Standard ordinances. Parking meters. Free parking area, 1st Ave. S. and 13th St.

Street Order and Numbering: Avenues N. and S., Streets E. and W.; Phillips Ave. is the dividing line between E. and W. for numbering and 9th St. for N. and S. Phillips Ave. and Main Ave. are the principal shopping districts.

Accommodations: Several hotels; tourist camps.

Information Service: Sioux Falls Chamber of Commerce, 100 W. 10th St. (US 16).

Newspaper: The Daily Argus-Leader.

Radio Stations: KELO (NBC—1320 kc.), KIHO (MBS—1270 kc.), KSOO (1140 kc.), KISD (1230 kc.)

Theatres: Special programs and road shows at Coliseum. Seven motion picture houses; two drive-in theatres.

Athletic Park: Howard Wood Field, E. 10th at Franklyn (baseball, football, track).

Swimming: Drake Springs pool, Indiana Ave. off E. 10th St.; Terrace Park, N. Menlo Ave. bet. 1st & 6th Sts.; wading pool at McKennan Park, S. 2nd Ave. bet. 21st & 26th Sts.

Golf: Elmwood Park, N. end of Elmwood Ave., (public) 27 holes; Country Club, W. end of 22nd St., (by invitation) 18 holes.

Tennis: McKennan Park and Terrace Park.

Annual Events: Elks Charity Pari-mutuel Races, July 3, 4, 5; Sioux Empire Fair, mid-August; Auto Show, Nov. 23–27.

SIOUX FALLS (1,422 alt.), named for the falls of the Big Sioux River, is the largest city in South Dakota and the most important industrial and distributing center in the State.

The natural beauty of the site upon which Sioux Falls is built contrasts with the rather monotonous undulating plains of the surrounding country. The river often designated by early-day chroniclers as "The Thick-Wooded River" but called "Wakpa-Ipaktan," the winding river, by the Sioux Indians, meanders in the form of a gigantic S through the center of the city. The business section follows the river flats from which the residential districts rise up the gradual slopes to the level of the surrounding plains. On the steep hill to the north is the State Penitentiary, its sturdy red and white stone walls dominating the landscape except for the twin spires of St. Joseph's Cathedral which loom infinitely graceful against the sky to the west. Although a dam built for power purposes has marred the original beauty of the falls, in springtime the swollen river tumbles and roars over a series of cascades. The upheaval of red quartzite in the rock-banked river is picturesque, for the stone has worn smooth and taken on orange, pink and purple hues to contrast with the blue-green river and its white foam.

The unusual coloring of the quartzite gives the town an individuality, for practically the whole of the city is underlaid by great deposits of this durable building material which outcrops in many places within the city limits; a number of business buildings, government edifices, churches, schools and residences are constructed of this stone.

Sioux Falls resembles a century-old Eastern City, more than one of Western flavor so commonly associated with South Dakota—the great trees that shade residential streets, the stately colleges, the numerous churches, and the attractive lawns and gardens. There are twelve well-kept, heavily wooded parks covering more than 500 acres.

The fertility of the surrounding prairie is the main reason for the existence and rapid growth of Sioux Falls. Products of the soil are manufactured and livestock processed; in turn the city has become a trading center for a large area and a distributing point. Trucks and freight trains make a steady trek to huge warehouses, stockyards and manufacturing concerns. This commerce is the life of the town, and Sioux Falls is called the clearing house of a prairie State.

The history of the white man in this region begins when Jean Nicollet was sent by the Government of Canada in 1839 to treat with several tribes of Indians. He published a sketch of his travels in the Northwest, wherein he gave a description of the falls of the Big Sioux River. A copy of this sketch found its way into the hands of Dr. George M. Staples of Dubuque, Iowa, who was so impressed by the natural advantages of the location that in 1865 he organized the Western Town Company of Dubuque, which the same year sent a party to take up land near the falls for a town site. They followed the east bank of the river from Sioux City and took undisturbed possession of the location. A legend that a band of Indians forced the white men to retrace their steps just as they came to the point on Penitentiary Hill where the falls are visible has been proved erroneous.

Speculation in lands and town sites was at high pitch and in the winter of 1856–7 the Dakota Land Company was chartered by an act of the Legislature of Minnesota Territory. The same act established the city of Sioux Falls. Representatives of this company also occupied land in the vicinity of the falls, and erected a log house, naming their settlement Sioux Falls City.

The population of Sioux Falls numbered at that time five persons, and although they were representatives of rival companies, they lived together in peace and harmony, fearing only their common enemy, the Sioux. They were not troubled, however, until late in July, when the Indians threatened the extermination of all the settlements on the Big Sioux River. The new settlers discreetly withdrew, leaving the Sioux Valley once more deserted by white men, but not for long.

On August 27, 1857, a party of men sent by the Western Town Company arrived in Sioux Falls after a ten days' trip from Sioux City. They brought by ox-team machinery for a sawmill and a large stock of provisions. The sawmill was built, and also a stone house and a store. Several of the party then went back to Sioux City, leaving only six men in the settlement until the middle of October, when the Dakota Land Company sent seven men to look after their interests in the settlement.

The settlers passed a fairly comfortable winter in three new dwelling houses. During the spring of 1858 a number of other settlers came, some taking land in the upper part of the Sioux Valley, among them the first white woman, a Mrs. Goodwin, who came early in May with her husband, to settle in the Territory.

In 1858 hostile Indians found the thirty-five settlers well fortified and left without molesting them. The white men did not know, however, that the enemy had gone, and remained close within their sod fort until they almost starved to death.

The initiative and the determination of the settlers is well shown by the two outstanding happenings of the year 1858. First, there was the acquisition of an old Smith printing press from St. Paul, Minn., a veteran machine that had seen long service and had already a colorful past of perilous travels through the wilderness, having come from Dubuque, Iowa, to Lancaster, Wis., before being hauled to St. Paul. On July 2, 1859, *The Democrat*, the first Sioux Falls newspaper, appeared. Secondly, there were the proceedings that took place in September 1858, when the 30 or 40 persons who made up the population held, in a most original manner, an election to select members of a Territorial Legislature. The situation of the settlers was a peculiar one, with the admission of Minnesota as a State, since that part of the present Dakotas lying east of the Missouri and the White River had no legal name or existence. On the morning of the election, the whole population divided into parties of three or four, appointed each other judges and clerks of election and then started out with their teams in whatever direction pleased their fancy. Every few miles they rested their horses and established an election precinct on that spot. With all the dignity that the occasion deserved, the members of the party cast their votes, and being determined to succeed in their high ambition to impress the Federal authorities with their numbers, they thought it only fair to cast also the votes of all their relatives and friends, being convinced that these absent ones, if they knew of the high purpose of the actual voters, would without doubt be favorable to the plan. The total balloting reached the hundreds; and soon afterwards the Legislature convened and a Governor and a speaker were chosen.

In April 1862, Company A., Dakota Cavalry, was organized and a detachment stationed at the Falls. In August an Indian uprising occurred. On the 25th Judge J. B. Amidon and his son were killed about a mile north of Sioux Falls while making hay. A party of Indians appeared on the bluffs northwest of the falls the next day but did not attack.

The settlers were alarmed and when two days later some messengers brought news of massacres on the frontier in Minnesota, and also orders from the Governor for the soldiers to proceed to Yankton and bring the settlers with them, the village was abandoned. The Indians then destroyed everything, setting fire to the buildings and throwing the old Smith press into the river. They carried the type away with them, however, and used the bits of metal for making inlaid decorations on the pipes carved from the celebrated pipestone, sung by Longfellow. Years later the old press was retrieved from the Big Sioux River, the platen now being on display in the Pettigrew Museum (*see below*) and the rest of the machine in the Minnesota Historical Society building at St. Paul. In 1950 the site of this first newspaper in Dakota Territory was marked at the west end of the 8th Street bridge. The trail over which the settlers fled to Yankton is also marked; a monument on the campus of Sioux Falls College indicates where ruts of the heavy wagons are still faintly visible.

For nearly three years the Sioux Valley remained almost deserted. On May 1, 1865, a military post, Fort Dakota, was established in rambling log and stone barracks built on what is now Phillips Ave., between Seventh and Eights Streets, and occupied by a company of soldiers on a military reservation five miles square, including the present site of the city. The sutler's store at the fort was the forerunner of the mercantile establishments of Sioux Falls.

Gradually the settlers returned, newcomers from the East joined them, and the town was established. In 1868 Minnehaha County was reorganized and the next year the hamlet of Sioux Falls had again reached a population equal to that of eleven years before.

In 1870 the military reservation was vacated and the land preempted by settlers, and for the next three years the devlopment of the valley stimulated the growth of the town, until in the fall of 1873 a census showed 593 inhabitants.

A scourge of grasshoppers the following year proved a calamity of such proportions that many people left the country and it took until 1876 for the struggling little town to regain 600 inhabitants.

In 1868 the first postmaster was appointed, and the office was kept in barracks, back rooms, stores, and like places, until in 1884 it was given permanent quarters. The city was the first in the Territory to have free carrier delivery.

In 1871 the first steps were taken towards the organization of a church. The first public school was taught in 1873 and a year later the first school building was erected, one teacher being sufficient. Fifteen years after the first venture, a second newspaper was established in Sioux Falls and from that time the city was never without one.

A grist mill built in 1873 proved to be the first successful attempt to use the power of the falls. The first shipment of stone took place in 1878 when the first railroad came in, and in 1881 the village trustees had lampposts erected for street lighting by kerosene.

The rigor of the climate added to the hardships of the pioneers, the winter of 1880–81 being the most noted for its severity. Snow fell in October and did not disappear until late the following spring. Railroads ceased operating; mail came only at rare intervals by sled; and corn, wheat, hay, and railroad ties were used for fuel. High water the following spring destroyed many buildings.

Because the laws governing divorce required only a short stay in the State to establish residence, Sioux Falls in the late 1890's and the first decade of the new century shone with the doubtful glory that has since been transferred to Reno, Nev. During that period Bob Fitzsimmons' wife came to seek a divorce from the heavyweight champion who was deeply in love with her. He pleaded his case so insistently that she relented. Elated, Bob set out to celebrate, not at saloons, but at a blacksmith shop where he forged horseshoes and distributed them among the crowd of admirers gathered around him. The floor of the old shop was worn and the supporting timbers rotten. Without warning the floor gave way and the entire group, together with the anvil and forge of live coals, crashed through to the basement. One boy was painfully burned, but no one else was hurt. The child was the son of a poor man and the next day Bob staged a benefit performance at a theater. A large crowd swelled the receipts; Bob gave the boy $250 and the rest of the money to the Children's Home.

With the disappearance of frontier ways, Sioux Falls began to be satisfactorily governed and policed. The advancement of the city has never been of the spasmodic variety that has characterized so many Western communities. Since 1876 the development has been continuous, keeping pace with that of the rich farm land of the surrounding region.

However, World War II had a tremendous effect on the city. In 1942 the War Department leased 1,582 acres from the city to build an Air Force Technical Radio School costing $13,000,000. For four years thousands of soldiers jammed the city, leaving behind millions of dollars and all the sources of night life and entertainment that thrived so gayly.

Meanwhile, a Sioux Falls flying Marine ace in the Pacific was awarded the coveted Congressional Medal of Honor, after shooting down 31 enemy aircraft. He was Joe Foss who, after the war, returned to establish a successful airplane business, serve in the State Legislature, and command the South Dakota Air National Guard.

The industrial life spread out when steel fabrication and millwork joined meat packing as major industries. Sioux Falls also has become a terminal for gasoline and natural gas piped from Texas, and three large tank farms supply oil transports that fan north and westward.

The city serves as the medical center for a large area. McKennan Hospital (Catholic) and Sioux Valley Hospital (independent) have a total of 354 beds, and the new Royal C. Johnson Veterans Memorial Hospital, with 300 beds, serves South Dakota and parts of Iowa, Nebraska, and Minnesota. To provide an orthopedic and polio center for the East-river area, citizens of 44 counties subscribed funds to build the Crippled Children's Hospital-School here.

POINTS OF INTEREST

1. CITY HALL, 9th St. and Dakota Ave., a modern building, designed by Harold Spitznagel, Sioux Falls architect, was opened in 1937. For more than a quarter-century Sioux Falls' officials occupied a wooden, barrack-like structure. In 1934 the old building was torn down and replaced by this modern three-story structure. The exterior is constructed of buff-colored brick with limestone copings, limestone and black aluminum spandrels, carved plaques and rainbow granite trim. The interior is finished in gray Kentucky marble. Palmer Eide, Sioux Falls artist, designed the carved ornaments on the exterior walls, and Edwin Boyd Johnson, Chicago, painted the three symbolic panels in the City Commisioners' room.

2. The CARNEGIE FREE PUBLIC LIBRARY, 10th St. and Dakota Ave. (*open weekdays 10—9; Sun. 2—6*), is constructed of

Sioux Falls quartzite. Begun with 100 volumes by the Ladies Club in 1879, the library now contains more than 50,000 volumes, including the J. W. Tuthill collection of history and biography, the Bishop O'Gorman collection of Catholic books, among them several first editions, and the Glidden Fine Arts collection which provides for the addition of the best books on art and music each year. An extensive collection of South Dakota works and reference materials are available, and the library also serves as a selective depository of government documents.

3. MASONIC LIBRARY, 415 S. Main Ave., (*open 8:30—4 daily, except Sat. and Sun.*), was begun in 1924 by George Pettigrew, grand secretary of the State Masonic organization. The library lists between 25,000 and 30,000 volumes including a chronological record of the proceedings of the Masonic Lodges in all the States of the Union. At the west end is a small museum, one large show case being filled with trophies from various Masonic group meetings. One feature is a stained glass window which was in the stair room at the Columbia Exposition in Chicago. A reproduction of King Solomon's temple, delicately carved, with decorative beads worked out in Mosaic pattern, is also in the library museum.

4. The MANCHESTER BISCUIT COMPANY, 205 E. 6th St. (*open weekdays 10 to 3, adm. free*), is the largest factory in Sioux Falls and employs 400 people. Intricate machines transform endless belts of dough into varied assortments of appetizing crackers, cookies, and wafers. L. D. Manchester started as a one-man establishment and delivered his products on a bicycle. Organized in 1900, the Manchester Biscuit Company grew rapidly and in 1915 the present six-story building of Sioux Falls granite was completed. Since then branches have been established in many large cities of the Middle West.

5. WASHINGTON HIGH SCHOOL, between Main and Dakota Aves., and 11th and 12th Sts., known as the "million dollar high school," was constructed of native pink quartzite stone, with the north wing trim and column portico of a black quartzite so rare that occasionally it has been dismantled and exhibited at expositions.

6. The COLISEUM and ANNEX, N. Main Ave. and 5th St. a brick building of simple neo-classic architecture, provides the city with an auditorium, a block long, a half-block wide and two stories high. The seating capacity of the Coliseum proper is about 3,000. A large variety of entertainments is included in the amusement program including road shows, operas, a flower show, automobile shows, recitals, athletic events, and college activities.

7. PETTIGREW MUSEUM, N. Duluth and 8th St. (*Adm.*

free; weekdays 10:30—12; 1:30—5; Wed. 7—9 p.m.; Sun. 2—4 p.m.) was formerly the private residence of U.S. Senator R. F. Pettigrew and was given to the city in 1928. Constructed of native stone it is designed in Romanesque style. Specimens of polished petrified wood form part of the wall near the north entrance. The museum contains a collection of Indian relics, among them a Sioux Council tipi made from the hides of seven buffalo, set up with poles exactly as the squaws erected similar shelters long ago. Wampum and tomahawks, bead work, war bonnets and peace pipes fill many glass cases. There is also on display one of the famous "ghost shirts" worn in the Battle of Wounded Knee. The shirt was believed to be impervious to the white men's bullets; but the lead slugs crashed through the fabric notwithstanding.

Among the numerous other exhibits are guns, knives, and the brutal hand-forged manacles used in early days. A large collection of mounted birds, snakes, and animals found in South Dakota is worthy of note.

8. MINNEHAHA COUNTY COURTHOUSE, Main Ave. and 6th St., was built in 1890, of Sioux Falls quartzite and is a good example of the Richardson Romanesque style of architecture. The square tower is especially distinctive and gives the building a medieval aspect that contrasts pleasingly with the modern business buildings of the downtown district. Murals in the building were painted in 1916, by O. G. Running, a local artist. The scenes depicted are early historical views of Sioux Falls, and incidents in the lives of the pioneers.

9. ALL SAINTS' SCHOOL (Episcopal), Philips and Dakota Aves., is a resident and day school for girls. The buildings, constructed of native stone, are surrounded by shade trees.

10. CALVARY CATHEDRAL (Episcopal), cor. Main Ave. and 13th St., was completed in 1889 as a memorial to Charlotte Augusta Astor whose husband, John Jacob Astor, donated funds for its construction. This handsome building of native stone, French Gothic in design, stands in contrast to the simple first church in Minnehaha County, the Calvary Episcopal Church erected in 1872, at the northwest corner of Main Ave. and 9th St., and since dismantled.

A cross made of jasper similar to that used in Conrad's Glorious Choir in Canterbury Cathedral, England, was placed upon the altar of Calvary Cathedral by Bishop William Hare, known throughout the State as the "Apostle to the Sioux" and the founder of the Episcopal Church in South Dakota.

Another cross, imbedded in the floor, a few feet in front of the altar, is formed of about 15 small stones taken from the foundation of St. Augustine Abbey, the oldest church in Britain. Every king, queen, and Archbishop of England, from the time of William the Conqueror to George VI, has stepped on or over the stones from which the fragments forming the small cross were taken.

11. ST. JOSEPH CATHEDRAL (Catholic), Duluth Ave. and 5th St., was opened Dec. 8, 1918. The building is one of the most imposing edifices in the State. Of modified Romanesque and French Renaissance styles of architecture, it is designed according to an Italian Basilican plan. The two spires are original with the architect, Masquerry. The nave is shorter and wider than in early cathedrals, bringing a large congregation within hearing distance of the pulpit. Huge transept arches, of Renaissance design, rising to a height of 50 feet, are among the most impressive features of the interior. The exterior of the building is entirely of white Bedford Limestone.

12. MORRELL PACKING PLANT, Weber Ave. and Rice St. (*free tours, one hour, weekdays 10 and 1:30*), from a small beginning in 1909, has developed into a great meat packing plant which buys more than 100 million dollars of livestock each year and employs about 4,000 people. An extensive building program has provided an auditorium at the information center and large storage buildings where thousands of carcasses of prime beef hang in orderly rows. The City of Sioux Falls operates a large stockyard across the road from the plant.

13. SEENEY ISLAND PARK and the FALLS OF THE BIG SIOUX RIVER, entrance at McClellan Ave. bridge SW. of Morrell plant, form a neglected area around which the city was built. The original falls were almost blasted away to form a power dam, although during high water the remaining cascades are beautiful as the fast water rushes and roars over the bed of red granite crags. Across the river is the towering abandoned flour mill of stone that once dominated the city. A garbage dump adjoined the falls until 1950, when efforts were started to set aside the granite cropped area as a park.

14. THE SOUTH DAKOTA SCHOOL FOR THE DEAF, end of 8th St. E., was founded in 1880 in a frame structure. In 1883, substantial stone buildings of Tudor Gothic design were erected.

The institution is maintained by the State for the purpose of providing individual instruction and special training for the deaf. In addition to intensive instruction and standard school courses, the girls are taught domestic science and needlecraft, and the boys dairying, manual training, and printing. Athletics are encouraged and the boys basketball teams compete with the high schools in the district. The boys are so trained that they notice simple signals and interchange gestures quickly. Spectators are unaware of the fact that the players are in any way handicapped.

15. SOUTH DAKOTA CHILDREN'S HOME, 1301 E. 10th St., was established as an orphanage in 1893, largely through the efforts of Masonic bodies. It is not a State institution. With a large nursery building added in 1950, an average of 90 children are cared for in the two main buildings of Sioux Falls granite. An early-day stable has been converted into a gymnasium and work shop for the children.

16. McKENNAN PARK, 21 St. bet. 2nd and 4th Aves., includes a 20-acre tract of which seven acres are wooded. It is fitted out with tennis courts, and has a swimming pool for children. The band shell provides facilities for regular concerts, and a greenhouse and rock garden enhance the beauty of the park.

17. SIOUX FALLS COLLEGE, 22nd St. and Prairie Ave., has buildings of Sioux Falls quartzite, and is of modified Gothic design. This college is the successor of the first Baptist school in South Dakota, which was established in 1883. The average enrollment is 350 students, with students from throughout the U. S. The campus of this four year liberal arts school is particularly attractive, with large shade trees almost secluding the buildings. A marker points out the preserved Yankton Trail which was used by the early settlers to evacuate Sioux Falls during the Indian uprising in 1862.

18. AUGUSTANA COLLEGE, at S. Summit Ave. between 28th and 33rd Sts., with buildings of Tudor Gothic, is the largest denominational school in South Dakota, offering all regular courses and extra-curricular activities. It moved four times before becoming permanently located in Sioux Falls. While the prime purpose of the institution was to provide opportunity for imparting Lutheran teachings, and to perpetuate the Norse language, non-Lutheran students are welcomed. In addition to the regular academic course, there is a School of Music that offers a four-year course leading to the degree of Bachelor of Music. The Augustana College Choir and the Augustana Symphony Orchestra have attained wide recognition.

The school, which has an average enrollment of 900 students, is supported and controlled by the Evangelical Lutheran Church. Athletic teams, known as the "Vikings" compete in the North Central Conference, with the university of South Dakota and State College as major rivals.

19. NORTH AMERICAN BAPTIST SEMINARY, S. Covell Ave. and 24th St., was constructed in 1950, of modern design. The Northern Baptist Convention moved its theological school to Sioux Falls from Rochester, N. Y., in 1948, and housed the students at Sioux Falls College.

20. PRESENTATION CHILDREN'S HOME, 15th St. and S. Western Ave., was opened in 1940, under the operation of the Presentation Nuns. An average of 85 children between the ages of

5 and 14 are cared for in order to keep family groups together. After completing the 8th grade at the home, the girls are sent to Notre Dame Academy at Mitchell or Mount Marty at Yankton, and the boys go to Boy's Town at Omaha for high school educations.

21. CRIPPLED CHILDREN'S HOSPITAL-SCHOOL, 26th St. between Holly and Elmwood Aves., is a philanthropic institution which was built in 1950, with funds raised entirely through voluntary gifts from 50,000 individuals and organizations of eastern South Dakota. No State or Federal funds were involved. It is designed as an "opportunity" center to combine treatment, training, and schooling under one roof. A crafts shop (*open to the public*) is operated by the children for display and sale of their handiwork.

22. VETERANS' ADMINISTRATION CENTER, 22nd St. between S. Western and Kiwanis Aves., includes the ROYAL C. JOHNSON VETERANS MEMORIAL HOSPITAL and the REGIONAL VA OFFICES. Situated on the 60-acre former campus of Columbus College, the several red brick buildings are dominated by the hospital with its nine-story tower.

The administrative offices moved into the attractive, rambling college-classroom and gym building in 1944. English Gothic architecture was followed in constructing the $3,842,000 hospital, which opened in 1949. The two buildings are connected by a corridor of the same design. The VA Center serves patients and handles veterans' affairs for South Dakota and parts of Iowa, Nebraska, and Minnesota.

The 300-bed hospital (*visiting hours 2 to 4 p.m. each day; 7 to 8:30 p.m. Sun., Mon., Tues., Wed.*) is designated by the Veterans' Administration as a General Medical and Surgical Hospital. The main floor includes the information center, out-patient examining rooms, various clinical offices, and the pharmacy. The fifth floor is devoted to surgery, with other floors used largely as patients' wards. The canteen is in the basement. A rear center wing houses special services facilities, including an auditorium, chapel, recreation rooms, library, and the dining halls.

On the grounds are several other permanent buildings, including the manager's residence, a four-plex for doctors, a nurses dormitory, laundry, garage, and shop.

The original school building has had many uses. Columbus College was opened here in 1921, as a Catholic men's school, having been started at Chamberlain. For several years the college was especially well known for its athletic teams which cut a wide swath in collegiate ranks of the region. However, bank and crop failures forced its closing in 1929, but that same fall the building was converted for use as a girls normal school. During the summer of 1934, the doors of the normal school were opened to the homeless children, whose orphanage at Turton had burned to the ground. In 1939, when the Presentation Children's Home was finished, the building was turned over to German refugee priests and students, who had escaped from the Nazi government. The building housed St. Bernards, a pre-seminary, until 1943, when the U. S. Army requisitioned it for an emergency hospital, although it was never used as such.

23. SHERMAN PARK AND ZOO, Kiwanis Ave. between 17th and 26th Sts., comprise 200 acres of tree-covered land along the Sioux River. It was set aside in 1900 to be developed as a park for picnics and recreation. Along Kiwanis Ave. and extending S. into the grounds of the Minnehaha Country Club several large, rounded mounds are prominent. Some of these have been excavated and indicate that a village of some early race of mound builders existed here. In addition to the stone implements and pottery artifacts, some of the mounds have yielded human skeletons, and US Cavalry trinkets which archaeologists claim were buried by the Sioux, without realizing that this was the burial ground of a more ancient people.

A zoo, featuring buffalo, deer, and bear, is at the foot of 18th St. There is a lighted bowling green to the W. of the zoo.

24. TERRACE PARK, at Covell Lake near 1st St. and Menlo Ave., has 52 acres of woodland. Covell Lake is a small, spring-fed lake occupying a depression of the granite bed that underlays this area. The lake is well stocked with fish and reserved exclusively for youngsters. The park has a series of terraces formed from native pink quartzite, with flower beds and walks around the large Community House. A large swimming pool, built for the use of soldiers when they were stationed at the adjacent airbase, and the tennis courts, are popular recreational facilities.

25. MUNICIPAL AIRPORT, with entrances off Minnesota and Prairie Aves. and Northwest St., has a variety of uses. It provides commercial airline facilities at the terminal building. There are also a flying school, a transient aircraft hangar, the S. D. Air National Guard wing, and the Naval Reserve headquarters. There is also a housing project operated by the city with barracks converted to 440 apartments. Former warehouses used by the Air Force Technical Radio School during the war were returned to the city in 1946, and now are manufacturing and storage establishments. The former Officers' Club is the Izaak Walton League clubhouse and a skeet shoot is operated in connection. The former service club has been moved toward Elmwood Ave. for use as the municipal golf course clubhouse, and part of the airbase has been made part of the course (*see below*).

26. ELMWOOD PARK, N. Kiwanis Ave. at Walnut St. in W.

Sioux Falls, is heavily wooded; most of the area being used for the 27-hole golf course operated by the city.

27. STATE PENITENTIARY, Main Ave. and Walnut St. on US 77 (*open by permission only*), is a somber fortress built of red Sioux Falls quartzite with white stone trim. The Penitentiary was established in 1881, most of the improvements and additions being erected by the prisoners, even to the huge wall that has made escape almost impossible. At intervals along the wall are towers in which guards keep constant watch, with a miniature arsenal beside them.

Behind the red granite walls a twine plant works a day and night shift, employing about 120 men during the day and 100 at night. The twine is sold to the farmers. Manila rope is also produced and the license plate plant manufactures all automobile, truck, and compensation plates used in South Dakota. A farm of about 1,200 acres is worked in connection with the institution. The buildings are modern and much of the stock, notably the cattle, is thoroughbred.

Despite the formidable barriers, there have been two serious breaks in the history of the prison. On Aug. 17, 1922, three convicts escaped. One was killed and the others recaptured. In March, 1936, two convicts, aided by an outsider, kidnaped the warden, Eugene Reiley, and won an hour's liberty. In the fight that ensued, the warden, a convict, and a civilian were killed and three persons were wounded.

POINTS OF INTEREST IN ENVIRONS

Wall Lake, recreation center, 12 m., Brandon Mounds, Indian burial ground, picturesque scenery, 19 m. (*see Tour 5A*); the Dells, beautiful scenery and unique formation 20 m. (*see Tour 9*); the Palisades State Recreation Area, 22 m. NW. (*see Tour 9A*).

Watertown

Railroad Stations: Chicago and North Western R.R., 122 N. Maple St.; Rock Island and Minneapolis and St. Louis R.R., 168 N. Broadway; Great Northern R.R., SW. edge of city.
Bus Station: Union Depot, 10 2nd St. SW. for Northland Greyhound, Jackrabbit, and Kyote lines.
Airport: Municipal, 3 m. NW. on State 20 for Mid-Continent Airlines and charter service.
Street Busses: Office, 305 4th Ave. SW.; service to all parts of city.
Traffic Regulations: Parking meters in downtown area.
Accommodations: Three hotels, numerous motels and trailer camps.
Information Service: Chamber of Commerce, Kemp Ave. off Broadway.
Radio Station: KWAT (950 kc.), Midland National Life Ins. Co. bldg., 1st St. and Maple Ave.
Moving Picture Houses: Three; also a drive-in theatre.
Swimming, boating, fishing: Lake Kampeska, 3 m. west.
Golf: Municipal Golf Course, Lake Kampeska, 18 holes; Country Club, Lake Kampeska, 18 holes.
Annual Events: State Amateur Baseball Tournament, 1st week in September; American Baseball Congress, western division, mid-September.

WATERTOWN (1,750 alt.) is an agricultural and recreational center on the Big Sioux River near Lake Kampeska. The sandy loam of the Coteau Des Prairie (hills of the prairie) makes the area surrounding Watertown an intensive farming region, especially for potato growing. With a large lake so close at hand, the town draws a heavy trade from vacationists during summer, and in the fall is headquarters for pheasant and duck hunters from adjoining States.

Watertown residents spend most of their spare time at Lake Kampeska, and a varied program of sports—ice boating, skating, fishing, swimming, sailing and golfing—goes on during the year.

Unlike most mid-western towns, Watertown has no long Main Street, but a concentrated business section. Almost treeless when founded, it has 300 shaded residential blocks.

When J. C. B. Harris of Yankton arrived at Lake Kampeska in 1873, he found mile after mile of rolling prairie with the lake alone breaking the monotonous landscape. The lake had always been a landmark for the Indians who computed distances from its shores; its clear waters were sought by the red men, since few springs were to be found in the region. After returning to Yankton, Harris obtained homestead rights to land about a mile east of the lake's outlet. In 1874 James P. Warner settled at the outlet, and homestead colonies were chartered along the lake. Colonies were organized in the

East "sight-unseen," and a village called Kampeska City was started; but a grasshopper invasion during the fall of 1874, destroyed the crops and the colony dissolved.

Harris returned in 1876, and found two other settlers, Ben Lovejoy and O. S. Jewell, on the west bank of the Big Sioux, where Watertown is now situated. Lovejoy had hauled rough boards, shingles and tarpaper from Marshall, Minn., and built the first frame house in the vicinity. The spring of 1878 witnessed an influx of homeseekers as the Winona and St. Peter Railroad extended its line to the new town. The county was organized and named for Rev. G. S. Codington, a member of the Dakota Territorial legislature. A violent dispute broke out over the selection of the county seat and the railroad, wanting it at the terminus of the line, offered free transportation excursions from nearby villages. Crowds gathered to vote on the question, and Watertown was selected. After the ballots were counted, railroad officials decided to christen the town Waterville. But John and Oscar Kemp after considerable argument persuaded officials to designate the town Watertown in honor of their former home in New York State.

Colonel Jacoby platted the town Sept. 1, 1878. The first sign of spring in 1879, brought many newcomers to Watertown, some seeking homesteads, others business opportunities. The drug store of O. H. Tarbell was moved by oxen from its location in Kampeska City at the outlet of the lake to what is now the SW. corner of Broadway and Kemp Avenue. During the early days a prairie fire, originating from a blacksmith forge in a shop where the Elks building is situated, razed almost the entire town, which then consisted of three stores and scattered homes.

Progress in building the new town went on as rapidly as men could be obtained; 100 carpenters working at the time of the snow blockade of 1878. During this time rail transportation was at a standstill. Ten feet, six inches of snow on the level, completely covered dwellings and made travel by foot impossible. Food and fuel supplies were meager. For flour, wheat was ground by hand in coffee mills. During the extreme weather residents burned railroad ties of the extension from the town to the outlet. The trestle bridge across the river was also torn down to provide fuel.

During the next two years the town's progress was rapid. In 1884 two railway lines were added, and the first edition of the present *Daily Public Opinion* was published in 1889.

In 1892 the Sisseton Reservation, north of Watertown, was opened for homesteading, and day after day long lines of men and women stood at the door of the Land Office in Watertown to register. The opening of the reservation was a great aid to the settlement of the surrounding country, since 1,500 avid land-seekers were on hand awaiting the starter's gun at noon of April 15.

POINTS OF INTEREST

1. MELLETTE HOME, (*open by permission*), 5th St. and 5th Ave. NW., is a show place reflecting the style of the 1880's, and also provides the setting for much of Watertown's current afternoon social life. The former Governor's Mansion is being restored and refurnished through the efforts of civic and women's clubs whose meetings are held there.

It was the residence of Arthur C. Mellette, last Governor of Dakota Territory and first Governor of South Dakota. Situated on the summit of Mellette Hill, it offers a fine view of the country to the west. The house is somewhat similar to the James Whitcomb Riley home in Indianapolis. It has block towers and an encircling porch, with a spiral staircase inside, which rises to the cupola, crowning the house, three stories above.

Mellette, who was appointed to the Territorial office by President Harrison in 1889, also served as Governor of the State until 1893, when he returned to Watertown to practice law. However, when he learned that his State Treasurer had absconded with public funds, Mellette turned over his entire fortune, including this house, to the State.

The house had many tenants, including the local radio station studios, before 1943, when an association was formed to restore the landmark. Meanwhile, all the furnishings, cupboards, doors, and even windows had been removed. The decaying building was condemned and sold to the association for $600.

Rooms have been redone in the style of the period, and antique furniture is being installed throughout.

2. SWIFT & CO. PLANT, along the Great Northern tracks on River St., is one of the largest meat packing plants in the State. Cattle, hogs, and sheep are processed here and shipped East. The plant has added to the city's commerce, besides employing a large number of workers.

3. CODINGTON COUNTY COURTHOUSE, 1st St. bet. Maple and Bdway., was constructed in 1928, of white Indiana limestone, and was one of the first courthouses in the State of modern architectural design. It is adorned with tapering columns, topped with Ionic volutes. Two murals representing "Wisdom and Mercy" and "Justice and Power," were painted by Vincent Aderentti of New York City. Indirect lighting sets off the decorated dome. County offices are on the first and second floors; the third floor is the State

headquarters of the American Legion. Architects of the building were Perkins, McWayne, and Freed.

4. ST. ANN HOSPITAL, 9th Ave. between 4th and 5th Sts. NW., was completed in 1950, at the cost of one million dollars. It is operated by the Bernardine Sisters of St. Francis. The 100-bed, four-story yellow brick building dominates the skyline of the city because of its hilltop location.

5. WATERTOWN STADIUM, W. Kemp Ave. at 14th St. SW., is a combination football and baseball field. The large concrete structure was built as a WPA project. In addition to being used for local sports contests, it is the scene of the annual State Amateur Baseball Tournament, and since 1949 has been the site of the western division championships of the American Baseball Congress.

LAKE KAMPESKA TOUR—6.8 m.

R. from Kemp Ave. on State 20.

6. BRAMBLE PARK, at 4th Ave. NW., provides a roadside picnic area, aviary, and zoo. The park is named for F. L. Bramble who was a leader in introducing into South Dakota the Chinese Ringneck pheasants, for which the State has become famous among sportsmen. The AVIARY includes these breeds of pheasants: Lady Amherst, golden, Reeves, silver, mutant, Mongolian, and white. There are also ducks and geese native to the region. The ZOO houses deer, coyotes, raccoons, red fox, silver badgers, and monkeys.

7. The MUNICIPAL AIRPORT, at 2.6 m. (L), was a U.S. Air Force base during World War II, serving as a ferrying point to the Aleutians. Some of the buildings are used for commercial airline services, as a supper club, and for housing. The large stone buildings at the airport were erected in 1937, as a WPA project.

L. from State 20 on Shore Line Drive.

8. KAMPESKA CITY MONUMENT, marking the site of the forerunner to Watertown. Until recent years a State Pike Hatchery was operated at the lake outlet here, but that, too, has been abandoned.

9. CITY PARK comprises 140 acres along Lake Kampeska, the lake's name having been taken from the Indian for *shining-shell-like.* A public bathhouse, picnic grounds, dance hall, playgrounds, and concessions are under municipal supervision.

10. LAKESHORE INN, near the Municipal Golf Course, doubles as a convention hall and night club. It was the Officers' Club when the airbase was used by the Air Forces.

11. STONEY POINT is a resort with bathing, boating, fishing, skating and other recreational facilities. Three hundred yards from

shore is MAIDEN'S ISLAND. A legend is told of a hunter and his daughter, Minnecotah, who made friends with the Sioux tribe. The young warriors of the tribe vied with each other to win the affection of the pretty maiden. She decided that whoever of them could hurl a stone farthest into the lake would be the recipient of her love. The man of her choice had journeyed to the west and was not expected to return for several months. The warriors hurled rocks and boulders, exerting every fibre of their muscles to outthrow their competitors, not realizing the wily diplomacy of Minnecotah in this contest. No one could judge the exact distance because of the waves. After days and nights of rock throwing the braves realized the trickery used on them. So many rocks and boulders had been thrown that a stone island had been formed a few hundred yards out from shore. The maiden was forcibly placed on the island without food or shelter, the Indians believing that her choice of one of them would be forced by suffering and exposure.

A great white pelican at night brought Minnecotah fish for food and saved her from starvation, and after many days her lover returned to learn of her predicament. Quietly paddling his canoe through the stillness of night, he took her from the stone island and escaped to the west. Upon finding the maiden gone the following morning, the braves decided that the white pelican had been sent by the sun god to transport her to other regions.

L. from Stony Point is U.S. 212, 1 m.; Shore Line Drive circles Lake Kampeska to St. 20 again.

12. MEMORIAL PARK, N. end of lake, is a memorial to the U.S.S. South Dakota which was used in World War I. Bathhouses, picnic grounds, and fishing equipment are available.

The Black Hills

Highways: E. and W.—US 212, northern foothills; US 14, northern Hills; US 16, south-central Hills; US 18, southern Hills. N. and S.—US 85 and US 85A, central Hills. Especially scenic connecting routes—Rushmore Memorial Highway (unnumbered), Needles Highway (State 87), and Spearfish Canyon Highway (State 89). Also network of alternate and side routes.
Many travelers combine portions of the above to make circular tours.
Railroads: The Milwaukee (C. M. St. P. & P.), the North Western (C. & N. W.), and the Burlington (C. B. & Q.) touch cities along the edge of the Hills. Passenger service is limited within the Hills proper.
Busses: Burlington Trailways connect most points. A sight-seeing bus line is operated out of Rapid City.
Airports: Rapid City Municipal Airport (*see Rapid City*) and Black Hills Airport near Spearfish (*see Tour 4*) served by Western Airlines. Rapid City Air Force Base for military aircraft only (*see Tour 5*). There are several local fields for transient and charter service in Hills area.
Accommodations: Hotels and motels in cities; dude ranches, lodges, and cabins along highways. Four State-owned and operated park-type inns, all in Custer State Park—Sylvan Lake Hotel, the Game Lodge, Legion Lake Lodge, and Blue Bell Lodge.
Camp Grounds: U. S. Forest Service maintains 34 public picnic and camp areas scattered throughout the Black Hills.
National Forests: Black Hills National Forest (Hqs., Deadwood) and Harney National Forest (Hqs., Custer).
National and State Park Areas: Mount Rushmore National Memorial, (*see Tours 5 and 5A*); Wind Cave National Park, (*see Tour 14*); Custer State Park and Federal Wildlife Sanctuary, (*see Tours 5, 5A, 5B, and 14A*); Jewel Cave National Monument (*see Tour 5*); and Fossil Cycad National Monument, (*see Tour 7*). Black Hills headquarters for the National Park Service at Rapid City; for Custer State Park at Superintendent's office near Game Lodge, US 16.
Recreational Facilities: Trout fishing and big game hunting in season (*see Recreation*). Winter sports being developed, especially in the Lead area. The several lakes have boating, fishing, swimming, and picnicking facilities. Hiking and horseback trails are well marked, and saddle horses are available at most towns and lodges.
The Black Hills Passion Play at Spearfish and the University of South Dakota Playhouse at Legion Lake give regularly scheduled productions during summer. Nearly every weekend throughout the summer there are special rodeo or frontier day programs in the various cities (*see Calendar of Events*).
Precautions: State law makes it a misdemeanor punishable by fine or imprisonment, for dropping or throwing from any vehicle burning matches, cigarettes, cigars, or pipe ashes; also failure to extinguish camp fires.
Information Center: Black Hills and Badlands Association, Sturgis.

PAUL BUNYAN BURYING THE BLUE OX
TO FORM THE BLACK HILLS

The Black Hills region is geographically, geologically, socially,
and economically a unit, differing from the rest of the State in each

of these regards. Its most common title is the "richest hundred square miles in the world," this chiefly in reference to its many valuable mineral deposits, the principal one of which is gold. But the region is more than that. It is one of the chief recreational areas of the Middle West, and its vacational facilities are being enjoyed by an ever-increasing throng of visitors.

This mountain region extends approximately 150 miles north and south, and 75 miles east and west. The western portion spills over into Wyoming where the adjacent Bear Lodge Mountains form a part of the same range.

While Rapid City is the metropolis of the Hills, there are several lively cities and towns, such as Spearfish, Belle Fourche, Deadwood, Sturgis, Lead, Custer, and Hot Springs. And there are the villages, some robust and others senile. Where Keystone and Hill City have reawakened with new mining activity and tourist invasions, such off-the-highway places as Rochford, Central City, and Silver City are gradually joining the ranks of Black Hills ghost towns.

With regard to the physical origin of the Black Hills, there is a wide diversity, not to say conflict, of ideas. According to the Paul Bunyan school of thought, it all came about through that mighty logger's Big Blue Ox, Babe, who was 42 ax handles and a plug of tobacco broad between the eyes. It seems that the Big Blue Ox ate a red hot stove—a stove with a griddle so big that Paul Bunyan had negro boys with hams strapped to their feet slide around on it and grease it. At any rate as soon as the ox had committed this gustatory indiscretion, he left for parts adjacent, contiguous, outlying and still more distant. It was while traveling the more distant parts, far out on the plains, that the ox finally fell down and died of exhaustion or heartburn or whatever oxen do die of when they eat red hot stoves. Paul Bunyan, meanwhile, had been in swift pursuit of his pet ox, but he arrived too late to do him any good. He could only weep floods of tears that flowed in all directions and then ran together to form the Big Missouri River. Then he set about burying the ox. It was out of the question to dig a grave big enough to hold him, so Paul began to heap earth and rocks upon him until he had covered all of the mighty bulk, making an immense mound at the place where the ox had died. But in time the rains came and washed gullies in it, and the wind and the birds carried seeds there and the mound became scored with gulches and canyons and covered with trees and grass. And so this great mound of earth and rocks which was heaped up to cover Paul Bunyan's ox became the Black Hills that we know today.

However there are certain quibbling and hair-splitting scientists who reject this reasonable theory altogether. According to them, these so-called "Hills" are in reality an old mountain chain. In very ancient times, even considering the age of the earth, a great dome or batholith like an overturned wash basin, was slowly thrust from the depths of the earth by some tremendous convulsion of nature. (*See NATURAL SETTING.*) The granite core, which formed the center of the mass, thrust aside, as it rose, all the sedimentary layers which had been deposited at the bottoms of successive oceans. Before the Alps and the Rocky Mountains were formed, and while the site of the present Himalayas was still a stagnant marsh, the Black Hills were already old. Thousands upon thousands of feet of sedimentary deposits have been washed off their summits leaving spires and crags of upthrust granite exposed. And while these ancient Hills do not have the snow capped peaks of the younger Alps nor the rugged grandeur to be seen in Glacier Park, nevertheless they have a charm and beauty all their own. The roads of the Hills lie through an almost primeval forest of pine, with rushing streams rather than mountain torrents, with unexpected parks and meadows, with glimpses of shy deer and industrious beaver. Or less frequented trails may be followed, trails that apparently lead into the wilderness, only to end at some abandoned mine. And beside them one may fish for trout in unspoiled streams, or spend whole days in solitude and contemplation of "Nature in her various forms."

The Black Hills and Harney National Forests, of slightly over half a million acres each, are for the most part in the same state in which nature left them. Their rolling hills and ridges are covered with ponderosa pine, which comprises 98 percent of their total timberage. For the remainder there are the silver trunks of birch, quaking aspen, and cottonwood, the slim gray shafts of ironwood, and thickets of plum, buffalo-berry and other bushes. Through the open forest glide the timid deer, venturing out into the parks and glades to graze at twilight. In the deepest fastness of the Hills may be heard the bugling of the seldom-seen elk, and the broad slap of the beaver's tail sounds like a pistol shot on many a mountain stream. Gamy and wary trout lurk in the shadows of the deepest pools, their number swelled from year to year by recruits from State and National hatcheries. The woodchuck ambles awkwardly across the road and the stupid porcupine stolidly strips the bark from the trees. The coyote skulks around, robbing a bird's nest or tearing at an ancient carcass with equal relish and gusto. Among the trees flit innumerable birds, while high over all soars the stately eagle, making his nest on inaccessible granite crags.

Great herds of buffalo graze in their natural habitat along the southern slope, sometimes challenging motorists to the right-of-way; but new to the Black Hills is a herd of Rocky Mountain goats. The herd started a few years ago when a male and female, being imported from a Canadian park for the zoo at Custer State Park, escaped during the unloading and fled to the rocky ledges. About 150 wild goats now inhabit the Harney Range, and occasionally one may be seen looking down curiously from atop the heads of the presidents carved on Mount Rushmore.

But while wildlife pursues its untrammeled course, the comforts of civilization are not lacking. At appropriate spots near the stream or scenic wonder, the Forest Service has provided camp sites, with conveniences that eliminate camping hardships. Here and there are artificial lakes, with bathing, boating, and still-water fishing adding their attractions. Footpaths lead intriguingly through the forest and horseback trails extend for miles through territory impossible of access by any other means. Throughout this region the visitor may be as primitive or civilized as he pleases. It is his to choose.

One of the most interesting phases of conservation work on the part of the Forest Service is represented by the lookout stations on various mountain peaks. There are five within the forest area. Of these the most accessible and most visited is that on Harney Peak (*see Tour 14A*). More than ten thousand people a year make this trip. The view amply repays the effort. The fire guard who is on constant duty will tell you that the question invariably asked him by visitors is "Don't you get lonesome up here all by yourself?" "And," he adds "I probably speak to more people a day than any of them."

Custer State Park, one of the largest State parks in the United States, contains more features of unusual interest than any similar area in the Black Hills. To name a few of them, there is the Mount Rushmore National Memorial, known as the Shrine of Democracy, where the heroic busts of four great Americans have been carved into the towering granite upthrust (*see Tour 5A*); the incomparable Needles, those cathedral-like spires pointing skyward above the tall pines (*see Tour 14A*); the luxurious Sylvan Lake Hotel, overlooking an Alpine lake setting, and rough, bald Harney Peak, with an elevation of more than 7,000 feet (*see Tour 14A*); the majestic Iron Mountain Highway, with its picture-framed tunnels and pigtail bridges, and lovely Stockade Lake, the largest in the park, lying near the historic Gordon Stockade (*see Tour 5*); and the wildlife and fishing haunts around Blue Bell Lodge (*see Tour 5B*).

This State park, together with the wildlife sanctuaries, covers 128,000 acres and is under the jurisdiction of the South Dakota Game, Fish and Parks Department. The main park, comprising 61,000 acres, was set aside in 1913 as a game refuge, and the Federal government has transferred additional areas since. Wind Cave National Park adjoins Custer State Park to the south.

Tours

WHETHER travel is by motor, train, or airplane, horseback or afoot, the tours that follow penetrate every region and community of the State, covering in all more than five thousand miles.

The main tours, connecting at the borders with like tours in surrounding states, crisscross South Dakota from north to south and from east to west, following in general the main Federal highways. These tours numbered from one to eight, such as Tour 2 (US 12), run from east to west, while those that run north and south are numbered from nine to fourteen. Tours bearing a number followed by a letter, such as Tour 5A (the road that passes Mt. Rushmore), indicate alternate routes, perhaps not as direct but often more interesting than the main tours. Side trips from the main highway are indicated by smaller type. The introduction to each tour is a description of the region through which that tour passes.

These tours may be followed in reverse order by subtracting the mileages given and by changing "right" to "left" and vice versa.

With the aid of the Key Tour Map, showing where the various routes cross one another, circular or regional tours may be planned.

The tours in this book are designed for South Dakotans as well as for visitors. Few people living in the Black Hills have visited the Lake Region; and it is said that more people from Illinois register at the Rushmore Memorial than from South Dakota during the summer months.

If in spite of the map and directions you suddenly find yourself lost, build a fire, throw in the book, and make smoke signals. There may be an Indian over the next ridge.

SOUTH DAKOTA
TOURS

KEY
TO

LEGEND
•••• State Boundary
—— Tour Routes
1   Tour Section ends
3b Tour Section Numbers
7a Independent Side Tour Number

Tour 1

(Browns Valley, Minn.)—Sisseton—Britton—Eureka—Junction with US 83.
State 10.

Minnesota Line to Junction with US 83, 172 m.

No railroads parallel the highway, but several branch lines are crossed.

Roadbed oil surfaced between Minn. line and US 281; graveled, except short stretches, western portion.

Hotel and tourist accommodations available at above towns, and at numerous lake resorts on or near the highway between Sisseton and Britton.

STATE 10 crosses northern South Dakota's lake region in the Coteau des Prairies and levels off through the James River Valley. In the northeast corner of the State is the Sisseton Indian Reservation, triangular in shape and bisected by State 10. This section is also dotted with lakes, spring-fed and tree-fringed. It is developing into a resort area slowly and with little fanfare; few people from other parts of the State have ever been there. Although the highway passes through an Indian Reservation, few Indian homes are seen, for it has been open for white settlement since 1892. Here the Indians and whites live and work side by side, observing no tribal or racial boundaries. Off the main highway, groups of Indian families are clustered along lake shores; large numbers loiter in the streets of Sisseton, agency headquarters.

Swedes, Norwegians, Poles, and Germans settled the eastern area through which State 10 passes, and farther west are communities of Finns, Russians, and Germans. In the Indian country, intermarriage between the whites and Indians has brought about many unusual names and degrees of color. There are dark-skinned, black-haired persons with Swedish, Norwegian, Polish, British, and German names, and clear-skinned, blue-eyed youths with Indian names.

State 10 crosses the South Dakota-Minnesota boundary, 0.5 m. W. of Browns Valley, Minn., between Big Stone Lake on the south and Lake Traverse on the north. When it rains on this road, the water falling on the south side is said to drain into the Gulf of Mexico, and that on the north into Hudson Bay. Lake Traverse, headwaters of the Red River, is famous in the history of the Northwest; from Big Stone Lake flows the Minnesota River, which later joins the Mississippi.

At 3 *m.* the SISSETON INDIAN RESERVATION extends westward. (*The boundary is not marked, and the reservation is open. The agency headquarters is at Sisseton.*)

The Sissetons and the Wahpetons (*dwellers among the leaves*), bands of the Sioux Nation, found this region of cool crystal lakes, wooded ravines, edible berries, buffalo, and fish an earthly paradise when they migrated westward (*see INDIANS*). Good hunters and fishermen, these peaceful people never strayed far. They welcomed the visits of Jean Duluth, Father De Smet, Francis Rondell, and Stephen Return Riggs, trading with Duluth and Rondell, and listening to the religious teachings of De Smet and Riggs.

Following the Minnesota Massacre at New Ulm, during the Civil War period, the Sissetons were advanced upon by troops from Fort Snelling, Minn. The tribal council made a law that all whites in their lake country would have to dress like Indians to keep from being massacred. Fleeing Indians, pursued by soldiers, came into the Sisseton country bringing their captives with them; the Sissetons were instrumental in having the captives released to the soldiers, and in return the military advance was discontinued. Another troop, however, came into the Indian country, burning gardens and tents. Attempts were made towards peace, but continued misunderstandings arose, followed by actual warfare. Old Indians enjoy relating how, while fleeing, they turned about so that the cannon would be brought into use. To their extreme amusement they dodged the baseball-sized cannonballs directed toward them. In 1863 the Sissetons, who had been driven W. across the Missouri River and into Canada, returned to their lake country. When they camped at Enemy Swim Lake (*see Tour 2B*), the soldiers surrounded them. There a treaty was made which, in Indian language, was to the effect: "There will be no more wars; we will be brothers."

With the help of the Indians, Fort Sisseton was established in 1864 (*see Tour 1A*), and in 1876 a treaty was made establishing the Sisseton Indian Reservation. The Indians settled around the lakes—Enemy Swim, Pickerel, Blue Dog, Red Iron, Piyas, Two Mile, Four Mile, Six Mile, and Nine Mile—in family groups. In 1892 the Federal Government purchased the reservation from the Indians, opening it to homesteaders. The Indians were allotted 160 acres for each individual; there is no unallotted land there at present. As families have grown, there has been no new land for the children, so that today one plot and one house serves an old man and his wife, together with their married children and families.

There are 2,728 Indians on the reservation roll, only 775 of which are full-blooded. A small annual increase in the Indian population is reported by the superintendent of the agency. The close proximity to the whites during the past 45 years has resulted not only in intermarriage, but adoption of white men's customs. The Sioux language is used at pow-wows, church, and meetings, but English is understood by nearly everyone. There is no tribal property; instead, 70,630 acres of Indian-owned land is rented, and 5,781 acres cultivated by Indian farmers. Native handicraft is no longer engaged in to any degree. Wild fruits are still gathered and processed by old methods; corn is dried on cheese cloth; and choke-

cherries and wild plums are ground with meat. There is still some
fishing, particularly in winter through the ice. "Store clothes" are
worn exclusively, and few old-time garments survive. At summer
pow-wows, the washtub has taken the place of the hide tom-tom,
and lipstick the place of war paint. There are 306 permanent
homes used by Indians and less than a dozen log cabins. A few
tents are seen in summer as temporary dwellings. There are about
200 Indian children in public schools on the reservation, 200 in
Federal boarding schools, and 100 in church boarding schools. The
churches—mostly Episcopal, Catholic, and Presbyterian—furnish
the social life. Wagons and old cars start toward church on Saturday, loaded with Indians, staying all night with friends or relatives who live near the edifice.

At 3.6 *m.* is a series of MOUNDS (R) whose origin is contro-
versia—whether built by Mound Builders, Ree Indians, or Sioux
(*see INDIANS*). The mounds have been excavated and the artifacts have not been preserved. It is generally agreed, however, by
archaeologists that they were burial grounds of that race known as
the Mound Builders.

At 5 *m.* is the junction with a graveled road.

Right on this road is LAKE TRAVERSE RECREATION DEVELOPMENT
AREA, 2.2 *m.* The South Dakota Game, Fish and Parks Department has set aside
30 acres along the lake to be developed as a public park and picnic area.

SISSETON, 12 *m.* (1,202 alt.), is the agency for the Sisseton
Indian Reservation and the trading center for a large diversified
farming area. The word Sisseton means in Sioux language, *dead fish,*
or less literally, *fishing village.* As the town is the administrative
center of the reservation, Indians are seen at any time on the streets.
There are a few older women who wear blankets or shawls, but for
the most part only their color differentiates the Indians from the
whites. The AGENCY is at the top of the Main Street hill, together with
the new INDIAN HOSPITAL operated by the U.S. Indian Service.

As the major town in the NE. corner of the State and the seat
of Roberts County, Sisseton has a public library, a city hall with
public meeting rooms, a golf course, an airport, and a large high
school. Pure spring water is piped from the Coteau Hills.

The progressive city suffered a series of set-backs in 1950 when
six major fires destroyed eleven business places, including the three-
story Stavig Brothers department store, a Sisseton landmark.

Sisseton has been the home of some interesting Indians, one of
whom was Asa Sweetcorn, a football player with Jim Thorpe at
Carlisle Institute. The giant Sweetcorn, who is supposed to have
worn a size 21 collar, was arrested 40 times for intoxication and
assault and battery during his varied career. One of his feats to
raise money was to bet he could ram his head through wooden
doors. On one occasion six splintered port holes in the side of a

barn were said to have been made by him following as many runs and dives into the wall. Another time Asa encountered his match in an impromptu wrestling engagement, and his opponent bit off his ear. Earless Asa carried the auditory appendage in his pocket four days before visiting a doctor. The heading in a local paper read: "Chews Sweetcorn Ear in Winter."

At Sisseton is the junction with US 81 (*see Tour 10*).

At 13.1 m. is the junction with a graveled road.

Left on this road is the TEKAKWITHA INDIAN MISSION (Catholic), 0.4 m. There are several modern-styled buildings, including a 45-bed hospital for both Indian and white patients. An orphanage and school built in 1938 accommodates 110 Indian children, and in 1946 a Cradle—known locally as the Papoose House— was built. A clinic was erected in 1947 to provide out-patient services for the Indians of the area. There are also the Mission office building, a rectory, and a dairy barn on the grounds.
The Oblate Fathers and the Sisters of the Divine Saviour operate the mission which began with an eight-room frame maternity hospital in the 1930's.

At 19 m. is the eastern edge of the COTEAU DES PRAIRIES (*hills of the prairies*). This range of hills rises abruptly above the level prairie, and the road winds through the hills with sharp curves and steep grades; going E. a car can coast 7 m. into Sisseton from the last hill.

At 20.2 m. is LONG HOLLOW, a deep wooded ravine which has been a gathering place for Indians since the Sioux first occupied the region. Late each summer members of the Sisseton band still gather there for pow-wows. A church has been built 2 m. N., and can be reached by walking up the draw. There is good pasture in the bottom-land and shelter from icy winds; tall trees cast cool shadows during the summer. When enemies came, the Sissetons often followed the long ravine S. into a deeper and more secluded gulch, known as BAD HOLLOW, called Siechie sica by the Indians.

At 23.3 m. is the junction with a graded road.

Left on this unnumbered road to the first of a chain of lakes, known as BUFFALO LAKES, 1 m., with the main lake at 5 m. On their sand beaches and thickly-wooded banks picnic places can be found. The lakes received their name from a variety of fish that abound there—buffalo fish, frying-pan-shaped and small-boned. This is also a popular duck and goose hunting region.

At 27.8 m. is RED IRON LAKE, divided by State 10 into two bodies of water. Privately operated resorts along the highway offer fishing, boating, swimming, and picnic facilities. Bluegills, perch, and pickerel are caught in the lake.

At 28.4 m. is CLEAR LAKE, which borders the highway. A public sand beach near the road is used by bathers. A resort with fishing supplies and bathing accommodations is in the wooded area (L). At 28.9 m. is the headquarters of a State Game Warden where hunting and fishing licenses can be secured (*see GENERAL INFORMATION*).

At 31.1 *m.* is a junction with a dirt road.

Right on this road is LONG LAKE, 0.6 *m.*, one of several lakes in the State by
that name. Somewhere on its shores there is, according to Indian legend, a cached
flour sack containing gold coins. Indians relate a story told by Gray Foot, a Santee,
who on his deathbed gathered his sons together and told them of the gold he had
buried at Long Lake. A band of Santees, he said, raided the agency at Martin,
Minn. during the Minnesota Massacre, killing some of the soldiers stationed there.
The payroll had recently arrived and gold coins were heaped on the table. Each
Indian took a share. Gray Foot had filled part of a flour sack and tied it on his
horse. When the War Department sent out notice that anyone found with gold in
his possession would be considered guilty of murder by that evidence, Gray Foot
buried his loot, he said, between two straight willows near the shore at the E. end.
But the treasure has never been found.

LAKE CITY, 33.3 *m.*, is a country village named for the surrounding lakes, particularly Cottonwood Lake on the N. edge of
town and Roy Lake to the S. (*see below*). A chain of lakes in the
vicinity bear the names Two Mile, Four Mile, Six Mile, and Nine
Mile—so named by soldiers at Old Fort Sisseton to the SW. (*see
Tour 1A*) because of the distance from the fort along a military trail.

Lake City is at the W. boundary of the Sisseton Indian Reservation (*see above*).

At Lake City is the junction with a graveled road.

Left on this road is the ROY LAKE RECREATION DEVELOPMENT AREA,
2 *m.* A 50-acre tract of hardwood timberland has been set aside by the State Game,
Fish and Parks Department for park use. There are also a number of cabins along
the lakeshore.
At 7.5 *m.* is EDEN, founded in 1909 by Polish immigrants. There are a large
Catholic church and school in Eden, and also a number of Polish Jews. During the
fall duck hunting season, this area is popular because of the numerous lakes and
sloughs.

At 34.8 *m.* is SIX MILE LAKE.

At 35.4 *m.* is SQUAW HILL (R), which was named about 100
years ago by the Sioux. A large group of Sioux women was picking berries. The men of the tribe had gone southward, trailing a
buffalo herd. One young woman, with a papoose on her back,
noticed a movement among the bushes. Peering closely she spied
a Chippewa man. Without showing alarm, she quietly dropped
word of the impending danger to the others, who were talking
loudly; seeing nothing, they accused the young woman of having
a vision. Slipping stealthily among the brush, the young squaw
worked her way to the lake and hid. The piercing war cry of the
Chippewa was followed by screams and crying. When all was quiet
the woman returned to the hill, only to find the bodies of the Sioux
women and babies mutilated and strewn about the hill. When the
Indian men returned from their hunting trip they found the bodies
and, amid great lamentation, buried them on the hill's summit.

At 36.2 *m.* is the SISSETON GAME PRESERVE, a sanctuary
for wild waterfowl.

At 37.4 *m.* is NINE MILE LAKE (R), last of the "mile chain."

At 40.1 *m.* is the junction with the Fort Sisseton Road (*see Tour 1A*).

State 10 winds through the western portion of the Coteau des Prairies (*see above*); beyond are flat plains, dotted with red and white farm buildings, green meadows, yellow fields, purple plowed patches, and a distant clump of town buildings at Britton.

At 48.2 *m.* is the junction with State 25.

Right on this road is the junction with a graded road at 6 *m.* R. here to another junction with a graded road; R. here to SWIFT'S PEAK, 16 *m.* (2,240 alt.), the highest point in the eastern half of the State. From the top is a view of a dozen towns in North and South Dakota. The lights of Aberdeen, more than 50 *m.* away, are visible at night. North from this point is WINDY MOUND, 22 *m.*, from which the Indians watched for buffalo on the plains. The North Dakota boundary is immediately to the N.

BRITTON, 52.1 *m.* (1,354 alt.), reflects the prosperity of a rich farm region where the soil is said to be as productive as any in the Northwest. The raising of purebred beef cattle is an important local industry. The town was named in honor of Col. Isaac Britton, its founder and the prime mover in the building of the Dakota and Great Southern R.R., which before completion became part of the C. M. St. P. & P. R.R. Britton has a municipal hospital. Because of its location in a hunting and fishing region, its stores feature outdoor supplies. It is the seat of Marshall Co.

HOUGHTON, 76.3 *m.* is a rural village where the farmers bring their produce to trade for staples.

At Houghton is the junction with State 37.

Right on this road is HECLA, 6 *m.*, HOME OF THE SCHENSE QUADRUPLETS. Jay, Jimmie, Jean, and Joan were born in an Aberdeen hospital on Jan. 13, 1931, to Mr. and Mrs. Fred Schense. They received nation-wide publicity until the arrival of the Dionne quintuplets. Schense, a tenant farmer, encountered considerable difficulty in providing for his increased family. When the quadruplets were little more than a year old he took them on an exhibition tour of county and State fairs through the Northwest. The venture yielded hardly sufficient remuneration to pay expenses, and they returned to Aberdeen destitute. Their mother died when the children were two years old, and a year later their father married the housekeeper.

At 78.2 *m.* the highway crosses the James River.

At 80.8 *m.* is the junction with a graveled road.

Left on this unnumbered road is SAND LAKE and the U.S. Fish and Wildlife Service Station, 0.4 *m.*, where a steel tower rises high in the air. The station supervises 2,400 acres of the Sand Lake Game Refuge. Boys in a CCC camp developed the refuge for waterfowl.

COLUMBIA, 8 *m.* (1,304 alt.), prior to 1900, was expected to be one of the largest cities in the State, but a series of events caused it to become a small, inconspicuous town. The town was started in June, 1879, by Byron Smith of Minneapolis, who led a party of settlers to the confluence of the James and Elm Rivers. The next year Brown Co. was organized, and Columbia became the county seat. A large lake was formed by damming the river at the western edge of the new town, and steamboats began to ply its waters, carrying grain and produce northward. The C. M. St. P. & P. R.R. chose to build its road through the thriving young town, but the city demanded a drawbridge over the lake. Then things began to happen. The railroad withdrew and built through Aberdeen; the dike and the lake disappeared; Aberdeen won the county seat, and the citizens of Columbia moved to the newer town. The first county courthouse is now used as a school building.

BARNARD, 92 *m.* is at the junction with US 281 (*see Tour 11*). At 94.2 *m.* is a junction with a dirt road.

Right on this road is the COLIN CAMPBELL TRADING POST SITE, 1.6 *m.*, marked by a monument. This stockaded post was established in 1822 by Colin Campbell for the Hudson's Bay Co., and was occupied six years. The Indians residing near the stockade were a band of Yanktonnais Sioux, of which Chappa (Red Thunder) was chief. His son Waanata was born there and became a prominent figure through his exploits in the War of 1812. Waanata distinguished himself at the battle of Fort Stephenson near Sandusky, Ohio; at the close of the battle it was found that nine bullets had hit him. He fought with the British Army, was cited for bravery, given a captain's commission, taken to England, and presented to the King. Waanata's last years were spent in North Dakota where he and his band exercised a protectorate over a band of Arikaras. In return for protection against the Sioux, Waanata demanded tribute from the Arikaras, which enabled him to live in comfort and comparative luxury. He was buried near Fort Yates, N. Dak.

LEOLA, 114 *m.* (1,587 alt.), was named for Leola Haynes, daughter of a pioneer family. The town was started in 1885 when a group of Russian-German immigrants and people from other midwestern States settled on the "flats" S. of Leola. A prairie fire in 1889 burned all but 12 of the 100 buildings, leaving the school, McPherson Co. courthouse, and other buildings of brick or stone. It was not until 1906 that Leola obtained railroad facilities for shipping the large amounts of grain and hogs raised in that area; but in 1936 the railroad inaugurated a truck line to supplant the trains. Duck hunting brings sportsmen to Leola each fall; there are a number of hills and marshes N. of the town.

Between Leola and Eureka is a part of the Russian-German community that settled in McPherson and Campbell Cos., prior to 1900. The vanguard of the immigrants arrived in 1884 from the southern part of the State; in 1889, trainloads of them arrived, having come direct from their homes in Russia, taking practically all land available for homestead entry in the whole Eureka section. While generally termed Russians, these people are descendants of Germans who had emigrated to Russia in the time of Catherine the Great. The older people use their native tongue at home and in the stores, but the young people have adopted the English language and American ways. A trace of the influence of Old World architecture is still seen among the farm houses (*see ARCHITECTURE*). The original buildings were long and narrow, designed to conserve wall space, and for convenience; one end of the building housed the family, the center was used to store grain, and the third section for the livestock. The entrance door to the house was divided, so that the top part might be swung open, leaving the bottom half closed to keep children in and animals out. Most of the immigrants have had a degree of prosperity, and now the long narrow buildings are used to house the family or livestock exclusively, and other buildings have been erected nearby. There is a South Russian influence still noticeable in the use of vivid, contrasting colors in painting houses. In the country and town purple houses are trimmed in green, pink houses have blue borders, yellow houses are decorated with orchid, and no lack of originality is discernible.

EUREKA, 151.7 m. (1,884 alt.), is an example of a small city founded and still peopled by European immigrants who have provided themselves with most of the conveniences and comforts of modern American towns. The soil was productive for these newcomers, and during the 1890's Eureka maintained that it was the largest primary wheat market in the world, 36 elevators being required to care for the flood of grain produced by the immigrant farmers. The town has a large number of retired farmers who, after acquiring a competence, have left their farms to sons and daughters. They brought with them the traditional German love for beer; before prohibition it required 18 saloons properly to satisfy the thirst of the Eureka community. With the legalizing of liquor sales in 1935, Eureka promptly voted to operate a municipal liquor store. German dishes can be had in the restaurants, but are not featured. Services in German are held in the Lutheran and Catholic churches.

At 172 m. is the junction with US 83 (see Tour 12), 3 m. N. of Mound City.

Tour 1A

State 10—Old Fort Sisseton. Unnumbered County highway.
Junction with State 10 to Fort Sisseton, 6.5 m.
Roadbed is graveled.

BRANCHING S. from State 10 (see Tour 1) 7 m. W. of Lake City, this road winds through hilly country and around the Fort, or Kettle Lakes that surround the old military post. Another approach is from Webster and US 12 (see Tour 2).

At 6.5 m. is OLD FORT SISSETON (public; no admission), maintained by the South Dakota Game, Fish and Parks Department. Originally a U. S. Army post during the Indian troubles, it since has been a playground for wealthy out-of-state sportsmen, duck hunting headquarters, and a sheep ranch. During the 1930's a restoration project was undertaken by Marshall County, the National Park Service, and the Works Progress Administration. Many of the old stone buildings were restored, electric lights were replaced by candles, faucets by buckets, and garages were filled with hay. Since then, however, the buildings again have fallen into disrepair and the State has purchased the grounds to preserve the historic site.

On the E. side of the quadrangle are the barracks and commissary; to the N. are the hospital, blockhouse, and stables; to the W. are the Commanding Officer's headquarters and officers' quarters; and to the S. the Quartermaster's office, saddle shop, guardhouse, chapel, and blockhouse (*see CHART*).

The fort was established, following the Minnesota Massacre in 1864, by Major John Clowney, commander of troops recruited in Wisconsin. Acting upon orders from General John Pope that the post be set up "not east of the James River," Major Clowney led his soldiers into Dakota Territory, which at that time was inhabited only by Indians and a few traders of French origin. The Sisseton-Wahpeton tribes of the Sioux Nation had surrendered peaceably the year before at Enemy Swim Lake (*see Tours 1 and 2B*), and when the soldiers entered their domain the Indians guided them to the advantageous fort site. It was, contrary to order, 40 m. E. of the James River.

Situated on the elevated tablelands known as the Coteau des Prairies, the fort was partly surrounded by the Kettle Lakes where lived 1,200 Sioux Indians. It was named Fort Wadsworth originally in honor of General James S. Wadsworth of New York, who died in the Battle of the Wilderness. During the time that Colonel W. D. Boyce, Chicago millionaire newspaper publisher, leased the fort a few years ago, Congressman James W. Wadsworth, a grandson of the man for whom the post was named, was a frequent visitor. In 1876 the fort took the name of the tribe living in that region, the name which it still bears.

Building a fort in an undeveloped country was no easy task. Supplies had to be brought 244 miles from St. Paul. Stones for the barracks, commissary, officers' quarters, and stables were dragged by oxen from as far as Wahpeton, N. Dak., although many native stones were used. In 1868 brick was brought in wagons drawn by oxen from St. Cloud, Minn., for the permanent buildings, including the hospital. Large oak trees were cut and sawed by a portable sawmill for the storehouse, which was 150 ft. long and built entirely of logs. The two towering blockhouses were also made of logs. The stone buildings, 240 ft. long and 36 ft. in width, caved in from lack of care, hard usage, and the effects of vandalism after the troops were withdrawn in 1888.

In the early 1880's Fort Sisseton was the social center of the eastern half of Dakota Territory. For a civilian in Watertown, Fargo, Webster, or Browns Valley to receive an invitation for dinner at the fort was considered a high honor. A silver service was used exclusively in the officers' quarters, with an orchestra playing for the dinners and balls. During vacations when the young men and women returned from Eastern schools, brilliant social functions were in order and delicacies were brought by pony express from St. Paul for the occasion.

The soldiers stationed at the fort, ready to quell Indian uprisings and protect the whites, were of Irish, German, and Scotch descent. Physical hardships were common during the hard winters, and many are the stories of heroism.

Old Indians like to recall the days when their fathers were scouts at the post. One man in particular is legend. He was Samuel J. Brown, the half-breed son of the first white trader in the region. In April 1866, word was received at Fort Sisseton that the Indians were crossing the James River near Jamestown to make raids on the settlers. Brown, who was chief of the scouts, was sent to Ruilliard's trading post, about 10 m. NE. of Aberdeen and 55 m. from the fort, to warn them. A large tribe was living on the Elm River near Ruilliard's post, and Brown was to persuade them not to join in the fighting. Brown left Fort Sisseton near sundown and rode hard, arriving during the night. He was told that Indian carriers, who were much swifter than the Government mailmen serving the fort, had brought word that President Johnson had signed a treaty to stop the soldiers from fighting the Indians. Brown knew that he had to get back to the fort before the troops left in the morning for Jamestown to meet the Indians; he decided, therefore, that he must retrace his steps before another Indian war should commence, with the soldiers at fault. So he traded horses with Ruilliard and started back for the fort. Soon after he left, a terrific blizzard began. He angled E. more than N. because of the stiff, cutting wind and found himself among the Waubay Lakes at daybreak. Having gone too far S , he turned due N. and spurred his plucky pony into the raging blizzard. Brown reached the fort in time to halt the troops, after riding steadily since he had left the evening before. When he was taken from his pony he was unable to move his limbs, stiffened by the cold weather and the wearisome 135-mile ride. He remained paralyzed until the end of his life!

After the Civil War two companies of hand-picked Negroes were stationed at Fort Sisseton. Despite the fact that every man was over six feet tall and an athlete, they did not relish their situation. First, they were afraid of the Indians; next, they were ridiculously out of place when wintery winds swept tons of snow across the prairie; then too, and worst of all, they were given the job of digging up the bodies of the soldiers who had been buried there, for removal to another fort! Many of the dead were deserters who had been shot and dragged back behind horses. One of the stories related by old-timers about the Negroes and their grave-digging activities is as follows: one big, husky Negro was standing on a rough box in a grave, loosening the dirt around the sides so that the box could be pulled out. A board gave way and the Negro's foot sank into the body of a dead soldier! A superhuman leap vaulted him out of the grave to the solid ground, where he emulated the feats of Jesse Owens and Ralph Metcalf for speed. He never returned to the fort, and his whereabouts have never been entered upon the records.

Between 1910 and 1927 the fort was in the hands of private interests. Hunting parties from Minneapolis and St. Paul found the neighboring passes perfect for hunting ducks and geese.

In 1920 Col. W. C. Boyce, Chicago newspaperman, leased the fort and hospital to be used as a dwelling house. Colonel Boyce began his newspaper career at Britton (*see Tour 1*). At the time of his death in 1928 he owned newspapers in Chicago and Indianapolis. One room in the renovated hospital was the poker room, where games continued day and night every fall during the hunting season. Many of the visitors hired hunters to do their shooting in order that they might have ducks to ship home. Jerry Wilson, professional Sisseton trapshooter, was hired at $25 a day to hunt for several of the visitors. Colonel Boyce, known as the man who started the Boy Scout movement in the United States, astonished Webster citizens once when, after arriving by train from the West Coast, he had his Rolls-Royce sent out from Chicago in an express car. Motor boats, a putting green on the parade grounds, and the poker table, furnished entertainment for most of the guests.

In 1935 a Federal transient camp was set up at Fort Sisseton as an Emergency Relief Administration activity, and work on the restoration of the fort was started. An error in the reconstruction was soon discovered when a hip-roof was placed on a building which originally had a straight, pointed roof. A WPA project, with the National Park Service providing supervision, continued the work. A ditch was dug around the fort to the same depth it was originally, and the dirt used, as was formerly done by the soldiers, to build a mound wall on the inside. Work was discontinued at the outset of World War II, after which Gov. M. Q. Sharpe arranged for the State to buy the 640-acre reserve from the county. The cost was $25,000.

The State Game, Fish and Parks Department also maintains a 240-acre public shooting ground near the fort, for duck hunters. It is known as PARSONS PASS, and provides some of the best migratory waterfowl shooting in the State.

Tour 2

(Benson, Minn.)—Milbank—Webster—Aberdeen—Mobridge—Lemmon—(Hettinger, N. Dak.). US 12.
Minnesota Line to North Dakota Line, 326 *m.*
The C. M. St. P. & P. R.R. parallels the highway throughout.
Roadbed hard-surfaced.
Hotel and tourist accommodations excellent in larger towns, with lakeside camping places in Lake Region.

US 12, known as the Yellowstone Trail, crosses northern South Dakota through the lake region, the James River valley, the Missouri River ranges, and the Buttes and Badlands section, each different from the others. The north-eastern part of the State is dotted with lakes, spring-fed and tree-surrounded, abounding in game fish and wild fowl. Unfortunately, when the railroad and highway were built an attempt was made to avoid as many lakes as possible, and only a few can be seen from US 12. With the coming of the homesteaders and the building of the railroad in the early 1880's, small towns sprang up almost overnight. The fertile land of the broad James River valley was settled quickly, and farms through that region are large and modern. In spring the valley is checkerboarded with green fields of grass and black plowed lands, with occasional clusters of trees, all of which have been planted by the farmers. In the fall the golden fields wave like the sea, with tall corn rows forming the shore. Here is a prairie country, vast and apparently endless telling a story of ceaseless labor to make things grow. Farther west, in the Missouri River breaks, the land is less suitable for grain crops and better for livestock purposes. Attempts to farm on a large scale have met with little success and cattle now roam the stone-studded hills. Beyond the Missouri River are the Badlands, fantastic in shape and spotted with ranches. Raising of cattle, sheep, and horses forms the basic industry, with a little farming to obtain feed.

US 12 crossed the Minnesota Line 40 m. W. of Benson, Minn. (see Minn. Tour 10), and touches the southern end of BIG STONE LAKE, which stretches northward for 36 m. On a windy day white-caps roll high, the lake turning into a frothy, greenish-gray, roaring sweep of water. The lake was named for the out-croppings of granite rocks nearby, and is on the boundary between Minnesota and South Dakota. It is stocked with game fish, particularly pickerel, pike, bluegills, sturgeon, perch, crappies, and sheepshead, a variety peculiar to this lake. There are numerous places here and along the lake shore where boats and fishing equipment can be rented. Trolling, casting, and still-fishing are all possible. The best swimming beaches are north along the west side, with several resorts open to the public.

US 12 passes over a 100-ft. dike between the States, known as the WHETSTONE DIVERSION PROJECT. A cooperative arrangement was made between the Minnesota and South Dakota governments, acting with the Works Progress Administration, to divert water from Whetstone River (L) into Big Stone Lake (R), which during the drought years was sadly depleted. For 50 years attempts had been made to divert the Whetstone River into the lake, which has as an outlet the Minnesota River. Work was started in October 1934, and in March 1937 water from the river began pouring into the lake. Residents of Big Stone City, S. Dak., and Ortonville, Minn., left their work to watch the lake level rise, and one onlooker—a pioneer—exclaimed, "By gad! It's flowing uphill after all."

At the eastern edge of Big Stone City is a CORN CANNERY, 0.5 m., that operates each fall when the corn from the surrounding fields has been picked. A corn king is crowned each year—the man who can eat the most corn on the cob.

BIG STONE CITY, 0.8 m. (979 alt.), overlooks the lake from which it takes its name, and, in addition to being a summer resort center, has a brick factory, corn cannery, and granite quarry; yet the normal population is small. During the summer and fall, however, it becomes considerably larger. The town was first known as Inkpa City, named for the renegade Indian, Inkpaduta, who held captive there several women, taken in the Spirit Lake massacre.

Right from the center of Big Stone City, on an improved road, is CHATAUQUA PARK, 1 m., a popular summer resort with cottages, boating facilities, swimming, and fishing. Sheltered by trees, the resort is a center for week-end picnics and camping parties. At 9 m. is LINDEN BEACH, in a setting of tall linden or bass-

The People at Work and Play

PRAIRIE FARMER

COMBINING
WHEAT

FISHING AT
BIG STONE LAKE.

SOD SHANTY

IMMIGRANT TRAIN, EUREKA

MENNONITE CHILDREN

HARDANGER WEDDING

MODERN GOLD PANNING

DEVIL'S GULCH

STRATOSPHERE
FLIGHT

wood trees. A trading-post, established in 1865 by Moses Moreau and Soloman Robar, once occupied the site but now a hotel and cabins with modern facilities have taken its place.

At 11 m. is HARTFORD BEACH STATE PARK, with an excellent sand beach, bathhouse, and an unusual assortment of boats. The large hardwood trees form a canopy over the extensive picnic and camp grounds, and there is a picturesque stream running through the park bearing the translation of the Indian name for "river of the white herons." A trading post was established here in 1818 by Hazen Mooers. At the W. end of the park are the Hartford Mounds, in which skeletons and artifacts of an early race have been found (*see Indians*).

At the western edge of Big Stone City, 1.2 *m.*, is a brick factory utilizing native clay.

At 1.9 *m.* the Whetstone River is crossed, and US 12 begins to wind over a range of low, rambling hills, where frequent, clean-looking farm buildings are set in groves of trees.

At 7.9 *m.* is a junction with a graveled road.

Left on this road is the DAKOTA GRANITE QUARRY, 0.5 *m.*, with its huge piles of stone, like a strange fortress. A few years ago a young man named Stringle obtained control of a quarry in which there was a quantity of mahogany granite. He built a cutting and polishing plant, and today carloads of gravestones are shipped to all parts of the United States. The various kinds of granite quarried here are Hunter, royal purple, and mahogany.

MILBANK, 13 *m.* (1,148 alt.), was named for Jeremiah Milbank, a director of the Milwaukee R.R., which was extended through the city in 1880. The railroad established a division headquarters here, which attracted many families of Irish and Dutch origin to work in the shops and on the line. A windmill, once used to grind grain from the surrounding country, has been moved to the center of the city, R. of US 12.

Milbank became the seat of Grant Co. after a heated three-town contest. In 1880 Big Stone City won the first election for county seat; but the next year Milbank had outgrown Big Stone City, so the latter induced Wilmot, a town nearby, to enter the contest. Milbank won by 25 votes, but Big Stone City officials charged fraudulent voting and retained the records; Milbank at the same time established itself as the county seat, and residents filed their papers in both towns, to be on the safe side. The case was taken to court and Milbank was recognized as the official seat. Big Stone City officials, however, refused to give up their records until they had been reimbursed for campaign funds.

Milbank granite, quarried within the city limits, is well known and widely used. The town has been long noted in the State for its high school athletic teams and for the All-conference and All-American football players it contributes to Midwestern universities.

The BIRTHPLACE OF AMERICAN LEGION JUNIOR BASEBALL is commemorated by a seven-ton granite marker in the parkway along US 12. The first game between Junior teams was played in Milbank at a State Legion convention in 1925, and the next year the National convention adopted the idea of Junior League baseball throughout the United States. By 1950, there were more than 15,000 teams in the nation-wide program under American Legion sponsorship. Frank McCormick, Sioux Falls, who for many years was director of athletics at the University of Minnesota, is generally credited with the idea. The eight-ft. shaft is made of locally quarried royal purple stone. It was installed on the 25th anniversary, August 10, 1950.

At Milbank is the N. terminus and junction of US 77 (*see Tour 9*). Here also is the junction with State 15 which was opened in 1950 to provide another route to HARTFORD BEACH STATE PARK, 14 *m.* (*see above*).

A project to straighten US 12 has caused the new highway to skirt the edge of several towns it used to bisect between Milbank and Aberdeen.

MARVIN, 28 *m.* (1,657 alt.), was originally known as Grade Siding, owing to its situation on the railroad; but in 1882 a post office was to be established and a more dignified name was needed. There was a Marvin safe in the railroad office and a local punster suggested that Marvin was a "good, safe name."

The BLUE CLOUD MONASTERY, a modern-designed three story stone structure with an impressive tower, was built here in 1950 by the order of St. Benedict. As the first Catholic monastery in South Dakota, it is a priory dependent upon St. Meinrad's Abbey in Indiana. The name honors Chief Blue Cloud, a Sioux Indian christianized by Father De Smet, early missionary to this region.

Between Marvin and Summit, US 12 winds into the Coteau des Prairies, *hills of the prairies,* so-named by early French explorers. The hills have gullies and draws lined with oak, ash, and elm trees. From the crests of the hills are splendid views of Big Stone Lake, Lake Traverse, and far into Minnesota, a jumble of purple, yellow, and green.

SUMMIT, 36.5 *m.* (L) (2,000 alt.), is the highest point along the railroad in the Coteau range, about 1,000 ft. above Big Stone Lake. Because the town had an altitude greater than any other between the Mississippi and Missouri Rivers, it was named Summit. Each year a celebration is held to observe the anniversary of the opening of the Sisseton Indian Reservation (*see INDIANS*). Although the reservation was opened April 15, 1892, the celebration occurs the latter part of June.

At 37.4 *m.* is a junction with US 81 (*see Tour 10*), which united with US 12 to 39.3 *m.* where US 81 branches S.

Although actually a part of the original Sisseton Indian Reservation, the lands in this rural area were ceded and sold to homesteaders, particularly Scandinavians, many years ago, so that few Indians live along the highway here. Most of them returned to their former haunts, the lake shores.

At 48.5 *m.* is the junction with the Lake Region Highway (*see Tour 2B*).

BLUEDOG LAKE lies to the R., with marshes extending along the highway. The lake bears the name of Chief Bluedog who, with his wives, lived beside the lake for many years (*see Tour 2B*).

WAUBAY, 49 *m.* (1,813 alt.), is the English corruption of the Indian word "wamay" (*where wild fowl build their nests*), first given to the chain of lakes NW. of Waubay. The town is popular with the Indians, many families making their homes in Waubay, one of the few towns in which Sioux Indians actually reside. On the streets are Indian women in shawls and blankets, old men in moccasins, but with regular "store clothes" or, commonly, overalls. The younger Indians have been so influenced by their white environment, chiefly through intermarriage, that they are difficult to distinguish. Being comparatively an old town, having been founded in 1880, Waubay has many frame buildings, holds square dances with old-time music as often as modern dances, and nearly every male resident is a good fisherman.

The highway bridges a bay of Bluedog Lake and the road is built up across RUSH LAKE, so called because of its tall rushes and boggy marshes. Muskrat houses—mounds of mud, sticks, and rushes—are in the water; ducks also nest and swim about the lake during the spring and summer. Often in spring great white pelicans are seen far out on the water. Hunting clubs from Chicago, Milwaukee, and Sioux City have lodges here for fall duck and goose hunting.

An Indian legend of Rush Lake relates how ducks and other waterfowl received their beautiful colors. A young warrior who had from childhood been very fond of gay, bright colors, walked far from camp, lured by the beautiful colors of Indian summer. Now and then he would stop and take from his pouch clay and oil which he mixed to make shades and tints to his liking. As the shadows began to lengthen, he suddenly realized that it would soon be time for the night fire, so he made his way to Rush Lake where he built a small lodge of rushes. As he sat looking at the setting sun, he heard the talk of waterfowl not far away. Then he saw before him, diving and playing, ducks, mallard, teal, gray geese, and loons. They were his friends and were always glad to see him, so he put his hands to his mouth and called to them. They were startled at first but they soon recognized him, and paddled to shore as fast as they could. The Indian invited them to his lodge, where they took turns telling of what they had done that day. When he told that he had been studying and mixing colors, the mallard became interested and said, "You are our friend; would you be so kind as to paint us with some of your beautiful colors?"

"I will," said the warrior. "Choose your colors."

The mallard said that he wanted a green head, a white stripe around his neck, a brown breast, and yellow legs. When he was painted, the mallard said, "Now I do not want my mate to have the same colors as I do." So she was painted mostly brown.

The teal had his family and himself painted as he desired. By this time the paints were almost gone, so there were no bright colors left for the goose and the loon.

At 54 *m.* is a junction with a graveled road leading into the Lake Region (*see Tour 2B*).

WEBSTER, 59.3 *m.* (1,842 alt.), is the seat of Day Co., and styles itself the "gateway to the Lake Region." Platted in 1880 and named for the first settler, J. B. Webster, the town attracted young businessmen to the new farm frontier. With a Norwegian farming community growing up around the town, a Scotchman, two Englishmen, a German, and a few others who came from eastern States, started business enterprises, namely, a livery, real estate office, jewelry store, grain elevator, bank, general store, newspaper, and saloon. The livery stable and old-style saloon are gone, but around the others a prosperous, civic-minded town has developed until now it has a paved main street, City Hall with a public library and community dining room, hospital, parks, golf course, and a large high school noted for State championship basketball teams.

HOLMQUIST, 65.8 *m.*, has three large white houses, pretentious in the 1890's, and identical in appearance. It is a safe wager that every third person in the community is named Holmquist, Olson, Peterson, Johnson, Helvig, Sundstrom, or Jensen.

BRISTOL, 70 *m.* (1,775 alt.), has the largest creamery in the region, the farms around having large dairy herds. The town was named for Bristol, England, in 1881, when it became the terminal of the Milwaukee R.R., but it was not until 1921 that it was actually incorporated. The village was the western terminal of the railroad for a year.

Between Bristol and Andover the range of hills dwindles to level prairie, and large wheat fields spread out in all directions. Occasionally early in the morning coyotes are seen on the hills near the road, and in the spring large flocks of geese feed in the cornfields along the highway.

At 78 *m.* is the junction with State 25, an oil highway.

Left on this road is LAKE PIERPONT STATE RECREATION AREA, 4 *m.* An artificial lake, formed during the drought period of the 1930's, has become a popular and pretty spot with 160 acres of trees planted for park purposes.

ANDOVER, 81.6 *m.* (1,475 alt.), was first known as Station 88 by railroad graders, but when the town was platted in 1881, it took its present name from Andover, Mass. This market town for a rich farming region has a large, old-fashioned hotel, the Waldorf.

GROTON, 93.2 *m.* (1,304 alt.), is a grain and implement market for a large portion of the James River valley. Groton was the birthplace of Earle Sande, a few years ago the premier jockey in American horse racing. As a youth he first rode ponies, and then farm horses, bareback, and eventually because of his experience and small stature, became a professional jockey.

In the winter of 1936–37, after drought had ravaged the crops, townsmen and farmers found a remunerative business in shooting jackrabbits, the fur from which is used in the manufacture of coats and hats. At Groton the Boy Scouts staged gunless rabbit round-ups, using clubs instead.

Between Groton and Aberdeen US 12 passes through the James River valley, one of the richest farming areas in the Middle West, the soil of which is a rich black loam, a deposit of the glacial period. Around each farm is a grove of trees, reminiscent of homestead days when a claim could be had for planting 20 acres in trees.

At 101 *m.* US 12 crosses the James River, in the spring, a clear, fast-flowing river, in the summer a sluggish stream, and in the fall often completely dry or consisting of a series of pools. Dikes can be seen along the banks, to keep the river from flooding the bottom-land in high water. During the drought period the river was dry most of the time. Pheasant hunting is especially good along the river, and the bright-colored ring-neck pheasants are to be seen any day, any season, somewhere along the highway. The river contains bullheads and a few pickerel (*see RECREATION*).

At 109.1 *m.* is SAUNDERS AIRPORT, the Aberdeen municipal field served by Northwest and Mid-Continent Airlines. The large, stone administration building was completed in 1950 and the airport named for Brig. Gen. Laverne Saunders of Aberdeen, an Air Force hero in World War II (*see Aberdeen, CITIES*).

ABERDEEN, 112 *m.* (1,300 alt.), (*see ABERDEEN*).

Northern State Teachers' College, Wylie and Melgaard Parks, Civic Auditorium-Arena.

Here is a junction with US 281 (*see Tour 11*).

At 122.4 *m.* are the Milwaukee R.R. STOCKYARDS, in which trainloads of cattle, sheep, and hogs from the ranch country of western North and South Dakota and Montana are unloaded for rest, water, and feed on their way to packing centers farther east. There are 150 pens for cattle, each holding a carload, and 109 pens for sheep. From 200 to 2,000 carloads of stock pass through the yards each month during the fall shipping season. The yards are interesting by day as well as by night, when trains unload under bright lights.

At 116.5 *m.* is a junction with a graveled road.

Right on this road is RICHMOND LAKE STATE RECREATION AREA, 4 *m.* The lake, which covers more than 1,000 acres, was formed as a WPA project, and is one of the largest man-made lakes in the State. Trees planted in the 1930's provide 300 acres of park along the hilly lake shore. A Youth Camp is maintained here.

At 126.3 *m.* US 12 crosses one prong of horseshoe-shaped LAKE

PARMLEY, also known as Mina Lake, formed by damming Dry Run Creek. LAKE PARMLEY STATE GAME REFUGE AND RECREATION AREA lies to the L. Construction of the dam was started early in the 1930's through public subscriptions raised by Aberdeen and Ipswich sportsmen. It was completed by Federal relief agencies under the sponsorship of the State Game, Fish and Parks Department. Its original name came from the nearby hamlet of Mina, but in 1949 the name was changed to honor Joseph W. Parmley of Ipswich, pioneer promotor of trunk highways in South Dakota. Another arm of the lake is crossed at 127 m. over a rock spillway.

IPSWICH, 139 m. (1,530 alt.), was named by Charles H. Prior, superintendent of the Milwaukee R.R., for the English city of that name. It is the seat of Edmunds Co., and has a new modern-style courthouse. A PUBLIC LIBRARY, presented to the city by the heirs of Marcus P. Beebe, pioneer resident, is built of native stone from the prairies. The first library was opened in a roller skating rink in 1886, with each member of the Ladies Library Association donating one book. The present library has 10,000 volumes.

The promotion of the Yellowstone Trail (US 12) from "Plymouth Rock to Puget Sound" was begun at Ipswich by Joseph W. Parmley, and the organization, now known as the U. S. No. 12 Association, still maintains its national headquarters here.

South of Ipswich, in Powell township, a colony of Welsh people settled and made their characteristic national contribution to the music of the region, three of them having been members of the Royal Welsh Glee Club which sang before the King and Queen of England.

Between Ipswich and Mobridge the glacially-formed hills rise like a rumpled blanket. Near the Missouri River there is more grassland, and grazing cattle are seen.

ROSCOE, 154.4 m. (1,826 alt.), is a trade center for a farming community, not unlike the small towns of the movies, with pool halls, tall red grain elevators, general stores, square houses, and large frame churches.

BOWDLE, 169 m. (1,995 alt.), came into being with the advent of the railroad, which was gradually pushing toward the Missouri River. The town was named for a banker who represented the railroad's interests in that region. Bowdle in the 1880's was an important sheep and wool shipping point, but with the coming of German farmers, diversified farming has become more important. Most of the businessmen in Bowdle are of German extraction, and the German language is used on the streets. Churches form an integral part of social life, both in town and in the rural communities.

A flour mill here ships milled, hard wheat to distant points, including South America, Europe, and the Philippines. One of Bowdle's favorite sons was Sam Barry, long-time basketball coach at the University of Southern California.

At 177.4 *m.* is the junction with a graveled road.

Right on this road is JAVA, 5 *m.*, which is visited by curious people who invariably ask "Is it coffee time?" or "Is the pot hot?"

At 188.1 *m.* is a junction with US 83 (*see Tour 12*); the two routes are united through Selby.

SELBY, 192 *m.* (1,877 alt.), was founded in 1899 when the town of Bangor, then county seat 5 *m.* S., was moved to the railroad line. Selby became the seat of Walworth Co. and the trade center of a large area in which cattle and horse raising is carried on extensively, as well as farming. Selby sends a large percentage of its high school graduates to college, and many of the residents are college graduates. It is the home of George T. Nickelson, Governor of South Dakota (1947-51).

Right from Selby is LAKE HIDDENWOOD STATE RECREATION AREA, a popular picnic ground with shade trees and an artificial lake as part of the park.

At 195.4 *m.* is a junction with US 83 (*see Tour 12*).

LAKE MOLSTAD STATE RECREATION AREA, 203 *m.* (R), has a picnic area with facilities for travelers.

At 211.5 *m.* the crest of the Missouri River breaks is reached, with a view of the river and bottom-land stretching N. and S., fringed with cedar, willow, and cottonwood trees. Here farming and livestock-raising are carried on together, and proposals for large irrigation projects are made annually. The most successful crops have been alfalfa and other forage plants. Thick timber, matted with dense underbrush along the river, gives testimony of what is possible where moisture is sufficient in this area, often classed as semi-arid.

MOBRIDGE, 213.7 *m.* (1,657 alt.), was formerly the site of Arikara and Sioux Indian villages, but it was not until 1906 that the present city was founded. At that time the Milwaukee R.R. built a a bridge across the Missouri River, and when a telegrapher used the contraction "Mo. Bridge" in his reports a name originated that has remained with the town. Several buildings were moved from Old Evarts, a town which had been started 8 *m.* S., now deserted. As the division headquarters for the Pacific extension of the railroad, the town grew rapidly. The railroad is the lifeline of the town, with an annual payroll of $900,000 here. On the grounds of the railroad station are two large stones called the CONQUEROR'S STONES. It is said that defeated Indian chiefs were forced to kneel on the stones, placing their hands in the hand-shaped grooves in token of submission to their captors. An excellent collection of Indian relics taken from Arikara village sites near Mobridge (*see below*) is displayed on Main St., by O. L. Lawein. Unlike towns along US 12 to the E., in Mobridge are seen ranchers with ten-gallon hats and cowboy boots, and Indians in overalls or shawls.

In the new City Hall are huge murals by Oscar Howe, Sioux

Indian artist, depicting historical events of the region. Howe is resident artist at Dakota Wesleyan University at Mitchell.

The city has an excellent park, including an outdoor swimming pool and athletic field.

At the western edge of the city is the NORTHWESTERN LUTHERAN ACADEMY, a sectarian school.

At 222.9 m. is a junction with a graveled road.

Right on this road is RIVERSIDE PARK and the FOOL SOLDIERS BAND MONUMENT, 2 m., erected in honor of the "Fool Band" of Indians who rescued a party of white prisoners. During the War of the Outbreak (see HISTORY), a band of Santee Indians attacked Shetek Lake, Minn., and took captive two women and seven children. The white captives were taken to the Missouri River, at its junction with Grand River. Word of their whereabouts came to Fort Pierre. A party of eleven young Indian men, known as the Fool Soldier Band because they had taken an oath to help the whites, set out with Martin Charger, reputedly a grandson of Capt. Merriwether Lewis, the explorer, as their leader. The other Indian men were Kills Game and Comes Back, Four Bear, Mad Bear, Pretty Bear, Sitting Bear, Swift Bird, One Rib, Strikes Fire, Red Dog, and Charging Dog. They found the Santee camp of White Lodge, leader of the hostile band, and bargained for the captives, offering horses, food, and weapons. Finally a trade was effected and on Nov. 20, 1862, the captives were released to the Fool Soldiers. Having traded all but two guns and one horse, the rescuers made a basket for the children to ride in and placed one of the women, who had been shot in the foot, on the horse. Martin Charger gave his moccasins to the other woman who had no shoes.

At 3 m., is an ARIKARA VILLAGE SITE, the outlines of which can be seen, as a different shade of grass fills the circle where the mud huts once stood. Each hut was from 20 to 30 ft. in diameter. Mounds are still visible beside each circle; these were refuse piles, and fragments of pottery are still found in these heaps. Several of the mounds were excavated by the Smithsonian Institution and the artifacts are on display in Washington, D. C.

At 216.6 m. is the Missouri River bridge built by the State in 1924. North of the bridge is the railroad bridge, which rests on piers sunk 90 ft. into the river bed.

From the highway bridge, up the river, ASHLEY ISLAND is visible (R). It was named for Gen. William H. Ashley, a partner in the Rocky Mountain Fur Co., who in the spring of 1823 conducted a party of 100 men and a cargo of merchandise up the Missouri River, on flat boats, to his trading post on the Yellowstone River in Montana. Arriving at the Arikara Indian villages opposite the island on May 30, he traded trinkets for horses. Some of the Ashley party planned to continue the trip overland the next day, but at dawn the Indians made a surprise attack, killing 12 men and wounding 11. The land party returned to the boats and, taking the dead and wounded, drifted down the river. The boats halted where the highway bridge now stands, and the journals record how Jedediah Smith made a "powerful prayer" for the wounded. It was the first recorded act of public worship in South Dakota. General Ashley sent a message with news of the massacre to Col. Henry Leavenworth at Fort Akinson, Kan., who immediately dispatched an expedition to punish the Rees. On the way the soldiers met a party of trappers under Major Pilcher, and the remainder of the Ashley party, augmented by several hundred Sioux, set out in search of the enemy. Major Pilcher and the Sioux went ahead to hold the Rees until the arrival of the artillery. Hostilities began, but the Rees, camped on on the E. side of the river, refused open battle. A six-pound howitzer, which had been brought and mounted on a nearby hill, began a bombardment of the Arikara village. The very first shot beheaded the chief. By noon the Rees sent a plea for peace, agreeing to return the goods stolen from the Ashley expedition. They returned a few buffalo robes, and further negotiations were postponed. In the morning it was discovered the Rees had escaped during the night with their belongings.

At the western end of the bridge the time meridian is crossed; W. of the bridge is mountain time, E. is central. (*Going W. turn watches back one hour; going E. turn them ahead one hour.*)

At 217 *m.* on top of a high hill, at the junction with State 8 (*see Tour 2A*), is the SACAJAWEA MONUMENT to the most famous of all Western Indian women. Sacajawea was a Shoshoni Indian girl who was captured by the Mandans at the age of 12, and later sold to a French trapper, Charbonneau, who married her. Charbonneau was hired by Lewis and Clark in 1805 to guide their expedition through the Rocky Mountains (*see HISTORY*). He took along with him his wife and infant son. Sacajawea, known as the Bird Woman, served as scout for most of the journey, and was also the nurse. On the return of the expedition in 1806 Sacajawea and her husband stayed with the Mandans for a while, but later, at the urgent invitation of Capt. Clark, visited him at St. Louis. He persuaded them to leave their son with him to be educated. Shortly after the return, according to two contemporary journals, a wife of Charbonneau died of fever, supposedly at Fort Manuel, on the Missouri River S. of the State line, and was buried there. There is some question, however, whether the wife referred to was Sacajawea. Charbonneau had more than one wife, and records of the Wind River Reservation in Wyoming offer evidence that a woman known as Sacajawea died there after having lived to a considerable age. Fort Manuel was destroyed during the war of 1812, and the site eroded into the Missouri River, so neither the fort nor the grave can be located accurately today.

The STANDING ROCK INDIAN RESERVATION, 220 *m.* covers the eastern half of Corson Co. in South Dakota, and extends into North Dakota, with the Agency at Fort Yates, N. Dak. (*No permission necessary to pass through open reservation; office of agent at Fort Yates, N. D.; Federal offense to transport intoxicating liquors into or through reservation.*)

There are 2,058 Sioux Indians on the reservation roll, 1,111 of which are listed as full-bloods by the South Dakota agency superintendent. The native bands within the Sioux Tribe (*see INDIANS*) on this reservation are: Hunkpapas, Yanktonai, Teton, Minneconjou, Itazibeo, Oohenupa, Sihasapa, Ogalala, Sicungu, and Isanyati. The

Indian population is increasing. All persons under 40 years of age can speak English, but many speak the native tongue at home. The native language is used by 90 percent of the people over 40, and by half the children of pre-school age. It is used very little by school children.

Rodeos are held at irregular intervals during the summer months.

From US 12 Indian farms are seen, but a better view of the life on the reservation is obtained on the winding, dirt side roads. There are 222 frame houses occupied by Indians on the reservation, but none have modern facilities; 426 families use log houses today. Nearly every family has a tent in addition to its regular home. "Store clothes" are worn by 80 percent of the tribe, while old time garments such as moccasins, shawls, and petticoats made of flannel, with many gathers for fullness, are still worn by older women. Skins are still dressed by removing the hair with wood ashes, soaking the hide in water, and greasing it; after this it is worked by hand until it is soft and pliable. Other surviving customs include the general "give away" when a death occurs in the family. Clothing, household articles, and furnishings are given away, and the survivors of the family are obliged to replace things as best they can. The social life on this reservation consists of much visiting and dancing. When families go visiting, they take their tents and camp on the premises of those they are visiting. Usually they bring their own bedding and, if they have it, their food. Old time dances such as square dances and waltzes are popular, as well as the kahomani and other Indian steps. The Sioux enjoy the fairs and rodeos in the summer, taking their tents to the celebration where they camp until everything is over. The traditional tribal music prevails, but there is no set time or place where it can be heard. Funeral songs, rain songs, war songs, songs for the rejected lover and for those who are downhearted are heard wherever a group gathers in the evening. Native cults are not active on the Standing Rock Reservation, and 99 percent of the Indians are affiliated with some Christian sect. The Catholic, Episcopal, and Congregational denominations are strongest in point of numbers.

A tribal council of 14 members has some administrative powers; and a tribal judiciary of two judges, appointed by the Government, holds court over crimes of minor nature. The inhabitants of the reservation participate in county and State administration, with usually two or three holding elective county offices. The tribal wealth is approximately $11,000, but the per capital wealth averages only about $20, not including land. All property is now individually owned, but there are 95,000 acres of unallotted land. About 320,000 acres of Indian-owned land are rented. There are 21 Indian-owned stock ranches. During the drought period, the farms have not been self-supporting. Several Indians have built up various types of individual businesses, including two newspapers, a creamery, a shoe repair shop, and two dance orchestras. There are cooperative livestock associations. Native handicraft forms a means of partial support, but it is not practiced extensively.

At 217.3 *m.* is the junction with a graveled road.

Right on this road at 10 *m.* is ST. ELIZABETH'S SCHOOL (R), an Episcopal boarding school for Indians. In front of the white buildings, situated on a high hill, is a monument erected to the early Christian leaders, and especially to the native minister, Rev. Philip Deloria.
WAKPALA (Ind., *stream*), 11.6 *m.* (1,633 alt.), is a settlement of whites and Indians. The one-street village, of dull frame buildings and a bright new community hall, has board sidewalks. A modern, brick schoolhouse contrasts with log cabins and tents in the wooded outskirts of the village.

At 242 *m.* is the junction with a graveled road.

Left on this road is ELK BUTTE, 5 *m.* (L), one of the old sacred hills of the Sioux People. At 6 *m.* is LITTLE EAGLE, an Indian village of cabins and tents. It was here that probably the last Sun Dance ever to be held by the Sioux was staged in 1936, in quest of rain. Chief White Bull, nephew of Sitting Bull, led the three-day dance. At Little Eagle is a monument to Indian soldiers who died in the World Wars, Little Eagle claims to have the only all-Indian American Legion post in the country. Right from Little Eagle at 9 *m.* is SITTING BULL PARK, where the Sioux chief was killed during the Messiah War. (Indian guide available during summer.)
It was during the early dawn of the crisp, frosty morning of Dec. 15, 1890, that Sitting Bull, last chief of the Hunkpapa Sioux, fell riddled with bullets at the hands of his own people, the Indian police, sent to arrest him. Here Sitting Bull last exhorted the wavering fragments of his once powerful band. Today the site of the medicine man's home is a public park, unimproved in order to preserve the actual setting. The sites of the cabins, the spots where each man fell, the common grave of the seven followers who died with Sitting Bull, and various relics of the famous "struggle in the dark" are preserved in this park.
The old chief spent most of his life in South Dakota, but his body was taken to Ft. Yates, N. Dak., the agency, for burial. There in a solitary grave, in a corner of the old army post cemetery, Sitting Bull sleeps; bodies of white men, once buried near him, have been removed.
Probably no figure in all Sioux history has caused more controversy, more uneasiness, was more colorful, more disliked, and more respected. When Sitting Bull was killed and his followers were dispersed on that cold, hazy morning, the dim lamp of hope that had flickered so long in Sioux breasts, suddenly flared crazily, resulting finally in the Battle of Wounded Knee and the pitiful crushing of the dying spirit of the Indians. The ghost dance had been the last straw at which the Indians, in their final stand against civilization, had grasped. Believing that the white men, "Wasicun" (pronounced waseeehun), would suffer for their greed and selfishness, the Sioux imagined a Messiah would soon come and punish their enemies. The Wasicun had crucified their saviour, and retribution, they were sure, would overtake them.
Many books have been written about this chief, part of whose influence rested on his fame as a medicine man. Some disparage him; others praise him. Those who knew him declare he was canny, treacherous, deceitful, and cowardly. He never was a brave warrior in battle. At the Little Bighorn battle he was busy making medicine in his tipi, while braver leaders were in the thick of the red tide, directing the extermination of Custer's detachment or engaged in driving Reno across the river. But, at any rate, he always exerted a powerful influence, and caused no end of worry to white authorities, especially Maj. James McLaughlin, for many years agent on the Standing Rock Reservation where Sitting Bull lived. When McLaughlin learned that Sitting Bull was preparing to leave the reservation, he deemed it wise to place him under arrest. Detailed for the uncertain and risky task were 43 Indian policemen, under the command of Lieutenant Bullhead, a cool and reliable man,

and an avowed enemy of Sitting Bull, as well as of his chief bodyguard, Catch-the-Bear.

The police approached Sitting Bull's camp quietly, at daybreak Dec. 15. The medicine man was sleeping when the police burst into his cabin, struck a light, and read to him the order of arrest. He consented to go with them and sent one of his wives to saddle his favorite mount, a trick circus horse he had brought back with him from Buffalo Bill's Wild West show, with which he had traveled at one time.

While the police were hurrying him into his clothes, word was spread about the camp of the arrival of the police, and quickly the medicine man's followers began to assemble about the cabin. The police, seeing the impending danger, hastened to get Sitting Bull out of the cabin and whisked away before bloodshed should occur, and half-dressed, he was dragged outside. Once out of the cabin and in view of all his loyal tribesmen, he hesitated; and while jibes from his young son, Crowfoot, from one of his wives, and others in the group, stung him deeply, he made up his mind that he would not be taken without a struggle. Lieutenant Bullhead and Sergt. Shave Head held Sitting Bull, each by an arm, Sergt. Red Tomahawk was guarding the rear, while the rest of the police (Metal Breasts the Sioux called them) were trying to clear a path through the barricade of menacing red bodies, which hemmed them against the cabin.

When Catch-the-Bear, rifle in hand, appeared among the warriors, shouting threats at Lieutenant Bullhead, his personal enemy, Sitting Bull cried out, "I am not going! I am not going!" Catch-the-Bear threw up his rifle and fired. Bullhead fell, a bullet in his leg. But as he fell he turned and sent a slug into the body of Sitting Bull, who was shot from behind at the same time by Red Tomahawk. Shave Head was struck simultaneously with a bullet, and the three—Sitting Bull, Bullhead, and Shave Head—all went down in a heap. Then began a terrible hand-to-hand struggle between 43 policemen and about 150 of Sitting Bull's warriors. It was no common fight; Indian against Indian, Hunkpapa against Hunkpapa, the result was frenzy, brutality—Indians clubbing, stabbing, choking each other. Some of the police were Yanktonnais and Black Feet; the rest were Hunkpapas, Sitting Bull's own people.

Soon after the firing started most of the police dodged behind the cabin where they had the advantage, while the enemy took refuge behind trees that fringed the stream nearby. They held each other at bay until the arrival of the troops.

An event that almost struck panic to the more superstitious of the Indian police was the behavior of the gray circus horse, which Sitting Bull had ordered saddled and brought to his door. During all the fighting he sat calmly down in the midst of the melee and lifted one hoof as he had been trained to do. Then he performed other tricks he had learned with Buffalo Bill's Wild West show. This spectacle frightened some of the police, who feared that the spirit of the dead Sitting Bull had been reincarnated in the horse and had returned to punish them for their deed. Despite the fact that the air was alive with bullets the old horse came through without a wound.

The seven warriors who had fallen with Sitting Bull on December 15, lay unburied for two weeks after the battle. Relatives were afraid to return because they thought the soldiers were still there. It was then that the Rev. T. L. Riggs, son of Stephen R. Riggs, pioneer missionary of South Dakota, volunteered to go with them and assist in the burial. They were placed in a common grave near the scene of the fight.

McLAUGHLIN, 248 m. (2,002 alt.), is a young town in a comparatively new country, and while its trade is largely with Indians, it reflects the effect of prosperous years in this ranching and farming community. The town was named for Col. James McLaughlin, Indian Inspector of the Bureau of Indian Affairs.

McINTOSH, 275 m. (2,276 alt.), is the oldest town in Corson Co., having been incorporated in 1910; it is also the county seat.

The town was named after the McIntosh brothers who were the subcontractors in charge of building the railroad grades through the Standing Rock Reservation.

Left from McIntosh, on a graded road; is the BLUE HORSE DAMSITE, 22 *m.*, on the Grand River, one of the reclamation and flood control projects in the Missouri River Basin Development program (*see HISTORY*).

Between McIntosh and Lemmon the rolling country breaks into occasional sharp buttes and grassless mud flats. Less than 30 years ago the prairie was covered with shacks, hastily put together by homesteaders who came, only to leave as soon as the land became theirs. The few who remain, living along the little streams, have gradually acquired herds of cattle. This country was once the paradise of cattlemen; it still is, but in a different sense. The cattleman must rent his land today; yesterday it belonged to anyone or no one. Here, where there are few towns and the roads are impassable in wet seasons, the temptation to go to town is less; families are large and live to themselves. Men and women are windburned the year around, and children are virtually raised in the saddle.

MORRISTOWN, 293.6 *m.* (2,240 alt.), named for the C-7 ranch proprietor, Nels Morris, supplies the surrounding ranchers with such supplies as they do not get from mail order houses.

THUNDER HAWK, 305.5 *m.,* has a general store where on Saturdays commodities, politics, and gossip are exchanged over the cracker and pickle barrels.

LEMMON, 315 *m.* (2,567 alt.), was named for "Ed" Lemmon, pioneer and cattleman, who for years was foreman of the large L7 cattle outfit. The town is the trade center for a large territory in both North and South Dakota, which produces grain, cattle, horses, and sheep. Thus, it is one of the few towns in the United States where cattlemen, sheepmen and farmers—each uncomplimentary to the other—meet on a common ground—the store, poolhall, bar, dancehall, or courtroom. Situated on the North Dakota Line, part of the town is actually in the adjoining State. It has enjoyed rapid growth during recent years, due to the fact that it is the only town of appreciable size within a wide area and commands a very large trade territory. Attempts at farming in the immediate vicinity have resulted in much distress during recent drought years, although the soil is exceptionally fertile.

Although Lemmon is the outstanding town in Perkins Co., it was forced to concede the county seat to Bison, an inland hamlet, about 40 m. SW.

The PETRIFIED WOOD PARK, on US 12, contains several buildings, and numerous curios, built entirely of petrified wood obtained toward the southern part of the county. With agates and petrified wood at hand, the manufacture of native stone jewelry is being developed as a local industry employing handicapped people.

Lemmon is widely known for its Clown Band which attends major festivals in the State and the annual St. Paul, Minn., Winter Carnival. Staid businessmen become gaily bedecked clown musicians, passing out lemon drops wherever they parade. The band has been pictured in national magazines. The town has the reputation in the area of being a lively recreation and entertainment center; there is a public swimming pool, lighted athletic field, and considerable nightclub life.

At Lemmon is the junction with State 73.

Left on this tarvia road is FLAT CREEK LAKE RECREATION DEVELOP-MENT AREA (R), 11 m. The 160-acre tract has been set aside by the State as a park area.
At 12 m. is the SHADEHILL DAM, a Federal reclamation project on Grand River. It is part of the Missouri River Basin Development Program (see HISTORY). The reservoir began to fill in 1950, and has been stocked with fish, mostly bass.
At 16 m., on a side road (R), is the HUGH GLASS MONUMENT (see Tour 2A).

WHITE BUTTE, 324 m., the last town in South Dakota on US 12, is a typical Western movie village, its few houses evidently built without much idea of the town's coherence. Since it is a rail-road town with a favorable location as a stock shipping point, it is a familiar sight to see cows or sheep dodging behind houses as the herds are driven to the stockyards for their long journey to market.

At 326 m. US 12 crosses the North Dakota Line, 15 m. SE. of Hettinger, N. Dak. (see N. Dak. Tour 9).

Tour 2A

Junction with US 12—Trail City—Timber Lake—Isabel—Bison—Buffalo—Camp Crook—(Miles City, Mont.). State 8.
Junction with US 12—Montana Line, 199 m.
Between junction with US 12 and Isabel this route parallels a branch of the C. M. St. P. & P. R.R.
Hotel and tourist accommodations at Timber Lake, Isabel, Bison, and Buffalo.
Roadbed graveled except for short stretches of oil surfacing.

WEST of the junction with US 12 the road goes through a more or less level country for 125 miles, but from that point on it is more picturesque. It passes through the Reva Gap of the Slim Buttes, and thence westward is never out of sight of pine-clad hills—whether the Slim Buttes, the Cave Hills, or the East and West Short Pines. For a number of miles west of the Slim Buttes the road parallels Grand River, although not always in sight of it.

State 8 branches W. from US 12 (see Tour 2) 3 m. W. of Mo-bridge.

To the S. lies the CHEYENNE RIVER INDIAN RESERVA-TION (see Tour 3), paralleling this highway for 75 miles at a dis-tance varying from five to 15 miles. Side roads leading S. go to

Indian villages, trading posts, and ranches along the Moreau River. Most ranches are operated by white families, on land leased from the Indians.

TRAIL CITY, 12 m. (2,143 alt.), is at the junction of two branches of the C. M. St. P. & P. R.R., running to Isabel and Faith (*see Tour 3*), respectively.

TIMBER LAKE, 32 m. (2,161 alt.), was built on the edge of Timber Lake, which, paradoxically, has virtually no timber. At times the lake, crossed by a bridge, has been almost dry. The town is the seat of Dewey Co.

Ranches in this vicinity raise horses for use in rodeos. The O'Leary Brothers Ranch ships wild horses throughout the United States to furnish bucking bronchos for rodeos.

FIRESTEEL, 41 m. (2,340 alt.), became wellknown for the State-operated coal mine there until its sale in 1936. Acres of ground around the town were excavated for lignite coal, veins of which are close to the surface. The State operated the leased mine at a severe loss, but during the "depression" years coal was given to needy, relief families. Coal beds are so common in the area from this point W. that coal is sold for $1.00 to $1.50 a ton at the mine.

On a cold winter night in February, 1950, half of the Firesteel business district burned to the ground, including the post office, telephone office, café, pool hall, and bar.

ISABEL, 49 m. (2,402 alt.), is the terminus of one branch of the C. M. St. P. & P. R.R. and serves a large territory to the W.

COAL SPRINGS, 85 m., is a general store and post office, and was originally a quarter of a mile N. of its present site.

At 94 m. is the junction with State 73.

Right on this graveled road 15 m.; L. on old scenic round-up trail to the SITE OF OLD SIEM, 18 m., a discontinued post office dating to range days. Left of Old Siem, across Grand River by ford and up a steep hill by footpath, is the HUGH GLASS MONUMENT, 19 m. Hugh Glass, in the summer of 1823, was a hunter and guide for a trading party under Gen. William A. Ashley, en route from the Missouri River, following the route of the earlier Astorians. Glass was scouting ahead of the main party near the forks of the Grand, when he came upon a grizzly and her cubs. He had no time to retreat, and a terrific battle ensued between him and the bear. When his companions found him, the bear was dead and Glass was unconscious, badly clawed about the face and mauled. Ashley left two men to stay and take care of him. They watched the unconscious man for four days and then, concluding that he would not live, they took his gun and ammunition, his knife, and even his matches, and left him. When they overtook the Ashley party, they reported that Glass had died and that they had buried him.

Glass recovered consciousness some time after they had left. He knew, by the campfires, that someone had been left to aid him, and he was enraged that they should have left him defenseless and deserted. When he tried to move, he found that his leg was broken. For several days he lived on what bear meat he could tear off with his teeth. Then the meat commenced to spoil and from that time he lived solely on roots and berries. He decided that if he were to save his life, he would have to crawl to the nearest white settlement, Ft. Kiowa on the Missouri River, over a hundred miles away. It took him weeks to accomplish this incredible feat, setting a record for grit and endurance.

HUGH GLASS AND BEAR

His wrath at the men who had betrayed him had grown to be a consuming fire, and, as soon as he was able to travel, he started in pursuit of them. He joined a keel-boat party bound for the mouth of the Yellowstone; but when they reached Mandan, the ice closed in and the party had to remain there for the winter. But Hugh Glass' anger would not let him wait. He started overland alone and he found the Ashley party at the mouth of the Big Horn. He strode into the cabin and demanded to be shown the men who had deserted him. One of them cowered against the wall. Glass covered him with his gun and, walking over to him, kicked him lightly. "Get up!" he said, "and wag your tail. I wouldn't kill a pup." He inquired after the other man, a youth whom he had befriended, and found that he had gone to Ft. Atkinson with dispatches. After a few weeks' rest Glass set out to find him; but when he reached the fort, he found that the man had gone up river again. He finally overtook him and in the end forgave him; "and that fact," Neihardt says, "raises his story to the level of sublimity." John G. Neihardt, poet laureate of Nebraska, immortalized this feat in "The Song of Hugh Glass." On the hill 0.5 m. S. of the forks of the Grand, is the monument with the following inscription:

1823–1923

This altar to courage was erected by the Neihardt club August 1, 1923, in memory of HUGH GLASS who, wounded and deserted here, began his crawl to Ft. Kiowa in the fall of 1823.

Also on State 73, at 18 m. (L), is the SHADEHILL DAM, one of the U.S. Bureau of Reclamation projects in the Missouri River Basin development program (see HISTORY). In addition to providing a flood control reservoir, by backing up Grand River, it serves as the water supply for the town of Lemmon (see Tour 1).

MEADOW, 96 *m.*, is a small prairie town with a garage, filling stations, and a few stores.

BISON, 108 *m.* (2,500 alt.), was named for the large shaggy animals that roamed the plains in countless thousands when the first white man came. It is a typical prairie town with one main street, from which the false front wooden stores of early days are not entirely lacking. The residence portion is more attractive; each house is surrounded by a large yard, and a beginning of tree planting has been made. Although towns like Bison are negligible in comparison with Eastern towns, they are economically much more important with relation to the region which they serve. Bison and Buffalo, its neighboring county seat to the W., each with a population of less than 300, are both on mail order house maps of the Northwest. Surrounding Bison are cattle ranches and large grain farms. This town is the seat of Perkins Co.

The BISON MUSEUM, which has been pictured in national publications, is unusual in construction and content. The neat, new building is made of rammed earth. On one outside wall are carved the cattle brands of the outfits that have been, or still are, associated with this range country. The museum was developed primarily by Fred Jennewin, a pioneer with a bent for preserving historical materials and geological specimens.

This area appears to have been a stamping ground for dinosaurs some 60 million years ago, for expeditions have unearthed footprints of gigantic creatures in and near Bison. More than 20 casts have been made of three-toed prints, including one 31 inches wide. Also uncovered by the South Dakota School of Mines and Technology workers are tracks of the Tyrannosaurus, a 20-ton prehistoric dinosaur estimated to have been 20 feet high, 40 feet long, and having a 20-ft. tail. The footprints were made when the dinosaurs stepped in mud which later filled with sand. Many dinosaur bones and pieces of petrified wood are found in the vicinity.

At 115 *m.* is the junction with a graded road.

Right on this road at 7 *m.* is a sign, "Petrified Tree"; L. here 3 *m.* to a PETRIFIED TREE, claimed to be the largest in the world. Competent observers have declared that there is no record of a larger mass of petrified wood all in one place. The tree, buried in a hill, was discovered only recently. Seventy-five feet of it have been uncovered and there is still more in the hill. At the base the diameter is 2 ft. There are several large knots where limbs once grew and rings indicating the growth of the tree are plainly visible. Scientists say that this gigantic tree is a member of the Sequoia family.

REVA, 146 *m.*, is a store and post office just E. of the Slim Buttes. At 146.5 *m.* is the junction with a graded road.

Left on this road is the post office, GILL, at the ROCK RANCH, 12 *m.* This ranch is remarkable for the beauty of its buildings and their setting. As the name implies, they are all of stone, and two stone arches give entrance to the parklike grounds. The stonework is interspersed with pieces of petrified wood and fossil specimens. Within the house are many fossil remains gathered in the surrounding hills. Here are fossil bones of the three-toed horse, the oreodon, and the cephalopod. There are also fossilized turtles and snails, and the imprints on rock of ferns and leaves that grew in early geologic ages.

At 16 *m.*, (R) up Deer Draw 0.5 *m.*, is a picnic ground. Here is a spring of good water and all camping facilities.

At 16.5 *m.* there is a gap in the Buttes known as CEDAR PASS. This is second only to Reva Gap in beauty. The view from the top of the pass over the prairies is remarkable, with Castle Rock and Square Top in the distance, and on the horizon the faint blue outlines of the Black Hills. To see sunlight and shadow chasing each other over fifty miles of prairie is a sight long to be remembered.

At 148.5 *m.* (L) is SLIM BUTTES BATTLEFIELD MONU-MENT, a simple shaft, eight ft. high, commemorating the Battle of Slim Buttes, which took place in the immediate vicinity. This was one of the three major conflicts between soldiers and Indians in the history of the State, the other two being the Battle of Wounded Knee and Colonel Leavenworth's campaign against the Rees.

The Battle of Slim Buttes was fought on Sept. 9, 1876. General Crook's troops were hastening S. to protect the settlers in the Black Hills, when an advance guard under Maj. Anson Mills encountered a small force of Indians in Reva Gap of the Slim Buttes. Major Mills held the Indians off until the arrival of reinforcements under General Crook. The Indians, meanwhile, had been reinforced by members of Crazy Horse's band. The two forces fought one entire day, at the end of which three white men and a dozen or more Indians had been killed, and a few Indians were taken captive. The battle was more or less of a stalemate, but the Indians withdrew during the night. The next morning General Crook burned what was left of the Indian villages and buried his own dead, causing his whole column to trample over their graves as he broke camp, to conceal their location from the Indians. Of the white men killed, one was a well-known scout, William White, a friend and follower of Buffalo Bill, whom he admired intensely. So noticeable was White's constant companionship with Buffalo Bill that General Sherman gave him the nickname "Buffalo Chips," because, he said, where you saw one you always saw the other.

At 150 *m.* is the boundary of CUSTER NATIONAL FOREST (*hqs.: Deadwood*), the highway crossing only a neck of L-shaped forest area. It is about three miles wide here, but extends about five miles N. and 20 S. to cover the Slim Buttes. This is one of four isolated areas in Harding County and adjoining Montana making up Custer National Forest.

At 150.5 *m.* the route enters the SLIM BUTTES, a long range of pine-topped hills, with limestone cliffs facing the W., and broken ridges and wooded valleys sloping to the E. For 20 m. this ridge stretches N. and S., and at the southern end it bends slightly SE. for another 15 m. towards an isolated peak known as Sheep Mountain. Through this entire stretch of 35 m., the range is never more than six miles wide, and more frequently two or three. It is this characteristic that has given it the name, Slim Buttes. The white limestone cliff to the W. is broken in three places: at Reva Gap near the N. end, at the JB Pass 10 m. S. of Reva Gap, and at the elbow where beautiful Cedar Pass permits passage (*see above*). These are the only points in the range where any kind of vehicle can cross.

The Slim Buttes have a history more replete with incident than any other part of this region. The first white men to see them were the members of the Astorian party under Wilson Price Hunt, who in 1811, followed Grand River from its junction with the Missouri in order to avoid the long northward curve of the larger stream. The traders marveled at the buttes and mentioned them in their journals. Next to see them were the members of the Ashley Party, who followed the trail of the Astorians in August 1823. This was the party of which Hugh Glass was guide, when he performed his almost incredible feat (*see above*). The next to note the Slim Buttes was a detachment of soldiers under Maj. Anson Mills who encountered a force of Indians in the Reva Gap and fought the Battle of Slim Buttes (*see above*).

At the north end of the Buttes is a sharp, detached rock rising to a peak, known as the Saddle Horn. There also are two great cliffs, 200 ft. high, facing each other across a deep draw. Farther S. along the western edge is a lofty knoll, rising above the skyline of the rim. This is called Government Knob, because on its summit is a marker of the Coast and Geodetic Survey, a brass-capped pipe thrust into the earth. This is the highest point in the county. From this and almost any other point along the Western rim, there is a really superb view. To the W. are the hills known as the East and West Short Pines, and beyond them the long blue line of the Long Pine Hills in Montana. To the NW. are the rounded shoulders of the Cave Hills. To the N. are jagged peaks that rise along the North Dakota border, and to the S., Castle Rock, Square Top and the faint blue outlines of the Black Hills, a hundred miles away.

South of the mile-wide Reva Gap the unbroken ridge extends for ten m. to the JB Gap, a lofty pass with scarcely a break in the line, but with an auto road descending its W. side with tortuous windings and terrific grades. This pass was named for the famous JB HORSE RANCH nearby (*open to visitors*), which has existed from the earliest days of white settlement.

A few miles S. the Buttes make their bend to the SE., and at this point is a break, beautiful Cedar Canyon (*see above*), down which the road winds on its way S. From Cedar Pass the Buttes extend 15 m. farther and then ease as abruptly as they began, with Sheep Mountain standing beyond, a lonely sentinel.

In general, the western edge of the buttes is abrupt and commanding, with limestone cliffs the entire distance; the eastern side is broken up into long sloping valleys, with jutting points between. Springs are found throughout the buttes, the grass is long and thick, the draws are wooded, and it is an ideal place in which to winter stock. As a part of the Custer National Forest, neighboring stockmen acquire the right from the Government to run stock on the Reserve, paying by the head.

The buttes are also rich in fossils. Bones of the three-toed horse, the oreodon, the cephalopod and the sabre-toothed tiger, turtle shells of unusual size, fossil tracks of animals, and other interesting specimens have been picked up. In Reva Gap Indian relics have been found, such as bones, arrows, and an abandoned tipi that gives its name to Tipi Canyon.

In the buttes are numerous outcroppings of lignite coal, and in Reva Gap there is a coal mine that has been worked for many years. It has been estimated that there are a quarter of a billion tons of lignite coal in Harding Co. alone, and that the whole Slim Buttes region is underlaid with it.

At 151.5 *m.* the crest of REVA GAP (3,100 alt.), of the Slim Buttes is reached. This is the beauty spot of Harding Co. South of the road strange formations of rock and clay rise perpendicularly in many different forms. One of the largest of them has been named Battleship Rock because of its resemblance to the prow of an enormous ship. Many other narrow formations stand out here and there, or in line. They resemble nothing so much as individual pieces of stage scenery waiting to be pushed into position. At the highest point of the pass (L) is a perpendicular column of rock and earth rising two or three hundred feet, with grass and trees on its summit. This has become known as Flag Rock. It is climbed, but with difficulty. Just W. of Flag Rock a dirt road turns off (L) and follows the crest of the divide for half a mile. Along this trail are many camp sites with permanent ovens and other conveniences. Water can be obtained from nearby ranches.

West of the crest of Reva Gap the road winds down a horseshoe curve to lower ground and out of CUSTER NATIONAL FOREST.

At 159 *m.* is the junction with a dirt road.

Left on this road; at 2 *m.* L. through gate; at 2.5 *m.* is the STATE ANTELOPE PRESERVE (visitors welcome).
This is the only place in the world where antelope in large numbers are reared in captivity, so that this interesting and deer-like creature may be preserved for future generations. A six-ft. fence of heavy-mesh wire topped by two strands of barbed wire surrounds the preserve; the heavy posts stand only a rod apart, a tubular steel post set in cement alternating with a pitch pine post, making a durable fence around this tract of over 14 sections.
Much of the land now enclosed was part of an old cattle ranch that dates back to the early 1890's, and the original ranch buildings are now the home of the Park Superintendent. It is the intent of the State Game and Fish Commission, under whose auspices the park exists, to preserve the buildings in the same form

as they were when the ranch was taken over, for there are comparatively few examples left of the ranch architecture of the early days. The main dwelling is a typical log ranch house, roomy, low-ceilinged, and homelike. This ranch is ideally situated on the banks of Squaw Creek, a spring-fed stream that flows the length of the park and, with its twists and turnings, supplies sufficient water to all parts of it. In a comparatively small enclosure near the ranch building, are the baby antelopes that are being reared by hand. Every year from a dozen to 20 young antelopes are picked up in the large pasture to be brought up as "bottle babies." A baby antelope three days old, or younger, can be picked up off the ground. Instinct tells the young antelope to trust to its power of concealment, and at this stage it flattens itself to the earth, with its long neck outstretched and only its eyes betray signs of life.

Antelopes are difficult to rear, being high-strung, delicate creatures. They must be fed often and a little at a time. They cannot take pure cow's milk at first, but must have it diluted with water. The proportion of milk is gradually increased until at about five weeks they are taking it undiluted.

The object of rearing a certain number by hand each year is twofold. They are kept in a smaller enclosure near the buildings, as an exhibit for visitors; also it is planned that the place with its increasing herd of antelopes (about 450) shall become a supply station for foundation herds of State and National Parks. The commission will not supply antelopes for municipal parks, because it has been repeatedly proven that these prairie animals will not live in close confinement; and the commission feels that to place them under conditions in which they cannot survive is to impose a needless cruelty.

As many as 175 antelopes in one band have been seen on the prairie just outside the fence. But they are much more likely to be seen in groups of six or a dozen, both inside the fence and out.

The antelope is a graceful, tawny creature, somewhat smaller than a deer, with a white rump which under excitement or fear flares out in all directions to twice its size and makes that antelope "flag" of glistening white which is seen for miles. It is their danger signal to one another, the sign that it is time to employ their great weapon of defense, their marvelous speed. They are said to be the speediest animal in the world. The coyotes are obliged to relay on them in order to catch them. They are protected by law, and are increasing outside the park as well as inside. Their flesh is dark and tender, even more so than deer meat.

A feature of the antelope preserve is a large dam that holds back some of the waters of Squaw Creek. In a lakeless country this dam has been very popular as a swimming place, with people coming for 20 m. Two bathhouses are conveniently placed near the dam face. The dam has also been stocked with fish and should afford good sport in time to come. The fish are of two kinds, bullheads and black bass. The former are intended for fishing by children and those who simply desire to get fish, while the black bass are for those who look on fishing as a sport and wish to pit their skill against a game fish.

From the junction with the road to the Antelope Preserve, State 8 runs for about three m. through the sheep ranch of A. H. Dean, for whom the author of *Sheep*, Archer B. Gilfillan, herded for 16 years. It was here that he obtained material for his book, which he wrote after he had herded sheep ten years. A graduate of an Eastern university, he drifted into herding through force of circumstances and continued the occupation because he liked it. The author described the antics of sheep and the foibles of women from the viewpoint of a bachelor. The book went through several printings, and Gilfillan became associated with the South Dakota Writers' Project for a time, later gaining a writing fellowship from the University of Minnesota.

At 168 *m.* is the junction with US 85 (*see Tour 13*). Between this point and Buffalo US 85 and State 8 are one route.

BUFFALO, 170 *m.* (2,800 alt.) (*see Tour 13*).

Here is a junction with US 85 (*see Tour 13*).

Within a radius of 50 m. of this point there are more sheep than in any similar area in the United States. Sheep wagons are seen on the top of many a hill, and bands of sheep graze along the roadside. A visit to one of these wagons will be of interest perhaps to anyone who has never seen one. But first locate the herder. He may object to strangers invading his home without permission. He will be somewhere close by with his sheep, and will gladly show how he, the last of the nomads, lives. But do not expect to find him different from anyone else who tends animals or works on a ranch. He wears no distinctive garb and talks no special "lingo."

The sheep wagon is reminiscent of the pioneer covered wagon, except that it is much shorter and the canvas is pulled taut, eliminating that ribbed appearance. Mounting a set of steps, or walking up the wagon tongue, to the doorway, the visitor sees before him a marvel of compact and convenient living quarters for one person. At the right, close to the door, is a small camp stove and above is a set of shelves for dishes and utensils. Along each side are benches, formed by extending the wagon bed over the wheels; in the center of each of these benches is a trapdoor that opens into a "grub box," extending down into the space between the front and back wheels. Here the herder keeps his bread, cereal, meat, and light groceries. The two benches terminate in a bed across the end of the wagon—a board bunk, which may or may not have a set of springs, but has a mattress and bedding such as is found in any bunkhouse. Under the bed is a recess which sometimes has a drop door in front. Here the herder keeps his potatoes and bulky articles; and here his dog sleeps at night—and retires to it in the daytime when the herder inadvertently steps on his foot. Over the bed is a small window, hinged at the top and manipulated by a rope attached to the bottom, so that the herder can open and hold it at any angle desired by simply tying the rope. This window, being at the opposite end of the wagon from the door, insures perfect ventilation and also permits the herder to look out over his sleeping flock at night without getting out of bed. For this reason the wagon is always placed with its door facing away from the bedground. The door is cut in two, crosswise in the middle, the upper and lower halves swinging independently on their own hinges, making it easier to keep the wagon at any temperature desired without a direct draft on the stove. There is no table in sight until the herder either swings it up from the front of the bed and props it with its one leg, or, more likely, pulls it out flat from beneath the bed, the exposed part being held firm by the part that remains beneath the bed.

SHEEP HERDER

Such is the herder's happy home, a model of compactness and convenience. His personal belongings are kept on a shelf above his bed. There is plenty of room in the wagon for one person, but two would crowd it. Perhaps that is the reason why there are so few married herders, or at least herders whose wives live with them in the wagon. There is distinctly no room for temperament, and the sheep wagon will probably continue to be in the future as it has been in the past, the refuge of the married man and the hiding-place of the bachelor.

On the tops of many hills in this part of the country are small monuments made of piled stone, often two or more on one hill. These monuments, locally called "stone Johnnies," are as characteristic of sheep country as the sheep themselves. They are the work of herders. Many explanations have been given for them. One, obviously unfair to the herder, is that when he feels himself mentally slipping, he piles up rocks in order to occupy his mind. Another theory is that by the shape or size of the monument he can assure himself of his location in case of fog or darkness. The fact that there are not half a dozen foggy days a year in this region would seem to argue against this theory. Perhaps the most reasonable explanation is that the monuments are the result of the conjunction of an idle hour and a convenient scattering of stones, which usually are found on hilltops. Herders spend much of their time on hilltops, since it is easier to watch the sheep from an elevation.

The country W. of the buttes is somewhat different from that to the E. It is rougher and the soil is lighter. There are few small farms, but large ranches. Often for miles there is not a house; but the landscape is more picturesque and varied. To the E. are the white, pine-topped cliffs of the Slim Buttes; to the W. are two shorter ranges of the same formation and appearance, the East and West Short Pine Hills. To the N. are the rounded outlines of the Cave Hills, from which the limestone cap has been worn away.

Petrified wood is also plentiful throughout this region; it is found in almost every creek bed and in Grand River, where it should be looked for on the riffles. There are isolated small patches of badlands where an occasional fossil specimen is picked up, although the best have been taken. In the mud buttes leaf impressions are found by those who know how to look for them.

At 191 m. is the region known as the JUMP-OFF. At this point is a junction with a prairie trail.

Left on this road, following the rim of the Jump-Off, which is really a fault in the earth's surface extending N. and S. for many miles, the country is much like the Badlands on a smaller scale. It is rough and broken, with many bare hills. Grotesque formations, washouts, and cut banks make it a very difficult country for travel. Along the rim of the western edge is a good view of this region, but only on foot or horseback can the remarkable formations be explored. As in the Slim Buttes, there have been found a considerable number of fossils, including dinosaur bones. Some of these are on exhibition at the Harding post office, and a number of them are in the School of Mines Museum in Rapid City (*see RAPID CITY*).

It was in the heart of the Jump-Off that Tipperary, South Dakota's most famous bucking horse, lived his entire life on the ranch of his owner, Charlie Wilson. He retired an undefeated champion and lived to be more than 20 years old. In spite of good care, he was caught in a severe winter storm and his remains were not found for many weeks.

At 194 m. is the junction with a dirt road.

Left on this road is the old town of HARDING, 12 m. in a most picturesque setting between the East and West Short Pine Hills. It consists of only a few stores, dwellings and post office, but in the early days it served a large territory and had a very good trade. There is a display of fossils at the postoffice (*see above*).
The SHORT PINE HILLS are so named to distinguish them from the Long Pine Hills of Montana, just across the line. The "Short" refers to the length of the hills and not to the pines. The hills are in two groups, the East and West Short Pines, respectively. They are limestone-capped ridges of the same general character as the Slim Buttes, and are a part of the Custer National Forest. These hills are covered with ponderosa pine, which upon designation by the forest ranger may be cut into lumber by the ranchers. The hills are easily accessible, and afford many delightful camp sites.

CAMP CROOK, 195 m., was named after Gen. George Crook, the Indian fighter of the middle '70's in this region. Like Harding, Camp Crook is an old pioneer town. Like Buffalo, it serves a very large ranching territory. Its trees make it more attractive than the average prairie town. There is bathing and fishing in the Little Missouri, on whose banks the town is built.

It was in this region that the last of the great northern herd of buffalo were killed. When the terrific slaughter of these animals by the hide hunters took place, they split into two great bands. The northern herd was slaughtered along the Little Missouri River.

At 199 m., State 8 crosses the Montana State Line, 129 m. SE. of Miles City, Mont.

Tour 2B

US 12 (Waubay)—Enemy Swim Lake—Pickerel Lake—Waubay Lakes—Junction with US 12.
Unnumbered road.
Waubay—Junction with US 12. 34 m.
Graveled roadbed.
Resort, hotel, and cabin accommodations at Enemy Swim and Pickerel Lakes.

THIS circular route passes through the lake region north of Waubay and Webster, where chains of small lakes weave through the hills. Fishing, swimming, motorboating, aquaplaning, camping, picnicking, waterfowl hunting, ice skating, ice boating, and skiing are popular sports, and lodges, resorts, and cottages have been built to promote these activities. This section has been visited little by people from other parts of South Dakota, largely because of its location; however, groups of people from Chicago, Milwaukee, and Akron spend weeks here each year. The route through this region is in the Sisseton Indian Reservation (*see INDIANS and Tour 1*).

The Sisseton and Wahpeton bands of the Sioux Nation found the lake country to their liking, withstood attacks from the Chippewas, and moved no farther until they were driven out by U.S. soldiers in 1862. They returned the next year and settled permanently around the lakes. The early settlement of the lake country is the story of white immigration and intermarriage with Indians. For instance, there was Albert Barse and E. P. Owens, a printer. After the Civil War, with jobs scarce, the two men sought employment from Horace Greeley, whose "Go West, Young Man" campaign was starting. The editor hired them to write stories of the Northwest, and the pair started on their adventure. Settling first at Graceville, Minn., they married twin cousins of One Road, a noted chief, in order to secure the confidence of the tribe. Barse used to relate how the women were afraid to stay with them because of their white color and unusual language, so One Road had to move in too. Later Barse moved to the Waubay Lakes (*see below*), and Owens homesteaded at Minnewasta. They never returned to New York; their descendants are still prominent in the lake region. An influx of Norwegian and Swedish homesteaders, followed by groups of Poles, came in the 1880's. The effect of hybridization through the marriages of whites and Indians is noticeable; most of the Indian families have mixed blood, and have taken the names of the white members.

From the junction with US 12 at WAUBAY (*see Tour 2*), this route runs along the E. side of BLUE DOG LAKE which was named for a Sisseton chief who used to live in a log house here, beside which were three smaller cabins—one for each of his wives. In Blue Dog Creek, which flows into the lake, are large yellow water lilies. Blue Dog Lake has mostly rough fish, such as bullheads, carp, and eels.

The road passes through a rolling, farming country; a small house, unpainted barn, several dogs, small garden, and two or three horses usually comprise an Indian home, while the more pretentious homesteads are those of white farmers. The Polish farms can be distinguished from the Indian homes by a two-story house and the color of the numerous children in the yard.

At 7.5 *m*. is a junction with a dirt road.

Right on this road is reputedly the BURIAL MOUND OF CHIEF BLUE DOG, 0.7 *m*., which has been opened by vandals who removed relics; at 1.4 *m*., is GUDERIAN BEACH, a small resort in a grove of linden and elm trees. At 1.7 *m*. is a canal to raise the level of CAMPBELL SLOUGH (R), a bass-spawning and waterfowl refuge.

From the highway ENEMY SWIM LAKE can be seen (R). The lake is the setting for a famous Indian legend which has several variations, but it is generally agreed that its name was derived from a battle between the Sioux and Chippewas. According to the old legend, handed down for generations, a band of Sisseton Sioux was camped in the woods of the peninsula which extends from the southeastern shore and almost reaches a long, high island. A powwow was in progress one evening and the squaws had been sent out for more firewood while the others sang and danced around the fire. Meanwhile a band of hostile Chippewas from the Mississippi country, who were on a hunting trip, saw the reflection of the fire in the sky and followed the light to the lake shore. Leaving their horses in the woods on the eastern side of the lake, the Chippewas planned a surprise attack on the village after the dance was over and all were asleep. Sioux guards being stationed on the mainland, the Chippewas quickly made rafts and landed on the island, which provided an approach from which no attack was expected. As the tom-toms beat loudly, the Chippewas quietly crossed the waistdeep neck to the peninsula and hid in the bushes waiting for the village to retire. But one of the squaws, picking up sticks, heard her dog growling; when she went to find it she saw a stranger in war paint crouching nearby. She screamed. There was no escape from the excited, war-whooping Sioux. The Chippewas splashed back to the island and, as the Sioux followed, they swam for the shore and their waiting horses. "Toka nuapi!" (*the enemy swim*), cried the Sisseton Chief. Some of the Sioux rode their horses around the bay and as the swimming enemies reached the shore they were trampled to death.

At 8 *m*. is the junction with a graveled road, where there is the small brown house of an Indian family, in which pow-wows are often held during the early fall on Saturday nights. Here the young Indian people gather for the rabbit dance, and legion dance, two favorites in which couples circle the room side by side while singing. A few white people, friends of the Indians, are often present and join in the dance. Unbuttered bread and coffee are served during the dancing, which lasts until a late hour and is followed in the morning by church.

Right on this road at 0.6 *m*. is the entrance to CAMP CHEKPA, regional Boy Scout Camp. Chekpa means "twin" in Sioux, and Chief Chekpa was noted in local history as a peaceful leader. The beach, known as SANDY BEACH, is excellent for swimming (open to the public). At 0.8 *m*. is a pond and private refuge for mallard ducks (R); L. is a bay full of stumps which in normal years is a fine bass-fishing region. The BIOLOGICAL STATION of Northern State Teachers College (see ABERDEEN), 1.2 *m*., holds summer classes in biology, zoology, and botany; women students live in cabins and men in tents.
Visitors seeking Indian relics can often find flint arrowheads along the beaches or high ground nearby. Diamond willows, stripped to make ornamental canes, are found near the lake shore, the most suitable being those from 6 to 10 ft. high. Buffalo beans and sweet-flag, the root of which is used by the Indians as an antidote for colds, grow on the hills beside the lake.

At 8.8 *m*. is an INDIAN CHURCH (Episcopal) and CEME-TERY. In 1863 when the Sissetons, who had fled W. across the Missouri into Canada, returned to their lake country and camped at Enemy Swim Lake, U.S. soldiers surrounded them (*see Tour 1*). Here a treaty was made, and on this ground where they agreed to "be brothers" with the whites, the church that was built still stands (R); but there is a new, glistening white edifice nearby. To the L. is the rectory, a house and barn, for the minister and his family.

In front of the church is the cemetery in which a variety of grave-stones mark the burial places. On many of the markers is a daguer-reotype set in stone, showing an old Indian dressed in the clothing of white men. Some of the graves are covered with brightly colored glass and others have flags to show their participation in wars. Several markers are for white men who have lived with the Indians, including Albert Barse (*see above*).

Between Enemy Swim and Pickerel Lakes the road cuts through a series of hills and draws.

At 11 *m.* is the junction with a graveled road.

Right on this road is PICKEREL LAKE, 1.3 *m.*, a slender, fish-shaped, tree-bordered lake about three miles long. Spring-fed and deep, its waters are cold even in summer, but swimming, aquaplaning, rowing, canoeing, motorboating, and sailing are popular and regular sports. Northern pike, pickerel, wall-eyed pike, black bass, silver bass, crappies, bluegills, perch, and steelhead trout are caught here. At the foot of the hill is SOUTH END, 1.5 *m.*, a village of summer cottages grouped around the shoreline for over a mile. A hotel and dining room are in the center. (The beach is public and boats, swimming suits, and fishing equipment are available at the hotel.)
1. Right from South End on a winding dirt road is a STATE FISH HATCHERY, 0.5 *m.*, where pike, pickerel, and lake trout are hatched for lakes in the region. The low white hatchery building is beside a stream which flows from a natural spring farther up the ravine. Behind the row of cottages along the lake are Indian homes.
2. Left from South End, on a dirt road between rows of cottages, is the PEA-BODY GARDEN, 0.6 *m.*, where an irrigated garden affords a botanical exhibit.
3. Behind the South End hotel is a path to a MOUND 1.1 *m.*, which overlooks both Enemy Swim Lake and Pickerel Lake. From this vantage point one can see the chain of Waubay Lakes (SW) and Webster, 25 m. away. The hill is sacred to the Indians, because it was here that the medicine men and holy men went to fast and have visions. Wailing for days, and without food, the men would fall into swoons and usually experienced hallucinations. These they would interpret to their tribe, and future plans would be made accordingly. Among the stories handed down from father to son is the prophecy of Tasonkesapa 200 years ago. He was asked to have an understanding with the Great Spirit about the coming of the white men, of whom they had met several. His reply was: "The Great Spirit answered, 'The buffalo and wild things will disappear'."

At 12.3 *m.* is a junction with a dirt road.

Right on this road is RAMONA BEACH, 1.2 *m.*, a private resort owned by Aberdeen people.

At 14.2 *m.* is the northern end of Pickerel Lake and a junction with a graveled road.

Right on this road is the ABERDEEN Y. M. C. A. CAMP, 0.6 *m.*, a summer camp for boys and young men. Across the narrow neck of water is ADAMS BEACH, a public resort.

This route turns L. at the junction with the graveled road and for a few miles crosses rolling prairie land. At 19 *m.* is a junction with a graded road where the route turns L. to GRENVILLE, 22 *m.*

(1,815 alt.), which was incorporated in 1918 as a town, but had been a village since 1885 when a group of Poles established a Catholic church there. The church has been rebuilt and an academy has been established for the Polish farm children.

East of Grenville the route passes between two bodies of water, known as Waubay Lakes. In the lake to the R. is an island which is frequented by white pelicans every spring during mating season.

At 27 m. is the HILDEBRANDT RANCH on an oak-covered hill, behind which is the site of the old BARSE TRADING POST.

The WAUBAY NATIONAL WILDLIFE REFUGE covers 5,372 acres of this area. Although it was established primarily as a waterfowl refuge, about 100 deer are in the unfenced area, having come there apparently for protection. The deer browse on wild grapes, chokecherries, June berries, and woody plants. A U.S. FISH AND WILDLIFE SERVICE STATION is maintained here, and there is a high observation tower (L).

At 28 m. are the main bodies of the WAUBAY LAKES which cover 3,600 acres in irregular bays and separated ponds.

At 30.4 m. is the junction with a dirt road.

Right on this road is HEDTKE PASS, 0.8 m., a natural shooting pass—a strip of land between two large, marshy lakes. The pass is owned by the State Game and Fish Commission and only restricted duck and goose shooting is allowed. On the western edge of the pass is a wooded area in which are clusters of bittersweet, a red berry with open orange peel, often used for decoration.

At 31.2 m. is another WAUBAY LAKE, in the middle of which is CORMORANT ISLAND, so called because of the number of long-necked black waterfowl that build nests there each spring, so close together that there is no room to walk. This lake is used in winter for ice boating because of its size, but it is not used for either swimming or fishing.

At 32.8 m. is LAKE MINNEWASTE (Ind., *good water*). This lovely lake is shaped like an hourglass. Although there are no public bathhouses, swimming is popular in summer and ice skating in winter.

At 34 m. is the junction with US 12 (*see Tour 2*), 5 m. W. of Waubay and 5 m. E. of Webster.

Tour 3

(Dawson, Minn.) — Watertown — Redfield — Gettysburg — Faith — Newell — Belle Fourche—(Alzeda, Mont.). US 212.
Minnesota Line to Wyoming Line, 424 m.
Between Watertown and Gettysburg US 212 is paralleled by the C. & N. W. R.R.; between Le Plant and Faith, by the C. M. St. P. & P.; and between Newell and Belle Fourche, by the C. & N. W.
Hotels and tourist camps at larger towns.
Roadbed hard-surfaced more than three-fourths of distance; remainder graveled.

US 212 is a direct route across South Dakota, touching the northern fringe of the Black Hills. It passes through part of the State's NE. lake region, over the plains westward to the Missouri River Valley Oahe reservoir project, through the Cheyenne River Indian Reservation, and across the "wide open spaces" of ranchland and steep-walled buttes. The dry cattle country gives way to irrigated fields north of the Black Hills, and from Belle Fourche a new road makes a tangent NW. extending US 212 across the corner of Wyoming and into Montana.

Between Faith and Newell there are towns in name only, for none of them can boast of much more than a store and post office. There are no hotel or tourist accommodations in this distance, although gasoline and oil can be purchased along the highway. Despite the fact that much of US 212 traverses a sparsely settled, open country, the route is picturesque, hills and buttes providing constantly changing scenery.

Section a. Minnesota Line-Cheyenne River Reservation, 210 m.

US 212 crosses the South Dakota line 15 *m.* W. of Dawson, Minn. (*see Minn. Tour 11*).

At 9 *m.* is the junction with US 77; the two routes are united for 5 *m.* (*see Tour 9*). Near the highway (L) is LAKE ALICE, one of the numerous bodies of water that form a belt of glacier-formed lakes from the North Dakota line to Madison and Brookings. Two Woods, School, and Round Lakes lie to the NW.

At 13.1 *m.* is the TUNERVILLE CORNER, which took its name from a comic strip some years ago, and the junction with US 77. As US 212 resumes an E-W course, the highway is paralleled by shelterbelts and farm tree-planting projects, designed to break the wind and retard erosion. Before 1935 most of this area was treeless.

KRANZBURG, 25.8 *m.*, consists of a few scattered buildings, including a night club, garage, gas stations, and a large church.

WATERTOWN, 35.8 *m.* (1,734 alt.), (*see WATERTOWN*).

Summer resort center at Lake Kampeska. Mellette Home, Bramble Park.

Here is the junction with US 81 (*see Tour 10*).

At 37.9 *m.* is PELICAN LAKE (L), which is a waterfowl habitat.

At 39.4 *m.* is the junction with a graveled rd. leading to LAKE KAMPESKA's Lake Shore Drive at Stony Point (*see WATERTOWN*).

US 212 skirts the S. end of LAKE KAMPESKA. At 42.5 *m.* is the junction with the hard-surfaced Lake Shoe Drive along with W. side of the lake.

At 49.5 *m.* is the junction with a graveled road.

Right on this road is MEDICINE LAKE, 8 *m.*, called in the Sioux Indian language "Min-ne-pe-juta." This small body of medicinal water covers approximately 400 acres and is fed by subterranean springs. A chemical analysis reveals that this lake contains chemicals similar to those found at French Lick, Ind.

Skin eruptions and irritations are relieved by these waters. The Indians who named the lake made use of its medicinal properties. Water from it is bottled and sold throughout the country. A short time ago a movement to establish a sanitarium was started, but as the lake is rurally located, funds were lacking for the completion of the project. A fine sand beach encircles the entire lake, and two resorts, one on the east and another on the west shore, provide bath-houses, lunches, and picnic grounds.

HENRY, 54.4 *m.* (1,812 alt.), takes on added life each fall because this section is popular with pheasant hunters.

Henry is one of the many towns that, during early railroad days, were given the names of railroad officials, their wives, daughters, or even sweethearts, other towns included in this list being Florence, Wallace, Lily, Bradley, Raymond, and Butler. Henry has a a well-equipped tourist park.

CLARK, 67.5 *m.* (1,779 alt.) seat of Clark Co., was founded in 1882 and has always been the center of a prosperous farming region. Its courthouse, completed in 1935, is one of the outstanding structures of its kind in northeastern South Dakota.

The town, which was first called Clark Center, took its name from the county which, in turn, was named for Newton Clark, a Territorial legislator and Sioux Falls school teacher. When the State's counties were created, the lawmakers adopted a you-scratch-my-back-and-I'll-scratch-yours attitude for the names of 25 counties read like the Legislature's roll call.

At 76 *m.* is the junction with a graveled road.

Left on this road is the FORDHAM LAKE RECREATION DEVELOPMENT AREA, a rural park project of the State Game, Fish and Parks Dept. The 90-acre artificial lake has an 80-acre planting of trees.

DOLAND, 86.2 *m.* (1,355 alt.), has a population composed of many nationalities, intermingled to such a degree that they can only be called Americans. The town has a large trade territory and is situated in a productive farming region.

FRANKFORT, 97.2 *m.* (1,296 alt.), is noted for the abundance of pheasants in the surrounding country. The town was named for the German city in honor of an early settler, Frank I. Fisher, who shot the last buffalo in Spink Co. The animal's head was mounted and is now displayed in the courthouse at Redfield.

At 100 *m.* is the junction with a graveled road.

Right on this road is FISHER GROVE STATE PARK, 0.2 *m.* A 160-acre stand of hardwood trees along the James River was turned over to the State Game, Fish and Parks Dept. in the 1940's to develop public picnicking and camping grounds and to preserve an old bridge used as a stage crossing before the railroad was built. Near here also is the site of the first bridge believed built in South Dakota, constructed by an expedition headed by Major Abercrombie in 1856, while charting a wagon road from Ft. Ridgely, Minnesota, to Fort Pierre.

REDFIELD, 108.4 *m.* (1,295 alt.), is the largest town on US 212 between Watertown and the Black Hills. Four hotels and a tourist park afford ample accommodations. In Redfield is the new EASTERN STAR HOME OF SOUTH DAKOTA, designed to take care of old and indigent members of the order. It is housed in the buildings formerly occupied by Redfield College, now non-existent. The town also is the home of PLEASANT VIEW ACADEMY, a denominational school.

Redfield has the distinction of having had to take up arms in a struggle over the site of the county seat, a fight which began in 1880, and was not permanently settled until 1886.

By the election of 1880, Redfield, then Stennett Junction, was selected as the seat of Spink Co., but for some reason the county records were not moved from Old Ashton. In the next election, 1884, there were more votes cast than there were people in the county. The towns contesting for the county seat sent delegations to attest to the voting in every polling place and it was believed that the totals were correct, but when the ballots were counted apparently dead men had voted, as well as all the railroad construction crews and others.

Following this fraudulent election there was much discussion as to where the county seat should really be, and a delegation from Redfield, sworn to secrecy, stole the county books and records, after picking the vault.

Feeling ran high, and before long word had been passed throughout the northeast part of the county, and in the early morning about 300 "Minute Men" gathered at Old Ashton, armed with various weapons.

On the morning of Dec. 7, 1884, an army of about 1,500 men from the northern section arrived at Redfield and made camp near where the Milwaukee depot now stands. Mayor Hunt of Redfield attempted to parley with the "Army of the North," but they sent the Redfield mayor a message that two hours would be allowed to get the women and children out of town, because at that time they would invade the town, take the records, and destroy the place if necessary.

Acting upon the suggestion of an attorney, that, inasmuch as Redfield had won the election of 1880, an injunction be applied for, to prevent the removal of the records, a Chicago & North Western engine was chartered for a trip to Watertown. From there the party went across country to Milbank to obtain the injunction. In the meantime marksmen were posted at convenient points as unrest became apparent in the ranks of the "Ashton Army." The arrival of the train bearing the injunction, which was promptly served, was perhaps the only thing that averted bloodshed.

Later, sixteen leading citizens of Redfield were named in warrants issued by Justice Bowman of Ashton. All gave bonds except one, who demanded immediate trial; the case was transferred to Athol and heard by Justice Oakland. Attorneys from Watertown, Huron, and Aberdeen appeared for the prosecution and the entire Redfield bar presented the defense. The defendant was dismissed with a word from the judge, "Not proven; but don't do it again."

Although Redfield continues to be the county seat, there are many old-timers who still hold strong opinions on this subject.

Since 1910, when the first large release of pheasants was made in this area, Redfield citizens have taken special interest in both the protection and the heavy hunting of the game birds. The town is practically closed up the first day of shooting each fall.

An artificial lake covering 400 acres was created in the 1930's to provide recreation during the summer, and a public bathhouse is operated by the city.

At Redfield is the junction with US 281 (*see Tour 11*).

Right from the center of town on a graded road that crosses Turtle Creek, is the STATE SCHOOL AND HOME FOR THE FEEBLE MINDED, 1 *m.* In connection with the school is an excellent herd of nearly 200 Holstein-Fresian cows, cared for by the institution. This herd has won national fame and received many awards. The spacious barns and other buildings of the school are visible for many miles.

At 111.9 *m.* is the junction with a graded road.

Left on this road are the SINK HOLES, 0.6 *m.,* large openings in the ground, partially filled with water. They were created while blasting for a spring several years ago. They are about 1,000 ft. from the point where the blasting occurred and their presence is attributed to an underground stream that probably washed out loose gravel beneath, the blast then causing the cave-in.

ROCKHAM, 125.5 *m.* (1,394 alt.), is a grain and produce market for the large and thrifty German community that surrounds it.

FAULKTON, 146.2 *m.* (1,595 alt.), seat of Faulk Co., also draws business from a large territory, as it is a considerable distance from any town of appreciable size. It was named for Andrew J. Faulk, an early governor of Dakota Territory.

Like many early towns, Faulkton also engaged in a county seat fight. The other contestant was LaFoon, now a ghost city, 5 m. east of Faulkton. LaFoon won the first election, but Faulkton became the permanent seat with the advent of the railroad in 1886. That sounded the death knell for the town of LaFoon, and its residents moved to Faulkton.

At 148.5 *m.* is the junction with a graveled road.

Left on this road is the LAKE FAULKTON RECREATION DEVELOPMENT AREA, 0.5 *m.* A 100-acre lake was created as a WPA project and taken over by the State Game, Fish and Parks Dept. to provide a public park in the county.

SENECA, 170.3 *m.* (1,911 alt.), is a short distance (R) from the road.

It was named for Seneca Falls, N. Y., by Eastern homesteaders. In 1936 a fire leveled many buildings here.

LEBANON, 182.5 *m.* (1,956 alt.), for many years was the thriving center of a prosperous farming area, but trucks and automobiles robbed it of much of its earlier business. The town has an excellent swimming pool and park.

GETTYSBURG, 194.1 *m.* (2,082 alt.), was named for the Pennsylvania battlefield by a group of Civil War veterans who first settled here. Founded in 1881, the town has kept its main street neat and attractive by considerable paving and the preservation of many old trees. Today several large cottonwoods protrude through the sidewalks and tower above the adjacent buildings.

The town presents a colorful sight, with visitors from farm, ranch and reservation. The Indians live at the Cheyenne Agency, headquarters for the officials of the Cheyenne River Reservation (*see below*). Gettysburg has a wide trade area and normally is the busy center of a prosperous farming section.

At 198.1 *m.* is the junction with US 83; the two routes are united to another junction at 199 *m.*

At 207 *m.* a dim but passable road leads R. through a gate over a small hill.

Right on this road to MEDICINE ROCK, 0.4 *m.*, long held sacred by the Indians, and a subject of controversy among scientists. On it are the imprints of three human feet, a hand, and many animal tracks. Although the footprints are of enormous size, they are perfect in outline. This fact caused Indians to tie bags of medicinal herbs on poles above the rock with the belief that the herbs would absorb additional powers. They also laid gifts upon the rock, offerings to the "Great Spirit." The presence of the rock was known before 1825, for on that date Gen. Henry Atkinson and Col. Benjamin O'Fallon, having heard of it, visited the site while on a trip up the Missouri River, and reported the fact to Washington.
For a long time it was generally believed that the imprints were made by some man of prodigious size who walked across the rock before the clay had hardened into stone. Some believed it was the work of an artist-jokester, who desired to give future generations something for speculation. However, scientists are now of the opinion that the prints were made by some sagacious medicine man who wanted further to impress his followers.

At 208.1 *m.* is the MISSOURI RIVER and OAHE RESER-VOIR, the latter formed by a dam near Pierre (*see Tour 4*). This point is known as Whitlock Crossing, the camp of the crews that built the first bridge across the river in 1924. Before there was a bridge, a ferryboat plied from Forest City to the Cheyenne Agency. Forest City, about 3 *m.* S., became a ghost town when the new road by-passed it. At 210 *m.* the edge of the Cheyenne River Indian Reservation is reached.

Section b. Cheyenne River Reservation-Wyoming Line, 214 m.

The CHEYENNE RIVER RESERVATION (*open to visitors*) is one of the nine Indian reservations in the State. A Federal law imposes severe penalties on persons convicted of selling or giving intoxicants to Indians. Possession of liquor and its transportation across a reservation are also prohibited. Order is preserved through a system of Indian police who have authority to arrest any law violators.

The reservation covers all of Armstrong and parts of Dewey and Ziebach Counties. Indian life, however, is not confined to these specific boundaries, there being many families in the adjacent territory. Here the "vanished American" is no longer vanishing; in the last 10 years there has been an annual increase of about 10 persons per 1,000 population.

There is now a total of 4,307 Indians on this reservation, of which only 1,898 are full bloods. Included in the group are numerous native bands designated by the names; Miniconjou, Sans Arc, Two Kettle, Blackfeet, Uncapapa, Upper and Lower Yanktonai, Oglala, and Sisseton. Nearly all the older Indians speak only the Sioux language, but with improved educational facilities on the reservation, only 2 percent of those between the ages of 20 and 40 use their tribal language exclusively.

With much of their land within the reservoir area of the Oahe project in the Missouri River development program, the Indians demanded the right to negotiate with the Federal Government for the sale of land being flooded. The U.S. Congress in 1950 made such a provision.

These Sioux, with few exceptions, have never been entirely self-supporting. At times the Government has made payments to them, but these have been from the sale of inherited lands or interest on tribal funds. Very little money accruing to them is given in a lump sum, but rather is divided into periodic payments. Various funds, which in most cases have their sources in treaties, include the Trust Fund, Three Percent Fund, and Sioux Benefit Funds. Their total wealth consists of $455,334 in tribal funds and $1,429,085 in tribal lands.

Farming is another source of income, although few of the Sioux have made much progress in this respect. Furthermore the reservation is not situated in the best agricultural section of the State. Some forage crops are raised along the Cheyenne River, but this treacherous stream has a habit of suddenly changing its course during flood periods, thus making the permanence of homes erected on its sandy bottoms decidedly uncertain.

Despite the fact that education and attempts to foster better living conditions have made noticeable inroads on old tribal customs, many of the Indians, especially the old ones, live in a manner similar to that of 40 or 50 years ago. Regardless of the fact that little credence is given to tales of the dog as a source of food, the custom still exists. Take away the dog and the Indian would be robbed of a major food source. Dog meat is never eaten except in soup, canine steaks being practically unknown.

After a wedding the parents of the bride and groom generally give a feast. Feasts are also given after funerals, often on the same day. This is an old custom, and unless the Indian observes it he rapidly loses the esteem of his fellows. Sometimes the more fortunate members of the tribe are persuaded to give a feast and invite their destitute friends. At these festivities the meal begins with meat. In addition there are bread, or biscuits, and perhaps a vegetable. Sometimes "wasna," a concoction of chokecherries, meat, and grease pounded together and dried, is served. Often there is "tipsla," or Indian turnips, dried in the fall and served in a kind of soup. If a guest cannot eat all that is served him, he wraps up the more solid food and takes it home to be consumed later.

Changes in habits of eating have come slowly on the reservation. Only in recent years has there been a tendency to buy canned milk, cereal, and fruit. The Sioux still use large amounts of lard, potatoes, onions, tomatoes, and baking powder; the last item has always been a consistent seller among post traders, for the Sioux like biscuits. Habits of dress have changed more rapidly than other customs, virtually all the Sioux dressing as do their white brothers.

Between 200 and 300 of the Indians have comfortable homes and a similar number own cabins and log houses; however, the average family spends much of its time roaming about the reservation, their home consisting of a tent, a few cooking utensils, and some bedding. Although nearly all have permanent homes, many of them prefer living in a tent much of the time.

Under the present system, a tribal council comprises the chief governing body among the Sioux. It consists of 15 members, and carries on negotiations with the Federal, State, and local governments; it presents and prosecutes claims and demands of the tribe; and it administers tribal lands, funds, and property within the control of the tribe.

Cattle and other property have been issued on the Cheyenne River Reservation, with the expectation that the Indians would be encouraged to start in business for themselves. Many have been in a measure successful, and figures show 376 Indian-owned ranches. Accustomed to a roaming life and looking upon cattle mainly as providing food for the moment, the Sioux, generally speaking, have not built up many herds.

CHEYENNE AGENCY, 1.7 *m.*, is the headquarters of the Cheyenne River Reservation. Living here are Government officials, traders, missionaries, school teachers, and Indians. Government officials at the agency will answer questions of visitors concerning all parts of the reservation.

Approximately 250 children attend the boarding school; and an up-to-date hospital, well-staffed, takes care of patients from all over the reservation.

In the western part of town is an INDIAN VILLAGE of log cabins and tents, typical of Indian life. School buildings are modern, and a large gymnasium aids pupils in competing with other towns in athletics. West of the school the Indians have erected a monument to their dead chiefs. There is a growing tendency among the Indians to mark spots of historical interest and to honor heroes of past generations.

LA PLANT, 21.6 *m.*, has long been known as a prairie trading post for Indians, cowboys, and ranchers. The village, strung haphazardly along a hillside, is representative of the towns of the transition era between the open-range and homestead periods.

Over this part of the country, before the advent of the homesteader, roamed great herds of cattle—released by large outfits who staked their chances of success on the favorable weather. Sometimes they lost; often they won. Occasionally the cattleman's fortune was wiped out in a few days. Such was the case in the memorable Thanksgiving blizzard of 1896 which raged three days, when thousands of head of livestock blindly drifted into draws and washouts, were covered with snow, and perished. Spring round-ups revealed that most of the cattle outfits had suffered more than a 50 percent loss.

For many miles US 212 winds and dips over the rolling prairie, with only occasional houses to lend assurance of the fact that human life is near, even if infrequent. There is no attraction in this region for anyone who sees it only on the surface. But to the Westerner or to anyone else with imagination it brings to mind loping herds of buffalo relentlessly pursued by bands of Indians, ponderous freight wagons, drawn by swaying teams of oxen; great herds of cattle; the decline of the big outfits and the rise of the nester; and the tide of homesteaders and their subsequent drift back East. All this is typical of the evolutionary process of western South Dakota. In some sections where climate and soil conditions permitted, the farmer came to stay; but generally speaking, this range country will remain for some time to come the realm of the stockman.

RIDGEVIEW, 30.4 *m.*, was so named because of its position on the divide between the Cheyenne and Moreau Rivers. The swift-flowing Cheyenne is the largest feeder of the Missouri in western South Dakota. Its hundreds of tributary creeks and draws reach out on either side, like the legs of a centipede, to cut sharp creases in its basin. The Moreau, a smaller stream, often dries up entirely in the course of an extremely dry season, but during rainy periods, or during the melting of heavy snows, it becomes a roaring and impetuous torrent.

US 212 passes through range country where the traveler may see genuine cowboys, round-ups, line camps, and branding existing today much as it did a half-century and more ago. Until after World War II, the Diamond A, South Dakota's largest cattle spread, operated here, with several ranches now taking over the holdings. At one time as many as 50,000 cattle wore the Diamond A brand and Capt. Burton C. Mossman, the chief owner, leased most of the land in Armstrong county and parts of two others.

EAGLE BUTTE, 52.5 m. (2,415 alt.), was named for a nearby butte on which Indians hunted eagles for feathers to make war bonnets. According to legend, deep pits were dug, covered with light branches, and a rabbit laid on them for bait. The trapper concealed himself in the pit and caught the eagle by the foot as it swooped down to get the rabbit. The town was started when the railroad was extended through the locality in 1910, and today is supported by a mixed population of farmers, ranchers, and Indians.

LANTRY, 63.6 m., was also founded in 1910 when the railroad entered the region, but did not enjoy the growth of the neighboring towns. Near here is a large dam used by the railroad as a water supply.

DUPREE, 70 m. (2,356 alt.), for 25 years after its founding retained its board sidewalks, typical of early cow towns. It was named for Fred Dupree, an early French trapper. Although founded largely through the influx of homesteaders, it has lost little of its Western color. Cowboys, Indians, and ranchers still give it most of its business.

Following its founding, the real estate business enjoyed a flourishing period, the first land office being in a tent on Main St. Pointing out the sites of surveyed quarter-sections to prospective homesteaders was a lucrative business in those days. The business was called "locating," and the newcomer, for a fee ranging from $25 to as much as he could be induced to pay, was taken out into the country where the corners of his prospective claim were pointed out to him. In those days the automobile had not yet displaced the horse as a means of conveyance; consequently nearly all of the "locating" was done by using a horse and buggy for transportation. Often a handkerchief was tied around a buggy spoke and the revolutions counted as a help in measuring the approximate distance to the next corner.

Every period has its attendant stories. One, told of homestead days, referred to the improvements required by law before the filee was given a patent to his land. One homesteader of lethargic tendencies, who was required to have broken a certain number of acres on his land, was asked how many he had plowed. He replied:

"Around twenty." Investigation showed that he had not lied, for he had broken a single furrow around 20 acres.

During normal years Dupree is a busy marketing center for live-stock, flax, and small grain. When the prairie was first broken, large yields of flax brought small fortunes to the early farmers. It was not an uncommon occurrence to have one crop of flax pay for the land.

Left from Dupree on an unnumbered graded dirt road is CHERRY CREEK, 35 *m.*, sub-agency of the Cheyenne River Reservation. During average times it is com-posed of a few Government buildings, two post traders' stores, and a hetero-geneous group of scattered Indian homes—log huts with dirt roofs, tents, tempo-rary homes of hundreds of Indians from all parts of the reservation. Cherry Creek was the home of Chief Hump, famous Sioux leader, and was a point of tension during the Messiah War of 1890. It was to Cherry Creek that Sitting Bull's fol-lowers fled after the old medicine man was killed on Grand River, and it was a few miles above the town that Big Foot and his band were first overhauled by soldiers prior to the Battle of Wounded Knee.
The village received prominence in South Dakota literature through the descriptive and colorful essay by former Governor Charles N. Herreid during one of his visits to Cherry Creek. The essay, called "The White Squaw," relates the tragic episode of a white woman in an Indian environment, besides presenting a vivid picture of the reservation town. It is reprinted in part by permission of O. W. Coursey's "Dakota Literature."
". . . It was ration-day at the agency. About 1,500 Indians belonged to this station and at this time, Indian fashion, most of them were camped in their tents and tipis—some on the plains and some on the heavily timbered bottom-lands—altogether forming an improvised, semi-barbarous, picturesque village.
"On the banks of the Cherry Creek and the Cheyenne immense quantities of red buffalo berries burdened the bushes—forming a most appropriate and artistic setting in the luxurious foliage, tinged with nature's announcement of the passing season. It was an ideal camping ground, an ideal fall day. It was Indian summer, Indian feast day. Indian village, Indian country. Smoky eyes, smoky complexions har-monized perfectly with smoky skies. Man and nature were attuned. The atmosphere was languid, peaceful, dreamy, melancholy. To me, with my intense love for the wilderness and sympathy for the Red Man it was a day of intense interest and enjoyment.
"The agent informed me that among the squaws was an old 'white' woman, who had lived among the Indians since infancy. This aroused my curiosity. I asked permission to see her and talk to her and a messenger was sent to find her. After some time the messenger returned saying he had found her, but that she refused to appear at the office of the Agent. The Chief of the Indian police, named Straight-head—a magnificent Indian—was sent out, with orders to bring her to the office. While waiting for developments I pictured to myself the helpless baby girl, snatched by savages from her tomahawked parents. I saw the restless pioneers leaving civilization; the emigrant train, traversing and trespassing upon the broad domain of the aborigines. I saw the wild attack of the red men, made ferocious by the resistless rush of the venturesome white men. I saw the red and white both dominated by the same powerful motives—the comfort and happiness of his family and himself.
"Presently the policeman ushered into the room a decrepit and most wretched-looking woman, apparently at least seventy years old. She shuffled into a corner, crouching upon the floor, trembling with fear. She knew that she was a white woman, that her folks had been killed in a skirmish on the plains; that she had been with the Indians since she was about one year old. She could not speak a word of English and, excepting her blue eyes and features, looked like the most degraded and miserable savage. The poor old woman did not show the least desire to know anything about her own people, nor to come in contact with white people or civilization."

FAITH, 94.5 *m.* (2,600 alt.), is at the end of a branch of the C. M. St. P. & P. R.R. It is another of the towns founded during the homesteading wave of 1910. It was named, according to a story, because an early resident expressed his belief that it required *faith* to live on the rolling, semi-arid prairie. The town has a trade territory reaching in four directions, extending into the expansive hinterland of the cattle and sheep country to the N., W. and S. and the farming region to the E. It is typically a town with Western flavor, dominated by ranchers and cowboys and colored by a mixture of Indians who come from the nearby reservation to trade.

Faith, which is 112 m. from its county seat at Sturgis, has modern facilities and no local tax levy. Profit from the municipal liquor store is used to operate the town government as well as helping to build the light, water, and sewer systems. Water is piped from Lake Durkee, an artificial pond built by the WPA 3 m. S. The State Game, Fish and Parks Dept. has set aside 160 acres there for the Durkee Lake Recreation Development Area.

The country between Faith and Newell is devoid of railroads, the region being a vast open-range domain of the cattle and sheepmen. There are no towns or even hamlets, but merely post offices and stores with gas pumps outside.

EDSON, 104 *m.*, FOX RIDGE, 117 *m.*, MAURINE, 122 *m.*, are merely hold-overs from homestead days, unable to muster much population because of lack of railroad facilities. Once busy little centers of the homesteader's trade, they now serve small groups of ranchers in their vicinity.

CEDAR CANYON, 127 *m.*, so named because of a nearby canyon with a thick growth of cedar trees, is the point where US 212 first crosses the OLD BISMARCK TRAIL, angling from the NE. This old historic trail, which formerly wound across 275 m. of broken, treeless country, uninhabited except for Indians, was the road over which an assorted throng of gold-seekers, adventurers, and get-rich-quick men of many types, lured by prospects of sudden wealth in the Black Hills, traveled in early days. The name of Ben Ash is closely associated with the Bismarck Trail, for it was he who first marked the route. In 1876, during the gold rush, it happened that Bismarck, N. Dak., was one of the railroad points nearest Deadwood.

Starting at Bismarck, there was first the Missouri River to be crossed, then the Cannon Ball, Grand, Moreau, and Belle Fourche Rivers, besides numerous creeks. The stagecoach furnished the transportation used by most of the people making the trip, and for those days the service was first class. There were stage stations at convenient points where drivers and horses were changed. The bullwhackers were the most picturesque characters who traveled the trail. With a wagon and trail wagon drawn by four or five yoke of oxen, and with several outfits traveling together for protection, these caravans traveled 10 or 15 m. per day. Unlike the stage drivers, the bull whackers made their own camp. If the weather was fair, they usually made the trip without mishap, but if it was rainy the long stretches of gumbo made traveling impossible. Although fields, fences, and roads have partly obliterated the old trail, the deep ruts made half a century ago are still visible in many places.

MUD BUTTE, 137.3 *m.*, was named for a butte that, with its absence of any vegetation, resembles a prodigious handful of dark mud slapped rudely upon the grassy prairie which surrounds it.

SULPHUR, 146 *m.*, is also on the old Bismarck Trail. The town was so called because it is near Sulphur Creek, the waters of which are heavily impregnated with sulphur. During the homestead period, when legal notices had to be published for proof of claims, a newspaper was printed here. In spirit of the times, it was called *The Sulphur Match.*

NEWELL, 175.3 *m.* (2,820 alt.), although in a dry section of the State, has streets lined with luxuriant trees, and shrubbery, and is surrounded by farms where green vegetation stands out in striking contrast with the dun prairies beyond. All this is because Newell is in the heart of the Government Reclamation Project, which brings water from the Belle Fourche Dam to irrigate the level areas lying along the Belle Fourche valley. Sugar beet production is the chief industry, while in wide, shallow valleys alfalfa is grown for forage and seed. Bear Butte, 25 m. to the S., is plainly visible from Newell. At Newell is the junction with State 79.

Right on State 79 is a sub-station of the STATE EXPERIMENT FARM, 1.5 *m.* (L), operated in connection with the principal experiment station at Brookings. It was established here because being in an irrigated region, numerous experiments can be carried on relative to irrigation problems. The station is also the headquarters of the U.S. Bureau of Reclamation and Belle Fourche Irrigation Project. A farm picnic is held here every year in July.

NISLAND, 184.5 *m.* (2,855 alt.), is another town in the irrigated section of South Dakota. In recent years the growing of cucumbers, made possible through fertile soil and abundant water, has been stimulated by a large pickle-salting station at Nisland. The town is also the scene of the annual Butte Co. Fair.

At 192.6 *m.* is the BELLE FOURCHE DAM (R)—locally called Orman Dam—is built on shale or heavy compact clay, locally known as gumbo, and is 6,200 ft. long, 115 feet high, and 19 ft. wide on top. The reservoir, approximately 10 m. long, with an average width of more than 2 m., supplies water to more than 75,000 acres in the Belle Fourche valley. The dam is on Owl Creek, but water is supplied by a diversion dam in the Belle Fourche River, which turns flood waters into the reservoir.

Construction was begun in 1905; in 1908 the first unit was opened for settlement, and water was applied to 12,000 acres. Extension of the work continued until 1917, when water became available for about 82,000 acres.

The Inlet Canal, constructed for the purpose of conducting the flood waters of the Belle Fourche River to the storage reservoir on Owl Creek, is 6½ m. long and has a capacity of 1,600 ft. per second of water.

The irrigation season extends from May to September, inclusive, although spring rains are generally sufficient to germinate crops, and often make irrigation unnecessary before June.

BELLE FOURCHE, 200 *m.* (3,013 alt.), (*see Tour 13*), is the junction with US 85 (*see Tour 13*).

US 212 continues NW. over a new improved road known as the Miles City Cut-Off.

At 214 *m.* is the Wyoming Line. US 212 sweeps for 14 m. across the corner of Wyoming without passing through any towns and crosses the Montana Line 4 m. from Alzeda (*see MONTANA STATE GUIDE, Tour 10*).

Tour 4

(Lake Benton, Minn.)—Brookings—Huron—Pierre—Rapid City—Sturgis—Spearfish—(Beulah, Wyo.), US 14

Minnesota Line to Wyoming Line, 458 m.

Except in a few places the Chicago & North Western R.R. parallels the route between the Minnesota line and Sturgis. Between Sturgis and the Wyoming line there is no parallel railroad.

All-weather roads.

Good hotel and tourist accommodations in larger towns and cities.

CROSSING a level, almost unforested plain for about 225 miles, with only a few tree-fringed lakes and occasional hills to break the monotonous expanses of prairie, US 14 drops abruptly into the Missouri River valley and winds over rolling country to the Black Hills. Appearing first dimly distant, the Black Hills rise sharply from the prairie land surrounding them. Within their pine-covered portals is a rugged, picturesque mountain region including many points of scenic and historic interest.

This highway traverses the State, east and west, and affords a composite picture of the eastern farming area, western grazing region, and mountain country. Yucca, cactus, buffalo berries, occasional prairie dog villages, magpies, eagles, and perhaps a coyote are seen west of the Missouri River.

Section a. Minnesota Line—Pierre, 211 m. US 14

US 14 crosses the Minnesota Line 8 m. W. of Lake Benton, Minn. (*see Minn. Tour 12*), and enters one of the best farming regions in South Dakota.

ELKTON, 2 *m.* (1,751 alt.), is at the junction of the C. & N. W. and the C. R. I. & P. R.R. Along the railroad track is a park with a band shell, walks, and elm trees; similar parks have been established in nearly every town along the line in eastern South Dakota, as a compliment to the railroads that brought the towns into being.

Free coinage of aluminum was tried in Elkton three years before the Presidential campaign of 1896, when William Jennings Bryan stumped the country for free coinage of silver. Suffering from a lack of anything to use as a medium of exchange, mainly because of hard times, Elkton businessmen concocted a plan to employ aluminum money in lieu of a more precious metal. Accordingly, they hired a St. Paul firm to "make money" for them. Thin strips of aluminum were cut to imitate the respective denominations of coins and the name of a firm was printed on one side.

The plan worked remarkably well for a time. When purchases were made with legal coin the substitute would be given out in exchange. Mr. Jones would take his change from the grocer and buy meat with it. The butcher would spend it in other stores or buy a calf or a hog from a farmer. But retribution was not far distant. A United States inspector dropped in one day and notified the businessmen that they must cease the practice. Furthermore, he told them that they were subject to a fine of $100 in real money for every aluminum coin dispensed. From Elkton the inspector went to St. Paul where he closed the money-making plant. Satisfied that the Elkton men had no fraudulent intent, he gave them time to call in the illegal coins. Eventually all the bogus money was redeemed, and Elkton returned to the gold standard.

AURORA, 14.2 m. (1,630 alt.), platted in 1880, at the time of the extension of the railroad into this part of the State, has tall red grain elevators, white houses, and a few towering cottonwood trees, which break the level expanse of rich farm land.

BROOKINGS, 20.3 m. (1,636 alt.), is the home of South Dakota State College and is the center of a prosperous and progressive farming area, much of it reflecting the experimentation provided by the agricultural school. The State's largest producer of field seeds has its headquarters here, with branches in much larger cities of the Midwest. One of the growing industries is the manufacture here of devices used for cleaning, counting, and planting seed. The college has had other influences also; for instance, Brookings is one of the few places in the State prohibiting the sale of liquor by bottle or drink, and the taverns that try to grow up around the edges of the town have short lives.

When Brookings was platted in 1879 it absorbed Medary, the first town site in Dakota Territory, which had been started in 1857 a few miles to the south. Brookings County and its seat of government both were named for Judge W. W. Brookings, one of the most remarkable men in the State's history. He came west in 1857 following his graduation from Bowdoin College, and during his first winter he froze both legs so badly they had to be amputated with a butcher knife. He went on to serve as president of the Territorial Council and as a Supreme Court Judge. He also superintended the building of the first wagon road to the Missouri River from the Minnesota line and promoted the first railroad. In fact, the first locomotive to enter what is now South Dakota was named the "Judge Brookings."

The city government has long been identified with municipal ownership enterprises. Owned and operated by the town are the power, telephone, water, and hospital facilities, with the light plant also offering steam heat to business places in the downtown district. The MUNICIPAL GOLF COURSE, at the N. edge of town, is operated by the American Legion. A new MUNICIPAL AIRPORT, at the SW. outskirts, was completed in 1950, at a cost of $400,000; it is served by Western Airlines. The city's ARMORY-AUDI-TORIUM on Main St. is used for road shows, conventions, exhibits, and dances.

Two excellent parks are maintained by the city. HILLCREST PARK, on US 14 at the E. edge of town, has a public swimming pool and bathhouse, baseball field, picnic grounds, and game area. PIO-NEER PARK, on US 12 at the W. edge of the city, has a band shell, picnic area, and athletic field.

The SOUTH DAKOTA STATE COLLEGE campus and experiment areas comprise the NE. portion of the town. It is a land grant college of agriculture and mechanic arts, with a variety of courses in allied fields (see EDUCATION). As the largest college in South Dakota, its annual homecoming "Hobo Day" is a time-honored event. As many as 35,000 people crowd the streets and the campus for the festivities which feature a parade and a football game. The ringing of cowbells accompanies all athletic contests here, and on Hobo Day this clamor is augmented by the appearance of the student body dressed as tramps and the men sporting beards which have been nursed along for months.

The campus is in the form of a quadrangle, with a mixture of old and new buildings. Most dominant is THE COUGHLIN CAM-PANILE, called the "Singing Silo" by students, which rises 165 ft. and dwarfs all other buildings in the city. Its chimes not only peal out the time, but fill the air with melodies. It was the gift of Charles L. Coughlin in 1930, on the occasion of the 20th anniversary of his graduation. He was a South Dakota farm boy from near Carthage, and became a prominent Milwaukee manufacturer.

The total cost of the tower was approximately $75,000. It measures 30 ft. square at the base, not including the approaches, and 47 ft. square with the approaches. It is built of white Indiana limestone, red brick, and concrete, to harmonize with the beautiful LINCOLN MEMORIAL LIBRARY and the COOLIDGE SYLVAN THEATRE nearby. There are 180 steps leading to the balcony, the highest point that can be reached by visitors. The balcony floor is 112 ft. above the ground, or almost exactly two-thirds the height of the tower.

A glass-covered hatchway in the ceiling of the balcony room permits a view of six of the eighteen tubular chimes, and also of Old

Faithful, a bell cast for State College in 1885, and one of the 8,000,000 candlepower beacon lights.

Another alumnus, Harvey Dunn, who began his art studies here, has returned 40 of his canvasses for hanging in the UNION BUILD-ING. They include oil paintings used as illustrations in the *Saturday Evening Post*, *American Legion* magazine, and other publications. In the Union is the bookstore and a cafeteria. Other buildings of special interest on the campus are the AGRICULTURAL HALL, the ARMORY, and the RURAL JOURNALISM AND PRINTING BUILDING.

State College athletic teams are known as the "Jackrabbits" and compete in the North Central Conference.

At Brookings is the junction with US 77 (*see Tour 9*).

VOLGA, 28.2 *m.* (1,636 alt.), was named for the Volga River in Russia, though the people of the community are not of Russian descent, but Scandinavian.

A story is still current in Volga about a salesman from Chicago who, in 1880, came to Volga for the first time. Learning of a trading post at the inland town of Oakwood, he hired a livery team and drove there. It was apparent that he expected to find the country wild and woolly, and during the evening some of the local men concluded that it would be too bad if he returned disappointed. He was taken to Charlie Porter's drug store, where a group of men were apparently gambling for high stakes under the influence of liquor. Suddenly a a violent quarrel started and Porter rushed behind the counter, returning with a huge cheese knife. Another man came reeling out of the back room, swinging a double-barreled shotgun. Three men rushed at him, when both barrels were discharged into the ceiling. This was too much for the salesman, who bolted out of the door for the livery barn, forgot about collecting his money, and never returned.

At Volga is the junction with a graveled road.

Right on this road is OAKWOOD LAKES STATE PARK, 9 *m.* This historic and scenic area was purchased by the South Dakota Game, Fish and Parks Department in 1947 to be developed as a public hunting grounds and 900-acre park. The shorelines, and particularly the peninsula at the north end, are timbered with oak, ash, elm, and hackberry groves. Picnic areas, with fireplaces, tables, water and toilet facilities have been set aside for picnickers and visitors.
When Nicollet and Frémont visited the region in 1838, they gave their maps the the notation "lakes of the grand lodge" because of the Indian villages here. Several burial and ceremonial grounds are prominent, and arrowheads, hammers, and other artifacts may be found. A fort was established in 1859, consisting of a large log building surrounded by earthen breastworks. Outlines of the fortification, with cannon corners, are visible.
A log cabin, believed to have been built in 1875, stands in good condition at the north end. It was the home of "Old Spot" Mortimer and his Indian wife. At one time there was a village called Oakwood, with a hotel, flour mill, drug store, and blacksmith shop. One of the pioneers, Ernest V. Sutton, wrote about the area in his book *A Life Worth Living*.

At 38 *m.* is the junction with US 81 (*see Tour 10*).

ARLINGTON, 40.4 *m.* (1,846 alt.), originally called Nordland because of the large number of Scandinavians who first settled here, has an artificial lake and a native rock island. Although a small, two-street town, people get confused in directions, as the streets are diagonal to the compass.

Here is the junction with US 81 (*see Tour 10*) .

HETLAND, 47 *m.*, is also the center of an extensive Scandinavian community, named for a settler by that name who came from Hetland, Norway.

The life of the homesteaders who settled in this prairie country in the 1880's was hard but often romantic. In the spring of 1880, Hod Phelps brought his family from Minnesota and filed on a homestead near here. As money was none too plentiful, he made a temporary home in a dugout in a steep bank that faced the east. He spent the summer breaking the prairie with his walking plow and horse, making a stable for his cow, digging a well, and putting up hay. During the same summer a young woman, May Wheeler, came from Baraboo, Wis., and filed on a homestead near the Phelps land, as she had known the family previously; however she returned to Wisconsin to earn more money before building. In the meantime, Mrs. Phelps' unmarried brother, Willis Atwater, came from the East and filed on a nearby homestead. In October a blizzard began on the morning of the 15th, followed by several storms until by mid-January travel and communication were cut off. On the last train to break through the snow blockade, Miss Wheeler arrived at Nordland (now Arlington). After buying lumber and equipment, she found she could not start building while the storms continued, and so she moved in with the Phelps. The storms increased in fury and frequency during the rest of January and February, and it was not long until there were 12 ft. of snow on the level. Each new storm buried the dugout completely, making it dark as night the day around. The kerosene supply was soon exhausted, and the only source of light was a saucer of grease with a rag in it. Wheat was ground in a coffee mill, and they burned hay and straw hauled by manpower on a home-made sled.

Through the long, cold winter a romance between Atwater and Miss Wheeler developed. The first thaw came on April 17, and the weather turned suddenly warm. Water flooded the land and ran in torrents through the ravines. Those who had vowed to leave during the winter now began making plans for their homes on the prairie. Among them were Atwater and his bride, who eventually built up a large and prosperous farm.

LAKE PRESTON, 54 *m.* (1,722 alt.), received its name from the lake nearby, which was discovered and named in 1839 by Gen. John C. Frémont, noted pathfinder, who surveyed the levels of the water on his journey through the Northwest. He named the lake for Senator Preston of North Carolina.

This area is an excellent farming region during normal years, its
prosperity attested by large barns and farmhouses.

DE SMET, 62 *m.* (1,726 alt.), first settled in 1879, was named
in honor of Father Peter J. De Smet, early apostle to the Indians
of South Dakota (*see HISTORY*). Lying in the heart of a dairying
section, it has been called the Cream City. Many of the merchants
and professional men in De Smet are sons of pioneers, and modern
buildings show the town's development.

An Old Settlers' Day highlights each summer. In 1950 Aubrey
Sherwood, editor of the *De Smet News,* persuaded Harvey Dunn, a
former resident (*see below*) to come and bring some of his paintings
of homestead and prairie scenes. Dunn brought 40 large canvases.
When placed on exhibit, they covered the walls of the Masonic
Hall and attracted so many visitors that Dunn stayed on for several
weeks. Finally, he moved the exhibit to State College at Brookings
(*see above*) and returned to New York.

At De Smet is the junction with State 25.

1. Right to the BIRTHPLACE OF ROSE WILDER LANE (1887–   ), the writer,
2.5 *m.* Only a few gnarled boxelder trees mark the place that was her home, although the remains of the sod shanty in which she was born are marked by two
slight elevations near the trees. Laura Ingles Wilder, author of children's stories and
mother of Rose Wilder Lane, came here as a bride. Rose Wilder Lane has said that
the pattern of her whole life was formed in that pioneer setting. At the age of six
she became so intensely interested in writing that she developed writer's cramp and
was taken out of school. For a time it was feared she would lose the use of her
arm. Leaving the country in a covered wagon at the age of seven, she remembered,
however, the prairies and the town, which have been used as the settings of her
books. The Earnestine Series of stories which were published in the "Saturday
Evening Post" had descriptions of De Smet and subtle characterizations of its early
inhabitants. In "Let The Hurricane Roar" the description of the blizzard and cold
is that of the Dakota prairie. In a recent book, "Old Home Town," De Smet can
easily be recognized.
2. Left from De Smet on State 25 to a junction with a graveled road, 8 *m.*; L.
on this road is LAKE THOMPSON, 10.7 *m.* (R), which covers an area of 20 sq. m.
LAKE HENRY (L) is a smaller body of water. It was at Lake Thompson in 1857
that a party of Santee Sioux overtook Inkpaduta, after he had committed numerous
depredations. A fierce battle ensued. Inkpaduta, chief objective of the long chase by
the Santees, escaped, but two of his sons were killed. South Dakota and Minnesota
history records the "high spots" in the life of Inkpaduta, infamous son of Wamdesapa,
whose cruel traits he inherited. Recently, human bones, thought to be those of
Indians, were unearthed in the vicinity.

Along US 14 is the DE SMET EXPERIMENTAL FOREST, an
80-acre demonstration planting sponsored by the South Dakota
Game, Fish and Parks Department.

At 70 *m.* is a junction with a graded road.

Left on this road, 2 *m.* (R), is the BIRTHPLACE OF HARVEY DUNN, the
artist. Only two mounds of dirt remain to mark the site of the sod house in which
he was born in 1882. At the age of 14, Harvey Dunn was doing a man's work on
the farm. In school the teacher made a practice of hiding the chalk, as Harvey
emptied the chalk box every day. His strong fingers sketched everything, from

delicate flowers to powerful locomotives. Harvey wished to study at the Art Institute in Chicago, but he was without funds. A De Smet landowner, Charles Dawley, offered to pay $2 an acre to summer-fallow 200 acres of land, and a deal was made. Working from sunup to sundown, Dunn saved his money and left for Chicago to attend school in 1902. Finishing his course in Chicago, he went to New York. When World War I began, Dunn was sent to France by the War Department to portray scenes of American activities as historical records. Many of his war pictures were on covers of the "American Legion Monthly" from 1928 to 1936. He has illustrated many magazine stories and articles. Among his best known paintings are: "Artillery in Action," "A Corner in Hell," "The Raiding Party," "In the Wire," "The Raid," "The Vigil," "The Homesite," "The Railsplitter," "Kamerad," "Armistice," and "Camouflage." The original painting of "The Sniper," cover design of the American Legion Monthly in 1928, is hung in the De Smet American Legion Post clubhouse

IROQUOIS, 77.3 m. (1,401 alt.), was named for the Iroquois Indian tribe.

LAKE IROQUOIS STATE RECREATION AREA (L) has camping and picnicking facilities around the artificial lake in a prairie setting.

At Iroquois is the junction with a graveled road.

Right on this road is LAKE OSCEOLA STATE RECREATION AREA, also maintained by the State Game, Fish and Parks Department. It is designed for use by the rural communities of the region.

CAVOUR, 86 m. (1,311 alt.), received its name from Count Cavour, Italian statesman and builder of railroads in Italy.

HURON, 95.5 m. (1,285 alt.), (see HURON).

Home of the State Fair, Huron College; meat-packing and farm-trading center.

Here is the junction with State 37 (see Tour 11A) running south.

Left on State 37 is the LAKE BYRON RECREATION DEVELOPMENT AREA and STATE FISH HATCHERY, 15 m. At 16 m. is the HURON MENNONITE COLONY, a religious sect that farms along the James River and lives in community buildings. The Mennonites wear drab, home-made clothing and married men are required to wear beards. They are friendly people, and while they welcome visitors they do not like to have their pictures taken.

It was in the vicinity of Huron that the dust storms of 1933 and 1934 were particularly devastating. Tumble weeds and shifting topsoil piled up against fences and the land was stripped of vegetation. Between Huron and Wolsey ditches were filled with silt, and whenever the wind blew a "black blizzard" developed. Soil conservation and shelterbelt projects were started to halt erosion and new drought-resistant crops were introduced.

The area between Huron and Miller is part of the U.S. Government's 750,000-acre Oahe Irrigation Project. Work was begun in 1950 on a dam in the Missouri River near Pierre (see below) to store water for the project along the west side of the James River. Headquarters are at Huron (see HURON).

At 107.1 *m*. is the junction with US 281 (*see Tour 11*) with which US 14 is united through the town of Wolsey.

WOLSEY, 110 *m*. (1,353 alt.), was named for Cardinal Thomas Wolsey of 16th century note. It was in Wolsey, according to a story related there, that the late Richard Sears, of Sears, Roebuck & Co., received the impetus that caused him to embark upon the mail order business. In 1882 he was the first railroad station agent at Wolsey. Having several small C.O.D. shipments of varied articles that remained unclaimed, he notified the consignors. A jewelry company suggested that he try to dispose of the articles on commission. This he did, and was so successful that he was soon doing a small mail order business. After two years he left Wolsey, found a partner, and organized one of the world's largest mail order houses.

North of Wolsey US 14 branches L.; US 281 R.

WESSINGTON, 124.5 *m*. (1,419 alt.), which received its name from the range of nearby hills, is often confused with Wessington Springs, located about 30 m. S. On its main street are often seen huge transportation trucks parked beside the teams and wagons that bring produce from the back country.

ST. LAWRENCE, 136.7 *m*. (1,580 alt.), is the center of a rather extensive dairying region, and at different times has led all other towns along this branch of the Chicago & North Western R. R. in shipment of cream.

MILLER, 139 *m*. (1,587 alt.), was named for its first settler, Henry Miller. The town has a large new SWIMMING POOL (*open to visitors; moderate charge*). On the second floor of the Hand Co. courthouse here is a free exhibit of Sioux and Arikara Indian relics.

At 145 *m*. is the junction with a graveled road.

Left on this road is MILLERDALE, a Hutterite colony established in 1948. This group is an offshot of the sect which lived at Milltown, a colony on the James River in Hutchinson Co., for many years before migrating to Canada during the war. Although they still spin wool from their own sheep for clothing, in their communal kitchen they use a refrigerator, deep freeze; mixer, electric bread slicer, and other modern appliances.

The flat haylands along US 14 produce blue grass seed (*see AGRICULTURE*). In mid-summer the prairies are rich red-brown until the stripping machines extract the seed and leave short yellow stems. The stripping does not damage the hay which is a valuable feed crop in this vast livestock growing area.

At 150 *m*. is the junction with a graveled road.

Right on this road is the LAKE LOUISE STATE RECREATION AREA, 6 *m*. A 320-acre park surrounds the lake which was formed as a WPA project by damming Wolf Creek. There are camping and picnicking facilities, and fishing is popular.

At 150.2 *m*. is a junction with a graded road.

Left is REE HEIGHTS, 0.8 *m.* (1,731 alt.), from which picnic trips to the Ree Hills can be taken.

The REE HILLS to the S. were named for the Arikara Indians, commonly known as the Rees. Wooded ravines and lookouts from which miles of country can be seen, were used in pioneer times as a hide-out by horse and cattle rustlers, according to tradition. Cattle and horses stolen as far south as Nebraska were brought into the Ree Hills and hidden; later they were taken in small bunches to various markets—Pierre, Bismarck, Aberdeen. When traffic on the trail to Fort Pierre became heavy, the hills were abandoned by the rustlers and were then used by bull-whackers as a place to rest and view the trail ahead.

HIGHMORE, 162 *m.* (1.890 alt.), seat of Hyde Co., received its name through a foreign railroad worker's imperfect command of English. The foreigner, attempting to inform his fellow workers that the land rises gradually to the W. of Ree Heights, announced repeatedly, "high more," and as a consequence named a growing community. A STATE EXPERIMENT FARM (*open*) on the highway (L) is used especially for testing leguminous crops.

Here is the junction with State 47 (*see Tour 4A*).

HOLABIRD, 170 *m.,* consists of a garage and oil stations along the highway.

HARROLD, 177 *m.* (1,801 alt.), was founded with the coming of the railroad in 1881, and might be termed a "mushroom village," as it grew to approximately its present population in about one month in 1883.

BLUNT, 190.2 *m.* (1,621 alt.), for more than 20 years was the center of a wide trade territory, and at one time had a population of more than 2,000. But with the building of a new railroad line to the N. in the early 1900's, the town's prosperity waned steadily.

At the W. edge of the village, a half-block off the highway, is the MENTOR GRAHAM HOUSE (*open; free*), being restored by the South Dakota Historical Society. It was the last home of one of Abraham Lincoln's teachers and the man who is said to have exerted tremendous influence on Lincoln's thinking. The house was purchased in 1947 at a tax sale and it is being refurnished in the style of the 1880's.

When Mentor Graham was a teacher in Sangamon County, Illinois, Lincoln lived in the Graham home for six months and is believed to have absorbed many of the teacher's opinions on slavery, temperance, religion, and government. Lincoln's first platform, when he ran for the Illinois Legislature, was written by Mentor Graham. When Lincoln was inaugurated president, Graham was invited to sit on the platform. After Lincoln's death, Graham continued to teach for several years, then moved to Dakota Territory in 1883 to join his son on a homestead near Blunt. He died in this house in 1886.

Blunt is also the locale of the novel *Prayer for Tomorrow* by Hyatt Downing.

At 194.4 *m.* is the junction with US 83 (*see Tour 12*); US 14 and US 83 are united to the W. approach of the Missouri River Bridge.

A streamlined highway to Pierre has replaced former US 14 which took a circuitous route over river buttes and through draws. At 208.2 *m.* is the junction with an improved road.

Left on this road is the PIERRE MUNICIPAL AIRPORT, 0.9 *m.*, and the U.S. ARMY CORPS OF ENGINEERS OAHE DISTRICT OFFICES. The airport was built by the U.S. Air Force during World War II and turned over to the City of Pierre. It has regular commercial airline service (Western Airlines). The Army established offices here in 1949, to supervise construction of the Oahe Dam across the Missouri River.
Near the airport is LAKE ARIKARA, an artificial body of water formed by damming a dry creek bed. To the N is the SITE OF AN ARIKARA INDIAN VILLAGE, marked by mounds and excavations.

At 210 *m.* is the junction with the Oahe Observation Road.

Right on this road at 1.5 *m.* is the CENTER MONUMENT, erected in 1923 to mark the center of South Dakota. It also is supposed to mark the approximate center of North America, in common with similar markers in North Dakota and Nebraska. This monument has been moved three times as roads have been changed. The long winding ridge on which the monument stands is called SNAKE BUTTE, the scene of another Indian legend of a brave young Ree who ran into an ambush of his arch enemies, the Sioux. Though mortally wounded and reeling with pain, he ran a lurching, swaying course until he dropped. In admiration of his bravery the Sioux placed a rock on every drop of blood that dripped as he ran. In the center they placed their own symbol, the turtle. The result is a winding line of rocks, nearly a half mile in length. A fence has been placed around the figure of the turtle. The OAHE DAM OBSERVATION POINT, 6 *m.*, overlooks the Missouri River Valley and the Oahe Reservoir area. Moving of earth for the gigantic dam was begun in 1950 as part of the Pick-Sloan plan for developing the Missouri Basin. It is one of a series of dams under U.S. Government construction designed to provide hydroelectric power, flood control, irrigation, and navigation control. Cost of the Oahe Dam is estimated at $281,000,000. Most directly affected by the project is nearby Pierre (*see CITIES*).
When completed the Oahe Dam will be the tallest of the Missouri River dams and its crest will stretch 2 miles between the high river bluffs on each side. The reservoir, when completely filled, is to be 250 miles long, reaching beyond Mobridge (*see Tour 2*). A supplemental irrigation project includes pumping of water to the area around Huron (*see CITIES*).
Lying to the N. of the Observation Pt., along the E. bank of the river, are several historic points of interest in the wake of the reservoir waters. They include the Oahe Chapel, built in 1877, the Harney Cabin which dates back to 1855, and numerous Lewis and Clark campsites.
Across the river, below the dam, is the SITE OF FT. PIERRE CHATEAU, built in 1831 as a fur trading post, forerunner of the present towns of Pierre and Fort Pierre. A winding road leads northward from the Observation point 16 *m.* to the SITE OF FORT SULLY, built in 1866 as a consolidation of the old and new forts of the same name. During the Messiah War of 1890 it was used as a central point for outfitting military expeditions. Mayor Fiorello H. La Guardia of New York lived here as a youth, while his father served as post bandmaster. Foundations of the old buildings are still almost intact and the several cisterns used there are in a good state of repair. (Note: Visitors are warned to watch for uncovered cisterns.) The buildings of the fort occupied the rim of a flat and extended along the slopes. On the hill is a monument recently erected to mark the historic site. The fort was abandoned in the early 1890's.
South of the site of the fort, 1.2 *m.* (R), are traces of an old Arikara Indian village, depressions and mounds. Pieces of pottery and occasionally arrowheads can be found.

US 14 descends into Pierre at 211 m.

Section b. Pierre—Rapid City, 180 m.

PIERRE, (1,440 alt.), (*see PIERRE*).

State Capitol, Memorial Hall, Riverside Park.

US 14 crosses the Missouri River at 1.2 m. At the bridge is a time change (*CST on the east side; MST on the west side*).

At 2 m. is the junction with US 83 (*see Tour 12*). The new highway misses Fort Pierre (*see Tour 12*) and follows the old route of the Deadwood Trail which served the Black Hills from this direction until the railroads built across the western half of the State in 1907.

Winding serpent-like across approximately 200 m. of prairie, the Deadwood Trail in gold-rush days served as the main artery of travel and transportation from Pierre to the feverish mining camps of the Black Hills. Over this trail passed the huge, slow freight wagons, the stagecoaches with their relays of fast horses, and the colorful, motley throng of adventurers, gold-seekers, cowboys, gamblers, and outlaws.

At 2.7 m. is the junction with the Oahe Access Road.

Right on this road is the SITE OF OLD FORT PIERRE 2.4 m. Relics of the early days, when fur traders, trappers, and soldiers made the vicinity their headquarters, can still be found. Several other so-called forts, actually only trading posts, were once established in this vicinity. They were designated on the map as Ft. Tecumseh, Ft. Galpin and Military Fort. Although the original fort was established near the site of the present town of Fort Pierre, it was moved to this point two years later.

Beyond the site of old Fort Pierre (L) is the HOME OF JAMES "SCOTTY" PHILIP, 3 m., formerly called the "buffalo king," because when the shaggy range lords were virtually exterminated, he purchased a small herd and built it up in a mammoth pasture near his home. At the time of Philip's death in 1911 there were nearly 1,000 buffaloes in the herd. In the yard around his home is his grave.

At 4 m. is the back of the OAHE DAM, including the spillway and outlet tunnels.

At 10.5 m. US 14 crosses WILLOW CREEK, which in freighting days, between Fort Pierre and the Black Hills, was an almost impassable hazard in wet weather, the heavy gumbo soil of its valley clinging to wagon wheels and paralyzing travel.

HAYES, 33 m., in the era of the big cattlemen, was a typical cowboy center with most of the characteristics of the "wild and woolly" days—saloon, dance hall, general store, hitching posts. The site of the original town was one-half mile S. of the present hamlet, and a tall, unpainted building was at one time used as a dance hall.

At 35.5 m. is the Methodist Episcopal LITTLE BROWN CHURCH ON THE HILL (R). Just as the town of Nashua, Iowa, became famous through its *Little Brown Church in the Vale,* immortalized in the hymn of Dr. William S. Pitts, this little prairie church is known in a lesser degree throughout most of western South Dakota. As the Church in the Vale earned wide attention for its many weddings each year, the Hayes Church is receiving similar note in its community, many couples having taken their marriage vows here since the present structure was erected in 1923. Beginning in 1908 with a handful of homesteaders as a nucleus, the church has weathered the years of depopulation caused by continued droughts, when settlers, discouraged, left their holdings to return East.

At 61.9 m., just before descending into the Bad River Valley at Midland, is the junction with a dirt road.

Left on this road is CAPA, 10 m., of interest because of its hot mineral baths. The source of the water for baths is a deep artesian well. The water is piped to a pool in the Capa Hotel, where treatments are given for all kinds of rheumatism and muscular pains.

MIDLAND, 62.2 m. (1,878 alt.), was given its name because it was supposed to be midway between the Missouri River and the south fork of the Cheyenne River. It was one of the towns engaged in a riotous county seat contest in 1914, when rambling Stanley Co. was divided (see PHILIP below). At the NW. edge of town is LAKE CHO-KA-YA, an artificial body of water where swimming and fishing are available.

At 85.1 m. is SUNSHINE LAKE (L), built under a Federal program to provide a water supply, a road grade, and swimming and fishing facilities for the community.

PHILIP, 88 m. (2,159 alt.), was named for James "Scotty" Philip, the "buffalo king" (see above). The town was started with the extension of the railroad to the Black Hills in 1907. With many new business houses and a large new auditorium, Philip is the center of a vast farming and ranching section, its trade territory extending N. as far as 50 m.

Always a thriving little town, it staged a lively campaign in 1914 in an effort to become the seat of the newly created Haakon Co. Almost overnight five towns in the county—Philip, Nowlin, Powell, Midland, and Lucerne, the last merely an inland post office in the center of the county—joined the race. The result was an easy victory for Philip.

At the County Fair Grounds on the western edge of town a graded dirt road makes a slight turn and then runs directly W.

On this road is the SILENT GUIDE MONUMENT, 8 m., a recent improvement on an original rude stone monument, built in early days by a sheepman to mark the location of a waterhole that never failed. It figured in many disputes between the sheep and cattle ranchers and was torn down and rebuilt several times during the range feuds between the two traditional enemies. It was customary for cowboys to express their contempt for sheepherders by roping the monument and toppling it over whenever they happened along. At last one sheepherder, imbued with more courage than the rest, mounted the monument with a rifle and threatened to shoot any cowboy who attempted to molest him. The monument, on a high hill near the road (L), is visible for miles. It was rebuilt in 1924 through public subscription.

US 14 turns L. at Philip, crosses Bad River and winds over a series of hills.

At 94 *m.* is the junction with US 16 (*see Tour 5*); US 14 and US 16 are united for 86 *m.*, between the junction and Rapid City, 180 *m.* (*See Tour 5, Section b.*)

Section c. Rapid City to Wyoming Line, 67 m.

RAPID CITY, (3,196 alt.). (*See RAPID CITY.*)

State School of Mines and Museum, Dinosaur Park, Alex Johnson Hotel, Canyon Lake, Hangman's Hill, U.S. Indian Museum, Dinosaur Park, Rapid City Air Force Base, and gold jewelry manufacture.

Here is the junction with US 16 (*see Tour 5*), and with the Rim Rock Trail (*see Tour 4B*).

From Rapid City, US 14 goes in a northerly direction, skirting the eastern edge of the Black Hills. The route parallels the old Sidney Trail which served the Deadwood and Lead gold camps with a stage coach line, pony express, and wagon freights from the railhead at Sidney, Neb.

At the outskirts of Rapid City is the SOUTH DAKOTA STATE CEMENT PLANT (R) (*see RAPID CITY and HISTORY*).

At 1.2 *m.* is the junction with a graveled road, a scenic drive connecting with US 85A (*see Tour 4C*).

The highway passes through rolling country of interesting soil formation. On one side of the road is red clay, and on the other is yellow, each making a sharp contrast with the grass and ever-greens. This area is alternately wooded and barren, with occasional small ranch houses.

At 5.6 *m.* is the BLACK HILLS KENNEL CLUB, a dog racing track, where pari-mutuel races are held nightly during the summer season. About 600 dogs are kept here during the summer for training and racing; the dogs are brought from Florida and are returned there each fall for the winter racing season.

BLACKHAWK, 7.6 *m.*, is a small town on Blackhawk Creek, with souvenir shops, gas stations, and a schoolhouse.

At 9.3 *m.* is a marker at the point where US 14 crosses the trail General Custer made as he was returning to Ft. Abraham Lincoln in North Dakota in 1874.

At 12.5 *m.* (R), near the highway, is a reproduction of the SID-NEY STOCKADE, an important stage station on the old Sidney-Deadwood and Pierre-Deadwood stage lines during gold rush days. It was the first station N. of Rapid City.

At 12.6 *m.* is a junction with a graded road, built on the roadbed of a narrow-gauge railroad used formerly by the Homestake Mining Co. to carry timber out of the Hills.

Left on this road to STAGE BARN CAVERNS, 2.2 *m.* (open; adm. fee; trip requires an hour). There are five openings, and the underground caves extend about one-half mile. The cave is situated in a limestone formation 500 ft. thick, and the walls show markings which indicate that the water remained at different levels for long periods of time. The rooms vary in height from a few feet to 20 ft. The walls are covered with calcite crystals and the cave has both stalactites and stalagmites. The cave is considered "alive," as its features are still in the process of formation. Various colors are present, and iron in solution gives many of the stalactites a reddish tinge.

At 13.8 *m.* is a junction with a graded road.

Right on this road is the TIMBER OF AGES, 1.2 *m.* (adm. charge), comprising a collection of petrified wood. The 60-acre tract has huge stumps and long logs which show the structure of trees in petrification, such as the limbs, roots, bark, growth rings, knotholes, indents of rot, mineral coloring, agate, crystals, and cycads. Small pieces are plentiful. This group of petrified trees is in the Minnewasta layer of the Dakota Sandstone, and, according to scientists who have examined the area, it is considered approximately 100 million years old.

PIEDMONT, 14.5 *m.*, furnishes supplies to ranches of the region and caters to tourists who stop there.

US 14 follows Elk River valley and crosses Elk Creek at 17.1 *m.*

BLACK HILLS ROCK MUSEUM, 17.3 *m.* (L), is a private collection of rocks, crystals, and petrified wood, some specimens of which are for sale.

At 17.4 *m.* is the junction with a graveled road.

Left on this road is the route to CRYSTAL CAVE, 5.5 *m.* (adm. fee. Free crystal souvenir to every visitor. Trips every half hour, day or night, year around.)
The cave has been compared in appearance to a huge sponge, with all its windings, galleries, rooms and turnings. Unlike the dead color of a sponge, each of these passages is lined with glittering crystals, above, below, and on the sides. Every projecting rock is covered and every recess lined with gleaming calcite crystals. In the wealth of crystals there is no monotony. In one room the formations are pointed and glittering; in another rounded and dull. Impurities have given some of them a deep yellowish tinge, and in one room they resemble a quantity of prodigious baked beans. Sometimes boxwork, deeply encrusted with crystals, is visible on the ceiling. The cave has 50 m. of explored rooms and 22 m. of paths.
In the lower room of the explored part—some of the cave is still inaccessible— there are pools of clear, cool water with stalactite and stalagmite formations, sometimes with a combination of the two. There are places where the crystals have been of necessity broken in making passages, the exposed rock resembling choice cuts of beef with streaks of fat running through. Occasionally a crack in the crystal walls will be marked by a thin red line where water seeping through has deposited iron and left it to oxidize.

At 17.6 *m.* is the junction with a graveled road.

Left on this road is WONDERLAND CAVE, 5.4 *m.* (adm. fee). Competent guides conduct regular trips through the cave, an hour and 15 minutes being required to make the trip.
Though not as large as some in the region, it has many strange and fantastic formations such as "The Sheep," "The Frozen River," "The Madonna and Her Child," "The Icicle Fence," and many other weird and beautiful forms, built through countless ages by the steady drip of mineral-laden water. The cave, discovered in 1931, is

now equipped with a complete electric lighting system. Stalactites hanging from the roof join with stalagmites reaching up from the floor.

At 24.5 *m*. is the FORT MEADE NATIONAL CEMETERY, established in 1948. Soldiers who lost their lives in Indian conflicts and were buried at the battlegrounds of the Northwest have been moved here, along with the dead of World War I and II from this area.

DEAD MAN CREEK, 28.5 *m*., is crossed just S. of Sturgis. On its banks (R) is a monument of varicolored stones to the memory of Charles Nolin, a pony mail carrier, who was killed and scalped by the Indians at this point. The monument is in the form of a shaft and is surrounded by an ornamental fence with posts constructed of like material. Behind the monument are five black walnut trees growing from the slips obtained from five historic American battle-fields including Gettysburg, Valley Forge, and Antietam.

STURGIS, 28.6 *m*. (3,432 alt.), was named by Maj. S. D. Sturgis, who was in command of nearby Fort Meade when the town-site was laid out in 1878, in honor of his son, Lt. J. G. Sturgis, a cavalry officer who lost his life with General Custer in the Battle of the Little Big Horn.

It is in the extreme southwestern portion of Meade Co., and it is said that many residents of the county, particularly in the north-eastern portion, have never visited their county seat. Meade Co. is the largest in the State, its area exceeding the combined areas of Rhode Island and Delaware.

The town was nicknamed "Scooptown," or "Scoop," from the fact that Sturgis was originally populated by the usual type of camp following. There was a saying among the soldiers that when you visited in town you were apt to get "scooped" or "cleaned out."

The early population of Sturgis was made up largely of bull-whackers, due to the large amount of supplies required by the military post and citizens. With the building of toll roads into Dead-wood from the N. in 1877–78, all heavy freighting was routed to circle the Hills along the eastern flank, this being a much easier route to follow. All travel from the S. came this way, and the route from Pierre was forked at the Cheyenne River to head in directly for Sturgis with all freight intended for Deadwood and the northern Hills. This made of Sturgis quite a metropolis in a very short time, so that its one main street was literally teeming with life all day long and most of the night.

Among the more colorful characters identified with Sturgis was a woman known as Poker Alice, the cigar-smoking madam of a popular brothel.

For 65 years Fort Meade was a cavalry post, but during World War II it was converted into a Veterans facility for those whom com-bat left with mental and nervous disorders. For a town that had grown up with rough and ready soldiers, Sturgis promptly made the care and comfort of these veterans its major project. The Fort Meade Veterans Hospital in 1951, had a capacity of 720 patients, and there were 410 employees.

Sturgis today is an important trade and tourist center. The Black Hills and Badlands Association maintains its headquarters here. People of the region consider Sturgis a gay "Saturday Night" town. Annual events include the Jack Pine Gypsy Tour and Motorcycle races in August, and the Key City Rodeo in early September.

1. Right from the center of Sturgis on State 24 is the FORT MEADE VETERANS HOSPITAL, 2 m. Since 1944 the buildings and grounds of the old cavalry post have been used by the Veterans Administration.

The fort was laid out in 1878 by Gen. Phil Sheridan who galloped over the prairie and pointed where he wanted each building. It was named in honor of Gen. George B. Meade, leader of the Union forces at the Battle of Gettysburg. Some of the original buildings still stand near the W. entrance, but they have been refaced with cut stone. The reservation consists of 13,127 acres.

The Seventh Cavalry at one time was stationed at Fort Meade. When Gen. George A. Custer led this regiment in the battle of the Little Big Horn, the Indians killed every living being except one horse, "Commanche," and he was found two days later, riddled with bullets, standing in a small stream of water. He was taken first to Fort Lincoln and later moved with the regiment to Fort Meade where he lived for 10 years. When the regiment was transferred to Fort Riley, Kan., he was moved also. When he died, at an advanced age, he was accorded military honors.

The Fourth Cavalry occupied the fort between World Wars I and II, boasting outstanding polo and jumping teams. Mechanized cavalry units were developed here and, for a time, the post was used for training airborne troops.

2. Right from the center of Sturgis on State 79 is an improved road to BEAR BUTTE, 5 m. (4,422 alt.). Rising like a huge mound of dirt dumped there by human hands, the Butte was named "Mato Paha" (Ind. bear hill) because to them it resembled a huge bear, as seen from the NE. Standing detached from the Black Hills proper, like a last outpost, this mass of earth rises 1,200 ft. above the prairie surrounding it. The N. and W. sides are so abrupt that they are inaccessible, even to experienced hikers; but the eastern slope is more gradual, and from this direction the summit can be reached.

At the base of the butte is BEAR BUTTE LAKE, formed by water from an artesian well sunk in an attempt to locate oil. There are swimming facilities here, and the area is part of a waterfowl refuge. A corral of donkeys is kept near here for rent to visitors who wish to be carried to the summit of Bear Butte. Legends of the Butte tell how different tribes held possession of this sacred mound, which was the goal of an annual pilgrimage of worship as well as their watch and signal tower. Traces on top show that fires have been kept burning for days at a time. Records were kept by different tribes by placing rocks in the forks of trees and thereby showing which tribe was in possession. The Mandans are said to have made annual pilgrimages to Bear Butte as long as they were permitted to do so. The Cheyennes took the territory from the Mandans, and later the Sioux absorbed the Cheyennes who held possession when the white man claimed it by treaty. The Mandans held an annual religious festival called "Mee-nee-ro-da-ha-sha" (sinking down or settling waters).

Nu-mahk-muck-a-nan, they believed, was the only man saved from a flood. He landed his canoe on a "high mountain in the West." Every year the Mandans believed they must make some sacrifice to the water, and this sacrifice must be of sharp-edged tools, as the canoe was made by similar instruments. They also believed they must visit the mountains or else another flood would come and no one would be saved. The time for pilgrimage was when the willow leaf was in full growth. According to tradition, a turtle dove was sent out from the canoe and it returned with a willow twig on which the leaves were in full growth. Therefore the dove was regarded as a medicine bird and the Indians considered its destruction a crime.

At Sturgis is the junction of US 14 and US 14A, the latter being an alternate, less-mountainous route to Spearfish.

Right on US 14A, an oil-surfaced road, are open prairie and foothills. WHITEWOOD CREEK is crossed at 6 m. The waters of this stream are black with mill tailings from the Homestake Gold Mine at Lead (*see CITIES*). WHITEWOOD, 7.1 *m*. (3,625 alt.), is a picturesque village, so named because of the extensive growth of aspen and birch trees in the vicinity. It was platted in 1888 when the C. & N.W. RR. by-passed bustling Crook City, just over the hill to the W. The ghost town of CROOK CITY has only a log cabin and an unkept, lonely cemetery left from its days of glory when it was one of the wildest towns of the Gold Rush era. On the Fourth of July 1876, the day began with gun play but it was decided not to bury the dead until after the races were over. At one time Crook City had a population of nearly three thousand. US 14A skirts the WHITEWOOD HILL, from which is a striking view of the mountain valleys leading out of the northern Black Hills. CENTENNIAL PRAIRIE, settled in 1876 by a group of Iowa farmers to provide vegetables for the mining camps, forms a broad valley over which the highway passes. At 12.4 m. US 14A rejoins US 14.

Between Sturgis and Deadwood, US 14 rises 1,000 ft. through BOULDER CANYON with its high limestone cliffs and heavy pine timber, a scenic drive.

At 34.5 *m.* is a boundary of the BLACK HILLS NATIONAL FOREST (*hqs. Deadwood*). Branching off the highway (L) are backwoods forest trails leading to logging camps, small mines, and hunting camps. Best known gulches off Boulder Canyon are Two Bit and Lost, both of which are pock-marked with mine diggings.

At 41.4 *m.*, at the E. edge of Deadwood (*see CITIES*), is a junction with US 85 (*see Tour 13*); US 14 and 85 are united to Spearfish.

At 42.4 *m*, at the summit of the hill above Deadwood, is PINE CREST CAMP. There are many cabins in a picturesque setting on a pine-covered slope. There are laundry facilities, a camp store, and playground equipment.

Left from this point is the CABIN OF DEADWOOD DICK, 0.3 *m.*, where Deadwood Dick of dime novel fame lived until his recent death. (Open to visitors; free.) Up the mountain side from the cabin, is a footpath to the summit of Sunrise Mountain, where, blasted out of solid rock, is the GRAVE OF DEADWOOD DICK. It is close to the junction of the old Bismarck Trail with the Pony Express trail between Pierre and Deadwood, and overlooks the town which is so closely associated with the romance of his name. From this point can be seen not only Deadwood and Lead, but also Terry Peak, Custer Peak, and Mt. Roosevelt, with Bear Butte in the distance.
Deadwood has always had a penchant for Deadwood Dicks. The original was Richard Clark, who is said to have driven the first stage into Deadwood. It was he who was the apocryphal hero of a thousand hair-raising, blood-and-thunder Wild West tales written in New York City and not intended to be believed by anyone. But they spread the fame of Deadwood and its mythical hero to the four corners of the country. Whether the occupant of the present "grave of Deadwood Dick" is the original of that name is beside the point.

At 43.3 *m.*, the crest of the hill, is the PREACHER SMITH MONUMENT. The Rev. Henry Weston Smith, a Methodist minister and itinerant preacher, was the first to exercise his profession in the Hills. On the 20th of August, 1876, he set out from Deadwood for Crook City, in spite of the fact that he had been warned that to do so was dangerous. Shortly after, word was brought to Crook City that he had been found, killed by Indians, five m. from Deadwood at a place called "The Rest." A party of men set out from Crook City and carried his body to Deadwood. On Aug. 20, 1914, exactly 38 years after he had been murdered, the Society of Black Hills Pioneers unveiled a monument to his memory on the spot where he met his fate. On each anniversary of his death, his last sermon is read at a memorial service.

From the Preacher Smith Monument the road runs for miles down a narrow winding gulch, and clings to the hillside above the creek, with thickly wooded hills on either side. Since most of the timber is pine, it is difficult to say whether the scenery is more attractive in summer or in winter when the pines show green against the snow. This is the far-famed DEADWOOD HILL, one of the memorable drives in the Black Hills.

At 46.5 m. is HALFWAY HOUSE, early-day stage station still in operation although methods of transportation have changed.

At 47.5 m. is the junction with US 14A (see above).

Here also is the junction with the St. Onge Road.

Right on this road is ST. ONGE, 5 m., settled as a French colony in 1881, and named for Pitoche St. Onge, prominent member of the group.

At 50 m. is the BLACK HILLS AIRPORT, dedicated in the summer of 1936 and serving the towns of Deadwood, Lead, and Spearfish. There are three main buildings constructed of native limestone quarried nearby. The main hangar has accommodation for thirty planes. There is a repair shop of almost the same size for the servicing of planes; also an administration building, with accommodations for pilots and passengers, a coffee shop, radio room, and lobby. Western Airlines stops here; and there is charter and transient aircraft service. In winter, local airplanes are equipped with skiis.

SPEARFISH, 54.5 m. (3,637 alt.), took its name from a rather apocryphal incident of the early days. One old-timer was supposed to have remarked to another as he stood on the banks of a stream, "This would be a good place to spear fish," and forthwith the creek and future town were named.

The nickname of Spearfish is "The Queen City," because the hills surround it like a diadem. To the E., overlooking the town, is the lofty peak of Lookout; to the W. is Crow Peak; and to the S. Spearfish Mountain.

The town lies on both sides of Spearfish Creek and at the mouth of beautiful Spearfish Canyon, one of the most popular scenic and recreational areas in the Black Hills (see Tour 13A).

Spearfish has a variety of interests. It is the home of a co-educa-
tional college and the widely-traveled Luenen religious drama group;
here, too, is a Federal fish hatchery, a large sawmill operated on the
prairie by a gold mining company, and California-like roadside fruit
markets.

The BLACK HILLS PASSION PLAY AMPHITHEATRE is
the scene of regular performances (*every Tuesday, Thursday, and
Sunday evening*) during the summer, of the production that originated in the Cappenberg Monastery at Luenen, Germany, in 1242.
Josef Meier, who portrays the part of Christus, brought the Passion
Play to America in the early 1930's because of Nazi interference, and
in 1938 selected Spearfish as the kind of community most like that
in which the play had been given since the 13th century. The natural
amphitheatre seats 8,000 persons. The stage is nearly three blocks
long. For the summer performances local residents make up a large
part of the cast of 250. The camels and other animals are kept at
Meier's farm nearby. Each winter the play tours the larger cities in
the U.S.

The campus of BLACK HILLS TEACHERS COLLEGE is
spread out on high ground overlooking the town, with shade trees
and a creek forming a park around the buildings. It was founded in
1883, as Spearfish Normal School and had a steady growth until the
1930's when, during a State economy wave, only a two-year course
was offered. However, it has been restored to a four-year school
offering a B.S. degree, and serves as a branch of the University of
South Dakota. A large men's dormitory was added in 1950. Its summer school draws students from throughout the country. Regional
art is fostered by the college. The athletic teams are known as the
Yellowjackets and the annual homecoming is Swarm Day.

In CITY PARK is the old DEADWOOD STAGECOACH, a
sturdy relic of the early days in the Black Hills. Harvey Fellows,
who had driven the stage more than 300,000 miles without an acci-
dent, fell from the coach during a parade and died.

The park is in two sections. One of these is a cabin camp just
opposite the U.S. Fish Hatchery. The other, without cabins, serves
as a city park as well as a place where tourists may pitch their tents
or park their trailers. It is one of the most attractive parks in the
Hills. Bordering Spearfish Creek and faced by a rock cliff on the
other side, it is shaded by great trees. Red squirrels and robins
glean the scraps that the visitors leave. Campers may catch trout
within a few yards of their tents.

There is also a community building with a good collection of
native and other curios. A store supplies the needs of the campers,
and gas for cooking, as well as laundry facilities are available. There
is a large dance pavilion in which dances for the townspeople are
held weekly.

Just S. of the city park is the u.s. fish hatchery (*open to
visitors*), established in 1899 for the purpose of hatching fish with

which to stock the streams and lakes of the Black Hills region. This hatchery is now engaged in the propagation of brook, rainbow, Loch-Leven, and black-spotted trout. A brood stock of rainbow and brook trout is maintained at the hatchery in open ponds. This stock supplies part of the eggs from which the small fish are hatched to be used in stocking streams. Additional eggs of these species are sometimes shipped to this hatchery from other States.

The Spearfish hatchery raises approximately 2½ million fish each year, varying in size from two to five inches. These fish are supplied to any person free of charge for stocking public waters. There is one commercial hatchery in Spearfish which sells trout to hotels and restaurants.

At the W. edge of town is the HOMESTAKE SAWMILL which turns out 50,000 board feet of lumber daily for use in gold mining operations. Logs are hauled by truck from forest areas and floated in the mill pond.

At Spearfish is the junction with the Spearfish Canyon Highway, State 89 (*see Tour 13A*).

US 14 and US 85 run north through orchards and irrigated gardens.

At 56.5 *m.* is the junction with US 85 (*see Tour 13*); U.S. 14 turns west. The Bear Lodge Mountains of Wyoming loom ahead.

At 67 *m.* US 14 crosses the Wyoming Line 2 m. E. of Beulah, Wyo. (*see Wyoming State Guide, Tour 10*).

Tour 4A

Highmore—Crow Creek Reservation—Fort Thompson—Lower Brule Reservation—Chamberlain. State 47.
Highmore to Chamberlain, 54 m.
No R.R. paralleling this route; no bus line.
Usual accommodations at Highmore and Chamberlain.
Graveled roadbed.

STATE 47 branches south from US 14 at Highmore, 0 *m.* (*see Tour 4*). Few houses are seen along the highway between Highmore and Fort Thompson. For the entire distance of 30 m. between the two towns the road is straight as a plumb line, and the topography, except when State 47 plunges down into the Missouri River valley, is level or gently rolling.

The CROW CREEK RESERVATION (*open to public*) is entered at 17.2 *m.*, and the region is featured by upland stretches covered with buffalo grass, where great herds of shaggy buffaloes grazed in the days of Indian hunters. During the hard winter of 1934, farmers in the country N. of this section drove their wagons over these flats and gathered loads of dried cow dung for fuel, just as in the early days homesteaders picked up "buffalo chips" to burn.

At the western edge of the reservation, in the pocket formed by the Big Bend of the Missouri River, are sheep and cattle ranches and small farms owned by both white and Indian settlers.

Although several Sioux tribes are represented on the reservation, the land was set aside by the government primarily for the Lower Yanktonais.

At 19.5 *m.* is STEPHAN, community center for the area and home of the IMMACULATE CONCEPTION MISSION (Catholic). The postoffice takes its name from Msgr. J. A. Stephan, director of the Bureau of Catholic Indian Missions. In 1886, the government granted 160 acres for a Catholic mission school and secular priests built a small frame building to serve as a school and dwelling. The next year Pius Boehm, a Benedictine monk, arrived with funds to start building a 2½ story school. Two Benedictine nuns assumed charge.

The mission has been beset by disasters to its buildings. In 1896 fire destroyed the newly-built school. By 1900 a church was built and the school rebuilt. Fire again swept through the mission in 1916. When Marty Hall was constructed, it was made fireproof. In 1924 the church was destroyed by a hurricane, and a new one built. An office building was erected in 1928, dormitories added in 1931, and more classrooms and laboratories provided in 1934. A prairie fire in 1943 destroyed the farm buildings, but the main mission buildings were saved.

There are usually about 250 Indian children attending the boarding school. The large chapel is the central church for the adult Catholic people of the surrounding country. The gymnasium is used as a center for community recreation. Sewing and work in Indian handicrafts are sponsored by the mission.

At Stephan is a junction with State 34, a new route across the reservation to Pierre.

FORT THOMPSON, 30.2 *m.*, is administrative headquarters for the Indians on the Crow Creek Reservation. As late as 1880 Crow Creek, as the post office was known, was an important stopping point on the stage route which began at Yankton and extended along the river, through Pierre, to northern posts. Traders' stores in Fort Thompson are typical of reservation posts—visiting and loafing places, as well as trading centers. Buildings are arranged in the form of a square, the office being in the center. The square is a holdover from the days when a stockade surrounded the group of buildings.

The fair grounds and exhibit hall are on the right of the entrance to the agency. All is quiet and deserted around this spot except on Fridays, when the Indians gather for business meetings of the tribe, or to engage in old Indian dances. In early September a fair is held here.

The reservation roll at the last census showed 1,132 Indians. As

Ranch, Range and Badlands

A BADLANDS WINDOW

BATTLESHIP BUTTE

ROUNDUP
CHUCKWAGON

BRANDING
SEASON

BRANDS MUSEUM,
BISON

RODEO AT
BELLE FOURCHE

SHEEP
COUNTRY

SIOUX MAIDENS

on other reservations, an Indian council governs many of the affairs of the tribe, the group holding regular meetings in the council room at the office building. The 10th and 25th of each month are ration days. At 8 a. m. on these days a food ration of flour, baking powder, coffee, sugar, pork, tomatoes, and prunes is given out at the commissary building to about 70 old and indigent Indians.

An excellent water supply plant was built in 1934 and pumps send purified water into the institutions and homes of the employes. The Indian population in general live in cabins, tents, and open-air shelters. Unsanitary conditions prevail, the water being hauled in open barrels to their homes.

A large proportion of the children of school age attend five schools on the reservation, the largest one of which is on the western edge.

A large collection of examples of old Indian art and craft work, decorated clothing and rude implements, is housed in the EPISCOPAL MISSION HOUSE (*open to public*). Modern pieces of beadwork and carving, products of a group of 20 Indians who use the name Crow Creek Crafts, are for sale.

Just W. of Fort Thompson SOLDIER CREEK marks the limits of the agency. On a bank of this creek, near the bridge, eight people were drowned in September 1933, when their house was carried away in a disastrous flood that rushed down the valley following a cloudburst.

Several small log and frame cabins in this vicinity are excellent examples of the type of houses that most Indians throughout the reservation occupy today. Sometimes a shade, or shelter, is built for summer use in front of these cabins. Shades are built of forked poles set in the ground, with more poles laid horizontally and thickly covered with leafy willows to form the roof. This well-ventilated room, sometimes called a "squaw cooler," is used as a special center for the family and visitors, its open-air sides enclosing a combined kitchen, dining-room, living room, bedroom and workshop. A village of white tents is generally seen in the vicinity of Fort Thompson. Round shades of bent willows, covered with fresh leaves, are set up in front of the tents to take advantage of the breeze and for additional sleeping quarters. Tuberculosis is prevalent here, as on other reservations.

At 32.2 *m.* is a junction with an unimproved dirt road.

Right on this road is a FERRY, 6.2 *m.*, reminiscent of the early days, which makes regular trips across the river to the LOWER BRULE RESERVATION, 6.9 *m.* The jurisdiction of this reservation has recently been combined with that of Crow Creek, only a sub-agency being maintained here now.
LOWER BRULE, 7.5 *m.*, is the headquarters for the little reservation on which barely 600 Indians reside. The small population was the chief reason for combining it with the Crow Creek reservation. Teton Sioux of the Sicangu tribe live on this reserve. "Brule" was derived by French traders from their translation of Sicangu (burned thighs). An old map of 1829 marks this area as occupied by "Tetons of

the Burntwood." These Indians are closely related to those of the Rosebud Reservation. Until 1890 the reservation extended S. to White River. When the reservation boundaries were changed, part of the Indians moved W. to Rosebud.

At Lower Brule is the lower end of the famous BIG BEND, a 45 m. loop, noted in the journals of every river explorer. At the time of the War of 1812, Manuel Lisa was made agent for all the Indians on the upper Missouri River. He established a strong trading post in the vicinity of Big Bend. When fur traders ascended the river, parties often left their boats at the turn and walked the 4 m. across the neck of the loop. The account of Elias J. Marsh (1859) tells how such a party had to wait overnight for their boat to navigate the distance around the bend to rejoin them. A Federal dam at Big Bend is part of the Missouri River Basin Development Program being undertaken in the State (*see History*).

From Lower Brule the dirt road winds a sinuous course along the rough, jumbled breaks of the Missouri River to IRON NATION, 12.3 *m.*, a store and post office situated near the river. Along the road, spread fanwise from Iron Nation, are the scattered homes of Indians comprising this community. A white church—Messiah Chapel, Episcopal—stands on a hill near the road. Below the hill a large spring has been walled in and a pump placed over it. Lower Brule Reservation is marked by scenes that vary little from those of a hundred years ago, the few Indian houses, rude outbuildings, and occasional barbwire fences, comprising the only advance upon the primitive.

The post office was named for Chief Iron Nation, leader of the Brules when this tribe began to adopt civilized ways. Over this area Iron Nation and his band roamed during the last days of the red man's untrammeled wanderings. Medicine Creek in this vicinity was the headquarters for the bands, as they sallied into the prairie country to hunt buffalo. Numerous dams, constructed under a Government works program, with many wells placed at advantageous points on the several reservations, have helped solve the water problem that periodically becomes acute. The average Sioux Indian is not particular about the source of his water supply, sanitation playing an insignificant role in his choice.

From Fort Thompson, State 47 spirals down the valley of the Missouri River, winding near the shores, dipping into hollows, and lifting over ridges. Remains of Indian life are still seen at various places near the road. Arrowhead seekers have found many relics of early days scattered along the valley. Trenches, used by the Ree or Arikara Indians more than a century ago for defense, are found in different places, and when State 47 was constructed it cut through a forgotten Indian burial ground.

At 40.1 *m.* is CROW CREEK, for which the reservation is named. Several miles of the valley can be seen from the highway along the hilltops, and many Indian homes are visible, the stream being a favorite camping ground of the Sioux. At the mouth of Crow Creek tribes once met for councils. The place is called the "Sioux Pass of the Three Rivers" in Lewis and Clark journals, because two other creeks, Elm and Campbell, empty into the Missouri River near here.

BEDASHOSHA LAKE (L), formed by damming Crow Creek, bears the Sioux equivalent of "roily waters." The 487-acre lake, which backs up 10 miles, holds back flood waters from the Missouri R. and provides a recreation area on the reservation. The earthen dam was constructed during the 1930's.

At 43 *m.* is the S. boundary of the Crow Creek Indian Reservation.

At 53.2 *m.* (R) is ST. JOSEPH'S INDIAN MISSION, a Catholic school for Indian children from the Crow Creek and Lower Brule reservations (*see Chamberlain*).

CHAMBERLAIN, 54 *m.* (1,363 alt.) (*see Tour 5*), is at the junction with US 16 (*see Tour 5*).

Tour 4B

Rapid City—Junction with US 85A (Pactola). An unnumbered road known as the Rim Rock Trail, 16 m.
Usual accommodations at Rapid City; dude ranches along route.
Roadbed graveled.

THIS road, known as the Rim Rock Trail, is primarily a scenic route, but it also affords a short cut between Rapid City and US 85A, 2 m. N. of Pactola. The views, after the road has climbed the hill above the valley of Rapid Creek, are exceptional. Typical Black Hills scenery, pines, parks, and mountain streams, are in evidence for the rest of the route.

With the abandonment after World War II of the colorful Rapid City, Black Hills & Western R.R., this route utilizes or crosses the railroad grade in places. While the little railroad followed Rapid Canyon for 35 tortuous miles, during which the creek was crossed 105 times, the highway parallels the picturesque canyon in which are found some of the best trout ponds in the Hills.

The Rim Rock Trail runs W. from Canyon Lake, which is just within the city limits of Rapid City (*see RAPID CITY*).

At 0.6 *m.* (L) is a STATE FISH HATCHERY (*adm. free*). Here several different kinds of trout are raised to "fingerling size" and then planted in the creeks. This service to fishermen has succeeded in keeping a normal supply of trout in the streams. The pools in the hatchery have been repaired and in some cases entirely remade to improve the rearing ponds. Full-grown rainbow and Loch-Leven trout are in the N. pond.

In Rapid Canyon are many large residences and a few public lodges.

At 1.9 *m.* is a junction with a graded road.

Right on this road is NAMELESS CAVE, 2 *m.,* (*adm. fee*). Like other caves in the Black Hills its many rooms contain beautiful crystalline formations. Here are stalactites and stalagmites—"The Frozen River," "Palisades," "The Devil's Kitchen," "Fairies Hallway," and many other unusual formations. Well-formed crystals and frostwork of crystal aggregates coat the rock surfaces in great profusion and delicacy. The cave is 75 ft. below the surface of the ground and is easily reached by a stairway.
The limestone formation in which the cave is found is said to be 290 million years old and contains fossils such as corals, gastropods, and brachiopods.

At 2.3 *m.* a road branches (L) into DARK CANYON, which is one of the natural phenomena of the region because a small stream has eroded such a deep rent into the rock that the sun seldom penetrates parts of the canyon.

The Rim Rock Road winds (R) upward, with the cliff faces showing strata running in several different directions, betokening some former violent convulsion of nature.

At 4.1 *m.* the road emerges upon the RIM ROCK, overlooking the valley below. Many beautiful views are obtainable along this stretch of road. Below lies the trail just traveled, and the creek which cuts its way along the bottom of the gorge.

At 4.8 *m.* the road enters the Black Hills National Forest and winds through the pines.

TRIANGLE I RANCH, 7.6 *m.*, established in 1882, is now a dude ranch and lodge for summer visitors.

Here is the junction with the Hisega Road.

Left on this road is the village of HISEGA, 1 *m.* It consists of a general store and numerous summer cabins. Many people suffering from hay fever and asthma spend their summers in the vicinity. In the fall, it is a mecca for deer hunters. The name was derived when, at the opening of a lodge here by Pierre citizens, the initials of the given names of the first six young women visitors were used; they happened to be named Helen, Ida, Sadie, Ethel, Grace, and Ada. Down Rapid Creek from Hisega about 2 m., on foot, the waters of the creek issue from a seven-ft. hole in a rocky wall. In 1878, when prospectors first sought the canyon, someone conceived the idea of draining the creek bed above the hole to obtain gold. So a tunnel was driven through a rocky wall in a bend, and the entire stream diverted through it. That the experiment was by no means in vain is evidenced by the fact that no less than $2,000,000 was paid by a Rapid City bank for gold taken from the stream at this point.

At 8 *m.* is a road leading L. to the power-house of the Dakota Power Co. At this point the water is returned to Rapid Creek after being used for the generation of electric power.

At 9.7 *m.* (L), in the creek, is a wheel used to bail out water for use on an irrigation project consisting of a small plot.

At 10.2 *m.* the highway approaches the FLUME (L), which carries the water from Pactola to Big Bend, to furnish power to operate the hydroelectric plant.

At Pactola a low dam backs up the water of Rapid Creek and turns it into the upper and open part of the flume. This part is 12,773 ft. in length, and is made of heavy planking in the form of an open trough. For most of its length it is supported on high trestles as the country through which it passes is very rough.

The flume follows, roughly, the course of Rapid Creek and the railroad right-of-way, but in many places it is far from both. It runs as an open ditch on the top of a tableland for 3,933 ft.; a pipe-line, about 5 ft. in diameter, extends 11,257 ft., and a tunnel, through solid rock, 612 ft. The penstock which conveys the water to the turbines is 724 ft. long. The flume, pipe-line, and ditch, are 5.5 m. in length, and have a drop of more than 300 ft. from Pactola to Big Bend, developing 2,000 horsepower.

The flume was first built in 1894 by the Pactola Placerville Mining Co., to convey water to placer mines between Pactola and Placerville, 2.5 m. below. It was then only an open flume and ditch. The mines did not produce as much gold as expected and the flume and ditch were taken over by the Dakota Power Co. in 1906, and they extended it to Big Ben.

The water drops 83 ft., generating electric power which is sent to Rapid City over steel towers and a 2,400 volt transmission line. Due to difficulty caused by freezing in winter, the plant and flume are shut down from about December 1 to March 15 each year.

At 10.6 m. (L) is a burned-over area which is beginning to be reforested.

At 10.7 m. (R) is JOHNSON SIDING, which consists of a covered platform like a station stop on an interurban electric line, an incongruous touch in this wild country. It was used by the Rapid City, Black Hills & Western R.R. until the line was discontinued in 1948.

Right here on a Forest Service Road is the Norris Peak Lookout (5,500 alt.), 1.5 m. It overlooks Wild Irishman Gulch and Loveland Canyon to the E. and S., and the Bogus Jim Creek area to the NW.

At 14 m. is the DEER CREEK PICNIC GROUND, set aside by the U.S. Forest Service.

At 16 m. is the junction with US 85A (see Tour 14), 2 m. N. of Pactola.

Tour 4C

Junction US 14 (Rapid City)—Nemo—Roubaix—Junction with US 85A (Pluma).
Junction US 14—Junction US 85A, 39.1 m.
Unnumbered, graveled road; not paralleled by railroad.

WINDING westward through one of the most scenic parts of the Black Hills, this route provides many points of interest. In order fully to appreciate the trip it is advisable to take plenty of time in driving the distance, stopping at the numerous points of attraction along the road. For one accustomed to riding, much of the route can be covered on horseback.

This road branches W. from US 14 (see Tour 4), 1.2 m. W. of RAPID CITY, 0 m. at junction indicated by a sign.

At 1.7 m. the road enters the cool, shady mouth of SOUTH CANYON, a deep gorge with tree-covered slopes flanking the road on either side. Occasionally sheer walls of solid limestone interrupt the green forest covering.

At 2 m. is a ranch house, where saddle horses are for hire by the hour or day. From the ranch several hiking and bridle trails can be taken.

Farther up the canyon, 4.3 *m.*, at the foot of a bluff (R), is a large cave extending back into the mountain. Ponderosa pine, oak, elm, aspen, boxelder, and spruce cover the hillsides and extend to the edge of the creek along most of the drive. Birch is seen frequently, but most of the white-barked trees are aspen.

At 6 *m.* the road passes over the divide between South Canyon and Box Elder Creek, the canyon walls merging gradually into picturesque valleys and farm land. At 9.7 *m.* the road crosses the boundary of the BLACK HILLS NATIONAL FOREST (*see THE BLACK HILLS*). There are numerous beaver dams along the creeks, where anglers may match their skill with the shrewdness of the elusive trout.

At 9.8 *m.* the highway strikes the TRAIL OF GENERAL CUSTER'S EXPEDITION on its return in 1874 from French Creek, near the present town of Custer, to Fort Abraham Lincoln, near Bismarck, N. Dak. General Sheridan secured permission from Washington in the spring of that year to send an expedition into the Black Hills for the purpose of exploration and scientific survey of the territory, to determine its mineral and geological possibilities. By the first of July Custer set out with about 1,000 soldiers, a supply train, and 300 beefs which were to be killed as needed.

Their route skirted the Montana-Dakota boundary to Mt. Inyan Kara, thence SE. to French Creek. Three exploration parties went out from the permanent camp, one down French Creek from which Charley Reynolds took dispatches to Fort Laramie. The return trip took the same course to Castle Creek, thence past Nemo and along Box Elder Creek to the point where it joins BOGUS JIM CREEK, 10 *m.* On this site Custer camped and while there, a story says, the expedition buried arms, ammunition, and some whiskey. However, no discovery of the reported cache ever verified the truth of the story.

The story of Bogus Jim dates back to early Black Hills days. When the region was the favorite haunt of gold prospectors, a certain Francis Calabogus located a mining claim and established a camp on the creek. From the contraction of Calabogus comes the name, Bogus Jim. Many claims were filed along the creek and farther back in the hills. Lead and silver ore were found in large quantities, and one or more copper veins were uncovered. But the prospectors wanted gold. There was little market for the other metals. Facilities for smelting were poor, transportation difficult, and most of the miners lacked the capital to develop their claims; consequently, there was little development of mineral resources in this part of the Hills.

Green Mountain, (5,101 alt.), highest peak in this region, commands a beautiful view of the surrounding forest and country. Rocky Point is another nearby attraction; it can be reached by a little hard climbing and affords a good view.

At 11.6 *m.* the highway passes CUSTER'S GAP through which

the expedition passed on the journey to Fort Abraham Lincoln. During the ascent of the gulch several wagons were overturned. Today there is still a wagon road up the gulch. The route follows Box Elder Creek through deeply-wooded canyons. At 13.1 *m.* (L) there is a dark streak, largely iron ore; and at 14.7 *m.* is a formation which resembles a castle wall with high battlements.

At 16 *m.* is a ranch house where rooms are rented to tourists.

At 16.4 *m.* is STEAMBOAT ROCK (R), so named because of its resemblance to the hull of a boat stranded upon a huge reef; with considerable effort and about a day's time one can reach the top, from which there is a broad view of the surrounding country. To the W. is Bogus Jim valley; to the NW., Custer Peak (6,794 alt.); to the N., the town of Nemo; while to the E. are rolling prairies and the distant Badlands.

The U.S. Forest Service has developed a picnic ground, 16.5 *m.*, at the foot of the mountain. Along the cliff (R) the formation of the rocky ledge resembles ancient castles. At 17 *m.* is a small store and filling station.

NEMO, 19.5 *m.* (4,616 alt.), is a quiet little village where the Homestake Mining Co., maintains a logging-camp and sawmill. There is also a ranger station here. Forest quietness, broken only by the occasional hum of a motor or the whistle of a sawmill, prevails. There is a LOG CHURCH (R) and across the street from the church is an old TOWN HALL. Just inside of the door of a shack along the board sidewalk is an old-fashioned fire hydrant and hose.

The first sale of timber by the U.S. government was made here Sept. 19, 1898, to the Homestake Mining Co., marking a new era in scientific forestry management for national forests. On the 50th anniversary, in 1948, Nemo was the scene of ceremonies bringing together conservation authorities from throughout the country.

W. of the Nemo Ranger Station, on a Forest Service road, is the BOXELDER FORKS PICNIC GROUND, with firewood furnished. There are some good trout ponds in the creeks that join here.

Beyond Nemo the country is more rugged, the steep slopes of the mountains having been swept by forest fires, and large excavation scars indicating abandoned mines.

At 21.5 *m.*, on each side of the road, are two abandoned mines, reminiscent of an earlier day.

At 22.5 *m.* is the BOXELDER ORGANIZATION CAMP, rented by the U.S. Forest Service to non-profit groups for summer camps, meetings, and clinics.

At 23.1 *m.* is a concrete-encased spring. The water is clear and cool and of the usual pure quality found in most Black Hills springs. Two miles farther there is a dam and a dry lake bed.

At 31.2 *m.* the road enters a forest of young trees with a distant glimpse of Custer Peak. The wooded area is often broken by out-croppings of schist and milk white quartz. This type of quartz contains gold in free-milling form.

The ANACONDA GOLD MINE is passed at the little Hamlet of ROUBAIX, 34.2 *m.* (5,392 alt.). The mine was discovered in the early 1880's and was first named the Uncle Sam Mining Co. The vein which the prospectors discovered contained what is known as free-milling gold. Simple stamping and washing was all that was necessary to recover the metal. This vein played out, and the property was later worked by the Clover Leaf Mining Co. until 1905, when the water broke through into the seventh level, about 700 ft. down. If the shaft leading to the pump had not broken, the mine could have been pumped out. The Anaconda Mining Co. acquired the property in 1934 and began operations to drain the mine. For months the draining of the mine went on until by late 1935 all seven levels were emptied. About 100 men were employed in the mine and stamp mills at the outset of World War II when all gold mines were closed by Federal order.

At 39.1 *m.* is the junction with US 85A, 5 m. S. of Pluma (*see Tour 14*).

Tour 5

(Luverne, Minn.)—Sioux Falls—Chamberlain—Rapid City—Custer—(Newcastle, Wyo.). US 16.
Minnesota Line to Wyoming Line, 463 m.
Roadbed hard-surfaced throughout.
Except for a few deviations the C. M. St. P. & P. R.R. roughly parallels the route between Sioux Falls and Rapid City.
Good hotel and cabin camp accommodations are available at the larger towns.

Passing through one of the best farming sections of South Dakota at the start, US 16 crosses the State westward through a gradually changing country. Tree-sequestered farm homes with many improvements slowly give way to farms with less pretentious buildings. Dairy herds and cornfields become less numerous, pasture land replaces improved fields. After the road descends into the Missouri River valley, the scene changes rapidly, and the road lifts again in long, easy spirals into the open West-river country, the "wide open spaces," marked by widely separated farms and grazing herds of cattle. The change becomes more pronounced as the route continues west. Winding snake-like over rolling prairie, touching the scenic Badlands, skirting ridges, sinking into hollows, the road finally abandons its sinuous course and heads straight for the Black Hills, At a distance of about 25 m. these unusual mountains are dimly visible, jutting from the horizon line like smoke-shrouded thunder clouds. The Black Hills region is vastly different from the prairie stretches to the east.

Section a. Minnesota Line—Junction with US 14, 294 m.

US 16 crosses the Minnesota Line 14 m. W. of Luverne, Minn. (*see Minn. Tour 13*), and passes through rolling country, with occasional groves along the highway. The oak trees are almost the last of that variety to be seen on the route, as farther west there are only a few, scattered along the Missouri River.

VALLEY SPRINGS, 1 *m.* (1,395 alt.), was settled in 1873 and had the first railroad station in Minnehaha Co. It received its name because of the number of springs along Beaver Creek.

At 3.1 *m.* is the junction with the Palisades Road, County H. (*See Tour 5A*).

At 4 *m.* is the BEAVER VALLEY CHURCH, the center of a Swedish community noted for its *smorgasbord*—a spectacular array of appetizers generally served as an evening meal at the community meetings held at the church. An enormous table is spread and loaded with Scandinavian specialties—herring, sardines, anchovies, cold ham, and several other cold meats, liver loaf, vegetable salads of every description, headcheese, and three or four other kinds of cheese, including getost, a chocolate-covered cheese made of goat's milk. A large dish of boiled lobsters is generally on the table, and with this course a generous supply of the Swedish national bread, flatbrod, is served. Some special fish is commonly used for the second course, perhaps herring in cream, or meat balls of a special Swedish type, with tea and marmalade, rye bread and Swedish rusks. For dessert frozen whipped cream is served with a bowl of strawberries when seasonable. Perhaps the most pleasant features of a Swedish smorgasbord are the coffee and the many varieties of sweet rolls and rings and fancy cookies that have helped make a reputation for Swedish cooking.

U.S. 16 sweeps across the Split Rock Creek valley, with out-croppings of the purple-hued Sioux Falls granite that underlies the region. To the N. along this creek are the Palisades, Devil's Gulch, and other interesting formations (*see Tour 9A*).

The mounds left by the Mound Builders, known locally as the BRANDON MOUNDS, 8.2 *m.* (R), are on a hill between the Split Rock and Big Sioux Rivers. There were originally 38 easily distinguishable mounds. Relic-seekers have opened several of them; but the only scientific investigation was made in October 1921, under the auspices of the Smithsonian Institution. William E. Meyer, who supervised it, died before his findings could be published. The Smithsonian has artifacts but no record of the investigation. Most of the available knowledge concerning the Brandon Mounds is based on the word and publications of Dr. W. H. Over, curator of the University of South Dakota Museum in Vermillion. Dr. Over was present when the excavation was made and carefully kept notes concerning all of the skeletons and artifacts which were uncovered.

It is thought that the Mound Builders migrated from the East. They are said to have been less inclined toward a nomadic life than the Sioux Indians, but eventually they crossed the width of Minnesota and settled near where the Split Rock River flows into the Big Sioux River. Modern Indians are of the opinion that the village could not have been very far from the mounds; and white settlers in the vicinity have found many arrowheads on the site; some rubbish-piles still exist.

The most unusual bit of information concerning the Brandon Mounds, disclosed by the investigation of 1921, was that the Sioux Indians reopened the mounds for their burials. At the depth of 7 or 8 ft. there were found the older remains and artifacts; and at the depth of 5 ft. the bones were in a better state of preservation. Some of the relics are made of metal.

The upper, shallow burials, are credited to the Sioux Indians, and the deep, lower burials are considered to have been those made by the Mound Builders.

SIOUX FALLS, 15.6 m. (1,422 alt.) (*see SIOUX FALLS*).

State's industrial center and largest city. State Penitentiary, Morrell Packing Plant, Manchester Biscuit Company, Pettigrew Museum, Terrace Park, Sherman Indian Mounds, Coliseum.

Here is a junction with US 77 (*see Tour 9*).
At 24.1 m. is the junction with a graveled road.

Left on this road is WALL LAKE, 1.5 m., one of the most popular resorts in Minnehaha Co. The lake covers about 240 acres and is included in a 960-acre game preserve. Stocked annually with fish, the lake gives up thousands of several different varieties each summer. Here are cottages for rent, two dance pavilions, a skating rink, bathhouse, refreshment stands, and boats for hire. A sandy beach and playground add to the many recreational facilities.

PUMPKIN CENTER, 33.6 m., unlike the mythical town of the Uncle Josh stories, has actually existed for many years at the crossroads of US 16 and State 19.

At 48.6 m. is STANLEY CORNERS and the junction with US 81 (*see Tour 10*).

BRIDGEWATER, 54.6 m. (1,420 alt.), was originally called Nation, for Carrie Nation, the prohibition-crusader who carried on a bottle-smashing campaign. According to stories, the present name was given because railroad workers were required to carry their drinking water across a bridge during the time the Milwaukee R.R. was being constructed. The town has received Nationwide publicity through its Colony Band, a group of musicians who dress in the garb of Mennonites while giving their programs at national American Legion conventions.

Bridgewater was another of the many towns in the State that engaged in a determined county seat fight. The town had won the honor in 1880, but it was claimed that their victory was the result of unfair practices. Accordingly, a group of Salem citizens drove to Bridgewater after dark and waited until it was safe to proceed with their business. The county clerk, in sympathy with the Salemites, left a window unlatched to expedite the coup d'Etat. The records were procured and the men returned to Salem where they set up an improvised courthouse. When the Bridgewater citizens learned of the loss, they went to Salem, heavily armed, expecting to retrieve the records; but at the latter town everyone feigned ignorance of the entire affair and the Bridgewater men returned home, defeated. Salem was later named the permanent county seat.

EMERY, 62.3 *m.*, since early days has been known for its musical societies, both in the schools and in the town.

It was through Emery that the old Sioux Falls-Black Hills Trail passed in the days of oxen and prairie schooners. The county was surveyed in 1876, and opened for settlement. Soon Easterners were pouring in, some remaining to take up claims, others continuing westward to the Black Hills, where the lure of gold had already precipitated a turbulent rush of fortune seekers.

ALEXANDRIA, 71.6 *m.* (1,352 alt.), seat of Hanson Co., is on the northern edge of a large German farm area. The many pretentious farm houses and substantial buildings in the community indicate years of thrift and thoroughness. It is still related in Alexandria that, in 1884, when a tornado swept through the town, a woman who took her children into the cellar came up after the storm, lifted the trapdoor, and found the house gone.

At Alexandria is a junction with a graveled road.

Left on this road is LAKE HANSON RECREATION DEVELOPMENT AREA, 1 *m.* An artificial lake, formed as a WPA project in the 1930's, has become a popular summer picnicking, swimming, and fishing area with the State Game, Fish and Parks Department planting trees for a park along the shore.

At 7.3 *m.*, along the James River, is the ROCKPORT MENNONITE COLONY, the home of a stern religious sect of Swiss-German people who had lived in Russia before settling here. They retain the curious dress, customs and beliefs of their ancestors, living in secluded rural colonies where their industry and thrift enable them to become prosperous farmers. In 1895 several groups of these people emigrated to this country from Russia to escape persecution and settled in colonies along the James river between Huron and Yankton.

The sect originated in Switzerland in 1530 when Menno Simons, a leader of the Anabaptists, founded a new branch which became known as Mennonites in his honor. Because of religious persecution they later emigrated to Austria and Germany. Near the close of the 18th century the Czarina of Russia offered them land and freedom from military service, so in 1774, followers of Jacob Hutter, one of their religious leaders, imigrated into Russia and the members became known as Hutterites. After several decades the Russian ruler repudiated her agreement and again they moved, this time coming to the United States.

Men in the colony never shave after they marry and thus are easily distinguished from the single members. Men and boys wear gray-black jackets and trousers, black felt hats in summer and fur caps in winter. Women and girls wear long, full, black calico dresses, and have shawls tied over their heads. Small children are cared for in a day nursery; the older ones receive religious training as well as grade school education. Large chalk-stone buildings house several families, with one room usually assigned for each. Household duties are divided among the women, and farm work among the men. An overseer or elder, who also serves as spiritual leader, is elected to supervise the work and commercial life. A treasurer handles all the money and makes all the purchases for the community. If one marries outside the colony, he forfeits his claim to a share of the wealth. One may join by turning over all his property to the colony and accepting its customs. Those who leave the colony are unable to recover their property or shares. Besides not believing in war, the Hutterites disapprove of the use of firearms, tobacco, and moving picture shows. They are efficient farmers, steady workers, and live with little thought for their modern neighbors. Man is king in the colony; at meals the men are served first and the women do not eat with them.

Imbued with deep religious convictions, the Hutterites devote Sundays mainly to spiritual teachings. In everyday life these people live up to their ideals. Physical punishment is unknown. If a member commits a minor offense, he may put himself in the good graces of the community by asking forgiveness from all members.

Proud of the fact that not once during the depression or drought did they seek help, the Hutterites continue to farm the fertile valley of the James River. It is especially noteworthy that these people of strange dress and customs are unusually polite and willingly explain the plan of their community. They permit pictures to be taken of their buildings and fields, but never of themselves.

At 74.3 *m.* is a junction with State 38, which parallels US 16 between this point and Sioux Falls (*see Tour 9*).

Right on this hard-surfaced road is SPENCER, 10.7 *m.* When harness and saddle shops closed throughout the Midwest with the advent of mechanized farming, Nichel and Son here enlarged. Harnesses and fancy saddles are shipped to all parts of the U. S. During World War II, the leather craftsmen turned to making scabbards for military use, and since have added the manufacture of canvas awnings and lawn furniture.

Along US 16 are several SHELTERBELT PROJECTS, planted during the dust storm and drought years of the 1930's by the U.S. Department of Agriculture. The rows of various kinds of hardy trees, including cottonwood, elm, Russian olive, and cedar, were set out in long east-west and north-south strips to break prairie winds and retard erosion.

At 82.9 *m.* the highway crosses the James River, a small dam to the S. of the bridge forming a pool popular with local fishermen. Firesteel Creek flows through the golf course of the Mitchell Country Club and into "the Jim" river here.

MITCHELL, 86.4 *m.* (1,301 alt.) (*see MITCHELL*).

Corn Palace, Lake Mitchell, Dakota Wesleyan University, Indian Village site.

Here is a junction with State 37 (*see Tour 11A*).

MOUNT VERNON, 98.6 *m.* (1,413 alt.), in 1889 was entirely destroyed by a prairie fire, fanned by a 60 m. gale that swept the town. The result was that original buildings were replaced by newer types of architecture. Much of the surrounding area is underlaid with Dakota sandstone, an excellent building material. In order to obtain a satisfactory well it is necessary to reach this sandstone, which sometimes is more than 700 ft. below the surface.

At 109.8 *m.*, just E. of the Plankinton city limits, is a junction with a graded road.

Right on this road is the SOUTH DAKOTA TRAINING SCHOOL, 0.8 *m.*, where incorrigible and delinquent children under the age of 18 are committed by law until they are 21, unless discharged by the Board of Charities and Corrections. The school opened in 1888 as the Dakota Territory Reform School. The main building is the three-story administration center and school, with a new wing for the boys' dormitory. There is a new girls' dormitory to the W.
The land, comprising 800 acres, is farmed by the boys. A dairy herd maintained by the school wins frequent prizes in State Fair competition. Girls are segregated in the school, with emphasis on housekeeping courses. Boys are trained in carpentry, metal working, and mechanics, as well as vocational agriculture.
The high school athletic teams are known as the Lincoln Loggers and play a regular schedule with surrounding public schools. The band, sponsored by the State "40 et 8," attends American Legion conventions and other affairs. Since 1940, nearly 90 per cent of the boys have gone on to college.

PLANKINTON, 110.8 *m.* (1,528 alt.), is the seat of Aurora Co. Although Mitchell is generally believed to have had the first corn palace, the honor in reality belongs to Plankinton, for in 1891 a grain festival was held here. The bold statement, "Dakota Feeds the World," was printed on the outside of the building, a plain wooden structure, its exterior covered with grains and grasses. A story of the event at the time related how people came from a wide area on foot and horseback, in buckboard and wagons, to see the grain palace, which was abandoned after 1892.
At Plankinton is the junction with US 281 (*see Tour 11*); US 16 and US 281 are united for 19 m.
At 117.5 *m.* is the junction with a graveled road.

Left on this road is the SITE OF THE STRATOSPHERE FLIGHT LANDING, 12 *m.* On Armistice Day, 1935, Explorer II, a tremendous balloon and its gondola bearing Capt. (later Col.) Albert W. Stevens and Capt. (later Maj. Gen.) Orville Anderson, made a successful landing here following a record ascent into the stratosphere of nearly 13 miles. The flight originated in the Black Hills (*see Section c, below*). An artificial pond near the marker was named Gondola Lake following the event.

WHITE LAKE, 123.2 *m.* (1,646 alt.), has had a variety of names. It was first known as Siding 36, because of its distance from Mitchell. The name was changed to Winsor in 1881, then to Yorktown in 1882, and finally was named for the lake that lies 4 miles N. The lake was named by early settlers who were impressed by the bright reflection of the sun off the water.
At 129.9 *m.* is the junction with US 281 (*see Tour 11*).
KIMBALL, 137 *m.* (1,789 alt.), founded in 1880, was first called Andover, which was later changed to Kimball in honor of a railroad commissioner.
At 147.5 *m.* is the junction with a graveled road.

Left on this road 0.1 *m.*, then again L. 0.1 *m.*, and finally R. 1.6 *m.*, is the NELSON ROADHOUSE, now called the Custer Farm, on the old trail from Yankton N. along the Missouri River. In early days a supply line started from this point, connecting with forts stationed in several places up the river. The house was constructed with timbers two ft. apart, which were then filled in with home-made mud bricks, used to build the chimney. The outside walls were boarded over and the inner brick covered with plaster. The roof was thatched with long grass cut in nearby lowlands. The house was later shingled and sided. It was here that Gen. George A. Custer and his troops stopped on their way to the Black Hills in 1875. The Nelson Roadhouse enjoyed a lucrative business during the gold rush days of the late 1870's.

PUKWANA (Ind., *peace-pipe smoke*), 149 *m.* (1,546 alt.), was well known for many years as the headquarters and shipping point for a device designed to save gasoline consumption in automobiles. With a large office force and trade territory which extended even to foreign countries, Pukwana became nationally known as the smallest town in the United States with a first-class post office. The business still operates on a small scale.

CHAMBERLAIN, 158 *m.* (1,363 alt.), like several other early towns on the Missouri River, was for many years a ferrying point for passengers and freight. Its picturesque location on the eastern slope of the river valley, its numerous park and recreational facilities, and its paved streets combine to make it one of the most attractive towns along the route. The fact that it is situated on the Missouri River, which is the approximate dividing line between the East-river farming region and West-river ranching country, gives the town an added touch of color, there being an intermingling of the characteristics of the two sections. On the extreme western edge of town is the new COMMUNITY HOSPITAL, which was opened in 1950. The site, in a grove of cedar trees overlooking the river, includes a rambling frame building which formerly housed a sanitarium sponsored by the Seventh Day Adventists. At the NE. edge of Chamberlain is ST. JOSEPH'S INDIAN MISSION (Catholic), a school for 200 Indian children from the Lower Brule and Crow Creek reservations (*see Tour 4A*). Originally, it was the site of Columbus College. The mission also serves as headquarters for field missionaries.

Chamberlain is host each fall to hundreds of hunters seeking geese and ducks; the area is especially noted for good goose hunting.

Land W. of the Missouri River was opened for settlement in 1890, and the sole means of crossing the river was by a ferry that was operated only at certain hours of the day. In 1893 a pontoon bridge was strung across the river at Chamberlain. This floating structure was so built that the deck of the bridge rested on flatboats tied side by side. When river steamers approached, one end of the pontoon was released from its anchorage on the bank and allowed to float free. Although unsafe, especially in high water or freezing weather, the pontoon served as the connecting link between the markets at Chamberlain and the open range westward. In 1905 the C. M. St. P. & P. R.R. built a bridge across the treacherous river, which continually threatens to change its course. In winter the only way in which teams and cars could cross the river was on the ice. In 1920 Charles Bolling and his wife of Oacoma were drowned, leaving nine helpless children, after which a drive was started to secure a highway bridge. In 1923 the State Legislature passed a bill to build five bridges over the Missouri, one of which was constructed at Chamberlain. Plans were begun in 1951 to move both the highway and railroad bridges to allow for the broadened river resulting from the Fort Randall dam about 60 m. to the S. (*see Tour 7*).

At Chamberlain is the junction with State 47 (*see Tour 4A*).

AMERICAN ISLAND, 158.8 *m.*, is a historic and popular recreational area scheduled to be partly flooded by the waters of Fort Randall Reservoir in the 1950's. In Municipal Park, cabins, a picnic area, and a swimming pool have been maintained for public use.

The history of the island dates back more than 125 years. In 1809 a trading post, called Fort Aux Cedras, was built here. Fort Recovery replaced it in 1822, following the burning of the former. The latter fort was afterwards abandoned.

In 1925 a re-enactment of the Custer massacre was staged on American Island to feature the completion of the bridge. About 5,000 Indians took part, and just as they were the first to cross the river before the white men came, they were also the first to cross the new bridge. Dressed in full Sioux regalia, they presented an impressive spectacle as they marched with moccasined tread, bells tinkling at every step, gaudy war bonnets flashing a half-dozen colors in the sun, the older Indians doubtless recalling the days when there was no bridge, no town, and no vestige of the white man. Indians came to the celebration in automobiles, on ponies, and in wagons loaded with camp equipment, in a seemingly endless line.

OACOMA (Ind., *place between*), 161 *m.* (1,338 alt.), was so named because it lies between the Missouri River and the bluffs beyond. Manganese was discovered in the hills NE. of the town, but the deposits have not been utilized to any extent, though some attempts have been made in this direction. Loss of the county seat to Kennebec, together with the completion of a highway bridge, which diverted much former trade to Chamberlain, caused a rapid decline in population. Today many empty buildings give the impression of a ghost town in the making.

A new highway climbs the bluffs along the Missouri River. During World War II the search for war materials caused the U.S. Bureau of Mines to establish a pilot mill here to test the manganese content of the deposits that protrude from the bare hills. The ore was found to be plentiful, but of too low grade for profitable commercial use (*see NATURAL RESOURCES*).

RELIANCE, 175.4 *m.* (1,780 alt.). A large artificial lake, which backs water nearly a mile, has given the town a much needed addition to its water supply as well as improved recreational facilities.

This section of the country was stimulated to a sudden growth in population in 1907, when the railroad was built, tying together the eastern and western parts of the State. Homesteaders took up the available land, and soon many thriving communities had developed. Some of the new residents were able to withstand the unusually dry years of 1911–12–13; others, unable to make a living, returned to the East. The deserted houses—generally small shacks—were soon appropriated by neighbors, sometimes for a financial consideration, sometimes for nothing. Today many homes comprise a group of shacks joined together to form a composite house—not the most graceful type of architecture.

KENNEBEC, 189.2 *m.* (1,687 alt.), seat of Lyman Co., boasts a new courthouse as a result of its victory in an exciting county seat race, with Presho and Oacoma as opponents. A large dam, built under the Federal Emergency Relief Administration, is NE. of the town. It is in a new game preserve.

PRESHO, 198.5 *m.* (1,764 alt.), was the "bedding down" place for extensive round-ups in the days of the large cattle outfits. Ample water and feed were usually found on Medicine Creek nearby. Twenty years ago it was considered one of the largest hay-baling and shipping points in the United States. At one time its mushroom population neared the 3,000 mark. According to a story, eight minutes after the first town lot was offered for sale in 1905, a bank, composed of two barrels and a plank, opened for business. At first the bank operated day and night in serving the frantic rush of homesteaders, and the cashier was compelled to carry a six-shooter and all the currency with him when he went to lunch.

At Presho is the junction and N. terminus of US 183 (*see Tour 12A*).

VIVIAN, 209.5 *m.*, is one of the many typical prairie towns on this route. Straggling along a slope of Medicine Creek, Vivian retains its board sidewalks and the roofed porches of 30 years ago.

At 210.9 *m.* is the junction with US 83 (*see Tour 12*); US 16 and US 83 are united to Murdo (*see below*).

DRAPER, 225.3 *m.* (2,230 alt.), perched on a hill, is visible for many miles in all directions. The name honors a railroad conductor.

MURDO, 232.2 *m.* (2,217 alt.), the largest town on the long, undulating stretch of prairie along US 16 between Chamberlain and Rapid City, was named for a pioneer cattleman, Murdo McKenzie.

The Texas Trail, over which thousands of cattle were brought N. each spring, had a branch to this point. The Matador Cattle Company of Texas ran about 20,000 head of cattle in western South Dakota with Murdo McKenzie as manager.

Murdo was founded in 1905 prior to the building of the railroad from Chamberlain, and when Jones County was created in 1916 Murdo became the county seat. Handicapped by a scarcity of water during dry years, an artificial lake was formed S. of town with the aid of a Federal project in the 1930's.

At Murdo is a junction with US 83 (*see Tour 12*).

Here also is a time change (CST going east; MST going west).

OKATON, 243.1 *m.*, and STAMFORD, 253 *m.*, are two small prairie hamlets that were founded when the railroad was extended to the Black Hills in 1906.

There have been periods when this area has produced large wheat crops, and farming has been attempted since homestead days. However, it probably will always remain principally a stock country, scanty rainfall combining with other natural conditions to render farming a doubtful venture.

BELVIDERE, 265.6 *m.* (2,308 alt.), invites the traveler to stop and enjoy bathing, boating, or fishing in Lake Belvidere, near the town and US 16 (L). South of Belvidere is the 30,000-acre cattle ranch of Tom Berry, South Dakota's "Cowboy Governor," 1933–37.

KADOKA (Ind. *hole in the wall*), 278.7 *m.* (2,467 alt.), was so named because the town is near the rim of the Badlands' wall.

Kadoka has been called the "jumping off place," not in the usual sense, but because W. of the town is an abrupt entrance to the scenic Badlands. The town is attractively built, clean looking, and has excellent tourist camps. It is the principal outfitting point for the Badlands.

At Kadoka is the junction with State 73.

Left on this highway is KODAK POINT, 14 *m.*, a vantage point from which the Badlands is viewed and photographed in three directions. After driving 12 m. the road follows the rim of a precipice, and in the distance the formations of the Badlands, with their many shapes and colors, stand out like strange spectral ruins of a vast medieval city.

At 285.1 *m.* is the junction with US 16A, the Badlands National Monument Highway (*see Tour 6*).

At 294 *m.* is PHILIP JUNCTION and the point where US 16 is joined with US 14 (*see Tour 4*).

Section b. Junction with US 14—Rapid City, 86 m.

US 14 and US 16 are united between the Philip Junction and Rapid City, passing through a hilly area marked by startling buttes and eroded gullies. Although much of the grazing area has been fenced, herds of cattle often take to the highway, especially at night, and form a serious hazard where vision between hills is limited.

Prior to the homesteading period early in the 20th century, this vast domain was the empire of large cattle operators whose herds were fed on the rich native buffalo grass before shipment to market. When this area was opened to homesteaders, the old range was quickly broken up by barbwire fences, plowed fields, and unsympathetic farmers. The soil was submarginal for farming, and during the dust storms of the 1930's the cycle was completed. The farmers moved out, plowed fields returned to grass, and the government formed huge grazing districts in which local cattlemen could run their cattle. The picturesque and cryptic brands have returned, as one will note not only on the cattle but on mailboxes and ranch gates as well.

COTTONWOOD, 12.4 m. (2,414 alt.), first called Ingham, was given its present name because of the groves of cottonwoods growing nearby. This has always been a favorite area for grouse and sage hens, rigid hunting laws having restored their numbers in recent years.

QUINN, 25.1 m. (2,607 ft. alt.), once was the trading points for a group of Jewish farmers and ranchers who settled nearby. Ruts of the old Deadwood Trail and an early telephone line are still visible 10 m. N. of the town, which was named for Michael Quinn, one of the early-day freighters.

WALL, 31.2 m. (2,713 alt.), received its name because of its situation near the edge of the Badlands. Its founding in July 1907 was marked by a lively celebration, an event which has become an annual affair. Called the "Gateway to the Badlands," the town is the trading center of a farming and stock-raising country.

The WALL DRUG STORE is one of the most advertised concerns in the State and, for many, one of the biggest disappointments. Highway signs are posted for hundreds of miles in all directions and during World War II signposts in N. Africa, France, Guam, and Australia pointed the way to this enterprising store.

At Wall is the junction with US 16A (see Tour 6).

West of Wall US 16 winds down into the valley of the Cheyenne River. Before the days of highway improvement, the breaks of this river were always a knotty problem to freighters, especially during wet weather.

At 46.4 m. is one of the forks of the Cheyenne River, the two branches of which envelop the Black Hills area and carry away the water from the numerous creeks that dash down from the mountains. Noted for its swift current, the river often becomes a swirling, roaring torrent, carrying with it trees, brush, and silt gathered from its many dry tributaries, each transformed into a rushing river following a heavy rain. The Cheyenne River is also noted for its treachery. During normal periods it can be forded by a team or on horseback, but it may rise two feet or more in an hour. Many instances have been known where a stranger to the wiles of the stream would attempt to cross, only to have his rig swept away by the swift waters, fortunate if he escaped with his life.

WASTA (Ind., good), 49.4 m. (2,320 alt.), was named by Doane Robinson, first State Historian. Nestling at the foot of massive gumbo bluffs, it is the trading center for a vast cattle country to the N. In the early 1880's this region was a vast range territory with large cattle outfits, their herds often numbering tens of thousands. Ranches were generally near some stream, and the cattle were turned loose to roam at will until round-up time called for a check-up.

Many youths with a desire for Western life obtain work on a modern ranch with the expectation of "cowboying," but to their dismay usually discover that the work in the main consists of endless drudgery—haying, chores, fencing, cleaning sheds, and other manual tasks similar to those on a farm. The boss is the one who usually does the "cowboying." There are two reasons for this. In the first place he likes to keep in daily touch with his stock, and in the second place it is the easiest work on the ranch. Fences, smaller herds, and the shrinkage of open range, have all combined to take the glamour from the once colorful role of the cow "waddy."

NEW UNDERWOOD, 65.7 *m.*, is situated on Box Elder Creek, one of the numerous streams that drain the Black Hills. Tumbling down from the mountains, the creeks gradually slow their pace as they stretch out across the plains before joining the Cheyenne River. The mouths of these little streams often provide good fishing.

At 77.1 *m.* is the junction with a military highway.

Right on this hard-surfaced road is the RAPID CITY AIR FORCE BASE, 1.3 *m.* (*Military Police at gate; stop for pass*). This field, designated as a permanent base by the U.S. Air Force, was built at the outset of World War II at a cost of $25 million. It was used primarily as a final stage training station for B-17 bomber crews. Following World War II, it became a B-29 base and then a B-36 wing headquarters. A CONCRETE HANGAR (L), described by the Corps of Engineers as "the world's largest monolithic concrete structure," will accommodate the biggest bombers contemplated by the Air Force. It is one of the largest aircraft hangers ever built, being designed for housing B-36 and similar-type bombers. It is 369' wide, 314' long, and 95' high at the top of the curved roof. When it was dedicated in 1950 more than 30,000 people danced inside the hangar as a name band attempted to make itself heard.

A four million dollar HOUSING PROJECT for 400 families of officers and enlisted men was begun at the E. edge of the base along Marginal Road.

For live bomb practice, the training crews use a huge gunnery range S. of Badlands National Monument (*see Tour 6A*).

RAPID CITY, 86 *m.* (3,196 alt.) (*see RAPID CITY*).

State School of Mines and Museum, Dinosaur Park, Halley Park and Indian Museum, Alex Johnson Hotel, Canyon Lake.

Here is a junction with US 14 (*see Tour 4*); and Rim Rock Trail (*see Tour 4B*).

Section c. Rapid City—Wyoming Line, 83 m.

US 16 through the Black Hills is a scenic route, with dense forests, wild game retreats, rustic park hotels, trout streams, unique mountain views, and only two towns. The Mount Rushmore National Memorial, South Dakota's most visited and widest known feature, is reached by this route and a short sideroad (*see Tour 5B*).

The portion of US 16 through Custer State Park is known as the Iron Mountain Road. In scaling the summit of Iron Mountain, travelers must pass through three tunnels focused on the sculptured figures on Mount Rushmore, negotiate corkscrew bridges, and take one-way lanes. An alternate route around Custer State Park, via 85A, has been designated as US 16A (*see below*).

From Rapid City, the highway strikes S. through foothills, with the mountains rising to the R. This area is popular with Hollywood motion picture companies for location filming of western backgrounds and Indian sequences.

At 2.8 *m.* is the REPTILE GARDENS, an exhibit of rattlesnakes and imported reptiles.

At 7.5 *m.* is SPRING CREEK. It was in connection with this stream, in gold rush days, that the tale of *When a Mule-Skinner Kisses a Mule* originated. There was a gold stampede in Rockerville, which was becoming a town almost overnight. The Indians had held up a mule train on the Sidney road between Rapid City and Spring Creek, and the next day a merchant approached one Johnny Hunt and asked him to haul a load of goods from Rapid City to Rockerville immediately. As Johnny and his mules would have to go over the road on which the Indian hold-up occurred, he asked the merchant if he thought the trip advisable. "Oh yes," said the merchant, "I'll go over with you, but you will have to come back alone."

After a lot of thinking on Johnny's part and a great amount of coaxing from the merchant, Johnny finally agreed to make the trip, but first went home for his 50-70 needle-gun. After he had delivered the goods, some miners told him of a new trail whereby he could save five miles. Although the new trail was treacherous, he was still worried about Indians and decided to try it. Everything went well until he came to Spring Creek Canyon. Here he found himself and the mules looking over a precipice of about 300 ft., inclined at a 45-degree angle. Not wishing to retrace his steps for 15 miles, and anxious to get back to Rapid City, he resolved to make the descent.

After chaining an old tree top to the rear end of the wagon to act as a brake, locking both rear wheels, and adding a little persuasion intermingled with much profanity, Johnny coaxed the mules to take off. They gathered momentum as they slid down, the wagon zigzagging and careening, the mules skidding along on their haunches. Johnny's mind had been centered on Indian raids so earnestly that he had forgotten to secure the wagon box to the chassis, and about halfway down the precipice it slid roughly onto the mules' backs. Johnny managed to hang on somehow until they reached the bottom, where he was catapulted over the dashboard ahead of his mules. Searching thoroughly for broken bones and finding none, he scrambled to his feet, walked over and jubilantly kissed the nose of one of his dour-faced mules. This was too much for the mule, which immediately broke away and bolted down the trail. About two hours afterwards he was found with his nose in the waters of the creek.

At 10.3 *m.* is a junction with a graded road.

Left on this road are the SITTING BULL CAVERNS, 1 *m.*, first known by the Sioux Indians as Two Bear Holes, from the fact that two large bears made their homes in the entrances. The location was popular, and old Indians recall that Sitting Bull's band used to camp there. The caves were not extensively explored until 1934, and in 1935 they were opened to the public.

At 11.5 *m.* is the boundary of HARNEY NATIONAL FOREST (*hqs. Custer*). This forest covers 706,525 acres in the southern portion of the Black Hills with 30 miles of forest trails. It was named for Harney Peak, highest point east of the Rockies (*see Tour 14A*).

At 11.8 *m.* is the STRATO RIM PICNIC GROUNDS (R), maintained by the U.S. Forest Service. From this vantage point is a view of the natural ampitheatre 425 ft. below which was used for balloon flights into the stratosphere.

At 12.2 *m.* is the junction with an unimproved dirt road.

Right on this road, through a gate, is the rim of the Stratosphere Bowl, 1 *m.* (see below). From this vantage point the entire bowl can be seen, including the floor, 425 ft. below.

At 13 *m.* is the junction with a dirt road.

Right on this road is the floor of the STRATOSPHERE BOWL, 1.3 *m.* (3,500 alt.). (Steep descent, drive in second gear, and sound horn at turns.) The bowl was used for the National Geographic Society-U. S. Army Air Corps record-breaking flights into the stratosphere. On Armistice Day, 1935, the balloon, "Explorer II," rose to a height of 13 *m.* from the rock-walled basin. The bowl was chosen because it is sheltered from surface winds in an area where cloudless days are frequent, and to the E., the direction in which the balloon was expected to travel, are hundreds of miles of level plains, assuring a good landing. Here for weeks scientists, balloonists, and Army troops toiled day and night in preparation for the flight. Finally, on November 10, the long-awaited high pressure area drifted in from the W., indicating the weather would be ideal for a flight the next day. All guests were barred from the bowl; truck loads of soldiers arrived from Fort Meade to hold the balloon in leash while the helium gas flowed into it. At night a huge battery of floodlights, placed in a circle around the floor of the basin, were turned on, lighting the bowl so brightly that it was possible to read a newspaper at any time during the night. Mooring ropes were attached to each of the points in the scalloped edge of a girdle encircling the balloon near the top, and these ropes were payed out by the soldiers as the balloon filled with gas. Soon after inflation began, some gas formed a pocket in the fabric underneath and caused a 17 ft. tear, resulting in more than an hour's delay while it was being mended. As the first streak of dawn was seen above the cliffs, the important task of fastening the gondola to the balloon was completed. The gondola, rolled out on a rubber-tired "dolly," was suspended below the bag with bridles of parachute webbing. The 40 bags of lead dust, the emergency parachute and heavy scientific equipment, which was later released and floated to earth by parachute as the balloon came down, could be seen hanging from the gondola's sides, as the craft was maneuvered to take advantage of favorable air currents. Inside were Capt. Albert W. Stevens, scientist, and Capt. Orvil A. Anderson, pilot, making last preparations.

At 7:01 a. m. word was given to cast off, and the giant balloon, clearing the rim of the bowl by only 50 ft., floated upward. Because of northwest winds blowing at the time, it was necessary to take off over the very highest cliffs. To lighten the load for quick ascent, 700 pounds of ballast were removed before the start. When the balloon was 100 ft. above the trees, a downward trend of air forced it earthward, but Capt. Anderson, who was standing on top of the gondola, quickly dumped 750 pounds of ballast. Immediately the immense bag rose rapidly, ascending to the height of 13.71 m. above sea level—exceeding all previous attempts to rise into the stratosphere.

After the balloon reached an altitude of 15,000 ft., Capt. Anderson slowed the rate of ascent so that Capt. Stevens could have an opportunity to rig the instruments which trailed underneath the gondola. The ports were then sealed and the pilot continued the ascent, maintaining as nearly as possible a speed of 400 ft. a minute. As they neared the ceiling and the balloon became fully expanded the rate of climb was reduced to 200 ft. a minute. The balloonists maintained their position at the ceiling for 1½ hours, making observations and collecting scientific data. In mid-afternoon, during the descent, a radio hook-up was arranged whereby the two men in the metal gondola talked to the commander of the China Clipper flying over the Pacific Ocean and also to a newspaper editor in London.

After remaining aloft for more than eight hours, and reaching an altitude of 72,395 ft., the two sky explorers managed a perfect landing in an open field near White Lake, S. Dak. (see above, section a), 240 m. E. of the natural amphitheatre from which the craft took off.

Explorer II, the world's largest balloon, was made of 2⅔ acres of cloth, had a capacity of 3,700 cu. ft. of gas, and weighed 15,000 pounds including the gondola, instruments and crew. Its height at the take-off was 316 ft.

The successful flight of 1935 was the third attempt and the second ascension, sponsored by the National Geographic Society and the United States Army Air Corps, to be made from the Stratosphere Bowl. The first flight took off at dawn, July 28, 1934. The balloon had attained a height of slightly over 60,000 ft., when the bag commenced to rip and the descent was begun. The flight ended that afternoon when the huge bag and the gondola crashed in a field near Holdredge, Neb. The balloonists saved their lives by using their parachutes. The second attempt to penetrate the upper air was disastrously halted when, an hour before the scheduled time for the take-off, the balloon ripped at the top, collapsed to the floor of the bowl, and its charge of helium escaped.

The results of the stratosphere tests of the pressurized cabin, wind velocities, temperatures, radio reception, and photography were used later by the Air Corps in designing aircraft and equipment for World War II high altitude flying.

ROCKERVILLE, 13.3 m. (4,371 alt.), has been almost completely abandoned, joining the ghosts of other old mining towns. It may not look prosperous now, with its rotting cabins and caved in walls, but during the first two years of Rockerville's existence (1876–78), $350,000 in gold was washed out of the wooden, cradle-like rockers used by the miners. By 1882 the placer mines had yielded more than one million dollars, and the town boasted a newspaper and the most boisterous saloons in the Hills. However, the rich diggings played out, lawsuits blocked water rights, and the newspaper editor followed the miners to new fields. A dance hall continues to provide social life.

The ROCKERVILLE PICNIC AREA (R) has Storm Mt. for a backdrop.

L. from Rockerville on a Forest Service road is the secluded FOSTER GULCH PICNIC GROUNDS, 1.3 m.

At 13.5 m. is the SILVER MT. CAMPGROUND. The Boulder

Hill Fire Lookout station (R) provides a good view of the forest area.

The mountainsides along the highway are scarred with mines, several of them actively producing feldspar, lithium, beryl, and some gold. In TEPEE GULCH, which the highway crosses, are the CALUMET (R) and the WEALTHY and KING OSCAR MINES (L), among others.

SAWMILLS, producing shingles from ponderosa pine logs, are operated along the highway under authority of the U.S. Forest Service.

At 18.5 *m.* is the junction with US 16A.

Right on this hard-surfaced highway to US 85A (*see Tour 14*), 6 *m.* At that point, US 16A joins US 85A, 4 m. N. of Hill City, and the two routes are united (*see Tour 14*) to the junction with US 16 at Custer (see below).

KEYSTONE, 22.1 *m.* (4,342 alt.), is one of the pioneer towns of the Hills. The older part follows the creek (L), with unpainted houses on one side and store buildings on the other. The newer part follows US 16 and caters to travelers with its markets and camps.

A FELDSPAR MILL (L) is at the fork of two roads, its large building covered with a coat of white dust. The plant has been operating day and night since repeal to furnish feldspar to be used in making glass, and also false teeth, bathtubs, linoleum, and other articles. Breaking naturally into cubes, the rock is ground with Belgian granite until it is pulverized. Some of the rock is reduced to a powder four times as fine as flour. The spar is mined from the mountain behind the mill, and other minerals are also extracted, particularly lithium, used in making soft drinks, and mica, used in the manufacture of isinglass.

The real mining community is off the highway, little changed from the days when it provided the setting for Stewart Edward White's novels *The Westerners* and *The Claim Jumpers*. White left the country when irate prospectors after reading about themselves, sought to place his neck in a noose.

Keystone is also the site of the famous HOLY TERROR GOLD MINE which was located in 1894, and produced ore assayed as high as $18,000 per ton. It was still nameless when the discoverer's wife suggested the mine be named for her. Her ire was salved somewhat when the Holy Terror's gold output amounted to $70,000 a week. For several years the mine was a sensational producer. Since then there has been flooding trouble and numerous changes in ownership. The mine was revived again after World War II.

Also in the Keystone vicinity are the ETTA and INGERSOLL MINES, the country's leading producers of lithium and beryl, respectively.

L. from Keystone is the HARNEY RANGER STATION, 1.3 *m.* and the BATTLE CREEK PICNIC GROUNDS, 1.6 *m.*

At 22.7 *m.* US 16 enters the HARNEY PEAK GAME SANC-
TUARY. A large crag of jesset is near the road (R) at 22.9 *m.*

At 23.1 *m.* US 16 enters the eastern end of CUSTER STATE
PARK, one of the largest State parks in the United States, comprising 128,000 acres. Created in 1913, with the exception of modern
hotels and improved highways, this park remains in a wilderness-like
state and is a wild-life sanctuary where over 600 buffaloes, 2,500 elk,
and 2,000 deer roam freely (*see THE BLACK HILLS*).

At 23.8 *m.* is the junction with the RUSHMORE MEMORIAL
HIGHWAY (*see Tour 5A*). From here US 16 traverses the Iron
Mountain Highway.

At 24 *m.* are the GRIZZLY PARK campgrounds, in rugged se-
clusion.

From the PIGTAIL BRIDGE, 24.3 *m.*, is an excellent view (R)
of Washington's face carved on Mt. Rushmore in the distance. At
25.2 *m.* is another Pigtail Bridge, claimed to be the longest spiral
bridge in America. The bridge is built so that each succeeding upward
curve passes over the last one until the road reaches a sufficient
height to take to the hillside in its upward climb.

A TUNNEL, 26.4 *m.*, is cut through solid granite for 176 ft. The
whole tunnel is focused on the Rushmore figures, the sides of the
tunnel forming a frame, and the whole making a most effective telescope; but the view is backward through the tunnel.

At the end of the tunnel the road forks into two one-way drives
through a grove of quaking aspen and birch.

At 26.7 *m.* another bridge approaches a tunnel, which again is
focused on Mt. Rushmore, but this time the view is straight ahead.
The road winds upward with sharp curves and pitches, and divides
again into one-way roads.

At 27.6 *m.* is the summit of IRON MOUNTAIN (5,500 alt.),
from which a view of surrounding mountains is available. To the
W. is Harney Peak, NW. is Mt. Rushmore, and E., through the trees,
are the yellow Badlands; below, the road drops away in ribbon-like
curves and loops. Iron Mountain is estimated to have 55 percent
iron content. Such a deposit is known as "Iron Hat."

At 28.6 *m.* is another tunnel, with a rear view focused on Mt.
Rushmore, and for the next few miles ironwood trees replace the
pine, until a treeless plain is reached.

At 32.4 *m.* is the junction with a dirt road.

Left on this road is the SPOKANE MINE, 1 *m.*, one of the mines reopened during
the gold boom

Continuing down the mountain side, US 16 recrosses Iron Creek
several times until the foot of the mountain is reached.

At 39.1 *m.* is a junction with State 36.

Left on this hard-surfaced road, through the Custer State Park gate, to the

BORGLUM RANCH STUDIO, 4.2 *m.* (*private*). At 7.1 *m.* is RUSHMORE CAVE, a crystalline cavern along Battle Creek.

HERMOSA (*beautiful*), 8 *m.* (3,278 alt.), was founded by the Pioneer Town Site Co. in 1886. The principal point of interest is the little white CONGREGATIONAL CHURCH (L) at the northern edge of town. Here President and Mrs. Coolidge attended service each Sunday during the summer of 1927, when the Summer White House was at the nearby State Game Lodge (*see below*). A student pastor had charge of the church that summer but President Coolidge was faithful in his attendance. At his request, no mention or reference was made to his presence at any time. The only formality was that after the service the congregation remained seated until the President had left the church. At the end of the summer the President and Mrs. Coolidge entertained the student pastor at dinner.

US 16 winds westward, and on the hillsides along the highway herds of elk and deer often are seen munching the grass.

GRACE COOLIDGE CREEK, 40.1 *m.*, was named for the wife of former President Calvin Coolidge, who spent the summer of 1927 in the Black Hills. It was previously called Squaw Creek.

At 41.5 *m.* (R) is the CUSTER STATE PARK ZOO (*open to public*). A variety of native animals, including bear, deer, elk, bobcats, mountain sheep, wolves, porcupines, foxes, coyote, and badgers, are kept on exhibit.

Here is the junction with the East Fire Guard Road.

Left on this road, in a southwesterly direction, through the BUFFALO PASTURE are many views of the animals grazing, sleeping, and fighting. Occasional buffalo round-ups are held in this area. The park herd, which numbers 600, roams free over the pastures. Usually buffalo remain in a herd, but sometimes the quiet, shaggy creatures are seen singly or in small groups beside the road. They pay little attention to passers-by, but as they possess agility and speed contradictory to their clumsy appearance it is advisable not to leave the car when they are near.

STATE GAME LODGE, 42 *m.* (4,225 alt.), is a State-owned hostelry built of native stone and pine. It gained national notice as "The Summer White House" of President and Mrs. Calvin Coolidge in 1927. The ground floor, with the exception of the dining room, contains a museum of Indian relics and geologic specimens. Noted for its Western hospitality, the popular lodge has been enlarged and renovated to accommodate more visitors and meetings. A number of modern housekeeping cabins have also been built. A store is maintained on the grounds.

Horseback trips are featured, with cowboy guides, from half-day rides to three-day pack trips into the heart of the Hills.

At 42.5 *m.* is the CUSTER STATE PARK MUSEUM (*open to public*), a low rambling rustic building constructed of native stone and lumber, built in 1934–5–6. The main exhibit room, is entered through a massive and attractive portico fronting the highway to the S. A pictorial record of Black Hills historic events is featured, with maps of the Custer Expedition, early trails, and present-day hiking and horseback trails. The geologic and forestry exhibits, as well as the historic group, were worked out under the supervision of the National Park Service.

The office of the Park Superintendent is near the Museum.

At 47.9 *m.* is the junction with the Needles Highway (*see Tour 14A*). Between the arms of the Y is the forester's residence.

LEGION LAKE, 48.5 *m.*, was formed by damming a creek and flooding the canyon. This lake, known for its striking beauty, has a huge, rounded rock at the south end. It has been stocked with lake trout and blue gills.

LEGION LAKE LODGE (L) is another State-owned inn. In addition to rooms in the hotel, there are a number of cabins for the public and a restaurant that features elk steaks and buffalobergers, made from ground buffalo meat. There is a good beach, and boats may be rented. A corral here has saddle horses. The lake and the lodge were named for the American Legion because the South Dakota department operated the hotel here at one time.

Here also is the BLACK HILLS PLAYHOUSE, summer theatre operated by the University of South Dakota (*mid-June through August*). The canvas-walled playhouse is a reproduction of Deadwood's first theatre, in which Jack Langrishe and his troupe entertained the miners during the gold rush of '76. This project was started in 1946 by Dr. Warren M. Lee, head of the department of dramatic art at the University. The casts are professional, and students from all parts of the country enroll in the summer classes connected with the theatre. The repertoire ranges from Broadway hits to melodramas; one of the most repeated is Dr. Lee's *The Legend of Devil's Gulch*. The troupe goes on tour to the various Hills cities with a regular play schedule during the summer.

East along the shore of Legion Lake, on the Barnes Canyon Road, is the secluded BADGER HOLE, 0 *m.*, home of Badger Clark, South Dakota poet laureate, and author of *Sun and Saddle Leather*, *Sky Lines and Wood Smoke*, *Spike*, and other collections. Beyond the house, down the canyon, is the ELK PASTURE.

US 16 winds westward through heavy pine forest. At night the car lights stop deer in their tracks, on and near the highway.

BALANCED ROCK, 48.6 *m.* (R), is a curiosity that causes many passersby to stop for a personal examination.

At 49.3 *m.* is the junction with State 87 (*see Tour 5B*).

At 51 *m.* is the junction with a graveled road.

Right on this road is the BISMARK LAKE ORGANIZATION CAMP 1.8 *m.*, a permanent camp area built by the U.S. Forest Service for use by organizations for summer outings. It is administered by the Harney National Forest hqs. at Custer.

At 51.5 *m.* US 16 reaches the east edge of STOCKADE LAKE (5,189 alt.), a long, narrow, 135-acre artificial lake, formed by damming French Creek. At the east end are a beach, diving tower, and boat dock (*open to public*). The road winds along the shore, over the dam and spillway. A pear-shaped peninsula extends into the lake to form an unusual scenic effect, and in the distant background rises the majestic Harney Range. The lake is stocked with trout.

The STOCKADE LAKE CAMPGROUND, a public picnic area maintained by the Forest Service, is in a stand of timber overlooking the lake.

ANNIE D. TALLENT MONUMENT, 53.4 *m.*, is a memorial to the first white woman in the Black Hills. Born in York, N. Y., and educated in the East, she came to the Black Hills with the Gordon Expedition in 1874. When all the trespassers were taken to Fort Laramie, Wyo., in 1875, she was transported on a government mule. She returned with another expedition a year later. She wrote a book, *Black Hills, or Last Hunting Grounds of the Dakotas,* in which she described the early days of the Black Hills. When she died in 1901, a special train was furnished by the Society of the Black Hills Pioneers to carry her body to Elgin, Ill.

At 53.5 *m.* US 16 passes the western edge of Stockade Lake opposite the old Gordon Stockade site; at this point is the junction with a dirt road.

Right on this road is a reproduction of the GORDON STOCKADE, 0.2 *m.*, originally built on the banks of historic French Creek in gold rush days.

Reports from the Custer expedition that penetrated the Black Hills in the summer of 1874 stated positively to the Government that there was "gold in them thar hills." The news created considerable excitement, especially at Sioux City, Iowa. Charles Collins became active in organizing an expedition to the new El Dorado. By October a small band of 26 men and a woman and her boy, together with six covered wagons, each drawn by four oxen, and with provisions enough for six months, were assembled for the trip.

The van started Oct. 6, with the pretense of having O'Neill, Neb., as their goal. After a few days it was deemed best to elect one of their number as leader and pilot. Their choice was John Gordon and his ability proved the wisdom of their selection. A few weeks after the train passed O'Neill one of their number, Moses Aaron, became seriously ill, died Nov. 27, and was buried that evening on a knoll near where the town of Wall now stands.

The expedition reached General Custer's old camping grounds on French Creek, about 2.5 m. E. of Custer, Dec. 23, 1874, after a trip of 78 days, marked by sufferings and privations. The weather turned extremely cold but, fortunately for the pioneers, fuel was handy. The large pine logs, filled with pitch, burned freely.

For protection against hostile Indians the band decided to build what later became known as the Gordon Stockade. US 16 now passes the place, and a signboard, about 200 yards distant, marks the spot where gold was first discovered July 27, 1874, by Horatio N. Ross and Wm. McKay, who were prospectors with Custer.

The stockade was, as the reproduction shows, an enclosure 80 ft. square, built of logs 12 to 14 in. in diameter, set 3 ft. in the ground, making a fence about 12 ft. high. The structure was placed on level ground beside French Creek, 400 ft. from either timber or rocks. Cracks were filled from the inside by smaller timbers. Bastions were built at the corners so that occupants could protect themselves by shooting along the outside of the fence in every direction. The double gate was made of 10-inch hewn logs and opened inside. A well seven ft. deep was sunk two rods from the gate.

Six log cabins were erected inside, and companions were chosen according to compatability. Some of the cabins had puncheon floors and the rest only the ground. Each cabin had a good fireplace built of rock and mud. The roofs were made by splitting 12-inch logs into halves and hollowing them out like a trough. Cracks in the roofs were filled with grass and mud. No nails were used.

After the stockade and cabins were finished, they began the search for gold, occasionally taking a day off to get a deer, elk, or mountain sheep, to keep up the supply of meat. By the end of January 1875 the miners had panned out $40 in gold, enough to prove the metal was there.

To keep their word with Collins, who organized the party, Gordon and Eaf Witcher started Feb. 3, 1875, for Sioux City with their gold for proof, and also to bring back reinforcements and provisions before the Indians should begin to come into the Hills in the spring.

In March the colonists were so sure they were making a permanent settlement that they laid out a town and named it Harney. It proved to be only another dream, for on April 3, 1875, two army officers accompanied by Rodger Williams and Red Dan McDonald appeared in camp to inform the band that they were under arrest and must prepare to move immediately to Fort Laramie. Confusion was rife at once, for they were to take only what was absolutely necessary. Many of the men hid their tools, so sure were they that they would be back. Of the 28 oxen they had turned out, only 15 would be rounded up. Camp was broken April 7, and the band started for Cheyenne.

Upon their arrival at Fort Laramie they were paroled, and were surprised to learn that their friend, Collins, had sent money for their transportation back to Sioux City. A few of the men went back, and when they arrived they were met at the depot by the mayor and thousands of citizens.

John Gordon was not daunted. Openly backed by thousands of citizens, he organized another expedition of 300 members and crossed the Missouri River three days before a special message from Washington reached Sioux City, forbidding anyone to leave for the Black Hills. When the wagon train reached the Indian reservation, Government troops overtook it, burned all the wagons and supplies that were not needed by the trespassers for their return trip, and placed Gordon under arrest at Fort Randall. Even this treatment did not stop the movement. Adventurers still sifted through until a treaty was signed and the restrictions raised.

Through the Commercial Club of Custer, the stockade was rebuilt in 1924. A huge mass of pegmatite, covering several acres at the base, rises behind the stockade to a height of about 500 ft.

At 53.6 m. is the W. boundary of the CUSTER STATE PARK GAME REFUGE.

CALAMITY PEAK, a pegmatite rock formation rising 1,200 ft. above French Creek, is R. of the highway. It was named for Martha Jane Canary Burke, universally known as Calamity Jane, a woman who cut a wide swath for herself in the Black Hills, at a time when men outnumbered the women 10,000 to one.

At 53.6 m. FRENCH CREEK is crossed. It was from this creek that the first gold in the Black Hills was panned, starting the gold rush of '76. Gold is still being panned in the creek, but with suction pumps and mercurized pans.

At 53.8 m. is a native-stone marker where Gen. George A. Custer's soldiers camped in 1874. Beside it is the grave of John Pommer, a private of the U.S. Cavalry.

The FIRST GOLD CLAIM, 54 m., was registered by soldiers and posted on this site.

At 56 m. is the junction with the Sylvan Lake Road (see Tour 14A).

CUSTER, 56.5 m. (5,301 alt.), seat of Custer Co., is the oldest town in the Hills. It is on French Creek near the place where gold was first discovered July 27, 1874, by Horatio N. Ross, a prospector with General Custer's expedition into the Hills. Although the discovery has resulted in an extraction of a half-billion dollars in gold in the Black Hills, neither Ross nor the town of Custer benefited greatly. Ross is buried in a pauper's grave, and richer gold fields were found elsewhere (*see DEADWOOD and LEAD*).

To see Custer spread out over a wide, green valley, with broad Main St. and in-town airfield, it is difficult to realize that here is a "mile-high" town, highest of any of the major Black Hills cities and towns. Seeking plenty of elbow room, Custer laid out its streets "so that a four yoke of oxen could be turned around without driving around the block."

The town was staked out in 1875 and named Stonewall in honor of the Confederate general, "Stonewall" Jackson. The group of miners first on the site, like the Gordon party that previously settled on French Creek and erected the Gordon Stockade, was ordered out because no treaty had as yet been signed with the Indians. In this case, however, the authorities permitted seven men to remain as custodians of the property of all. Many of those who left never returned. After the withdrawal of the Federal troops, leaving the country open to settlement, the town was named Custer at a miners' meeting and lots were divided among the miners present. Immigrants began to come in great numbers, and by April 1876 the population had increased to 5,000. After the discovery of the rich placer mines at Deadwood, in the short space of three weeks the 5,000 population had dwindled to less than 100 residents. But Custer had been publicized throughout the East, and its natural advantages of location in the hills, abundance of water for placer mining in the French Creek valley and neighboring gulches, and the discovery of large quantities of mica, all tended to render the city important once more in the eyes of settlers.

The first post office in Custer, and in the entire Black Hills region, was a spacious cave in the rock just a mile W. of town, on the N. side of the road. Here, in the earliest days of placer mining, everyone who came in from the "outside" deposited the mail he brought. And there the miners would come, each one sorting out his own mail and leaving the rest. The next post office, in the rear of a general store in Custer, consisted of an apple box into which all mail was thrown and from which each person took what belonged to him. This was satisfactory to all until the arrival of a U.S. postal inspector. Horrified at this unorthodox handling of the mail, the inspector in no uncertain terms told the storekeeper just what he could and could not do. As he left the building, the irate merchant overtook him on the porch and thrust the apple box into his arms. "Here's your darned post office!" he said, "Take it with you."

Between the years 1881 and 1890 the town began to build for permanency, several brick structures being erected. In 1890 with the arrival of the railroad, Custer was at last connected with the world outside its little valley. Today, because of its proximity to such points

Heights and Depths of the Black Hills

MOUNT RUSHMORE NATIONAL MEMORIAL

WASHINGTON'S PROFILE

CARVING LINCOLN'S NOSE

STOCKADE LAKE NEAR CUSTER

ROCK SKYSCRAPER, NEEDLES HIGHWAY

ROUGHLOCK FALLS, SPEARFISH CANYON

WIND CAVE NATIONAL PARK
BOXWORK
CALCITE CRYSTALS

CRYSTAL CAVE

as the Needles, Harney Peak, Sylvan Lake, and other scenic spots, the town has become a mecca for tourists. A historical pageant (*see below*), held on the anniversary of the discovery of gold in French Creek, attracts increasing thousands of people yearly. Situated in a favorable hunting region, the town is a gathering place for deer hunters during the fall open season. There is still some placer mining being done in Custer, while local and nearby lumber mills bring in a considerable amount of trade. A feldspar mill at the edge of town ships several carloads of ore weekly. In addition, quartz, gold, mica, beryl, tantalite, amblygonite, soda spar, tourmaline, and gypsum are shipped in commercial quantities. During World War II a mica fabricating plant was opened where sheets of this isinglass mineral are prepared for use in electrical equipment.

The GOLD DISCOVERY DAYS PAGEANT GROUNDS, on a grassy tree-bordered slope at the SE. edge of town, are the scene of part of a two-day celebration held each year, July 27–28, to commemorate the discovery of gold on French Creek in 1874 (*see HISTORY*). The pageant, held on the actual date of the discovery (July 27) presents, first, an allegorical representation of creation, with costumed groups of children symbolizing flowers, young girls representing the stately pines, and with small boys, dressed as gnomes, planting gold in the earth. The following scenes show the Custer expedition, the arrival and removal of the Gordon Party, the gold rush, the Metz massacre, the hanging of Fly Speck Billy, Indian battles, and an attack on a stagecoach. All the white actors in the drama are residents of Custer, while a large number of Indians from Pine Ridge Reservation play historic roles. The production is in charge of the Women's Civic Club of Custer, and the author of the script is a life-long resident of the city. Besides the pageant, there are rodeos and Indian dances in an arena NE. of town, and a street carnival.

SCOTT'S ROSE QUARTZ CO. STORE is housed in a large concrete building near US 16 at the east end of town. The cement doorstep to the salesroom is inlaid with small pieces of rose quartz, laid in parallel lines spaced about a foot apart. In the salesroom are displayed different kinds of mosaic work and stones, all on sale. The articles are made in the workshop in the rear of the salesroom. Outside is a rock garden, its borders and paths outlined with large slabs of petrified wood.

The LOG CABIN MUSEUM, on Main St., opposite the courthouse, is the oldest standing building in the Black Hills. It was built by General Crook's soldiers under Captain Pallock of the Fifth Cavalry in 1875. It stands in Way City Park, which was named for Harry E. Way, pioneer resident and antiquarian, who donated the park and museum, originally his private collection, to the city. The building, constructed of hewn logs, is 16 ft. wide and 20 ft. long. Loopholes in the walls are bullet-scarred at the outer ends. Since it was first built a fireplace and floor have been added, and the roof has been shingled. It contains a collection of stuffed animals and birds—hawks, a mounted lion, bobcats, and eagles—and also a large collection of mineral specimens and historical relics dealing with the history of Custer and the Black Hills.

The ROSS MONUMENT, just a short distance W. of the Log Cabin Museum in the park, was erected in 1921 by the Association of Black Hills Pioneers in honor of Horatio N. Ross, who first discovered gold on French Creek. The monument is composed of rocks set in cement, the rocks being contributed by pioneers and friends of Ross. One crystal was taken from the post office room in Wind Cave 50 years ago. Among other rocks are diamond drill ores, rose quartz, tourmaline, purple and yellow lapidolite, petrified moss, calcite crystals, mica, and gold and copper ore.

At Custer is the junction with US 85A (*see Tour 14*) and US 16A (*see above*).

At 60.8 *m.* is FOUR MILE RANCH, a resting place on the old Cheyenne Trail; here is a junction with a graded dirt road which follows the old trail down the valley.

Left on this road is HEUMPHREUS' TWELVE MILE RANCH, 8 *m.*, one of the oldest ranches in the southern Hills, so named because it is 12 m. from Custer on the Custer-Cheyenne Trail. It was a favorite stopping place in the early days and its hospitality has always been proverbial. In these latter days when the swift auto has replaced the slow freight wagon, the old traditions are upheld by the presence of numerous rustic cabins clinging to the hillside underneath the pines. At the foot of the hill sprawls the comfortable old ranch house, with the barns and corrals that identify it for the cattle ranch that it is. There are three collections at the ranch that are well worth seeing—books, mineral specimens, and art objects. The library, one of the largest in this section, is especially rich in books on the botany and geology of the region. The mineral collection is unusually valuable and complete. There are over 1,000 specimens of minerals and fossils gathered in the Black Hills and vicinity, all named and identified. The art collection contains 70 drawings in color of the native wild flowers of the region, together with numerous wood carvings of exquisite artistry done in native juniper wood; also drawings and oil paintings of Indian, pioneer, and Western life.

At 65 *m.* is LIGHTENING CREEK PICNIC GROUND, set aside by the U.S. Forest Service and supplied with firewood and drinking water.

At 69.5 *m.* is the Entrance to JEWEL CAVE NATIONAL MONUMENT, supervised by the National Park Service. The cave is best known for its colorful crystal formations. Since 1934, when it was acquired by the Federal Government, there has been considerable exploration of the underground routes. Jasper Cave has also been included in the monument area, and is in the process of development. Jewel Cave was first discovered by Albert and Frank Michaud while prospecting and was retained by them as a mineral claim until 1928, when the Custer Commercial Club and the Lions Club of Newcastle, Wyo., took it over to preserve the underground formations. Jasper Cave was discovered when some mountain lion cubs were tracked to the entrance.

US 16 winds down Tepee Canyon; the TEPEE CANYON RANGER STATION is (L).

At 70.1 *m.* US 16 crosses HELL'S CANYON (5,092 alt.), so named by frontiersmen because it was "hell to cross."

At 72.2 *m.* begins a mile stretch where trees have been uprooted by a tornado. Stumps are all that remain to mark the scene of the catastrophe; the timber was logged and the debris burned.

The heavy timber is being gradually replaced by smaller trees, and the top of the tableland is covered with sagebrush.

At 83 *m.* US 16 crosses the Wyoming Line, 8.2 m. SE. of Newcastle, Wyo. (*see Wyo. Tour 8*).

Tour 5A

Junction with US 16 (Keystone)—Mount Rushmore National Memorial—Horsethief Lake—Junction with Needles Highway. Rushmore Memorial Highway (unnumbered). Junction with US 16—Junction with Needles Highway (State 87), 13.7 m. Roadbed hard-surfaced through Rushmore Reservation; W. portion is graveled.

THIS dramatic route provides comparative close-up views of the Mount Rushmore National Memorial, also known as the Shrine of Democracy. The huge sculpture may be viewed effectively at most any hour and any season, for it was designed by Gutzon Borglum to catch the earliest and last rays of the sun each day; at night flood lights are cast upon the lofty faces.

The road continues across the Rushmore Reservation, a 1,800-acre natural area designated by the Congress as a "land of perpetual wilderness, never to be improved in any form or manner."

Beyond are picnic grounds, a picturesque lake, nature trails, unique formations, and dude ranches. At places the road branches into separated one-way lanes through aspen groves and around rock upthrusts.

The Rushmore Memorial Highway branches W. from US 16, 1 m. S. of Keystone (*see Tour 5, Sec. c.*). The ascent is steep and twisting. At several turns the chiseled faces stand out in silvery profile, towering above surrounding mountain peaks.

At 0.3 *m.* is a spring (R); springs are numerous along the route and many of them are piped to the road so that the traveler can lean from his car for a drink.

At 0.9 *m.* is another spring and camping area.

At 1.8 *m.* is DOANE MOUNTAIN and a parking space for the MOUNT RUSHMORE STUDIO (5,500 alt.). Doane Mountain was named for Doane Robinson, for a quarter-century South Dakota's State Historian, who conceived the idea for the Mount Rushmore Memorial in 1924. The large, stained-log studio (*free*), which was built recently to accommodate more visitors than Borglum's original studio, houses the working model of the four figures—Presidents George Washington, Thomas Jefferson, Abraham Lincoln, and Theodore Roosevelt. Through the use of a plumb bob and compass, the directions and measurements were transmitted by telephone to the workers on the mountainside opposite. Here also is a large model of the Hall of Records, part of which has been cut out of the rock behind the figures.

The National Park Service, which supervises the memorial, has converted the old studio into a public lunch room.

At several convenient points along the studio porch and road are telescopes through which one may bring the sculpture to closer inspection.

The MOUNT RUSHMORE NATIONAL MEMORIAL (6,040 alt.), across the sharp valley, is said to be the largest sculpture undertaken since the time of the ancient Egyptians; the gigantic figures in granite are carved to the proportion of men 465 ft. tall. George Washington's carved face is 60 ft. from hair line to chin, and one can stand in Jefferson's eye. The forehead of Lincoln is 17 ft. from the eyebrows to the unruly lock of hair, and his mouth is 22 ft. wide. The Roosevelt figure is set deep into the mountain, and even the spectacles have been faithfully reproduced. Together they perpetuate a memorial to the founding, the expansion, the preservation, and the unification of the United States.

Funds to start the project were raised by public subscription, largely through dime contributions of South Dakota school children and gifts from outside the State. Although the State Legislature granted permission to create the memorial, it carefully refrained from making any appropriations. Gutzon Borglum, who already had more than 150 works of art prominently displayed through the world, undertook the job. President Calvin Coolidge dedicated Mount Rushmore, August 10, 1927, during his vacation in the Black Hills, and blasting began. The funds were depleted in 1928 and, largely through the efforts of President Coolidge, the Congress appropriated $250,000 for the memorial on February 22, 1929. The Mount Rushmore National Memorial Commission was created to administer the project.

Meanwhile, the face of Washington was chiseled, and the features of Jefferson, to Washington's right, became prominent. However, when a deep fissure in the rock was discovered the face of Jefferson was blasted out. Borglum was forced to regroup the figures, placing Jefferson at Washington's left and deeper into the mountain.

In 1936, President Franklin D. Roosevelt visited the memorial and dedicated the sculptured portrait of Jefferson, who is shown here at the age of 33 when he wrote the Declaration of Independence. The Abraham Lincoln head in the rotunda of the nation's capitol at Washington, D. C., which was executed by Borglum, served as his Rushmore model except that Lincoln is shown here with a beard.

The face of Theodore Roosevelt was taking shape when Gutzon Borglum died in February, 1941. His son, Lincoln, who had worked on the project since he was 16 and is an outstanding sculptor in his own right took charge and completed the faces.

The night-lighting system was dedicated in June, 1950. Drew Pearson, the columnist, and Van Heflin, who was with a Hollywood film company making a picture in the Black Hills, presided.

The magnitude of the figures carved in the mountainside necessitated engineering as well as sculptural skill. After the surface rock had been blasted, large drills operated by compressed air cut out the features. Holes were bored into the rock to the desired depth and pieces between broken out. Another air drill, with a chisel point, took off the rough surfaces. Polishing was the last job.

The workers were let down in small seats by gear-rigged cables over the edge of the mountain, and used their feet to push them away from the rocks. Scaffolds to hold several men were also built on the figures. The regular staff consisted of 36 men, about 19 of whom operated the carving drills. There was a blacksmith to sharpen the drills, engineers to operate the three large compressors, a powder man to blast the rough work, and hoisting men to lower the carvers on the mountain face.

The stone is a greyish-white granite with black flecks in it. Outlines are drawn on the rock in red to show where the rock is to be cut away, and the faces are chiseled out from top to bottom.

Most visitors inquire about the significance of the name Mount Rushmore. Following the gold rush period of the late 1870's, Charles E. Rushmore, an attorney from New York, visited the Black Hills in the interests of his mining clients. While touring the Hills, by horse and buggy, the attorney inquired the name of the granite-crested mountain. One of the party jokingly answered: "Why that is Mount Rushmore." And it still bears that name.

From the studio is a footpath leading to the Hall of Records behind the sculptured figures. A stairway of 400 steps is part of the ascent through a crevice in the rock near the summit.

From Doane Mountain, Rushmore Memorial Highway twists below the figures.

At 2.1 m. a person can stand directly under the nose of Washington, 500 ft. above, and sense the magnitude of the project.

The road winds behind Mount Rushmore through Starling Canyon, named for Colonel Edmund W. Starling, White House Secret Service agent, who was particularly impressed with this natural area since set aside as RUSHMORE RESERVATION. It extends N. from here. Mountain goats are sometimes seen scrambling on the high rock formations.

NEEDLES EYE, 3.1 m., is a granite formation with a great slit, shaped to suggest the eye of a needle.

At 3.2 m. (R) is the LEANING ROCK, another granite formation, appearing to lean dangerously toward the road.

At 3.5 *m.* (L) there is a beautiful view of the northern hills.

At 4.6 *m.* (R) is a huge GRANITE FORMATION. These particular formations seem to rear up out of the earth, a surprising contrast with the forest lands surrounding them.

At 4.8 *m.* is HORSETHIEF LAKE in a pine setting. Along the shores of this pretty lake a public camp ground is maintained by the U.S. Forest Service, and there are facilities for swimming, boating, and fishing. It was so named because Lame Johnny, an infamous robber of the early 1880's, is supposed to have cached in this area some of the gold and jewelry taken in Black Hills stagecoach holdups. While the dam was being built by boys in the Civilian Conservation Corps during the 1930's, they searched in vain for the treasures.

At 6 *m.* is the ELKHORN SPRING PICNIC GROUND, a Forest Service recreation area. From here is a NATURE TRAIL, well-marked for hikers, around Elkhorn Mt. (L) to Harney Peak. This area abounds in wild game.

At 9.7 *m.* is the PALMER GULCH HORSEBACK TRAIL to Harney Peak.

PALMER GULCH LODGE, 10 *m.,* is a dude ranch which caters to summer vacationists and draws most of its guests from Chicago and the Twin Cities. Several writers and librarians usually make their headquarters here.

At 11 *m.* (L) is an excellent view of Harney Peak.

At 11.7 *m.* begins a one-way road which crosses an area of thick timber, spruce and aspen predominating.

At 12.3 *m.* is an area of dead trees skirting the road, the trees having died from an attack of beetles.

At 13.1 *m.* (L) is the GRIZZLY BEAR HORSEBACK TRAIL. Here also is the approximate center of a burned area 1 m. long.

At 13.7 *m.* is the junction of Rushmore Memorial Highway with the Needles Highway (State 87), 3.5 m. N. of Sylvan Lake Hotel (*see Tour 14A*) and 2.5 m. S. of the junction with US 85A (*see Tour 14*).

Tour 5B

Junction with US 16 (Custer State Park)—Mt. Coolidge—Blue Bell State Lodge—Wind Cave National Park—Junction with US 85A. State 87.
Junction with US 16—Junction with US 85A, 16.5 m.
Roadbed graveled.

THIS is a scenic route and short-cut within the W. portion of Custer State Park between US 16 and Hot Springs (*see Tours 7 and 14*). It passes through a rugged, forested area noted for good trout fishing, and at the S. end is the range for bison herds of Wind Cave National Park.

State 87 turns S. from US 16 at a junction 0.8 m. W. of Legion Lake.

At 1.6 *m.* (R) is the MT. COOLIDGE LOOKOUT (6,400 alt.; visitors welcome in tower). Originally known as Sheep Mountain, the peak was renamed in 1927, in honor of President Coolidge. Because of the remarkable view of the entire southern Hills, the State maintains a year-around ranger station to operate a central control radio system for fire fighting. Forest fires are a constant threat and lookouts are constantly on watch, especially during the tourist season. Visitors who make the steep climb to the glass-enclosed tower platform are rewarded with a panoramic view extending far beyond the mountains.

BLUE BELL LODGE, 4.7 *m.*, is a State-owned resort hotel with a cluster of modern cabins half hidden in the pines. The two-story log hotel, on the banks of historic French Creek, has a large public dining room and lounges on the main floor. It was built in 1925 by Chris Jensen, Hot Springs telephone line owner, who named it for the Bell Telephone company's sign rather than the bluebell flowers that grow in profusion here. Blue Bell is an official postoffice, and there is quite a summer community along the creek. Horses and cowboy guides are available for trail rides and pack trips.

At Blue Bell is the junction with the Lame Johnny Trail.

Left on this fire-guard road through rough country along French Creek is the NARROWS PICNIC AREA, 1 *m.* Here are fireplaces and picnic tables in the woods. A path leads (L) to the OVERLOOK, a rock ledge above a long, deep pool of clear water. The Narrows proper can be negotiated only on foot; this wild gorge is noted for its plant and animal life. Beyond the picnic area, the road passes over a ridge and into the valley of LAME JOHNNY CREEK, which was the scene of the execution of the bandit, Lame Johnny. Like most mountainous or forest regions, the Black Hills became the hiding place for many fugitives from the law, and the rendezvous of various gangs who preyed upon travelers, miners, prospectors, and settlers. Lame Johnny, who walked with a limp, was one of the most ambitious thieves of the Hills' country. A college man, he wandered into Texas from the East and engaged in the profitable trade of stealing horses from the Indians. After a time he moved into the Black Hills and took up the well-ordered life of the average pioneer, serving as deputy sheriff of Custer Co. and then for a time worked in the Homestake Mining Co. office, where an acquaintance recognized him as a horse thief from Texas. Soon there was a rumor that he was back at his old trade of running off Indian horses as well as those belonging to white men. In the fall of 1878 he and his gang engaged in the holdup of a coach on Gilme and Sanlabury stage line on Lame Johnny Creek in Custer Co.; shortly after the robbery Lame Johnny was arrested on a charge of horse stealing previous to this time. Later it developed that he was wanted for the stagecoach robbery and was put on a coach at Red Cloud to be brought into Deadwood for trial. A short distance from Buffalo Gap when the coach reached the small creek that now bears his name, Lame Johnny was taken from the coach and hanged to the limb of an elm tree, at the place where he and his gang had robbed the coach.

At 7.2 *m.* is a BOY SCOUT CAMP.

At 8.3 *m.* is the junction with the South Fire Guard Road (L) through the buffalo pasture of Custer State Park.

At 11 *m.*, is the boundary between CUSTER STATE PARK and the FEDERAL GAME SANCTUARY, a part of WIND CAVE NATIONAL PARK.

Winding through canyons, State 87 traverses one of the pig-tailed bridges where the inevitable remark is heard: "We're meeting ourselves coming back."

At 16.5 *m*. is the junction with US 85A, 13 m. N. of Hot Springs (*see Tour 14*).

Tour 6

Junction with US 16—Badlands National Monument—Wall. US 16A.
Junction with US 16 (W. off Kadoka) to Junction with US 16 (at Wall), 53 m.
Accommodations at Cedar Pass Lodge and Pinnacles Camp.
All-weather roadbed.

US 16A is a scenic route through the most picturesque portion of the Badlands National Monument (*no admission fee*). The 150,000-acre area was set aside in 1939 by Presidential proclamation and is supervised by the National Park Service. It is a major part of the White River, or Big Badlands, of South Dakota, scene of numerous scientific expeditions into this graveyard of prehistoric wildlife. It also serves occasionally as a setting for motion pictures.

This drive is most pleasant and the region is best viewed in early morning or evening, rather than during the heat of the day. Shadows add to the eerie beauty, and under moonlight the Badlands are especially effective.

US 16A branches W. from US 16 (*see Tour 5*), 7 m. W. of Kadoka.

At 13 *m*. freak formations begin to rise beside the highway and the Badlands Wall looms ahead, a range of grassless, eroded peaks with different layers of various colors—gray, tan, buff, olive, cream, and deep rose. The cathedral-like spires rise above the more eroded rounded domes, with washed-out gaps forming windows and new vistas.

At 15 *m*. is a boundary of BADLANDS NATIONAL MONUMENT.

"Mako (*land*) sica (*bad*)" was the expression used by the Indians to describe the strip of barren land, ghostly peaks, lofty pinnacles, spires, and terraces that make up the White River Badlands of southwestern South Dakota.

"Mauvaise terres" (*bad lands*), said the early French explorers of this region when confronted with the problem of travel through this fantastically weird country, with its countless formations of marvelous size and structure, its varied shapes and colors.

"A part of Hell with the fires burned out" was the way Gen. George A. Custer described them.

Frank Lloyd Wright, the noted architect, had this to say of the Badlands:

"As we rode, or seemed to be floating upon a splendid winding road that seemed to understand it all and just where to go, we rose and fell between its delicate parallels of rose and cream and sublime shapes, chalk white, fretted against a blue sky with high floating clouds—the sky itself seemed only there to cleanse and light the vast harmonious building scheme. Here, for once, comes complete release from materiality. Communion with what man often calls 'God' is inevitable in this place."

In developing this region, it is the aim of the Government to preserve its pristine freshness, and to restore the animal life that formerly abounded there. While they cannot bring back the dinosaur and the triceratops, the oreodon and tyrannosaurus rex, they plan to have the Rocky Mountain sheep once more look down from the jagged pinnacles, as they have done within the memory of man, while the Rocky Mountain goats sit staring to windward for hours from some inaccessible mountain shelf. On the plains at the base of the white-walled formations, wary antelope and deer will once more roam, and the lumbering buffalo will file through the passes and browse in the draws. Only the slinking coyote will be banned, the robber of birds' nests and the killer of defenseless young animals. So the region will return to a primitive state, almost as it was perhaps when the little three-toed horse roamed the plains "unrestrained by the nearest rider, fifty million years away."

Millions of years ago this part of the earth was probably covered by a great marsh. Amidst the terrific, steaming heat, huge, lumbering animals and reptiles lived and fought and died, to be covered with sediment deposited through many centuries. New species of animals appeared upon the scene—a three-toed horse, a small camel, a saber-tooth tiger.

As time rolled on the many animals and reptiles of those dim ages died, leaving almost no visible trace of their existence. Then the forces of erosion began to operate. As centuries passed, slowly and steadily the numerous growing streams carved their way into the soft, yielding soil, molding the present Badlands formation and uncovering in places the prehistoric skeletons that are rich sources of information to the modern scientist. After a heavy rain, fossilized bones are often found lying exposed on the ground. The Badlands are a treasure storehouse of ancient animal life, and specimens and skeletons from this region have found their way into museums all over the world. One of the largest collections of Badlands fossils is at the South Dakota State School of Mines and Technology at Rapid City (*see RAPID CITY*).

US 16A penetrates the Badlands Wall through a corridor that cuts a downhill swath into CEDAR PASS, 17.2 *m.*, which opens onto the vast White River flats below. The Pass itself has a few scrub Cedar trees and a parking and picnicking area (R), surrounded by serrated peaks of the Badland's interior.

Left from Cedar Pass is a hiking and horseback trail (*saddle horses available at Cedar Pass Lodge; see below*).

Fossil remains are exposed from time to time as the formation weathers away, and they fall or are washed to the bottom of it. When several bits of bone are found close together, it is often possible to trace them to their source directly above where they lie. Whole bones are rare, but fossil teeth are not uncommon, either embedded in part of the jaw or singly.

Along this stretch of wall, at 1 m., are various low places called "windows," which look out over that desolate region aptly termed DANTE'S INFERNO. Through these windows are seen a series of striking views, each different from the rest. The infinite variety of scene is one of the most striking characteristics of the Badlands, and even the same place looks quite different when viewed at dawn or at twilight, in the glare of the noonday sun or by moonlight.

A climb to the top of the formation at any point is difficult but well rewarded. Here are rows of barren ridges, with sheer sides and thin walls, a welter of chaos and desolation. In either direction is seen mile after mile of Badlands wall. The highway winds downward and directly ahead (R) is VAMPIRE PEAK, so old in legend that even the oldest residents of the section do not know why it was so named. It is a tall, majestic peak, circular at its base and growing slimmer until capped by twin spikes. Nearer at hand are a few scattered clumps of cedar trees growing upon the peaks or springing from the fissures, all that remains of the heavy growth of trees that once gave the pass its name.

At 18.5 m. is CEDAR PASS LODGE (*hotel, restaurant, cabins, saddle horses*), spread out on the grassy floor of the Badlands. The modern public lodge buildings of rustic architecture utilize the materials of the area. Floors are made of polished agates and other colorful stone, walls are tinted with natural clays, and unique fossils and Sioux designs provide some of the decoration. The setting is particularly impressive.

Half a mile away is a skyline with a broken and serrated edge as sharply etched against the sky as if just struck off by the sculptor's chisel. The broken edges of this skyline assume every conceivable shape and form, with here a minaret and there a castle, here a a pyramid and there a tower, and here a projection that started out to be a peak and became a glistening candelabrum; this fantastic skyline stretches in both directions as far as the eye can see, with infinite variation.

Likewise, there is no sameness in the mighty wall below. At one point the clay has been whipped by wind or water into a series of fluted columns supporting a giant table. At another, a sheer wall rises to a peak in a gigantic pyramid of dazzling whiteness. Here and there are subtle bands of color, harmonizing with one another, and yet distinct; while at intervals is a band of red. And sometimes upon the benches there is a touch of green where grass or shrub is striving for a foothold, or where the stunted cedars raise their wizened heads against the white wall behind them.

Between the lodge and the wall are patches of prickly pear cactus, which blooms profusely, and of Mariposa lilies.

At 19 m. is the junction with State 40 (*see Tour 6A*).

For 20 m. US 16A winds through the heart of the Badlands, one of the most scenic stretches of road in the State. Now it skirts the base of the formation, now it winds up narrow canyons with towering peaks of white clay on either side, and now it climbs the almost vertical wall by a steady grade, and then follows the snake-like contour of the formation's brink for miles, with all the panorama of the Badlands spread out below, with the breaks of White River visible to the S., and to the N. and W. the level plains stretching to the distant Black Hills. Far to the W. Sheep Mountain stands like a lone sentinel, marking the end of the Badlands.

At 28 m. (R) is BIG FOOT PASS. It was through this natural opening that the wily Indian chief, Big Foot, led his band of 400 warriors, eluding the United States soldiers who had thought every possible pass was guarded. John J. Pershing, then a captain, was one of the soldiers attempting to stop Big Foot. After penetrating the Badlands, Big Foot and his warriors met a disastrous end at the Battle of Wounded Knee (see Tour 7) when he and almost all of his band were annihilated in the last conflict between the whites and the Indians, the culmination of the Messiah War.

After a steep, circling climb up Big Foot Pass the road follows the freakish wall until Dillon Pass leads down into another, perhaps a more wonderful, region, the PINNACLES, where likenesses of huge ancient cathedrals, turrets, spires, and altars are seen. After a few winding miles among the foothills of the Pinnacles, the road passes through the upper tunnel to the Great Wall.

The Badlands Wall takes a heavy toll of range cattle and horses whenever a winter blizzard hits suddenly. There have been few such storms, but the threat is a constant worry to stockmen. In January of 1949, 56 horses plunged over a 150-ft. precipice in the West-river's worst storm since 1888. Eleven of the horses were saved through hoist operations. At another place along the wall, 75 cattle perished; only a calf was saved by hoisting it back to safety.

At 40 m. is the PINNACLE POINT TOURIST CAMP, overlooking the great formations of the Badlands; here the gorgeous coloring at sunrise, once seen, is never forgotten. At the edge of the wall the view commands a bewildering maze of valleys, ravines, and jutting peaks, like the ruins of an ancient city. There are furnished cabins, a dining room, and other conveniences.

At 40.1 m. is the junction with an unnumbered road (see Tour 6A).

From Pinnacle Point the road runs northward, and at 53 m. forms a junction with US 16 at WALL (see Tour 5).

Tour 6 A

Junction with US 16A—Interior—Scenic—Pinnacles. State 40 and unnumbered road.
Junction with US 16A—Pinnacles, 61.8 m.
Chicago, Milwaukee, St. Paul and Pacific R.R. parellels this route for 30 m.
Limited accommodations.
Roadbed graded; good in dry weather only.

THIS is an "off the beaten path" route skirting the Badlands, with offshoots into regions of lonely isolation. The area S. of the road between Interior and Scenic has been designated an Air Force Gunnery Range; during bombing practice the area is posted with warnings.

State 40 twists westward from its junction with US 16A, the Badlands National Monument Highway, just W. of Cedar Pass Lodge. From Scenic an unnumbered road winds northward along the outer side of the Badlands Wall.

INTERIOR, 1.8 m. (2,381 alt.), is so named because of its position within the Badlands wall. It is an old town for this region, having been founded in 1891. Although it is in a ranching country, its principal source of income is derived from catering to the wants of tourists, who flock to the Badlands in increasing numbers.

At 3.8 m. is a junction with a dirt road.

Left on this road at 2 m. is WHITE RIVER, named for the white clay that washes off the hills and colors its waters in flood time a milky white. Here is a fork, L. up the hill winding through the breaks, past log and sod shanties, to the HEADLEE RANCH, 18.2 m., a country store and post office. At 21.2 m. in a draw is a windmill, the landmark for a prairie trail (R) which winds 1.4 m. to RATTLE-SNAKE or DEVIL BUTTES. It is advisable to park on the W. side of the second butte and walk to the summit 100 ft. (Boots should be worn for protection from rattlesnakes). The only known SAND CRYSTAL BED in North America is atop the western butte. The unusual cylindrical, pipe-like crystals occur only on this butte. Exposed banks of the crystals jut out of the hill and extend several yards; the crystals, varying in size from ¼ inch to 15 inches, are hard, whether lying singly on the ground or in large masses. Six or eight inches under the surface, the sand becomes wet—like the beach of a seashore—although in a semiarid region and at the highest elevation of that area. In the wet sand are lumps which, when delicately excavated, assume the appearance of a group of ill-proportioned fingers. Although easily broken while damp, the crystals harden quickly on exposure to the air. They are 60 per cent sand and 40 per cent calcium carbonate, the former occurring as an inclusion and the latter as a mineralizing and crystallizing agent. In this bed of sand, less than 3 ft. thick, the sand crystals occur in numbers measured in tons. Every form, from solitary hexagonal crystals to crowded bunches of multiplets, can be obtained. The formation discloses evidence of internal molecular or crystalline arrangement, and weathered specimens show a radiate or rosetted structure, owing to the tendency of lime salts to crystallize according to the laws governing calcite.

CONATA, 13.8 m. is in a picturesque ranching area.

SCENIC, 31.8 m. (2,812 alt.), was so named because of its situation in the shadow of Sheep Mountain among Badlands formations. The place was founded in 1907 as a station of the C. M. St. P. & P. R.R., with a boxcar for a depot and a cluster of tar paper shacks for residences. For 26 years water was hauled a distance of 10 *m.;* since 1933 it has been piped 2 m. from springs. The town has a fossil and rock MUSEUM (*free*). Nearby scenic attractions are Castle Rock and "Hell's Ten Thousand Acres."

At Scenic is a junction with a dirt road.

Left from Scenic on this road, at 1.5 *m.* is the foot of SHEEP MOUNTAIN. An extremely steep hill leads to the plateau above and cars should be put in low gear before attempting it. At the top is a gate. After passing through the gate a trail completely encircles the rim of the plateau a mile in circumference, which comprises the top of Sheep Mountain. From every point along this road are splendid views of the Badlands. Their vast extent and varied character can perhaps be better determined here than from any other point. At the base of Sheep Mountain the State School of Mines and Technology (see RAPID CITY) maintains a permanent camp to which a party of students, in charge of a faculty member, comes every summer to excavate fossils, further to enrich the School of Mines Museum. This immediate territory is peculiarly rich in fossil remains, even for the Badlands. A roster of visitors to the Badlands reads like an international scientific "Who's Who," as scientists from every country have come here to inspect this rich storehouse of paleontological treasures and secrets. Even for the visiting layman, a scramble in the surrounding formations will be richly repaid.

North of Scenic the road winds through an almost deserted region to the junction with the Badlands Monument Highway, 61.8 *m.* (*see Tour 6*), 9 m. S. of Wall (*see Tour 5*).

Tour 7

(Inwood, Iowa)—Canton—Lake Andes—Winner—Hot Springs—Edgemont—(Lusk, Wyo.). US 18.
Iowa Line to Wyoming Line, 458.4 m.
C. & N. W. R.R. parallels US 18 between St. Charles and Winner; C. B. & Q., between Hot Springs and Edgemont.
Roadbed oil-surfaced almost throughout.
Good accommodations east of Missouri River; fair, west of river as far as Winner. Gas and oil available west of Winner, but few lodging accommodations.

US 18 is an interesting route across southern South Dakota which has been improved only recently. It is not widely advertised nor heavily traveled as there are no major cities along the route. But the towns along this highway remain typically western, and there are long stretches of Indian country between the Missouri River and the Black Hills. It passes through two Sioux reservations (the Rosebud and the Pine Ridge) and skirts another (the Yankton); two of the Missouri River Basin Development projects—Fort Randall and Angostura—have changed the topography and the economy in the areas surrounding these Federal hydro-electric and irrigation programs.

After pursuing a level course for many miles in Iowa, US 18 crosses the Iowa Line 6 m. west of Inwood, Iowa (*see Iowa Tour 11*), and passes through the valley of the Big Sioux River. Rising in the Coteau des Prairies of northeastern South Dakota, the river drains an extensive territory. The Selkirk colonists en route from Winnipeg, Canada, to St. Louis, Mo., followed the valley, which was first explored by Nicollet and Frémont in 1838. The Sioux Indians named the river Can-ka-sda-ta (*where-they-paddle-softly-by-the-woods*).

Section a. Iowa Line—Junction US 281, 133.3 m.

After crossing the Big Sioux River, US 18 traverses wooded flats, luxuriant with vegetation, rising again to resume a level prairie course.

At 0.5 m. the upper structure of the Sioux Valley Ski Slide is visible ahead (L).

At 1.2 m. is the junction with a graveled road.

Left on this road is the SIOUX VALLEY SKI SLIDE, 0.7 m., which has been the scene of State, regional, and several national championship tournaments. The slide measures 600 ft. from the top of the scaffold to the bottom of the hill, and provides speed for expert jumpers of 60 to 100-m. per hour at the take-off. The surrounding hills provide excellent runs for cross-country ski races.

During the summer, these hills are used by the Sioux Valley Cycle Club for motorcycle climbs and exhibitions.

At 1.7 m. is a road leading (R) to the CANTON-INWOOD MEMORIAL HOSPITAL, serving the adjacent Iowa and South Dakota communities. The main building has had a varied history. It was built in 1901, to care for insane Indians, and for several years it was the only institution of its kind in the United States. Then, during the 1930's, the Hiawatha Indian Asylum was closed, following charges of carelessness and neglect. Next it became a branch of the State Penitentiary to house first-term lawbreakers. In 1946 the Federal government gave the city of Canton the title to the run-down institution and a square mile of property. The city promptly installed a public golf course, an airport, a trap shoot, and converted two barns for 4-H club use. Public subscriptions provided for improvements to the hospital, which was dedicated in May, 1950.

CANTON, 3.2 m. (1,244 alt.), owes its name to the belief by early settlers that it is situated diametrically opposite Canton, China. Founded in 1860, the town has become the center of an extensive Scandinavian community, with productive farms and substantial buildings.

It was in this section that the settings of two books, O. E. Rölvaag's *Giants in the Earth* and Phil LeMar Anderson's *Courthouse Square*, were laid. Central characters in Rölvaag's widely read saga of pioneer life are six brothers, named Berdahl, whose combined ages total 488 years. The oldest is 88 and the youngest 68 years old.

Rölvaag, who is a son-in-law of the eldest brother, vividly describes many of their adventures. The Berdahls and several other families came to Dakota Territory in early days to obtain free land.

Canton is the seat of Lincoln County. There are a number of fine old homes here, and the town is popular with antique hunters.

The AUGUSTANA ACADEMY, a Lutheran school, has buildings that are striking examples of the use of native Sioux Falls quartzite in construction. It formerly was a normal school.

Only after arriving in the town does the stranger discover that the tall, odd-looking cylindrical object, jutting above all other structures near it, is the city water tower, practical but unattractive.

At Canton is the junction with the Newton Hills Road.

Left on this graveled road is the NEWTON HILLS STATE PARK, 4 m. This 650-acre park was created in 1947, when the South Dakota Game, Fish and Parks Department purchased several tracts of beautifully wooded area adjacent to the Big Sioux River. Camping and picnicking facilities are maintained. According to local legend, the area was a favorite hideout and rendezvous for early day outlaws, including the notorious James Brothers. Jesse and Frank James are supposed to have hid in the Newton Hills country following the robbery of the Northfield, Minn., bank. They "traded" some horses stolen from Nils Nelson in Minnehaha County for fresh mounts here, without the formality of dealing with the owners.

At 10.4 m. is the junction with US 77 (see Tour 9) and the two highways are united for 5 m.

The early settlers in the State took up land in this southeastern section and during those pioneering years they were faced with many hardships. In 1881, following the ever-memorable blizzard of 1880, there was considerable snow; and when this melted the valleys throughout the region held sweeping torrents. Even the Vermillion River, normally a small stream, became a veritable Mississippi, as it swelled to cut a mile-wide swath along its course. Bridges were washed out, homes flooded, and settlers were forced to flee to higher ground.

In 1885 a prairie fire swept through the center of Turner Co. Fanned by a furious gale, the blaze licked up the long grass, catching occasional haystacks and hurling the burning straw high into the air, as it wiped out farm homes in a relentless holocaust.

The blizzard of 1888, while not as severe as that of 1880, took a great toll of life over a wide area. Jan. 12, 1888, broke dark and lowering; a light steady snow was added to the foot that had already fallen. By 10 o'clock the region was blanketed with fog. Suddenly, without warning, the wind changed and the temperature tobogganed nearly 70 degrees. The wind continued to rise and soon a 60-mile gale was howling mercilessly across the open expanses. Steel-like snow in blinding eddies was hurled with withering intensity at whatever object happened to be in its path. So thick was the snow, and so sudden was the onslaught of the storm, that there was little opportunity for preparation. The devastating blast continued with unabated fury, choking and blinding victims unfortunate enough to be caught away from shelter. When the storm had subsided, it had written a pitiful tale of suffering and death across its icy pages. About 200 persons perished in South Dakota and adjoining States; men, women, and children, singly and in groups, lay where they had first fallen, unable to combat the cruel elements. Some were found in a sitting posture; some lying as though they had fallen, exhausted; some were propped against haystacks.

At 11.6 m. is the junction with a graveled road.

Right on this road is WORTHING, 0.6 m. (1,364 alt.), one of the early towns in this part of the State. Its proximity to Sioux Falls and Canton has retarded its growth and forced it to remain a small town. A fertile agricultural region surrounds it.

At 15.5 m. is the junction with US 77 (see Tour 9).

DAVIS, 29.8 m. (1,253 alt.), has a well-kept city park and a new municipal building. It is a prominent grain shipping point in a productive farming area.

At 32.2 m. is the junction with State 19.

Left on this hard-surfaced road is SWAN LAKE, 1.5 m., a popular picnic spot. At 4.0 m. is VIBORG, founded by a group of Danes and named for their home town in Denmark. At 14.9 is CENTERVILLE, a prosperous community of large scale cattle buyers who fatten western steers on local corn.
Right on this paved road is HURLEY, 2.1 m., and PARKER, 10.0 m., seat of Turner County.

At 41.1 m. is TURKEY RIDGE, a country community with a blacksmith shop, filling station, store, and a trap shoot. On the Sunday before Thanksgiving Day each year, the surrounding farmers gather for a trap shoot for turkeys and other fowl.

At 49.0 m. is the junction with US 81 (see Tour 10).

MENNO, 57.8 m. (1,325 alt.), is a contraction of Mennonite, there being many members of this sect in the surrounding territory (see Tour 5). Although there is no exclusive Mennonite colony near Menno, there are many descendants of the original German-Russian families, principally E. of the James River Valley.

At 62.0 m. the James River is crossed. This lazy, meandering stream moves along so idly and indifferently that it appears to be absorbing the full value of the scenery along its muddy banks as it crawls listlessly to join the impetuous cloudy waters of the Missouri. During 1934, the period when the drought was most severe, the water along most of its course receded to mere pot holes and finally dried up entirely. Fish were trapped in these holes, but most of them were rescued by the Game and Fish Department and transferred to other places until water again returned to the abandoned river bed.

OLIVET, 62.4 m. (1,221 alt.), though without railroad connections, is the seat of Hutchinson Co., a distinction it has had since 1871. Despite numerous efforts to move the seat of the county government, Olivet hangs tenaciously to the prize it has held so long. In 1878 the Free Methodists built a sod church at the town site, while they were doing missionary work in this part of the State. In this crude building court was held until a courthouse was constructed.

At 64.3 *m.* is the junction with State 35.

Left on this oiled highway is SCOTLAND, 5.0 *m.*, which was settled by pioneers of Scottish ancestry. Gen. Charles T. Campbell, a Civil War veteran, provided the townsite in 1879, on his homestead along the Firesteel Trail between Yankton and Fort Thompson on the Missouri River.
The soil in this region is of clay origin, and the country gradually becomes more hilly as US 18 moves westward. There are many curves and dips, and fast driving is not advisable.

At 67 *m.* the highway rises over a divide which separates the flow of the small feeders of the Missouri and James Rivers, respectively. From the divide, the streams flow SW. to join the "Big Muddy" in its long pilgrimage to the Mississippi.

TRIPP, 77.9 *m.* (1,563 alt.), stands on the brow of a hill in the SW. corner of Hutchinson Co. The town is modern in every respect, and its school buildings, with school busses covering the surrounding country, provides good educational facilities. The Hutchinson Co. Fair is held here annually, and its grounds cover 34 acres, with grandstand, pavilions, and exhibit buildings, comparing favorably with the leading fairs of the State.

The greater part of the city's population is of German-Russian ancestry.

At Tripp is the junction of State 37; the two routes are united to 80.8 *m.* (*see Tour 11A*).

DELMONT, 88.2 *m.* (1,488 alt.), is a well kept village and cattle shipping point.

At 98.1 *m.* is the junction with State 41.

Right on this oil-surfaced road is ARMOUR, 3.0 *m.* (1,521 alt.), seat of Douglas County. It was named for Philip D. Armour, meat packer and railroad director, who reciprocated by furnishing a bell for the church in town. NE. of Armour is LAKE CORSICA STATE RECREATION AREA, a 120-acre tract planted with trees, around an artificial lake.

At 107.2 *m.* is the junction with State 50 (*see Tour 8*).

RAVINIA, 111.3 *m.* (1,490 alt.), is a quiet village patronized by Indian farm families from the Yankton Reservation to the south.

At Ravinia is the junction with a graveled road.

Left on this road is ST. PAUL INDIAN MISSION at Marty, 10 *m.* This Catholic mission includes a large boarding and vocational school, an orphanage, the only community of Indian nuns in the U.S., and a beautiful church that attracts worshippers and visitors from long distances.
The original mission was started in 1913 when a $1,100 legacy was received from a New York seamstress for land and a chapel on the Yankton Indian Reservation.

It was without a resident priest until 1921, when Father Sylvester, a Benedictine, arrived. He was met by a delegation of Indians who raised $400 for a larger church. An old frame building at Wagner, 13 miles away, was purchased; it took three months of arduous labor to haul the structure across the prairie.

Three sisters of the Blessed Sacrament converted the old chapel into a school, which has now grown to several modern brick buildings and an enrollment of 400 grade school children and 90 high school students. They represent sixteen tribes from surrounding states as well as South Dakota.

Funds are raised through a publication entitled *The Little Bronze Angel* which has a wide circulation. Its popularity led to the printing also of the *Catholic Indian Herald*. Because of these two publications, printing has become a major course in the school, and has resulted in Marty becoming an important post office although no town exists. The Indians petitioned the name in memory of Abbot Martin Marty, who became the first Bishop of South Dakota. The Indian Oblate Sisters, fostered by the Sisters of the Blessed Sacrament, form a unique community. They have their own chapel, home, and superior; assist in the school and serve the surrounding Indian country.

Sioux Arts and crafts made at the school are for sale. A farm and ranch also are operated in connection with the school. A new church, consecrated in 1942, was built by the Indians who made their own bricks, cut stone, and made the decorations. The spire rises 167 feet.

At 112.2 *m.* is the junction with a dirt road.

Left on this road is the Site of the Pawnee House, 8.3 *m.*, the first house built by a white man within the present confines of South Dakota. It was a rough structure erected by Jean Baptiste Trudeau, a fur trader from St. Louis, in 1794, along the chalk cliffs of the Missouri River. It is also known as the Trudeau House.

US 18 parallels LAKE ANDES (R) for about 3 m. It is a shallow, boot-shaped body of water covering 6,400 acres. It was first known as Handy's Lake, named for an early fur trapper, but somehow the "H" was dropped and the "y" changed to "e." Along Owen's Bay is the 360-acre LAKE ANDES MIGRATORY WATERFOWL REFUGE of the U.S. Fish and Wildlife Service. Two artesian wells furnish an independent water supply for the nesting area and feeding grounds. A STATE FISH HATCHERY is operated by the South Dakota Game, Fish and Parks Department. Bass are propagated here for stocking lakes throughout the State.

During drought years, Lake Andes almost dried up. Through the efforts of a Civilian Conservation Corps camp, a canal was dug to drain an extended watershed into the lake bed. There are several resorts with cabins along the shore.

LAKE ANDES, 116.1 *m.* (1,441 alt.), is the seat of Charles Mix County. A lively trade center resulted from the construction of the nearby Fort Randall Dam and Reservoir Project (*see below*). It has always been a town offering amusement and recreation for the surrounding territory. A new auditorium was built in 1950, to provide more entertainment facilities.

The town is picturesquely situated on the slope near the toe of the lake's boot, and has a neat, well improved park. The courthouse, which dominates the town, symbolized a 37-year struggle for the seat of the county's government. The river port of Wheeler (*see below*) became the county seat in 1879, before the other towns were platted. Then as Lake Andes, Geddes, Platte, and Wagner fought among themselves, Wheeler continued to hold the honor. Finally in 1916, Lake Andes mustered enough votes to win.

At Lake Andes is the junction with the Fort Randall Highway. (US 18 and US 281 will be routed via this highway and over the top of Fort Randall dam when it is completed.)

Left on this hard-surfaced road is PICKSTOWN, 6.5 *m*. This orderly new town was laid out by the U.S. Army Corps of Engineers in the late 1940's and named for Maj. Gen. Lewis Pick, chief promoter of the Missouri River Basin Development plan. This government-built town, situated atop leveled river bluffs, has tree-lined streets, neat houses, schools, churches, cafeterias, food markets, a recreation hall, and a hotel.

From the General Pick Hotel, in the center of the village, is a winding road (R) to the FORT RANDALL OBSERVATION PROMONTORY, 0.5 *m*. A panoramic view of the huge dam, spillway, power units, reservoir, and old Fort Randall is available from this high vantage point. The Missouri River at this point was originally a mile and a half wide.

The Fort Randall dam is a major unit in "the authorized comprehensive Missouri River Development program" created by the U.S. Congress. The dam is designed to create a reservoir covering 167 square miles up-river, extending beyond Chamberlain on US 16. It will hold back six million acre-feet of water at high level, to be released as needed for navigation from Sioux City, Iowa, to New Orleans. A power plant capable of producing 320,000 kilowatts has for its intake twelve tunnels cut through Niobrara chalk rock under the dam. Each tunnel is 900 feet long and 22 feet in diameter. The spillway gates support the bridge for the highway. To the NE. of the dam is the proposed RECREATION AREA, with facilities for boating, camping, and swimming.

Across the dam is the SITE OF FORT RANDALL (L). The fort was established in 1856, on a site selected by General William S. Harney in 1855, when he led an expedition into Dakota Territory for the purpose of seeking a treaty with the Sioux. It was named for Col. Daniel Randall, an Army paymaster. During the Indian wars, the Fort was visited by Generals Sheridan, Sherman, Custer, Sully, and Terry. For a time, following the Custer battle in 1876, Sitting Bull was held prisoner there following his surrender in Canada. The post was abandoned in 1884, and the buildings auctioned. Only a yellow stone church, built in 1875 by soldiers of the 1st Infantry, remained. It was spared during the dam construction and plans were formulated in 1950, to restore the old structure.

US 18 (temporary) sweeps west from Lake Andes to WHEELER, 133.3 *m*., a ghost village destined to be buried under the waters of the Fort Randall reservoir. The courthouse building, which served for many years as the seat of county government, was relegated to the less dignified role of a granary.

At Wheeler is the junction with US 281 (*see Tour 11*); at this point the two highways unite and follow one road for 10 *m*.

Section b. Junction with US 281—Hot Springs, 285 m.

At 0.4 *m*. the united routes cross the MISSOURI RIVER, the story of which, with its tributaries, is essentially a story of the State. River traffic began in the early 1830's and continued until late in the 19th century when the railroads displaced this mode of transportation. As many as 40 steamers plied up and down the

Missouri River, sometimes 20 or more being tied up at a single landing point.

From the earliest days of settlement in South Dakota, the rivers of this valley have overflowed occasionally, causing suffering and damage. In March 1862, an ice gorge formed near the mouth of the James River, flooding the entire valley to a width as great as 12 m. in several places.

The flood causing the most damage came in the spring of 1881, the climax of a winter of unusual severity. Oct. 14, 1880, a slow drizzle began and soon turned to snow that sailed in on a strong wind. The storm lasted three days, blocking all communication with the outside world for weeks. Frequent snows followed, and held the valley in an ice-locked grip for five bitter months. On March 27, 1881, the ice began to move downstream, the melting snows soon swelling the river until it overflowed the banks and covered the bottom-land from bluff to bluff. An ice gorge formed near Yankton, and ice congested the stream as far as Springfield, more than 30 m. away. The following day the gorge suddenly broke, releasing millions of tons of ice that moved with slow, irresistible force down the river, sweeping everything in its path. Masses of ice were hurled against steamships, helplessly docked, crushing them like eggshells. The sudden rise of the water sent residents of the valley scurrying to higher ground to watch the roaring, impetuous flood swallow up their belongings—homes, livestock, machinery—and hurl them downstream. A village called Green Island was completely devoured by the swirling waters. Within two hours after the first masses of ice crashed into the village, every building was drifting with the current as it joined the growing procession of debris gathered along the river's course. Even the church was wrested from its foundation, and settlers 30 m. downstream told of seeing a building float by and of hearing bells tolling uncannily as the structure bobbed up and down in the surging river. The loss of human life was not high, but the loss of homes and all other belongings, wrought hardships that required years to overcome.

At 1 m. US 18 enters the eastern end of the ROSEBUD INDIAN RESERVATION, named for the wild roses that still cover large areas of this section. It was originally a part of the Sioux Reservation, which was set aside under the treaty of 1868 (see INDIANS). Modifications of this treaty subdivided the area, setting up the present boundaries. Although the reservation extends E. to the Missouri River, the actual closed boundaries have been reduced to Todd Co. only, the remaining area being open to white settlement, with the laws governing the Indians applying to all parts. With a total Indian population of about 9,470 the reservation roll shows about one-half to be full-bloods; the native language is used by nearly 90 per cent of the inhabitants.

The reservation section, like the western half of the State, has many sharp draws and jutting buttes; the topography is not ironed out like the land E. of the Missouri River. The tillable grazing country has a very sandy soil which is subject to erosion by the wind when native vegetation is disturbed by cultivation or over-grazing.

In June 1934, the Wheeler-Howard Act, giving the Indians a greater degree of self-government, became a law, and the Indians voted to accept the act. Severe drought has caused critical conditions on this reservation as well as on others. While the average Indian does not rate high as a farmer, the fertile soil of the region usually produces crops that supplement the aid given by the Government through benefits accruing as a result of past treaties. Despite incomes from tribal sources, leases, and land sales, approximately half the families on the reservation depend almost entirely upon some form of Government relief. Most farm plots consist of a small patch of weedy corn, potatoes, and smaller vegetables.

Home conditions in a majority of cases are poor; the bulk of the population lives in shacks and tents that have few sanitary facilities.

Order is preserved on the reservation through a system of Indian police, aided by honorary law enforcement officers, who serve without pay, and help maintain order at dances and other functions where the most prevalent law violation—drunkenness—arises. It is unlawful to sell or give an Indian liquor although it is sold to whites on the open part of the reservation. It is unlawful to have liquor in one's possession in the restricted area. Drunkenness and adultery rank first and second, respectively, among the criminal charges on the reservation.

Meandering up from the Missouri River bottom, US 18 enters a gently rolling region.

At 10.1 *m.* is the junction with US 281 (*see Tour 11*).

BONESTEEL, 13.2 *m.* (2,009 alt.), like other towns along US 18, sprang up when it was known that the C. & N. W. R.R. planned to extend W. of the Missouri River. With this in mind, Bonesteel, named for an early resident, gradually took on the semblance of a town and when the railroad actually came, the population increased rapidly. However, it never boomed to the extent that some of the other towns along the route did. It has now settled down to the humdrum existence of the average small town, its tides of fortune ebbing and flowing with the current conditions of its surrounding territory.

ST. CHARLES, 20.2 *m.,* consists of a few scattered houses and a business district typical of a small hamlet. Never affected to any extent by the influx of homesteaders, the village was stifled in its infancy by the diversion of most of the business to Gregory and Dallas.

HERRICK, 25.8 *m.,* was named for Samuel Herrick, an attorney who was instrumental in opening the Rosebud Reservation to white settlement. This was effected in 1904 and a great wave of homeseekers flooded the new and promising territory. Gregory Co. suddenly became the mecca for families of all types. Some had lost all their worldly goods in the East, or perhaps never had any; some were college graduates, many of them adventurers, others were health-seekers; some were of substantial Scandinavian or German stock, looking for sites for homes.

At 31.2 *m.* is the BURKE LAKE RECREATION DEVELOPMENT AREA, consisting of a picnic area and 160 acres planted with trees, around the artificial lake. It is a South Dakota Game, Fish and Parks Department project.

BURKE, 34.6 *m.* (2,251 alt.), was named in honor of Charles Burke of Pierre, one-time Commissioner of Indian Affairs. Its beginning is traced to the pre-railroad days when the extension of the lines became a certainty. The 1910 census shows a population of 311, and the town has experienced a slow but steady growth since then. While many of the towns decreased in population, Burke was able to hold its own. It was settled largely by persons who planned to stay in the country, and was less affected by the influx of homesteaders than other towns of the semiarid region when the exceptionally dry years of 1911–12–13 ravaged the country. It still is a lively little center, deriving its business from farmers, ranchers, and Indians.

GREGORY, 42.5 *m.* (2,216 alt.), prior to 1904 was merely a town in the offing, but with the opening of the county for white settlement, houses were hastily built, and a busy village was an actuality in a few weeks. Today it vies with Winner as the chief trading center of the Rosebud country, the two towns eclipsing all others in the area in size. With a varied population, comprising a mixed Indian, ranching, and farming group, Gregory has the distinction of being a melting pot for different types of people. Western flavor is mixed with modern, Eastern customs. The frontier spirit of the West still dominates, and the people are noted for their liberal tendencies. When they have money, they are willing to spend it; when hard times come, they accept their plight without murmuring. Here, as well as in other western South Dakota towns, is a friendliness and hospitality that will evoke a glow of warmth in the most blasé visitor.

DALLAS, 46.2 *m.* (2,238 alt.), was originally built about 10 m. distant from the present line of the railroad when the latter was extended W. of the Missouri River. To remedy this the citizens moved their little village to a location at the end of the proposed extension of the railroad. Their "hunch" proved correct and in 1907 the first train whistled into the infant town, gateway to the region that was next slated for opening.

Launching the new land boom with profuse and widespread advertising, Dallas became one of the most "heard-of" towns in the Middle West. Thousands of landseekers came to this section in the next few years, and the population of Dallas shot upward until it crowded the 2,000 figure. Seven churches, a library, water system, electric lights, and three blocks of business district marked this flourishing town. The cattleman saw his range divided and subdivided, saw with dismay the virgin prairie turned to brown as the branding iron was melted into the plowshare. The range days were gone; cowboys would live only in books and in the movies; the old regime must succumb to the progressive spirit of the New West. Farm machinery was sold by the carloads, and soon rippling grainfields replaced endless stretches of dun prairie. Such was the setting of Dallas for a few years.

But the halcyon days of its prosperity were numbered. The meteoric rise that had wafted the little prairie town to heights of prosperity was quickly reversed and financial doldrums settled upon the community. Drought, crop failures, dust storms, low prices, and several disastrous fires wrought their havoc. Dallas today is but a fragment of its former self, although it still maintains many of the features that accompanied its early prosperity—churches, library, modern improvements.

COLOME, 57.1 *m.*, was named for the Colome brothers, of part Sioux Indian parentage. The founders of the town, looking into the future, located a town site on the railroad right-of-way and in 1909, following the opening of Tripp Co. for white settlement, the influx of settlers began. The county developed so quickly that the railroad was extended to Winner, in the heart of the new region, within three years after it reached Colome. Although successful farming is hampered by occasional dry periods, the productive soil of the area enables the people, through combination dirt-farming and stockraising, to earn a comfortable livelihood during normal times.

At Colome is the junction with US 183 (*see Tour 12A*); the two routes are united for 20 m.

WINNER, 68 *m.* (1,860 alt.), one of the newest towns in the State, is also one of the most typically Western in color. Founded following the rush of homesteaders, which began in 1908, Winner grew up mushroom-fashion, becoming the busiest trading point along the entire stretch of US 18 across South Dakota.

Modern Winner has 48 blocks of paved streets, and in appearance its business district resembles a much larger city. Besides the usual types of business, Winner has an ice cream factory, a powdered soap and cleaner factory, and an awning factory. A few years ago one Winner business man bought more than 20,000 rabbit skins in one season, gathered from the surrounding country. The town is also a shipping point for turkeys and other poultry raised in the adjacent territory.

As a pheasant hunting center, Winner teems with activity each fall. On opening day as many as 28 transient airplanes check in at the airport and more than a thousand out-of-state licenses are sold. Sports celebrities are special guests, and nation-wide radio programs sometimes originate there. Winner takes its baseball seriously, having one of the best parks in the State and a payroll that includes ex-major leaguers. The town also has a fine children's playground and a community hospital, each of which would do credit to larger cities.

Visitors are reminded by townspeople that Frank Leahy, Notre Dame football coach, attended Winner High School.

One block (L) from Main St. is the OUTLAW TRADING POST, a well known store of the West-river country. Started during the early days of Winner, the store was named by Ben Butts, the founder, who was called "the outlaw down the alley" by competitors, because of his large scale operations in buying goods in carload lots and selling them at cut prices. Covering most of a square block, the general store for years was unpretentious in appearance and amazing for its disorganized and varied stock. However, it has followed the streamline influence, and warehouses now hold the carloads of merchandise that used to crowd the store.

JORDAN, 77.2 m., is at the junction with US 183 (see Tour 12A). Its nearness to Winner precludes the possibility of its becoming a town of appreciable size.

CARTER, 86 m., with its present few inhabitants, represents a dream that never came true. With the opening of Tripp Co. for settlement, the Western Town Site Co. made arrangements with the C. & N. W. R.R. to extend its line W. of Dallas. Seven towns were slated to be on the extension of the line. After a delay of two years, the proposed extension was begun, but advanced only as far as Winner. Not until a few years ago was it built farther W. and then it missed Carter by taking a more northern route.

As originally planned, Carter would have been the gateway to the great undeveloped country to the W., a gateway through which all settlers moving into the new country would pass. As a result this region became known as the "jumping off place." A novel, *The Jumping Off Place,* by Marian Hurd McNeely, has as its setting this Rosebud country during homestead days, and the characters were drawn from life.

At 87 m. is the eastern edge of the Rosebud Reservation proper; this part of the reservation is not open to white settlement.

OKREEK, 95 m., is typical of the many small communities that are scattered through the Indian reservations, towns that are centers of the social life of their districts.

Many of the houses in Okreek are typical of the social status of the Indian families on this reservation. The Superintendent's annual report of the Rosebud Reservation tersely states: "The home conditions of the Indian families are for the majority very poor. Their homes are far from sanitary. Undoubtedly this contributes a great deal to the high rate of tuberculosis that is prevalent among the Indian population."

HAYSTACK BUTTE (R) is visible for several miles along the route. Long noted for its rattlesnake dens, the butte is visited each spring and fall by scores of persons either interested scientifically, or merely curious.

Rattlesnakes, while not prevalent and rarely seen unless looked for, hibernate and emerge in the spring when the temperature approaches the 80-degree mark. Then they scatter, but rarely venture more than four or five miles from their dens. Men who understand the habits of the reptiles visit the dens every day during the first balmy days of spring, and snare them as they crawl to the sunlight, or drag them from their holes with a specially devised hook. Often writhing balls of the reptiles, entwined around each other and comprising as many as 25 or 30 snakes, are dragged out. Rattlesnakes, authorities say, are one of the worst enemies of nesting birds, their ability to find nests and devour fledglings, often the mother bird and the eggs, results in a huge loss each year.

At 108.1 *m.* is a large INDIAN BOARDING SCHOOL, maintained by the Government for the Indian children of the Rosebud Reservation. About 200 children are enrolled and classes range from the first to the tenth grades.

MISSION, 111 *m.* (2,150 alt.), is a trading point for Indians and white settlers of the neighborhood. A 12-grade public school is attended by both white and Indian children. The Episcopal church maintains a dormitory and school farm. The Lutheran church operates a day-school. There are Lutheran and Episcopal chapels in the town, and the Catholic chapel is near the agency.

An excellent CABIN CAMP and a small artificial lake, where swimming and fishing are available, are open to the public.

At Mission is the junction with US 83 (*see Tour 12*); the two routes are united for 3 m.

All through this part of the country Indian homes can be seen, each standing alone on its individual 160-acre allotment. There is little variety in the style of architecture of the homes of the Sioux. A one or two-room log house, plastered usually with mud, with a roof composed of poles, hay, and dirt, is the usual type; one or two small windows carry the burden of admitting light; the floors are often of dirt, while a small stove, frequently of sheet-iron, provides the heat that is generated from the burning of wrist-size sticks of wood. The Indians spend much time in tents, even during the bitterest winter weather.

The white men have attempted to eradicate Indian habits and practices of centuries. Superstitions, fetishes, and customs, however, defy the forces of change. Legends that have been handed down from one generation to another are still treasured by the Sioux. One that is told by wrinkled old squaws to their children and grandchildren, and which undoubtedly will continue to be handed down to future generations, describes the origin of the rainbow.

One bright summer day when all the flowers were nodding their heads in the breeze and proudly exhibiting their many beautiful colors, the Great Spirit, who watches over all the little earthlings, heard this conversation between two of the older flowers.

"I wonder where we will go when winter comes and we all have to die? It doesn't seem fair; we do our share to make the earth a beautiful place to live in. It would only be fair if we, too, should go to a happy hunting ground of our own."

The Great Spirit considered this idea and decided that they should not die when winter came. And so now, according to the legend, after a refreshing shower all the many-hued flowers are seen in the sky, making a beautiful arc across the heavens.

At 119 *m.* is the junction with a graveled road.

Left on this road is the ROSEBUD AGENCY, 6 *m.* It is in a rough part of the country with some of the agency buildings on Rosebud Creek and some on the steep hills opposite. On the flat N. of the agency are old corrals and a fairground. About two m. NW. of the corrals, Sugar Loaf Butte projects its cone-shaped top above the flat prairie. On this flat, herds of issue cattle were turned loose every ten days in olden times. This was the beef issued to the Indians on the hoof; there was sport as well as food in shooting down one's own beef.

A celebration is sometimes held here on the Fourth of July, and the annual fair is early in September. Riding, roping, Indian dancing and singing, baseball games, races, and often the old Indian game of shinny, give much local color. Beyond the flat is a sharp turn through a deep cut known to the Indians as the "Big Hole." At this point the whole agency comes into view. Below, on the hillside, is the Government hospital. At the top of the hill (R) lies an old BURIAL GROUND. The white shaft in this cemetery marks the grave of Spotted Tail, the chief for whom this agency was first named. Spotted Tail was friendly to the whites and his own people mistrusted this friendship. A group of the headmen of the neighboring Indian bands drew lots to determine who should kill him. Crow Dog drew the fatal lot and killed Spotted Tail from ambush. Afterwards Crow Dog was ostracized by his own people and scorned by the white men.

The name, Spotted Tail Agency, was used until 1871. This place was heavily guarded during the Messiah War; and in 1890 the soldiers dug rifle pits on the hill for the protection of the agency. This hill overlooking the agency is still called Soldier Hill. The Government buildings are close together on the bench, in the form of a square. The general office building is on the southwestern corner. Long established traders' stores carry candles, bright beads, gay calico, broad-brimmed Stetsons, and sheep-lined coats. Rows of canned goods give evidence of the derivation of the Indian word "mazopiye" (*the place where things are put away in tins*). The 25 members of the tribal council meet here for deliberations, and the Indian court of three men, appointed by the Superintendent, sits here to judge minor offenses. Below the hill the Indians live in cabins, or camp out, while transacting business for a few days. SW. from the Rosebud Agency is ST. FRANCIS MISSION, one of the largest Catholic Indian boarding schools in the U.S. It was started in 1885 on a site selected by the Indians and named in honor of Francis A. Drexel. A gothic-styled church, built of prairie stone hauled by the Indians, is impressive. The large school building is in the shape of an F. Basketball teams from St. Francis are prominent in State high school athletics.

US 18 passes through rough country, with ravines and steep hillsides spotted with dark jackpines. The Little White River, fed by clear springs, is crossed as the highway sweeps westward.

At 132 *m.* is the junction with a graveled road.

Right on this road is PARMALEE, 3*m.*, an Indian town on the flat prairie. Ever since the days when He-Dog's band camped in this district, Parmalee has been a Government issue station and a trading post. The post office of Parmalee was named for Dave Parmalee, rancher, trader, and pioneer of this region. The old Indian name for the section was Cut-Meat, from the Indian word Wososo (*where they cut the buffalo meat into little strips*). The creek half a mile beyond Parmalee still bears the same name, Cut-Meat. There is an old story among the Indians that the Indian hunters used to drive the buffalo over the steep banks of this stream.

He-Dog and his followers camped on this creek and, when homes were built by the Government for the chiefs, He-Dog's house was erected on the flat, 9 m. beyond Parmalee, where it can be seen from the highway. A new consolidated school, called He-Dog School, is 8 m. W. of Parmalee. It is typical of the fine new day schools the Department of the Interior is now building as community centers in Indian country.

At 145.1 m. US 18 crosses the western boundary of the closed area of the Rosebud Reservation and continues through more Indian country—the open area of the Pine Ridge Reservation—ceded territory, containing isolated tracts of trust land.

VETAL, 152 m., is another roadside trading center to which the scattered population of the sparsely settled neighboring area come to buy their "grub" and other necessities. At Vetal on busy days can be seen three types of vehicles—team and wagon, battered Fords of the Model T variety, and modern automobiles, with the first type most prevalent.

MARTIN, 173.5 m. (3,250 alt.), called the "metropolis of the Pine Ridge Reservation country" because of its surprisingly large population in such a thinly settled country, was founded in 1912 at the time Bennett Co. was organized, and has since remained the county seat. Indians, interspersed with cowboys, farmers, and white-collared men, make a composite picture that is truly Western and colorful. At fair time and on celebration days, the Indians appear in native dress and perform tribal dances, sing their songs, and go through other ceremonies.

Bennett Co., despite its lack of railroad facilities, has thousands of acres of good grazing and agricultural land with abundant water, good roads, and full-course schools.

Left from Martin on State 73 is the LA CREEK TEAL AND MIGRATORY FOWL REFUGE, 12 m., a series of long dams impounding water in several artificial lakes.

BATESLAND, 194 m., consists of a small residence and business district, the appearance of the town as a whole giving the impression of a group of buildings huddled together in the prairie hinterland for mutual protection.

Here the Indian character of the country becomes more strongly pronounced, for US 18 is entering the PINE RIDGE RESERVATION. Living within its borders are more Indians than on any other reservation in South Dakota, a total of more than 10,207 having been recorded at the 1948 count. Indian customs and characteristics are similar on all reservations W. of the Missouri River. (*See Tours 2, 3, and KOSEBUD RESERVATION, above*).

The extent of this reservation makes it difficult for the visitor with little time to see many parts of it. The old Indian life can best be studied in remote villages, where the Sioux pursue their old tribal customs, unchanged by white influence. The native language is used by 85 per cent of the population. A tribal council performs numerous duties including the management of tribal affairs, recommendations for positions, the settlement of domestic difficulties, the leasing of tribal lands, and the investigation of complaints against personnel or departments.

Few Indians on the Pine Ridge Reservation are successful farmers, virtually none of them producing enough from their tracts to support their families. Considerable handiwork is carried on, and, in 1937, the sale of articles was started. In wooded areas trees are often cut up and sold as fuel, although the Indians derive little income from this source. In gathering his own firewood, he usually seeks the smaller dead trees or branches of larger ones, full-grown timber being left until a scarcity of the other kind forces him to depart from his customary practice.

There are 33 separate Indian communities on the Pine Ridge Reservation, each designated by a tribal name.

At 203 *m.* is the junction with State 75.

Left (S) on this oil-surfaced road is the NEB.-S.D. Line, 4 m., the highway continuing to Gordon, Neb., popular trade center for this area.

At 211 *m.* is the junction with a graveled road.

Right (N) on this road is the WOUNDED KNEE TRADING POST, 6 *m.* A road leads up the hill behind the store to the WOUNDED KNEE BATTLEFIELD, 0.4 *m.* where on Dec. 29, 1890, occurred the last important conflict between the whites and Indians. The battle marked the end of the Messiah craze, which for months had been deluding the Indians and terrifying white residents on and near South Dakota reservations. (*see HISTORY*).

Although today referred to as a battle, many insist the affair was nothing short of a massacre in which non-combatants—squaws with infants on their backs, boys and girls—were pursued and ruthlessly shot down by maddened soldiers long after resistance had ceased and nearly every warrior lay dead or dying on the field. Pictures taken on the battlefield two days after the encounter and before the Indians had been buried showed bodies scattered for 2 m. along the creek, mute testimony of the relentlessness of the pursuit.

Today, near the battlefield, is a monument and cement curbing, indicating a common grave, a rude trench, in which the bodies of the slain Indians—men, women, and children alike—were hastily buried.

The chief ritual of the Messiah delusion was a ghost dance, conceived and introduced to the tribes by a Nevada Paiute Indian named Wovoka, whose Christian upbringing had little effect on his Indian superstitions. He claimed to have seen a vision, following an eclipse of the sun in 1889, in which the buffalo were restored to the prairie and the whites driven from the earth. He declared he had seen the glory of the Indians returned to them as it was in the days before the white men came. This vision Wovoka began to relate among the tribes near his home. Word of the supposed revelation spread like a prairie fire, and soon every tribe in North America had heard of it and many were practicing its teaching. It took deepest root among South Dakota tribes where two skilled exhorters, Kicking Bear and Short Bull, became imbued with the belief and began preaching it among their followers. Soon hundreds had flocked turbulently into camps to take part in the weird ceremonies. During the ceremonial dance the Indian men wore a special garb, consisting principally of a calico garment, called a "ghost shirt." The ritual started with the participants joining hands and shuffling around in circles, slowly at first, and careening crazily until one by one fell exhausted. The medicine men pronounced them dead, but said that after a visit to the Great Spirit they would return to tell what they had seen. Needless to say, what they told was imaginary. "The buffalo are coming back!" they cried. They saw the whites at the mercy of the Indians; sickness had vanished from the earth; the red man's paradise was returning. They believed the bullets of the whites could no longer harm them.

Short Bull's band of dancers hurried away to the fastnesses of the Badlands to engage in further ceremonies (see Tour 2). In the meantime the implacable Sitting Bull had been killed, and his followers fled to join Big Foot's band of dancers on the Cheyenne River. Soldiers sent to arrest Big Foot found him willing to submit, but in the night he and his band escaped and reached the badlands. He was overtaken at Wounded Knee Creek.

The soldiers were ordered to disarm the warriors, but found them wretchedly equipped with a few out-of-date rifles of little value. Dissatisfied with the results, the soldiers were ordered closer to the tipis, where a more thorough search was instituted. In the meantime Yellow Bird, a medicine man, was haranguing the Indians telling them the ghost shirts were impervious to the bullets of the enemy. As Yellow Bird spoke in the Sioux tongue, the soldiers did not realize the import of his talk. When one of the searchers began to examine the blankets of the Indians Black Fox jumped to his feet, drawing his gun as he rose, and fired at the soldiers. The rest of the warriors, as if waiting for a signal joined in so quickly that the attendant volley sounded almost like one report. The soldiers immediately returned the fire and for a few minutes the carnage was terrible. So close together were the combatants that many discharged rifles into the faces of their foes. When the firing started, a battery of Hotchkiss guns, firing two pounds at each charge and at the rate of nearly one a second, raked the camp, shattering and setting fire to the tipis and killing everyone within range.

The superior numbers of the soldiers, who were equipped with modern rifles and aided by artillery, soon routed the Indians; only a handful escaped through the lines of the whites and took refuge in ravines and depressions of a fringe of hills nearby. Meanwhile the tipis were burning above the dead and dying within them, and the rest of the Indians—women mostly, carrying small infants on their backs—were fleeing in wild panic, as soldiers cut them down ruthlessly and left them scattered over the plain. Big Foot was killed; his son died beside him, and most of the warriors killed in the melee fell near the chief's tipi. The members of the burial party, who came with wagons three days later to bury the dead Indians, found several live babies wrapped in shawls close to the cold bodies of their lifeless mothers, though temperature during the interval had been near zero. The bodies of the dead Indians were placed in wagons and hauled, several in each load, to a large grave where they were placed without ceremony.

PINE RIDGE AGENCY, 220.5 m., was so named because of the abundance of dark pines that clothe the hills and line the ravines nearby. Until 1878 it was called Red Cloud Agency, for the chief of one of the leading bands in this territory. Of the 33 bands, identified by family relationships and living on this reservation today, one is listed as the Chief James H. Red Cloud Band. The outstanding indications of the new order are the Government buildings, the school, the hospital, and the administrative buildings. In the school, native arts and crafts are taught, and some of the older members of the tribe are called in to teach tribal history and native folkways; at the same time teachers, under Government employ, give the Indian children an education like that provided for white children. The hospital employs a staff of eight nurses and, in addition, there are four field nurses and five doctors in the reservation.

Indian men with long hair and soft moccasins, and Indian women wearing full, bright-colored skirts, shawls, and headscarfs, can always be seen near the Council Hall, at the Agency office, and on the steps of the traders' stores. There are also young Indian students neatly dressed in dark suits, light shirts, and polished shoes, and girls dressed in the latest fashion.

Indian dances take place often and an annual rodeo is staged in August. A small fee is sometimes charged for permission to use cameras.

At Pine Ridge Agency a business in Indian arts and crafts is being developed, and groups of Indians are often employed to travel with shows in the summer season; a number went to the Chicago Exposition in 1933, and it was reported that 30 families went to Paris on the same errand in 1936. Thus these people are turning their knowledge of old Indian customs into a means of earning a living. Many of them have been to Hollywood to act in motion pictures, and hundreds have appeared as extras in films made in and near the Black Hills.

From this agency W. to Oglala many Indian homes can be seen. There are still more than 1,500 log houses on this reservation. Many have dirt roofs and dirt floors. The 1880 report of the Indian agent says, "The people have taken to house building to a remarkable degree. In the past year they have erected by their own labor, or employed others to build them, between 300 and 400 log houses with dirt roofs." In the past 60 years little has been done to encourage these people in their house building. The primitive houses were, unfortunately, one of the causes of the high incidence of tuberculosis among the people who had been accustomed to outdoor living.

HOLY ROSARY MISSION, 225 m., was started in 1883, by the Jesuits, to provide a Catholic school for the Pine Ridge Reservation. A kiln was constructed to manufacture bricks for the buildings, and school opened in 1888. Dormitories, a gymnasium, and other buildings have been added. Since 1939 a full four-year high school has been in operation. This is also headquarters for the twenty-two chapels on the reservation.

OGLALA, 235 m., is known mainly for its large Indian boarding school, attended by children from many parts of the reservation. Oglala (Ind., *to scatter one's own*) is the name of one of the many tribes of the Sioux nation. In recent years Indian pupils at various schools, combining native athletic grace with sinewy litheness and speed, have threatened the accustomed supremacy of whites in modern sports. In 1936 the Oglala Indian school basketball team won the State Class B tournament, the first time in history that an Indian athletic squad has won a South Dakota title of such importance. Comfortable buildings, good playgrounds, gymnasium, and all modern equipment aid the school's program of diversified education.

At 245 *m.* the main fork of White River is crossed. Although a small stream, it often rises to surprising proportions during periods of hard and continued rains. Its source is in northern Nebraska.

At 258.5 *m.* US 18 crosses the Shannon-Fall River Co. line and winds snakelike over a high sloping ledge that tops a wasteland of rolling prairie, broken only by small humps or knolls that appear like scattered grass huts.

SMITHWICK, 265 *m.*, was at one time the center of a cattle-grazing country and a fair-sized cow town, but with the division of a part of the prairie to the S. into farms, its prosperity waned.

From Smithwick the road continues over a hilly section to the junction with State 79 (*see Tour 14*), which is reached at 271 *m.*, the two routes are united between this point and Hot Springs.

At 276.5 *m.* is the junction with the Angostura Road.

Left on this road is the new ANGOSTURA DAM AND IRRIGATION PROJECT, 5 *m.*, which is part of the vast Missouri Basin development and flood control program sponsored by the U.S. Bureau of Reclamation (*see HISTORY*). Construction of the dam across the Cheyenne River was begun in August, 1946, when U.S. Rep. Francis Case of Custer set off the first dynamite charge. The dam was completed in December, 1949. It provides a reservoir that extends E. to State 79 and W. to State 87, a distance of about 11 m. Designed to provide irrigation and flood control, the reservoir will provide water to irrigate 16,000 acres of semiarid land S. of Hot Springs.
The Smithsonian Institution made excavations in the area before it was flooded, and uncovered a number of stone javelin heads. Some petroglyphs are above the water line.

At 276.8 *m.* is the junction with a dirt road.

Left on this road is the HOT SPRINGS AIRPORT, 1.2 *m.* The hangar is an attractive building of native stone.

At 277.5 *m.* US 18 crosses the Cheyenne River and enters the Cheyenne breaks. From here to Hot Springs the road is oiled, a black ribbon of wide, well-guarded curves, rolling and weaving through the irregular country.

At 278.5 *m.* the highway skirts a ridge and drops down a steep hill. Gushing from a steep hillside (R) are artificial falls caused by discharge of water from the flume of the water and light plant at Hot Springs. At this point US 18 enters FALL RIVER CANYON, its breadth divided by the green Fall River. With forested slopes casting queer, dull shadows on the bare, standstone cliffs below, and the thin blue ribbon of highway threading beyond, the Fall River valley drive is one of the most picturesque along the entire course of US 18 across the State.

At 278.8 *m.* (R) is FALL RIVER FALLS, a series of small cascades surging down over sandstone ledges; and (L) at 279 *m.* is the EVANS QUARRY, from which sandstone is taken and shipped for building and other purposes.

At 279.5 *m.* is the Eagle's Nest Curve, and high up on a ledge overlooking the road is an EAGLE'S NEST, discernible from the highway.

At 283 *m.* is the junction with State 87.

Left on this road; paralleling it (L) are seven peaks of sandstone, so similar in appearance as to height and slope from the N. that they were long ago named the SEVEN SISTERS by some of the earlier settlers.

Near the top of the Seven Sisters Range, are the SUNKEN WELLS—holes in the ground, ranging from 15 to 40 ft. deep. The wells are caused by underground water eroding the limestone layers, leaving an unsupported roof which in time drops.

At 13 *m.* is the interesting ghost town of CASCADE, started as a resort center to provide Eastern health seekers with peace and quiet. The large sandstone hotel and the other buildings are quiet enough, having been deserted when Hot Springs became a more accessible spa. The CASCADE FALLS here originate in a few large springs of warm water that tumble over a 15-ft. cliff.

At 285 *m.* is the junction with US 85A in Hot Springs (*see Tour 14*).

Section c. Hot Springs—Wyoming Line, 40.1 m. US 18.

HOT SPRINGS, o *m.* (3,443 alt.), in the foothills of the southern Hills, has a mild, bracing climate. On the S. is the Saw-Tooth range, on the E., Battle Mountain, and on the W. and N., the southern end of the main Black Hills range, locally known as Evans Heights and College Hill, at the base of which flows warm Fall River. In the business section all stores are on one side of the main street and on the other side is the river.

Although the Indians had been making health pilgrimages to the springs for many years, it was not until 1879 that the first permanent white settler arrived. By 1881 a few more people had moved into the canyon and it was then proposed to divide the town, first named Minnekahta, into two parts, because of the narrowness of the canyon. Today, although each section has its residential and business blocks and they are called "upper town" and "lower town," Hot Springs is one unit. In 1891 the courthouse was built fixing the seat of Fall River Co. at Hot Springs.

The growth and development of Hot Springs has never been of the boom variety. The first settlers were interested in agriculture and cattle raising, but through the promotion of the Dakota Hot Springs Co., composed largely of professional men from other towns in the Hills, Hot Springs has developed into a health resort and tourist town. Badger Clark, in his book, *When Hot Springs Was a Pup,* relates that Dr. R. D. Jennings built a shed over a natural bathtub and the spring, and in this place the first white patient took his treatments. This is the INDIAN BATHTUB, now in the Hot Springs Hotel bathhouse. The tub was supposedly used first by an old squaw, who was cured of rheumatism. It is the result of erosion and excavation of the solid rock over one spring.

The South Dakota Beauty Pageant, at which the candidate for Miss America honors is selected, highlights the summer season. Horse racing is the favorite local sport; and pari-mutuel races are held in July.

Fall River, the warm stream famous for the water that never varies in temperature from season to season, is formed by the union of the spring-fed Hot and Cold Brooks on the northern border of Hot Springs, and flows S. through the length of the town.

The largest spring in the Black Hills is MAMMOTH SPRING, two blocks N. of the Evans Plunge on Court St. Some years ago the city purchased this spring and later deeded certain water rights to the National Home for Disabled Veterans. The rest was put at the disposal of the Water, Light & Power Co. At its source this spring has a temperature between 95 and 100 degrees F. The EVANS PLUNGE SPRING, just outside the Evans Plunge building, furnishes the major part of the water for the plunge. Through the Evans Plunge pour 5000 gallons of crystal clear mineral water every hour, at a temperature of 90 degrees. The plunge is open to the public summer and winter, and is subject to none of the disadvantages of open air pools.

The HYGEA SPRING, in the center of town, has long been visited by people who drink its sulphurous water for the alleviation of various disorders. The BRAUN SPRING, on Court St., was the incentive for the building of the Braun Hotel and bathhouse. Over the MINNE-KAHTA SPRING the Hot Springs Hotel has been built. It not only provides bath treatments, but also recreation in the HOT SPRINGS PLUNGE, which, though smaller than that of the Evans, has both indoor and outdoor swimming.

The STATE SOLDIERS' HOME was established in 1889, and ten Civil War veterans were the first patients. Several additions have been made to the original building. Veterans of five wars—Civil, Indian, Spanish-American, and both World Wars—are now admitted, and the wives and widows of these men are taken, if they have only a limited amount of property and are 60 years old or more.

High on the slope of Battle Mountain is the BATTLE MOUNTAIN SANITARIUM (Veterans Administration Facility), home of disabled war veterans. The main buildings of Spanish-style architecture, constructed of native pink sandstone, form a wheel-like design, each building opening upon the beautifully kept acreage of the reservation. The hospital has 270 beds for acute cases and a domiciliary is maintained with 548 beds for chronic patients. Plans in 1951 are to increase the domiciliary facilities. Of the 388 persons employed at the Sanitarium, 298 are connected with the hospital and 90 with the domiciliary.

Others besides war veterans come to Hot Springs seeking health.

For these, two general hospitals are maintained, OUR LADY OF LOURDES (Catholic) and the LUTHERAN HOSPITAL AND SANITARIUM. A polio epidemic in the West-river area in 1946, prompted a public fund-raising campaign for a Crippled Children's Polio Center in connection with the Lutheran Hospital; and construction was started in 1950.

The quarrying of stone is one of the town's major industries. Begun before the year 1900, 5 m. SE. of town, the quarry has been operated for many years for the purpose of obtaining pink sandstone, which is used in local and State-wide construction work. Other quarries in the vicinity have produced large quantities of buff Dakota sandstone and red Dakota sandstone, both used in many of the buildings in Hot Springs.

At 5 m. (R) is the JOHN ROBERTSON MEMORIAL, consisting of a suitably marked Black Hills boulder. It was dedicated July 18, 1935, by the South Dakota State Horticultural Association, in recognition of the work done by John Robertson since 1896, until his death in 1937, in the improvement of the hardier fruits. It has been proposed to set aside a three-acre plot near the boulder as a park for the purpose of planting native trees, flowers, and shrubs.

MINNEKAHTA (Ind., hot water), 6.8 m., is a small railroad junction of the C. B. & Q.

At 11.8 m. (L) is PARKER PEAK (4,848 alt.), one of the oldest landmarks in the history of the Black Hills; when approached from the E., it looks small and unpretentious in comparison with other peaks in the Saw-Tooth range surrounding it. But from a greater distance, Parker Peak appears high above all others. This appearance is perhaps caused by the fact that the blunt-topped summit is shaped much like a loaf of bread and the surrounding peaks, which are much lower, are jagged.

At 14.8 m. is the junction with a dirt road.

Left on this road to the FOSSIL CYCAD NATIONAL MONUMENT, 1 m., an area containing large deposits of the fossil remains of fern-like plants of the Mesozoic period. It is said to be the best fossil cycad bed so far discovered, the specimens having been perfectly preserved. This region consists of a plowed field, the cycads having been removed to Yale University. If any cycads remain, they lie buried beneath the surface in the cretaceous beds known locally as the Dakota formation, a grayish-white sandstone, 30 ft. in thickness.

The fossil cycad is a member of the dacotensis family and the genus Cucadoidea. It has been proven that this species bore flowers millions of years ago when large egg-laying monsters such as the dinosaurs roamed the earth. The height to which the trunks of these plants grew depended upon the species and upon climatic conditions. The more intemperate and adverse the conditions were for this plant, the shorter the trunk. The fruit resembled a pineapple in appearance and became fossilized easily. Some specimens have been found in the Minnekahta fossil bed and have been removed to museums.

The beds were first discovered in 1892, when F. H. Cole of Hot Springs saw a resemblance between these fossils and certain plants growing in the tropics. He immediately sent photographs to the Smithsonian Institution in Washington. Prof. Henry Newton, geologist, was put in charge of the investigation and found them to be the "fossil cycadean trunks." The area was set aside by Presidential proclamation in 1922.

At 17.7 *m.* is FLINT HILL (L), on which is an old Indian flint quarry.

At 25.8 *m.* is the junction with a dirt road.

Right on this road, which follows the course of Pleasant Valley Creek through Red Canyon, are the mysterious PAINTED ROCKS, 7.1 *m.* The small parking space (L), from which the rocks are reached, is not marked, but a clump of cottonwood trees, a washout, high cutbank (R), and the 200-ft. cliff (L) are landmarks. Across the creek bed a steep path (L) leads up the face of the cliff to a pole with several cross-boards. On the smooth face of the rock, at a height of seven or eight ft., are the faint outlines of crudely drawn figures cut into the rock. Deer, goats, beetles, crosses, and other figures can be distinguished. The animals have oval-shaped bodies and crude heads, with straight lines representing legs, tails, horns, and antlers. Some of the characters are simply a string of ooooo, while others look like the family wash hanging on the line. Especially interesting are the crosses, used both as a symbol and an instrument of torture in ancient Mexico and far back into antiquity. The pictures are probably of Indian origin.

At 27 *m.* US 18 crosses the Cheyenne River again.

EDGEMONT, 28.4 *m.* (3,449 alt.), was given the name because of its proximity to the Black Hills. The town originated with the building of the railroad, and has been developed by railroad men and their families. It is the trading center for the surrounding area.

Edgemont boasts an excellent BAND HALL, a half-dome in shape, with a white interior, so that colored lights can be used as a background for the musicians. The walls are constructed of native stone from a quarry situated a few miles north of Edgemont.

At the EDGEMONT HOT WATER SULPHUR BATH SANITARIUM baths are given in water that comes directly from a well in town. The water that gushes from this well ranges in temperature from 116 to 120 degrees at all times. The sanitarium is a well-equipped building, with dining facilities and rooms for many patients.

At Edgemont is the junction with an oil-surfaced highway.

Left on this road is the BLACK HILLS ORDNANCE DEPOT, 5 *m.* (*Pass required at military gate; no matches or lighters permitted*) and the village of IGLOO inside the fence. This U.S. Army installation was built during World War II as an ammunition storage area covering 30,875 acres, converting the prairie desert into a $73,000,000 ordnance supply depot. There are 275 miles of hardsurfaced roads, 48 miles of military railroad, and 1,276 buildings, not counting the hundreds of storage magazines, known as "igloos." They are arched concrete structures set into the earth. With grass growing on top, they are invisible from the air.

Igloo is a government town with military and civilian personnel working in the depot. There are churches, a large school, recreation hall, library, cafeteria, store, and transient dormitories. About 2,000 persons are permanently employed on the project.

Near Edgemont are large quantities of fossils and petrified wood.

At 28.9 *m.* US 18 passes the FALL RIVER FAIR GROUNDS (L). In the early fall every year, the Fall River Co. Fair is held at Edgemont, with a good racing program and exhibits from all parts of the county. The fair has been held annually for the last 24 years.

Indians from the Pine Ridge Reservation lend a gay and colorful touch.

At 30.6 *m*. Parker Peak again stands out (L) in bold relief against the sky, high above the surrounding Edgemont Valley.

At 40.1 *m*. US 18 crosses the Wyoming Line, 50 m. E. of Lusk, Wyo.

Tour 8

Junction US 77 (Elk Point)—Vermillion—Yankton—Wagner—Junction US 18 (Lake Andes). State 50.
Junction with US 77 to Junction with US 18, 97 m.
The C. M. St. P. & P. R.R. parallels this route throughout.
Roadbed hard-surfaced throughout.
Accommodations in towns above.

STATE 50, branching W. from US 77 10 miles N. of Elk Point, passes through the oldest and one of the richest agricultural sections of South Dakota. With the Sioux, Vermillion, and James River valleys, the southeastern section has become an intensive livestock-feeding area, producing tall corn and forage crops for fattening cattle and hogs. It is a virtual continuation of Iowa farmland, with large modern houses, groves of trees, and big red barns. Farther west a gradual transition takes place; the farmers base their hopes on large wheat tracts, which one year may yield thousands of dollars and the next give them no return for their seed and labor. The farms and towns here are newer and less numerous; the valleys give way to rugged, rolling hills. The Yankton Indian Reservation is along the Missouri River toward the western end of this route.

This highway serves as an arterial to the Ft. Randall Dam, government hydro-electric project in the Missouri River.

At o *m*. is JUNCTION CITY, a cluster of roadhouses and filling stations.

Between the junction with US 77 and Vermillion, State 50 passes through a flat country, where farmers haul their produce and livestock to markets in large trucks two and three times a week.

VERMILLION, 9 *m*. (1,131 alt.), the seat of the University of South Dakota, is situated on the bluffs above the peaceful Vermillion River, and also overlooks the turbulent Missouri. The town was so named because of the red clay obtained from the banks of the river.

In 1835 a trading post called Fort Vermillion was built by the American Fur Co. on the banks of the Missouri River, and in 1843 Audubon, the famous naturalist, visited the post and the trail now known as the Ravine Road in the present city. A colony of Mormons, en route to the Rocky Mountains, spent the winter at the fort in 1845–46, but the site of the fort has been washed away by the bank-eroding Missouri.

When the Homestead Act went into effect Jan. 1, 1863, settlers moved in to stake claims along the valley. A settlement was started on the flat where the Vermillion and Missouri Rivers join, and the new town boomed. But in 1881, a flood roared down through the lowlands, sweeping away 150 buildings in the young city and leaving the rest in ruins. There was not a single life lost, however, as residents climbed to the high bluff and watched their belongings and five bridges float down the swirling river. The result of the flood was twofold: a new city was built high on the bluffs, and the Missouri cut a new channel four miles South, creating a large island.

The UNIVERSITY OF SOUTH DAKOTA, adjacent to State 50 on Dakota St., is an important factor in the development and growth of the State (*see EDUCATION*). Through the research work of its laboratories and the expert services of its staff, the University contributes widely to the development of wealth and culture in the State.

In 1862 the first Territorial Legislature established the University, but failed to provide any funds. Succeeding legislatures refused to make an appropriation, and 20 years later the citizens of Vermillion decided to take energetic action. The site was selected and the first 10 acres donated by Judge Jefferson Kidder. The county commissioners called an election to approve a $10,000 bond issue for the construction of one building. Although the building was not yet finished, the fall term opened in 1882 in the court house. The faculty consisted of one man, Dr. Ephriam N. Epstein, a Russian Jew who had become a Baptist clergyman; the student body numbered 39, but increased to 69 before the end of the first year. The next year the faculty was doubled, and the Territorial Legislature voted its support to the extent of $30,000.

The original plan for the campus was a semicircle, but the founders failed to realize the space needs of future growth. The buildings are now arranged on the 69-acre campus with more regard to convenience than symmetry. There is no uniform type of architecture. English tendencies are noticeable in some of the buildings. Centered in the semicircle is venerable UNIVERSITY HALL, built of Sioux Falls pink quartzite, in 1882. Of similar stone and design is EAST HALL (R.), a dormitory for women. Another women's dormitory, DAKOTA HALL, built of dark brick, joins the older building. To the (L.) of University Hall is the fortress-like OLD ARMORY, now the women's gym, and SCIENCE HALL. The MAIN LIBRARY and the SCHOOL OF LAW, flanking the entrances to the campus, are of Colonial type in Bedford limestone. Other buildings are of brick.

The ADMINISTRATION BUILDING, which includes Slagle Auditorium and the W. H. Over Museum (*see below*), dominates the grouping. Near it is a reproduction of the LOG SCHOOLHOUSE which was built originally by U.S. soldiers at the foot of Ravine Hill (*see EDUCATION*).

The newer portion of the campus lies to the W. The SOUTH

DAKOTA UNION houses student and alumni lounges, book store, snack shop, publication offices, and studios of KUSD, university radio station. JULIAN HALL, a large dormitory for men, was opened in 1950. Other buildings in this area are CHEMISTRY, APPLIED SCIENCE, the ARMORY-GYMNASIUM, and INMAN STADIUM. The new SCHOOL OF MEDICINE building is to the S.

Fraternity and sorority houses border the campus, with a few in the near-downtown district.

The main public event of the year is Dakota Day (homecoming) in October. University athletic teams are known as the Coyotes and compete in the North Central Conference.

The W. H. OVER MUSEUM (*free: open 9 a.m. to 4:30 p.m. weekdays*), in the Administration Building, has more than 30,000 labeled exhibits. The Indian Room includes articles of the Sioux Indians, and also artifacts excavated from the various pre-historic Indian villages and mounds in South Dakota. The Morrow Memorial Room has collections of photographs and stereoptic cards of early South Dakota historical subjects and events. The Pioneer Room contains hand-made looms, musical instruments, glassware, furniture, and clothing brought into the State by early settlers. In Firearm Hall is a very large collection of ancient and modern firearms, swords, and articles of warfare. One of the largest shotguns in existence is exhibited here. The Bird Room contains mounted specimens of nearly every bird that lives or migrates through the State. There is also a very large collection of birds' eggs. The Mammal Room is devoted primarily to mounted animals of South Dakota. In the West Room are found collections of reptiles, fish, shells, both marine and land, and exhibits of butterflies and insects. In the Geology Room are fossil and mineral collections from the Black Hills and Badlands.

AUDUBON PARK, S. Dakota St., borders the Ravine Road from the bluff to the flat, and is heavily wooded with natural timber. A monument to the first permanent schoolhouse in South Dakota (*see EDUCATION*), together with a miniature reproduction of the building, stands at the foot of the hill, across from which is a memorial to the first Masonic chapter in the State.

PRENTISS PARK, E. Main St., has a large municipal swimming pool (*open daily during summer*).

At the western end of Main St. is a junction with State 19.

Right on State 19 to SPIRIT MOUND, 3 *m.*, a high hill rising from a level plain, and believed sacred by the Indians. Lewis and Clark stopped in 1804 to investigate the stories told by the Sioux of mysterious little people who inhabited the mound and shot arrows at anyone who approached. The explorers found neither inhabitants nor any evidence of their activities. There was nothing of unusual interest except the mound, which is approximately 300 ft. long, 70 ft. wide, and 65 ft. high.

At 10.4 *m.* the Vermillion River is crossed.

At 10.6 *m.* is a junction with a graded road leading to a ferry, 3 *m.*

A V-shaped valley between the Vermillion and Missouri Rivers, with high bluffs rising from the far sides of each, has productive and well-cultivated farms. To the S. the rugged bluffs form part of the Nebraska boundary.

MECKLING, 16.8 *m.* (1,156 alt.), has one of the largest consolidated schools in the State.

At 27.5 *m.* the WNAX radio station transmitter looms (R.), its 927 ft. tower being one of the world's tallest.

At 30.3 *m.* the James River is crossed. The SITE OF THE FROST-TODD TRADING POST, which served the Indians and early-day trappers, is (R).

YANKTON, 34 *m.* (1,157 alt.), was the capital of Dakota Territory before South Dakota and North Dakota were divided, and much of the State's early history had Yankton as its setting (*see HISTORY*).

Yankton has an air of quiet dignity, and the reputation for being a prosperous business center. It is the seat of two colleges, Yankton and Mount Marty, and two large hospitals, Sacred Heart and the State's hospital for the insane. In 1951 the city's tempo increased as plans went forward to build a Federal dam and power project at Gavins Point in the Missouri River, four miles W. of Yankton (*see below*).

In March 1858, George D. Fiske, representative of a fur company, pitched his tent near the Missouri River, becoming the city's first permanent white settler. Sixteen cedar rafts were floated down the river from Fort Pierre, out of which a trading post was built near the present Meridian Highway bridge. The Yankton Sioux Indians, led by Smutty Bear, gathered at Yankton in 1859 to protest being removed to reservations. A satisfactory agreement was reached, with the presentation of some trinkets by the U.S. Agent, and settlers moved into the region. The town was surveyed in August 1859, and construction of more buildings was begun to augment the two log cabins there. On Christmas Day, 1859, the first tavern was opened where the Merchants Hotel now stands; in fact, the original structure is part of the present building.

An unusual character of those days was James Witherspoon, a bachelor, locally known as Limber Jim; it is said that he walked to Washington, D. C., to procure the patent to his land, now known as the Witherspoon Addition.

Yankton was selected capital of Dakota Territory in 1861, and when the first Legislature met, was nicknamed "The Pony Congress," the upper house convened in the William Tripp residence (*see below*). The lower house met in the Episcopal chapel. The first copy of the *Weekly Dakotan* was printed June 6, 1861.

An Indian uprising in 1862 resulted in the erection of a stockade, 450 ft. square, at Third and Broadway, and residents of Sioux

Falls and Yankton gathered there for protection. After the excitement subsided, the prosperous city grew steadily.

In 1873 the Dakota Southern Railroad (now the C. M. St. P. & P.) reached Yankton to connect the capital with the "outside world." Soon Yankton became the outfitting point for parties heading for the Black Hills in search of gold. When a man from Yankton, John B. Pearson, discovered the first rich lode in Deadwood Gulch in 1875, the rush was on. Steamboats lined up along lower Levee St. to carry passengers and freight up the Missouri River as far as Fort Pierre, and wagon trains rumbled along the old Fort Randall Trail (*see below*).

FIRST HOUSE IN YANKTON

There are many fine old houses in Yankton, dating back to Territorial days. Some of the older business buildings are made of chalk rock quarried along the Missouri River; other old structures, such as the Phil Kearney Memorial Hall, reflect the military motif and brass ornamentation of the period. Yankton's streets are unusually wide, some 130 ft., with boulevards of flowers and shrubbery. There are several large parks having excellent picnicking and recreational facilities.

Throughout South Dakota and adjoining States, Yankton is best known for its radio station, WNAX, which was among the first powerful stations in the midwest. Studios are in the House of Gurney, a unique farm store here, and also at Sioux City, Iowa. The station is owned by the publishers of *Look* and *Quick* magazines and the *Minneapolis Star and Tribune*.

The SITE OF THE CAPITOL OF DAKOTA TERRITORY is marked by a bronze tablet on polished granite at Capital and Fourth Sts. The original two-story building was frame.

TERRITORIAL COUNCIL CHAMBER (*free*), in Waterworks Park along the Missouri River, has been restored as a museum by the Yankton chapter of the Daughters of the American Revolution. Originally the home of William Tripp, the house served as the first meeting place for the upper chamber of the Dakota Territorial Legislature (*see HISTORY*). In 1893 the old frame building was moved away and forgotten. It was not until 1935 that townspeople began searching for the historic structure, finding it in use as a granary on a nearby farm. To the W. of the Council Chamber building is INSPIRATION POINT, also known as Pierre Dorian Hill, from which is a broad view of the Missouri River, with the Nebraska hills in the distance.

The YANKTON BRIDGE, at the foot of Walnut St., carries US 81 (*see Tour 10*) and crosses the Missouri River to Nebraska. It was built entirely by private capital raised in the vicinity. It is a double-deck, seven-span draw bridge, and was formerly known as the Meridian Highway Bridge.

PRESS AND DAKOTAN BUILDING, Walnut St. between 3rd and 4th Sts., is the home of the oldest daily newspaper in the State. The first issue was published April 26, 1875, during the Black Hills gold rush. One of its big news stories appeared on the morning of July 7, 1876, under a headline of "TELEGRAPHIC: DEATH." A sub-head read: "Custer and His Entire Command Swept out of Existence by the Wards of the Nation and the Special Pets of Eastern Orators." The story told about the Battle of the Little Big Horn which had been fought two weeks earlier.

The building was erected in 1878 by the German Turnverein (society) and was used as an Opera House before the newspaper moved into it.

CARNEGIE LIBRARY, Capital and 4th Sts., has several valuable collections, among which is the Roane Memorial Collection of 1,000 volumes; a South Dakota Collection of 900 volumes; and a genealogical department consisting of 300 books.

YANKTON COLLEGE (Congregational) is the oldest institution of high learning in the Dakotas, having been founded in 1881 by Dr. Joseph Ward. The Conservatory of Music is considered one of the best in the Midwest. The college has an attractive campus. NASH AUDITORIUM, built following World War II, is used for college athletic events, city affairs, and farm programs. The GARDEN TERRACE THEATRE, an out-of-doors amphitheatre, has a seating capacity of 5,000. It is the scene of college dramatic productions and spring festivities.

Yankton College athletic teams are known as the Greyhounds, and "Pioneer Day" is the annual fall homecoming.

BENEDICTINE SISTERS' CORPORATION, W. end of 4th St. (State 50), is the Motherhouse of the order and includes SACRED HEART HOSPITAL, MOUNT MARTY COLLEGE, and the new BISHOP MARTY MEMORIAL CHAPEL. The convent and a new nurses home are other major buildings; and there is a men's dormitory for the workers who operate the farm in connection with the convent.

The convent was begun in 1887, through the efforts of Bishop Marty, first bishop of South Dakota, who brought a small group of Benedictine nuns to Dakota Territory. The first hospital was opened in 1897, in a building which served as the first Catholic cathedral in the Territory. A new 100-bed hospital was erected in 1915, and added to in 1929, 1940, and 1947. Sacred Heart is now the largest hospital in the State. The new four-story nurses home includes a swimming pool.

Mount Marty is a four-year college and high school for girls. The enrollment is about 200.

The Bishop Marty Memorial Chapel, consecrated in 1950, is considered one of the most beautiful in the country. Of modified Gothic architecture, it was constructed of carved limestone and lannum stone at a cost of more than a million dollars. The activities of the Benedictines are depicted in the large window at the entrance. The chapel is built on two levels. One room is devoted to souvenirs of Bishop Marty.

The convent has a department of Ecclesiastical art embroidery (*open to public*) in which vestments are made and sent throughout the world.

YANKTON STATE HOSPITAL, N. on Broadway Ave. (US 81), is a State institution for the insane, senile, and alcoholic. Until 1878 the insane persons of Dakota Territory were cared for, by special arrangements, in Nebraska and Minnesota institutions. When Gov. William A. Howard found the institutions in the other States overcrowded, and insane persons numerous within the State, he used his own funds to secure land and provide shelter at Yankton. The institution was almost immediately overcrowded. With 57 women packed in a cottage originally built for a laundry, fire broke out and 17 patients perished, the others escaping with only their night apparel.

The hospital owns 1,700 acres of land, 1,400 of which are under cultivation. Fine, new buildings have been constructed to make it one of the outstanding institutions in the State.

A collection of pictures, including 273 water colors, 27 oil paintings and 35 etchings, is on exhibition at the hospital.

At Yankton is the junction with US 81 (*see Tour 10*).

W. from Yankton, on what is known as The Lower Road which follows the route of the historic Fort Randall Trail, is the SITE OF THE GAVINS POINT DAM, 4 *m.*, one of the major projects in the Federal government's Missouri River Basin Development program (*see NATURAL RESOURCES and HISTORY*). It is the farthest downstream of the series of dams in the Missouri River schedule; the Fort Randall dam is 78 miles up-river. The Corps of Engineers, U.S. Army, designated this peninsula for a rolled earthen dam 72 ft. high and 10,500 ft. long between South Dakota and Nebraska.

One of its major purposes is to release water for river navigation below Sioux City, Iowa. The project also calls for a hydro-electric power plant here. Prior to 1950, a sum of $668,000 was expended in the planning phase of the project; when completed, the cost is estimated at $44,900,000. Acquisition of land and preparing access road and rail facilities were begun in 1951.

Bordering the Missouri River are the interesting CHALK ROCK CLIFFS. When first excavated, the rock is soft enough to be cut with a knife, but hardens soon after exposure to air. When weathered it makes a fair building material. A cement plant to utilize the rock was operated here at one time.

From the Chalk Rock Cliffs is a road N. known as the Postman's Road to State 50.

At 41.5 m. is the junction with the Postman's Road (*see above*).

At 47.5 m. is the junction with a graveled road.

Left on this road is the BON HOMME HUTTERITE COLONY, 4 m. It takes its name from Bon Homme (good man) Island in the Missouri River which was named by a French trapper. The county bears the same name. The colony is one of several in the State in which this religious sect operates extensive farm holdings (*see Tours 4 and 5*).

The WALTER A. BURLEIGH HOUSE, one of the oldest in the State, is in the colony. Half frame and half chalk rock, the joined buildings were built originally in the early 1860's by Dr. Burleigh. He was a physician who came to Dakota Territory from Pennsylvania in 1861, to serve as agent to the Yankton Indians. He operated a ranch on the land which is now used by the colony. Dr. Burleigh defeated Capt. J. B. S. Todd, cousin of Mrs. Abraham Lincoln, for Dakota Territorial delegate to the U.S. Congress in 1864. He is reported to have given away 1,000 sheep and 500 barrels of flour during his successful campaign.

TABOR, 51 m., is the center of a Bohemian, or Czech, settlement. Most of the town's population, as well as that of the surrounding farming area, bear the names of their nationality, and many old customs are observed. In 1939, several relatives of Eduard Bénes, president of Czechoslovakia, took up donations in the community to send to their homeland at the time of the Nazi invasion. Noted for fun-loving tendencies, they hold their "Sokols" several times each year. A Sokol is the performance of setting-up exercises similar to those practiced in the army; the Bohemians enter into them with great zest, every summer holding a contest in a spirit of keen competition. They also have the old folk dances, the best known and most difficult of which is the Beseda. This requires 20 couples and the participants are always dressed in native costumes.

A Bohemian wedding is a festive occasion. The entire neighborhood is invited; there is plenty to eat and drink, and the air is filled with music and laughter. A dance always follows the wedding.

Housewives here are noted for the quality and quantity of food they prepare. Their best known food is kolach, a small biscuit filled with fruit or with poppy seed. Bohemians are heavy meat eaters, with pork heading the list. Potato dumplings and sauerkraut, with pitchers of beer, are often included in their menus.

TYNDALL, 64 m. (1,418 alt.), is the seat of Bon Homme Co. and the center of a prosperous farming community, largely of Bohemian and German origin. The town was founded in 1879 when the depot was built by the Milwaukee railroad. The first shipment to be received was a box of rabbits.

Tyndall has a library, auditorium, and swimming pool for public use.

At 66.5 *m.* is a junction with State 37.

Left on this hard-surfaced highway is SPRINGFIELD, 10 *m.* (1,234 alt.), which was incorporated by the first Territorial Legislature in 1862. The town was not platted, however, until 1869 when Gov. John A. Burbank purchased the site. *The Springfield Times,* which began publication on July 27, 1871, is the oldest surviving weekly newspaper in the State, the earlier ones having been consolidated or abandoned. At Springfield is SOUTHERN STATE TEACHERS COLLEGE. The institution was established as Springfield Normal School in 1881, but it was not until 1897 that it actually opened. It began with an enrollment of 21 students and a faculty of four. In recent years the Board of Regents have enlarged the trade and vocational training facilities. On the campus of 40 acres are a main building, a science hall-gymnasium, mechanical shops, and dormitories. Athletic teams are known as the Pointers, and the annual home-coming celebration is Founders Day.
Also at Springfield is ST. MARY'S (Episcopal), only exclusively all-Indian girls' high school in the United States. It was founded as a mission in 1873, by Bishop William Hobart Hare. The main hall was built in 1884. An average of 50 students, from reservations throughout the country, are enrolled. School records show that 95 per cent of the graduates go to college, or enter nursing or business schools. A 3,000-volume library has orange crates for stacks, and all the girls help in the maintenance of the school because of limited funds.
From Springfield is a graveled road S. to RUNNING WATER, a ferry landing on the Missouri River making connections to Nebraska highway State 14.

At 70.2 *m.* is a junction with State 37 which runs N. (*see Tour 11A*).

AVON, 74.8 *m.*, was named by early settlers for Avon., N. Y., the town from which they had migrated. It has a fine, shady park and unusually good drinking water.

At 79 *m.* is a deep gully, lined with oak trees, which virtually marks the dividing line between the rich farming region and an area of larger grain farms in which weather conditions determine the wealth of the people. The country beyond is more rolling, and the view far reaching.

DANTE, 83.1 *m.*, was first called Mayo, in honor of E. O. Mayo, owner of the town site, but when it was learned that there was a post office in the Black Hills by the same name, Mayo renamed the town for his favorite author, Dante. The town was founded in 1908, when the railroad put in a siding to accommodate farmers who shipped large quantities of livestock. For a town of its size, it has one of the largest Catholic parishes in the State.

WAGNER, 91.2 *m.* (1,442 alt.), is a picturesque trading center for the Indians who live on the Yankton Reservation, and is a live Western town. Indians are seen every day loitering on the street, the women dressed in shawls and blankets and the men in overalls. An annual Labor Day celebration is held, featuring Indian dances.

A Government INDIAN HOSPITAL, costing $85,000, was opened in 1937, to take care of Indians on the Yankton Reservation needing hospitalization. The hospital is a one-story building, with wards in the wings, so that all rooms receive sunshine. Indian labor was used in constructing the building.

At Wagner is a junction with a graveled road.

Turn L. on this road, which goes through Indian country; along this route are improved and well-kept Indian homes, as well as shacks with "squaw coolers," four posts in a square with a roof of branches and leaves.

At 14 *m.* is a small graveyard where a group of Sioux members of the Peyote cult have been buried.

Old Indians like to recall an incident that happened along this road when it was only a foot trail. An Indian had gone about 5 m. to Greenwood Agency for supplies. While there he also purchased a new hat, which he put on immediately, and with his sack of groceries thrown over his shoulder he started for home. Night was coming on so he walked rapidly. After traveling some distance he noticed an object directly in front of him, and finally became alarmed when he noticed it popping up before him, no matter where he looked. Speeding up his pace, he started across country; but still the bobbing object continued to make its appearance. Frightened by the evil-appearing demon, he tried vainly to go around it. So he set out at full speed, zig-zagging and stumbling as he sped through brush and undergrowth. Finally he saw a light glimmering through the dusk and breathlessly made a last desperate effort to elude his pursuer which, strangely, was behind him whenever he looked back. He dashed on, falling exhausted against the door, battered and bruised by his swinging sack of supplies. After being taken in and revived, he was relieved to discover the demon was no longer before him. When he put on his hat, there it was again. Then he saw that the demon had been the heavy hat cord hanging over the brim of his hat in front.

At 18 *m.* is GREENWOOD, which until recently was the Yankton Indian Agency. A boss farmer now has charge of the Indians there, under the direction of the Agent at Rosebud Agency (see Tour 7). Greenwood is on the banks of the Missouri River and has several large frame buildings no longer in use. Most families of the agency haul their water from the river in barrels. An incident of 1889 illustrates the difficulties confronted by the United States Government during the territorial period. At that time the Government took steps to allot the lands, but the measure was resisted by an Indian, Big Tobacco, and his band. Troops were called out and bloodshed almost ensued before the band consented to the allotment. Bobona, another Indian, opposed the act but surrendered after a 15-m. chase by soldiers with bayonets. A legend Greenwood Indians tell concerns the origin of the sunflower. A certain boy early in life developed a deep affection for the sun. For hours each day he would sit and gaze at the flaming disc on its journey across the heavens. He would sing weird songs praising the object of his affections. And because of his strange communion with the sun he was named Sun Gazer. In time he became blind, and because he ate very sparingly his body wasted away. One evening when he did not return from his favorite spot on a nearby hill, a party was sent out after sundown to find him. They came upon him facing W.; though blind, he had by force of habit followed the sun on its course as he did when he still had his eyesight.. When they came closer to him they found that the last spark of life had left along with the last ray of light. They buried him on that very spot. The next morning they returned to the grave, they found that a flower had grown from the mound; as they watched it, they saw that it, too, followed the course of the sun.

At 97 *m.* is the junction with US 18 (*see Tour 7*), 9 m. E. of Lake Andes.

Tour 9

Milbank—Brookings—Sioux Falls—Elk Point—(Sioux City, Iowa) US 77.
Milbank to Iowa Line, 208.1 m.
Except at intervals, US 77 is not paralleled by railroads.
All-weather roads.
Good hotel and tourist accommodations.

US 77 passes through South Dakota's richest farming region—a region of ample rainfall, characterized by diversified agriculture. Bisecting the heart of the State's dairy section at the start, the road first crosses an area where small grains lead other crops, then touches a region of moderate livestock production, and finally passes through the portion where intensive livestock-feeding dominates. Incidentally, Deuel County on this route is the only County in the State where oats form the leading crop.

While the general character of the country is level, numerous hills and occasional tree-fringed lakes interrupt the monotony of the landscape. The northern half of US 77 touches the section known as the Lake Region, and the southern half the Sioux Valley region. Much of the soil is of a rich black loam quality, capable of producing abundant crops and able to withstand considerable drought.

The eastern section of the State was the first to be occupied, earliest settlers coming from Minnesota. The region is quite typically eastern, the descendants of the first settlers remaining on the farms during succeeding generations. There are pretentious farm homes, surrounded by large substantial buildings, in groves of trees.

MILBANK, 0. *m.* (1,148 alt.), (*see Tour 2*), is at the junction with US 12.

US 77 sweeps S. over a new, straight highway through semi-hilly country with a multitude of grass tufted knolls.

At 19.9. *m.* is the junction with US 212 (*see Tour 3*); the two routes are united to the TUNERVILLE CORNER, 25 *m.* US 77 continues S.

At 28.2 *m.* is the junction with an oiled road.

Right on this road is ALTAMONT, 0.5 *m.* (1,834 alt.). Situated among the hills, the town has one of the highest altitudes of any town in this part of the State.

CLEAR LAKE, 34.8 *m.* (1,800 alt.), was named for the once clear lake E. of town (*see below*). As the county seat and trade center for a large area, the town has a new COMMUNITY HOSPITAL and operates its municipal liquor store and library on the equitable basis of having them share the front rooms of the City Hall.

The county's new COURTHOUSE, built of Bedford limestone, is

one of the outstanding structures in Deuel Co. This handsome building is a far cry from the first courthouse that figured in a prolonged
and bitter county seat war, settled finally in 1890. Gary, where the
State School for the Blind is located, and Clear Lake were the princi-
pals in the contest. Clear Lake was situated in the approximate center
of the county; but Gary was the older town, and in addition, had
been presented with a new courthouse by the Chicago & North Western R.R. When the battle ended, Clear Lake had won, and Gary's
new courthouse slowly began to fall into a state of desuetude. Today
it is used as a chicken house at the State School for the Blind.

An annual rodeo is held in late June at the nearby Crystal Springs
Ranch which has a natural bowl. Events include wild horse races,
wild cow milking contests, saddle and bareback bronc riding, calf
roping, bulldogging, and bull fighting.

At Clear Lake is the junction with State 22.

Left on this road at 0.5 m. is Clear Lake for which the town was named. Early
settlers remember its transparent, sparkling water and clean sandy bottom; they
also recall that about 1910, following a drought period, a ditch was dug to augment
the water supply. Since then Clear Lake has become a depository for eroded soil
from the hillsides along the ditch.

At 14 m. is GARY, a quiet, tree-shaded town built on three
levels of ground, with many dignified houses, and the SOUTH
DAKOTA SCHOOL FOR THE BLIND. The school consists of a
large dormitory and classroom building and several smaller workshop and farm buildings. Railings of pipe on the grounds help the
boys and girls to find their way about. The children are trained in
crafts and their work is displayed here.

The first railroad built into the State was a spur to GARY built
in 1871, by the Winona and St. Peter R. R. The village was called
State Line because of its location on the Minnesota-South Dakota
border; then for a time it was called Headquarters, because the railroad contractor maintained his office here. Later it was named in
honor of H. B. Gary, the mail agent; he reciprocated by presenting
the postoffice with a stamping machine.

Despite the fact that US 77 traverses a rich farming section between Clear Lake and Brookings, there is not a single town on the
highway along the 35-m. stretch.

At 47.2 m. is the junction with State 28.

Left on this road is the village of TORONTO, 2 m. and several popular lakes,
including FISH LAKE, OAK LAKE, and LAKE HENDRICKS.

At 49.1 m. is the junction with a graveled road.

Right on this road through BRUCE, 5 m., is OAKWOOD LAKES STATE PARK,
12 m. (see Tour 4, Sec. a).

At 69.1 *m.* is the Brookings GOLF COURSE, and a short distance beyond is the ATHLETIC FIELD of South Dakota State College.

BROOKINGS, 70 *m.* (1,636 alt.), (*see Tour 4*), is at the junction with US 14.

At 78.1 *m.*, a few feet from the road (R), is the MEDARY MONUMENT, erected to commemorate the first townsite in Dakota Territory in 1857. Nothing is left of this little settlement of three-quarters of a century ago, but a rather unostentatious pillar of cobblestone on a base of gray stone and concrete.

US 77 crosses the Big Sioux River in a wooded area known as CONSERVATION PARK.

At 80.2 *m.* is the junction with a graveled road.

Right on this road is LAKE CAMPBELL, 3.5 *m.*, a summer resort area (*fishing, boating, swimming*). The Brookings Country Club maintains a golf course here (*green fees*).

At 96 *m.* is the LONE TREE CORNER, so named because of a large, stately cottonwood tree which has been the subject of controversy for many years. The tree was planted by a pioneer in 1876, and became a prominent landmark in the vicinity. As roads were built, it stood in the center of a crossroad. However, traffic was diverted around the tree until the paving contract was let. Then the State Highway Department announced that "the tree must go." The storm of protest that followed reverberated through the newspapers. Nature lovers from all over the United States were aroused. Officials reversed themselves, but the concrete was run so close around the old tree that no water could reach its roots. Although it was declared officially dead in 1950, any sly hints that it would be cut down were still being met with editorials and readers' letters daring the Highway Department to as much as chip the bark.

Left from Lone Tree on State 34 is FLANDREAU, 14 *m.* (1,565 alt.), which was first settled in 1857 but destroyed the following year when Indians frightened the settlers away. In 1859 a band of Santee Sioux disregarded the dictates of the Government and settled "like white men" on homesteads in the Big Sioux River valley. In 1874 both Episcopal and Presbyterian churches were built, and in 1878 Flandreau was again settled by white people. Flandreau is the seat of Moody Co., and the home of the FLANDREAU INDIAN VOCATIONAL HIGH SCHOOL, (open; student guides). The school is situated in an Indian community at the western edge of the city. Its campus comprises 481 acres and 54 buildings. Here 420 Indian students receive both academic and vocational training. Native arts and crafts are given a prominent place in the curriculum—weaving, carving, and beadwork; articles made from native pipestone are featured. The craft work is for sale. The vocational department offers courses in auto mechanics, welding, millwork, cabinet making, engineering, book making, library work, nursing, sewing and commercial work. In the community surrounding the school, 75 per cent of the people use the Dakota, or Sioux language. Few traces of Indian habits of life and customs of dress remain, however. The Indian women operate a garment factory where they manufacture about 15,000 dresses annually for the Indian service.

At 109.5 *m.* (R.) is the ODD FELLOWS HOME, a short distance from the road. At this institution old and indigent members of the lodge are taken care of.

DELL RAPIDS, 108.2 *m.* (1,489 alt.), first settled in 1864 is one of the most picturesque towns in south-eastern South Dakota. It was so named because of the dells and rapids of the Big Sioux River that flows through the town. CITY PARK, which is bisected by the highway, has swimming and picnicking facilities. There is also a large dance hall.

The DELLS OF THE SIOUX are at the SW. edge of the town, a striking gorge cut through the pink and purple quartzite rock underlying this region. A road parallels the Dells which extend about a mile, but there are paths along the edge and steps to some of the formations. Sunlight, evening shades, and moonlight all produce different and picturesque effects.

The rock in the Dells juts to the surface through a thin layer of earth for many feet from the edge of the chasm. Below is the swift-flowing Big Sioux River, which divides into two channels above the Dells to join again below. About halfway along the Dells is PULPIT ROCK, a small amphitheatre with a smooth floor of red stone at the top of the cliffs. This queer natural formation actually served as a place of worship in early days before churches were built, the congregation occasionally being subjected to a drenching because of the lack of a roof.

The road passes a spot where iron rails guard a deep crevice that joins the main gorge. From natural platforms of rock S. and N. of this point are impressive views; toward the S., visible for a long distance, is the river valley, its walls, red and purple in the sunlight. Through the gorge is a view of pastures and small groves and a glimpse of the vast prairie country.

These gorges were formed by torrents which came down the Big Sioux Valley when the glaciers melted thousands of years ago. Coming from the N., the waters forced themselves over the barrier of Sioux Falls quartzite at Dell Rapids. The channel here was narrow and the rock more resistant than the drift through which the stream cut the wider part of the valley. The steep walls of the gorge are due to the method by which the stream cut its valley.

When a strong current crosses a formation like the Sioux quartzite which is broken by many cracks and fissures, a process known as "plucking" takes place. Instead of being worked off bit by bit, the blocks of rock are lifted out bodily and carried away by the force of the water. The strong current of the Big Sioux River carried everything before it, including any rock projections that may have been formed, and thus left the walls smooth.

The Dells are city-owned and no admission is charged.

The Dell Rapids POST OFFICE, established in 1871, began operations in a rude shanty with an old trunk for equipment. The town then was called "Dell" and the postmaster, Albion Thorne, played an aggressive part in its development. The post office was established on Dec. 11, and on Christmas the first mail arrived from Sioux Falls. Celebrating the two events, the entire population, 13 in number, gathered at Thorne's shanty for Christmas dinner. The mail carrier often made the trip on foot, sometimes on horseback, and during times of deep snow used a cutter or light sled with tall, narrow runners. A grain sack served as a mail bag during the first trips. For his first 18 months service as postmaster Thorne was paid $18.

At 113 m. is the junction with a graveled road.

Left on this road is BALTIC, 2 m. (1,471 alt.), a town in which nearly every resident is of Norwegian descent. In "Little Norway," as the community is often called, many customs of the mother country are still observed by the residents. The Norwegian Lutheran church is the only place of worship in town. The village was first named St. Olaf; later the name Keyes was adopted; and this in turn was changed to the present name. May 17, the Norwegians' Independence Day, is celebrated each year. The town claims to have the oldest grain elevator in the State, erected in 1887. Two dams built across the Sioux River have created two lakes where fish abound. A Government nursery here raises many varieties of shrubs and trees used in the shelterbelt. Baltic has a cooperative funeral home and a cooperative telephone company.

In Baltic, as in many typical Norwegian communities, there is a branch of the Hardanger Lag, a national organization composed of Scandinavians throughout the United States who have emigrated from the community of Hardanger in Norway. Each year they hold a two-day wedding festival for the purpose of perpetuating the customs of rural Norway. The first Hardanger wedding in this part of the country took place in Sioux Falls in 1911. Since that time these weddings have taken place in different parts of the State, including Garretson, Colton, and Canton.

Beginning the ceremony the toastmaster enters with a violin player. The latter makes a very striking picture dressed in knee breeches and white silk coat, elaborately trimmed in bright colors. Tassels and buttons decorate the costume. The violin player is followed closely by the bridesmaid, best man, and maid of honor. A company of 50 girls follows, dressed in silk costumes with red waists, black skirts, and white aprons. The girls march in front of the stage and form an entrance for the bride and groom. The bride wears a high silver crown upon her head and a black skirt trimmed elaborately with beads and beautiful lace. The bodice of her waist is covered with minute decorations in contrasting colors. Over the skirt she wears a white apron heavily trimmed with several panels of lace. In her hand she carries a beautiful corsage of roses. As the bride and groom stand upon the stage, a song is usually sung by a "mandskor."

Following the ceremony a hugh banquet is served. The tables are decorated with American and Norwegian flags and banners, and a huge basket of apples is always present as a centerpiece. Apples are used because of the great abundance of especially delicious varieties in this region. The menu served usually consists of "krootakoka," flat-bread, "blodpotse" (blood bologna), mutton, rutabagas, potatoes, cream mush, "primost," and several other kinds of cheese.

At 116 m. is MIDWAY JUNCTION. L. is a hard-surfaced highway to Palisades State Recreation Area and Garretson (see Tour 9A).

At 123.1 m. is the junction with State 38, a new paved highway connecting Sioux Falls and Mitchell as an alternate route for US 16 (see Tour 5).

SIOUX FALLS, 127 m. (1,422 alt.), (see SIOUX FALLS).

State's industrial center and largest city, State Penitentiary, Morrell Packing Plant, Manchester Biscuit Company, Pettigrew Museum, Terrace Park, Sherman Indian Mounds, Big Sioux River, Coliseum, Veterans Hospital, two colleges.

At Sioux Falls is the junction with US 16 (*see Tour 5*).

SOUTH SIOUX FALLS, 128.8 *m.*, is an independent village that mushroomed, following World War II, as a pipeline and trucking terminal.

At 142.2 *m.* is the junction with State 44.

Right on this road is WORTHING, 2 *m.*, and LENOX, 8 *m.*, the latter a prosperous town and winter headquarters for carnival companies that provide midway rides and sideshow attractions at Midwest fairs and celebrations.

At 144.1 *m.* is the junction with US 18 (*see Tour 7*); the two routes are united to 149 m. (*see Tour 7*).

At 160 *m.* (L) is the BETHESDA HOME, operated since 1914 by the Evangelical Lutheran Church for the aged and for children. In 1950 a new addition enlarged the capacity to 80 persons.

BERESFORD, 166 *m.* (1,505 alt.), was named for Admiral Lord Charles Beresford of England.

It was in the fertile region in this section of the State that early settlers first made their homes. Beresford is in the heart of the corn-raising section of South Dakota, approximately 50 per cent of the acreage under cultivation being devoted to this crop. With so many natural advantages, there is little wonder that prosperous farms have grown up in this section.

At Beresford is the junction with State 46.

Right on this hard-surfaced highway is CENTERVILLE, 12 *m.*, a town of wide streets and large homes. It is the center of a concentrated livestock feeding area. Clinton P. Anderson, Secretary of Agriculture under President Truman and U.S. Senator from New Mexico, was born here Oct. 23, 1895. His father was sheriff of the county for a time.

At 172 *m.* is UNION COUNTY STATE PARK (L), a 124-acre forested area maintained by the South Dakota Game, Fish and Parks Department for picnics, community rallies, and large family gatherings. There is a community building with electric lights and tables for use during inclement weather.

This is part of an area surveyed in 1861, at the direction of President Lincoln, prior to the opening of Dakota Territory for homestead settlement. The first homestead in the State, and possibly the first in the United States, was filed just 10 miles SE. of the park when Mahlon Gore took out the first claim at 12:01 a.m. January 1, 1863.

At 182.4 *m.* is the junction with State 50 (*see Tour 8*).

ELK POINT, 198.5 *m.* (1,126 alt.), was given that name because of the large number of elk seen near the original townsite, and it was in this vicinity that Lewis and Clark shot their first deer.

Beginning in 1889, an old settlers' picnic has been held every year. Most of these reunions are featured by inspirational programs, and, until the last few years, a field mass was held in commemoration of the ceremonies in 1877, to rid the country of the grasshopper scourge. (See JEFFERSON below.)

While the population of Elk Point, like that of other towns in this part of the State, has fluctuated little in the last 20 years, the town has lost considerable trade because of paved roads over which residents in the vicinity can, in less than half an hour, reach Sioux City, for a shopping tour.

JEFFERSON, 208 *m.* (1,114 alt.), claims a prominent place in the early settlement of Union Co. This beautiful and level tract, covered with lush grass and many trees, attracted pioneer homeseekers as early as 1859. The town was first started at the 14-MILE HOUSE, 2.5 m. NW., which was a stopping place for settlers as they pushed farther into Dakota Territory. An old post office building of early days is now used as a residence at the former townsite.

A large BLACK CROSS in the cemetery dates back to 1877 when grasshoppers ravaged the State. A few old-timers in the community still remember this devastating plague that swept the territory, leaving in its wake stark desolation, blighted hopes, and starvation. There were few inhabitants, then, but this part of the Territory was more thickly settled than other sections. Coming in hordes so dense that the sky was darkened and the sun nearly obscured, the grasshoppers devoured the scanty crops, already stunted by drought.

Frenzied with grief, the settlers, after exhausting all human efforts to rid themselves of the grasshoppers, decided to ask Divine aid. The pastor of the Catholic Church announced at mass that a retreat was to take place the next day. Messages were dispatched as quickly as possible to all the people of the country and community. Protestants and Catholics alike came to the church next morning. Many of them were barefoot.

The priest carried a cross and led the procession that formed two m. S. of town. From here the group marched N. 6 m., then proceeded from E. to W. in the form of a cross. At each of the four points they placed a simple cross and, in the cemetery at Jefferson, a larger one. The ceremonies connected with the procession were solemn, men, women, and children joining in prayer. Not long after the event great heaps of dead grasshoppers were found along the Sioux and Missouri Rivers.

At 208 *m.* is STEVENS, consisting of taverns and liquor stores patronized largely by Sioux City people because Iowa laws are more stringent.

At 208.1 *m.* the Iowa line is crossed at the Big Sioux River, 4 m. N. of Sioux City, (*see Iowa State Guide, Tour 10*).

Tour 9A

Junction with US 77—Palisades State Recreation Area—Devil's Gulch—Garretson.
Unnumbered highway and State 11.
Junction with US 77 (at Midway)—Garretson, 11 m.
Hard-surfaced highway.

THIS route branches E. from US 77 at Midway Junction, 11 *m*. N. of Sioux Falls, and leads to a region of bizarre beauty along deeply gorged Split Rock Creek.

At 9.5 *m*. is the junction with the Palisades Road.

Right on this graded road is the PALISADES STATE RECREATION AREA, 2 *m*., a 44-acre scenic park (*free*). It is under the supervision of the South Dakota Game, Fish and Parks Commission.

Split Rock River adds the magic of dark, silent waters to the bizarre, entrancing picture made by the great pillars of granite-like stone—red, gray, and purple— that tower high above the many trees, like ruins of a gigantic palace. The nature of the formation creates this striking illusion, for the quartzite is marked into regular blocks by lines and surface fissures, so evenly distributed from top to bottom that it resembles skilled masonry work. Cedars—dark blue, almost black against the sky—cling to the bare rock.

Westward from the bridge that spans the river at the entrance of the park, a path, shaded by oaks and elms, winds around masses of tumbled blocks of rock that have fallen from the cliffs to the R., over projections of jutting stone worn smooth by the elements, and along the water's edge of the King and Queen Rocks, their cedar-crowned heads more than 100 ft. above the mirror-like water. The view from these perilous points of vantage is so thrilling that the exertion necessary to reach their summits is amply rewarded. For those who are not in mountain-climbing trim, an easier path to the R. is available for ascending the cliff. However, the beauty of the many colored, cedar-topped walls on the other side can be enjoyed from the water's edge, where the coolness of the air that blows from the river and the shade refresh those who do not care for climbing in the hot sun.

BALANCE ROCK, on the opposite side of the river, is a formation that seems to defy the laws of gravity, for it stands on a narrow base at the top of a cliff and looms larger above, apparently lopsided. The mass of alternating red and gray stone, seems to hang precariously—on the verge of crashing to the depths below; yet the rock has evidently been there for ages, a bold sentinel against the sky, defying wind storms, lightning, and raging blizzards.

Other attractions in the park include the DEVIL'S KITCHEN, an enclosure walled in by red rock where queerly-shaped stones, jutting through the floor, might be imagined as some banished devil's store and kitchen furniture.

CHIMNEY ROCK is sometimes missed because part of its bulk is hidden by tall trees; the color of the stone is a deep vivid red.

On both sides of the stream are paths that are full of surprises, leading to unexpected crevices and queerly-shaped rocks. Cool places for picnics are available, with tables provided. Excellent fishing can be enjoyed during the season, the cold waters yielding channel catfish, speckled trout, black bass, rock bass, and pickerel.

GARRETSON, 11 *m*. (1,492 alt.), is the center of a rich farming community and a region of unusual scenic spots, providing a spectacular little world of its own off the main highways. The town was incorporated in 1891 and prospered as the Great Northern R.R. and a grist mill were kept busy. The American Legion Hall is built to resemble a camouflaged battlefield dugout. Since World War II, the town has built a new Community Hall and rebuilt a dam across Split Rock Creek to form a pond in the public park.

One block E. of Main St. is a graveled road.

Right on this road to the tree-hidden canyon called DEVIL'S GULCH, 0.4 *m.*, often referred to as "Spirit Canyon." Its fascination lies in its weird beauty, solemn and almost oppressive. A jagged wound, burnished by nature's hand, across the gently rolling plain, Devil's Gulch is a sanctuary of charm and inspiration. The chasm is featured by bold walls of pink and purple rock, cleft by crevices, some so deep that they are thought to be bottomless; mysterious green water reflects the cedars clinging to the stone and the fronds of ferns that thrive in the moist, cool air.

Surrounding this gulch is a park, maintained by the town's authorities. However, aside from providing tables and seats for the convenience of picnickers and building the footbridges, nothing has been done to disturb the beauties of nature. The winding paths follow a natural way among the rocks and from the peak of the last one a glimpse of the red rock can be caught through the branches of many varieties of trees and shrubs that thrive there.

The footbridge, protected with iron guard rails, affords a splendid point from which to view the perpendicular cliffs of quartzite. Striking is the coloring of the rock in the sun and shadow, red in the light and purple in the shade. Bushes and ferns grow wherever a little earth has become lodged in the narrow ledges, but the cedars cling to the bare rocks in a fantastic manner. These beautiful trees grow luxuriantly on the very top of the cliffs where nothing but bare, weather-beaten stone can be seen, and the wonder is that they grow nowhere else in the vicinity except on similar formations at the Palisades (see above), and at the Dells (see Tour 9).

Just under the bridge is the BOTTOMLESS PIT. The water is dark and oily and seems to have no current, but there is a powerful undertow that forces the plumb line against some projection of the walls, so that no one has been able to measure the depth below 600 ft. under water level.

Crossing the bridge, the path leads along the edge of the canyon. Many platforms of smooth, bare rocks afford points of observation to those who can stand on the very brink of the chasm without becoming dizzy. The black shadows on the water at the foot of the cliff opposite create an illusion that the great wall overhangs a deep cave, and if one gazes fixedly for a moment at that dark reflection, the cliff seems to approach silently and menacingly, as if it had become the prow of a giant ship. At the head of the gulch is the famed DEVIL'S STAIRWAY. Only those with strong muscles, steady heads, and sound hearts are advised to attempt the descent. There are several long jumps and huge steps; but those who are brave will be well rewarded. From the bottom, the view is almost bewildering. The contrast of blue sky and dark green waters and the red, pink, and purple cliffs overhanging threateningly would delight an artist. Seen from below, the cedars and ferns seem to cling to the rock by some inexplicable magic. The strange moaning of the wind adds to the feeling of being in the abode of some unearthly being. At night, or when a storm rages and thunder echoes and reechoes within the walls, one can easily imagine that the devil of the Indian legend is about to emerge from some dark crevice to gather in another soul. The climb upward is easier than the descent. The visitor, slowly retracing his steps along the canyon, discovers new rocks and new platforms, each with new and startling effects.

North of Garretson, on State 11, is a sign (R) bearing the legend: "Jesse James' Cave."

Right on this road to a farmhouse, 3 *m.*, where inquiries must be made for the route to JESSE JAMES' CAVE, 0.4 *m.*, (adm. free).

This reputed hide-out of Jesse James has no sunken lake, underground river, or sparkling stalactites, but it is the only cave in this part of the country, and from the entrance is a magnificent view to the N.

Twenty-five years ago a farm hand, who was working for the farmer owning the land on which is the cave, found the name, Jesse James, carved in the wall of the strange hole in the rocky cliff of the Split Rock River. Early settlers knew of the place, and there was a sort of legend about the notorious desperado having hidden there after the robbery of the bank at Northfield, Minn.

No one unacquainted with the area could find the beginning of the rough and slightly dangerous stairway made of coarse blocks of stone in the cliff. Extreme care must be taken while descending this steep incline, as the rocks are slippery and no rail or guard of any sort is provided.

The only way to the cave from the foot of the natural stairs is through a narrow tunnel, a little more than 3 ft. in diameter and perhaps 12 ft. in length. One must crawl through, but the walls are smooth quartzite and the floor solid. There is no danger. It must be understood that the cave is not at the bottom of the cliff, where the clear water of Split Rock River flows noiselessly, but halfway down, about 30 ft. from the base.

The little tunnel gives access to a sort of ledge, a level platform of red granite about 10 ft. square, from which is a beautiful view of the valley. The scenery is fascinating with color effects of red, purple, and gray cliffs, blue sky and mirror-like water. Directly across the river, green meadows extend to the broken cliffs, which resemble ruins of a gigantic wall. Cedars clinging to the bare rocks, and groups of thickly foliaged trees growing where the cliffs have collapsed, add to the beauty of the picture.

The cave itself is quickly explored. A flashlight is necessary, because of many jutting rocks and projecting ledges. Legend has it that Jesse James used to creep in the shadows and hide on one of the high shelves when enemies came near.

Tour 10

(Fairmount, North Dakota)—Sisseton—Watertown—Madison—Yankton—(Crofton, Nebr.). US 81.
North Dakota Line to Nebraska Line, 249 m.
All-weather roadbed.
Suitable hotel and tourist accommodations at towns above.

US 81, known as the Meridian Highway, crosses eastern South Dakota through a country long popular with the hunting Sioux Indian tribes because of its lakes, creeks, and grassy hills; but now, less than a century later, it is mostly an area of intensive farming. Indians still reside in the northern region, which is part of the Sisseton Indian Reservation (*see INDIANS and Tour 1*), and along US 81 are occasional Indian farm houses, squat, frame buildings, and barns, with a few horses nearby. This hilly country, known as the Coteau des Prairies, was once the habitat of buffalo herds, and the Sioux lived many happy years in the ravines and along the lakes. Few towns have sprung up and most of the country has been untouched by the plow. Farther S. the country is a rolling prairie with occasional shallow lakes and frequent groves of trees. These were planted by homesteaders around what are now modern farm homes, built up, despite years of cold, snow-bound winters, hot, dry summers, drought, and depression. When railroads were built, towns sprang up along the sidings; in recent years new highways have been built to shorten routes and these towns no longer are on the main routes of travel. US 81 passes through few towns, but is bordered by filling stations that have sprung up to take care of increasing traffic.

Nine m. S. of Fairmount, N. Dak., in the Red River Valley (*see N. Dak. Tour 1*), US 81 crosses the North Dakota Line, and enters the SISSETON INDIAN RESERVATION (agency at Sisseton). The reservation has been opened to white settlement since 1892 (*see INDIANS and Tour 1*). (*Visitors are cautioned against giving or selling liquor to Indians; this is a Federal offense.*)

At 1 m. is a junction with a graveled road.

Left on the road is WHITE ROCK, 1.8 m., a village in the extreme northeast corner of the State, bordering North Dakota and Minnesota. The Red River, also called the Bois De Sioux, flows through the edge of the village, on its way from Lake Traverse northward to Hudson Bay.

US 81 parallels a neck of LAKE TRAVERSE at 2.2 m., the northern end of this narrow lake, which is over 30 m. long.

At 5.3 m. is the TRAVERSE-BOIS DE SIOUX GOVERN-MENT DAM which controls the flow of water from Lake Traverse into the Red River.

ROSHOLT, 10 m., was not founded until 1913 when the rich farming area needed a trade and market center. Julius Rosholt was constructing a short-line railroad with which to transport farm commodities to Fairmount, when the Soo Line purchased his enterprise, and the town was named for him. The train which serves the town is known as a mixed train, carrying freight cars and a passenger coach. Blacksmith shops are fast becoming extinct elsewhere, but Rosholt still has two.

At 14.3 m. is a marsh-banked lake called COTTONWOOD LAKE, one of several in the State by that name. The popularity and prevalence of the fast-growing cottonwood trees account for the repetition.

NEW EFFINGTON, 25 m. (1,305 alt.), was founded in 1913. The surrounding community is made up of Scandinavians, Germans, and a few Indians.

Between New Effington and Sisseton is an intensive farming region.

SISSETON, 39 m. (1,202 alt.), (*see Tour 1*), is at the junction with State 10.

A new highway between Sisseton and US 12 has replaced the "Hogback Road" to the W., so called because it straddled the range of Coteau Hills (R). In many of the wooded draws of these barren-appearing hills are Indian homes. US 81 takes a level course through the Big Stone Valley.

At 47 m. is the junction with a graveled crossroad.

(1) Right on this road at 1.2 m. is the abandoned SISSETON AGENCY, a few white frame buildings, that once served as the headquarters for the reservation; the agency was moved to Sisseton. Along the road are chokecherry and wild plum thickets.

At 2.4 m. is the RENVILLE MONUMENT, which was erected in memory of Gabriel Renville, treaty chief of the Sisseton tribe from 1862 to 1892, during which time the whites and Indians were often at odds. Renville, a half-breed, was one of the noted personalities of early Territorial days. The first Renville came from France to the Great Lakes in 1775, later marrying the daughter of Captain Crawford, who served the British at Prairie du Chien. An uncle, Joseph, who married an Indian, was guide and interpreter for the Zebulon Pike expedition and fought in the War of 1812 with the British. Gabriel Renville joined General Sibley's troops during the Minnesota Massacre, and because of his bravery and loyalty was made chief of scouts in 1864. With other Indians, Renville began an attempt to secure a permanent closed reservation for his tribe. He traveled to Washington several times to plead with officials, but in the year of his death, 1892, the Sisseton Reservation was opened for settlement. He had three wives and 20 children, so that many Renvilles are found living in the Lake Region today.

(2) Left is PEEVER, 3.1 m. a small village of whites, half-breeds, and Indians.

Left from Peever on a graveled road to the THUNDER BIRD ROCK 7.3 m., the scene of a Sioux legend. When the lightning flashes and thunder rolls, the Sioux say that the mysterious power is revealing itself to them. Just before rain falls, two white birds are said to fly across the darkened sky. These are the signs of a mysterious power. On this high rock the Thunder Bird left his track—a clear, deep imprint of a bird's foot.

At 52.2 m. is a junction with a graded road.

Right on this winding road, which was built by Indians as a part of the Federal Emergency Relief program, to ASCENSION CHURCH, 0.9 m., first Indian church on the Sisseton Reservation. It was built of logs in 1862 in BIG COULEE, and a frame structure has since replaced it. Services are held here Sundays.

At 58 m. is the junction with a graveled crossroad.

(1) Right to HURRICANE LAKE, 5 m. According to Indian legend, a hunter was riding his pony along the lake shore when he saw a lone buffalo feeding on the thick grass on the lowland. The hunter took good aim with his bow and arrow, wounding the buffalo above the front leg. In pain, the buffalo turned and pursued the hunter's horse, which became excited by the sudden charge, stumbled and broke his leg. The hunter jumped from the back of the horse to the buffalo and rode him, holding on by the tail. The buffalo ran in circles until he became exhausted and bled to death from the wound.

(2) Left to WILMOT, 10 m. At 18 m. is BIG STONE LAKE, with numerous resorts (fishing, boating, swimming) along the 30-mile shoreline. At 20.5 is HARTFORD BEACH STATE PARK (see Tour 2).

At 63 m. is the junction with US 12 (see Tour 2); from this point US 81 and US 12 are one route for 3 m.

At 66 m. is the junction with US 12 (see Tour 2).

Between the junction with US 12 and Watertown, US 81 passes through a level farming country, which was developed in the 1880's by farmers from other midwestern States who followed the farming frontier.

At 81 *m.* is the junction with a graveled road.

Left on this unnumbered road is PUNISHED WOMAN'S LAKE, 6 *m.* At this point is the junction with a graveled road. Right on this road is SOUTH SHORE, 6.2 *m.*, a country hamlet. At 8.3 *m.* is the PUNISHED WOMAN EFFIGY. The two huge rocks are supposed to represent the legendary figures of Wewake, a Sioux maiden, and Wapskasimucwah, a young brave. The girl had spurned the favors of Chemoki, a 60-year old chieftain, for the young lover. The chief, enraged by her resistance, killed Wapskasimucwah and bound the woman to a tree on the north shore of the lake, now known as the Punished Woman's Lake. The bodies were placed on a nearby knoll and the chief, while making an angry speech exhorting his people to fear the example of his erstwhile love and her slain lover, was struck by a bolt of lightning out of a clear sky. The effigy of Chemoki in repentance was placed at the feet of the two lovers.

WATERTOWN, 94 *m.* (1,750 alt.), (*see WATERTOWN*).

Lake Kampeska, Mellette House, Bramble Park, Stadium.

Watertown is at the junction with US 212 (*see Tour 3*).

At 96.9 *m.* is CHAPMAN HILL, the only hill in the region, which was used to test automobiles years ago. A car that could make this slight hill on high was considered good, and many a sale was made on its summit.

At 102.5 *m.* (L) is a large lake bed. This region has scores of lakes—sometimes brimming full, and then completely dry a year or two later. This phenomenon is the result of the pressure and weight of glaciers that caused depressions and deposited waste around the edges as they melted. There are no springs, creeks, or rivers flowing into the lakes to maintain a water level against evaporation, local rains being the only water supply.

At 103.4 *m.* is CLEAR LAKE (R), one of three lakes by that name in the NE. corner of the State.

At 111 *m.* is a junction with an oiled road.

Right on this road is HAYTI, 3.8 *m.*, a village that was named in 1880 when twisted hay, known as "haytie," was used as fuel during the winter. At 4.1 *m.* is MARSH LAKE, a popular hunting region.

At 117 *m.* is the junction with a graveled road.

Left on this road is STONE BRIDGE, 4 *m.*, a resort center on LAKE POINSETT. Lakes extend on both sides of the bridge.

At 118 *m.* is the junction with State 28.

Right on this road is LAKE NORDEN, 5 *m.*, popular with pheasant and duck hunters. Lakes Norden and St. John surround the town.

US 81 skirts the shore of LAKE POINSETT, with several public resorts (boats and fishing tackle). This large lake, which covers more than 8,000 acres, was named by John C. Frémont during his exploration of the region in 1839, in honor of Joel Roberts Poinsett, Secretary of State. Nearly every year someone is drowned in this lake because sudden winds capsize fishing boats far from shore.

From the SW. shore of Lake Poinsett, the highway sweeps over a hill and parallels LAKE ALBERT (R). The lake was named for Col. J. J. Abert by John C. Frémont, but settlers of the area inserted an "L."

At 127 m. is the junction with a graveled road.

Left on this road is OAKWOOD LAKES STATE PARK, 9 m. (*see Tour 4*).

ARLINGTON, 133 m. (1,846 alt.), (*see Tour 4*), is at a junction with US 14; the routes are united 2 miles (*see Tour 4*).

At 148 m. is a junction with a graded road.

Right on this road is LAKE BADUS, 1 m., and around the small lake are families of the LEGIA GREISCHA COLONY. In 1875, 30 families came from Switzerland to America because they wanted more land and better opportunities for their children. They settled first near Stillwater, Minn., and then sent out representatives to locate suitable land for a colony. A lake, about one sq. m. in size, was found and promptly named Lake Badus for a mountain lake in their home country. In 1879 the group moved to Lake Badus and each man over 21 years old filed two claims—a homestead and a tree claim. In order to provide shore-lines for as many homesteads as possible, each homestead was only 80 rods wide and a mile long. A cooperative system was followed, and a community store was operated. The schoolhouse built by the original colonists is still in use. While some of the men built houses, others plowed the fields. Joseph Muggli, leader of the group, and his descendants have remained on the original homestead, and the Tuors, Derungs, and Cajacobs are prominent names in the farming region of Lake Badus, although it has lost its old-world atmosphere.
The cooperative principle was discontinued as soon as each of the group became self-supporting, and many of the younger men have entered private businesses in surrounding towns. The only old custom still observed in the community is that at funerals the pall-bearers carry the casket from the church to the cemetery instead of conveying it in a hearse. A few years ago each family made Swiss cheese expertly; but that too is almost a thing of the past.

MADISON, 157 m. (1,669 alt.), founded in 1875, attracted early settlers because of its proximity to lakes and the abundance of game and fish within easy reach. Its environs reminded the pioneers so much of the capital of Wisconsin that they gave the embryonic town the same name. Soon it became a trading post, although at that time it was situated 4½ m. E. of the present site. Madison and Herman competed for the county seat, but a compromise was effected and both villages moved to a halfway point, merging and taking the name of Madison.

Noted chiefly for its teachers college, its proximity to two popular lakes, and as the center of a well-developed farming section, Madison has experienced a slow, steady growth ever since its beginning. Never considered a city of great commercial possibilities, it has nevertheless enjoyed a large trade in flour, dairy products, and thoroughbred livestock.

Its pioneers endured the hardships attendant on life on the prairie —drought, grasshoppers, fuel shortage, severe winters—although Madison, like many other eastern South Dakota cities lacks the glamorous, romantic history common to cities and towns in the western section. It began as an agricultural area, agriculture developed it, and agriculture supports it today.

Before the advent of the white man, this region was a favorite camping ground of Indians. It was near the site of the present city that Wamdesapa (Black Eagle), renegade Indian chief, lived after being ostracized by his people in Minnesota for killing his brother, who was much loved by the tribe.

Established in 1881, GENERAL BEADLE STATE TEACHERS COLLEGE is the oldest institution of its kind in South Dakota. The first structure was destroyed by fire in 1885, but the campus now has six buildings. It has been known as Madison Normal and Eastern State Normal School, but when a four-year course was accredited during the 1940's, the name was changed to honor Brig. Gen. William Henry Harrison Beadle, who had been president of the school from 1889 to 1906. Beadle had also been Territorial superintendent of public instruction, founder of the South Dakota Education Association, and a prominent attorney. His statue has been placed in Statuary Hall of the Capitol in Washington, D. C., and in the rotunda of the Statehouse at Pierre. There is a high school in connection with the normal school, which uses it for practice teaching; the institution has a 15,000-volume library, one of the largest in the State. The GYM-NASIUM is near the athletic field. The GARDEN THEATER, with a seating capacity of 2,000, has an orchestra pit and wings on a stage shut in by clever landscaping. At the school is an extensive COLLECTION of stuffed birds (*open to public*).

Other large buildings and institutions in the city include the POST OFFICE, the new county COURTHOUSE, erected at a cost of $128,000, the COMMUNITY HOSPITAL, the ARMORY-AUDITORIUM, and the CARNEGIE LIBRARY. Industries include a packing plant and a creamery.

At the south end of Main St. is the junction with State 19.

Left on this road to LAKE MADISON, 2 *m*. In normal years it is one of eastern South Dakota's most popular resorts. A dancing pavilion and facilities for all kinds of water sports have contributed to its popularity. On the N. side are about 125 cottages. On the western side is IDLEWOOD PARK, near the site of old Madison. WENTWORTH PARK with its small group of cottages is on the eastern shore.

US 81 runs W. from Madison, being joined by State 34.

At 159.5 *m*. the highway curves around the N. end of LAKE HERMAN (*fishing, swimming, boating, picnicking, golf*). Near the highway, on the E. side of the lake, is LAKE HERMAN STATE PARK, a recreational and historical area being developed by the

South Dakota Game, Fish and Parks Department. In the heavily-wooded 160-acre tract is the log house built by Herman Luce, after whom the lake was named. The massive oak timbers are well preserved. Stones marking several graves have been found near the cabin, and Indian arrowheads and stone hammers are still being found in the area. Lake Herman was the scene of the rescue of a white woman taken captive by Inkpaduta and his band of renegades following the Spirit Lake Massacre in 1857. All the men of the Iowa settlement had been killed and four women carried away by the Indians. One of the women was killed near Flandreau and the others were brought here. Two Christian Indians met the outlaw chief in this vicinity and affected a ransom of two women. The fourth, a 13-year old girl, was rescued near Redfield; the site is marked by the Abigail Gardner Monument. (*see Tour 11*).

The MADISON COUNTRY CLUB GOLF COURSE and some organizational camps are also maintained along the shores of Lake Herman.

JUNIUS, 163 *m.*, is a small farming community, the few houses appearing to have been set in their present places in order that the occupants might have a closer social contact than if they remained on their farms.

WINFRED, 169 *m.* (1,500 alt.), exemplified the growing co-operative movement in South Dakota communities; its telephone exchange, the Winfred Telephone Co., is an unusual type of the mutual association, the majority of which control elevators, creameries, general stores, and lumber yards.

At 170 *m.* US 81 turns S. at the junction with State 34.

Straight ahead on State 34 is HOWARD, 7 *m.* (1,564 alt.), seat of government for Miner Co.

SALEM, 188 *m.* (1,520 alt.), during the years 1880–1881, became known as the most important railroad point between Sioux Falls and Mitchell. It was a flourishing town in early days, although much of its original prosperity has been lost because of its location between large cities. Crop failures, acute financial pains from the over-inflation period, and depression have reduced Salem to the condition of hundreds of other small towns.

The town has a large, well-equipped school, with the classrooms, as someone once remarked, "built around the gymnasium." The gymnasium has helped to develop the interest in athletics that has carried Salem basketball teams to an enviable record over a long period of years. Playing games for many years in a frame building which competitors dubbed a "sheep shed," Salem won the State basketball championship in 1914 and came within one point of winning it the next year. The team finished third in championship tournaments in 1912, 1913, 1923, and 1927. As runner-up in 1925, it was invited to the National Tournament in Chicago, and lost to

342   SOUTH DAKOTA

Clarkston, Wash. In 1926 it won the State championship, and lost
the National Tournament to Fitchburg, Mass., the ultimate national
winner, 17 to 16, in an overtime period. Besides the public schools,
Salem has a Catholic boarding grade school and high school.

STANLEY CORNERS, 201 m. (sometimes called the Four
Corners), consisting of two filling stations, is at the junction with
US 16 (see Tour 5).

At 209.5 m. is one of the few remaining PIONEER HOUSE-
BARNS built by Russo-German settlers to conserve materials and
provide protection against prairie storms. The N. end of the building
housed livestock and grain, while the S. portion provided the
family's living quarters.

At 216 m. is FREEDOM CORNER and the junction with an
oiled road.

Right on this road is FREEMAN, 0.8 m. (1,511 alt.) center of a large Mennonite
community. Although coming to the United States from Russia, they are of German
descent. Most confusing is the fact that so many families bear the same names.
Freeman is a flourishing town in the center of a rich farming section. The farmers
in the community are hard-working, thrifty, and competent, and use the latest
farming methods. An annual grain and poultry show is the climax to the season's
harvest.
The FREEMAN JUNIOR COLLEGE, which is affiliated with the Mennonite
Church, is at the S. of Main St. Augmenting the older classroom building and girls
dormitory is the new GYMNASIUM-HALL to serve the college and community.
Following World War II, when the Army discontinued the Sioux Falls Air Base,
the college purchased the frame theatre building and two barracks for $960. With
volunteer labor, the buildings were dismantled and carted to Freeman. The men
of the community used the materials in building the hall which has a 2,500 seating
capacity and a dining room in the basement. Enough materials were left over for
a boys dormitory.
This area is known for its exotic and imported recipes. Some of the cafes and roadhouses feature *Sheshlyk*, mutton roasted on a skewer. It is a dish that was
brought from Persia (Iran) via Russia by the early immigrants whose travels were
extensive because of religious persecution. *Fleischhuehnel*, a sort of hamburger rolled
in dough and fried in fat, is another popular dish. One of the Freeman bakeries is
noted for its *Poppyseed Pie*, made from locally grown seed.

At 223 m. is the junction with US 18 (see Tour 7).

At 236 m. the James River is crossed. The valley, as at other
points along its course, is gently sloping and the roads dip down
into it with little previous warning. The river meanders lazily across
the State, unlike the Missouri River and all streams W. of it, which
are swift, restless, and with roughly-broken valleys.

At 246.3 m. is a marker designating where Jack McCall was
hanged for the murder of Wild Bill Hickok at Deadwood in 1876 (see
Deadwood, CITIES).

At 246.5 m. is the junction with a crossroad.

1. Right is YANKTON STATE HOSPITAL, an institution for mental patients
(see YANKTON, Tour 8).
2. Left is the YANKTON MUNICIPAL AIRPORT, 0.8 m. It is served by Mid-
West Airlines; transient aircraft service available.

YANKTON, 248.7 m. (1,157 alt.), (*see Tour 8*), is at the junction
with State 50.

At 249 m. US 81 crosses the Nebraska Line over the MERIDIAN
HIGHWAY BRIDGE (*50c for car and driver; 10c for each additional passenger*), 16 m. NE. of Crofton, Nebr. (*see Nebr. Tour 3*).

Tour 11

(Ellendale, N. Dak.)—Aberdeen—Redfield—Platte—(Butte, Nebr.) US 281.
North Dakota Line—Nebraska Line, 234.5 m.
C. M. St. P. & P. R.R. parallels the route between Aberdeen and Tulare.
Roadbed hard-surfaced from N.D. line to US 14; graveled roadbed most of southern
portion.
Usual accommodations; most towns small.

FOLLOWING the almost level basin of the James River Valley south
to Wolsey, midway on the route, US 281 crosses a level plain with
little timber. Along this almost straight highway there are few hills
north of the valley of the Missouri River.

The James (commonly called "Jim") River has been referred to
as the "longest unnavigable river in the world"; its lethargic fingers
reach into North Dakota for the source of its waters. So gentle is the
valley of the river that it appears to be merely an irregular crease
bisecting a flat surface. There is very little current, and in flood times
the stream looks more like a long serpentine lake than a river, so
imperceptible is its flow. The river drains most of east-central South
Dakota, where large, diversified farms predominate and yields of
small grain are normally high.

The North Dakota Line is crossed 5 m. S. of Ellendale, N. Dak.
(*see N. Dak. Tour 2*).

FREDERICK, 6.8 m. (1,371 alt.), was named for the son of a
railroad official when the branch line and town site were established
in 1881. Although the town was settled by families from Illinois and
Wisconsin, the rural population is largely Finnish. At Savo Hall each
May Day there are labor celebrations, often resulting in serious disorder. Among the business enterprises in Frederick is a COOPERATIVE
STORE, owned and operated by farmers of the community.

SIMMONS PARK is a recreational and scenic point having an arch
built of unusual stones from the Black Hills, Badlands, and other
parts of the State. Of special interest are two meteorites about 20 in.
in diameter, one at each end of the park. There are also a bathing
beach, bathhouse, and picnic grounds. It was near Frederick that
Waanata, noted Indian chief, lived at one time during his career (*see
Tour 1*).

BARNARD, 14.2 m., though consisting of only a few business
houses and residences, has an elaborate consolidated school, attended
by pupils from a wide neighboring territory. In a neat row near the
school are several cottages where teachers live during the school year.

At Barnard is the junction with State 10 (*see Tour 1*).

WESTPORT, 19.7 *m.*, is one of several towns in the Aberdeen territory that have been stifled by proximity to the larger city. Despite the variation in the sizes of the towns, all the upper James River Valley region is quite similar, there being little difference in the soil texture, land contour, and industries. The country has known its fat and lean years, the latter coming with periodic dry seasons.

It was during the summer of 1893, after a period of relentless drought, that this country was invaded by the "rainmakers," a small group of shrewd promoters who attempted to exploit the misfortunes of the farmers. Ridden by despair as they watched their green fields wither and brown under the blistering glare of the sun, farmers of the early 1890's were ready to welcome any scheme, no matter how impractical, that might bring precious moisture from cloudless skies. Descending like a welcome Moses upon a thirsty land, a Kansas man named Morris promised to bring water from the heavens instead of coaxing it from a rock, as the Israelitish leader did. He guaranteed to bring water to any community within five days, provided suitable remunerations were forthcoming from the inhabitants.

His first engagement was by the farmers on the eastern slope of the James River valley, where he guaranteed to produce a half-inch of rain over an area of 300 sq. m. within five days, or receive nothing; if successful, he was to be paid $500. Soon after he began operations, dark clouds hovered overhead and the farmers were jubilant. But on the second day a brisk wind sprang up, sweeping the clouds eastward. That evening Watertown, 50 m. distant, received a drenching downpour. The rainmaker said this was his rain and that the wind had carried it away. Undismayed by his first defeat, Morris persisted in his efforts, and on the evening of the last day the promised area had received a full half-inch of rain, and the rainmaker his $500.

Flushed with victory, Morris was besieged with offers from all over the State. He next moved into Aberdeen but found entrenched there a rival named Capt. Hauser, who had begun operations in the top story of a business building, erecting on the roof a long pipe that emitted a stream of evil-smelling gases day and night. With both rainmakers working desperately, Brown Co. residents fully expected a cloudburst. But three days wore away and no rain fell. Capt. Hauser's time was up, but Morris still had two days left. On the last day Morris once more brought rain, dampening the Fourth of July picnics. The thirsty soil received more than .5 in., and Morris again collected $500.

There were three general schools of rainmaking. One group used the artificial explosion method, such as artillery or dynamite. This was supposed to cause condensation and the falling of water. Many communities in North and South Dakota tried to bring rain through their own efforts, and instead of paying the rainmakers $500, bought dynamite and ammunition with which they bombarded the upper air.

Most reputed rainmakers favored the hydrogen method, which consisted of the emission of this light gas in large quantities. A combination of the two methods was used in the most desperate cases. Even a school for rainmakers was started, but history fails to reveal that the school had sufficient graduates to form an alumni association.

Later experiments of rainmakers were not so successful and they lost the confidence of the public. When drought struck the following year, the mayor of Aberdeen set aside a day of prayer for rain, and the rainmakers were forgotten. Rainmaking in the modern manner was attempted during the dry summer of 1950, in the foothills area, east of the Black Hills. At the suggestion of U.S. Senator Francis Case, the *Rapid City Daily Journal* sponsored the "planting" of dry ice crystals in slight cloud formations, at high altitude, by airplane. Broad claims were made for the rainfall that followed.

At 24.5 *m.* is a junction with a graded road.

Left on this road is the HAMLIN GARLAND HOMESTEAD SITE, 4.6 *m.*, where the author began his writing career as a young man, and where he lived, intermittently, from 1881 to 1884. It was while stacking wheat in a field adjacent to the homestead that his ambition for a literary career was born. Writing in "A Son of the Middle Border" concerning this incident, he says, "Every detail of the daily life on the farm now assumed literary significance in my mind." Garland's poem, "The Color in the Wheat," had the homestead as its setting. "Mrs. Ripley's Trip," his first short story, was followed by "Main Traveled Roads," his first book, the characters of which were his neighbors. After this first book, other works followed, among them numerous short stories. "I began writing when there was no special market," he said. His favorite short story from his own pen is "The Return of a Private," which was based on the return of his father to the Wisconsin farm after the Civil War. "Under the Lion's Paw," another short story, was the outgrowth of a prairie incident. "Ideas for stories come in various ways," he said. Always imbued with a strict sense of right and wrong, he has said, "To spread the reign of justice everywhere should be the aim of the artist."
Biographical studies reveal the deep and lasting influence that Garland's residence in Brown Co. had upon his subsequent career as a man of letters. References to Ordway, Columbia, and Aberdeen abound in his writings, (see ABERDEEN).
For his work "A Daughter of the Middle Border," he received the Pulitzer prize for the best biography in 1921. His last trip to the old homestead was in 1915. The last years of his life he divided between New York and Hollywood. The site of the homestead is marked by a 12-ton boulder which was placed there in July, 1936, at a ceremony sponsored by the South Dakota Writers' League and the Ordway Community Club. A biography, "Hamlin Garland," has been written by the South Dakota Writers' League. In 1940 the poet and author died.
Southwest of the Hamlin Garland Homestead Site is ORDWAY, 6.1 *m.*, so small in population that it is not recorded in census records. Founded in 1881, Ordway enjoyed a meteoric growth, its citizens firm in the belief that Gov. Ordway of Dakota Territory would influence the choosing of the town as the capital. With this stimulus a Chicago syndicate bought land and platted it near Ordway in preparation for the boom. The town flourished for a time until Bismarck was chosen as the capital. The result was a sudden bursting of the bubble and today Ordway is one of the State's many "wide places in the road."

ABERDEEN, 33.2 *m.* (1,300 alt.) (*See ABERDEEN*).

Northern State Teachers' College, Baseball Park, Stockyards, Melgaard Park, Wylie Park.

Aberdeen is at the junction with US 12 (*see Tour 2*).
At 49.9 *m.* is a junction with a graveled road.

(1) Left on this unnumbered road is DUXBURY, 1 *m.*, a grain elevator; at 8 *m.* is RONDELL PARK and the OAKWOOD TRADING POST. The park, owned by the John Firey family, pioneer residents, is on the James River and consists of a grove of large oak trees, one of the few groves of natural oak in the State. The willows and oaks along the river are usually covered with wild grape vines, and in the fall with grapes. It is a popular picnicking place. To the left of the road, across the bridge, is a large prairie boulder with a bronze tablet, marking the site of a trading post established by Major Joseph R. Brown in 1835. The Indian trading post was first occupied by Pierre LeBlanc, but he had trouble with an Indian customer and was murdered. Francis Rondell, a young Frenchman, took charge of the post in 1842, and lived there for nine years, marrying an Indian woman. Rondell named his first son Felix. The latter, in his old age, recalled that as a youth he was taken in a buckboard to St. Paul to enter a boarding school, but the restricted life there did not appeal to him and he actually ran home, about 300 m., returning ahead of his father. Francis Rondell established other trading posts later (see Tours 1 and 2B). Left of the marker, erected by the Aberdeen chapter of the D.A.R., is the scuffed and worn doorsill, the only relic of the trading post. Along the river was a prison camp in which Omaha or Pawnee Indians were held as hostages by the Sioux. These Indians who had come from the Mississippi River, built mud huts, known as dirt lodges, and occasionally artifacts are found along the river banks. The enemy Indians were held for ransom, sold as slaves, and made to work in the gardens by the Sioux, according to stories told by old Indians to Francis Rondell.
(2) Right on this road, through Mansfield, 1.5 *m.*, is SCATTERWOOD LAKE, 9.4 *m.* This 200-acre natural lake is one of the few in the area. It has sand beaches and is a popular spot for farm picnics. The lake was named by the Frémont and Nicollet expedition in 1839, the "Lake of the Scattered Small Wood."

At 54 *m.* is a junction with a graded dirt road.

Left on this road is the James River, 4.4 *m.*; at this point in 1856 Major Abercrombie built a bridge, which was used on the route from Fort Ridgely, Minn., to Fort Pierre. It was never again used for military purposes, however. At 4.9 *m.* is the SITE OF FOSTER CITY, no longer existent. A store and several log houses once stood by the Foster homestead. In 1879 the C. M. St. P. & P. R.R. surveyed a line through the town, but it was never built, as it was expected the land would become part of the proposed Drifting Goose Indian Reservation. A bridge has been built where the banks were cut down years ago for an Indian Ford, 5.1 *m.*, and ARMADALE PARK is entered there. The park is in a horseshoe shape, having 120 heavily-timbered acres of cottonwood, willow, ash, elm, and boxelder trees.
The older cottonwoods are 2 and 3 ft. thick. The Upper Yanktonnais tribe of Sioux Indians camped on the island as late as 1879, caching food there for summer camps. In the center of the island is a PAVILION and RACING TRACK, 5.4 *m.*, where Fourth of July celebrations are held each year, as are club and lodge picnics.

At 65.8 *m.* is a junction with a graveled road.

Left on this road is ASHTON, 1 *m.* (1,296 alt.), which replaced Old Ashton, first town in Spink Co. and the first county seat. It was Old Ashton that figured in the county seat race with Redfield (see Tour 3).
At 2.8 *m.* is the junction with an unimproved dirt road. Right on this road is the ABIGAIL GARDNER RESCUE SITE, 3.8 *m.*, at the confluence of the James River and Snake Creek. Here was effected the rescue of Abigail Gardner, a 13-year-old girl who was held captive by a band of Yankton Sioux Indians following the Spirit Lake

Massacre of 1857. She and three women were captured and taken north by the Indian party. One of the four was tortured to death near Flandreau and another murdered by Roaring Cloud, son of the ruthless Inkpaduta, who figured in the Spirit Lake Massacre. A third was rescued by two Christian Indians, while Abigail Gardner's freedom was obtained through two missionaries, Riggs and Williamson, and three Christian Indians, after she had been subjected to long and severe torture.

At 76 *m.* the institutional buildings of the SOUTH DAKOTA STATE SCHOOL AND HOME FOR THE FEEBLE MINDED are passed (R) at the N. edge of Redfield.

REDFIELD, 76.9 *m.* (1,295 alt.) (*see Tour 3*), is at the junction with US 212.

At 80.5 *m.* is the junction with a graveled road.

Right on this road is COTTONWOOD LAKE 8 *m.*, a large, shallow body of water with numerous summer cottages and a STATE FISH HATCHERY (*open to public*). It is one of eight lakes in the State bearing that name.

At 83 *m.* the highway passes (R) the first two of two sets of TWIN LAKES (*see below*).

TULARE, 86.3 *m.* (1,317 alt.), accounts for its name in two different ways. According to one version, it was named for an Indian chief. The other version, more interesting but probably less authentic, is that the name was the outgrowth of a series of "tall" stories told by two brothers to passengers on trains that halted on an uphill grade near the present town. So persistent were they in their gross exaggerations, that after a few trips over the route it became customary for passengers to refer to the brothers as the "two liars." From this, the story says, the two words were contracted into "Tulare."

BONILLA, 96.4 *m.*, has for many years been a feeding ground for pheasants. William Hale Thompson, while mayor of Chicago, came here with a group of sportsmen to hunt.

At 104.1 *m.* is the junction with US 14 (*see Tour 4*), the two highways following the same route for 7 m.

WOLSEY, 108 *m.* (1,353 alt.) (*see Tour 4*).

At 111.3 *m.* is the junction with US 14 (*see Tours 4 aud 11A*). US 281 continues through generally level country, with much of the broken ground showing the effects of erosion by dust storms. In this vicinity the Federal Government is carrying on soil conservation work, as much as 6 in. of top-soil having been blown away by persistent winds during the drought period. With this top soil has also gone the nitrogen so essential to crop nourishment.

This region also lies in the shelterbelt area. In the spring of 1936, approximately one million trees were planted. Those adapted to this particular soil were chosen.

At 135 *m.* is the junction with State 34.

Right on this hard-surfaced highway is WESSINGTON SPRINGS, 5 *m.* (1,410 alt.), set picturesquely in the recesses of the Wessington Hills. The town took its name from the hills and from the copious springs that are here. It was founded in 1880, by a small group of settlers under the Rev. A. B. Smart, who conceived the idea of starting the town on a "strong, pure basis of temperance, education, and Christianity." WESSINGTON SPRINGS COLLEGE, a junior college and high school operated by the S.D. Conference of the Free Methodist Church, was started in 1887 as a seminary. First classes were held on the second floor of a store building. The college now has a 125-acre campus on a wooded hillside, with several large buildings. On the campus is the SHAKESPEARE GARDEN, which has 150 varieties of flowers and shrubs, and the ANN HATHAWAY COTTAGE. The college does not participate in any interscholastic or intercollegiate athletics.

People from several counties gathered at Wessington Springs during the summer of 1893, to see a balloon ascension. The balloonist sat on a trapeze below the gas bag. He sought to improve his act by tying a hard slipknot to release the parachute instead of using a knife. As the band played the balloonist ascended. He first hung by his toes, then by one hand, and finally by his toes. When he prepared to come back to earth he discovered to his dismay that the knot would not slip. Up and up he went until he became a mere speck against the blue. Eventually the gases cooled and he landed only a few hundred yards from his starting point.

The WESSINGTON HILLS—a long, narrow range extending approximately 50 m. —were named for a man who was tortured to death by the Indians in 1863. These hills in early days were a hide-out of bands of horse rustlers and other renegades, the timber-lined draws affording excellent concealment for their movements, and the summits enabling them to discern approaching parties. Three m. N. of Wessington Springs is TURTLE PEAK, a long, high hill rising 500 ft. above the surrounding lowlands. It was named for an Indian chief. From this point distant towns—Woonsocket, Alpena, Huron—can be seen on clear days. Upon the highest portion of the hill (the whole range is a glacial moraine) is a low, broad mound of earth, 50 ft. in diameter and about 3 ft. high. Upon its southern slope is the gigantic figure of a turtle. The figure is constructed of stone 4 to 6 in. in diameter. There are many picnic and camping spots in the fastnesses of the hills, used by school classes and other groups for summer outings.

US 281 continues S. through a diversified farming section, not a single town being passed in 23 m.

At 139.1 m. is the junction with a graveled road.

Left on this road to TWIN LAKES and the STATE FISH HATCHERY (*open to public*).

At 144 m. is the junction with a graveled road.

Right on this road is LAKE WILMARTH RECREATION DEVELOPMENT AREA, a park project of the State Game, Fish and Parks Dept.

PLANKINTON, 158.3 m. (1,528 alt.) (*see Tour 5*), is at the junction with US 16.

West of Plankinton US 281 and US 16 are united for 19 m. (*see Tour 5*).

At 177.2 m. US 281 again turns (L); US 16 continues W. (R). The nature of the country has been gradually, almost imperceptibly, changing. In this section farms are less numerous than farther N. and E., and rainfall is normally lighter. It is between the eastern farming section and the western ranching country.

PLATTE, 201.1 m., was first settled in 1882, by a colony of Hollanders, and many descendants of the original immigrants still live in the vicinity. Situated at the end of a railroad line and in the center of a wide trade territory, Platte has many business houses, including a large creamery and flour mill. Its paved Main St. is a long landscaped boulevard. There are many attractive homes here, and a large, well-equipped school provides excellent educational facilities. The annual county fair held in Platte each fall is one of the outstanding fairs in the State. Northwest of town is LAKE PLATTE, where both swimming and fishing are available.

South of Platte the country becomes more hilly as the breaks of the Missouri River valley are reached. There are many dips and turns as the highway weaves its course down to the river bottom. From the heights above the river is a scenic view of the winding, indomitable Big Muddy, its green, tree-fringed shores standing out in sharp contrast with the light-colored sand bars between which the stream winds its restless way.

At 218 m. is the junction with US 18 (*temporary*); when the Ft. Randall dam is completed, the highway will pass over it (*see Tour 7*). US 281 (*temporary*) and US 18 (*temporary*) cross the Wheeler Bridge and are joined for 10 m.

At 228 m. is the junction with US 18 (*see Tour 7*); US 281 continues S.

FAIRFAX, 232.4 m., was settled following the opening of the Rosebud Indian Reservation in 1890. Formerly this region was all Indian country but the closed area of the reservation has been reduced, now covering only Todd Co.; within its former boundaries, however, are many Indians, living under approximately the same regulations as those in the restricted part (*see INDIANS*). The country S. and E. of Fairfax is quite sandy, and soil erosion is prevalent during drought years when the grass has been grazed short or the crops are poor.

In normal years the light, sandy soil grows good crops, especially of corn and potatoes.

At 234.5 m. US 281 crosses the Nebraska Line, 10 m. N. of Butte, Nebr. (*see Nebr. Tour 4*).

Tour 11*A*

Junction with US 281—Huron—Mitchell—Junction with State 50. US 14 and State 37.
Junction with US 281 to Junction with State 50, 114.3 m.
Paralleled roughly by C. M. St. P. & P. R.R.
Roadbed hard-surfaced throughout.
Accommodations at all towns.

THIS route runs through the center of the east-central section of South Dakota, following roughly the fertile James River valley. The country is alternatingly level and slightly rolling, and is crossed or touched by four east-west highways. There are few curves in the road, which is featured by many miles of well-improved, "plumb line" stretches.

From the junction with US 281 (*see Tour 11*), 3 m. south of Wolsey this route is united with US 14 (*see Tour 4*) to Huron.

HURON, 11 m. (1,288 alt.) (*see HURON*).

State Fair Grounds, Huron College, Municipal Airport.

At Huron is the junction with State 37; this route leaves US 14 (*see Tour 4*) and turns S. (R) on State 37.

South of Huron the road crosses a level country, glimpses of distant hills breaking the otherwise unvarying prairie expanse.

At 32 m. is the junction with State 34.

Right on this hard-surfaced road 3 m. to WOONSOCKET (Ind., City of mists) (1,308 alt.), named for Woonsocket, R. I. The most noteworthy feature of the town is picturesque LAKE PRIOR, an artificial body of water covering several acres in the center of the town. The lake was made many years ago by flooding a natural depression, and has been several times improved. A Government aid project made possible the facing of the shores with multicolored rock, improvement of swimming facilities, and restocking with fish. An island in the center of the lake is reached by an arched bridge.

Woonsocket at one time boasted the world's most powerful artesian well, from which a stream of water rocketed 96 ft. into the air. Because the water could not be controlled on account of the enormous pressure, and after numerous villagers had been drenched when the wind suddenly veered, the well was closed. Woonsocket is in one of the best artesian basins in the State, and many farms obtain their water supply by such wells. The town is noted for its excellent water, both hard and soft, depending on the depth to which a well is dug.

The town missed an opportunity in early days to have an important cereal factory —that of Post—when the governing body became skeptical of the intentions of a stranger who wanted the town to give him land on which to build his factory. Post considered Woonsocket a good site—in "the heart of the grain belt," as he said,— but because he was refused, he took his proposal to Battle Creek, Mich., where he opened business

Woonsocket is the center of an area peopled by Scandinavians, Irish, and Germans. It has one of the largest Catholic churches in the State, and a parochial school.

At 39 m. is the junction with a graded road.

Right on this dirt road to the SAND HILLS, 4 m. These hills, topped with trees, are a popular goal of picnickers and hikers during the spring and fall. There is a story that the hills were once a rendezvous for horse thieves, the elevation making them a vantage point for rustlers who could see approaching parties for considerable distances. Residents of the vicinity tell of Horse Thief Cave, supposedly in the fastnesses of these hills, but no one has ever been able to find it.

FORESTBURG, 39.2 m., was so named because of the number of trees near the town site.

The soil along the James River in this vicinity is noted for its fertility and its adaptability to the raising of watermelons and muskmelons. Every fall roadside stands are built along the highway and rarely a mile is passed without seeing one. Here the melons are dispensed to customers without the necessity of a "middleman." Besides local sales, tons are shipped each year to other regions.

The brush and trees fringing the course of the James River harbor many pheasants and rabbits, the latter often becoming so numerous that concerted drives are staged and hundreds of the little animals are killed in an afternoon. When too numerous, they become destructive to small trees and other vegetation. The rabbits are usually shipped East, where the pelts are made into coats and other garments for women, the original name of rabbit being discarded for a trade name—lapin—upon the appearance of the coats in shop windows.

At 41.1 *m.* is a junction with a graded but winding road.

Right on this road is RUSKIN PARK, 0.8 *m.*, in a large wooded horseshoe bend of the James River. With 50 cottages of from one to four rooms, with fishing, camping, and other recreational facilities, Ruskin Park is a popular spot during summer months. Dancing, roller-skating, baseball, boating, horse-racing, and automobile racing constitute the diversified amusements available to the public. A recent survey showed some of the trees in the park to be 150 years old; there is one elm with a trunk so large that it cannot be encircled by three men joining hands. A large dance pavilion, the sides constructed of prism glass doors 12 ft. high, is at the northern edge of the park. The material employed was used in some of the buildings at the World's Fair in Chicago in 1893.

At 43.3 *m.* State 37 turn R. at the junction with State 34.

At 62.5 *m.* LAKE MITCHELL is passed, the highway describing an arc and crossing the wall of the dam that impounds this large artificially formed body of water (*see MITCHELL*).

MITCHELL, 64.1 *m.* (1,312 alt.), (*see MITCHELL*).

Corn Palace, Lake Mitchell, Indian Village, Hackberry Trees.

Mitchell is at the junction with US 16 (*see Tour 5*).

DIMOCK, 81.2 *m.*, is the center of a community of mixed nationalities, many of the residents being of German-Russian descent.

At the northern outskirts of Dimock is the junction with a graveled road.

Left on this road is the NEW ELM SPRINGS MENNONITE COLONY, 8 *m.*, on the banks of the James River. Following the unsuccessful migration to Canada, more than a hundred Mennonites returned to South Dakota late in 1936 and resettled here, beginning an attempt to regain their once prosperous financial status through their thrifty methods of community living. (See Tour 5, ROCKPORT MENNONITE COLONY).

PARKSTON, 87.3 *m.* (1,400 alt.), the largest town in Hutchinson Co., is surrounded by well-improved farms. Many farmers of the section are of German and Bohemian ancestry, their thrift and industrious habits having created substantial homes. Drought years have taken their toll here as elsewhere, but, as residents of the neighboring communities say, many of the long-time farmers in the vicinity have considerable money "in the sock," sufficient to tide them over until good times return.

TRIPP, 99.3 *m.* (1,563 alt.) (*see Tour 7*), is at the junction with US 18.

At 114.3 *m.* is a junction with State 50 (*see Tour 8*), 5 m. W. of Tyndall.

Tour 12

(Linton, N. Dak.)—Selby—Pierre—Murdo—(Valentine, Neb.) US 83.
North Dakota Line to Nebraska Line, 249 m.
This route is not paralleled by any railroads, but crosses several.
Roadbed hard-surfaced N. two-thirds; graveled S. third.
Hotel and tourist accommodations at towns above.

THIS highway bisects the State, passing over a rolling, treeless stretch of prairie, much of it virgin, especially S. of Murdo where the newly-designated route crosses the Rosebud Indian Reservation. US 83 forms a direct connecting link between the North Dakota capital, Bismarck, and Pierre, capital of South Dakota; travel by air or rail requires triangulation.

US 83 roughly parallels the Missouri River Oahe Reservoir between the North Dakota Line and Ft. Pierre.

Although the Missouri River is one of the largest in the world, its valley is very narrow—from two to three miles—and is bordered by steep bluffs and breaks. The present course of the river marks the western edge of the last ice sheet. Consequently the soil E. of the river is composed of glacial drift and studded with stones; to the W. is Pierre clay, or gumbo. (*See GEOLOGY*).

Most of the State's early history took place along the banks of the Missouri River, which was the thoroughfare traveled by explorer, trapper, and missionary. In the middle of the 18th century the Arikaras occupied the banks of the river and its tributaries. Then the Sioux waged a 75-year fight against them and finally drove them northward out of the State. The Verendrye brothers' expedition followed the river southward in 1743, leaving the first record of white men in the State at Ft. Pierre (*see HISTORY*). The Lewis and Clark expedition went up the Missouri in 1804 and returned in 1806; the Astorians traveled the course in 1811. The early history centered around the fur trade, and this in turn centered on the banks of the Missouri. The fur trade decreased with the growing scarcity of fur, and was finally disrupted by the Civil War.

US 83 crosses the North Dakota Line, 7 m. S. of Hull, N. Dak. (*see N. Dak. Tour 3*).

HERREID, 7 *m.,* was named for the late Gov. Charles Herreid when the town was founded in 1901. There are German-Russian families in the community and their native tongues are used to a large extent in business places, as well as in the homes.

At 11.7 *m.* is the junction with State 10 (*see Tour 1*).

MOUND CITY, 14.8 *m.*, is one of the five inland county seats in South Dakota. When the Minneapolis, St. Paul & Sault Saint Marie R.R. was built to Herreid in 1901, most of the population of Mound City moved there. The first court was held in an old machine shop, while the second session was given quarters in a haymow. On the north edge of the town there is a draw in which insignia of soldiers and Indian relics have been found together, indicating an unrecorded pursuit, probably in 1863 or 1864.

To provide recreational facilities for Mound City and Campbell County, the LAKE CAMPBELL RECREATIONAL DEVELOPMENT AREA is maintained by the State Game, Fish and Parks Department.

At 28 *m.* is a junction with US 12 (*see Tour 2*); the two routes are united for 7 m.

SELBY, 30.3 *m.* (1,877 alt.) (*see Tour 3*), is at the junction with US 12.

At 35.5 *m.* is the junction with US 12 (*see Tour 2*).

Between the junction with US 12 and Pierre, the road passes through the Missouri River ranges, where undulating, treeless prairies are broken by sharp, irregular hills rising from deep river bottoms, and where only an occasional farm is seen. For miles not a house is visible, and only here and there a fence. At the summit of each ridge a panorama of the immediate sections suddenly unfolds, and at the top of the next the scene is surprisingly similar.

At 44.2 *m.* is the junction with a graveled road.

Right on this road and past AKASKA, is old LE BEAU, 17 *m.*, one of the many ghost towns on the South Dakota prairies that owe their deserted state to some cruel quirk of fate beyond the control of the people who lived there. In the case of Le Beau it was not one disaster, it was several—fires, disappearance of the open range, abandonment of the railroad. Once a flourishing and boisterous cattle-shipping point of 500 population, Le Beau, in 10 years, faded to a mere wraith. For years a ferryboat plied across the clay-colored waters of the Missouri River, bringing cattle from the western range for shipment East. When the river was low, ranchers "swam" the stock across. The town, too, was a distributing point for Indian cattle. Every fall when the big cattle shipments were made, the town was packed with Indians and cowboys. The cowboys were bent on a good time and were willing to pay for it. Then in 1910 a fire wiped out most of the town and much of it was never rebuilt. This was the first of a series of disasters for the luckless village, for in 1911 a second fire destroyed most of the remaining buildings. By this time the range was disappearing, homesteaders were scarring the prairie with their plows, and large cattle outfits were folding up. Many of the buildings were torn down and moved elsewhere, although the railroad company continued sending trains quite regularly over the line until 1918 to pick up stock. After 1918 the trips became more and more infrequent and finally stopped. The rails were torn up, the trading post was moved away, and Le Beau was left with a lone building—a monument to the prosperity the town once enjoyed.

GENERAL STORE

At 45 *m.* is the junction with a graveled road.

Left on this road is LOWRY, 4 *m.*, with two grain elevators and a corral for cattle. E. of Lowry is SWAN LAKE.

At 49.1 *m.* is the junction with State 20.

Left on this graveled road is HOVEN, 14 *m.*, with a large Catholic church, school, and hospital.

At 64 *m.* is a junction with US 212 (*see Tour 3*); US 212 and US 83 are united to 66.1 m.

AGAR, at 72 *m.*, is a cattle-shipping point with a general store and a few houses.

Right from Agar, 12 *m.*, is the junction with a dirt road leading (R) to the SUTTON RANCH, 6 *m.*, which has a private herd of about 100 buffalo. Starting with three head from the "Scotty" Philip herd several years ago, the group has increased by propagation and additional purchase to the present number. Among the group are two "cattalos" (a cross between buffaloes and native cattle), smooth-haired animals with the characteristic buffalo hump above the shoulders. The buffalo are allowed to run at will along the Missouri River breaks and bottom land, their "rustling" ability carrying them through the bitterest winters with only range grass to sustain them. These animals have largely forsaken the nomadic tendencies of their ancestors and are generally content to remain the year around on the home range. Only occasionally does one wander away. Such was the case in 1936 when an old buffalo appeared in a farmer's yard near Witten in the Rosebud country. The children screamed and climbed the windmill; the excited parents called the neighbors on the party telephone line, and soon all were there with automobiles. Using cars, the farmers chased the decrepit old buffalo until he fell exhausted and died.
The Sutton Ranch, one of the largest in the State, comprises more than 15 sections over which approximately 1,100 cattle roam. Every year a rodeo is held at the ranch and a few of the more skilled broncho "twisters" ride, or attempt to ride, some of the buffaloes. A buffalo team drawing a wagon is another feature of the celebration. On the ranch was the largest tree in the State—a giant cottonwood, measuring nearly 40 ft. in circumference at the base. It was blown down during a gale a number of years ago.

ONIDA, 87.3 *m.* (1,878 alt.), was the center of a homestead boom in the early 1880's during which settlers came by ox trains into the new, rough country. Houses sprang up almost overnight in 1883, and several former New York State residents gave the town its name, a modification of Oneida. Small patches of land were broken here and there by those who had horses or mules, and the yield of garden and grain crops amounted to a bumper harvest the first year. Mail arrived once a week by stage from Sioux City, Iowa.

The Onida residents in 1883 began a movement to secure the county seat, competing with Clifton. The citizens of the county went to the polls, and the result was Onida 504 votes, Clifton 499. However, nine men did not vote in the election but declared themselves in favor of Clifton, after which the case was taken to court. On April 9, 1885, a group of Onida men appeared in Clifton at noon and marched off with the safe and county records, depositing them in the Onida Hotel. A few days later the county sheriff, a Clifton supporter, and a group came for the records, which were given up without resistance. Two weeks later the case was heard in district court at Pierre, and the judge ruled in favor of Onida. As it was too late in the day, attendants from each town retired to the hotel. However, one Onida man slipped out, hired a team and drove to Onida, spreading the word along in Paul Revere fashion. Early the next morning a large party of Onida people hitched up their teams and drove to Clifton, arriving before the Clifton men returned from Pierre. In half an hour the safe and records were loaded and carried back to Onida, where they have since remained.

At Onida is a junction with a graveled road.

Right on this road is LAKE SULLY RECREATION DEVELOPMENT AREA, where 60 acres have been planted with trees, and picnic facilities were built by the State Game, Fish and Parks Department.

At 100.5 m. is the junction (R) with a graveled road to the Oahe Dam Missouri River Reservoir Project (see Tour 4, Sec. a).

At 101 m. is the junction with US 14 (see Tour 4); US 83 and US 14 are united between this point and the W. side of the Missouri River bridge (see Tour 4).

PIERRE, 118.3 m. (1,442 alt.) (see PIERRE).

State Capital, Memorial Building and Museum, Farm Island, Indian School.

At 120.1 m. is the junction with US 14 (see Tour 4, Sec. b). US 83 branches S.

FORT PIERRE, 121.3 m. (1,437 alt.), at the confluence of the Missouri and Bad Rivers, has a history crammed with events of first importance in the annals of South Dakota. Perhaps no other point in the State boasts as many "firsts" as this quiet little town, which still retains a touch of the days when it was the boisterous center of a far-reaching cow country. Fort Pierre represents the eastern edge of the range country, and is approximately on the dividing line between the agricultural east and prairie west of the State.

Because of the buried Verendrye Plate (see VERENDRYE HILL below), Fort Pierre claims to be on the site of the first spot visited by white men on South Dakota soil. The establishment of a fort, near the site of the present town, by Joseph La Framboise in 1817, marked the beginning of the oldest continuous settlement in the State. In 1840 the Rev. Stephen R. Riggs, a missionary from Minnesota, preached the first sermon delivered in the Dakotas. In 1855 the Government bought Fort Pierre and General Harney moved 1,200 troops to that point. In 1865 the Indian War of the Outbreak was settled by a treaty at Fort Pierre.

With the building of the railroad to Pierre in 1880, Fort Pierre became the starting point for freight outfits on their long overland

trek to the Black Hills. It was also here that the river steamers
unloaded their cargoes for the Black Hills haul.

With the rise of Pierre, the importance of the older town declined.
Today it is a rambling, sleepy village, filled with memories of voyageurs and trappers.

After dark, however, Fort Pierre provides much of the night life
for the government employees from nearby Pierre and the cowboys
from the range westward. Some of the finest cocktail bars and the
roughest taverns in the State are found here.

Many of the nation's top rodeo performers come from this area.
Casey Tibbs won the International Rodeo Association's world bronc
riding championship in 1949, and repeated in 1950. First of the local
riders to gain fame was Bill Obele who was the champion in 1919.
Several others have been event winners in rodeos from Madison
Square Garden in New York to the celebrated Cow Palace in San
Francisco.

From the center of Fort Pierre an oil-surfaced road winds up the
bluffs overlooking the village.

Left is the VERENDRYE HILL AND MONUMENT. It was on this gumbo knoll,
overlooking the Missouri and Bad Rivers, that the Verendrye brothers—Louis and
Francois—in 1743 buried a lead plate and claimed a vast territory for France. This
is the first record of white men on Dakota soil.

In 1742 the Verendrye brothers set out from Canada to seek a route to the western
sea. After reaching what is now central Montana, they turned back, arriving at the
Missouri River near Ft. Pierre on March 15, 1743. They remained here with a band
of the Little Cherry Indians until April 2. While camped here, they buried a lead
and zinc plate bearing the date March 30, 1743. Here, at the joining of Waksicha, or
Bad River, and the Missouri, later centered the activities of the river trade which
were of commercial and historical importance.

The burial spot of the plate was marked by a rough pyramid of stones. The French-
men told the Indians the stones were a memorial for they did not want them to know
of the plate. The late William Frost said that a pile of stones, probably part of the
pyramid, was on this hill when he came to Fort Pierre in 1877. Other early residents
have spoken of hauling stones from there to use in building.

The years passed, bringing changes in the growth and development of the little town
of Ft. Pierre. The new school building was erected nearby and the school children
made this hill their playground. One Sunday, February 17, 1913, as a crowd of boys
and girls were walking about, one of the girls, Hattie Foster, noticed something protruding from the earth and pulled it from the ground. The children could see it was
a flat piece of metal but so covered with dirt that all they could read of the writing
was the date. Not knowing its value, they made laughing comments and speculations
as to what it might be, and were about to throw the plate away, when one of the
boys, George O'Reilly, took possession of it. He showed it to his father, William
O'Reilly, who had a collection of pioneer articles, and he got in touch with members
of the Historical Society. Historians had been searching for the location of the buried
plate, mentioned in the Verendrye journals, and the finding of this one caused much
excitement and speculation. Deciphering of the carving disclosed on one side the
following inscription in Latin:

> "In the 26th year of the reign of Louis XV the
> most illustrious Lord, the Lord Marquis of
> Beauhurnois being viceroy, 1741, Peter de La
> Verendrye placed this."

and on the reverse side, in French:

> "Placed by the Chevalier de La Verendrye
> Lo (Louis) Jost (Joseph Verendrye)
> Louis La Londette
> A Miotte
> The 30th March 1743."

The plate, 8½ inches long, 6½ inches wide, and ⅛ of an inch thick, was purchased by the Historical Society for $700 and is now in the Historical Museum of the Memorial Building in Pierre. The scene of this historic discovery was left unmarked for 20 years. On September 1, 1933, a monument was dedicated by the South Dakota Historical Society and the Fort Pierre Commercial Club on the opening day of the Stanley County Fall Festival. The French Government took official notice of the event and sent René Weiller, consul in Chicago, to represent that country. After a historic pageant, which wound through the town to the summit of the hill, the monument was formally dedicated with speeches by Gutzon Borglum, the sculptor, George Philip, nephew of "Scotty" Philip, and Lawrence Fox, State Historian. Among the honored guests was John Stanage of Yankton, born at Ft. Pierre in 1857, the first white boy in old Dakota Territory.

A few rods to the NE. of the Verendrye Monument is the concrete and stone map of South Dakota constructed of stones from each county, gathered by the Young Citizens League. It was dedicated on the last day of the Y.C.L. Convention in May 1935.

South of Ft. Pierre, US 83 crosses Bad River, so named because of its destructive activities in the spring season. The river drains part of the badlands and large stretches of rolling prairie; but when it reaches the Missouri River during high water, it backs up, causing frequent floods. At other seasons, it is a small, sluggish stream.

At the S. end of the bridge is a graded street.

Left on this graded road is LEWIS AND CLARK PARK, 0.5 *m.*, at the confluence of the Missouri and Bad Rivers. At this site the Lewis and Clark expedition stopped and visited an Indian village in 1804. So anxious were the Indians to have the explorers remain, that blood was nearly shed before they were allowed to proceed up the river. On the return trip the party slipped past the place without stopping. A recreational park, with outdoor fireplaces, has been laid out here.

At 133.2 *m.* GUMBO BUTTES rise abruptly along the E. side of US 83, exposing a black shale formation almost devoid of vegetation. Yucca plants, commonly known as Spanish bayonets, cling to the hillsides, and in spring have a wax-like pink and yellow blossom. Magpies, although native to more mountainous regions, are often seen along the road.

Bullsnakes may be seen sunning themselves on the tarvia roadbed; the grassy buttes and knolls along the highway are favorite haunts of rattlesnakes.

At 154.1 *m.* is the junction with US 16 (*see Tour 5*); US 16 and US 83 are joined W. to Murdo (*see Tour 5*); alternate route, via US 183 (*see Tour 12A*).

MURDO, 175.5 *m.* (2,217 alt.) (*see Tour 5*).

S. from Murdo US 83 follows the old Texas Trail, over which thousands of cattle were driven northward each spring to feed during the days of the open range.

At 181.8 *m.* the highway crosses White River which drains the Badlands region (*see Tour 6*). Here is a time change, CST to MST.

WHITE RIVER, 202 *m.* (2,136 alt.), a genuine "cowtown" little changed from the old West tradition. On Saturdays, ranchers, cow-pokes, and Indian families line the streets of the Mellette County seat.

At 217.7 *m.* is the N. boundary of the ROSEBUD INDIAN RESERVATION (*see INDIANS and Tour 7*).

At 222.3 *m.* is the junction with US 18 (*see Tour 7*); the two routes are united 3 m.

MISSION, 225.4 (*see Tour 7*); from here US 83 continues S. through Sioux country. Most of the Indians live in log cabins in winter and tents in summer, running a few head of cattle and keep-ing a small garden.

At 249 *m.* is the NEBRASKA LINE, N. of Valentine, Neb.

Tour 12A

Junction with US 16—Winner—(Bassett, Neb.) US 183.
Junction with US 16 to Nebraska Line, 78 m.
Roadbed hard-surfaced most of distance.
Accommodations at Winner.

US 183, formerly US 83 which parallels this route to the W. (*see Tour 12*), has its N. terminus at Presho on US 16 (*see Tour 5*). The route passes through the Winner area, known for its pheasant hunting.

PRESHO, 0 m. (1,764 alt.), (*see Tour 5*).

The highway runs S. through a range country with scattered houses, crossing the White River at 14.1 m., its tree-lined banks breaking the prairie landscape. During the summer, Indian families are often camped along the river.

At 37.2 *m.* is a junction with US 18 (*see Tour 7*); US 183 and US 18 are united for 20 m. (*see Tour 7*).

WINNER, 46.4 *m.* (1,860 alt.), (*see Tour 7*).

COLOME, 57 *m.* (*see Tour 7*).

At Colome is a junction with US 18 (*see Tour 7*).

US 183 continues S., with TURTLE BUTTE humped to the W.

At 68.5 *m.* is a junction with a graveled road.

Right on this road is the RAHN LAKE RECREATION DEVELOPMENT AREA, 7 *m.* A picnic area is maintained by the State Game, Fish and Parks Department.

The Keyapaha River is crossed at 75.7 *m.*

WEWELA, 76 *m.*, is a trading post, reminiscent of the Old West.

At 78 *m.* US 183 crosses the Nebraska Line 15 m. N. of Spring-view, Neb. (*see Neb. Tour 5*).

Tour 13

(Bowman, N. Dak.)—Buffalo—Belle Fourche—Spearfish—Deadwood—Lead—(New-castle, Wyo.) US 85.
North Dakota Line—Wyoming Line, 164.1 m.
Not paralleled by any R.R.
Roadbed graveled N. of Belle Fourche; hard-surfaced through Black Hills.
Between Buffalo and Belle Fourche, a distance of 74 m., there are no towns and only two filling stations. Motorists should check their gas and water carefully before entering upon this stretch.
Hotel and tourist accommodations available at above-named towns.

US 85 offers a wide variety of scenery from the North Dakota line southward. It passes through the eastern edge of the Cave Hills, and crosses numerous picturesquely named creeks, redolent of sage-brush and prairie. Between Bowman and the Black Hills are Spring Creek, Cold Turkey, Alkali, North Grand River, Crooked Creek, Big Nasty, Bull Creek, Jones Creek, Box Elder, Sheep Creek, South Grand, Buffalo Creek, Clark's Fork, North Moreau, Sand Creek, South Moreau, Four Mile, Twelve Mile, Antelope Creek, Indian Creek, Owl Creek, Crow Creek, and the Belle Fourche River. The territory between the State Line and Macy is primarily a ranching country, well-watered, well-grassed, and with sufficient shelter for stock. North of Macy the road runs through a sandy-loam region. Between Macy and Belle Fourche US 85 crosses the desolate gumbo, 40 miles wide. South of Belle Fourche it skirts the edge of the Black Hills, a pleasant region of scattered groves and prosperous farms, and continues through the wooded Hills to the Wyoming Line. The region between the North Dakota Line and Belle Fourche is antelope coun-try, and glimpses of these beautiful animals are occasionally caught.

Section a. North Dakota Line to Junction with US 14, 133 m.

Eighteen miles S. of Bowman, N. Dak., US 85 crosses the North Dakota Line and leaves the broad flats of North Grand River behind (*see N. Dak., Tour 4*). Passing over the divide between North Grand River and Crooked Creek, it climbs through the eastern edge of Cave Hills.

At 7 *m.* is the junction with the Cave Hills Road.

Right on this road is the CUSTER NATIONAL FOREST (*Hqs. Deadwood*), 4 *m.*, covering the wooded area of the NORTH CAVE HILLS. These hills, unlike the nearby Slim Buttes and Short Pines (*see Tour 2A*), have lost their limestone caps. They have rounded tops and a sprinkling of pine trees. With this small area, about 12 *m.* long, is a picnic ground, a scenic spot known as Riley Pass, and LUDLOW CAVE. This cave, for which the hills were named, has an opening about 20 ft. wide and extends into a sandstone cliffside for about 300 ft. When the Custer Expedition visited the Cave Hills in 1874, General Custer named the cave for Maj. William Ludlow, his engineering officer. The cave has no special significance other than the fact that some of the artifacts removed by University of South Dakota Museum archaeologists indicate a link between the Indians of the Rocky Mountains and the Great Plains (*see Vermillion, Tour 8*).

LUDLOW, 8 *m.*, consists of a store, post office, and school beside the road. Around the school yard is a high, metal-mesh fence, and the children are forbidden to go outside this fence during school hours. This is for protection against the cars that customarily go by in a cloud of dust and gravel.

South of Ludlow the road runs in a general southwesterly direction through a hilly, well-watered and well-grassed country. For several miles the highway parallels the SOUTH CAVE HILLS.

BUFFALO, 30.5 *m.* (2,800 alt.), the seat of Harding Co., is the center of a large ranching region, divided about equally between cattle and sheep (*see Tour 2A*). It serves a very large trade territory for a town its size.

Buffalo, a typical prairie town, is a lineal descendant of homestead days. Almost every inhabitant of the town who was of age in 1909–10, including the professional men, proved up on a claim. But it is not only a prairie town; it is still a range town. Big hats are the rule and other cowboy accoutrements are not uncommon; although anyone appearing in full cowboy regalia, as exemplified in the movies, would either be laughed out of town or placed under observation.

In 1909 the town of Buffalo was laid out on the N. bank of Grand River, in the geographical center of the county, with the idea of its becoming the seat of the newly organized county. But its ambition did not go unchallenged. Camp Crook (*see Tour 2A*), on the western edge of the county, situated on the banks of the Little Missouri River, was already an old town and was not at all backward about asserting its prior claim to county seat honors. Parties from both towns toured the county to secure votes, and their arguments were reinforced by certain liquid inducements to enable the voters to think more clearly. While the battle was at its height, a widely known and well-liked ranch hand from the eastern edge of the county staged an individual celebration in Camp Crook and was locked in the town jail overnight. In the morning he was found dead; the resentment of the eastern half of the county at the occurrence was sufficient to swing the victory to the rival town.

Buffalo, like other prairie towns, is a blending of the old and new. There are still small frame stores, with flamboyant high square fronts, and also substantial modern buildings—a new hotel, a surprisingly large garage and filling station, and good restaurants. The courthouse is wooden, as are the dwelling houses; a beginning of tree planting has been made, and the town is outgrowing its cruder stage.

Buffalo still retains the spirit of the pioneer days. Hospitality and friendliness are the rule. No one enters the town for the second time as a stranger. The fact that it is 50 m. from the nearest railroad has perhaps served to preserve the pioneer flavor.

Buffalo is at the junction with State 8 (*see Tour 2A*) going W.

At 32.5 *m.* is the junction with State 8 (*see Tour 2A*) going E.

REDIG, 52.8 *m.*, consists of a store and post office.

At 54.8 *m.* are the Crow Buttes, a group of lofty mud buttes where a fierce battle between the Sioux and Crow Indians was fought before the coming of the white men. This is an opportunity to study that curious phenomenon, a mud butte. Formed of gumbo and clay, rising abruptly from the plain without a spear of vegetation, every rain that washes off its sides is thick with gumbo detritus, and it seems strange that it is not thus made level with the surrounding plain. It is often possible to pick up fossils around its base, since the formation is somewhat similar to that of the Badlands (*see GEOLOGY*).

At 57.2 *m.* is the junction with State 79, a graveled road.

Left on State 79 is MASON, 5.6 *m.*, a general store and post office.
At 5.9 *m.* State 79 turns R. and follows the same section line for 30 *m.*, those lines which checkerboard the country, one mile apart, according to the original U.S. survey. Within this distance there is a correction line, a jog to compensate for expanding meridians. The road occasionally swings R. or L. a little to keep to the wind-swept ridges; but it always returns to the same section line.
At 18.4 *m.* (R) there is an extremely high hill rising from the level plain. On Government maps it is marked HAYSTACK BUTTE, but every old-timer knows it as SQUARE TOP. It is shaped roughly like a ridge-poled tent.
At 21.7 *m.* (L) is a lofty ridge with a rocky crest which gives its name of CASTLE ROCK; a splendid view is obtained from its summit.
In the distance (L), are two conical hills, very appropriately named DEER'S EARS.
CASTLE ROCK, 23.6 *m.*, is a store and post office.
At 37.2 *m.* is a very good view of Newell and the Belle Fourche irrigation project.
NEWELL, 41.6 *m.* (2,820 alt.), is at the junction with US 212 (see Tour 3).

At 63.5 *m.* (L) is the old abandoned post office of MACY. This former post office dates back to the earliest days of the country's settlement. Macy was an Englishman who homesteaded on the South Moreau River, and was reported to have written back to England that he had an estate of 160 acres entirely planted to sage. People used to travel long distances to get their mail at Macy. Some of the Macy family still live there.

Between Buffalo and Macy the country is somewhat flatter than that farther N., but is well-grassed and a good sheep region. Macy, however, is on the northern edge of a gumbo belt 40 m. wide, which deserves special mention and description.

THE GUMBO, as it is universally called, is a desolate region looking like a sea with long rollers that have suddenly become petrified. Few people make their homes here the year round. It is too bleak, and the soil conditions are too obstinate. Gumbo, geologically known as Pierre Clay, is a black soil of almost unbelievable viscosity when wet. In the days of freight wagons, the freighters were obliged to remove their brake blocks as soon as the gumbo began to "roll." It is characteristic of gumbo to "ball up," and the feet of unlucky humans or animals forced to travel in it seem to grow continually larger. It is practically impossible to move stock across it when wet. Gen. Crook and his cavalry, coming from the Battle of Slim Buttes, tried to cross the gumbo in a ten-day rain. Before they reached the Belle Fourche River half of the horses were dead of exhaustion, and they had to kill and eat many others. Gen. Crook in his report said that he doubted whether in the annals of the American Army there had been a journey involving so much hardship and suffering.

The gumbo, when dry, is creased with innumerable wrinkles, like the face of a very old man. When rain comes, these wrinkles disappear and the soil flows together in a sea of mud. It is difficult to farm when it is too dry, and impossible to work when wet. Therefore, the farmer's activities are apt to be somewhat curtailed at inconvenient times.

On the gumbo there is no sod. Each spear of grass grows independently from its own root. Compared with sod grass, gumbo grass is sparse; but in content it is much richer. Gumbo lambs always outweigh the sand lambs in the fall. In the summer the gumbo is apt to be covered with herds of cattle and bunches of sheep from the surrounding regions. Lack of water is the chief difficulty, but dams are solving that problem where water holes are not available.

At 99 *m.* US 85 leads over a series of steep gumbo hills, from the last of which there is a splendid view of the fertile Belle Fourche Valley. The contrast between the greenness of the irrigated valley and the brown of the gumbo is most striking.

BELLE FOURCHE (Bell Foosh), 104.1 *m.* (3,013 alt.), takes its name (beautiful fork) from its site at the fork of the Belle Fourche River and Redwater Creek. It is the scene of the Black Hills Round-Up (*see below*), and has historical associations and a commercial importance out of all proportion to its size, husky young city though it is. Its selection as a town site by the Frémont, Elkhorn and Missouri Valley R.R. was the signal for the demise of its rival, old Minnesela 3½ m. away (*see below*).

Belle Fourche is the unofficial capital of a far-flung cattle and sheep empire, serving not only the northwest section of South Dakota but parts of Wyoming and Montana as well. At one time, it was the greatest primary cattle-shipping point in the world; until the Milwaukee Railroad was built through to the West Coast, the nearest railroad was the Northern Pacific running through the center of North Dakota. Today as many as 2,300 carloads of cattle are still being shipped annually from here.

Sheep now share the range with cattle, and Belle Fourche has also become a sheep and wool marketing center. There are two large wool warehouses, and sheep as well as cattle chutes are in the stockyards. The sheepman is almost as much a part of the local scene as the cowboy, and only occasionally does the old rivalry break out. In the modern version of the cattleman-sheepherder feud, sheepmen were convicted in a Belle Fourche court of roping a rival cowboy and tying him to the tail of a spirited horse. The enraged horse took off over cactus beds and rocky creek bottoms, dragging the cowhand for a painful ride.

The refining of sugar, the mining of bentonite, and the manufacture of bricks are growing industries.

A $2,000,000 sugar beet crop is raised and processed here each year. The BLACK HILLS SUGAR PLANT, with a five-story main building, can produce as much as 350,000 pounds of sugar a day. From 1912 until 1917, sugar beets were grown experimentally in the Belle Fourche Valley, and in 1927 the plant, which now covers eight acres, was opened.

About 500 farmers in the surrounding country participate in the beet-growing industry. Under a contract, the grower receives one-half of the total value of the sugar extracted from the beets, minus the cost of manufacturing his share. The present beet acreage in the Black Hills district is about 9,500 acres and lies to the E. (see Tour 3). Large groups of Mexicans or Jamaicans are imported to do the harvesting each fall. These imported migratory workers, follow the beet harvests northward, and harvest the crops on a contract or weight basis.

One of the largest known deposits of bentonite in the world (see NATURAL SETTING) is found along the banks of Middle Creek, a small stream that flows past the Belle Fourche stockyards. Much of this ore is exposed. Three BENTONITE PLANTS are in active operation, mining the gelatin-like clay for shipment to Eastern markets for use in reactivating molding sands in steel foundaries, as well as in the making of cosmetics, cleansers, and paints. In 1950, bentonite ranked second to gold in South Dakota mineral production (see Minerals).

The BELLE FOURCHE RESERVOIR known locally as Orman Dam, is E. of town and is one of the top wall-eye pike fishing spots in the State (see Tour 3 and Recreation).

The Black Hills Round-up, a three-day celebration, is held in Belle Fourche each year on July 3, 4 and 5. This annual celebration began in 1918, and was first planned as a benefit entertainment for war funds, the United States being then engaged in its second year of the World War. So overwhelming was the success of the first year's show that the board of directors decided to make an annual event of the rodeo. Its proceeds since then have been used for various community and regional enterprises, no private profit being taken from the sale of tickets. The program is considerably varied from year to year, the usual events being bucking contests, bull-dogging, steer-roping, and wild-horse racing. Women as well as men vie for elaborate prizes in these daring sports. One of the three days of festivities is usually set aside as Governor's Day.

Left from Belle Fourche on St. Onge road; at 3.5 *m.* turn L on the E. side of the Redwater bridge; at 4 *m.* is OLD MINNESELA, one of the few ghost towns of this region. This was a flourishing town for some time before Belle Fourche was born. It had many stores, including a drug store, a blacksmith shop, a large hotel, dwelling houses, a schoolhouse, a church, and several saloons. When it was evident that the railroad company was going to select a town site at the fork of the Belle Fourche River and intended to hold a sale of lots on a certain day, the enterprising citizens of Minnesela got out a map of the region showing their town as the general railroad center of this part of the country; listed on the back of the map were 40 or 50 reasons why Minnesela was destined to be the metropolis of this region. The citizens of Minnesela met the train bearing the prospective buyers, distributed the map freely, and not a lot was sold on the Belle Fourche town site that day. But the railroad won in the end; and one by one the business houses accepted the inevitable and removed to the new location. Only one man clung to the old location to the last. He took over the old hotel, cut it down to one-third its size, and converted it into a farmhouse with plenty of spare bedrooms. He made a success of farming and created a beautiful yard and garden. And there he lived until 1936, when he was laid to rest.

At Belle Fourche is the junction with US 212 (*see Tour 3*).

South of Belle Fourche US 85 goes through the Belle Fourche Redwater, and Spearfish valleys. Previously the road has been traversing the barren prairies, but now it crosses a series of wooded ridges interspersed with crop-covered valleys.

At 110.6 *m.* Red Water Creek is crossed.

At 112.4 *m.* Spearfish Creek is reached, and the road roughly parallels the creek through the rich LOWER SPEARFISH VALLEY, a region of prosperous farms and substantial buildings. Sugar beets and garden produce mingle with the small grains. But when the road swings into UPPER SPEARFISH VALLEY and heads directly toward Spearfish, a most unusual sight is encountered. Picture a long, straight tarvia road, shaded by large trees on either side; small, irrigated fruit and vegetable farms to the R. and L.; little stands in front of each, loaded with produce and attended by some member of the family—such is the entrance to Spearfish, a ROADSIDE MARKET PLACE that is known throughout all this region. The miners from Lead, the ranchers from the range country to the N., who do not have time to raise the vegetables they need, the housewives of surrounding towns, all come to Upper Spearfish Valley for fruits and vegetables which are replaced on the stand as fast as they are sold. There are apple trees on every farm, large orchards on some, and in the spring when the apple blossoms are out this lane is a pathway of beauty.

At 116.5 *m.* is a junction with US 14 (*see Tour 4*); the two routes are joined through Spearfish.

SPEARFISH, 118.7 *m.* (3,637 alt.), (*see Tour 4*). Here is the junction with the Spearfish Canyon Road, State 89 (*see Tour 13A*).

US 85 and US 14 are united to a junction at 133 *m.*, at the NE. edge of Deadwood (*see Tour 4*).

Section b. Junction with US 14 to Wyoming Line, 31.1 m.

Southwest of the junction with US 14, US 85 goes through the principal mining section of the Black Hills.

DEADWOOD (4,534 alt.) (*see DEADWOOD*).

Roosevelt Monument. Graves of Wild Bill, Calamity Jane, Seth Bullock, and Preacher Smith. Adams Memorial Museum.

At PLUMA, 2.5 *m.*, are a group of tourist cabins, filling stations, a night club, and a unit of the Homestake Mining Company's plant. Here is the junction with US 85A (*see Tour 14*).
LEAD, 4 *m.* (5,320 alt.) (*see LEAD*).

Homestake Mine. Open Cut. Grier Park.

At the W. edge of Lead is the junction with the Old Central Road.

Right on this road is TERRAVILLE, 1 *m.*, in 1876 a mining camp, but now a suburb of Lead. The village, in Bobtail Gulch, grew up around the Golden Terra Mine which was located by J. B. Pearson, discoverer of the first gold in Deadwood Gulch. It was sold to the Homestake Mining Co. in 1877 for $90,000.
At 1.6 *m.* is CENTRAL CITY, which today looks much like the movie setting of an old-time Western town. Situated on Deadwood Creek, the village has the old false-front stores and saloons of its heyday, although there are many gaping holes where buildings have burned down or have been moved away. Up on the cliffsides are the unused narrow gauge tracks and trestles, together with remains of old mills, that hummed with activity when this was a gold mine town. Today most of the men work in nearby Lead and Deadwood, and the town has gained considerable attention because women are in charge of garages, saloons, stores, shops, and town offices.
An old cyanide plant near Central City has been converted into an indoor ICE SKATING RINK (*open to public; adm. fee*).

At 5.5 *m.* is the junction with a graveled road.

Right on this road, along the slope of BALD MOUNTAIN (7,000 alt.), is the mining village of TERRY, 2 *m.*, reminiscent of the gold rush days. At the height of its prosperity, about 1893, Terry had a population of 1,000 residents, and was a station of the Burlington R.R. Today a few miners and their families occupy scattered cabins along the gulch in which the old, rip-roaring gold camp was situated. Most of the stores, saloons, and other buildings have been moved or have fallen into ruins.
At 3.5 *m.* is TROJAN where the Bald Mountain Mine has resumed operations; in 1950 its gold production jumped 71 per cent over the previous year. It is second to the Homestake in the Black Hills area.

At 10.7 *m.*, after a climb of almost 9 m., the highest point of the road is reached (6,702 alt.).
At 10.8 *m.* is a junction with a graveled road.

Right on this road to the summit of TERRY PEAK (7,071 alt.). Named for Gen. Terry, it is the fourth highest peak in the Hills, and from its summit is a remarkable view.
From Nov. to Apr. this is a WINTER SPORTS AREA, offering skiing and bob-sledding. There are three splendid slopes: the Stewart Slide, 2700 ft.; the Holy Terror Slide, 1500 ft., and the Tail Race Run, each of which is served by a motor-operated tow. There are several cross-country runs, one of the most popular being from the

top of Terry Peak into Spearfish Canyon, a distance of 4.5 m., with a drop of 1800 ft. A Club House is open to visitors. This winter sports area has been developed since 1945, as a community enterprise, with the Homestake Mining Co. providing most of the facilities.

At 10.9 m. the road enters ICE BOX CANYON, and descends steadily. The canyon was so named by early-day freighters, who found a welcome coolness in its tree-shaded depths.

At 14.3 m. is the CHEYENNE CROSSING, where the old Cheyenne Trail crossed Spearfish Creek; here is the junction with the Spearfish Canyon road (see Tour 13A).

The road follows the W. branch of Spearfish Creek for some distance, through scenes of unusual beauty. The undergrowth has been cleared out, and between the straight trunks of the pines are glimpses of the swift-flowing brook. The grass and moss make a carpet of green and the pine boughs a canopy overhead. It is a scene that lingers in the memory.

Hellsgate, Deadhorse, and Dead Ox gulches open (R) along the highway, and up each gulch one may find wild flowers and berries, bristling porcupines and startled deer, and mine diggings, new or old. A small picnic area is along Dead Ox Creek.

US 85 passes through a recently burned-over area where the devastating effect of forest fires is in evidence. Although the U.S. Forest Service keeps a constant vigil, there are several fires each summer and more than half are man-caused.

At 26 m., near the Hardy Ranger Station, is a junction with a Forest Service road.

Left on this graded road is the junction with another road, 3 m.
(1) Left is the Crooks Tower Road to HEADWATERS SPRING CAMP GROUND, 4.5 m. Here at the spring that feeds the S. fork of Rapid Creek, at the foot of CROOKS TOWER (7,114 alt.), is a camping area set aside by the Forest Service for those who seek an off-the-highway retreat in a spruce setting. At 6.5 m. is BLACK FOX CAMP GROUND and at 8 m. is DEER DALE CAMP GROUND, both noted for the good trout fishing nearby. This road continues to Rochford (see Tour 14).
(2) Right is the Moon Road, along the W. slope of the Limestone Plateau, wildest portion of the Black Hills. For 20 m., to the MOON PICNIC GROUND, the forest trail passes through country seldom traveled by "outsiders"—those who do not live along it.

At 31.1 m. US 85 crosses the Wyoming Line, 30.5 m. N. of Newcastle, Wyo. (see Wyo. Tour 1).

Tour 13A

Cheyenne Crossing—Savoy—Maurice—Spearfish. State 89.
Cheyenne Crossing—Spearfish, 19 m.
No railroad parallels this route.
Roadbed hard-surfaced almost throughout.
Lodges and cabins along route.

ONE of the most attractive routes in the Black Hills is that through Spearfish Canyon. This trip should be made down the canyon from south to north rather than in the reverse direction, since the fall of Spearfish Creek is pronounced, and the road quite steep in places. The upper portion of the canyon is comparatively shallow and open, but, farther down, the rock walls on both sides are higher and steeper; in the very depths of the canyon, the sun strikes the road and the creek bed for only a brief interval each day. This region lies in the so-called Deadwood Formation, made up of gray to red sandstone, greenish shale, and both slab and pebble limestone. The canyon, lined on both sides with cliffs of this material or at least a rimrock, is filled with constantly changing color, which varies still more in different lights. Here also is green pine, interspersed with the slim white trunks of birch, poplar, and quaking-aspen. Fishing is good at many points throughout the canyon and, for those who are not deterred by the temperature of mountain streams, swimming is available.

State 16 branches N. from US 85 (*see Tour 13*) at CHEYENNE CROSSING (3,310 alt.).

As the road dips into the canyon along the creek banks, there is a rearing pond for young trout, which are released by the U.S. Fish Hatchery from time to time (*see Spearfish, Tour 13*).

Between 1 m. and 3 m. are public lodges and cabin camps at which cottages may be rented by the day, week, or season. Meals are available also. Raspberry, Sweet Betsy, and Annie Gulches open along the E. side of the road, and to the W. are the mouths of Jackass and Timber Gulches.

At 4 *m.* is a DIVERSION DAM and intake of the Homestake Mining Co. At this point the waters of Spearfish Creek enter a wooden stave pipe and are conveyed in it for 6 m. to the hydro-electric plant at Maurice; for a corresponding distance the bed of the creek is practically dry.

SAVOY, 5.5 *m.* (5,012 alt.), consists of a maintenance station of the Homestake Mining Co., and LATCHSTRING INN, a summer and hunting resort which has been in operation since 1907. There are inn and cabin accommodations for 70 persons, and a large dining room. On both sides of the canyon limestone (*paha sapa*) cliffs tower 1,000 feet.

Left from Savoy on a crushed stone road, paralleling Little Spearfish Creek, is ROUGHLOCK FALLS, 1 *m.* From a parking space beside the road (L) there is a short path with foot bridges over three branches of the creek above the falls. The water circles a tree and falls about 30 feet, below which there is a series of cascades. A footpath parallels the creek for 100 feet. Roughlock is perhaps the most beautiful falls in the Hills. Above the falls is the ROUGHLOCK FALLS PICNIC GROUND, maintained by the U.S. Forest Service.
At 5 *m.* is the SPEARFISH RANGER STATION, and at 5.7 m. is the TINTON PICNIC GROUND, on Little Spearfish Creek at the mouth of Schoolhouse Gulch. It is a popular Sunday spot for families, since the Forest Service has provided a playground here.

At 7.2 *m.* is the junction with a crushed rock road.

Left on this road, which parallels Deer Creek, is IRON CREEK LAKE, 4 *m.* The lake was formed by damming Iron Creek in 1937, and covers about five acres. When the WPA began building the dam, the beavers that inhabited the creek watched the operations several days and then rebuilt their house a half-mile up the creek. When the lake filled, the beaver house was ideally situated in the shallow end of the lake. At 6 *m.* is a dam formed by beavers in Beaver Creek which has become so permanent that official maps bear the legend BEAVER CROSSING. At 7.5 *m.* is the village of TINTON, founded in 1876, when gold miners discovered deposits of tin. A mine is now operated here by the Fan Steel Co. Rising W. of Tinton is a peak named NIGGER HILL. In 1876 a group of Negroes joining in the gold rush inquired about a likely spot to try some mining. Practical jokers sent them to this unlikely place where the necessary water for a placer claim would have to be carried up the mountainside. They struck a rich ore pocket, and returned rich

MAURICE, 7.5 *m.* (4,472 alt.). Here is HYDROELECTRIC PLANT NO. 2 of the Homestake Mining Co. There is a flight of 800 wooden steps leading to the point at which the wooden stave pipe pitches downward to the plant. Just below the plant are the dwellings of those who man it. At this point the full flow of Spearfish Creek is returned to the creek bed and runs for a mile before being taken out at another diversion dam to be carried in pipes to Hydroelectric Plant No. 1 at Spearfish. This mile of stream is kept stocked with trout by the hatchery, and there is good fishing.
At 8.5 *m.* (R) is BRIDAL VEIL FALLS. The water comes down over a rock-face from a considerable height and it is a beautiful spot to stop for a picnic lunch or get a cool drink of pure water.
RIM ROCK, 9.5 *m.*, is a combined tourist and children's vacation camp in a remarkable setting. The walls of the canyon are very high and at their foot, a little distance above the road, is the main lodge. It is decorated with skins and curios and here the guests gather for their meals. Higher up on the slope is a large community hall, and still higher, on a rocky point jutting out a hundred feet above the road and creek bed, are cabins, with a splendid view up and down the canyon. For a part of each summer it is used as a children's vacation camp.
At 11.5 *m.* is the junction with a footpath (R).

Right on the trail is WILDCAT CAVE, 0.3 *m.*, reached by a scramble up the steep hillside; the deep cavern is underneath a shelving rock, with a trickle of water running down the face of it. It is worth the climb to rest under the deep recess and look out over the still woods.

At 19 *m.* Spearfish Canyon widens out into Spearfish Valley, and at the mouth is HYDROELECTRIC PLANT NO. 1 of the Homestake Mining Co. At this point the water is finally returned to Spearfish Creek. But the busy waters of this stream are not through with their work yet: all through Spearfish Canyon and just below it, laterals lead the water out to irrigate the thirsty soil and to make the Upper and Lower Spearfish Valley both a garden spot and a market produce center for the region (*see Tour 13*).

The Canyon road winds through beautiful woods and at 20 *m.* (R) is the MUNICIPAL CABIN CAMP of Spearfish.

At 20.2 *m.* (L) is a U.S. FISH HATCHERY (*see Tour 13*).

SPEARFISH, 20.5 *m.* (3,637 alt.), (*see Tour 13*), is at the junction with US 85.

Tour 14

Junction with US 85—(Pluma)—Hill City—Custer—Hot Springs—Oelrichs—(Wayside, Neb.). US 85A and State 79.
Junction with US 85—Nebraska Line, 129 m.
The Chicago, Burlington & Quincy R.R. parallels this route between Junction with US 85 and Custer.
Roadbed hard-surfaced throughout.
Lodge and cabin accommodations along route and in towns.

US 85A traverses the backbone of the Black Hills range between the Deadwood-Lead area of the northern Hills, and Hot Springs at the southern fringe. For more than 60 miles this route cuts through the scenic and historic region known locally as "The Heart of the Hills."

US 85A also serves as a connecting link between the east-west highways and cut-offs (*see Tours 4, 4B, 4C, 5, 5A, 7, 13, and 14A*); and off US 85A are numerous other sideroads into the inner recesses and retreats of the mountain region.

Included in this tour is the south approach to the Black Hills from Nebraska, via State 79.

Section a. Junction with US 85—Hot Springs, 88 m. US 85A.

PLUMA, 0 *m.*, is a tourist junction and dividing point between Lead and Deadwood (*see CITIES*). It was here on a March night in 1877, that Sam Bass, a frontier bandit, and his gang tried to rob the Cheyenne-Deadwood stage bearing 11 passengers and $15,000. The hold-up failed when the horses bolted during the shotgun shooting of the coach driver. Although Sam Bass did not live long, his deeds live in Western folk songs.

US 85A winds up STRAWBERRY HILL, and the huge, silvery hoists of the Homestake Mine loom (R).

At 5.3 *m.* is the STRAWBERRY HILL PICNIC GROUND, maintained by the U.S. Forest Service. It is a good skiing area in winter.

At 6 *m.* is the junction with the Roubaix-Nemo Road (*see Tour 4C*).

The TOMAHAWK GOLF COURSE (*public; greens fee*), 7 *m.*, is a sporty, nine-hole layout built around a mountain, providing a variety of natural hazards. It has been described by Johnny Goodman, one-time U.S. Amateur champion, as "the toughest course I have ever played." The clubhouse and course are operated by the Deadwood Country Club.

At 7.9 *m.* the road crosses Elk Creek and for 2 m. winds upward through the forest.

At 9.8 *m.* is a junction with a dirt road.

Right on this road is CUSTER PEAK (6,794 alt.), 3 *m.* Although this is not the highest peak in the Black Hills, it affords a wider view than any other. It was named for Gen. George A. Custer, who stopped close to this peak while leading an exploration party through the Black Hills in 1874. A trail of the same name passes near the peak.

At 13.9 *m.* (R) is a marker to show where the highway crosses the trail made by Custer on his way to Fort Abraham Lincoln, N. Dak., from French Creek in 1874.

At 15 *m.* is the ROUBAIX LAKE CAMP GROUND, with a large shelterhouse and playground along the banks of the small artificial lake formed in the 1930's by damming a fork in Boxelder Creek.

At 20.1 *m.* is the Merrit Ranger Station and the junction with the Rochford Road.

Right on this graveled road is ROCHFORD (5,307 alt.), 12 *m.* This sleepy village has the weather-beaten landmarks of a ghost town, but it is a typical back-country community which has survived the rush of modern living. The country surrounding Rochford provides some of the best trout fishing and deer hunting in the Black Hills. The MOONSHINE GULCH PICNIC GROUND is just E. of town, and there are several public camping areas in the "Limestone Country" to the W. The Rochford Ranger Station here should be contacted by strangers before attempting to penetrate wilderness areas.

It was a group of hunters, headed by M. D. Rochford, who found gold-bearing ore in this vicinity in 1877. Within two years the STANDBY MINE, underwritten by Eastern capitalists, was in full operation. Several things happened to close down the big mine and stamp mill. The superintendent's house and the main buildings still stand, their loose clapboards flapping in the wind.

At 24 *m.* is the junction with the Rim Rock Road (*see Tour 4B*).

At 26.2 *m.* is the junction with a dirt road.

Right on this road, up Boarding House Gulch, is the METHODIST CAMP, 2 *m.*, a summer camp of the Methodist Church.

At 26.4 *m.* is Flavin's Corner, and the junction with a graded road.

Right on this road is the SPRUCE TREE PICNIC GROUNDS, a public area set aside by the U.S. Forest Service.

At 4 *m.* is SILVER CITY (4,594 alt.), one of the ghost towns of the Hills. The general store and neat, white-painted Catholic Church are in striking contrast with the rough, unpainted board shacks that still stand, eloquent of the days when mining was the chief industry, and the hope of wealth beat high in the heart of every miner and prospector in the Hills. Today, the only evidences of the old mining days are a huge hoisting drum and the dismantled engine that turned it, now lying beside the railroad track and not valuable enough to pay the freight for their removal. Silver City was founded in 1876, at the time of the gold rush along Rapid Creek. Jack, Tom, and Luke Gorman were the real founders of the town, although other prospectors had located ores in the hills and along the creek before their arrival. The Gorman brothers located the first mines on the hillsides, one called The Diana, and the other, The Lady of the Hills. These mines had a heavy yield of silver, combined with some gold and other metals. The camp was called Camp Gorman at first, but a company of seven men was organized and they platted a town site, had it patented, and named it Silver City. It grew to a community of several hundred inhabitants, and the hills and gulches surrounding it were thronged with searchers after precious metals. An Eastern syndicate sent representatives to try to buy the holdings of the Gorman brothers, offering them $300,000. The brothers were ignorant and uneducated men who could not figure whether the offer was more or less than a million dollars, which they insisted was their price. They delayed their decision till one night their cabin caught fire and the eldest brother was burned to death. The other two brothers disappeared. Their heirs in the East, still hold title to the property.

Left from Silver City is a trail leading into THE UNKNOWN LAND. This is only a foot trail, since in many places it is overgrown with brush, blocked by fallen trees, and gullied out. The Unknown Land is a region bounded roughly on the N. by Rapid Creek, on the W. by the Burlington R.R., on the S. by Spring Creek and the National Forest Boundary, and on the E. by US 85A.

There is no public land within this territory. It is all United States Forest Reserve and staked mining claims that have been proved up and patented.

This whole region is practically inaccessible except to hikers and horseback riders, and in many places it is hard for a horse to find footing. High mountains, deep canyons, and tall timber are the principal features. The region abounds in game, being the home of most of the blacktail deer, outside the Game Preserves, in the Hills. Sometimes elk may be found hiding in some dark gulch. There are no streams of any size; hence there is no fishing; but springs of pure sparkling water are found in all the gulches.

Little lumbering has been done except along the edges, as the rough nature of the country prevents the transportation of timber without expensive roads or railroads. The hiker or hunter who penetrates these hills and valleys to make his camp finds himself in woods and mountains much as they were in the days of '76.

In 1876-79, many prospectors located mining claims along the bars of Rapid Creek from Pactola westward. They found gold, but no very rich strikes were made, and they concluded that the "mother lode" must be somewhere in the hills to the S. and W., along the course of the stream. Some of the miners, more hardy than the rest, set out to prospect the hills, and penetrated into the wilderness seeking the source of the placer gold. They failed to find mines of any great value, although a number of quartz veins were discovered that yielded low grade ore. In the meantime the Homestake Mine was discovered at Lead, and most of the mining activity was transferred to that locality.

In 1879, however, O. F. Johnson located a mining claim in this territory and uncovered a vein of quartz 150 ft. wide and 3 m. long. Expecting to develop it, he succeeded in interesting a group of New York investors who gained control of the property, but never developed it. Ore from the vein assayed about $3 or $4 per ton, but various difficulties have so far prevented development.

About this time three brothers, named Scruton, built a cabin near the foot of the highest peak in this section which is still called Scruton Mountain. They had a mine somewhere in the vicinity and from time to time brought out gold, but they never told where the mine was located, nor did any one else ever discover it. They died without disclosing its location. It was this lost mine that gave the territory its name, The Unknown Land.

PACTOLA, 27.3 *m.* (4,461 alt.), one of the oldest settlements in Pennington Co., is a center of recreational activity. Soon after the discovery of gold in the creek beds, prospectors and miners began to flock into this pleasant valley until it became a populous, thriving community. Owing to its isolation in the heart of the Hills, there was little law enforcement and the valley became the hiding place for many who, for various reasons, did not wish their whereabouts known. The miners made and administered their own law, but the two things they would not tolerate were claim-jumping and horse-stealing.

At first the valley was called "O" Valley, because of its round shape. In 1876 General Crook with his United States Cavalry, on their way to fight the Indians, made his headquarters here and called it Camp Crook. The development of placer mines, together with the establishment of the first post office in Pennington Co., and a tri-weekly stage service, made things boom; so the populace decided that the camp should have a more appropriate name. A mass meeting was called, and a lawyer who had recently moved into the community was asked to make the nominating speech. Having had a number of drinks and feeling fanciful he recited the legend of Midas, whose touch turned everything to gold; and he proposed, in view of the gold being taken from the sands of Rapid Creek, that the place should be called Pactola, for the Lydian river Pactolus, whose golden sands were believed to be the source of the wealth of Croesus.

Since 1945 Pactola has become a popular stopping place for travelers, and headquarters for fishermen and hunters because of the improved accommodations.

At Pactola is a U.S. Forest Service Ranger Station and a public picnic grounds.

At 30.4 *m.* are visible (L) the BALD HILLS, so called because there are no trees growing upon them. They extend SE. to within a few miles of Sheridan Lake (*see below*).

At 33.5 *m.* the road leaves the Black Hills National Forest and enters the Harney National Forest Reserve.

SHERIDAN LAKE, 34 *m.*, which has existed only since the early 1940's, is one of the most popular recreation areas of the Black Hills. US 85A has been relocated along its W. bank, and along the shore of the 400-acre lake the Forest Service has provided camping areas, and permitted boating and fishing concessions. Construction of a dam across Spring Creek was started in 1938, by a Civilian Conservation Corps camp; the work was completed by other agencies with the approach of World War II. It bore the name Lake of the Pines until 1945, when it was named for the historic town of Sheridan which lies buried beneath 40 ft. of water.

SHERIDAN, started as a mining camp called Golden City when, in 1875, prospectors locating claims along Spring Creek found rich placer deposits of gold in the meadows. The bars of the creek proved unexpectedly rich. "If a man's claim yielded less then $20 per day in gold dust, he abandoned it and moved to a new location." Golden City was the usual type of mining camp of that day. Saloons, dance halls, and gambling places flourished, with all the accompanying excitement of a prosperous mining community. A general store, which carried miners' supplies, food, and clothing, did a thriving business.

In 1876 a feeling of civic pride began to manifest itself. The citizens felt that some kind of permanent social responsibility ought to take the place of the irresponsible recklessness and excitement of gold rush days. A meeting was called and it was decided to rename the place Sheridan. Pennington Co. had just been organized and the county seat was established here. The Federal Government then established the first Federal Court W. of the Missouri River, and a log courthouse was built.

Sheridan became an important station on the Deadwood-Denver stage line. It was a regular stopping place for General Crook and his troops on their patrols through the Black Hills and the NW. It seemed destined to become one of the leading cities of the Hills, and a permanent community. But in 1878 the county seat was moved to Rapid City. With the coming of the railroads, the stage line gradually lost its patronage and was discontinued. The productiveness of placer mines began to lessen. The troops were withdrawn from the Hills. So Sheridan, which depended on all these things for its prosperity, gradually became an almost deserted village.

US 85A parallels Spring Creek, noted for its trout pools. High cliffs of serrated slate rock and other unusual formations rise beside the road. In the open spaces are ranch buildings, with their corrals and ox-yoke gates.

At 38 m. is the junction with US 16A (see Tour 5, Section c); the two routes are united to Custer (see below).

MITCHELL LAKE, 40 m., is a widened version of Spring Creek; it is popular for roadside picnics and fishing parties.

At 41.5 m. is the REDER RANGER STATION and MAJOR LAKE, a small pond with a public picnic area.

HILL CITY, 42 m. (4,945 alt.), lies in a small valley completely surrounded by pine-clad mountains. Discovery of tin, gold, and copper brought Hill City's first settlers in 1876. The town shows little of the British influence of the 1880's when a group of Englishmen spent $5,000,000 here to mine and mill casserite, or tin, deposits. Today the board sidewalks and hitching posts along Main Street are used by cowhands, lumbermen, and a few prospectors, mixed with dudes from nearby lodges. A number of mines, principally tungsten, have reopened in this vicinity, including the Empire, Ceko, Eldorado, and Tungsten.

Ghosts of the Past

GHOST TOWN

MAIN STREET
IN ROCHFORD

CUSTER STATE
PARK MUSEUM

HAND-HEWN CABIN

GRIST MILL, MILBANK

NEEDLE'S EYE

GRAVE OF CALAMITY JANE

DINOSAUR
PARK,
RAPID CITY

At Hill City is the junction with the Deerfield-Mystic Road.

Right on this graded road into the "Limestone Country"—a rugged area fingered by fireguard roads but sparsely settled—is the NEWTON FORKS PICNIC GROUND, 3 m.
At 5 m. is TIGERVILLE, the relic of a mining town once having 500 inhabitants. Several old rock chimneys mark the site. It was named for the Bengal Tiger Mine here, which was closed in 1887, but was reopened in 1938.
The road forks here; L. to Deerfield and R. to Mystic.
(1). Left, through part of the burned over area caused by the McVey forest fire in 1939, is DEERFIELD, 13.5 m. This remote hamlet serves as headquarters for a few ranchers and for the fishermen and hunters who come into the region. Near here on Castle Creek is DEERFIELD DAM, built by the U.S. Reclamation Bureau as a flood control project in 1946. It is stocked with trout.
(2). Right from the Tigerville Junction is MYSTIC, 9 m. From 1906 to 1948, this crossroads community was the W. terminus of the Rapid City, Black Hills & Western R.R. and a favorite holiday headquarters. The McCahan Memorial Chapel is a lovely log-cabin church, the bell for which came from the railroad engine that served the hamlet for many years. When the railroad was sold for junk in 1949, the bell was sent to Mystic.

At 45 m. is the junction with the Needles Highway, State 87 (see Tour 14A); part of this route, which was US 85A until 1949, also may be taken to Custer (see below).
US 85A and US 16A branch R. along the Burlington R.R. tracks on a new road known as the Oreville Cutoff. While the new route misses Custer State Park, there are no sharp turns or steep grades.
At 52 m. (L) is the CRAZY HORSE SIOUX MEMORIAL (adm. fee), a 30-year sculpturing project undertaken in 1948, by Korczak Ziolkowski, a Boston sculptor, who once worked on the Mount Rushmore Memorial. Beyond his ranch-studio is towering Thunderhead Mountain, on which the figure of Crazy Horse, noted Sioux chieftain, is being fashioned astride a running stallion. The granite cap will provide a sculpture 400 ft. long. One of Ziolkowski's works is the 13-ft. marble statue of Noah Webster in West Hartford, Conn.
A beautifully executed model is exhibited at the studio.
Visitors are permitted to take part in the daily blasting operation to remove surplus rock from the figure.
At 53 m. is the junction with a Forest Service Road.

Right on this road, past the rotting cabins of BUGTOWN, an abandoned mining camp at 3.5 m., is a fork at 7 m.
(1) The N. fork, up Sourdough Gulch, leads to the summit of BEAR MOUNTAIN at 11.5 m. With an elevation of 7,172 ft., compared to Harney Peak's 7,242, Bear Mountain not only missed being the highest point east of the Rockies by a scant margin, but also is visited only by a handful of people each year. From the lookout tower on this densely forested peak is a generous view of the Limestone region, the Needles, and the surrounding valleys.
(2) The W. fork enters the rugged Limestone country, noted for its wild game. At 8.5 m. is the BULL SPRINGS HUNTING CAMP, a public lodge for deer and elk hunters. At 12.5 m. is SIGNAL HILL LOOKOUT (6,500 alt.), from which deer can be watched as they seek the salt licks toward dusk.

At 54 *m.*, in the Custer Cemetery, is the GRAVE OF HORATIO N. ROSS, who first discovered gold in the Black Hills, and who died a pauper (*see Custer*).

CUSTER, 56 *m.* (5,303 alt.) (*see Tour 5*), is at the junction with US 16.

At 56.4 *m.* (L) is a FELDSPAR MILL, where rock is ground finer than flour for use in making enamel, glass, and polishes.

At 58.4 *m.* is the GRAY ROCKS resort, at which mineral specimens and souvenirs are exhibited.

At 61.6 *m.* (L) is the STATE SANATORIUM (5,340 alt.). This institution is set back a short distance from the road in a grove of pines. It is in the Harney National Forest Reserve and its grounds comprise 171 acres. Founded in 1909 by Dr. Batti of Custer, for the treatment of tuberculosis, it was later taken over by the State.

Sanator, as the place is known, was officially opened in 1911 with facilities to accommodate 14 patients. By 1950, as the institution was enlarged, more than 3,600 patients had been cared for. Present capacity is about 200.

PRINGLE, 68 *m.* (4,879 alt.), was originally called Point of Rocks, because of outstanding rocks nearby. The first post office, in 1886, was called Rocks. In the autumn of 1890 the Burlington R.R. reached the town and the station was called Pringle in honor of the owners of the water rights.

Here is the Pringle Ranger Station.

At 74.5 *m.* is the boundary of WIND CAVE NATIONAL PARK. Just inside the park is a junction with State 87 (*see Tour 5B.*)

At 76 *m.* the road crosses a dam which impounds the waters of Cold Spring Creek. The resultant lake (R) is named in honor of the late Sen. Peter Norbeck, who did so much to conserve the beauties of the Black Hills. From this point the road proceeds over small hills, around wide curves, and through an open buffalo pasture where buffalo can be seen grazing.

At 78 *m.* (L) is the headquarters building of WIND CAVE NATIONAL PARK (*trips every hour from 7 a.m. to 7 p.m. during summer; once a day the remainder of the year, adm. fee*). It is a long rambling building, containing a combined souvenir room and lunch counter; across the open arcade, which divides the building, is the general office and waiting room. From the arcade a series of steps leads down the slopes of the canyon to the entrance of the cave.

Wind Cave Park, with its game sanctuary, its beautifully landscaped hillsides, its rustic-looking residences for the officers and rangers, its attractive administration building, and especially its subterranean cavern, has become, in spite of its modest size of 18½ sq. m., one of the more attractive of our national parks. It was officially made a national park January 9, 1903.

The question of the discoverer of Wind Cave is a controversial one, inasmuch as the event dates back to a period in the history of the

Black Hills region when few records were kept. But the credit is given to Tom Bingham, a pioneer, who, while hunting deer over the rolling hills in 1881, was attracted by a singular hissing sound issuing from some undergrowth and, upon investigation, he found a small hole in the rocks. This hole, not more than 10 inches in diameter, is the only natural opening to the cave so far discovered. It is just a few steps behind the present cave entrance building.

Another story is that a cowboy, riding the range on a calm day, suddenly had his hat blown off, and on investigating found the natural opening.

The present cavern entrance leads into corridors and galleries, appropriately named for their similarity to such subjects as the Bridal Chamber, Post Office, Opera Hall, Queen's Drawing Room, Monte Cristo Palace, and Garden of Eden. These natural hallways and chambers show a variety of crystal formations, called boxwork or frost work, which is composed of delicately colored crystal fins arranged in honeycomb pattern—tiny white crystals on a pink background, hanging in clusters from ceilings and ledges. The formations here differ from those in most caverns, stalactites and stalagmites being almost nonexistent. This peculiar boxwork formation is said to have been caused by rain water seeping down from the surface through decaying vegetation and absorbing carbon dioxide. This carbon-dioxide-bearing water first took some of the limestone into solution, then deposited it in cracks or crevices below and, upon evaporation, formed the boxlike fins. Later the more soluble limestone between the fins of the boxwork was dissolved and carried away, leaving the boxwork as it is seen today.

Wind Cave is a limestone cavern, and the limestone layer in which the cave is formed is known as the Pahasapa formation, a local variety of Mississippian, which was deposited in a great inland sea perhaps 300 million years ago. Following the deposit of this limestone, there occurred several periods of elevation and subsidence. During these periods of submergence the Pahasapa limestone was overlaid several hundred feet by other sediment. The final upthrust of the land occurred about 60 million years ago, and the beginning of Wind Cave probably dated from that time.

The principal routes in the cave are lighted by indirect illumination, producing a soft glow which sets off the different formations to advantage. A large elevator lowers visitors to the floor of the cave. The temperature of the cave is 47 degrees and does not vary with the different seasons.

All trips through the cave are under the guidance of competent park rangers. The shorter route through the cave requires approximately two hours and the longer one about three hours.

The game preserve, formerly under the U.S. Biological Survey, is now under the supervision of the National Park Service. Big game in this park is estimated as follows: 225 buffalo, 70 elk, 60 deer, and

30 antelope. Since June 1936 these animals have been free to roam at large throughout the park instead of being confined to certain areas, and each seeks his own natural habitat.

No hotels or tourist cabins are located in the park; however, there is a public camp ground, with free wood and water, near headquarters.

A 81 *m.* is the southern entrance to Wind Cave Park.

At 81.5 *m.* is GOBBLER'S KNOB, (4,233 alt.), and just ahead is BUFFALO GAP, through which buffaloes formerly came in droves.

At 83 *m.* is the junction with State 79, and the route continues on this highway to the Nebraska Line.

HOT SPRINGS, 88 *m.* (3,433 alt.) (*see Tour 7*), is at the junction with US 18.

US 85A is united with US 18 between Hot Springs and Mule Creek Junction in Wyoming where it rejoins US 85 (*see Tour 7*).

Section b. Hot Springs—Nebraska Line, 41.2 m. State 79.

Southeast of Hot Springs, State 79 and US 18 are united for 15 m. (*see Tour 7*). At this point State 79 continues S. through a gently rolling country.

At 16.5 *m.* the road crosses Horse Head Creek, and at 27.2 *m.* Lonewell Creek.

OELRICHS, 28.3 *m.,* was named for a prominent rancher living nearby.

At 33.9 *m.* the road again crosses Horse Head Creek.

At 41.2 *m.* State 79 crosses the Nebraska Line 1 m. N. of Wayside, Nebr. (*see Nebr. Tour 6*).

Tour 14A

Junction with US 85A—Sylvan Lake—Needles—Junction with US 16. Needles Highway, State 87.
Junction with US 85A—Junction with US 16—20 m.
Roadbed hard-surfaced. This is a road with sharp curves and steep grades.
Excellent accommodations at Sylvan Lake.

ALTHOUGH this route through Custer State Park is short, it presents unusual views of the Black Hills. From either direction there is a climb of several miles to the crest facing Harney Peak, highest point in the U.S. east of the Rocky Mountains. There are switchbacks and tunnels, with ever-changing vistas of granite spires, dense forests, peaceful lakes, and tumbling creeks.

The Needles formation is unique in the State. Composed of the original granite core of the Hills, which thrust up from somewhere in the interior of the earth and pushed aside all sedimentary formations above (*see GEOLOGY*), it has been eroded by the action of countless centuries of wind and weather. According to Gutzon Borg-

lum, the granite face of Rushmore will weather less than an inch in
40,000 years. It has taken ages to weather away the granite that left
only graceful spires where solid rock must once have been. Countless centuries went into the making of the Needle's Eye in which a
thousand pine trees could be threaded with room to spare.

While this scenic highway was being built, the late Sen. Peter
Norbeck tramped on foot over every mile of this rough country and
wherever he found a particularly striking view, he would say to the
engineers, "Run the road here." They would assure him that it was
impossible, to which he would reply, "Put it there anyway." And they
did. This man did more than any other to make the natural beauties
of the Black Hills region available and accessible to all.

The Needles Highway (State 87) branches SE. from US 85A and
US 16A 3 m. S. of Hill City (*see Tour 14*).

At 1.6 m. is the boundary of the CUSTER STATE PARK
FEDERAL GAME SANCTUARY (*see The BLACK HILLS*).

At 2.5 *m.* is the junction with the Mount Rushmore Memorial
Highway (*see Tour 5A*).

As the highway ascends Sunday Gulch and the slope of St. Elmo
Peak, there are excellent views of the granite capped Harney Range
(L). The road makes a series of FOUR SWITCHBACKS, or hairpin
turns, so that five sections of the road lie one above the other.

At 5.6 *m.* is a TUNNEL cut through solid granite. As the highway reaches the crest, the elevation is about 6,300 ft.

The NEW SYLVAN LAKE HOTEL, 6 *m.* (L), overlooks a
placid mountain lake and faces Harney Peak. The hotel was built
by the Custer State Park Board and Public Works Administration
in 1936–37, replacing a wooden structure which formerly stood on
the lake shore and was destroyed by fire in 1936. The new hotel is
considered an excellent example of modern park-hotel architecture.
The architect was Harold Spitznagel of Sioux Falls. The hotel appears a continuation of the timbered granite-crested cliff on which it
stands. Slabs of rough, moss-covered pegmatite, above which is siding
of native pine, make up the exterior of the rambling building. A wide
flagstone terrace overlooks Sylvan Lake and the Harney Peak range
to the E., and extends around the north wall of the building. Brown,
with harmonizing blue and coral, predominate in the color scheme of
the furnishings. The diamond motif is used extensively in design, as
shown in huge columns that support the porte cochere. The fireplace
in the dining room is faced with Hot Springs calico sandstone. On
the walls of the dining room above the red cedar wainscoting are
Indian murals, painted by Erika Lohmann, New York artist. In the
lounge, only wooden pegs have been employed in the construction
of knotty pine walls and exposed beams and rafters. Into the grayish-
tan monks cloth draperies have been woven Indian designs, by
women of the Flandreau Indian school. The eight walls of the octag-
onal shaped lobby are of panelled California redwood, and Indian
thunder birds are molded in relief against the ceiling.

Modern housekeeping cabins are scattered among the tall Ponderosa pines. Rates of the State-owned hotel and cabins are moderate. At 6.2 *m.* is the junction with Custer Cutoff.

Right on this graveled road, formerly US 85A, is a seven-mile descent to Custer and US 16 (*see Tour 5*).

The Needles Highway swings down a ravine to the shore of SLYVAN LAKE, 6.4 *m.* No one viewing this beautiful body of water would imagine that it was anything but a work of nature. It is only after going through a natural chasm in the rock and emerging below the lake that the inconspicuous wall holding back the waters of a mountain brook is seen. But there is no surface indication to mar the beauty of this little lake, reflecting in its quiet mirror the rock walls that rise abruptly from its depths and those other rocks that jut from its placid surface to form picturesque islets. Overlooking it is the new State-owned hotel, seeming like a continuation of the rock itself. At a broad wharf are boats in which one may idle away a summer's afternoon, fishing from the rocky islands or from the boat itself.

Sylvan Lake was created in 1891–92, by C. C. Crary and the Reder Brothers, the latter operating a sawmill here. They cut the lumber for the original hotel which stood along the shore near the dam.

At the S. end of the lake is a campground with a store, tables, and fireplaces. At 0.2 *m.* is a stable where burros for the climb to HARNEY PEAK (7,242 alt.) may be obtained. At 0.5 *m.* the road comes to an end and cars must be parked. From this point a footpath leads three m. through the woods on a gradual upward slope to the base of Harney Peak. It is a beautiful, winding, shaded path, sometimes buried deep in the woods, sometimes skirting the edge of a precipice with views of distant peaks and of pine-covered slopes and the granite spires of the Needles thrusting upward through the foliage. Halfway to the peak there is a wayside spring. The remainder of the path is a little steeper; the final pitches lead out of the trees to the foot of a ladder in a granite crevice, at the top of which a final short scramble over the rocks leads to the lookout station on the bare granite crag that forms Harney's summit. And here is unfolded a view that repays any weariness the climb may have occasioned.

Far down, over the trail just traveled, are ridge after ridge with wooded hollows between, with stretches of granite cliff-face and jagged granite peaks. To the E., three m. away, a granite wall rises abruptly. It is on the other face of this wall that the great stone carving of Rushmore has taken form. Beyond, the ridges become ever lower until they flatten out into the plain, which in turn reaches out to the blue horizon line. To the S. is Mt. Coolidge with its tower, and to the N. the peaks of Terry and Custer. All about is what seems to be primeval wilderness.

Harney Peak is not only the highest point in the Black Hills and South Dakota, but it is the highest point in the United States east of the Rocky Mountains. It was named for an army officer, General Harney, who in 1857 led a small force of men from Laramie to Ft. Pierre, passing through this territory. In the glass-walled lookout station on Harney's summit sits a fire guard during most of the summer season. With a swivel telescope swinging over a map, he can instantly and accurately locate the first wisp of smoke that curls upward from a fire. A telephone keeps him in constant communication with the ranger stations throughout the Hills. Of the 10,000 people who climb the peak annually, almost every one asks the fire guard, "Don't you get awfully lonesome up here, all by yourself?"

At 7.5 *m.* (R) the road passes the TRAFFIC COP, a huge boulder that Nature has carved in the likeness of a hard-boiled Irish policeman.

At 7.6 *m.* the Needles Highway widens for a parking space. To the R. is that curious natural formation, the Needle's Eye, a huge upright fissure in a granite cliff, closed at the top as well as bottom. To the L. the road pierces a jutting promontory of granite and comes out upon one of the best views to be had in the Needles. Pinnacles and spires, strange and uncanny, reach into the blue of the sky hundreds of feet above their forested base, and multitudes of fanciful shapes lend to the whole a marvelous harmony. They are overtowered by massive Mt. Harney on the N., but their craggy heights, silhouetted against the sky, show across long distances from the E. and SE., even from far out on the prairie 50 *m.* away. This maze of sculptured granite, with its magic shapes of needles, organ pipes, cathedral spires, and castellated rocks, is impressive when viewed from Mt. Harney; but the peculiar individuality and sheer splendor of each formation appear to best advantage when viewed from the midst of the peaks; precipice and height alternate as granite formations spring with startling suddenness from the clinging forest of spruce and pine.

A TUNNEL, at 7.6 *m.*, is a popular photographic subject because of the trees that seem to grow out of the solid granite.

At 7.8 *m.* is another parking place where there is a wide view to the S., with Custer and Mt. Coolidge in the distance.

At 8.3 *m.* is a view to the N. of close-set pinnacles like organ pipes.

At 8.5 *m.* are two hairpin turns, with Skyscraper Rock just below (R).

As the road drops to lower levels, there are more birch and aspen trees. BALANCED ROCK (L) teeters at 11.5 *m.*, and at 12.6 *m.* is another TUNNEL. In Iron Creek, which races beside the highway, are a series of beaver dams.

At 14.2 *m.* is the junction with the Remington Road.

Left on this road is CAMP REMINGTON, 1 *m.*, a summer retreat maintained by the Episcopal Church in South Dakota.

At 17.1 *m.* is the junction with the Mills Cut-Off Road.

Left on this road is CENTER LAKE, 1 *m.*, an uncommercialized little lake considered by many people to be the most beautiful in the Hills. Trout spawning beds were built under supervision of the National Park Service before the waters were backed up by the dam.

At 20 *m.* is the junction with US 16, 8 *m.* E. of Custer (*see Tour 5*).

Cities and Towns

(Population of 1,000 or more, 1950 Federal Census)

Aberdeen	20,976	Lemmon	2,756
Arlington	1,090	Lennox	1,219
Belle Fourche	3,517	Madison	5,142
Beresford	1,678	Milbank	2,981
Britton	1,404	Miller	1,902
Brookings	7,730	Mitchell	12,062
Canton	2,532	Mobridge	3,747
Centerville	1,051	Parker	1,145
Chamberlain	1,912	Parkston	1,358
Clark	1,471	Pierre	5,690
Clear Lake	1,106	Platte	1,070
Custer	2,019	Rapid City	25,179
Deadwood	3,270	Redfield	2,642
Dell Rapids	1,650	Salem	1,107
De Smet	1,184	Scotland	1,188
Edgemont	1,151	Sisseton	2,873
Elk Point	1,366	Sioux Falls	52,161
Eureka	1,579	S. Sioux Falls	1,585
Flandreau	2,197	Spearfish	2,750
Gettysburg	1,550	Sturgis	3,461
Gregory	1,376	Tyndall	1,289
Groton	1,072	Vermillion	5,328
Highmore	1,158	Wagner	1,518
Hot Springs	4,980	Watertown	12,662
Howard	1,246	Webster	2,506
Huron	12,713	Wessington Springs	1,450
Ipswich	1,046	Winner	3,239
Lake Andes	1,844	Woonsocket	1,041
Lead	6,419	Yankton	7,704

Bibliography

SOUTH DAKOTA TODAY

Atherton, Loren G. and Atherton, Nora M. *South Dakota Geography*. Sioux Falls, Will A. Beach, 1936. 150 p. il.
Faris, John Thompson. *Roaming the Rockies*. New York, Farrar & Rinehart, 1930. 333 p. il.
Nelson, Bruce. *Land of the Dakotahs*. Minneapolis, University of Minnesota Press, 1946. 343 p.
Peterson, Purl D. *Through the Black Hills and Bad Lands of South Dakota*. Pierre, Olander, 1929. 189 p. il.
Reeves, George S. *A Man from South Dakota*. New York, E. P. Dutton & Co., 1950. 256 p.
Smith, H. Allen. *We Went Thataway*. New York, Doubleday & Co., 1949. 256 p.
South Dakota. State Planning Board. *State Finance in South Dakota*. Brookings, 1937. 65 p.
South Dakota. State Planning Board. *The People of South Dakota, A Preliminary Study of Population*. Brookings, 1936. 46 p.
South Dakota State School of Mines. *Black Hills Engineer, Badlands Number*. Rapid City, South Dakota State School of Mines, 1926. 65 p. il.
Visher, S. S. *Geography of South Dakota*. Vermillion, University of South Dakota, 1918. 189 p. il.
Warren, Lieut. G. K. *Preliminary Report of Exploration in Nebraska and Dakota in the Years 1855–56–57*. Washington, Government Printing Office, 1875. 125 p. maps. (U.S. Army. Topographical Engineers)
White, John M. *The Newer Northwest*. St. Louis, Self-Culture Publishing Co., 1894. 205 p. il.

NATURAL SETTING

a. Mineral

O'Harra, Cleophas C. and Connolly, Joseph P. *Mineral Wealth of the Black Hills*. Rapid City, South Dakota State School of Mines, 1929. 482 p. il.
O'Harra, Cleophas C. *Mineral Resources of South Dakota*. Rapid City, South Dakota State School of Mines. 88 p. il.

O'Harra, Cleophas C. *The White River Badlands*. Rapid City, South
Dakota State School of Mines, 1920. 277 p. il.
South Dakota. State Planning Board. *Portland Cement, Gypsum,
and Lime Industries in South Dakota*. Brookings, 1936. 71 p.
South Dakota. State Planning Board. *Tin Deposits in South Dakota*.
Brookings, 1936. 35 p.
South Dakota State Planning Board. *Tungsten Mining in South
Dakota*. Brookings, 1936. 32 p.

b. Water

South Dakota. State Planning Board. *Artesian Well Flow in South
Dakota*. Brookings, 1937. 138 p.
South Dakota. State Planning Board. *Dams in South Dakota*. Brook-
ings, 1937 179 p.
South Dakota. State Planning Board. *Water Resources of South
Dakota*. 14 bulletins. Brookings, 1937.

c. Flora and Fauna

Atherton, Loren G. and Atherton, Nora M. *Dakota Birds*. Pierre,
Olander, 1926. 238 p. il.
Audubon, Maria R. *Audubon and His Journals*. New York, Scrib-
ner, 1897. 2 vols. il.
Churchill, Edward and Over, W. H. *Fishes of South Dakota*. Pierre,
South Dakota Game and Fish Commission, 1935. 87 p. il.
Hornaday, William T. *The American Natural History*. New York,
Scribner, 1904.
Johnson, Floyd A. *4-H Club Guide and Wild Life Conservation*.
Pierre, South Dakota Game and Fish Commission, 1935. 52 p. il.
Over, William H. *Amphibians and Reptiles of South Dakota*. Ver-
million, University of South Dakota, 1932. 51 p. il.
Over, William H. and Thomas, Craig. *Birds of South Dakota*. Ver-
million, University of South Dakota, 1921. 142 p. il.
Over, William H. *Flora of South Dakota, An Illustrated Checklist
of Flowering Plants, Shrubs and Trees of South Dakota*. Ver-
million, University of South Dakota, 1932. 161 p. il.
South Dakota State School of Mines. *Black Hills Engineer, Black
Hills Plants. Description of Black Hills Flora*. Rapid City, South
Dakota State School of Mines, May 1931. 123 p. il.
Terrell, Claude B. *Wild Fowl and Fish Attractions*. Pierre, South
Dakota Game and Fish Commission, 1932. 72 p. il.

INDIANS AND INDIAN LIFE

Barton, Winifred (Williamson). *John P. Williamson*. New York,
Revell, 1919. 269 p. il.
Byrne, Patrick Edward. *Soldiers of the Plains*. New York, Minton,
Balch, 1926. 260 p.
Catlin, George. *The North American Indians*. Philadelphia, Leary,
1913. 2 vols. il.

DeLand, Charles Edmund. *The Aborigines of South Dakota.* S. Dak. Historical Collections, Vol. III, 267–586; Vol. IV, 275–730.

DeLand, Charles Edmund. *The Sioux Wars.* S. Dak. Historical Collections, Vol. XV, 9–730; Vol. XVI, 175–552.

Drift, Ivan (Iktomi Licala). *America Needs Indians.* Denver, Bradford-Robinson, 1937. 424 p. il. A young Indian, educated by the white man, attempts to solve the "Indian Problem."

Duratschek, Sister Mary Claudia. *Crusading Along Sioux Trails.* Yankton, S. D., Benedictine Convent of the Sacred Heart, 1947. 316 p.

Eastman, Charles Alexander. *From the Deep Woods to Civilization.* Boston, Little, Brown, 1916. 206 p. il.

Eastman, Charles Alexander. *Indian Boyhood.* New York, McClure, 1920. 289 p. il.

Eastman, Charles Alexander. *Red Hunters and the Animal People.* New York, Harper, 1904. 249 p. front.

Eastman, Charles Alexander. *Wigwam Evenings.* Animal Tales. Boston, Little, Brown, 1930. 250 p. il.

Ellis, Edward S. *Indian Wars of the United States.* Chicago, Kenyon, 1902. 484 p. il.

Gessner, Robert. *Broken Arrow.* New York, Farrar & Rinehart, 1933. 280 p.

Gessner, Robert. *Massacre, A Survey of Today's American Indian.* New York, Cape and Smith, 1931. 418 p. il.

Gilmore, Melvin Randolph. *Prairie Smoke.* New York, Columbia University Press, 1919. 80 p. front.

Hans, Fred M. *The Great Sioux Nation.* Chicago, Donohue, 1907. 575 p. il.

Holley, F. C. *Once Their Home: or, Our Legacy from the Dakotahs.* Historical, biographical and incidental material. Chicago, Donohue, 1890. 423 p. il.

Hyde, George E. *Red Cloud's Folk.* Norman, University of Oklahoma Press, 1937. 331 p. front.

Lange, Dietrich. *The Threat of Sitting Bull.* Boston, Lothrop, 1920. 370 p. front.

Macgregor, Gordon. *Warriors without Weapons.* A study of the Society and Personality Development of the Pine Ridge Sioux. Chicago, University of Chicago Press. 228 p. illus.

McCreight, M. I. *Firewater and Forked Tongues.* Pasadena, Cal., Trail's End Pub. Co., 1947. 170 p.

McGillicuddy, Julia B. *McGillicuddy, Agent.* Palo Alto, Cal., Stanford University Press, 1941.

McLaughlin, James. *My Friend the Indian.* Boston, Houghton Mifflin, 1926. 417 p. il.

Neihardt, John G. *Black Elk Speaks, Being the Life Story of an Holy Man of the Ogalala Sioux.* New York, Morrow, 1932. 280 p. il.

Olden, Sarah Emilia. *The People of Tipi Sapa (The Dakotas).* Milwaukee, Morehouse, 1918. 158 p. il.

Riggs, Stephen Return. *Mary and I. Forty Years with the Sioux.* Chicago, W. G. Holmes, 1880. 388 p. il.

Sandoz, Mari. *Crazy Horse, the Strange Man of the Oglalas.* New York, Alfred A. Knopf, 1942. 428 p.

Schultz, James Willard. *Bird Woman (Sacajawea), The Guide of Lewis and Clark.* Boston, Houghton Mifflin, 1918. 235 p. il.

Shetrone, Henry Clyde. *The Mound Builders.* New York, Appleton, 1930. 508 p. il.

South Dakota. State Planning Board. *Indians of South Dakota.* Brookings, 1937. 97 p.

South Dakota Writers' Project (Montana L. Reese, editor). *Legends of the Mighty Sioux.* Chicago, Albert Whitman & Co., 1941. 158 p.

Vestal, Stanley. *New Sources of Indian History, 1850–91.* Norman, University of Oklahoma Press, 1934. 351 p. il.

Vestal, Stanley. *Sitting Bull, Champion of the Sioux.* Boston, Houghton Mifflin, 1932. 350 p. front.

Vestal, Stanley. *Warpath.* Boston, Houghton Mifflin, 1934. 291 p. il.

Will, George F. *Archaeology of the Missouri Valley.* New York, American Museum Press, 1924. 59 p. (Anthropological Papers of the American Museum of Natural History, Vol. 22, Part 6.)

Wellman, Paul I. *Death on the Prairie. The Thirty Years' Struggle for the Western Plains.* New York, Macmillan, 1934. 298 p. il.

Zitkala-sa. *Old Indian Legends.* New York, Ginn, 1901. 165 p. il.

HISTORY

a. General

Andreas, A. T. *Andreas' Historical Atlas of Dakota.* Chicago, Donnelley, 1884. 246 p. il.

Armstrong, M. K. *Early Empire Builders of the Great West.* St. Paul, Porter, 1901. 446 p. il.

Casey, Robert J. and Douglas, W. A. S. *Pioneer Railroad,* the story of the Chicago and Northwestern System. New York, McGraw-Hill, 1948. 334 p.

Driscoll, R. E. *Seventy Years of Banking.* Rapid City, (Private) 1948. 85 p.

Dunham, N. J. *History of Mitchell Corn Palace.* Mitchell, Mitchell Gazette, 1914. 48 p. il.

Fite, Gilbert Courtland. *Peter Norbeck: Prairie Statesman.* Columbia, Mo., University of Missouri, 1948. 208 p.

Gering, John J. *After Fifty Years.* Marion, Pine Hill Printery, 1924. 60 p. il.

Hebert, Frank. *Forty Years Prospecting in the Black Hills of South Dakota.* Rapid City, Rapid City Daily Journal, 1921. 199 p. il.

Humphrey, Seth K. *Following the Prairie Frontier.* Minneapolis, University Press, 1931. 265 p. front.

Hunkins, Ralph V. and Lindsey, John. *South Dakota; Its Past, Present, and Future.* A school history. New York, Macmillan, 1932. 312 p. il.

Hunt, Frazier. *Custer; the Last of the Cavaliers.* New York, Cosmopolitan, 1928. 209 p. il.

Lowe, Barrett. *Heroes and Hero Tales of South Dakota.* Minneapolis, Hale, 1931. 196 p. il.

Lowe, Barrett. *Twenty Million Acres; The Story of America's First Conservationist, William Henry Harrison Beadle.* Mitchell, Educator Supply Co., 1937. 465 p. il.

Putney, E. F. *In the South Dakota Country.* Mitchell, Educator Supply Co., 1922. 2 vols. il.

Ransom, Frank L. *The Sunshine State.* Mitchell, Educator Supply Co., 1922. 159 p. il.

Robinson, Doane, *Brief History of South Dakota.* A school history. New York, American Book Co., 1926. 232 p. il.

Robinson, Doane. *History of South Dakota.* Chicago, Bowen, 1904. 2 vols. il.

Robinson, Doane. *History of South Dakota.* Chicago, American Historical Society, Inc., 1930. 3 vols. il.

Rosen, Peter. *Pa-ha-sa-pa,* or *The Black Hills of South Dakota.* St. Louis, Nixon, 1895. 645 p. il.

Schell, Herbert S. *South Dakota: Its Beginnings and Growth.* New York, American Book, 1942. 359 p.

Simmons, Walter. *Joe Foss Flying Marine.* New York, E. P. Dutton & Co., 1943. 160 p.

Smith, Charles A. *Minnehaha County History.* Mitchell, Educator Supply Co., 1949. 501 p.

South Dakota. Department of History. *South Dakota Historical Collections, compiled by the State Historical Society.* Historical documents, and articles pertaining to South Dakota history. Vol. 1–18. A valuable series; a volume is issued every two years.

South Dakota Historical Society. *South Dakota Historical Review.* A quarterly magazine. Oct., 1935.

South Dakota State School of Mines. *Black Hills Engineer, Semi-Centennial Number.* Rapid City, South Dakota State School of Mines, 1924. 82 p. il.

Sutley, Zack T. *Last Frontier.* New York, Macmillan, 1930. 350 p.

Sutton, Ernest V. *A Life Worth Living.* Pasadena, Cal., Trail's End Pub. Co., 1948. 350 p.

Taber, Clarence Wilbur. *Breaking Sod on the Prairie.* Yonkers-on-Hudson, World Book Company, 1924. 292 p. il.

Tallent, Annie D. *The Black Hills, The Last Hunting Ground of the Dakotahs.* St. Louis, Nixon, 1899. 713 p. il.

Van de Water, Frederic F. *Glory-Hunter; a Life of General Custer.* Indianapolis, Bobbs-Merrill, 1934. 394 p. il.

Young, Gertrude Stickney. *South Dakota, an Appreciation.* Brookings (Private), 1944. 127 p.

b. Early Settlement

Aikman, Duncan. *Calamity Jane and the Other Lady Wildcats.* New York, Holt, 1927. 347 p. il.

388   SOUTH DAKOTA

Aken, David. *Pioneers of the Black Hills, or Gordon's Stockade Party of 1874.* 151 p. il.

Bennett, Estelline. *Old Deadwood Days.* New York, Scribner, 1928. 300 p. il.

Brown, Jesse and Willard, A.M. *The Black Hills Trails.* A history of the Black Hills region. Rapid City, Rapid City Journal, 1924. 572 p. il.

Chittenden, Capt. Hiram Martin. *History of the American Fur Trade of the Far West.* New York, Press of the Pioneers, 1935. 2 vols.

Chittenden, Capt. Hiram Martin. *History of Early Steamboat Navigation on the Missouri River.* New York, Francis P. Harper, 1903. 2 vols.

Connelly, William Elsey. *Wild Bill and His Era.* A standard work dealing with the life and times of James Butler "Wild Bill" Hickok. New York, Press of the Pioneers, 1933. 229 p. il.

Coursey, O. W. *A Complete Biographical Sketch of General William Henry Harrison Beadle.* Mitchell, Educator Supply Co., 1916. 99 p. il.

Coursey, O. W. *Biography of Senator Alfred Beard Kittredge, His Complete Life Work.* Mitchell, Educator Supply Co., 1915. 224 p. il.

Coursey, O. W. (compiler and editor). *The First Woman in the Black Hills. As Told by Herself, Mrs. Annie D. Tallent.* Mitchell, Educator Supply Co., 1923. 181 p. front.

Coursey, O. W. *Wild Bill (James Butler Hickok).* Mitchell, Educator Supply Co., 1924. 80 p. il.

Custer, Mrs. Elizabeth Bacon. *"Boots and Saddles"; or, Life in Dakota with General Custer.* New York, Harper, 1885. 312 p. il.

Dye, Eva Emery. *The Conquest. The True Story of Lewis and Clark.* Chicago, McClurg, 1903. 443 p. front.

Finerty, John F. *War-Path and Bivouac, or the Conquest of the Sioux.* Chicago, Donohue, 1890. 460 p. il.

Hanson, Joseph Mills. *Conquest of the Missouri, Being the Story of the Life and Exploits of Captain Grant Marsh.* Chicago, McClurg, 1909. 458 p. il.

Irving, Washington. *Astoria.* New York, Putnam, 1902. 519 p. il.

King, Capt. Charles. *Campaigning with Crook; and Stories of Army Life.* New York, Harper, 1890. 295 p. il.

Kingsbury, G. W. *History of Dakota Territory.* Chicago, Clarke Publishing Co., 1915. 5 vols. il.

Rapid City Journal. *Holiday Greeting from Rapid City.* Rapid City, Rapid City Journal, 1915. 148 p. il.

Reese, John B *Some Pioneers and Pilgrims on the Prairies of Dakota, or From the Ox Team to the Aeroplane.* Mitchell, Author, 1920. 94 p. il.

Rhoads, William. *Recollections of Dakota Territory.* Pierre, State Publishing Co., 1931. 52 p.

Stokes, George W. *Deadwood Gold.* History of early gold mining in the northern Black Hills. Yonkers-on-Hudson, World Book Co., 1926. 163 p. il.

Torrey, E. C. *Early Days in Dakota*. Minneapolis, Farnham Printing and Stationery Co., 1925.

Vestal, Stanley. *Mountain Men*. Boston, Houghton Mifflin, 1937. 296 p. il.

Waldo, Edna LaMoore. *Dakota, Scenes from Pioneer Days in the Dakotas*. Caldwell, Ida, Caxton Printers, 1936. 459 p.

Wilstach, Frank J. *Wild Bill Hickok; the Prince of Pistoleers*. Garden City, Doubleday, 1928. 304 p. il.

c. Statehood and Government

Atherton, Loren G. *The Government of South Dakota, State and Local*. Pierre, Olander, 1927. 328 p.

Johnson, Willis E. *South Dakota, A Republic of Friends*. Mitchell, Educator Supply Co., 1923. 334 p. il.

Johnson, Willis E. *The State and Nation*. Mitchell, Educator Supply Co., 1922. 273 p. il.

Smith, G. M. and Young, C. M. *History and Government of South Dakota*. New York, American Book Co., 1913. 339 p.

AGRICULTURE

Byers, Horace G. *Selenium Occurrence in Certain Soils in the United States with a Discussion of Related Topics*. U.S. Dept. of Agriculture. Technical Bulletin No. 482. August, 1935.

Cheever, Lawrence Oakley. *The House of Morrell*. Cedar Rapids, Ia., The Torch Press, 1948. 283 p.

Crop and Livestock Reporting Service. *South Dakota Agriculture, 1949*. 1950. 40 p.

South Dakota. State Planning Board. *Agricultural Resources: a Preliminary Report*. Brookings, 1935–1936.

South Dakota. State Planning Board. *Land Ownership in South Dakota*. Brookings, 1937. 176 p.

South Dakota. State Planning Board. *Noxious Weeds in South Dakota*. Brookings, 1937. 38 p.

South Dakota. State Planning Board. *Selenium Problems in South Dakota*. Brookings, 1937. 30 p.

TRANSPORTATION

South Dakota. State Planning Board. *Transportation in South Dakota*. Brookings, 1937. 2 vols.

RACIAL ELEMENTS AND FOLKLORE

Shephard, Esther, *Paul Bunyan*. Collection of Paul Bunyan folk tales. New York, Harcourt, 1924.

EDUCATION AND RELIGION

Coursey, O. W. *A History of Dakota Wesleyan University for Fifty*

Years (1885–1935). Mitchell, Dakota Wesleyan University, 1935. il.
Durand, George Harrison. *Joseph Ward of Dakota*. A biography. Boston, Pilgrim Press, 1913. 252 p. il.
Howe, M.A. De Wolfe. *Life and Labors of Bishop Hare, Apostle to the Sioux*. New York, Sturgis & Walton, 1911. 417 p. il.
Kraushaar, R. W. and others. *Studies in South Dakota Education*. South Dakota Historical Collections, Vol. XVIII, 638 p. il.
McMurtry, William John. *Yankton College, A Historical Sketch*. Yankton, 1907. 160 p.
Powers, W. H. *History of South Dakota State College*. Brookings, South Dakota State College, 1931. 146 p. il.
South Dakota. State Planning Board. *Elementary and Secondary Education in South Dakota*. Brookings, 1937. 165 p.
Stewart, Edgar I. *Yankton College, The Second Twenty-five Years*. Yankton, 1932. 220 p.

LITERATURE

Boyles, Kate and Virgil D. *Langford of the Three Bars*. Chicago, McClurg, 1907. 278 p. il.
Boyles, Kate and Virgil D. *The Homesteaders*. Chicago, McClurg, 1909. 346 p. il.
Briggs, William Harlowe. *Dakota in the Morning*. New York, Farrar & Rinehart, 1942. 277 p.
Burleigh, B. W. and Wenzlaff, G. G. *A Book of Dakota Rhymes*. Yankton, Yankton Printing Co., 1907. 168 p.
Carr, Robert V. *Black Hills Ballads*. Denver, Reed Publishing Co., 1902. 175 p. front.
Castle, Marian. *Deborah*. New York, William Morrow & Co., 1946. 372 p.
Clark, Anna Morris. *Sylvia of the Hills*. Custer, Chronicle Shop, 1936. 140 p. il.
Clark, Badger. *Skylines and Wood Smoke*. Custer, Chronicle Shop, 1935. 73 p.
Clark, Badger. *Spike*. Boston, Badger, 1925. 215 p. il.
Clark, Badger. *Sun and Saddle Leather including "Grass Grown Trails" and new Poems*. Boston, Richard G. Badger, 1922. 221 p. il.
Coursey, O. W. *Literature of South Dakota*. Mitchell, Educator Supply Co., 1916. 201 p. il.
Dahl, Borghild. *Karen*. New York, Random House, 1947. 313 p.
Downing, J. Hyatt. *A Prayer for Tomorrow*. New York, G. P. Putnam's Sons, 1938. 342 p.
Downing, J. Hyatt. *The Harvest Is Late*. New York, William Morrow & Co., 1944. 304 p.
Fargo, Lucile F. *Prairie Girl*. New York, Dodd, Mead, 1937.
Federal Writers' Project. *Hamlin Garland Memorial: A Biography*. Mitchell, South Dakota Writers' League, 1939. 32 p.

Federal Writers' Project. *Hamlin Garland, Memorial Dedication.* Pierre, Federal Writers' Project, 1936. 12 p.

Federal Writers' Project. *MSS (Manuscripts).* Pierre and Custer, South Dakota Writers' League, 1936–37. 8 issues. il.

Feikema, Feike. *The Golden Bowl.* St. Paul, Webb Pub. Co., 1944. 226 p.

Feikema, Feike. *This Is the Year.* New York, Doubleday, 1947. 623 p.

Feikema, Feike. *The Chokecherry Tree.* New York, Doubleday, 1948. 270 p.

Garland, Hamlin. *A Daughter of the Middle Border.* New York, Macmillan, 1921. 405 p.

Garland, Hamlin. *Afternoon Neighbors. Further Excerpts from a Literary Log.* New York, Macmillan, 1934. 589 p. front.

Garland, Hamlin. *Back-trailers from the Middle Border.* New York, Macmillan, 1928. 379 p. il.

Garland, Hamlin. *Main Traveled Roads.* New York, Harper, 1930. 377 p.

Garland, Hamlin. *Prairie Folks.* New York, Macmillan, 1899. 283 p.

Garland, Hamlin. *A Son of the Middle Border.* New York, Macmillan, 1928. 467 p. front.

Gates, Mary. *Out of This Nettle.* New York, Crowell, 1936.

Gilfillan, Archer B. *A Shepherd's Holiday.* Collection of humorous Sketches. Custer, Chronicle Shop, 1936. 39 p. il.

Gilfillan, Archer B. *Sheep.* A modern treatment of an ancient industry. Boston, Little, Brown, 1929. 276 p. il.

Harris, Kennett. *Meet Mr. Stegg.* Black Hills stories. New York, Holt, 1920. 320 p. front.

Howie, Edith. *Cry Murder.* New York, M. S. Mill Co., 1944. 272 p.

Howie, Edith. *The Band Played Murder.* New York, M. S. Mill Co., 1946. 243 p.

Hueston, Ethel. *Blithe Baldwin.* Indianapolis, Bobbs-Merrill, 1933. 320 p.

Hueston, Ethel. *Good Times.* Indianapolis, Bobbs-Merrill Co., 1932. 315 p.

Hueston, Ethel. *Calamity Jane.* Indianapolis, Bobbs-Merrill, 1937.

Kirk, Murray Ketcham. *The Beacon Light and Other Poems.* New York, Vinal, 1927. 66 p.

Kramer, Horace. *Marginal Land.* New York, J. B. Lippincott Co., 1939. 426 p.

Lane, Rose Wilder. *Let the Hurricane Roar.* New York, Longmans, 1933. 152 p. front.

Lillibridge, Will. *The Dissolving Circle.* New York, Dodd, Mead, 1907. 314 p. front.

Lillibridge, Will. *Where the Trail Divides.* Chicago, Burt, 1907. 302 p. front.

Lindberg, J. C. (editor). *Fifteen South Dakota Poets.* New York, Harrison, 1930. 96 p.

Lindberg, J. C. & Gunderson, Gertrude B. *An Anthology of South Dakota Poetry.* Mitchell, Educator Supply Co., 1928. Second Anthology, 1935.

McNeeley, Marian Hurd. *The Jumping-Off Place.* New York, Longmans, 1930. 308 p. il.

Neihardt, John G. *Song of Hugh Glass.* New York, Macmillan, 1915.

Neihardt, John G. *The Splendid Wayfaring.* A trip down the Missouri River. New York, Macmillan, 1920. 290 p. il.

Palmer, Roy. *Marie of Circle A.* Boston, Meader, 1928.

Patton, Don. *The Bunch Quitter.* Philadelphia, Macrae, 1935.

Pendexter, Hugh. *Pay Gravel.* Indianapolis, Bobbs-Merrill, 1923. 353 p. front.

Richardson, Mabel K. *Killdeer.* Philadelphia, Dorrance, 1936. 97 p.

Rölvaag, O. E. *Giants in the Earth.* New York, Harper, 1927. 465 p.

Rölvaag, O. E. *Peder Victorious.* New York, Harper, 1929. 350 p.

Rölvaag, O. E. *Their Fathers' God.* New York, Harper, 1931. 338 p.

South Dakota Poetry Society. *Prairie Poets: an Anthology of Verse.* Minneapolis, Lund Press, 1949. 209 p.

Waller, Leslie. *Show Me the Way.* New York, The Viking Press, 1947. 322 p.

White, Stewart Edward. *Gold.* Garden City, Doubleday, 1913. 449 p.

White, Stewart Edward. *The Claim Jumpers.* New York, McClure, 1901. 284 p.

White, Stewart Edward. *The Westerners.* New York, Doubleday, 1917. 344 p. front.

SPORTS AND RECREATION

Case, Lee. *The Black Hills and Badlands.* Sturgis, (Private), 1949.

Casey, Robert J. *The Black Hills and Their Incredible Characters.* Indianapolis, Bobbs-Merrill, 1949. 371 p.

Dean, Robert. *Living Granite.* New York, Viking Press, 1949. 128 p.

Jennewein, J. Leonard. *Dakota Square Dance.* Huron, S. Dak., (Private), 1950. 93 p.

South Dakota. Game, Fish and Parks Commission, Pierre, *Game and Fish Laws. 1949–51.* 138 p.

South Dakota. State Planning Board. *Recreation in South Dakota.* Brookings, 1936. 184 p.

South Dakota Writers' Project. *Fifty Million Pheasants.* Pierre, South Dakota Game, Fish and Parks Dept., 1941. 90 p.

Spring, Agnes Wright. *The Cheyenne and Black Hills Stage and Express Routes.* Glendale, Cal., Arthur H. Clark, 1949. 418 p.

CITIES

Case, Francis, et al. *Black Hills Engineer. Hot Springs Number.* Rapid City, South Dakota State School of Mines, 1928. 97 p. il.

Clark, Badger. *When Hot Springs Was a Pup.* Hot Springs, Kiwanis Club, 1927. 53 p. il.

Federal Writers' Project. *Guide to Pierre, The Capital City and*

Vicinity. Pierre, City of Pierre and Chamber of Commerce, 1937. 24 p. il.
Federal Writers' Project. *Pioneer Mitchell.* Mitchell, Parent-Teachers Association of Mitchell, 1937. 16 p. il.

BLACK HILLS RECREATIONAL AREA

Anonymous. *Black Hills, South Dakota.* Casper, Wyo., Prairie Publishing Co., 1937. 32 p. il.
Baldwin, George P. (editor). *Black Hills Illustrated.* (Edited for Black Hills Mining Men's Association). 207 p. il.
Coursey, O. W. *Beautiful Black Hills.* Mitchell, Educator Supply Co., 1926. 265 p. il.
Federal Writers' Project. *Vacation Guide to Custer State Park.* Custer State Park Board, 1937. 36 p. il.
Lange, Dietrich. *The Lure of the Black Hills.* Boston, Lothrop, 1916.
O'Harra, Cleophas C. and Connolly, Joseph P. *The Geology, Mineralogy, and Scenic Features of Custer State Park, South Dakota.* Rapid City, South Dakota State School of Mines, 1926. 242 p. il.
Price, Sam Goodale. *Black Hills, the Land of Legend.* Los Angeles, DeVoras, 1935.
Sanford, Rev. John I. (compiler). *The Black Hills Souvenir, A Pictorial and Historic Description of the Black Hills.* Denver, Williamson-Hafner, 1902. 222 p. il.
U.S. Department of Agriculture, Forest Service. *National Forests of the Black Hills of South Dakota and Wyoming.* Washington, Government Printing Office, 1935. 48 p. il.

General Reference

Coursey, O. W. *Who's Who in South Dakota.* Mitchell, Educator Supply Co., 1916.
Fox, Lawrence K. *Fox's Who's Who Among South Dakotans.* Pierre, Statewide Service Co., 1924–28. 2 vols.
Robinson, Doane. *Doane Robinson's Encyclopedia of South Dakota.* Pierre, Robinson, 1925. 1003 p.
Sampson, York, editor. *South Dakota, Fifty Years of Progress, 1889–1939.* Sioux Falls, S. Dak., Golden Anniversary Book Co., 1939. 107 p.—picture section.
South Dakota Writers' Project. *South Dakota Place-Names.* Vermillion, University of South Dakota, 1941. 689 p. (Mimeo.)

MAP OF
SOUTH DAKOTA
IN EIGHT SECTIONS

KEY

COUNTY LINE	U.S. HIGHWAYS
INDIAN RESERVATION LINE	STATE HIGHWAYS
POINTS OF INTEREST	RAILROADS
EDUCATIONAL INSTITUTIONS	AIR ROUTES
RELIGIOUS INSTITUTIONS	AIRPORTS
PARKS	STATE LINE
DAMS	

SECTIONAL DIVISION OF STATE MAP

MILES
0 10 20 30 40

N

III V VII
II IV VI VIII

SECTION
I

NORTH DAKOTA

WOLF BUTTE   White Butte

MONUMENT TO
HUGH GLASS

CUSTER
NAT'L
FOREST
HILLS

Ludlow

SHEEP WAGONS

85

JUMP-OFF
COUNTRY

BATTLE OF
SLIM BUTTES

PETRIFIED TREE

8   Buffalo

ANTELOPE RESERVE
SLIM BUTTES

MONTANA

CUSTER
NAT'L
FOREST

BATTLESHIP ROCK

CUSTER SHORT PINE
NAT'L   BUTTES
FOREST

BAD LANDS

Redig

SIOUX-CROW
BATTLEGROUND, 1862

85
HAYSTACK
BUTTE

DEER'S EAR
BUTTE

Edson

Cedar Canyon   Maurine

CASTLE ROCK
BUTTE

Castle Rock

Mud Butte   Fox Ridge

Sulphur

212
BELLE FOURCHE
DAM

Belle
Fourche
Reservoir

Newell

212

WYOMING

Belle Fourche

Fruitdale   Nisland

14

BLACK
HILLS
TEACHERS
COLLEGE

398

MILES

0 10 20 30 40

I	III	V	VII
	IV	VI	VIII

SECTION
II

N

MILES
0 10 20 30 40

N

SECTION
III

I	III	V	VII
II	IV	VI	VIII

NORTH DAKOTA

Lemmon
Thunder Hawk   Morristown
PETRIFIED WOOD
MUSEUM & PARK
SHADEHILL
DAM
TO
BUFFALO BONES

Mc Intosh   Walker
HUMP BUTTE

Cadillac
Mc Laughlin   STANDING   ROCK   FORT MANUEL
INDIAN   RESERVATION
ELK BUTTE
NATIVE BAT
BATTLEGROUND   GRAVE OF
WORLD WAR MONUMENT   CHIEF
INDIAN SOLDIERS   SITTING BULL
Wakpala

Pollock

ASH FY ISLAND
MASSACRE 1823

Mobridge
Graham

LIGNITE
COAL FIELDS
Isabel   C. M. ST. P. & P.
SAKAKAWEA
MONUMENT
MONUMENT TO
FOOL SOLDIERS BAND

THUNDER BUTTE

River
ANTOINE LE BEAU'S
SETTLEMENT

WHITTAGE POINT
SCENIC
OBSERVATION

CHEYENNE   RIVER   INDIAN   RESERVATION
La Plant
INDIAN VILLAGE
SCHOOL

Red Elm
River

Edson   Faith   C. M. ST. P. & P.
Dupree   Lantry   Eagle Butte   Mossman   Ridgeview   Cheyenne Agency

RATTLESNAKE
BUTTE

CHEYENNE   RIVER
INDIAN   RESERVATION

FOREST
CITY

RIVER

CHEYENNE   RIVER
WOLF CAVE   INDIAN   RESERVATION
River
EPISCOPAL
INDIAN SCHOOL

INDIAN   RESERVATION
Cherry Creek
INDIAN PEAK
STANDING BUTTE
OIL WELL

FORT SULLY

400

SECTION V

SECTION VI

MILES
0 10 20 30 40

I III V VII
II IV VI VIII

SECTION
VIII

N

MINNESOTA

IOWA

NEBRASKA

INDIAN
BATTLEFIELD
INDIAN VILLAGE
Oldham
Carthage
Ramona
Lake
Boda
81
77
Ward
INDIAN SCHOOL
STATE TEACHERS
COLLEGE
Flandreau
Egan
37
Lake
Pret.
Woonsocket
MUSKIN PARK
Artesian
Roswell
Howard
Madison
Wentworth
Colman
Forestburg
Winfred
Junius
Lake
Herman
Madison
Lake
77
Trent
ANNUAL
LUDEFISK
DINNER
Letcher
Canova
Dell Rapids
THE DELLS
Sherman
Colton
Baltic
THE PALISADES
DEVIL'S GULCH
Garretson
Lake
Mitchell
Salem
Spencer
Montrose
Humboldt
Hartford
Mt. Vernon
Mitchell
Alexandria
Canistota
Valley Springs
MENNONITE
COLONY
Emery
Bridgewater
Stanley
Corners
16
Pumpkin
Center
Sioux Falls
Ethan
Monroe
C.J.KAUFFMAN
MUSEUM
Harrisburg
Dimock
MILLTOWN
ISLAND PARK
OLD TRADING POST
Parkston
Freeman
Parker
Chancellor
Lennox
Worthing
Canton
SKI SLIDE
18
Delmont
Tripp
Olivet
Menno
Hurley
Davis
NEWTON HILLS
STATE PARK
77
18
Vibora
Scotland
81
Centerville
LEVON WEST
BIRTHPLACE
Hudson
Wagner
37
Lasterville
Irene
Beresford
Alcester
Dante
Tyndall
Avon
Wakonda
Volin
INDIAN TREATY
MONUMENT
Tabor
MONUMENT TO FIRST
SCHOOLHOUSE IN
DAKOTA TERR.
Yankton
Gayville
50
Mackling
SPIRIT
MOUND
UNIVERSITY
OF S.D. MUSEUM
FIRST
HOMESTEAD
FILING IN U. S.
CHALK CLIFFS
GAVIN POINT DAM
Vermilion
Springfield
SOUTHERN
NORMAL
Elk Point
FIRST DAKOTA CAMP
OF LEWIS & CLARK
1804
Jefferson

405

BLACK HILLS

CUSTER STATE PARK

—2—	U. S. Highways
—3—	State Highways
+—+—+	Railroads
— · · —	State Line
— · —	County Line

☼	Airports
⚑	Tourist Camps
555	Ski Slides
⚒	Mines
■	Points of Interest

0 1 2 3 4 5 10
MILES

SHEET 1

406

SHEET 2

BLACK HILLS
CUSTER STATE PARK

2 U. S. Highways	☼ Airports
3 State Highways	⚑ Tourist Camps
Railroads	sss Ski Slides
State Line	⚒ Mines
County Line	▪ Points of Interest

MILES
0 1 2 3 4 5   10

Index